Lecture Notes in Computer Science   11594

Commenced Publication in 1973
Founding and Former Series Editors:
Gerhard Goos, Juris Hartmanis, and Jan van Leeuwen

More information about this series at http://www.springer.com/series/7409

Abbas Moallem (Ed.)

HCI for Cybersecurity, Privacy and Trust

First International Conference, HCI-CPT 2019
Held as Part of the 21st HCI International Conference, HCII 2019
Orlando, FL, USA, July 26–31, 2019
Proceedings

 Springer

Editor
Abbas Moallem
San Jose State University
San Jose, CA, USA

ISSN 0302-9743   ISSN 1611-3349   (electronic)
Lecture Notes in Computer Science
ISBN 978-3-030-22350-2   ISBN 978-3-030-22351-9   (eBook)
https://doi.org/10.1007/978-3-030-22351-9

LNCS Sublibrary: SL3 – Information Systems and Applications, incl. Internet/Web, and HCI

This Springer imprint is published by the registered company Springer Nature Switzerland AG
The registered company address is: Gewerbestrasse 11, 6330 Cham, Switzerland

Foreword

The 21st International Conference on Human-Computer Interaction, HCI International 2019, was held in Orlando, FL, USA, during July 26–31, 2019. The event incorporated the 18 thematic areas and affiliated conferences listed on the following page.

A total of 5,029 individuals from academia, research institutes, industry, and governmental agencies from 73 countries submitted contributions, and 1,274 papers and 209 posters were included in the pre-conference proceedings. These contributions address the latest research and development efforts and highlight the human aspects of design and use of computing systems. The contributions thoroughly cover the entire field of human-computer interaction, addressing major advances in knowledge and effective use of computers in a variety of application areas. The volumes constituting the full set of the pre-conference proceedings are listed in the following pages.

This year the HCI International (HCII) conference introduced the new option of "late-breaking work." This applies both for papers and posters and the corresponding volume(s) of the proceedings will be published just after the conference. Full papers will be included in the *HCII 2019 Late-Breaking Work Papers Proceedings* volume of the proceedings to be published in the Springer LNCS series, while poster extended abstracts will be included as short papers in the HCII 2019 *Late-Breaking Work Poster Extended Abstracts* volume to be published in the Springer CCIS series.

I would like to thank the program board chairs and the members of the program boards of all thematic areas and affiliated conferences for their contribution to the highest scientific quality and the overall success of the HCI International 2019 conference.

This conference would not have been possible without the continuous and unwavering support and advice of the founder, Conference General Chair Emeritus and Conference Scientific Advisor Prof. Gavriel Salvendy. For his outstanding efforts, I would like to express my appreciation to the communications chair and editor of *HCI International News,* Dr. Abbas Moallem.

July 2019   Constantine Stephanidis

HCI International 2019 Thematic Areas
and Affiliated Conferences

Thematic areas:

- HCI 2019: Human-Computer Interaction
- HIMI 2019: Human Interface and the Management of Information

Affiliated conferences:

- EPCE 2019: 16th International Conference on Engineering Psychology and Cognitive Ergonomics
- UAHCI 2019: 13th International Conference on Universal Access in Human-Computer Interaction
- VAMR 2019: 11th International Conference on Virtual, Augmented and Mixed Reality
- CCD 2019: 11th International Conference on Cross-Cultural Design
- SCSM 2019: 11th International Conference on Social Computing and Social Media
- AC 2019: 13th International Conference on Augmented Cognition
- DHM 2019: 10th International Conference on Digital Human Modeling and Applications in Health, Safety, Ergonomics and Risk Management
- DUXU 2019: 8th International Conference on Design, User Experience, and Usability
- DAPI 2019: 7th International Conference on Distributed, Ambient and Pervasive Interactions
- HCIBGO 2019: 6th International Conference on HCI in Business, Government and Organizations
- LCT 2019: 6th International Conference on Learning and Collaboration Technologies
- ITAP 2019: 5th International Conference on Human Aspects of IT for the Aged Population
- HCI-CPT 2019: First International Conference on HCI for Cybersecurity, Privacy and Trust
- HCI-Games 2019: First International Conference on HCI in Games
- MobiTAS 2019: First International Conference on HCI in Mobility, Transport, and Automotive Systems
- AIS 2019: First International Conference on Adaptive Instructional Systems

Pre-conference Proceedings Volumes Full List

34. CCIS 1033, HCI International 2019 - Posters (Part II), edited by Constantine Stephanidis
35. CCIS 1034, HCI International 2019 - Posters (Part III), edited by Constantine Stephanidis

http://2019.hci.international/proceedings

First International Conference on HCI for Cybersecurity, Privacy and Trust (HCI-CPT 2019)

Program Board Chair(s): **Abbas Moallem**, *USA*

- Mohd Anwar, USA
- Budi Arief, UK
- Brita Bayatmakou, USA
- Jorge Bernal Bernabe, Spain
- Wojciech Cellary, Poland
- Ulku Clark, USA
- Francisco Corella, USA
- Tarek Elsaleh, UK
- Steven Furnell, UK
- Paul Grace, UK
- Aqeel Kazmi, Ireland
- Dan Kim, USA
- Jorge Lanza, Spain
- Nathan Lau, USA
- Karen Lewison, USA
- Albena Mihovska, Denmark
- George Moldovan, Romania
- Jason Nurse, UK
- Maria Papadaki, UK
- Henrich C. Pöhls, Germany
- Sascha Preibisch, Canada
- Gerald Quirchmayr, Austria
- Kazue Sako, Japan
- David Schuster, USA
- Ralf C. Staudemeyer, Germany
- Elias Tragos, Ireland
- Adam Wójtowicz, Poland
- Sherali Zeadally, USA

The full list with the Program Board Chairs and the members of the Program Boards of all thematic areas and affiliated conferences is available online at:

http://www.hci.international/board-members-2019.php

HCI International 2020

The 22nd International Conference on Human-Computer Interaction, HCI International 2020, will be held jointly with the affiliated conferences in Copenhagen, Denmark, at the Bella Center Copenhagen, July 19–24, 2020. It will cover a broad spectrum of themes related to HCI, including theoretical issues, methods, tools, processes, and case studies in HCI design, as well as novel interaction techniques, interfaces, and applications. The proceedings will be published by Springer. More information will be available on the conference website: http://2020.hci.international/.

General Chair
Prof. Constantine Stephanidis
University of Crete and ICS-FORTH
Heraklion, Crete, Greece
E-mail: general_chair@hcii2020.org

http://2020.hci.international/

Contents

Security and Usability

Privacy and Trust

Authentication

Grid Authentication: A Memorability and User Sentiment Study

Paul Biocco and Mohd Anwar[✉]

North Carolina A&T University, Greensboro, NC, USA
manwar@ncat.edu

Abstract. Despite being one of the most crucial parts of online transactions, the most used authentication system, the username and password system, has shown to be weaker than ever. With the increase of processing power within computers, offline password attacks such as dictionary attacks, rainbow tables, and hash tables have become more effective against divulging account information from stolen databases. This has led to alternative solutions being proposed, such as logging in with a social media account or password managers, which do not replace the password entirely. Graphical alternatives have previously proposed, but none of them have become widely used. In a previous paper we proposed our own alternative called "Grid Authentication", which would allow users to authenticate using a sequence of clicks on a colored Grid, shown to be resistant against offline password attacks. Now we have implemented and tested Grid Authentication's memorability and recorded user sentiment data. Participants logged in using a newly created password, an 8-character password randomly generated for them, as well as used Grid Authentication scheme for three days each, once per day. We found that overall, Grid Authentication's memorability was like a user chosen password, and far superior to the randomly generated 8-character password. We also observed that user's overall sentiment towards Grid Authentication increased significantly after three days of regular use. Despite this, while sentiment over the system was overall positive, users perceived that they remembered the password more easily, perhaps given hints as to why alternative authentication types have not become widely used.

Keywords: Authentication · Memory · Grid Authentication · Security

1 Introduction

With the expansion of internet usage, verification of a user's identity has become a critical process for both privacy and security. The amount of personal information associated with both social media and business accounts has steadily increased as the internet has become more critical for daily activities. The most common verification process used online is the username and password, which allows a user to authenticate themselves with a public alias and a private string of characters. Unfortunately, this method has become vulnerable to cyber-attacks.

As technology has expanded and as both computational and processing power has increased, passwords have become significantly less effective at preventing passwords breaches. Both password breaches, such as the RockYou [1] and LinkedIn [2] breaches,

© Springer Nature Switzerland AG 2019
A. Moallem (Ed.): HCII 2019, LNCS 11594, pp. 3–18, 2019.
https://doi.org/10.1007/978-3-030-22351-9_1

and academic research has allowed us to understand human tendencies when creating passwords [3]. The combination of increased knowledge about password tendencies and database breaches have made offline password attacks extremely effective. Some rigs have even been able to crack all keyboard-typeable 8-character passwords within a single day [4]. Breaching an account can result in first names, last names, phone numbers, bank account numbers, and even credit card information. The username and password scheme must either be significantly reinforced or replaced entirely to ensure future confidentiality of a users' personal accounts.

Passwords have several critical issues that put users at risk. The primary problem stems from memory. Passwords commonly have words, phrases, and personal information. While this helps users memorize their password, this also gives attackers hints and tools to breach an account. The use of words and phrases within passwords allow offline password attacks such as dictionary attacks and hash tables more effective than if they were made of random characters. Secure passwords often must be long, randomized, contain symbols, and unique. These passwords tend to take a significant time to remember [5]. When a user creates a complex password, they tend to reuse the password over multiple accounts [6]. Alternatively, users may write them their passwords down and leave them in potentially insecure locations [7].

Companies have attempted to mitigate poor password security by creating security standards such as forcing users to create complex passwords and have them constantly change their passwords. At face value, these protocols were thought to help secure the system. Research has observed otherwise. Instead, these measures have led to written down passwords and create passwords easily derived from previous passwords, such as changing a single number [7].

Multiple solutions have been suggested to assist in solving the password crisis. Some solutions, such as social login and password managers fail to solve the problem. They create a bottleneck where if one password is breached, then all accounts can be accessed and pose significant downsides such as privacy issues with social logins [8] and insecure implementation with password managers [9, 10]. Other mechanisms such as fingerprint and iris scanning require significant amounts of processing power and have their own separate privacy issues, requiring companies to store biometric data [11].

Graphical authentication methods may hold a solution. Significant research has been done within this topic. However, despite multiple variations of this type of system, showing users can memorize graphical passwords, these types of alternatives have yet to be widely implemented. In a paper we proposed a graphical system that would prevent offline password attacks while without sacrificing memorability, called Grid Authentication [12]. To understand memorability and user sentiment towards Grid authentication, we recruited users from both offline and through Mechanical Turk. In our experiment, users logged into an experimental system using three methods: a password they chose, a randomly generated password, and Grid authentication. Fifty-five users entered the initial experiment, and 46 users completed the entire experiment.

This paper's purpose is to show that our system is as memorable as a user-created password and gather user sentiment data on such. The rest of this paper is organized as follows: Sect. 2 covers related works about graphical authentication, Sect. 3 presents our implementation of Grid Authentication, Sect. 4 describes the memory experiment we conducted, Sect. 5 covers the results of the experiment, Sect. 6 offers discussion and interpretation of the results, and Sect. 6 covers the limitation of our study as well as concludes the paper.

2 Related Works

In reviewing other graphical authentication systems, we found three primary categories: locimetric systems, cognometric systems, and drawmetric systems [13]. Cognometric systems primarily focused on users recognizing a preselected target to authenticate themselves. Locimetric systems focus on identifying a specific point within a predefined image. Drawmetric systems require the users to write something freehand or with a guide.

Locimetric authentication systems often was observed to have predictability issues. When focusing on singular points on an image, users projected their focuses into predictable areas [14]. When picking a specific area of an image, it was found that users notice heavily selected brighter areas of a picture, influencing points chosen [15]. Furthermore, users struggled to remember exact locations within the image. Instead, they were able to remember relative locations. An experiment done with Jiminy templates, which used a thin plastic square with small holes found that when placed on a grid of letters, one third of the participants were not able to give exact locations after a month but remembered general locations [16]. GrIDSure, a one-time pin mechanism which used a grid of numbers had similar issues. This system would have users login by entering a pin designated by predetermined locations in a predetermined order. Research observed that the relative shape of the pattern was memorized, but often the specific order was incorrect, further reinforcing the conclusions made within the Jiminy template study. Overall, these systems seem to have both predictability issues and memorability issues.

Cognometric systems rely primarily on user recognition over memorization. Users would remember a target image and recognize it later. Passfaces, a technique that uses a Grid of faces, is a primary example of a Cognometric system. Users would select a face, then choose it amongst distractors to login. This system was shown to be memorable but had no clear advantage over traditional authentication systems [13]. Further studies showed that users tended to select faces of their own gender and race, causing a predictability issue [17]. Another example of this type of system is Déjà Vu [18]. This system used abstract images over faces, and instead of using a single image, they used five selections instead of one. Users seemed to like this system more than passwords after a week of interactions [13], but it was also observed that the results were not fully substantiated [19]. These types of systems, if properly implemented, may make a viable password replacement.

Drawmetric systems have considered to have significantly larger password space than passwords, but fails in both memorability and accuracy. Draw-a-Secret is a clear example of this. It authenticates a user using a sequence of pen strokes on a blank grid, accounting for both the order and locations of where lines were crossed [20].

User evaluation of this method found that this mechanism was less memorable than traditional authentication systems [21]. Scribble-a-Secret is another system which fore-goes the grid and uses machine learning to approximate a user's design instead [22]. The best accuracy ratings they were able to achieve was 2.6% false acceptance rate and a 2.8% false rejection rate. The registration process took significantly longer, requiring a training period. In conclusion, Drawmetric systems are not viable password replacements.

3   Grid Authentication Experiment Design

We created a three-part experiment that took place over ten days to gain insight on user sentiment about Grid authentication and to test its memorability. Users registered with an experimental website that instructed the user to login to their account using various login methods. They are given instructions on the main area of the site each day as shown in Fig. 1. Participants created an account with a username and a password they chose. At this point, they were explicitly instructed to not use passwords and usernames for other accounts. It was also explicitly mentioned that they should not write down any authentication information beyond their username.

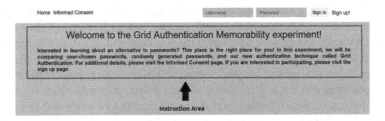

Fig. 1. This figure is a screenshot of the instruction area of our website that users were presented information.

The first day was an initial day that simply set participants up within the website. Through this, they would familiarize themselves with how they would get instructions. We compared Grid Authentication to both passwords that users would regularly use and randomized passwords that would be harder to break.

A one day waiting period would be initialized before we started them on their first day of logging in. After waiting the initial period, on days one through three, users logged into our website using their user-chosen password. On day three, each user was provided an 8-character password that was randomly generated using all 95-character symbols on the keyboard. To ensure that the difficulty remained consistent between all users, each user was given the same 8-character password. On days four through six, they logged in using this randomized password. On day six, users were introduced to Grid Authentication, implemented as specified in Sect. 4 of this paper. They reregistered on a different portion of the same website using Grid Authentication's registration process. Finally, on day seven through nine, they logged in using Grid Authentication.

To gain insight on user sentiment we asked users to partake in a survey both after their initial registration and after the experiment. We asked questions about user's overall opinion on the registration process, the login process, perceived login speed, and their overall sentiment of Grid Authentication.

Since we wanted to see if users could remember a particular password at all, no password reset function was provided within the website. Users were instructed to attempt logging in up until 5 attempts (and were told to contact a support email if they used more attempts). The system recorded if a user attempted to log in, and how many times they attempted to log in. Once the count reached 5 attempts, the user was allowed into the website while being given their displayed password or click sequence in the instruction area.

4 Grid Authentication Implementation

To display a user's Grid, we use a modal which is accessed through a "log in" button at the top right of the website. Visual examples of both the registration page and login area can be viewed in the Appendix. To implement this system, we created a basic PHP website supported by a MySQL database.

Our design of Grid Authentication primarily comes from our previous paper [12]. Figure 2 depicts both a technical view and a user view of Grid Authentication's interface. From the technical perspective, Grid Authentication consists of a table structure which contains a set number of characters. Each character is randomly generated via a predetermined mechanism. The total set of characters used to generate the Grid will be referred to as the "character set". To create a user's "password" which we will refer to as a "click sequence", a user would interact with a set of tiles, which would be concatenated together in the order they were interacted with. In the example below, three letters are used per box, and there were 6 user interactions resulting in an 18-character long click sequence. From the user view, we can see that each box is colored, and the characters are hidden. In this implementation of Grid Authentication scheme, users were able to choose their own coloration by using JavaScript color chooser. This allows users to focus on the Grid's coloration instead of trying to memorize a long string of characters. The set of colors that were chosen for a particular Grid will be further referred to as a "color set". Finally, for storage purposes, the character set, click sequence, and color set are all associated with an identifier during storage. An example of how Grid Authentication information was stored in an SQL table and an alternative implementation using Firebase is shown in Fig. 3.

The registration and login processes for Grid Authentication act similarly to usernames and passwords. During the registration process, the user creates some set of information they must memorize and correspond it to a username. Then when the user logs in, they must repeat the same task. The main differences from the user perspective is registration adds a level of customization and the users create and enter click sequences instead of traditional password.

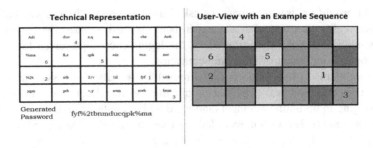

Fig. 2. A technical and user-view representation of Grid Authentication's core concept. The numbers within the user view represent clicked locations and are not usually seen during login.

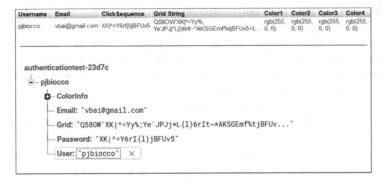

Fig. 3. On the top is an SQL entry example of Grid Authentication's database. On the bottom is a firebase storage example as an alternative to SQL.

However, from the server-side perspective, there are some major differences within the registration process and login process. Figures 4 and 5 explain these processes in detail. As shown in Fig. 4, during registration, a random generation process must occur. Then after the user chooses their tiles, the tile locations must be transferred to the server and the click sequence must be generated and stored. Because of the customizability during the registration, this means that a user cannot log in with a single form. Instead, visitors input their username and are given their corresponding Grid color set. From here, as shown in Fig. 5, the Grid with the appropriate color set is given. The creates their pattern. Individual tiles are converted to their click sequence and is compared to the one within the database. If the converted click sequence is the same as the one stored within the database, the user can log in.

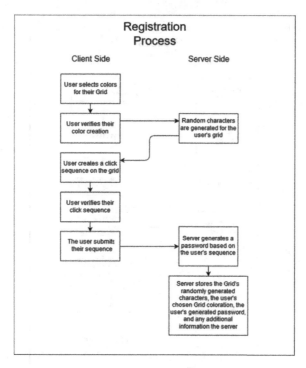

Fig. 4. Flow chart of Grid Authentication's Registration process from server/client point of view.

5   Results

Our study protocol was reviewed and approved by our Institutional Review Board (IRB). In our experiment, we had a total 71 users registered through the website, 49 users registered within the Grid Authentication site, and 46 users completed the entire study. Seventy percent of our participants were male, and 30% were female. A significant percentage of the participants had several of online accounts, over 80% having seven or more accounts. However, this group also tended to use repeated passwords when prompted about their password usage. Fifty-six percent of participants held between 3–6 passwords despite most users having over seven accounts. We asked these questions to reestablish why a password alternative is needed.

5.1   Memory Experiment

Users were generally able to remember their click sequences and user-chosen passwords easily. Randomly generated passwords were harder to remember than the click sequence and user-chosen passwords. Table 1 shows the number of login-attempts and the number of login failures. There was a significant spike in users who forgot their password on day 4 through 6 when the passwords switched to randomly generated, 26 users not able to remember their password on day 4. User chosen passwords and Grid

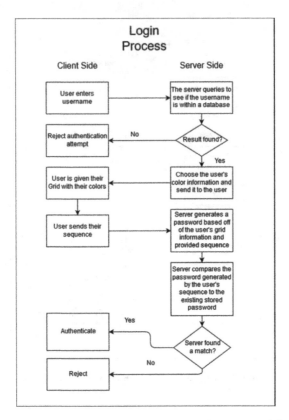

Fig. 5. Flow chart of Grid Authentication's Login process from a server/client point of view.

Table 1. The table below shows how many users attempted to log in per day and how many times they failed. Day 1–3 is user chosen passwords, Day 4–6 is 8-character randomized password, and Day 7–9 used Grid Authentication.

	Day1	Day2	Day3	Day4	Day5	Day6	Day7	Day8	Day9
Single Attempts:	48	50	46	11	18	18	31	33	30
1 Failure	4	3	5	3	3	7	8	7	11
2 Failures	0	0	2	4	2	1	3	0	2
3 Failures	0	0	0	1	0	0	0	0	2
4 Failures	0	0	0	2	0	1	0	1	0
5 Failures	3	1	1	26	25	21	2	3	0
Total Users	55	54	54	47	48	48	44	44	45
Could not remember	5.455	1.852	1.852	55.319	52.083	43.75	4.545	6.818	0

Authentication click sequences had only five instances of users not remembering their passwords throughout the entire experiment. Notably, we observed users of Grid Authentication were more likely to incorrectly log in at least once in comparison to traditional passwords, likely due to the new user experience.

When we asked about login performance within the survey, user opinion lined up with data collected through the website. We asked users how long it took to remember each login mechanism. As shown in Table 2, users claimed that they were able to remember Grid Authentication and chosen passwords were both mostly memorized within one to three hours from choosing their passwords, and most users claimed that they were not able to remember the randomized password at all.

Despite performance being similar between both mechanisms, when asked to participants to rate all three systems in memorability, user-chosen passwords clearly were chosen over Grid Authentication both after registration and after the experiment. Out of 41 responses, 11 users stated Grid Authentication was easiest to remember, 2 users stated the randomized password was easiest to remember, and 28 users stated that their chosen password was easiest to remember. Five users found that Grid Authentication was the hardest system to remember, 36 users found the randomized password was the hardest to remember, and no users found their user-chosen password the hardest to remember. In the middle, 25 users believed that Grid Authentication was the second most memorable, 2 users believed that the randomized password was the second most memorable, and 14 users said that their chosen password was the second most memorable.

As an additional point, we asked participants if their Grid's coloration assisted them in memorizing their click sequence. Out of 46 responses, 28 participants stated that it significantly helped, 9 users said it somewhat helped, 3 had no opinion, and 6 users stated that coloration did not help in memorizing their click sequence.

Table 2. User self-reported results of how long it took to remember their Grid Authentication Click sequence, randomly generated password, and self-chosen password.

	Grid	Random	Chosen
1-3 hours	38	7	40
4-12 hours	3	3	0
1 day	1	7	2
2 days	3	8	1
3 days	1	4	2
Did not remember	0	17	0
Total users	46	46	45

5.2 Sentiment Analysis

We asked several questions about user's reaction to Grid Authentication. First, we specifically asked them to rate Grid Authentication's naturalness from 0 to 10. As shown in Figs. 6 and 7, initially, most of the 46 users that responded were neutral or positive. The collective group gave an average of 6.282, giving Grid Authentication's initial rating slightly above neutral. However, there were some users who felt Grid Authentication was completely unnatural. User Sentiment significantly increased post experiment. With 46 responses, the average user rating increased from 6.282 to 8.0 and no users rated Grid Authentication below a 4.

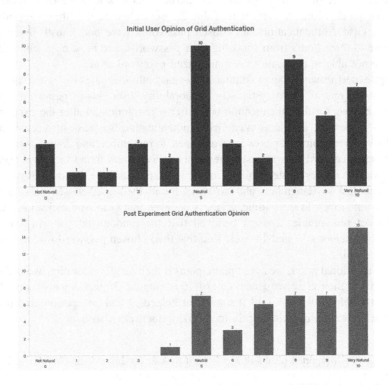

Fig. 6. The blue graph shows user's initial impression how natural Grid Authentication feels, which takes place on day 6. The red graph shows user's impression on Grid Authentication's naturalness post experiment, after participants have used Grid Authentication for three days. (Color figure online)

In addition to asking users for the overall naturalness of Grid Authentication, we also asked users specifically about the registration process and login process. First, we asked users how easy it was to create an account both after their first login and after the experiment to see if their sentiment changed over time. Out of 48 post-registration responses, 18 users found registration extremely easy, 22 users found it somewhat easy, 6 users rated it neutral, and 2 users rated it as somewhat difficult. Out of 46 post-experiment responses, 18 users felt that the registration process was very easy, 17 found it somewhat easy, 6 users rated it neutral, and 5 users rated it as somewhat difficult. Second, we asked users if the login process felt natural. Out of 48 post-registration responses, 18 stated Grid Authentication's login process was very natural, 17 users stated it was somewhat natural, 7 felt neutral, and 5 users felt it

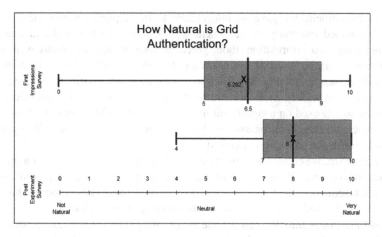

Fig. 7. Box and whisker plots for the users' first impression survey and their post experiment sentiment survey.

somewhat unnatural, and 1 user felt it was very unnatural. Responding to the same question again post experiment, positive sentiment about the login process significantly increased over time. Twenty-six users said the login process felt very natural, 15 users said it felt somewhat natural, 2 users were neutral, and three felt that Grid Authentication was somewhat unnatural. Overall, users felt the system was more natural after extended use.

Finally, to see if users felt like their use of Grid Authentication was improving, we asked users about their impressions of improving their login speeds. In the initial impressions survey, we asked users how much they agreed with the following statement: "With practice, I could authenticate with Grid Authentication quickly." Of 48 responses, 32 users strongly agreed, 12 users somewhat agreed, 3 users were neutral, 1 somewhat disagreed, and 1 strongly disagreed. In post survey, we asked if they had improved their login times. Of 46 responses, 26 believed their speed increased significantly, 15 users felt their speed increase slightly, 2 users stayed neutral, and 3 users said their login times believed their speeds did not improve.

6 Discussion and Conclusion

Overall, we found that users were able to login with Grid Authentication with similar success rates to passwords. However, users still seemed to favor their own user-chosen password over Grid Authentications despite their similar performances. Passwords are already well established, giving users a sense of familiarity. Human nature shows that users tend to prefer systems they are familiar with [23], which makes viable alternative authentication system significantly harder to become mainstream. We can see that as familiarity to us was built up user sentiment regarding the login process increased on average after extended use.

In this experiment, we gave no information to participants on how Grid Authentication functioned internally, so sentiment was only based off visual and functional appearance only. No information about potential security improvements were given, nor were telling users how this system translates on the backend may help increase user's positive sentiment. For any alternate authentication system to become mainstream, it must be widely available and well supported, such as the Android pattern lock, which now is used on a significant number of phones [24]. Not only does it have to have some advantage over passwords, but it also must be marketed well to get users to interact with it for an extended period.

To summarize, we created a memorability and sentiment experiment for a graphical authentication system. We observed that users were able to remember Grid Authentication click sequences just as well their own created passwords. Despite this, users still felt that Grid Authentication was less memorable than traditional passwords. We also found that users initially had a wide range of opinions, the average naturalness rating of Grid Authentication being just above neutral. The overall naturalness rating increased significantly after three days of interacting with Grid Authentication overall. Lastly, we conclude that to create a viable authentication alternative, in addition to having some advantage over a traditional password, it must be implemented and advertised widely to gain user's initial interest.

Appendix

See Figs. 8, 9, 10, 11, 12 and 13.

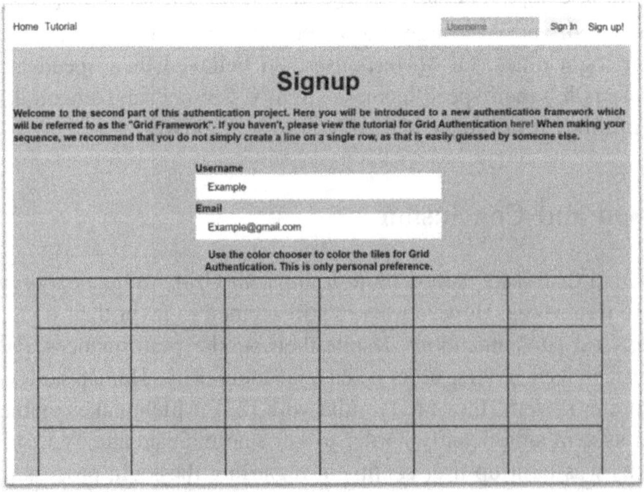

Fig. 8. Grid Authentication website registration

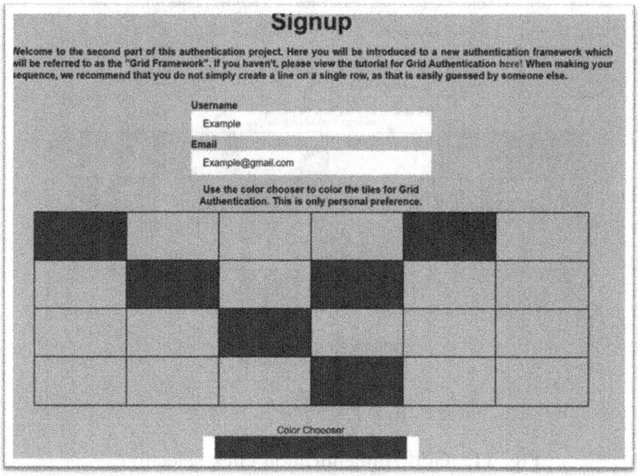

Fig. 9. Grid Authentication color application.

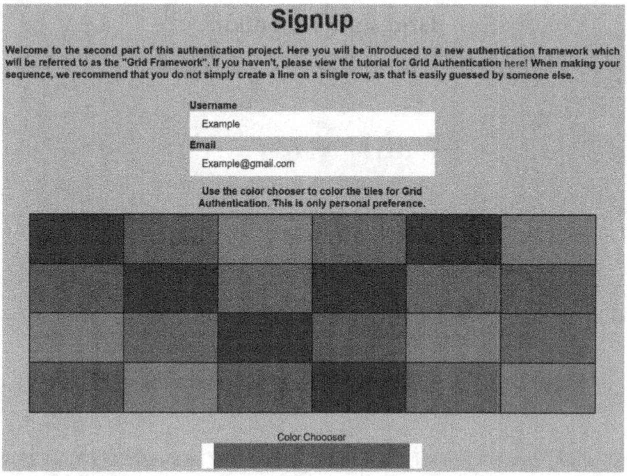

Fig. 10. Grid Authentication color application (completed).

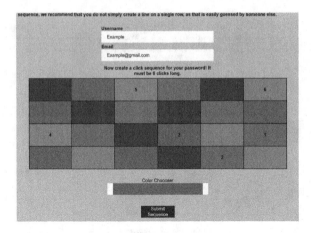

Fig. 11. Grid Authentication click selection.

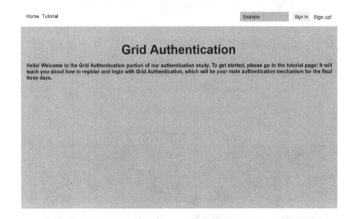

Fig. 12. Grid Authentication website login initial page.

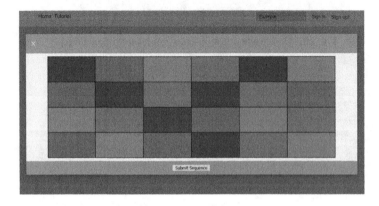

Fig. 13. Grid Authentication grid login modal.

References

1. Weir, M., Aggarwal, S., Collins, M., Stern, H.: Testing metrics for password creation policies by attacking large sets of revealed passwords. In: Proceedings of CCS (2010)
2. Walters, R.: Cyber attacks on US companies in 2014. Heritage Found. **4289**, 1–5 (2014)
3. Florencio, D., Herley, C.: A large-scale study of web password habits. In: Proceedings of the 16th International Conference on World Wide Web, pp. 657–666. ACM, May 2007
4. Goodin, D.: 25-GPU cluster cracks every standard Windows password in, 9 December 2012. https://arstechnica.com/information-technology/2012/12/25-gpu-cluster-cracks-every-standard-windows-password-in-6-hours/. Accessed 27 Oct 2018
5. Yan, J., Blackwell, A., Anderson, R., Grant, A.: Password memorability and security: empirical results. IEEE Secur. Priv. **2**(5), 25–31 (2004)
6. Bonneau, J.: Measuring password re-use empirically. Light Blue Touchpaper (2011)
7. Zviran, M., Haga, W.J.: Password security: an empirical study. J. Manag. Inf. Syst. **15**(4), 161–185 (1999)
8. Gafni, R., Nissim, D.: To social login or not login? Exploring factors affecting the decision. Issues Informing Sci. Inf. Technol. **11**(1), 057–072 (2014)
9. Silver, D., Jana, S., Boneh, D., Chen, E.Y., Jackson, C.: Password managers: attacks and defenses. In: USENIX Security Symposium, pp. 449–464, August 2014
10. Belenko, A., Sklyarov, D.: "Secure Password Managers" and "Military-Grade Encryption" on Smartphones: Oh, Really? Blackhat Europe (2012)
11. Prabhakar, S., Pankanti, S., Jain, A.K.: Biometric recognition: Security and privacy concerns. IEEE Secur. Priv. **2**, 33–42 (2003)
12. Biocco, P., Anwar, M.: Grid framework to address password memorability issues and offline password attacks. In: Nicholson, D. (ed.) AHFE 2017. AISC, vol. 593, pp. 52–61. Springer, Cham (2018). https://doi.org/10.1007/978-3-319-60585-2_6
13. De Angeli, A., Coventry, L., Johnson, G., Renaud, K.: Is a picture really worth a thousand words? Exploring the feasibility of graphical authentication systems. Int. J. Hum Comput Stud. **63**(1–2), 128–152 (2005)
14. Renaud, K., De Angeli, A.: My password is here! An investigation into visuo-spatial authentication mechanisms. Interact. Comput. **16**(6), 1017–1041 (2004)
15. Baik, M., Suk, H.J., Lee, J., Choi, K.: Investigation of eye-catching colors using eye tracking. In: IS&T/SPIE Electronic Imaging, p. 86510W. International Society for Optics and Photonics, 14 March 2013
16. Renaud, K., Smith, E.: Jiminy: helping users to remember their passwords (2001)
17. Davis, D., Monrose, F., Reiter, M.K.: On user choice in graphical password schemes. In: USENIX Security Symposium, vol. 13, p. 11, August 2004
18. Dhamija, R., Perrig, A.: Deja Vu-A user study: using images for authentication. In: USENIX Security Symposium, vol. 9, p. 4, August 2000
19. De Angeli, A., Coutts, M., Coventry, L., Johnson, G.I., Cameron, D., Fischer, M.H.: VIP: a visual approach to user authentication. In: Proceedings of the Working Conference on Advanced Visual Interfaces, pp. 316–323. ACM, May 2002
20. Jermyn, I.H., Mayer, A., Monrose, F., Reiter, M.K., Rubin, A.D.: The design and analysis of graphical passwords. USENIX Association (1999)
21. Goldberg, J., Hagman, J., Sazawal, V.: Doodling our way to better authentication. In: CHI 2002 Extended Abstracts on Human Factors in Computing Systems, pp. 868–869. ACM, April 2002

22. Oka, M., Kato, K., Xu, Y., Liang, L., Wen, F.: Scribble-a-secret: similarity-based password authentication using sketches. In: 19th International Conference on Pattern Recognition, ICPR 2008, pp. 1–4. IEEE, December 2008
23. Harrison, D.A., Mohammed, S., McGrath, J.E., Florey, A.T., Vanderstoep, S.W.: Time matters in team performance: effects of member familiarity, entrainment, and task discontinuity on speed and quality. Pers. Psychol. 56(3), 633–669 (2003)
24. Sun, C., Wang, Y., Zheng, J.: Dissecting pattern unlock: the effect of pattern strength meter on pattern selection. J. Inf. Secur. Appl. 19(4–5), 308–320 (2014)

Consonant-Vowel-Consonants
for Error-Free Code Entry

Nikola K. Blanchard[1]([✉]), Leila Gabasova[2], and Ted Selker[3]

[1] Institut de Recherche en Informatique Fondamentale,
Université Paris Diderot, Paris, France
nikola.k.blanchard@gmail.com
[2] Institut de Planétologie et d'Astrophysique de Grenoble,
Saint-Martin-d'Héres, France
[3] University of Maryland, Baltimore County, USA
http://www.koliaza.com

Abstract. Codes and passwords are the bane of user experiences: even small mistakes can delay desired activities, causing undue frustration. Work on codes has focused on security instead of people's ability to enter them error-free. Difficulties observed in a security demonstration motivated this investigation of code transcription difficulty. A pilot study with 33 subjects and a follow-up study with 267 subjects from 24 countries measured performance and preference for codes of varying lengths, patterns, and character sets.

We found that, for users of all languages, long codes with alternating consonant - vowel patterns were more accurately transcribed and are preferred over shorter numeric or alphabetic codes. Mixed-case and alphanumeric character sets both increased transcription errors.

The proposed CVC^6 code design composed of six Consonant-Vowel-Consonant trigrams is faster to enter, more secure, preferred by users, and more impervious to user error when compared to codes typically used for security purposes. An extension integrates error detection and correction, essentially eliminating typos.

Keywords: Usable-security · Error correcting codes · Authentication · User study

1 Introduction

People all have different codes for their driver's license, social security, government ID, and bank accounts, and passwords to access email, social media, and each online transaction or community system they use. These codes are now central to protecting our identities. Passwords are codes used in conjunction with logins to authenticate users.

The most frequent answer to our increasing security needs [17,31] has been to add more passwords, increase length and character complexity with

© Springer Nature Switzerland AG 2019
A. Moallem (Ed.): HCII 2019, LNCS 11594, pp. 19–37, 2019.
https://doi.org/10.1007/978-3-030-22351-9_2

upper- and lower-case characters and special characters [8], and change them frequently, counter-productively making them even harder to remember [10].

Biometrics have been considered a candidate solution to those problems for a long time, but finger prints, iris detection, and face recognition systems have all been shown to be hackable [9,22,27]. Passwords have the advantage of being pure information, hence easier to create and share with a trusted party, but they have become an arms race with no predictable outcome [21].

We are required to come up with and/or enter codes with a variety of patterns, from copying credit card numbers to Wi-Fi codes to account passwords. Much progress has been presented on usable security, to study the perception of complexity and counter the failures of user-created passwords [13,24,29,30]. Yan's paper [32] was an important first exploration into password memorability. It showed that mnemonics can help memorability of passwords [3] while not compromising security strength, leading to additional work in that direction [14,18,20,26].

But how well do people succeed when using codes and how can their success be improved? We all enter codes many times a day, typing our name and well-practised passwords much faster than new character strings (especially automatically generated ones). Many of us forget or misenter codes while needing to get access to our resources [7].

Creating codes adapted to their use, whether it is memorability, ease of entry, or speed can greatly reduce stress and breakage in everyone's work. Trade-offs are inherent in privacy and security [1], and a single compromised password can be catastrophic [15]. Typical systems might require people to use at least 8 characters, upper- and lower-case, numbers, and special characters, although some have started questioning if people gain actual security with the added complexity [10,11]. In one illustrative example, frustration and confusion with character recognition in a code-based voting system caused at least 10% additional abstention [5].

User-created codes versus single-use or automatically generated codes present very different challenges for usability. Automatically-generated codes depend on multiple frequent assumptions that haven't been extensively questioned. Does increased character set complexity [25] make better codes? Does separation of a code into multiple fragments (in this paper called 'chunking' a code) with spaces in between reduce errors? Are nonsense patterns of alphanumerics for security better than syllabic codes or even words? This paper tests usability and security together for codes that are not user-created.

Are there trade-offs between length, character sets and structural patterns that can improve people's ability to use codes? How do these trade-offs change when considering the ability to reduce transcription errors for one-time codes? Can techniques for making codes easier to enter work across cultures or even languages?

The rest of the paper is organised as follows. After presenting the main results, we introduce the experimental protocol for the two crowd-sourced tests of usability and transcribability via a web-based approach. Experimental Results presents data from the pilot and main experiments, showing links between length and type of code trade-offs. The implications of these findings are developed. Inspired by the results, the paper then introduces CVC^6, a 6-trigram code design for higher-entropy higher-usability codes always composed of 6 consonant-vowel-consonant trigrams. An extension of CVC^6 is also presented that includes error detection/correction, CVC^{6++}. The paper concludes by showing how more work could be done to further explore the design of cross-cultural, easy-to-transcribe, high-entropy codes everyone finds themselves using several times a day.

1.1 Definitions

The experiments included randomly-generated codes composed of sequences of the following type:

- numeric: numbers from 0 to 9.
- alphabetic: lower-case Latin letters (excluding diacritics).
- alphanumeric: numbers, lower-case, and upper-case alphabetic characters, containing at least one of each.
- CVCs: consonant-vowel-consonant alphabetic trigrams in lower-case. Vowels are a, i, e, o, u and y. Consonants go from b to z, excluding y as well as q due to demonstrated discrimination problems between y, q and g.

2 Main Results

This paper has 4 main experimental observations, and one theoretical contribution.

- Transcribing codes takes concentration and is highly dependent on the code's structure. This work found that, for a given length, code structure can reduce transcription error rates from 16.9% to 1.9%.
- A majority of code transcription errors can be eliminated by using a set of unambiguous alphabetic characters (excluding visually ambiguous g/q/y and i/l), eliminating mixed case to prevent upper-case/lower-case confusions, and eliminating numbers.
- The relationship between code length and time needed to enter it strongly depends on the code's structure; spaces can help for long alphanumeric codes but can be confusing for others. Using a consonant-vowel-consonant (CVC) pattern in codes can reduce time to transcribe even with codes twice as long.
- People have a 75% chance of recognising a code they had seen 2 to 5 min earlier. However, they will correctly reject a novel code they haven't seen in 87% of cases.

Based on these findings, the protocol, CVC^6 is proposed that is easier and faster to transcribe, with fewer mistakes and increased security. We also introduce CVC^{6++}, an extension that includes error detection and correction.

3   Experiment Design

The following experiments have the goal of demonstrating trade-offs between character sets, number of characters, and patterns of characters to create easy-to-enter secure codes. A web-based interface was developed in Javascript to sequentially present discrete code transcription problems. It was iteratively tested in a pilot experiment and then improved and extended for a main experiment. The goal was to have people type codes in the kinds of places they typically are when using online services. To understand how codes can be improved in the wild, experiments were conducted wherever a person was (real-life conditions, not a laboratory environment). Our analyses generally avoid raw averages and focus on trimmed averages and medians to eliminate anomalies (such as one participant taking close to 5 h to answer a single question).

3.1   Pilot Experiment

A protocol was developed that would take no more than a few minutes and test transcription of code length, character sets, and spaces. Engagement was initially solicited personally by a docent from 33 random attendants of the science fiction conference Worldcon 75 in August 2017 for a pilot experiment. The initial design did not adequately distinguish capitalisation problems and issues around the way input is entered on smart phones. Unfortunately it also didn't correctly disable auto-correct. Despite those setbacks, the data still showed that codes following syllabic patterns had many advantages and laid the groundwork for changes to put into the experiment (Fig. 1).

While several of the pilot experiment's results were statistically significant, the main experiment corroborates and extends these on a larger and more diverse sample. The pilot helped validate and improve the Javascript protocol and show where more data was needed. Results below detail only the main experiment (data will be available for both studies in a public online repository).

Fig. 1. Screenshots from the experiment's interface

3.2   General Protocol

Participants were individuals that responded to an opportunity to volunteer online. They were told that they could quit the experiment at any time. Their data was only collected (through FormSpree) if they confirmed submission at the end. The total time taken generally varied from 3 to 10 min.

For security as well as privacy, all code executed was on the user's device and visible to the user, and only recorded their final answers and timestamps.

The study was presented as a sequence of web forms with an introduction and three main sections, designed to measure transcription performance, preferences between different kinds of codes, and ability to remember the codes shown in the first section.

Sections

- Welcome and basic respondent information
- Transcription: Nine codes of different length to transcribe into a prompt
- Choice: Nine pairs of codes varying from 9 to 22 characters in length and type (alphabetic, alphanumeric, and Consonant-Vowel-Consonant (CVC)) where the participant was asked to choose and transcribe the easiest.
- Memory: Participants were presented with seven codes and asked if they had seen this code earlier. They were also asked to give an estimate of the number of codes they had transcribed.
- Accept: Participants were asked to upload their answers and given the choice of adding their email to be kept informed.

Introduction and Basic Information. The welcome page presented the experiment as an opportunity to help research, and informed participants that they could leave at any time. It took care not to prime them with research goals. It asked their age, country, main language used, self-rating of their ability to remember passwords and strings of numbers/letters, as well as whether they were using a mobile device or a numeric keypad in the experiment. Optionally, participants could submit their email to receive the experiment results once published. Those emails were stored securely and separately from the data that was analysed. Participants were not asked their gender or other personal characteristics as they were not pertinent to the research.

Transcription. The codes were grouped by length (9, 12, and 15 characters), each group presenting three types of code trials in the following order: numeric, CVC, and alphanumeric. This gave a baseline error rate from which to replicate standard findings [12,16] such as the prevalence of the g/q/y error. It also gave rates for other types of errors, allowing the comparison of different code structures. Participants were not informed of errors they had committed and had a single try for each code.

Choice. Each trial included choosing to type in a 10 alphanumeric control code or a second code. The codes were grouped by character sets used – 3 using numeric, 3 CVCs, and finally 3 alphabetic. Trials were given in order of increasing length for each type.

Memory. Every question included a code participants had seen earlier, or a randomly generated code of the same type and length, with probability 0.5 for each. The types were numeric of length 9, and CVCs and alphanumeric of length 9, 12, and 15.

Randomisation. A between-subjects approach was used to observe priming and learning. Half the participants did the Choice section first, and the other half started with the Transcription. Half the participants also received the Transcription questions in reversed order.

For the Choice section, the order in which the two codes were presented was also randomised to avoid preference for the one on the left or right. The 9 codes in the Choice section were presented in order of increasing length. The pilot experiment seemed to indicate a tipping point close to 18, so we bracketed by testing codes of length going from 15 to 22. As this phase was already the most time-consuming for the participant, having one code for each length would have made the experiment too long. Hence, it was broken up in A/B testing giving participants two codes of length respectively 15 and 20, and one of random length between 16 and 22.

Times. Time taken was measured for each question, as well as the time spent reading the different sets of instructions. As the protocol was self-administered and self-paced, some people took breaks, ranging from a few minutes to five hours. Large delays on a single question were observed in around 15% of respondents. Taking breaks or getting distracted is part of life; long breaks alone did not disqualify all trials from analysis. Data for each question was independently evaluated and the abnormally short and abnormally long responses were removed (top and bottom 10%). Medians were consistently 5–10% under the trimmed averages and are not shown as they lead to the same conclusions.

Chunking. The Transcription section codes were split into "chunks" of 3, 4, or 5 characters followed by a space. In the Choice section, chunks of 3 were used. For lengths not divisible by 3, the last chunk had between 2 and 4 characters, and the 10-character alphanumeric codes avoided a 1-character last chunk by using a 4-character central chunk.

3.3   Demographics

The main experiment included 267 respondents, with some skipping a few questions[1]. Participants were solicited for the main experiment using three methods, creating three groups. The web links followed to get to the experiment identified which group a participant was in. The first group was international in scope, spread through Facebook and totalled 61 respondents.

The second was mostly French, using a translated form, and was composed in majority of software developers, as it was spread through a French computer engineering school's social network and Internet Relay Chat, with 91 respondents. Members of this group were highly tech-savvy compared to the other two groups (due to how they were recruited).

The third was overwhelmingly composed of people from the USA, with 115 respondents recruited through a website indexing psychological and social experiments often used by college students (http://psych.hanover.edu/research/exponnet.html).

All three groups included a wide range of ages, with the youngest being 19 years old for the pilot and 13 for the main experiment[2]. The eldest were respectively 70 and 73 years old, with most participants between 18 and 32.

People from 24 different countries and speaking 14 languages participated, including a few who were used to scripts written from right to left. English was the most frequent language indicated (129 people), with French second (114 people), and 34 participants indicating other main languages.

The goal in this recruitment method was to avoid having anomalies coming from a bias stemming from a single recruitment process. The results shown are only the ones that are consistent among all groups.

4   Main Experimental Data

4.1   Error Typology

The first section acted as a control to get a transcribing performance baseline, and allowed different patterns in transcribing behaviour to be observed. The following Fig. 2 shows the different error types observed in both sections – which differ as the text to transcribe varies. Underneath are the definitions for the error types.

- *Missing/added char*: a single character is either missing or was duplicated, which changes the length of the code.
- *Similarity*: confusion due to the similar shape of two characters, most commonly where one writes 0 instead of O, g instead of q or y (mostly present in the pilot), or confuses I with l and 1.

---

[1] This accounts for less than 3% of questions and is generally caused by a double-click on the "next" button, as timestamps show the participants spending a few hundred milliseconds on a page.

[2] The three participants who were younger than 16 all came through the psychological study website.

- *Transposition*: the order of two characters was reversed.
- *Adjacent key*: a key next to the target was hit, such as g instead of h. This mostly happens with horizontally adjacent keys.
- *Capitalisation*: an upper-case letter is written in lower-case, or vice-versa – this nearly only happens with alphanumeric codes.
- *Autocorrect*: despite our disabling of autocorrect via JavaScript, 2% of participants showed repeated revealing mistakes where whole words were changed.

4.2 Transcription Trial

Figure 3 shows the error rates for each code (structure/length) couple, for each group. Figure 4 shows the time taken (trimmed average) for those.

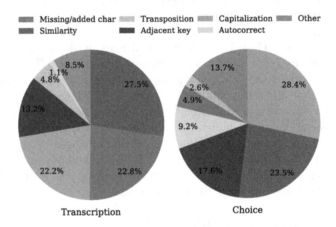

Fig. 2. Proportion of error types in each trial

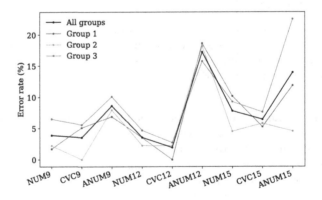

Fig. 3. Error rate, by code type and length

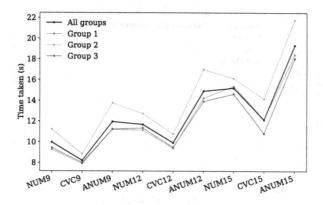

Fig. 4. Time taken to transcribe, by code type and length

4.3   Choice Trial

Figure 5 shows the proportion of people who chose to transcribe different code structures of varying lengths over a 10-character alphanumeric string.

Figure 6 shows the time taken for each structure by length, and the average time taken by the people who chose the 10-character alphanumeric.

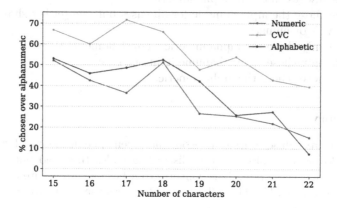

Fig. 5. Percentage of participants preferring alternative codes to 10-character alphanumeric ones, by code type and length

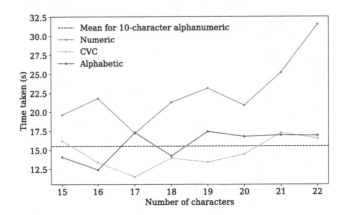

Fig. 6. Time taken by code length for each code type, Choice section

4.4 Strategies

Many people appeared to follow a strategy to choose which code to transcribe. Across 267 participants we identified 121 different patterns, of which here are the 5 most common ones (accounting for more than a third of participants):

- 31 people always chose the alphanumeric.
- 24 people chose the alphanumeric for all cases but one (either short or mid-length CVCs or numeric).
- 18 people only chose the alphanumeric against numeric codes.
- 12 people only chose the alphanumeric in one case.
- 11 people never chose the alphanumeric.

4.5 Memory

The ability to recognise codes that people had seen once in the past few minutes was 75%. People were also good at discarding codes they had not previously seen, with 87% success rate. This converts to a false negative rate of 25%, and false positive rate of 13%. The following table shows the error rate for each type of memory question:

NUM9	CVC9	CVC12	CVC15	ANUM9	ANUM12	ANUM15
22.5	28.8	8.6	14.4	29.2	12.0	16.7

The answer to the question asking them to estimate the number of codes they had written was relatively precise when we look at the trimmed average (18.7 for a true value of 18), but not with a simple average or a median (both at 20.0–20.1), because of a large variance, a strong tendency to write 20 (more than a quarter of participants) and the 8% of people who overestimated by a factor between 2 and 6.

5   Analysis

Here are the main effects observed:

- CVC codes were less error-prone than alphanumeric ones for all lengths ($p < 0.005$).
- Participants preferred CVCs of length at most 20 over 10-character alphanumeric codes, with rates varying between 72% and 48% in the worst case ($p < 10^{-4}$).
- 10-character alphanumeric codes were preferred to alphabetic and numeric codes of lengths greater than 19 ($p < 10^{-4}$). Only 7.4% chose the alphabetic code of length 22 over the alphanumeric alternative. They were preferred or equivalent for shorter lengths (with at most 53% choosing alphabetic codes over alphanumeric ones).
- For each length, CVCs were faster to type than numeric. Those were in turn faster to type than alphanumeric ($p < 0.05$ to $p < 10^{-4}$ depending on the couple). The speed increased by up to 59% for CVCs as opposed to alphanumeric.
- When presented with chunked codes (with spaces between groups of characters), 91% of participants wrote the spaces in the codes they typed.
- Chunked codes were faster to enter ($p < 0.015$) by an average of 8% (with a maximum of 14%).
- Chunking in three-character groups only statistically lowered the error rate for alphanumeric codes ($p = 0.033$).
- People were better at rejecting codes they hadn't seen than at confirming that they'd seen a specific code, ($p < 10^{-4}$, the false negative rate was more than twice the false positive rate).
- The typing speed and the error rate were not statistically correlated (both when considered by participant and by individual code).

Other significant effects presented themselves as well:

- There was no statistically significant difference on error rates between numeric and CVC codes.
- A great variability in typing speed was observed, with 20% of people typing above 1.34 characters per second, and 20% typing below 0.75 c/s (within the normal bounds for non-professional typists [19]). The top 5% entered codes more than three times faster than the bottom 5%.
- Recognition ability was correlated with self-rating in the memory section. Two cohesive clusters appeared, one around 28% error rate for people who rated their memory 1 or 2, and one between 16% and 18% for those who rated it higher ($p < 10^{-4}$).
- A learning effect was observed ($p < 10^{-4}$), with people reaching up to 18% higher speeds by the time they finished the transcription section. A/B testing compensated for this, making its effects negligible in other results.
- There was a recognition peak around length 12 for both CVCs and alphanumeric codes, strongly reducing both false positive and false negative rates ($p < 10^{-4}$).

6   Discussion

Pronounceable codes such as CVC are faster to type and more accurate than random alphanumeric ones. The crucial point is that the magnitude of the effect is such that it renders longer codes a viable alternative, even in contexts where security is the objective.

11 of the 31 errors present in the transcription phase of CVC were preventable by checking the length. An additional 4 could be automatically fixed by checking whether the letter typed was a vowel or a consonant. Among the 106 errors found in alphanumeric codes, only 7 were preventable in such ways. This motivated the development of CVC[6] below.

Chunking the codes in groups of 3 characters only reduced errors for alphanumeric codes (numeric codes seemed to benefit from chunking, although not enough for statistical significance). This might be explained from people's instinctive chunking of CVCs even without spaces. There was some confusion on whether to add the spaces between the chunks, but despite this and the added characters, the speed still improved overall for all codes.

Directly analysing error rates and speeds is difficult in the Choice section as they depended on the participants' strategies. Depending on the choice they faced, the average time taken by people who chose the alphanumeric code varied between 13.5 and 20.8 s. Presenting them with long numeric codes did slow them by up to 7 s, even for the people who ignored those long codes.

Memory was strongly influenced by length. The structure of the code did not visibly affect its memorability. Simple considerations of ability to discern two codes and memorability of long codes seem insufficient to explain a recognition peak at length 12 as they should differently affect false positive and false negative rates. When asked to estimate the number of questions, there was a tendency to answer with multiples of 5, in 76% of participants.

The three groups, with their different demographics and methods of recruitment, showed some variations in their performances. However, all the effects mentioned so far are observed not only in the general data, but also within each group, increasing their ecological validity as they do not depend on recruitment peculiarities. The most salient difference was that group 2 took more time but made fewer errors than the other groups. This could come from a variety of things such as their supposedly higher technical expertise (being mostly computer engineering students) or different keyboard layouts. The effect is also observed when we cluster by language (although the overlap is big between those two clustering methods).

7   CVC^6

The goal was to design a code that is easier and faster to enter, as well as more secure. CVC^6 codes are composed of 6 CVC trigrams, as in the following example:

$$cab \quad dij \quad kap \quad pod \quad myn \quad ret$$

7.1   Advantages

From a security standpoint (for use as passwords), CVC^6 has high entropy, with 1.03×10^{20} total possibilities, or 66.5 bits of entropy. This is following Kerckhoff's principle with the adversary knowing the format of the code used (against a blind brute-force, it would instead correspond to 2.95×10^{25} possibilities or 86 bits). Current standards for passwords are between 8 and 10-character alphanumeric codes, which are not necessarily randomly generated. Those have at most 48 and 59.5 bits of entropy, meaning that CVC^6 takes at least 100 times more effort to brute-force, assuming the adversary already knows which system is used.

Nearly two thirds (66%) of the study's participants perceived CVC^6 as easier than both equivalent alphanumeric and alphabetic codes.

Despite its length, CVC^6 is faster to type than other codes of similar or lower entropy. In the Choice section, CVC codes demonstrated average and median speeds higher by 10% to 80% compared to equivalent code structures. This is despite entropies being as low as 59.5 bits for alphanumeric and 50 bits for numeric (the trade-off meaning that a lower entropy generally implies a faster typing speed).

The error rate is already more than a third lower in CVCs than in comparable codes, but this can be improved even further. CVC^6 can get under 5% error by eliminating the following sources of error:

- Capitalisation errors, as the code isn't case-sensitive
- Symbol confusions, which would almost entirely disappear, leaving only v/w (which is very rare)
- Thanks to the alternating consonant and vowel pattern, character deletion and transposition would be immediately detectable by the system and visible to the user. This would also apply to 10% of near misses.

This can be additionally improved by handling error correction, shown below with the improved CVC^{6++} approach.

8   CVC^{6++}

Getting an error when typing in a code frustrates most users, and not being able to find its location even drives some to abandon whatever task was at hand.

One improvement of considerable value would then be for the system to detect an error and point it out, possibly indicating what the error was. This would eliminate mistakes CVC^6 is vulnerable to (mostly near misses and phonetically similar characters). It would have eliminated all of the 495 errors in this paper's experiments. Only double or triple errors wouldn't be corrected, and the three double errors observed in the transcribed CVC codes would have been detected correctly. Error detection, localisation, and/or correction would reduce user confusion and input time. A natural extension to CVC[6] achieves all of those.

8.1   Protocol

The extended error detection/correction protocol is shown on Fig. 7 and works as follows:

- To add correction without compromising on entropy, one last chunk "YZ" of two consonants after the last trigram is added to the code.
- To detect, localise, and correct the error:
  - Values from 0 to 18 are assigned to each consonant: b = 0, c = 1, d = 2 etc. Since consonants and vowels are not used in the same position, numbers can be reused by vowels: a = 0, e = 1, i = 2, o = 3, u = 4.
  - Y is computed by summing all the values modulo 19.
  - Z is computed by summing all the values, multiplied by their position in the code, modulo 19.

Suppose that there is an error concerning a single character in position $i \leq 18$ (i.e. the error is not on Y or Z). If the value of the entered Y differs from the sum computed from the input, the error is detected. $d \times i$ mod 19 is the difference between the computed Z and the Z' entered with an error. The difference d between the character entered and the correct one is also calculated. The combination of those two directly shows the unique possibility for a single-character error. This is where having a base 19 system is crucial, as only prime bases allow this (as the multiplication modulo 19 is bijective). In the case where the single error concerns Y or Z, the other one is correct, which cannot happen in normal cases, so the system knows that the error concerns either Y or Z (and can ignore it).

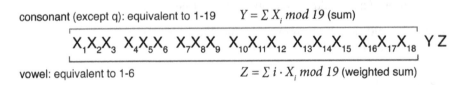

consonant (except q): equivalent to 1-19 $Y = \Sigma\, X_i \; mod\; 19$ (sum)

$$X_1X_2X_3 \; X_4X_5X_6 \; X_7X_8X_9 \; X_{10}X_{11}X_{12} \; X_{13}X_{14}X_{15} \; X_{16}X_{17}X_{18} \; Y\, Z$$

vowel: equivalent to 1-6 $Z = \Sigma\, i \cdot X_i \; mod\; 19$ (weighted sum)

Fig. 7. Error correction in CVC[6++]

8.2 Advantages and Limitations

The obvious advantage of CVC^{6++} is that it allows the system to automatically identify/correct the code and avoid wasting the time of a frustrated user. This automatic correction should not be used where correcting a double error into a different code would be strongly detrimental, such as voting. Instead, the system could indicate the location of the error to the user, to allow them to quickly check and correct it themselves.

The second advantage lies in its use in conjunction with cryptographic electronic voting, where one person can vote by proxy by giving a code to a trusted third party. This third party does not have access to the list of valid codes and would normally have no way to notice if something went wrong during the transmission of the code. As they have an obligation to make a selection, the only solution to an error would be a system that would allow them to quickly detect this error. A public website checking valid CVC^{6++} is available at www.koliaza. com/CVC.

The main limitation of CVC^{6++} is that it cannot work as naturally for CVCs longer than 6 trigrams, as multiple conflicting correction possibilities would appear. Probabilistic error correction could solve this, or an extension of the last two letters to a larger character-set.

Its length (for the same level of security) would also make it less popular than CVC^6, although a majority in our experiments would still prefer it to alphanumeric codes.

9 Conclusion

This paper explores how transcription of codes such as passwords can be affected by length, character sets, and structure. Results come from an experiment involving 267 subjects from 24 countries. The online experiments showed how large improvements to speed, transcription, and memorability can be made without compromising security for usable codes.

The value of generating passwords in general is discussed in the introduction but the original motivation behind this paper came from problems in electronic voting experiments which use automatically generated passwords. The results of this work are already helping in the ongoing voting technology experiments.

Discrete transcription trials showed that, as they are often found in words, codes based on CVC trigrams are preferred, faster, and less error-prone than alphanumeric, alphabetic, or numeric codes.

Most errors came from a few easily identifiable factors. Ambiguous shapes such as 0 and O, g, y and q, or l, i and 1 account for more than a quarter of errors. Along with wrong capitalisation, they explain why standard alphanumeric codes have much higher error rates than ones using simpler character sets. Moreover, when compared to language-like codes, they are much slower to enter, more than offsetting their increased security per character.

Although codes with simple syllabic patterns had better performance on all fronts, care has to be taken to prevent phonetic errors, and to avoid disadvantaging certain cultures in which some syllabic patterns are absent. This is especially important for codes used by diverse groups and in critical activities such as voting.

As a large majority of errors could be prevented by a simple pattern, a single length, and unambiguous characters, we propose a protocol, CVC^6, that is easier and faster to transcribe, with fewer mistakes and increased security. We also introduce CVC^{6++}, an extension that includes error detection/correction. Such codes could have wide-ranging applications, from voting technology to more accessible routers.

Finally, the memorability of codes was shown to depend strongly on pattern and length, albeit not in a trivial way. Subjects had a 75% chance of recognising a code they had seen 2 to 5 min earlier but correctly rejected a code they hadn't seen in 87% of cases.

We are hopeful that the increased reliability and usability of code-creation methods described here, together with new evaluation metrics for usable security [10], can help users create much more effective passwords and other codes, for improved security and usability.

9.1 Future Work

This study raises new questions on transcribing ability and code structure. Interesting follow-up experiments could be motivated by the following questions:

- Fonts have been shown to strongly impact reading ability [4]. What is the impact of font, spacing, and case on codes?
- Is there a cost associated with not typing spaces? Is the speed increase for chunking hampered by having to enter an extra space character? Why doesn't it increase transcribing ability? How would chunked input zones affect it?
- Other surface features also have important effects on memory and language learning [28]. How would the colour and texture coding of chunks affect transcribing ability?
- Different syllabic patterns, such as CCVC or CVCC, have higher entropy, but are less frequent and even absent in certain languages [2,6,23]. Could they constitute viable alternatives to CVC and would they be less language-dependent? Even further, could chunks made of real words be used, and would they be worth the entropy loss for English speakers?
- Some letters (like q or x) being less frequent in many languages, would transcribing ability increase with an even smaller alphabet? Could this compensate the entropy loss?
- The memory performance measured purposefully avoided tricky codes that were close to ones the subject had seen. What makes codes distinguishable? For goals of privacy, can easily transcribable but not memorable codes be formulated?

- The different error patterns shown are quite predictable, and could potentially be used for a CAPTCHA system where the error would be human. Could one game such a system?
- What is the impact of differences in typing ability among people who are used to a different alphabet (such as Ge'ez, Hiragana, or Cyrillic), non-alphabetic languages (Mandarin Chinese) or right-to-left writing systems?

This work also shows that new metrics might be needed to correctly analyse the benefits of code structure, depending on the application. Such metrics would need to include memorability, error probability and effect in case of error, typing speed, perceived ease, and cultural dependency.

The authors would like to thank Florentin Waligorski for his help with data analysis.

References

1. Acquisti, A., et al.: Nudges for privacy and security: understanding and assisting users choices online. ACM Comput. Surv. **50**(3), 1–41 (2017)
2. Adsett, C.R., Marchand, Y.: Syllabic complexity: a computational evaluation of nine European languages. J. Quant. Linguist. **17**(4), 269–290 (2010). https://doi.org/10.1080/09296174.2010.512161
3. Bellezza, F.S.: Mnemonic devices and memory schemas. In: McDaniel, M.A., Pressley, M. (eds.) Imagery and Related Mnemonic Processes, pp. 34–55. Springer, New York (1987). https://doi.org/10.1007/978-1-4612-4676-3_2
4. Bernard, M., Liao, C.H., Mills, M.: The effects of font type and size on the legibility and reading time of online text by older adults. In: CHI 2001 Extended Abstracts on Human Factors in Computing Systems, CHI EA 2001, pp. 175–176. ACM, New York (2001). http://doi.acm.org/10.1145/634067.634173
5. Blanchard, N.K.: Building trust for sample voting. International Journal of Decision Support System Technology (2018)
6. Borleffs, E., Maassen, B.A.M., Lyytinen, H., Zwarts, F.: Measuring orthographic transparency and morphological-syllabic complexity in alphabetic orthographies: a narrative review. Read. Writ. **30**(8), 1617–1638 (2017). https://doi.org/10.1007/s11145-017-9741-5
7. Brostoff, S., Sasse, M.A.: Are passfaces more usable than passwords? a field trial investigation. In: McDonald, S., Waern, Y., Cockton, G. (eds.) People and Computers XIV – Usability or Else!, pp. 405–424. Springer, London (2000). https://doi.org/10.1007/978-1-4471-0515-2_27
8. Burr, W.E., et al.: Electronic Authentication Guideline: Recommendations of the National Institute of Standards and Technology - Special Publication 800–63-1. CreateSpace Independent Publishing Platform, USA, U.S. Department of Commerce and National Institute of Standards and Technology (2012)
9. Cao, K., Jain, A.K.: Hacking mobile phones using 2D printed fingerprints. Technical report, Michigan State University (2016)
10. Cranor, L.F.: Time to rethink mandatory password changes (2016). https://www.ftc.gov/news-events/blogs/techftc/2016/03/time-rethink-mandatory-password-changes

11. Garfinkel, S., Lipford, H.R.: Usable Security: History, Themes, and Challenges. Synthesis Lectures on Information Security, Privacy, and Trust. Morgan & Claypool Publishers, San Rafael (2014). https://books.google.fr/books?id=HPS9BAAAQBAJ

12. Grissinger, M.: Avoiding confusion with alphanumeric characters. Pharm. Ther. **37**(12), 663–665 (2012)

13. Hausawi, Y.M., Allen, W.H.: An assessment framework for usable-security based on decision science. In: Tryfonas, T., Askoxylakis, I. (eds.) HAS 2014. LNCS, vol. 8533, pp. 33–44. Springer, Cham (2014). https://doi.org/10.1007/978-3-319-07620-1_4

14. Huh, J.H., Kim, H., Bobba, R.B., Bashir, M.N., Beznosov, K.: On the memorability of system-generated pins: Can chunking help? In: Eleventh Symposium On Usable Privacy and Security (SOUPS 2015), pp. 197–209. USENIX Association, Ottawa (2015)

15. Ives, B., Walsh, K.R., Schneider, H.: The domino effect of password reuse. Commun. ACM **47**(4), 75–78 (2004). https://doi.org/10.1145/975817.975820

16. Keren, G., Baggen, S.: Recognition models of alphanumeric characters. Percept. Psychophys. **29**(3), 234–246 (1981)

17. de Leeuw, K.M.M., Bergstra, J.: The History of Information Security: A Comprehensive Handbook. Elsevier Science, Amsterdam (2007). https://books.google.fr/books?id=pQBrsonDp6cC

18. McCabe, J.A.: Learning and memory strategy demonstrations for the psychology classroom (2014). http://goblues.org/faculty/professionaldevelopment/files/2012/01/McCabe-2014-Learning-Memory-Demos1.pdf

19. Norman, D.A., Fisher, D.: Why alphabetic keyboards are not easy to use: keyboard layout doesn't much matter. Hum. Factors **24**(5), 509–519 (1982). https://doi.org/10.1177/001872088202400502

20. Pilar, D.R., Jaeger, A., Gomes, C.F.A., Stein, L.M.: Passwords usage and human memory limitations: a survey across age and educational background. PLoS One **7**(12), (2012). http://www.ncbi.nlm.nih.gov/pmc/articles/PMC3515440/. pONE-D-12-21406[PII]

21. Reddy, P.V., Kumar, A., Rahman, S., Mundra, T.S.: A new antispoofing approach for biometric devices. IEEE Trans. Biomed. Circuits Syst. **2**(4), 328–37 (2008)

22. Ruiz-Albacete, V., Tome-Gonzalez, P., Alonso-Fernandez, F., Galbally, J., Fierrez, J., Ortega-Garcia, J.: Direct attacks using fake images in iris verification. In: Schouten, B., Juul, N.C., Drygajlo, A., Tistarelli, M. (eds.) BioID 2008. LNCS, vol. 5372, pp. 181–190. Springer, Heidelberg (2008). https://doi.org/10.1007/978-3-540-89991-4_19

23. Schiller, N.O.: Masked priming of sublexical units segments vs syllables. In: Steiner, F. (ed.) Advances in Phonetics : Proceedings of the International Phonetic Sciences Conference (IPS) (1999)

24. Shay, R., et al.: Correct horse battery staple: exploring the usability of system-assigned passphrases. In: Proceedings of the Eighth Symposium on Usable Privacy and Security, p. 7. ACM (2012)

25. Shay, R., et al.: Designing password policies for strength and usability. ACM Trans. Inf. Syst. Secur. **18**(4), 1–34 (2016). https://doi.org/10.1145/2891411

26. Shay, R., et al.: Encountering stronger password requirements: user attitudes and behaviors. In: Proceedings of the Sixth Symposium on Usable Privacy and Security, SOUPS 2010, pp. 1–20. ACM, New York (2010). http://doi.acm.org/10.1145/1837110.1837113

27. Smith, D.F., Wiliem, A., Lovell, B.C.: Face recognition on consumer devices: reflections on replay attacks. IEEE Trans. Inf. Forensics Secur. **10**, 736–745 (2015)

28. Stenton, A.: The contribution of the computer to improving L2 oral production. an examination of the applied and theoretical research behind the swans authoring programme. Etudes en Didactique des Langues (19) (2012)

29. Ur, B., et al.: Design and evaluation of a data-driven password meter. In: Proceedings of the 2017 CHI Conference on Human Factors in Computing Systems, CHI 2017, pp. 3775–3786. ACM, New York (2017)

30. Ur, B., Bees, J., Segreti, S.M., Bauer, L., Christin, N., Cranor, L.F.: Do users' perceptions of password security match reality? In: Proceedings of the 2016 CHI Conference on Human Factors in Computing Systems, CHI 2016, pp. 3748–3760. ACM, New York (2016)

31. Whitman, M.E., Mattord, H.J.: Principles of Information Security, 4th edn. Course Technology Press, Boston (2011)

32. Yan, J., Blackwell, A., Anderson, R., Grant, A.: Password memorability and security: empirical results. IEEE Secur. Priv. **2**(5), 25–31 (2004). https://doi.org/10.1109/MSP.2004.81

Two-Factor Authentication Using Leap Motion and Numeric Keypad

Tomoki Manabe[1(✉)] and Hayato Yamana[2,3(✉)]

[1] Graduate School of Fundamental Science and Engineering,
Waseda University, Shinjuku-ku, Tokyo, Japan
tomoki_manabe@yama.info.waseda.ac.jp
[2] Faculty of Science and Engineering,
Waseda University, Shinjuku-ku, Tokyo, Japan
yamana@yama.info.waseda.ac.jp
[3] National Institute of Informatics, Chiyoda-ku, Tokyo, Japan

Abstract. Biometric authentication has become popular in modern society. It takes less time and effort for users when compared to conventional password authentication. Furthermore, biometric authentication was considered more secure than password authentication because it was more difficult to steal biometric information when compared to passwords. However, given the development of high-spec cameras and image recognition technology, the risk of the theft of biometric information, such as fingerprints, is increasing. Additionally, biometric authentication exhibits lower and less stable accuracy than that of password authentication. To solve the aforementioned issues, we propose two-factor authentication combining password-input and biometric authentication of the hand. We adopt Leap Motion to measure physical and behavioral features related to hands. Subsequently, a random forest classifier determines whether the hand features belongs to a genuine user. Our authentication system architecture completes the biometric authentication by using a limited amount of data obtained within a few seconds when a user enters a password. The advantage of the proposed method is that it prevents intrusion by biometric authentication even if a password is stolen. Our experimental results for 21 testers exhibit 94.98% authentication accuracy in a limited duration, 2.52 s on an average while inputting a password.

Keywords: Hand-based authentication · Multi-factor authentication · Behavioral biometrics

1 Introduction

Recently, extant studies note the vulnerability of password authentication [1]. Although there is an increase in incidents caused by password leakage (such as SNS account hacking), biometric authentication systems are common as a new authentication method. A few biometric authentication methods are practically used, such as fingerprint authentication, iris authentication, and face authentication, which are implemented on smartphones. Biometric authentication involves less time and effort for users when compared with conventional password authentication. Furthermore, biometric

© Springer Nature Switzerland AG 2019
A. Moallem (Ed.): HCII 2019, LNCS 11594, pp. 38–51, 2019.
https://doi.org/10.1007/978-3-030-22351-9_3

authentication was considered more secure than password authentication because it was more difficult to steal biometric information when compared to passwords [2]. However, the risk of theft of biometric information is increasing with the development of high-spec cameras and image recognition technology. For example, smartphones that use fingerprint authentication are unlocked by a fake fingerprint created from fingerprints that remain on the touch screens [3]. In contrast to passwords, biometric information cannot be changed, and thus it is difficult to reuse biometric information as an authentication key once it is stolen. Another problem is that the authentication accuracy is lower and less stable than the password authentication because biometric authentication uses a device such as a camera or an infrared sensor. More specifically, even with the same authentication device, the authentication accuracy can be affected by sunlight or dirt on the device [4].

To solve the aforementioned problems, behavioral features are used for biometric authentication. Chan et al. [5] proposed a biometric authentication system that uses Leap Motion [6], and the method of [5] adopted the geometric structure and movement of a user's hand as physical and behavioral features. Experimental results for 16 testers indicated 99.97% classification accuracy. Although they achieved a low error rate, it took more than 25 s for the authentication. Other biometric authentication methods [7–10] using behavioral features of hand were also examined. They used motion for handwriting and signatures written in air. However, the studies exhibit less accuracy when compared to that of [5] and is approximately in the range of 86.57% to 98.82%.

The remaining problem is that extant studies [5, 7, 9] require a long time for authentication. To shorten the authentication time without decreasing accuracy, we propose a new method that enables authentication in a limited duration by simultaneously extracting both features, i.e., physical and behavioral features of hand. Our authentication system architecture completes biometric authentication by using a limited amount of data obtained within a few seconds when a user enters a password, i.e., two-factor authentication combining password-input and biometric authentication of hand. We adopt Leap Motion to measure physical and behavioral data of hands. Subsequently, random forest classifiers determine whether hand data belongs to a genuine user. The advantage of the proposed method is that it prevents intrusion via biometric authentication even if a password is stolen.

The structure of the study is as follows. In Sect. 2, we provide an overview of Leap Motion. In Sect. 3, we describe biometrics research that uses Leap Motion. In Sect. 4, we explain the outline of the proposed method. In Sect. 5, we discuss details of experiments, results of the system evaluation, and results. Finally, the study is summarized in Sect. 6.

2 Overview of Leap Motion

Leap Motion is an optical 3D sensor that tracks the geometric structure of hand and finger movements. In hand tracking, Leap Motion first irradiates infrared rays to an object as tracked. Subsequently, Leap Motion acquires the data related to the hand and fingers by measuring the reflection time of irradiated infrared rays. Leap Motion is normally placed vertically upwards in a horizontal place. Leap Motion can recognize both hands and ten fingers independently in units of 0.01 mm.

In this paper, we used Leap Motion to measure the length of hand bones, width of fingers, and velocity vectors of each finger based on the tip of a finger. In the study environment, Leap Motion is performed 60 times per second. Thus, Leap Motion can measure a user's hand data 60 times per second and save the measurement result. In the study, the time taken by Leap Motion to measure hand data once is expressed in units corresponding to "frame". Hence, a frame is 1/60 s in the study (Fig. 1).

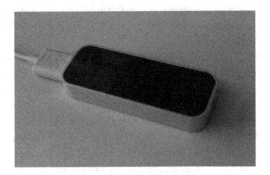

Fig. 1. Leap motion

3   Related Work

In the section, we describe related studies on biometric authentication using Leap Motion.

3.1   Biometric Authentication Using Gesture

Chan et al. [5] proposed a biometric authentication system using gestures for authentication at login of personal computer and on-line authentication in 2015. Their study consisted of two parts. The first part involved temporary authentication assuming scenes where users use Leap Motion for login authentication. The second part discussed online authentication. The on-line authentication assumes that the user browses web pages as a situation of practical use.

With respect to temporary authentication at login, a user initially holds his hands over the Leap Motion for 25 s. Subsequently, the system determines who the user is by analyzing physical features of his/her hands. When the user is determined as a genuine user, the user is requested to draw a circle with one finger to obtain behavioral features. The physical features consist of the width and length of the hands, arms, metacarpals, and phalanges of each finger. The behavioral features include the radius of the drawn circle, time taken for the gesture, and acceleration of finger movements. The results for the experiments with 16 testers indicate that the authentication accuracy (1 – Equal Error Rate) of static authentication using the random forest algorithm corresponds to 99.97%.

In online authentication, a user engages in an application run on a PC to control both cursors and seek bars via gestures. Both physical and behavioral features related to the hand are recorded to authenticate. The results of the experiments for 10 testers indicate that the value of authentication accuracy (1 - EER) corresponds to 98.39% in online authentication.

3.2 Biometric Authentication Using Handwriting in Air

Tian et al. [7] proposed a challenge-response authentication method using in-air handwriting in 2017. Their proposed method (hereafter, MoCRA) aims to deal with insider attacks by combining challenge-response authentication and biometric authentication. In its authentication phase, MoCRA asks a user to write a randomly chosen string in air to capture the movements of his/her hand via Leap Motion. Specifically, the random string corresponds to "challenge" in challenge-response authentication. After completing the writing part, MoCRA extracts the user's features as "response" in challenge-response authentication. By using the behavioral feature of users as a part of the "response," MoCRA can prevent imposter's attacks, while normal challenge-response authentication is unable to deal with attacks from an individual who knows the password. Experimental results for 24 testers indicate 98.82% authentication accuracy although a persistent issue is that it takes an average of 17.5 s to write the requested string.

In the same year (2017), Kamaishi et al. [8] proposed a biometric authentication system by adopting handwritten signatures. The biometric authentication combined a handwritten signature itself and features obtained from the hand when a user signs in air. The aim involved realizing changeable biometric authentication via adopting a handwritten password (i.e., signature) and biometric information. In the proposed method, the trait and speed of fingers measured by Leap Motion was used for authentication purposes. In [8], they performed experiments to track simple movements of a finger drawing (i.e., a straight line) as the initial stage of the proposed method. The results indicate that their system achieved 86.57% authentication accuracy.

Another example of handwritten signature biometrics system corresponded to the study by Xiao et al. (2016) [9]. They conducted experiments to examine the effect of user authentication using physical and behavioral features captured via Leap Motion. They initially constructed a system that authenticates based on biometric data of the user's hand structure and behavioral features when a user provided their signature in front of the sensor. The experimental data was collected from 10 testers, and the experimental results were evaluated via false rejection rate (FRR), false acceptance rate (FAR), and equal error rate (EER). Specifically, EER corresponds to the error rate when FRR and FAR are equal. The result of experiments indicated that they achieved an average EER of 34.80% by using physical features of the hand and an average EER of 3.75% by using behavioral data for handwriting. However, in the method, users can begin to provide their signature only when Leap Motion recognizes a maximum of two fingers because the method assumes that a user only extends their index finger or thumb. Hence, [9] may involve a long time period for authentication.

Additionally, Nigam et al. [10] proposed a system that is combined with handwritten signature and face authentication in 2014. By combining handwritten signature and face authentication, they intended to increase the accuracy of authentication compared to handwritten signature or face authentication only. In their experiments, they collected data from 60 testers and achieved a genuine acceptance rate (GAR) of 91.43%.

3.3 Summary of Related Work

Figure 2 shows the graph of the classification accuracy (1 - EER) values in previous studies [5, 7–10]. The result of EER was not described in the study by [10], and thus value of GAR of [10] was graphed as a reference.

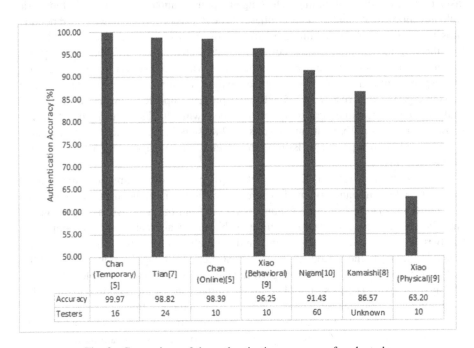

Fig. 2. Comparison of the authentication accuracy of each study

As shown in Fig. 2, Chan et al. [5] achieved the highest accuracy by adopting both the hand structure recognized by Leap Motion and the random forest classifier. The results indicated that the hand structure is indispensable for authentication and that the random forest classifier works well. However, the main three studies exhibit the disadvantage wherein the authentication is a time-consuming process.

4 Proposed Method

4.1 Overview of the Proposed Method

We propose two-factor authentication with Leap Motion and numeric keypad termed as *Hand and Password Combination Authentication* (hereafter, HPCA). Specifically, we assume the environments where a user inputs a numeric password into a system such as an ATM and door locker keypad. Figure 3 shows the flowchart of HPCA. In HPCA, Leap Motion simultaneously acquires hand geometry data and hand movement data. When the password is completely input, the system initially determines whether the password is correct or not. Subsequently, random forest classifier determines whether or not a user is an imposter based on the data obtained from Leap Motion.

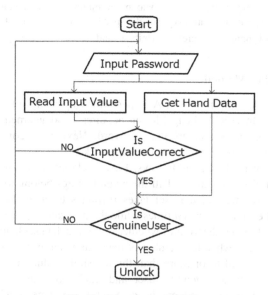

Fig. 3. Flowchart of HPCA

4.2 Purpose of HPCA

As a scene for the practical use of HPCA, we assume a situation such as unlocking doors or using an ATM. Although extant studies [5] realize high recognition accuracy of 99.97%, a potential issue is that authentication takes at least 25 s. Therefore, the aim involves shortening the time required for authentication and subsequently improving its practicality. Specifically, we aim to construct a system that can perform biometric authentication with a limited amount of data that is collected within a short time period while a user enters a password into a numeric keypad.

To enable authentication in a short time, we only adopt the features that are obtained during password input (such as within a few seconds) to authenticate. Table 1 shows the features used for our biometric authentication. While the password is input into a numeric keypad, it is essential to prevent the invasion of a third party. Therefore, we focus on reducing a false acceptance rate (FAR) among authentication errors. The errors in authentication include false rejection (FR) that falsely recognizes a genuine user as a third party and false acceptance (FA) that falsely recognizes a third party as a genuine user. Specifically, the objective involves decreasing the false acceptance rate (FAR) by allowing classifiers to learn the maximum possible number of other individuals' data.

Table 1. Features used for authentication (40 features)

Feature	Explanation
Length of phalanges and metacarpals (19 features)	Length (mm) of the distal phalanx, median phalanx, and basal bone of each finger Length of metacarpal bone other than thumb (mm)
Width of each finger (5 features)	Unit: mm
Maximum, minimum, and average value of each finger speed (15 features)	Maximum, minimum, and average value (mm/s) of the speed of the tip of each finger
Duration of password input (1 feature)	Unit: second

4.3 Authentication Method

In this section, we describe how HPCA is performed by using information obtained from Leap Motion. In HPCA, Leap Motion acquires hand geometry data and hand movement data when a user enters the password. Next, a random forest classifier determines whether the user has the right to open a key.

The classification method is as follows: First, a classifier is constructed for each genuine user. Each classifier outputs 1 iff the given features belong to the genuine user and 0 iff not. We assume that the user takes n frames to enter the password, Leap motion measures the same features n times while the user enters password. For each of the n data sets, the classifier determines whether or not the data set belongs to a genuine user. Subsequently, only when the number of data sets wherein the user is determined as a genuine user is equal to or more than the threshold value th, then the classifier concludes that the user is a genuine user and finally outputs 1. Specifically, the parameter th is determined based on the data set for parameter adjustment. While concluding that the user is not a genuine user, the classifier outputs 0.

4.4 Summary of the Proposed Method

In the section, we explain the outline and objective of HPCA. Our proposed method corresponds to two-factor authentication with Leap Motion and numeric keypad. We assume that unlocking a door or using an ATM corresponds to a scene where HPCA is practically used. The purpose of HPCA involves improving safety when compared to password authentication by itself by combining biometric authentication with password authentication. To achieve the purpose of the study, we consider a method to realize *short-term authentication* and *low FAR*. To shorten the authentication time, we adopt the data that is sufficiently obtained in a short time while entering password to authenticate. Additionally, to achieve low FAR, various individuals' data are used in learning as third party data to train the classifier.

5 Experimental Evaluation

5.1 Data Collection

Figure 4 shows the experimental environment to collect biometric data. In the experiment, 21 testers were asked to perform three trials of authentication procedure to input random four digit numbers displayed on the screen 25 times via a numeric keypad. Specifically, the random numbers are assumed as the password and they simulate a random key pad to eliminate any side-effects of input key positions. The three sets of procedures (i.e., three sets of inputs were considered 25 times wherein each asks a tester to input random four digit numbers) were prepared to examine the difference when testers possessed more experience related to inputting the password.

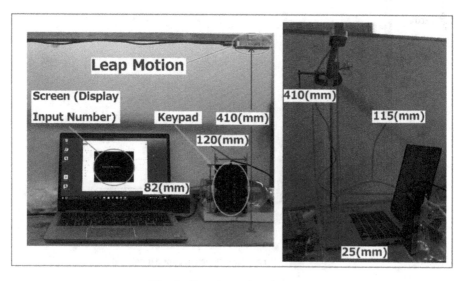

Fig. 4. Experimental environment

When the testers input passwords, the physical and behavioral data related to their hands were measured. The physical and behavioral data consist of 40 features as shown in Table 1. We constructed 21 random forest classifiers wherein each is trained to determine whether or not the given data belongs to a genuine user.

5.2 Verification of Measurement Error Range of Leap Motion

As a preliminary experiment, we examine the measurement error range of Leap Motion by using data collected from testers to confirm whether we can adopt the lengths of the phalanges and metacarpals as features. In the verification, we used input data obtained from 21 testers 525 times (i.e., 25 inputs per person). Specifically, each input data consists of 19 features because the total number of phalanges and metacarpals is 19 per hand. Furthermore, each input data consists of several frames because Leap Motion output data is observed 60 times per second. Thus, we term each observed data as a frame data.

With respect to each set of frame data when inputting a password, we calculate the difference between the maximum and minimum values of the lengths of the phalanges and metacarpals. Subsequently, we assume the difference as measurement error. Leap Motion recognizes hand in units of 0.01 mm based on its specification, and thus we separate the measurement error less than 0.01 mm and above. Figure 5 shows the result of the distribution of measurement errors. The verification results indicate that the ratio above an error of 0.01 mm is 15.09%.

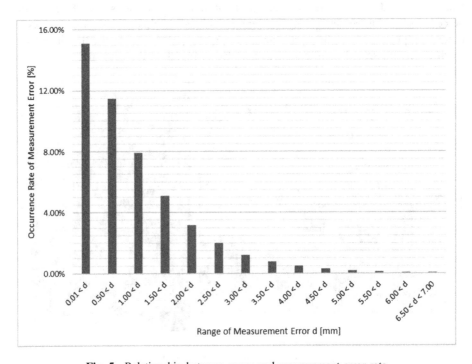

Fig. 5. Relationship between range and measurement error rate

Specifically, we reconsider whether the lengths of the phalanges and metacarpals as measured by Leap Motion during password input are useful as biometric authentication features. The results indicate that (1) the length of the phalanges and metacarpals of adults approximately corresponds to several tens of millimeters, (2) the rate at which the measurement error in the password input corresponds to 0.01 mm or less is 84.91%, (3) the maximum measurement error is less than 7 mm, and (4) the ratio of the measurement error of 1 mm or less is 92.09%. Hence, it is determined that the measurement results of Leap Motion with respect to the user's hand during password input can be adopted as the features of biometric authentication.

5.3   Evaluation of HPCA

With respect to the evaluation of HPCA, the classification accuracy of the classifiers is verified.

Evaluation Criteria. We calculate FRR, FAR, and error rate (ER) as evaluation indexes of the system. Specifically, nTrue, nFalse, nFR, and nFA are defined as follows:

nTrue: number of test data of genuine users
nFalse: number of test data of third parties
nFR: number of FRs that occur
nFA: number of FAs that occur

Subsequently, FRR, FAR, and ER are expressed as follows.

$$FRR = \frac{nFR}{nTrue} \tag{1}$$

$$FAR = \frac{nFA}{nFalse} \tag{2}$$

$$ER = \frac{nFR + nFA}{nTrue + nFalse} \tag{3}$$

In the study, classification accuracy is expressed as a percentage (%) of 1 - ER.

Features. We adopt 40 features as shown in Table 1. In the experiment, the cue to finish the password input is defined as pressing the enter key after inputting a random four-digit password. It also corresponds to the cue to display the next password on the display to ask a tester to input the next password. If it takes n frames (where 1 frame is 1/60 s) from the beginning to the end while inputting the password, then the number of frame data generated for a password input corresponds to n. Each frame data consists of both the length of the bones of the fingers and the width of each finger. Besides, the maximum, minimum, and average values of the speed of the finger movement and duration of password input are calculated after the password input is completed.

Training. We construct 21 random forest classifiers with m decision trees ($m = 1, 2, ..., 200$). Each classifier is trained by the training data set which consists of a genuine data and the other 19 users' data, each of which includes 20 password input data. Here, in each password input, we use the first five frames as training data to shorten the training phase. Here, we have confirmed the accuracy stays same even if we increase the number of flames. During the training, we exclude the remaining one user's data because it is used as other user's test data which is not included in the training data.

Test. We examine the accuracy of 21 random forest classifiers with m decision trees ($m = 1, 2, ..., 200$). Each classifier is evaluated by the test data set which consists of a genuine data and other user's data that were not used for training. Here, each user's data includes 5 password input data that exclude 20 password input data already used for training. In each password input, we use the first 70 flames, because the minimum value of time for testers to enter a 4-digit password was 1.22 s (>73 frames) in the experiment. Then, the accuracy was averaged by whole test.

Effectiveness of Each Feature. We examine the effectiveness of each feature used on classification. First, we exclude the i ($1 \leq i \leq 40$) th feature from the data set used in evaluation experiment. Subsequently, both training and test are performed in the same procedure as the evaluation experiment in the case of 40 features. Let A be the maximum value of the classification accuracy with 40 features and let A_i [%] be the classification accuracy in the case where the i-th feature is excluded. Specifically, the effectiveness of the i-th feature is defined as follows:

$$A - A_i[\%] \tag{4}$$

As shown in Eq. (4), it is considered that the feature with larger effectiveness more contributes to improving classification accuracy.

5.4   Experimental Result

In the section, we first discuss the evaluation results of the classification accuracy of HPCA with 40 features and without features having negative effectiveness value. Subsequently, we detail the evaluation results of effectiveness of each feature.

Classification Accuracy. Table 2 summarizes the classification accuracy with all features and without features with a negative effectiveness value. As shown in Table 2, FAR worsens although FRR and total accuracy improve if negative features are excluded.

Table 2. Classification accuracy

Experiments	All features (P)			w/o negative features (Q)			Diff. of
	Accuracy [%]	FAR [%]	FRR [%]	Accuracy [%]	FAR [%]	FRR [%]	Acc. Q-P [%]
First trial	90.19	1.78	17.84	90.37	5.4	13.87	0.18
Second trial	89.65	2.32	18.38	91.02	5.61	12.34	1.38
Third trial	93.98	1.49	10.54	94.98	1.93	8.11	1.00

Analysis of the Effectiveness of Each Feature. Figures 6 and 7 show the effectiveness of each feature. Generally, physical features are more effective than behavioral features. Specifically, behavioral features are effective when users get used to the password input, i.e., at the third trial, three out of 11 behavioral features contribute to increase the total accuracy.

5.5   Discussion

As mentioned in Sect. 4.2, the study focuses on preventing invasion of third parties. In the section, we consider practicality and safety of HPCA based on the experimental results.

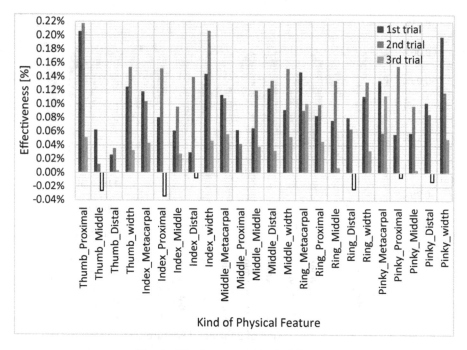

Fig. 6. Effectiveness of physical features

As shown in Table 2, FRR worsens (18.38%) when we use the dataset in the second trial with all features. However, the probability that false rejection occurs n consecutive times is represented as follows:

$$(0.1838)^n \tag{5}$$

Thus, the probability of being rejected twice consecutively corresponds to 3.38%, and the probability of being rejected three consecutive times corresponds to 0.62%. Thus, even when FRR is 18.38%, it is sufficiently possible to unlock by reentering the password several times.

Conversely, the optimal value of FAR corresponds to 1.49% and the worst value of FAR corresponds to 5.61%. If the probability that a third party is accepted by a one-time input is $p\%$, then the probability that a third party is rejected n consecutive times when the third party inputs the correct password n times is as follows:

$$(1 - p)^n \tag{6}$$

Figure 8 shows the relationship between the number of inputs and the rejection rate of others.

As shown in Fig. 8, when a third party enters the correct password 50 times, the probability of breaking through the key is 52.79% in the case of the optimal FAR and 94.42% in the case of the worst FAR. However, in the case of the optimal FAR, the

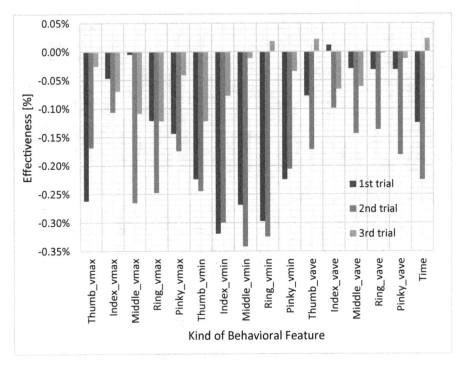

Fig. 7. Effectiveness of behavioral features

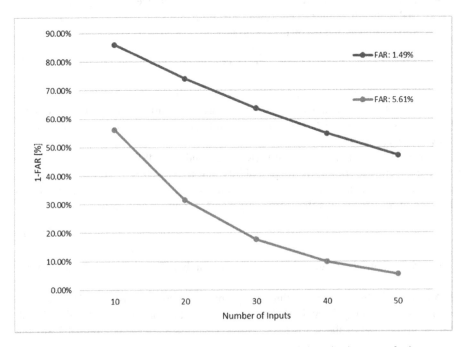

Fig. 8. Relationship between the number of inputs and the rejection rate of others

probability of preventing a third party from breaking through the key from 10 to 50 times is superior to that in the case of the worst FAR by 41.01% on an average.

6 Conclusion

In the study, we first described a previous study on biometric authentication using Leap Motion. In the case of biometric authentication using Leap Motion, previous studies realized recognition accuracy exceeding 99%, and this shows that Leap Motion can be used for biometric authentication. However, increases in the accuracy required increase in the time necessary to perform authentication.

The aim of the study is to perform biometric authentication using limited data obtained from Leap Motion while entering the password. In the experiment, we confirmed whether authentication can be performed with data obtained in a short time. Thus, the results indicated that our proposed method can perform biometric authentication with an accuracy of 94.98% by using the data obtained within the limited time while entering the password.

A future study will further investigate biometric authentication using Leap Motion and improve the authentication method so that it is more useful.

References

1. Masuno, R.: Passwords and cognitive psychology. IPSJ CSCE **49**(5), 1–6 (2010)
2. Biometric market to grow 21% by 2014 – SecureIDNews. https://www.secureidnews.com/news-item/biometric-market-to-grow-21-by-2014/. Accessed 30 Dec 2018
3. Chaos Computer Club breaks Apple TouchID – Chaos Computer Club. http://www.ccc.de/en/updates/2013/ccc-breaks-apple-touchid. Accessed 2 Jan 2018
4. Kawahara, H., Kouno, A., Nakamoto, A., Endo, J., Yasuhiro, M.: High speed/high accuracy face recognition sensor corresponding to ambient light. In: Technical Report of Panasonic Electric Works, vol. 57 (2), pp. 10–15. (2009)
5. Chan, A., Halevi, T., Memon, N.: Leap motion controller for authentication via hand geometry and gestures. In: Tryfonas, T., Askoxylakis, I. (eds.) HAS 2015. LNCS, vol. 9190, pp. 13–22. Springer, Cham (2015). https://doi.org/10.1007/978-3-319-20376-8_2
6. Leap Motion – LEAP MOTION, Inc. https://www.leapmotion.com/. Accessed 2 Jan 2018
7. Tian, J., Cao, U., Xu, W., Wang, S.: Challenge-response authentication using in-air-handwriting style verification. IEEE Trans. Dependable Secure Comput. (2017) https://doi.org/10.1109/tdsc.2017.2752164
8. Kamaishi, S., Uda, R.: Biometric authentication by handwriting with single direction using self-organizing maps. In: Proceedings of the 11th International Conference on Ubiquitous Information Management and Communication, Article No. 106 (2017)
9. Xiao, G., Milanova, M., Xie, M.: Secure behavioral biometric authentication with Leap Motion. In: Proceedings of IEEE 4th ISDFS 2016, Article No. 7473528 (2016)
10. Nigam, I., Vatsa, M., Singh, R.: Leap signature recognition using HOOF and HOT features. In: Proceedings of 2014 IEEE International Conference on Image Processing, pp. 5012–5016 (2014)

Identity Verification Using Face Recognition for Artificial-Intelligence Electronic Forms with Speech Interaction

Akitoshi Okumura[✉], Shuji Komeiji, Motohiko Sakaguchi,
Masahiro Tabuchi, and Hiroaki Hattori

NEC Solution Innovators, Ltd., Kawasaki, Japan
a-okumura@bx.jp.nec.com

Abstract. Concern over the decline in Japan's manufacturing competitiveness has increased in recent years. In particular, falsification of inspection data is a social problem that could undermine Japan's manufacturing industry, which is founded on a dedication to high quality. Falsification could be prevented by ensuring transparency of the inspection process by visualizing the process. End-to-end visualization facilitates early detection and prevention of various law infractions. In the workplace, visualization requires an efficient low-cost identity-verification method that ensures ease of visual confirmability for product traceability. We previously developed AI-forms, i.e., artificial-intelligence electronic forms, that provides a speech interface as a means of improving the standard work process in workplaces by making operations more efficient and visualizing processes. AI-forms improves production efficiency and visualizes the collected operation records by enhancing the readability and writability of records and handover operations that are not sufficiently supported by traditional electronic forms. To prevent falsification of inspections, it is necessary to use a widely deployed device and verification method in the workplace. We propose an identity-verification method for applying face recognition to AI-forms and developed a smartphone app for AI-forms. Preliminary feasibility testing involving 11 workers in an actual workplace confirmed that identity verification is possible when face recognition is carried out with frontal images of workers who are not wearing face masks. The face-recognition process completed within 0.4 s, enabling workers to seamlessly begin work with AI-forms. Recording both collation photos and worker names during identity verification also made it possible for a human to visually confirm a worker's identity. Discussion with workers and supervisors after the feasibility tests provided findings for improving our face-recognition app for closer integration of AI-forms and our identity-verification method at arbitrary times.

Keywords: AI forms · Data inspection · Face recognition · Biometrics · Identity verification · Falsifying inspection data

A. Moallem (Ed.): HCII 2019, LNCS 11594, pp. 52–66, 2019.
https://doi.org/10.1007/978-3-030-22351-9_4

1 Introduction

Concern over the decline in Japan's manufacturing competitiveness has increased in recent years. In particular, falsification of inspection data is a social problem that could undermine Japan's manufacturing industry, which is founded on a dedication to high quality [1]. Product quality ensures safety and customer satisfaction with products and services, so a decline in quality reduces trust in producers and distributors, causing great economic loss. As the complexity of products and services and awareness of personal safety increase, the importance of inspection also increases. Inspection is an essential process in the certification of product quality and prevention of quality decline, so the data obtained from inspection must be appropriate and accurate. The four types of inspection dishonesty are listed below [2]:

(1) The specified inspection is not carried out or some of the required inspection items are omitted.
(2) The inspection results are changed or fabricated.
(3) The inspection conditions are changed to produce a passing result.
(4) The inspection is repeated until a passing result is obtained.

To prevent such fraudulent inspection practices, transparency in the inspection process is necessary, that is, the process must be "made visible". Thorough "visualization" facilitates the early detection and prevention of various dishonest practices and may provide a solution that is highly effective in preventing such practices. We previously developed AI-forms, i.e., artificial-intelligence electronic forms, that interacts through speech as a solution for improving the standard work process in workplaces [3]. AI-forms is intended to increase efficiency and visibility in the inspection process and has brought about improvement at production-site workplaces with Internet of Things management systems. AI-forms improves both productivity (efficiency) and collection of operation records (visibility) by using speech interaction to achieve "ease of reading and writing", "ease of operations such as work handover", etc., which are often problems with conventional electronic forms. AI-forms improves the efficiency of the procedures for checking task descriptions and inputting task results based on the concept of a natural user interface (NUI). An NUI enables a person to operate a machine using his/her senses and perform actions naturally [4]. The NUI of AI-forms increases productivity by enabling hands- and eyes-free operation through speaking and listening via a light-weight intercom device that can be used for long periods without fatigue. The results of an evaluation conducted in a telecom equipment factory over a period of about two years verified a 2/3 reduction in training cost, 20% increase in productivity, and shortening of the worker skill-improvement cycle by a factor of about 40 [3]. For "visibility", the effectiveness of AI-forms in enabling real-time collective management of inspection results was also demonstrated. For example, the starting and ending times of the task results input by speech are automatically appended to the inspection data as "when" data. This makes it possible to visualize the variance in task time that is latent in the standard work procedures and enables rapid understanding of what should be improved to increase efficiency. To further improve efficiency and reduce dishonesty, we previously proposed an identity-verification method that uses a hearable device (terminal that integrates earphones and a microphone) for AI-forms to enable natural acquisition of "by who" information [5]. Using the hearable device as an inter-com makes it possible to verify personal identity with an ear-authentication technique, which measures the unique acoustic characteristics of a person's ear canal when sound from the headphone is reflected and picked up by the microphone. This technique makes it possible to capture "by who" information in addition to "when" information, which enables visualization of the work time for each worker and provides a means of increasing efficiency. It also prevents impersonation and provides a measure against inspection being carried out by unqualified workers, which has recently become a problem [5]. Clarifying the responsibility for inspection data makes it possible to prevent failure in performing inspection or omission of inspection items due to dishonesty. Although the hearable device is an excellent NUI, the technology is at the prototype stage and is not yet widely available on the market. Because the prevention of dishonest inspection is an urgent issue that requires immediate response in the workplace, it is necessary to use other devices and means that are widely available. Sound reflected within the ear canal can be recorded and saved for use in validating the ear-authentication results. For use in confirming inspection results and traceability, the recorded data should be easy to check by humans. To meet these requirements, we propose an identity-verification method with face recognition to be used with AI-forms. The face-recognition function of our method can be implemented with the camera of a smartphone. AI-forms can also be implemented with a smartphone. Because the image of a worker's face can be recorded for confirmation, the authentication result can easily be visually checked by a human, providing excellent confirmability for product traceability.

The proposed method involves integrating face recognition into a worker's workflow, i.e., introducing a security mechanism to human computer interaction. Though our method should be compared with a conventional method that does not include face recognition, the testing methodology and conditions are not self-evident. Therefore, we plan to evaluate the proposed method with the following testing steps: (1) feasibility tests for identity verification of workers, (2) large-scale tests for identity verification of workers, and (3) large-scale tests for comparing our method with a conventional method.

The remainder of the paper is as follows. In Sect. 2, we introduce current identity-verification methods that include face recognition. In Sect. 3, we present our proposed identity-verification method for applying face recognition to AI-forms after describing issues concerning identity verification in the workplace, objectives of identity verification through face recognition, and an outline of our smartphone app that integrates our identity-verification method with AI-forms. We also explain the three testing steps of our evaluation plan. In Sect. 4, we report on the results of conducting preliminary feasibility tests for the first step of our evaluation plan regarding the face-recognition accuracy of 99 photos taken under various conditions. In Sect. 5, we discuss the feasibility and problems with our proposed method. In Sect. 6, we consider future issues. We conclude the paper in Sect. 6.

2 Related Work

Legally verifying a person's identity requires verifying two points: that "the person actually exists (reality)" and "the person is who he/she claims to be (identity)" [6]. In Japan, the foundation of reality is the family registry. There are limited situations in which "reality" needs to be strictly confirmed, but there are many situations in which "identity" needs to be verified. This personal-authentication confirmation is called "identity" and is often used in the same sense as verification. Current personal authentication can be done using three methods: (1) knowledge certification using information only the person in question knows, such as a password or personal identification number, (2) possession of certification, i.e., such as an ID card or driver's license, and (3) biometric authentication by confirming a person's fingerprints, face, etc. Although knowledge certification and possession of certification are widely used, such as at ATMs and in e-commerce, identity can be transferrable with both methods when the knowledge and certification are lent out or stolen. Therefore, neither can be effective in preventing individuals from impersonating others. Many anticipate that biometric authentication can be a means of solving these problems [7, 8]. One advantage of biometric authentication is that there is no risk of biological information being lost or forgotten. Also, biometric authentication can be considered a means to prevent individuals from impersonating others because it involves using person-specific biological information. Biometric authentication verifies identity by matching preregistered biometric information and collation information obtained through a sensor. For example, both vein authentication used in financial institutions [9] and fingerprint authentication used in national and local governments [10] require dedicated biometric-information sensors. For identity verification in the workplace, it is necessary for workers to register biometric information and be able to verify it at various locations, indoors and outdoors. It is therefore desirable to use a sensor that is as highly portable and widely available as possible. Additional requirements are ease of confirmation in the workplace and traceability for stored recorded data. Face recognition can be accomplished using the camera of a smartphone or other such devices that can be easily handled by workers. Practicality of operation [11] and verification testing [12] regarding accuracy have been reported, and many face-recognition software and application programs have been developed [13].

We previously developed a system of verifying the identity of ticket holders at large-scale events using face recognition, which is called the Ticket ID System [17]. Its effectiveness was demonstrated at over 100 concerts [18]. The face-recognition software that the Ticket ID System uses is the high-speed and high-precision commercial product NeoFace [15]. NeoFace exhibited the highest performance evaluation in the Face Recognition Vendor Test 2014 conducted by the U.S. National Institute of Standards and Technology (NIST) [14]. NeoFace achieved the lowest false reject rate (FRR) of 0.3% in processing the passport/visa photo image database at a false accept rate (FAR) of 0.1% for the NIST personal identity searches [16]. The face-recognition process is outlined in Fig. 1. In this process, registration photos are compared with collation photos to determine whether they show the same person [16]. The Ticket ID System compares registered photos of applicants with collation photos of individuals entering the event venue. First, face detection is executed by detecting and processing the facial areas for each photo. Next the facial-feature points of the detected areas, e.g., the eyes, nose, and mouth edges, are processed to carry out facial-point detection. Finally, the obtained facial-point positions are used to normalize the size and positions of the facial areas and measure their similarity between a registered and collation photo during the collation process. When the similarity measure exceeds a certain threshold, the face recognition is regarded as successful. When NeoFace is implemented in a commercially available tablet terminal, the recognition result is displayed with regard to the facial-photo information of 100,000 people within about 0.5 s [17]. We developed a prototype system that uses attendees' selfies as input photos for face recognition, which succeeded in simplifying ID equipment by only requiring smartphone cameras [19]. Face recognition is also expected to be effective for identity verification in the workplace.

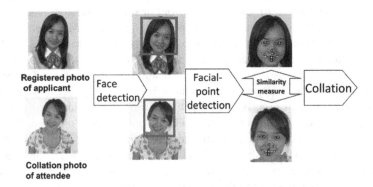

Fig. 1. Outline of face-recognition process

3   Methods

3.1   Verification of Worker's Identity in Workplaces

Figure 2 shows a conventional verification method of worker's identity and operation-record visualization that are used in the workplace. Initial identity verification is personal identification conducted by a supervisor or other responsible individuals by visually checking a worker's photograph on a certificate of qualification or ID card. On-demand identity verification is the same type of personal identification conducted when workers are working. The verification is required during shift changes. After the verification, workers input their names to AI-forms by tapping their names on the panel, as shown in Fig. 3. The verification should be carefully conducted because a worker may erroneously tap the name of another person.

Operation-record visualization is provided with AI-forms, which makes it possible for a supervisor or productivity analyst to verify operation-records, such as product IDs, working process and time, and workers' names, for checking the productivity of workers and confirmability for product traceability [3]. AI-forms provides a speech

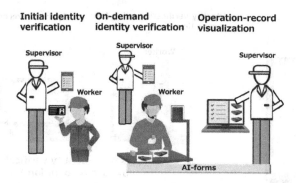

Fig. 2. Conventional verification method of worker's identity and operation-record visualization with AI-form

interface as a means of improving the standard work process in workplaces by making operations more efficient and visualizing processes. AI-forms improves production efficiency and visualizes the collected operation records by enhancing the readability and writability of records and handover operations that are not sufficiently supported by traditional electronic forms.

The initial and on-demand verification method is effective against impersonation and work being done by an unqualified person, but it is not efficient because of the time needed to confirm each person. In workplaces where many workers cooperate in performing a task, work efficiency declines when the time required for worker identification is long. If more people are assigned to carry out worker identification, cost becomes a problem. An identity-verification method that effectively and efficiently prevents impersonation while suppressing cost is needed. The use of an ID card reader or a device for inputting at identification number can be considered an efficient identity-verification method to prevent work being started unless a person has been identified as qualified. As noted in Sect. 2, however, identification by certification of knowledge or possession may not effectively prevent impersonation because either can be passed on to other people. Other identity-verification methods that are highly effective in preventing impersonation are required. Biometric authentication is effective against impersonation, but the cost of registering authentication data and installing special sensors and devices at all work sites are implementation problems. Biometric authentication using fingerprints, iris patterns, blood vessel patterns, etc. requires special sensors, and the registered data and comparison data cannot be easily confirmed by humans, so ease of confirmation is another problem. As mentioned above, we previously developed an identity-verification method that uses a hearable device to enable ear authentication [5]. However, this method has problems concerning currently low adoption rate as a device and ease of confirming ear authentication, so its introduction to the workplace will have to wait. As also noted above, the main issue for identity verification in the workplace is to efficiently and effectively prevent impersonation at low cost and in a way that can be easily confirmed by humans.

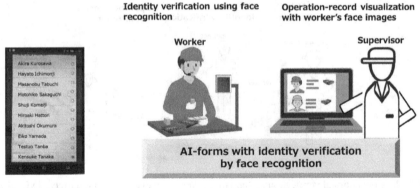

Fig. 3. Worker name selection for AI forms

Fig. 4. Proposed identity-verification method of workers identity and operation-record visualization

3.2 Identity Verification by Face Recognition

To improve verification of worker identity and operation-record visualization in workplaces, we propose an identity-verification method that includes face recognition to be used with AI-forms, as shown in Fig. 4. Face recognition is used for initial and on-demand identity verification of workers instead of a supervisor or other responsible individuals, which is integrated with AI-forms [3]. AI-forms stores workers' facial images for operation-record visualization and confirmability for product traceability.

Specifically, we aim at achieving the functions listed below using NeoFace for selecting worker names in AI-forms.

(1) Efficient identity verification

   With NeoFace running on a smartphone, face recognition processing can be completed within 0.4 s [17]. Replacing the worker selection of a name with face recognition enables efficient identity verification while maintaining the functionality of AI-forms.

(2) Effective prevention of impersonation

   Face recognition is effective protection against impersonation because lending, transferring, or misplacing is extremely unlikely. NeoFace provides highly accurate recognition and has a long track record of practical use [15, 16]; thus, it is a highly effective means of preventing impersonation.

(3) Low cost and ease of visual confirmation

   Face recognition is carried out using a photo of a worker's face taken with a smartphone camera as a collation photo by using a smartphone app. Because AI-forms is also implemented as a smartphone app, it is not necessary to introduce new equipment at the worksite, so this function can be implemented at low cost. Traceability is also excellent because facial images can be confirmed visually. Even if a worker falsifies a name, the facial image can be checked against the registered photo, so a high deterrence can be expected. The workplace identity-verification methods described in the previous section are compared in Table 1.

Table 1. Comparison of identity-verification methods

	Deterrent effect	Verification efficiency	Visual confirmability	Cost
Visual check by supervisors	High	Low	Low	High
Authentication with knowledge or possession	Low	High	Low	High
Authentication with fingerprint, iris, veins, or ear	High	High	Low	High
Face recognition	High	High	High	Low

3.3 AI-Forms

The concept of AI-forms is illustrated in Fig. 5 [3]. AI-forms is an interactive application composed of an AI-form class, virtual tray, and speech-interaction controller. The worker starts AI-forms in the workplace, as shown in Fig. 6, selects a name on the screen, as shown in Fig. 3, and creates or modifies the form. The AI-form class is an object definition that implements the reading and writing of form data by speech interaction with the worker, controls the workflow, including work handover, pausing, and restarting of work, and measures the duration of each work procedure according to a standard task definition. The AI-form class stores the form data and work status in internal states and has functions for dialog-scenario control and time measurement. An AI-form instance corresponds to the execution state of a standard task, which is to say a single form. The user creates an AI-form class by registering a work procedure and dialog scenario described in the specified Excel® format in the system. The virtual tray provides the user with a visualization of the AI-form class, AI-form instance of the uncompleted task, and AI-form instance of the completed task. By visualizing the task status, the virtual tray displays a list of the names of the registered forms (classes) of the AI-form class and displays the uncompleted and completed task trays. By managing the AI-form instance, the virtual tray also manages a "current tray" for each AI-form instance and changes the "current tray" to the uncompleted task tray if the task is interrupted or to the completed task tray if the task is completed. If an AI-form instance in the uncompleted task tray is specified by speech interaction or a touch operation when restarting a task, the task status is changed to in-progress and the task is restarted. Also, AI-form instance management involves managing combinations of AI-form instances and workers or items (product components), so the handing of a task over to other workers or order-memos attached to such items is implemented by a combination-change operation. The speech-interaction controller implements task-flow control by speech interaction such as the creation of AI-form instances, reading and writing of form data for AI-form instances that have been saved, and task handover, pausing, and restarting. In speech-interaction control, the user creates an AI-form instance by speaking an AI-form class name and sets the AI-form instance to the execution state. In the execution state, the AI-form instance controls speech synthesis for reading of the task procedure, automatically records the task results by speech recognition, repeats the recognition result, and measures the working time based on the AI-form class definition.

The workflow can also be controlled by speaking control words such as 'pause' and 'restart', and an AI-form instance can be placed in or removed from a virtual tray.

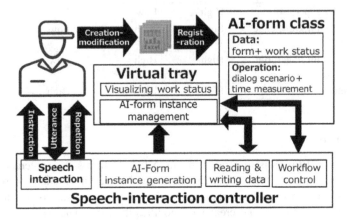

Fig. 5. Conceptual model of artificial-intelligence electronic forms (AI-forms) with speech interaction

Fig. 6. Workers using AI-forms at manufacturing workplace

3.4   Identity Verification by Face Recognition in AI-Forms

Our proposed identity-verification method works together with AI-forms through the installation of the NeoFace face recognition software on a smartphone on which AI-forms is installed. As described in Sect. 3.3, AI-forms enables form-data reading and writing by speech interaction with a worker as well as task-flow control such as work handover, task interruption, and task restarting, and total time accounting for each work procedure. Identity verification is carried out at the time of work handover and task restarting as well as just at the beginning of the task. The process of identity verification is shown in Fig. 7. A worker opens the identity-verification app, which takes a photo of his or her face and collates the photo with the registered photo. The acquired image of the worker's face is recorded in AI-forms regardless of the recognition results. The identity-verification screen is shown on the left of Fig. 8. If the identification is successful, the screen shown on the right of Fig. 8 is displayed. The worker is then authenticated as being qualified for the task and begins the task using AI-forms.

The name of the authenticated worker is recorded in AI-forms. If the identification fails, the worker can select his/her name from the conventional list of workers. The name of the worker that is selected is also recorded. The worker's name can be visually checked with his/her facial photos by a supervisor, as shown in Fig. 4.

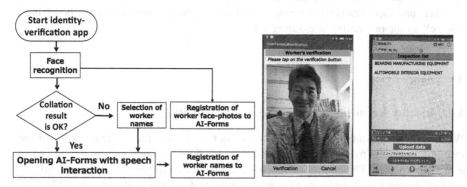

Fig. 7. Flowchart of verification process

Fig. 8. Screenshots of face recognition (left) and AI-forms (right)

3.5 Evaluation Plan

The proposed method should be evaluated through comparison with a conventional method that does not include face recognition from the view-points of identity verification and visual confirmability. The main issue for identity verification in the workplace is to efficiently and effectively prevent impersonation at low cost and in a way that can be easily confirmed by humans. The following testing steps are planned for such an evaluation:

Step 1: Feasibility tests for identity verification of workers
There are no findings on applying recognition technology for identity-verification of workers in actual workplace environments. First, it is necessary to clarify parameters of face recognition for this purpose through feasibility tests before applying the proposed method for large-scale tests. It is also necessary to examine what type of facial photos can be acquired for face recognition in certain environments. Feasibility check for visual confirmability, i.e., whether a supervisor or other responsible individuals can recognize workers' faces with their facial photos is required for product traceability.

Step 2: Large-scale tests for identity verification of workers
NeoFace achieved the lowest FRR of 0.3% in processing the passport/visa photo image database at a FAR of 0.1% for the NIST personal identity searches [16]. However, FRR and FAR should be evaluated in workplace environments because they are completely different from those of NIST searches. It is also necessary to evaluate the total time necessary for worker verification because supervisors should visually check workers' names and their facial photos when the workers selected their names for themselves.

Step 3: Large-scale tests for comparing our method with a conventional method
The proposed method should be compared with a conventional verification method regarding workers identity and operation-record visualization with AI-forms, as shown in Fig. 2. Specifically, we measure productivity change in the same way as conducted in a telecom equipment factory [3]. We will investigate the burdens on workers and supervisors where security and service quality assurance must be ensured as well as for preventing fraudulent acts.

4   Tests

4.1   Identity Verification and Visual Confirmability

We are currently conducting the first step of our evaluation plan. The accuracy of the recognition results must be verified before the proposed method can be introduced to actual workplaces. The control parameters for identity verification include internal and external parameters related to face recognition and operating parameters [17]. The internal parameters are physical properties of the face and are independent of the observer. Examples include caps, facial expressions, hair, eyeglasses, and makeup. The external parameters relate to how the face is seen and the situation, including face direction, lighting, background, and image resolution. The operating parameters relate to the operations performed for face recognition in the workplace. Examples include whether the camera is installed in a fixed location, whether the worker performs the operation manually, whether the worker is stationary or moving, and how many times face recognition is carried out.

Our method will be used at a factory workplace where AI-forms has been introduced. Workers may be required to wear caps, glasses, or face masks in the workplace, so whether such items are being worn is considered an internal parameter. External parameters, such as those related to changes in illumination and background, may have practical importance [19]. If the level of illumination is low, face detection may not be possible, and the faces of other workers that appear in the background may be detected [19]. Because the workplace that we considered for this study is indoors, the lighting is fully adequate for face recognition. Although there are various types of equipment and facilities at the site, a workspace for each worker is ensured, so the possibility of other workers' faces appearing in the recognition image is low. Therefore, deviation in a worker's face direction to the left or right or up or down from looking straight at the camera is considered an external parameter. Concerning the operating parameters, the worker remains stationary facing a smartphone camera, and the face-recognition process is carried out once. Facial images acquired for face recognition are confirmed whether they are useful for a supervisor or other responsible individuals who visually check workers' photos and names.

4.2   Test Method

Preliminary testing was conducted with the proposed identity-verification method integrated with AI-forms at the NEC Platforms Fukushima Plant. In this workplace, tasks are performed by up to ten qualified workers. For testing, facial images were registered for 11 workers as qualified workers and the method was evaluated for accurate recognition of those workers. The workers first confirmed that the images of their faces appeared on the screen of a smartphone placed within their reach beside their work tables. The workers then tapped a button on the screen to photograph their faces, and face recognition was carried out.

First, 44 facial images were acquired by photographing 11 workers under four conditions: bare face (wearing no cap, glasses, or face mask), wearing a cap, wearing glasses, and wearing a face mask. Workers may be required to wear both a cap and glasses in the workplace, so an additional 11 images in which the 11 workers were wearing both cap and glasses were acquired, making a total of 55 images for the recognition testing. In some workplaces, it may be difficult to acquire images in which the worker is facing straight toward the camera. For example, it may not be possible to position the smartphone directly in front of a worker, so the camera may be offset upward or downward or to the left or right to some extent. We therefore acquired an additional 44 images in which the faces of the 11 workers were photographed from four directions at about a 45° angle (within the range in which both eyes are included) to serve as non-frontal evaluation images. The grand total of images used in the evaluation was therefore 99.

4.3 Test Results

(1) Efficiency of identity verification

Beginning from when the worker opened the app, face recognition was completed within 0.4 s for each of the 99 evaluation images. When recognition was successful, the worker was able to use AI-forms with speech interaction seamlessly. When recognition failed, it was possible to use AI-forms by selecting the worker's name from a list in a conventional manner. Regardless of the recognition result, the facial image acquired during identity verification was recorded correctly together with the name in AI-forms.

(2) Accuracy of identity verification

The face-recognition accuracies for the 55 images in which the workers were wearing certain items are presented in Table 2. There were no cases of recognition failure due to insufficient illumination or faces of other workers appearing in the background. For recognition using front-facing images, identity was verified for all workers except for the images in which the worker was wearing a face mask; thus, recognition was not possible when a face mask was being worn because the face-recognition software uses features associated with the mouth. Because a worker begins a task using AI-forms after identity verification, we plan to address this problem with a work rule, such as face masks should be put on after identity verification. The recognition accuracies for the 44 non-frontal images are presented in Table 3. All workers were identified from the images of upward and downward face directions. The recognition accuracy was 18% for leftward and 27% for rightward. For vertical changes in facial direction, facial symmetry was maintained, but the loss of left-right symmetry with changes in the horizontal direction may have affected the recognition results. We consider two solutions to address the low recognition accuracy regarding deviations from the frontal direction when the face is photographed from the left or right. The first is addressing the camera operation by considering installation positions where it is not a burden on the worker to turn to face the camera directly. In cases in which it is not possible to properly position the camera and non-frontal facial images cannot be avoided, identity verification is carried out with additional non-frontal registered photos. Multiple registered photos including left and right deviations can improve the recognition accuracy of identity verification.

Table 2. Accuracy of faces with cap, glasses, and face mask [%]

No cap, glasses, or face mask	Cap	Glasses	Face mask	Cap and glasses
100	100	100	0	100

(3) Visual confirmability

Images acquired for identity verification were recorded in AI-forms together with worker names, including cases in which recognition failed. It was confirmed that all acquired images were recorded when discrimination by human visual examination was possible. However, visual confirmation could not be easy when a worker wear a face mask. This problem could be addressed with a work rule, such as face masks should be put on after identity verification.

Table 3. Accuracy of non-frontal faces [%]

Leftward	Rightward	Downward	Upward
18	27	100	100

5   Discussion

These preliminary tests showed the initial feasibility of our identity-verification method using frontal facial images of workers who are not wearing face masks in the factory workplace where use of the method is planned. The following improvement issues were clarified through discussion with workers and supervisors after the tests:

(1) Closer integration of AI-forms and identity-verification

There was a request from workers to reduce as much movement regarding the line of sight from the work location as possible for the identity-verification process during task handover or restarting a work task. Thus, the objective is to enable continuous concentration on a task in a nearly eyes-free state. To achieve this objective, it is necessary to consider placement of the camera used for identity verification in the same line of sight as the task. This will be taken into considering during the large-scale tests of the second step of our evaluation plan.

(2) Identity-verification at arbitrary times

There was a request from supervisors that the identity-verification process be carried out at arbitrary times in the work process and without workers being aware. Thus, the objectives are thoroughness in preventing impersonation and not hindering concentration on the task. Currently, facial images for identification are acquired at the beginning of a task and during work handover or restarting, but we are considering arbitrarily acquiring photographs when a task is being carried out and recording them together with the identification results. When workers are not aware of being photographed, they may have their eyes closed. Closed eyes cause face recognition to fail [18]. To avoid such failure, the face-recognition app will be improved to take two photos of workers after an interval of about 0.5 s to obtain facial photos with their eyes open. Few people spontaneously keep their eyes closed longer than 0.5 s because human blink duration is on average between 0.1 and 0.4 s [20]. Few people spontaneously blink twice in 0.5 s because human blink rate is between 7 and 17 per minute [21]. Either photo can be properly collated with their registered photos. The improvement will be taken into consideration during the large-scale tests of the second step of our evaluation plan.

(3) Preventing impersonation

Supervisors require thoroughness in preventing impersonation. Our proposed method principally trusts workers to self-assert as the correct worker if the smartphone app does not recognize them properly though a supervisor visually verifies workers' names and facial photos. For verification, the most important defense against this is when an adversary inserts an image of someone who is not one of the qualified workers, he/she is identified as a non-match.\

6 Conclusion

We proposed an identity-verification method for applying face recognition to AI-forms and developed a smartphone app for AI-forms. Preliminary feasibility testing involving 11 workers in an actual workplace confirmed that identity verification is possible when face recognition is carried out with frontal images of workers who are not wearing face masks. The face-recognition process completed within 0.4 s, enabling workers to seamlessly begin work with AI-forms. Recording both collation photos and worker names during identity verification also made it possible for a human to visually confirm a worker's identity. Discussion with workers and supervisors after the feasibility tests provided findings for improving our face-recognition app and evaluation plan. For future work, we will improve our face-recognition app for closer integration of AI-forms and our identity-verification method at arbitrary times.

References

1. The Mainichi Editorial: Quality control scandals endangering the 'Japan brand', October 2017. https://mainichi.jp/english/articles/20171028/p2a/00m/0na/014000c
2. How Workplaces Falsify Data, 12 December 2017. http://techon.nikkeibp.co.jp/atcl/feature/15/122200045/102300193/. (in Japanese)

3. Tabuchi, M., Sakaguchi, M., Hattori, H., Okumura, A.: Artificial-intelligence powered, voice-activated electronic forms for a standard process improvement solution. J. Inf. Process. **8**(2), 13–23 (2018). (in Japanese)
4. Tokyo Polytechnic University: Survey on natural user interface, December 2017. https://www.t-kougei.ac.jp/static/file/nui.pdf. (in Japanese)
5. Komeiji, S., Sakaguchi, M., Tabuchi, M., Hattori, H., Okumura, A.: An approach to realize an artificial-intelligence voice-activated electronic forms having cheat deterrent effect - a proposal of multi-layer speaker adaptation. J. Inf. Process. **8**(3) (2018). (in Japanese)
6. Japan Information Economic and Social Promotion Association: 2012 information security promotion business survey report, Survey research on social infrastructure construction using attribute information for identification, p. 16, March 2013. (in Japanese)
7. Imaoka, H., Mizoguchi, M., Hara, M.: Biometrics technology to preserve safety and security. Inf. Process. **51**(12), 1547–1554 (2010). (in Japanese)
8. Seto, Y.: Trends and prospects in biometric security authentication technology. Inf. Process. **47**(6), 571–576 (2006). (in Japanese)
9. Soto, M.: Using biometric authentication technology in Japanese financial institutions. Inf. Process. **47**(6), 577–582 (2006)
10. Sakamoto, S.: Present status and prospects of biometric products and solutions, NEC Tech. Rep. **5**(3) (2010). http://www.nec.com/en/global/techrep/journal/g10/n03/pdf/100303.pdf
11. IPA (Information-technology Promotion Agency, Japan): Guide for introduction and operation of biometric authentication, pp. 19–21, January 2013. (in Japanese)
12. Face Recognition Technology Evaluation Committee for Immigration: Demonstration experiment results on face recognition technology for Japanese going and returning from abroad, 18 November 2014. http://www.moj.go.jp/content/001128805.pdf. (in Japanese)
13. Face Recognition Homepage Vendors. http://www.face-rec.org/vendors/
14. NIST: Face projects. https://www.nist.gov/programs-projects/face-projects
15. NEC: NeoFace facial recognition – solutions. https://au.nec.com/en_AU/solutions/security-and-public-safety/biometrics/neoface-facial-recognition-solutions.html
16. Imaoka, H.: NEC's face recognition technology and applications, IPSG SIG Technical report, vol. 2013-CVIM-187, no. 38, pp. 1–4 (2013). (in Japanese)
17. Okumura, A., Hoshino, T., Handa, S., Nishiyama, Y., Tabuchi, M.: Identity verification of ticket holders at large-scale events using face recognition. J. Inf. Process. **25**, 448–458 (2017)
18. Okumura, A., Hoshino, T., Handa, S., Nishiyama, Y., Tabuchi, M.: Improving identity verification for ticket holders of large-scale events using non-stop face recognition system. J. Inf. Process. **8**(1), 1–8 (2018). (in Japanese)
19. Okumura, A., Hoshino, T., Handa, S., Yamada, E. Tabuchi, M.: Identity verification for attendees of large-scale events using face recognition of selfies taken with smartphone cameras. J. Inf. Process. **8**(3) (2018)
20. Bentivoglio, A.R., Bressman, S.B., Cassetta, E., Carretta, D., Tonali, P., Albanese, A.: Analysis of blink rate patterns in normal subjects. Mov Disord. **12**(6), 1028–1034 (1997)
21. Nosch, D.S., Pult, H., Albon, J., Purslow, C., Murphy, P.J.: Relationship between corneal sensation, blinking, and tear film quality. Optom. Vis. Sci. **93**(5), 471–481 (2016)

BREAKING: Password Entry Is Fine

Catlin Pidel[✉] and Stephan Neuhaus

Zurich University of Applied Sciences, Zurich, Switzerland
{catlin.pidel,stephan.neuhaus}@zhaw.ch

Abstract. In our digital world, we have become well acquainted with the login form—username shown in plaintext, password shown in asterisks or dots. This design dates back to the early days of terminal computing, and despite huge changes in nearly every other area, the humble login form remains largely untouched. When coupled with the ubiquity of smartphones, this means we often find ourselves entering complex passwords on a tiny touchscreen keyboard with little or no visual feedback on what is being typed. This paper explores how password masking on mobile devices affects the error rate for password entry. We created an app where users entered selected passwords into masked and unmasked password fields, measuring various metrics such as typing speed, error rate, and number of backspaces. We then did an exploratory analysis of the data. Our findings show that, perhaps unexpectedly, there is no significant difference between masked and unmasked passwords for any of these metrics.

Keywords: Security · Passwords · Data entry errors · Mobile security · Mobile usability

1 Introduction

The average person logs into 7–25 accounts every day [4], and the vast majority of people memorize their passwords, meaning reuse of identical or similar passwords is common [13]. This stands in opposition to traditional security advice, which dictates that passwords should be long, random strings full of complex characters, changed regularly, and never reused across accounts. This can really only be done by using a password manager, which only 3% of Americans use consistently [13]. What is more, in the smartphone era, tiny keyboards with separate screens for letters and special characters can turn a strong password into a usability nightmare: mobile users mistype their passwords twice as often as desktop users, and mobile password entry also takes 20% longer [12].

Password unmasking is the practice of displaying passwords rather than masking them with asterisks or dots. Is this a viable alternative? Usability experts claim that masking passwords is an unnecessary complication that causes confusion and frustration. But some security experts warn against the dangers of shoulder surfing (stealing passwords by looking over people's shoulders as

© Springer Nature Switzerland AG 2019
A. Moallem (Ed.): HCII 2019, LNCS 11594, pp. 67–80, 2019.
https://doi.org/10.1007/978-3-030-22351-9_5

they type). While there are a number of articles and blog posts espousing one view or the other, there is little evidence on how much password masking actually hinders usability. This paper aims to take on a small part of this overlying issue: how does the error rate for password entry compare between masked and unmasked passwords, specifically for smartphone users?

1.1   The Origins of Password Masking

Password masking comes from terminal computing, when every command was printed out on paper [9]. In those days, it made sense not to echo passwords at all, or at least to replace them with asterisks. Without it, anyone with access to the computer printouts could easily harvest someone else's login info. However, the days of such paper trails are long gone, and this rationale no longer applies. This begs the question: does password masking still serve a purpose, or is it simply there because it always has been?

1.2   Contributions

Despite having been pronounced dead many times [9], passwords are the most used authentication mechanism on the Internet today [10]. Similarly, mobile phones are ubiquitous, so gaining a deeper understanding of entering a password on a mobile device is a relevant issue. For as long as passwords have been around, we are still in a "data poor" research state [1,10], so this study contributes to password research as well as the growing intersection between usability and security research. We specifically make the following contributions:

- We compare the error rates of different types of passwords on mobile phones.
- We tested two different types of password fields: masked and unmasked.
- Additionally, we tested these logins with different types of passwords to see what role the password length and density of special characters play in this.

2   Related Work

2.1   Usability and Security of Password Masking

In the early days of computers, password masking helped communicate that a password was sensitive information [19], but this is now common knowledge, and not necessarily an argument for its continued use. From a modern usability perspective, the lack of visual feedback makes it difficult to find and correct mistakes in masked passwords, leading to unnecessary frustration. Usability expert Jakob Nielsen [15] and security expert Schneier [19] have argued that masking passwords causes users to choose easier (and therefore less secure) passwords, reuse passwords across accounts, or even copy and paste them from a file.

That said, password masking is also what the user has come to expect. A small-scale user study showed that unmasking passwords undermined the user's trust—even though masking is a purely cosmetic fix, 60% of participants became suspicious of a site when their passwords were displayed in plaintext [11]. There's also a perceived security threat of unmasking passwords. What if someone looks over your shoulder without your knowing? Additionally, how do you navigate the trust dynamics of entering a password with someone else present? Is it alright to ask your boss, your partner, or your child to avert their eyes from your login form [19]?

The most common security threat associated with plaintext passwords is shoulder surfing. Both Schneier and Nielsen have downplayed this risk, a point which many of the commenters on these articles disagreed with [15,19]. It is much harder to snoop a password typed onto a smartphone screen, and with mobile internet usage recently overtaking desktop traffic [4], the threat of shoulder surfing is becoming less common compared to the nuisance of repeatedly typing a password [20]. However, dissenters argue that there are still plenty of scenarios where password masking provides a necessary layer of security. Using a computer in a public setting like a coffee shop, for example, as well as needing to enter a password during a presentation, are legitimate use cases where plaintext passwords fall short.

Despite the considerable debate, we were unable to find research directly comparing the error rate between masked and unmasked password fields.

2.2   Usability and Security of Different Types of Logins

There is a fair amount of research into alternatives for the username and password combination, such as the usability of click-based graphical passwords [2] and password managers [3]. One study generated a "profile" of how the user types their password, based off of the time a key is held down and the time between key presses [17]. When the profiles of valid users were compared against those of impostors entering the same password, this additional metric helped filter out unauthorized users. However, typos and the subsequent use of backspace interfere with this metric, making it infeasible for large-scale adoption. Another study explored an alternative to password masking, the TransparentMask [8]. This combines the typical black dots with symbols that represent a hash of the last n characters of a password. The idea is that since humans can easily recognize sequences of symbols, it would provide a way to alert the user to typos without providing as much of a security risk as a fully unmasked password (Fig. 1).

While these ideas are fascinating, the likelihood for their widespread adoption is unlikely, and may also lead to user confusion. According to one survey of web tools [14], login forms are among the least standardized website components. Introducing new paradigms, however well-intentioned, may only serve to muddy the waters. Additionally, while the typical login form is not as interesting, its persistence in our digital world demands more research than has currently been done on the subject [1,10].

Fig. 1. Transparent Mask example inspired by Gruschka and Iacono's paper [8]. The colorful symbols (blue star, green diamond) represent a hash of the previous characters in a password. A typo in the preceding characters would result in a different symbol appearing, as shown when the "w" is mistyped as a "v". (Color figure online)

2.3 Mobile Password Entry

As mobile phone usage continues to increase [4], passwords are increasingly being entered on mobile devices. And while mobile devices are often cited as a reason why password unmasking is important (tiny keyboards leading to an increased likelihood of typos, for example), we did not find studies measuring how much masked password fields affect usability on mobile devices. One dissertation provides an in-depth analysis of password entry on mobile devices—what influences the user typing speed (such as switching keyboards to find special characters), and the most commonly made mistakes [5]. Prior research also explored the error rate of typing passwords on mobile phones compared to desktops [12], as well as an analysis of the "number and nature of errors committed during password entry" and whether the user notices these errors before submitting the password [7]. Our work provides another facet to the question of mobile password entry by studying the error rates for both masked and unmasked login prompts.

From a security perspective, Schaub et al. [18] examined how the design of different smartphone keyboards (iOS, Windows, Android, and others) can make shoulder surfing easier or more difficult. There has also been research into how the platform (mobile, tablet, desktop) affects the makeup of the password created [21], but not whether certain types of passwords are more or less error-prone in daily mobile use.

3   Methodology

This study aims to answer two questions: how password masking affects the error rate of password entry on mobile devices, and how the makeup of a password influences the aforementioned error rate.

3.1   Effects of Password Masking

We tested two different login forms—one with typical mobile password masking (where the password is masked except for the most recently typed character), and a fully unmasked password, displayed in plaintext. We also considered testing a third option where the user has the choice to mask or unmask their password with a checkbox, but we ultimately decided that this was better tested in a separate study concerned with whether users will choose to change the default masking of a password.

3.2   Effects of Password Makeup

There is a lot of variation in passwords, but we have identified four main categories:

- **Pass phrases**: multiple words separated by spaces ("`cats are fantastic friends`")
- **Typical passwords**: a single (in our case, English) word with letters replaced by numbers and special characters ("`C@terp!11ar2018`").
- **Randomized**: a fully randomized string of characters, such as those used by password managers ("`nBqzEcP2A}Q8,jG`")
- **Bad passwords**: passwords often seen in password leaks ("`password123`")

Of these four types, we are not interested in "bad passwords" because they have already been shown to be a security threat. For the 3 more secure alternatives, we generated a list of 10 passwords at equivalent password strength (as measured by our chosen software, 1Password). Our hypothesis is that the error rate for password entry varies both by type of password and by whether the password field is masked.

3.3   Study Structure

Our study measures the error rate of password entry using a custom-built app, PasswordResearcher[1]. This app is built in Unity and deployed to both iPhone and Android, and is available with either English or German keyboards depending on the preferences of the user. This is to mitigate any errors that could arise from using an unfamiliar keyboard layout.

Each session has two parts: one half where the passwords are masked and the other with passwords unmasked. We alternate whether the participant starts with the masked or unmasked task each time. To ensure there is no overlap of passwords between these two portions, the app randomly chooses four passwords from each of the three categories and splits them into two groups of six passwords (two from each category). For each half of the study, the participant sees each given password three times with all passwords shuffled in a random order. Entering the password multiple times is intended to elicit a learning response

---

[1] https://github.com/catiejo/PasswordResearcher.

since participants learn to type their passwords more quickly and consistently over time. Additionally, the random shuffling allows us to test all three password types under similar conditions—it controls for participants getting bored and therefore less careful over time, or alternatively, getting more used to typing and getting better.

The passwords are displayed on the screen as an image so it is not possible to copy-paste the on-screen password, and also so the user does not need to memorize the password. We were careful not to mention that we were interested in the error rate of password entry since this could change their natural behavior and skew our results.

3.4   Data Collected

We used a recruiting agency, TestingTime[2], to recruit ten participants. For each password attempt, we recorded:

- Expected password
- Actual (typed) password
- Entry time
- Password type (phrase, random, or typical)
- Participant ID
- Overall attempt number (1 to 18 for each half)
- Password attempt number (1 to 3)
- Operating system (Android or iOS)

We also collected qualitative exit questions from each participant:

- Do you remember any of the passwords you typed?
- Which of the password types, if any, did you feel were quicker to type?
- Which of the password types, if any, did you feel were easier or more difficult to type?

It is worth noting that this study is only concerned with whether a login attempt would be successful or not, so we are measuring errors on submission rather than incremental errors made while typing. The latter has potential for a follow-up study, but is outside the scope of the present one.

4   Results and Analysis

We defined an incorrect password attempt as one where the actual password entered by the user does not match the expected password. We used the Levenshtein edit distance to further quantify the correctness of a password and to give a lower bound on the actual number of mistakes that were made by the user.

After collecting the data, we removed any attempts that took more than 100 s. This happened occasionally when participants set down the phone to come ask

---

[2] https://www.testingtime.com/en/.

a question. Similarly, we removed any attempts with more than ten mistakes, which sometimes happened when participants accidentally pressed the enter key too soon.

Using this data, we calculated the error rates, which we defined as the total number of incorrect attempts (where the expected and actual passwords are not the same) divided by the total number of attempts for each of the following metrics:

- Masked error rate: 18%
- Unmasked error rate: 15%
- Phrase password error rate: 15%
- Typical password error rate: 22%
- Random password error rate: 12%
- Overall error rate: 16%

While there are differences in these error rates (especially between random and typical passwords), the pseudoreplication and small sample size of this study prevent them from being statistically significant. We therefore opted to explore and visualize results without trying to prove statistical significance (see Sect. 6). The conclusions below are our subjective interpretation of the data.

4.1   Password Masking Versus Error Rate

Going into this study, we expected to see a lower error rate on unmasked passwords. This made sense logically—participants can visually inspect an unmasked password for errors, whereas masked passwords seem more prone to "fat finger" mistakes (touching an adjacent key without realizing it). Unmasked passwords did indeed have a lower error rate, but not nearly as dramatically as we would have expected–a 3% difference between masked and unmasked for a sample size of n = 10.

We plotted the data, looking for a difference between masked and unmasked passwords. There was definitely a pretty broad range in the time it took to enter a password, but masked and unmasked data points are nearly perfectly interleaved. We also compared the overall entry time for masked and unmasked passwords (Fig. 3, below), and while there was a difference, it was very small.

4.2   Device Type Versus Error Rate

It seemed clear that the difference between the error rates for masked and unmasked passwords was very small, so we started looking for other interesting features of the data. We had participants using both iPhone and Android devices—was one platform less prone to mistakes? (See Fig. 4).

Visually inspecting the plots, it was hard to see a difference between the Android and iOS columns.

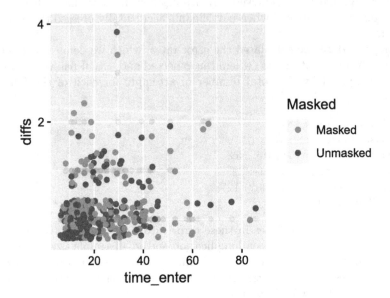

Fig. 2. Time to enter a password versus the number of differences between the expected and actual password. Jitter is added to the points in order to show the clustering of the data, but all differences are integer-valued.

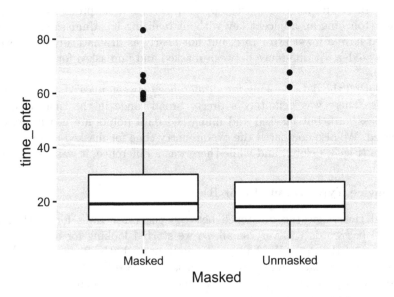

Fig. 3. Boxplot of the time it took to enter passwords with each password masking.

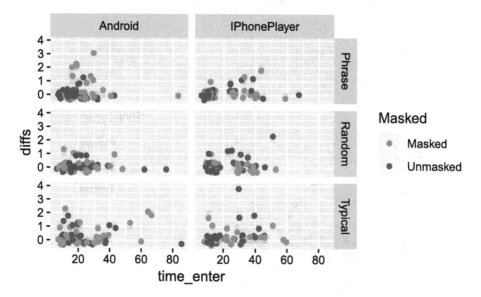

Fig. 4. Number of mistakes versus entry time, split by OS and password type. Points are jittered, y values are integers.

4.3 Password Type Versus Error Rate

Neither password masking nor device type affected the error rate more than is expected by chance. We were also curious about each of the password types—since a random password is much shorter than a multi-word password, we decided to compare the masked and unmasked entry times per password type. Given that all the passwords chosen for the study were equivalently secure, was a certain type of password more error prone? We plotted the same graph as shown in Fig. 2, this time coloring the points by the password type instead of whether it was masked or unmasked (See Fig. 5).

Visual inspection showed, once again, that there was no real difference, so we turned ourselves towards one last metric: was a certain password type faster to type than the others? (See Fig. 6).

Answer: not really. Even comparing each participant's typing speeds, the graphs for each password were more or less the same. This is actually interesting, given the difference in length between an 11-character random password and an upwards-of- 20-character multi-word password. This also aligns with similar research, which shows random passwords with special characters took considerably longer to type than standard text of the same length [5]. As for why this occurs, our qualitative results were in agreement with the previous work: users have to spend considerable time hunting for special characters.

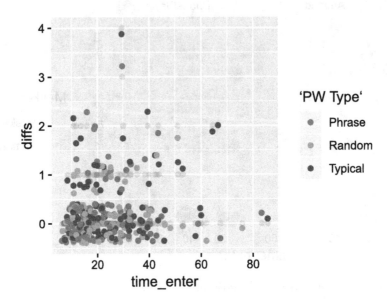

Fig. 5. Number of mistakes versus entry time, split by password type. Points are jittered, y values are integers.

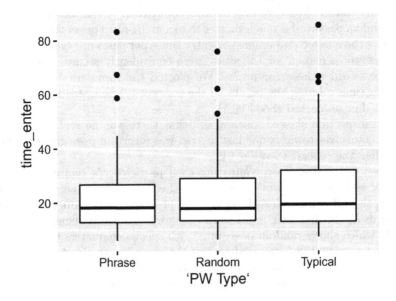

Fig. 6. Entry time versus password type.

4.4 Qualitative Analysis

Following each user session, we asked the same three exit questions.

Do you remember any of the passwords you typed? One participant could name nearly half the passwords, even some random ones, letter for letter. Another could not name a single thing they typed. The random passwords were definitely the least remembered, and while people could usually remember parts of the other two types, there were frequent mistakes. For example, they would confuse the order of words in a multiword password, or mix the words up between multiword passwords. For more typical passwords, they often remembered words, but would make mistakes on the exact placement of special characters, such as confusing "Cr@ck3rJacked" as "Cr@ckerJack3d".

Which of the password types, if any, did you feel were quicker to type? Nearly everyone said that the multiword passwords were easiest to type. We were surprised, however, that several participants also added, unprompted, that they would not choose such passwords since the lack of special characters and numbers made them less secure.

Which of these password types, if any, did you feel were easier or more difficult to type? For this question, we showed them a list of the passwords they had typed for the study, and asked them to point out any passwords that were particularly easy or difficult, and why. There was one password that was significantly longer than the other passwords, "jubilant wineshop sceptic cadenza", which was nearly always pointed out as difficult when participants encountered it. They would also point out characters they found ambiguous (such as a lower case 'l' and the upper case vowel, 'I').

5 Discussion

We observed a 3% higher error rate when passwords are masked versus unmasked. Based on the study size, we do not claim that this difference is real. We also could not find any groups or subgroups that had different error rates. If our data is at all typical, it seems that users are simply too good at entering passwords for it to matter whether or not they can see what they are typing, and thus we cannot reject the null hypothesis that masking or unmasking passwords makes no difference to the entry error rate.

6 Threats to Validity

This study was carried out as a small academic project, and as such, does not have a large time or financial budget. So while this project is intended to serve as a proof-of-concept for later work, it is not an exhaustive answer to the questions at hand.

6.1   Participants

The first threat is our sampling and number of participants. Our user study used a recruitment agency rather than surveying random students, which was done expressly to limit selection bias. While we had a good variety of ages, genders, and smartphone experience, candidates from this agency are often unemployed (which makes sense, given that the study took place on a weekday morning and afternoon). We also excluded UI/UX experts from our selection. Neither of these factors were a problem for the purposes of our work, but it does mean that the selection was not truly random. And even if selection were indeed random, the small number of participants ($n = 10$) limits the extensibility of our results.

It is also important to note only one participant was an English native speaker. While everyone was fluent enough to converse and they could use their keyboard of choice, both the "typical" and "multiword" passwords were based off of english words. This easily could have affected the entry time and error rate—unknown words take longer to visually parse, and are much easier to make mistakes when re-typing due to this lack of familiarity. This also could have made them more difficult to remember, thus hindering the learning response.

6.2   App

The app used for the study had some issues. One participant found a bug where pressing the back button would cause the keyboard to flicker on and off for several seconds, preventing the user from entering text. This did not happen a lot, but it still affected the password entry times. The font choice also proved to be problematic. We chose a monospace font with the goal that it would be easily readable, but one participant had considerable trouble with the glyph for the zero digit, and ended up looking for a special symbol that was an exact match to the font choice. Others asked about ambiguous characters, and still others just made their best guess and moved on.

The app was built specifically for this study. Therefore, it was not feasible to place the app directly onto participants' phones. Participants therefore had to use phones that were potentially unfamiliar to them. Typing on an unfamiliar device may lead to both more typing time and errors, and while we hoped to prevent this as much as possible, we could not completely remove the problem.

There is also the problem of the password selection used in the app. The random and multiword passwords used for the study were all generated by 1Password, and the typical passwords were generated by hand. The 1Password password strength metric was used to measure all three password types (to make sure they were roughly equivalent security-wise). However, 1Password is very clear that a strength metric can only test the strength of passwords for which it understands the underlying system that created them [6], meaning it could not accurately assess the security of our typical passwords.

6.3 Analysis

With $n = 10$, this study is clearly underpowered. Additionally, the number of ways we have looked at the data makes it very difficult to draw interesting conclusions, especially given the small sample size. Even if we did find a few interesting trends, we did so many other comparisons that the necessary corrections to any p-values would, in our opinion, render any hypothesis test dubious.

7 Conclusions

After all the debate over the tradeoff between the usability of unmasking passwords and the security of keeping them hidden, it seems that password entry is mostly working as-intended. There were slight differences in the error rates of masked passwords and their unmasked counterparts, but this difference was not statistically significant, nor were any of the other ways we sliced and diced the data. People are simply too good at typing passwords for it to matter whether they can see all the characters.

To replicate the research and the figures, download the raw data file (with participant names anonymised) and the R [16] scripts used to produce the figures from https://github.com/sten13/password-masking-data. The PasswordResearcher app is also available from https://github.com/catiejo/PasswordResearcher.

Acknowledgments. The authors wish to thank Bernhard Tellenbach of the Information Security group, Jürgen Spielberger of the Distributed Systems Group and Marc Rennhard of the Institute of Applied Information Systems at the Zurich University of Applied Sciences for funding this research.

References

1. Bonneau, J., Preibusch, S.: The password thicket: technical and market failures in human authentication on the web. In: Proceedings of the Workshop of Economics in Information Security (2010)
2. Chiasson, S., Forget, A., Biddle, R., van Oorschot, P.C.: User interface design affects security: patterns in click-based graphical passwords. Int. J. Inf. Secur. **8**(6), 387–398 (2009). https://doi.org/10.1007/s10207-009-0080-7
3. Chiasson, S., Oorschot, P.C.V., Biddle, R.: A usability study and critique of two password managers. In: Proceedings of the 15th USENIX Security Symposium, pp. 1–16 (2006)
4. Enge, E.: Mobile vs desktop usage in 2018: mobile widens the gap, April 2018. https://www.stonetemple.com/mobile-vs-desktop-usage-study/
5. Gallagher, M.A.: Modeling password entry on mobile devices: please check your password and try again. Ph.D. thesis, Rice University, May 2015
6. Goldberg, J.: Toward better master passwords, August 2018. https://blog.1password.com/toward-better-master-passwords/

7. Greene, K.K., Kelsey, J., Frankli, J.M.: Measuring the usability and security of permuted passwords on mobile platforms. Technical report NISTIR 8040, National Institute of Standards and Technology, Information Access Division, Information Technology Laboratory, 100 Bureau Drive (Mail Stop 8940) Gaithersburg, MD 20899-8940, April 2016

8. Gruschka, N., Iacono, L.L.: Password visualization beyond password masking. In: Bleimann, U., Dowland, P., Furnell, S., Schneider, O. (eds.) Proceedings of the Eighth International Network Conference (INC 2010), Heidelberg, Germany, 6–8 July 2010, pp. 179–188. University of Plymouth (2010). http://www.cscan.org/?page=openaccess&id=111

9. Gutmann, P.: Engineering Security (February 2014, in publication)

10. Herley, C., Oorschot, P.C.V.: A research agenda acknowledging the persistence of passwords. IEEE Secur. Priv. **10**(2), 28–36 (2012)

11. Holmes, J.: Stop password masking, September 2014. http://passwordmasking.com/

12. Melicher, W., et al.: Usability and security of text passwords on mobile devices. In: Proceedings of the 2016 CHI Conference on Human Factors in Computing Systems, CHI 2016, pp. 527–539. ACM, New York (2016). http://dx.doi.org/10.1145/2858036.2858384, http://doi.acm.org/10.1145/2858036.2858384

13. Mitchell, T.: Americans, password management and mobile security, January 2017. http://www.pewinternet.org/2017/01/26/2-password-management-and-mobile-security

14. Nielsen, J.: The need for web design standards, September 2004. https://www.nngroup.com/articles/the-need-for-web-design-standards/

15. Nielsen, J.: Stop password masking, June 2009. https://www.nngroup.com/articles/stop-password-masking/

16. R Core Team: R: A language and environment for statistical computing. R foundation for statistical computing, Vienna, Austria (2018). https://www.R-project.org/

17. Robinson, J.A., Liang, V.W., Chambers, J.A., MacKenzie, C.L.: Computer user verification using login string keystroke dynamics. Trans. Sys. Man Cyber. Part A **28**(2), 236–241 (1998). https://doi.org/10.1109/3468.661150

18. Schaub, F., Deyhle, R., Weber, M.: Password entry usability and shoulder surfing susceptibility on different smartphone platforms. In: Proceedings of the 11th International Conference on Mobile and Ubiquitous Multimedia, MUM 2012, pp. 13:1–13:10. ACM, New York (2012). http://dx.doi.org/10.1145/2406367.2406384, http://doi.acm.org/10.1145/2406367.2406384

19. Schneier, B.: The pros and cons of password masking, July 2009. https://www.schneier.com/blog/archives/2009/07/the_pros_and_co.html

20. Wroblewski, L.: Mobile design details: hide/show passwords, November 2012. https://www.lukew.com/ff/entry.asp?1653

21. Yang, Y., Lindqvist, J., Oulasvirta, A.: Text entry method affects password security. In: The LASER Workshop: Learning from Authoritative Security Experiment Results (LASER 2014). USENIX Association, Arlington (2014). https://www.usenix.org/conference/laser2014/program/agenda/presentation/yang

Explore-a-Nation: Combining Graphical and Alphanumeric Authentication

Lauren N. Tiller$^{(\boxtimes)}$, Catherine A. Angelini, Sarah C. Leibner,
and Jeremiah D. Still

Department of Psychology, Old Dominion University, Norfolk, VA, USA
{LTill002, CAnge001, SSort001, JStill}@odu.edu

Abstract. Graphical authentication has been a proposed solution to the usability and memorability issues seen with traditional alphanumeric passwords. However, graphical authentication schemes are often criticized for their susceptibility to Over-the-Shoulder Attacks (OSAs). This research proposes and evaluates Explore-a-Nation (EaN), a unique hybrid authentication scheme that attempts to bridge the gap between graphical authentication passcodes and strong alphanumeric passwords. EaN takes advantage of the known security and efficiency associated with passwords along with the enhanced recognition benefit of graphical schemes. The EaN scheme provides users with a static image consisting of a map wherein an icon passcode path is hidden amongst other distractor icons. Following the icon path allows users to generate their strong password. This study compared our EaN prototype to alphanumeric password standards and to Use Your Illusion (UYI) across the dimensions of efficiency, accuracy, OSA resistance, and subjective usability. User login times for both EaN and UYI met the efficiency usability standards established by alphanumeric passwords. Results for UYI (99%) login accuracy were significantly better than EaN (91%). And, UYI obtained a significantly higher Subjective Usability Survey score than EaN, with both schemes exceeding our usability requirement. Notably, EaN was shown to be resistant to OSAs while UYI was not. We suggest EaN might prove to be an effective next-generation authentication scheme for both frequent and intermittent users.

Keywords: Cybersecurity · Graphical authentication ·
Alphanumeric authentication · Over-the-Shoulder Attack

1 Introduction

Authentication is performed by a computing system in an attempt to verify a user's identity. The intent is to protect a user's valuable information (e.g., banking information, medical records). The most common form of authentication is the knowledge-based alphanumeric password [1]. However, to be effective, passwords must meet an array of requirements. Strong passwords ought to be long, contain numbers and symbols, and not use common dictionary words. Further, they should be different for every account, changed often, and not written down [2]. However, security requirements often make passwords hard to remember. This often leads to users employing workarounds and creating weak passwords. It has been suggested that the competition

© Springer Nature Switzerland AG 2019
A. Moallem (Ed.): HCII 2019, LNCS 11594, pp. 81–95, 2019.
https://doi.org/10.1007/978-3-030-22351-9_6

between usability and security can be resolved by using innovate authentication schemes [3]. For example, graphical authentication passcodes are easy to remember by taking advantage of humans' affinity for encoding and recognizing visual objects (e.g., picture superiority effect). Unlike letters and numbers, images are encoded both visually and semantically into long-term memory [4]. Research has shown that pictures are easier to encode into long-term memory than an alphanumeric string [5]. Graphical authentication takes advantage of the fact that the user can make more meaningful associations with novel images compared with novel character strings. Graphical encoding allows the user to formulate context around the image and the richer this contextual information, the more strongly the image will be encoded in long term memory [6]. The increased strength of encoding images leads to a decrease in the decay of memory over time when compared to a less meaningful alphanumeric password. Clearly, the graphical authentication literature has demonstrated the memorability benefits of employing visual objects over alphanumeric characters. Though, developers are still searching for ways to overcome security concerns like Over-the-Shoulder Attacks (OSAs).

Cyber attacks are an issue for any authentication system. Alphanumeric passwords must beware of brute force attacks, which occur when an attacker inputs multiple password combinations until they gain access [7]. Conversely, graphical authentication schemes have often been criticized for their vulnerability to OSAs. This occurs when a casual attacker looks over the shoulder of someone employing a graphical authentication scheme in a shared space. And, both alphanumeric and graphical passcodes are vulnerable to a social engineering attack. If users create their own passcode, an attacker could produce an educated guess by learning more about a user (e.g., exploring social media posts to determine a pet's name or visual appearance). But, clearly, the most common criticism of graphical authentication schemes is their susceptibility to OSAs.

To defend against OSAs, researchers tend to use one of four strategies: grouping targets among distractors, disguising targets, using gaze-based input, or translating targets to another location [8]. For instance, the graphical authentication scheme, Passpoints, implements a grouping targets among distractors OSA defense strategy by allowing users to click on specific points within a picture [9]. The Use Your Illusion (UYI) graphical scheme, involves users recognizing a distorted target image from a set of distorted distractor images; this disguising targets technique interferes with the attacker's perception of the passcode [8, 10]. Other graphical schemes use gazed based input requiring users to select passcode targets using their eyes, thus making passcode observation difficult [11]. To further bolster security, some graphical schemes require users to translate target information to another location after the passcode target is recognized (WYSWYE) [12].

Again, graphical authentication employment of visual objects increases a user's ability to easily remember a passcode. Beyond the picture superiority effect, users only have to recognize their graphical passcode amongst a set of icons (c.f., multiple choice question) and not produce them like in an alphanumeric scheme (c.f., essay exam question). But, this benefit for easy memory retrieval comes at the cost of login efficiency. Visually searching for icons amongst distractors takes time. However, entering a well-practiced alphanumeric password is effortless and only takes a couple of seconds.

Uniquely, we attempt to take advantage of the memorability of graphical authentication schemes and the known efficiency of alphanumeric passwords. We proposed a new graphical authentication scheme Explore-a-Nation (EaN) that bridges the gap between graphical authentication passcodes and alphanumeric passwords. The EaN scheme uses the translating targets to another location OSA defense strategy. EaN provides users with a static image consisting of a map with context themed icons wherein an icon passcode path is hidden amongst other distractor icons. To improve memorability, the information provided by the passcode path icons is leveraged as clues that translate to a strong alphanumeric password. The user types the password that corresponds to the icons along their passcode path. The typed alphanumeric password consists of the first two letters of the target icon waypoints along the user's

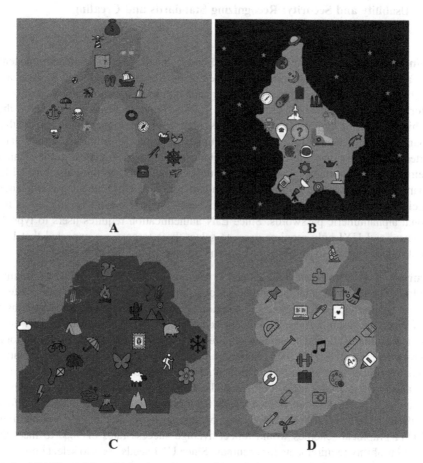

Fig. 1. (A) Blaze Map Passcode: treasure, feet, airplane, wheel, coconut, ? (Password: trfeaiwhco?). (B) Martian Map Passcode: gas, telescope, boot, !, rocket, home (Password: gatebo!roho). (C) Serendipity Map Passcode: @, pig, flower, sheep, umbrella, tent (Password: @piflshumte). (D) School Extravaganza Map Passcode: broom, eraser, ruler, dumbbell, camera, $ (Password: brerruduca$).

passcode path, except for one target icon that serves as a hint to the special character (see Fig. 1). As noted by Al Ameen [13], the cognitive abilities for both encoding and retrieval stages of memory are leveraged when users can view targets. Notably, if the user knows their password, it can simply be entered. The slower graphical scheme interactions only serve as a memory aid and are not a requirement of authentication. Therefore, the proposed EaN scheme ought to facilitate efficiency with sufficient practice.

The current study compared EaN to UYI a popular graphical scheme that disguises targets to prevent OSAs [10]. The purpose of our research was to assess the security requirements and usability of the EaN scheme across the dimensions of efficiency, accuracy, and subjective usability.

1.1 Usability and Security: Recognizing Standards and Creating Requirements

Login Efficiency. According to Still, Cain, and Schuster [3], authentication systems must allow for quick access in order to be efficient. Research conducted by Braz and Robert [14], revealed that the standard for alphanumeric password entry should be performed with login times that range from 7–20 s. Previous research has shown that graphical authentication passcode schemes tend to have longer login times than alphanumeric passwords [9]. Ideal alphanumeric alternative solutions should have shorter login times than those of some previously proposed graphical authentication schemes. More importantly, login times should be comparable to those established for alphanumeric passwords. To meet the standard usability requirement for efficiency, participants needed to be able to consistently enter their password as quickly as traditional alphanumeric passwords. Since EaN authentication requires users to type 11 characters and UYI only requires users to select three targets, we expected that UYI would reflect quicker login times given users are entering a novel passcode.

Accuracy. For a graphical authentication system to be usable, intensive training should not be required, and appropriate actions should be apparent for a wide range of users to ensure successful logins [3]. Previous research has shown that UYI consistently meets the usability requirement for accuracy [8, 10]. Additionally, a PIN entry graphical authentication scheme, that requires interactions similar to UYI, found login accuracy rates of 91% [15]. Perkovic and colleagues [16] found that their translating targets to another location graphical authentication scheme had login times of 8 s and 93% accuracy. A recent study compared the failure rates of graphical passcodes to alphanumeric passwords and yielded results for login inaccuracy rates that ranged from 11.59% to 13.01% [17]. We reasoned that participant login attempts for both the EaN and UYI graphical schemes would reflect average success rates of 90% to meet the standard usability requirements for accuracy. Since UYI needs users to select only three correct targets, while EaN requires users to correctly type 11 characters, we expected that accuracy would be higher for UYI login.

Subjective Usability. The Subjective Usability Scale (SUS) was used as a subjective measure of participant's usability experience [18]. If a login system is perceived as less usable, it may deter a user from using a website or program that employs that login method. Cain and Still [8] found that when users experience UYI for the first time they rated their experience with a SUS score of 65. We predicted EaN and UYI would follow the user requirement standards of 'OK' (e.g., SUS score of 51) or 'Good' (e.g., SUS score of 71) [19]. Since UYI uses a more familiar interaction metaphor, PIN entry, it would be rated as more usable.

OSA Resistance. Previous research suggests that the relative OSA resistance of a given graphical scheme can vary depending on the type of OSA defense strategy being implemented [8]. UYI disguises targets using image distortion in order to prevent OSAs [8]. Previous research proposes that images distorted at the optimal distortion level will simultaneously help users maintain recognition of targets and make the scheme more resistant to OSAs [20]. However, UYI has been shown to be vulnerable to OSAs when an attacker is permitted three or more viewings [8]. Research examining graphical schemes using a translating targets to another location OSA defense often find that when participants are asked to take the role of an attacker, they are unsuccessful at stealing a given passcode [21, 22]. We predicted the security of EaN will provide users with the same OSA resistance. Therefore, attackers will have 0% success in stealing an EaN password when given an unlimited number of views.

2 Method

2.1 Participants

Twenty-five undergraduate students (13 females, 2 left-handed, 24 reported English as their native language) were recruited from introductory psychology courses and were compensated with class research credit for their participation. Participants' daily computing device usage ranged from 2 to 15 h ($M = 5.54$, $SD = 2.94$). Ages ranged from 18 to 25 years ($M = 19.24$, $SD = 1.81$). Twenty-three students indicated that they would accept additional authentication entry effort in order to prevent an OSA.

2.2 Materials Stimuli and Apparatus

Explore-a-Nation Map Prototype. The EaN prototype consisted of four different themed maps that were created using Adobe Photoshop and flat icons (retrieved from https://icons8.com/icon/set/map/all). Each map theme was comprised of a unique set of icons that pertained to a fictitious website's theme: Blaze (beach), Martian (outer space), School Extravaganza, and Serendipity (outdoors) (see Fig. 1). Each map consisted of 23 unique icons matching the website's novel theme, 17 distractor and 6 target icons. Two of the 23 icons contained an embedded special character. During EaN map creation, a temporary grid was placed on each map wherein each grid square was assigned a number. The icons were placed using the grid and a random number generator. After all icons were placed, the passcodes for each map were developed using the same grid and random number generator method. The passcodes consisted of a start and end icon with four icon waypoints in between, one of which contained an embedded special symbol. All passcode icons served as a reference to the associated alphanumeric password. The alphanumeric passwords consisted of the first two letters of each icon waypoint along the user's passcode path, except for one waypoint which served as a special character clue (see Fig. 1). Each strong password had 11 characters, contained no dictionary words, and had a special character (e.g., @piflshumte).

The EaN prototype authentication instructions were created for each map theme. Participants were shown both the targets and distractors on the map with an arrow highlighting the passcode path. The instructions went step by step for each passcode icon waypoint, informing users about the target icon and what characters should be translated into the typed password field (see Fig. 2). Participants were encouraged not to point to their passcode icons on the screen. Participants were informed that an image of the map would always be visible during login. Finally, they were given the complete alphanumeric password and instructed to type the password into the password field during login.

E-Prime 2 software was used to create the EaN authentication prototypes (see Fig. 3). The prototype was programmed to display asterisks during password entry. The prototype provided participants with feedback after they typed a password by displaying either "correct" or "incorrect". The E-Prime 2 software recorded login times in milliseconds from the start of password entry to submission and recorded user accuracy.

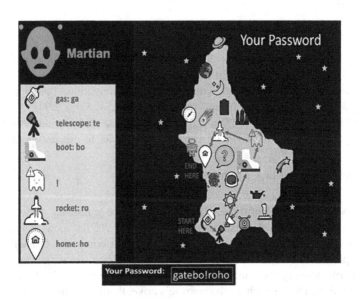

Fig. 2. A summarized representation of the Martian's website authentication instructions provided to participants in Microsoft PowerPoint.

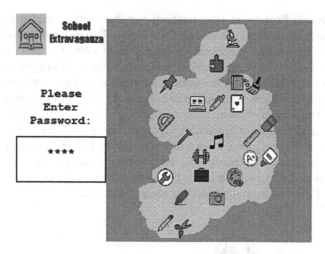

Fig. 3. A screenshot of the School Extravaganza EaN website authentication prototype implemented in the E-Prime experimental software.

Explore-a-Nation Over-the-Shoulder Attack Video. To test resistance against OSAs, a video of a researcher logging in to a fictitious food website, Craveology, was created and displayed to participants (see Fig. 4). The video was recorded with an iPhone 7 and captured the computer screen, the keyboard, and researcher's hands. The Craveology website was created using E-prime 2 software and followed the same creation procedure that was used when creating the EaN experimental prototype. A picture of the Craveology login screen was printed out and given to participants to refer to while viewing the video (see Fig. 4). The video was shown to participants in full-screen mode.

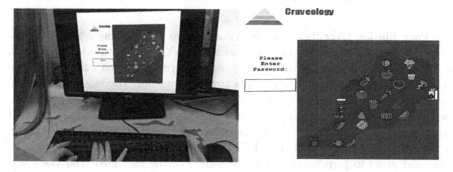

Fig. 4. The left image is a screenshot of the EaN OSA video which displays computer monitor and keyboard. The right image depicts the sheet printed and provided to participants while watching the video.

Use Your Illusion Prototype. Four fictitious websites were created using Paradigm software: Knitted Frog, Bean, GreenTech, and Hoppy Easter. Each website used UYI to authenticate. Each UYI website prototype was created with 27 images (24 distractors and 3 targets). Each website contained an independent set of 27 images. During login, participants were presented with the website information and given the passcode. The instruction depicted both the undistorted and distorted versions of the passcode images (see Fig. 5). Participants viewed three consecutive 3 × 3 grids. Each 3 × 3 grid contained one target and eight distractor images (see Fig. 5). All images were placed on the grid using a random number generator. The passcode targets were also selected using a random number generator. The Paradigm software recorded login times in milliseconds as well as participant input. The researchers verbally informed participants whether or not they successfully input the correct passcode.

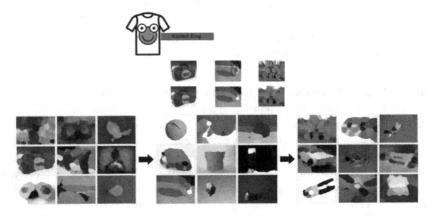

Fig. 5. The top image depicts a general version of what the instruction screen looked like for a given website theme. The bottom three images depict an example of the three 3 × 3 consecutive UYI prototype grids that would be shown during authentication.

Use Your Illusion Over-the-Shoulder Attack Video. To evaluate UYI OSA resistance, a video of a researcher logging in using the UYI system was created. Since a visible mouse cursor is used to select UYI passcode targets, the video was created using Tiny Take's screen recording feature on a computer monitor. The video captured the mouse clicking on the targets within the 3 consecutive 3 × 3 grids. The UYI prototype for the video was created using the same random placement method as the UYI experimental prototype. The set of 27 images used for the UYI OSA video was unique. A picture of all 27 images used in the UYI OSA video was printed on a single piece of paper and given to participants to refer to while viewing the video. The video was shown to participants in full-screen mode.

Usability Satisfaction Survey. Participant's subjective usability satisfaction was measured using the SUS after authenticating with both the EaN and UYI prototypes. The SUS is comprised of 10 items, and each question was scored using a Likert scale from 1 to 5 [18]. The SUS has been shown to have high reliability [23], and good correlation with performance measures [24].

2.3 Experimental Design and Procedure

Participants filled out an informed consent document and a demographics questionnaire. A fully within-subjects experimental design was used to compare the EaN and UYI. The experiment required participants to interact with the four different EaN website maps (Blaze, Martian, Serendipity, and School Extravaganza) and four different UYI websites (Knitted Frog, GreenTech, Bean, and Hoppy Easter). In addition, participants completed the associated SUS ratings and attempted to determine passwords from watching the OSA videos.

When participants interacted with EaN and UYI, they always assumed the role of the user first. To begin, they were shown a website's authentication screen and provided instructions. Participants informed the researchers when they had confidently memorized a password. Participants logged-in using a map 10 times for practice, followed by 10 logins that were recorded. These steps were repeated for all the maps for each prototype in the same presentation sequence. Participants rated their satisfaction of an EaN and UYI authentication experience by completing the SUS questionnaire.

Participants then assumed the role of an over-the-shoulder attacker. Participants were instructed to view the OSA video of an individual logging in to a website using the EaN authentication scheme. They were given the printed sheet of the website screen seen in the video and were informed they could view the video as many times as they desired. Participants informed the researcher when they were ready to guess the password. The researcher recorded the number of times the video was viewed and the participants' password guess.

3 Results

3.1 Authentication Login Efficiency

The data were cleaned by evaluating the EaN login efficiency data to determine if the different EaN website themes (e.g., Blaze, Martian, Serendipity, and School Extravaganza) had an effect on participant login time. The UYI login efficiency data were also cleaned by determining if the different website themes (e.g., Knitted Frog, Bean, GreenTech, and Hoppy Easter) affected participant login time. Boxplots were used to assess outliers and data discrepancies. Data cleaning resulted in removing data for three participants because their login data indicated times exceeding two standard deviations of the mean for the first EaN Blaze map. Additionally, an error in the EaN program allowed individuals to press ENTER without entering a password. This led to two trials where participants had login times of 100 ms. This accounted for less than 1% of the trials. Missing reaction times for these trials were replaced with the average reaction time for that participant on that map.

The researchers evaluated the login efficiency data to determine if the EaN and UYI authentication schemes had an effect on participant login time measured in seconds. The results indicated login speeds for EaN ($M = 8.09$, $SD = 2.75$) were significantly longer than the login speeds for UYI ($M = 3.56$, $SD = 0.52$), $t(24) = 8.33$, $p < .001$, $d = 1.67$. Longer login times for EaN were expected due to users having to type 11 characters versus only selecting 3 images for UYI. Overall, both authentication schemes obtained login times that met the usability standards for login efficiency (see Fig. 6).

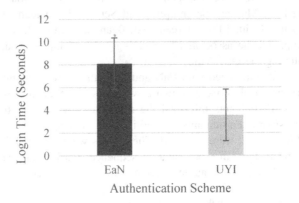

Fig. 6. Mean login times for EaN and UYI. Error bars represent standard error of the mean.

3.2   Authentication Accuracy

The data were cleaned by evaluating the login accuracy data to determine if the different themes affected authentication success. Boxplots were used to assess data discrepancies and outliers. There were outliers; however, excluding them did not significantly affect analyses. A one-way repeated measures ANOVA comparing accuracy for the four different maps indicated there was no difference in accuracy for the different EaN maps, $F(3, 72) = 0.45$, $p = .718$, partial $\eta^2 = .05$.

The researchers evaluated the login accuracy data to determine if the EaN and UYI authentication schemes affected accuracy. Users achieved significantly more accurate

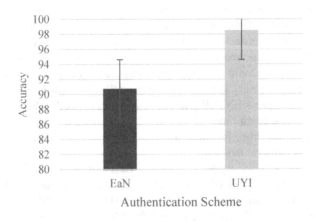

Fig. 7. Mean login accuracy for EaN and UYI. Error bars represent standard error of the mean.

logins using UYI logins (M = 99%, SD = 6%), when compared to the accuracy of EaN logins (M = 91%, SD = 9.7%), $t(24)$ = 3.44, p = .002, d = .69. Overall, both authentication schemes obtained high authentication success rates that exceeded our 90% login accuracy usability requirement (see Fig. 7).

3.3 Casual Over-the-Shoulder Attacker Role

The researchers evaluated OSA data to determine if the EaN and UYI authentication schemes affected attacker success. Boxplots were used to assess data discrepancies and outliers. EaN was uniformly distributed at 0% success, while UYI was uniformly distributed at 100% success with a few, expected outliers when participants did not succeed in guessing the password. Excluding the UYI outliers did not significantly affect analyses. A paired-samples t-test revealed that OSA attempts were significantly more successful for UYI (M = 80%, SD = 41%) when compared to EaN attacker success (M = 0%, SD = 0%), $t(24)$ = 9.80, p < .001, d = 1.96.

When participants attempted OSAs, they viewed the EaN login video (M = 7.60, SD = 3.95) significantly more times than the UYI video (M = 3.16, SD = 1.03), t (24) = 5.50, p < .001, d = 1.10. Overall, OSA attempts resulted in 0 accurate guesses for EaN despite more than twice as many average views compared to UYI (see Fig. 8).

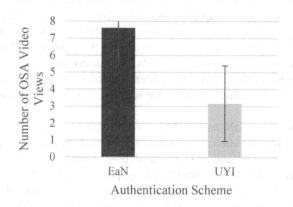

Fig. 8. Mean number of OSA video views of EaN and UYI authentication. Error bars represent standard error of the mean.

3.4 Subjective Usability Satisfaction

The researchers evaluated the SUS data to determine if the EaN and UYI authentication schemes affected satisfaction. Boxplots were used to assess data discrepancies and outliers. There were no outliers in the SUS data. A paired-samples t-test revealed that SUS scores for UYI (M = 81.90, SD = 10.78) were significantly higher than EaN (M = 69.60, SD = 16.56), $t(24)$ = 4.692, p = .010, d = .92. Overall, both authentication schemes obtained SUS scores that surpassed our usability requirement (see Fig. 9).

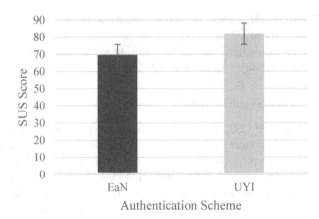

Fig. 9. Mean SUS scores for EaN and UYI. Error bars represent standard error of the mean.

4 Discussions

We proposed and evaluated EaN, a hybrid authentication scheme that combines a conventional strong password with a graphical authentication scheme. The EaN graphical scheme displays a map populated with icons which provides the user with clues for entering their strong password. We evaluated the usability and security of the proposed EaN graphical scheme by comparing it to the popular UYI scheme and to traditional alphanumeric password standards. We determined relative usability by evaluating user performance across the dimensions of efficiency, accuracy, and subjective satisfaction. Authentication security was measured by evaluating a schemes OSA resistance.

We found that both EaN and UYI allowed for quick authentication and met the usability standard for efficiency with login times falling between 7 and 20 s [14]. The login times for both EaN and UYI revealed users needed a maximum of 10 s to authenticate successfully. When compared to graphical schemes that use a translating targets to another location OSA defense, we determined EaN allowed more efficient account access than other schemes (c.f. WYSWYE and SSSL) [12, 16]. Our results for UYI were inconsistent with previous literature. We found that users needed between 2.9 and 5.3 s to login. Hayashi and colleagues found authentication UYI times between 11.5 and 24.7 s [10].

The accuracy usability requirement was determined by evaluating the rate of successful user authentication. To successfully authenticate, EaN login required users to type 11 characters correctly. On the other hand, UYI login only required users to select 3 targets correctly. As expected, we found that users were significantly more accurate when authenticating with UYI. EaN results indicated users achieved 91% accuracy rates on average. EaN accuracy met our usability requirement of 90%. However, UYI demonstrated near ceiling performance. It is important to acknowledge that UYI interactions can be mapped onto PIN entry authentication making its use more intuitive compared to our novel scheme [25].

Both EaN and UYI achieved SUS scores that exceed our usability requirement. Future EaN research should also look at other methods for collecting subjective data beyond the SUS. For example, interview questions could help pinpoint the aspects of the EaN authentication process where users felt improvements were needed.

To reach the authentication security requirements, we determined that casual attackers in the laboratory ought to ideally have 0% success performing an OSA when given one guess and unlimited views. And, indeed, the EaN resisted OSAs success-fully. Results indicated the number of EaN OSA video views ranged from 2 to 19, regardless, 0% of participants playing the role of an attacker were able to guess the correct EaN password. These findings were consistent with results reported for schemes that also deploy translation to another location OSA defense strategies [21, 22]. However, the UYI scheme prevented OSAs only 20% of the time. UYI results indi-cated when participants view the UYI OSA video 1 to 5 times, they would successfully perform an OSA 80% of the time. These findings were consistent with previous lit-erature that indicated UYI fails to prevent OSAs when attackers are given 3 or more OSA viewings [8].

Uniquely, the EaN scheme can equally provide a good usability experience for both frequent and intermittent users. In this study, authentication performance reflected first-time users who were required to learn how to use new schemes for authentication. According to Shneiderman and Plaisant [26], first-time users know the given task concept but lack the abilities resulting from extended practice. Typical graphical authentication requires users to complete a visual search. The targets being searched for are randomly placed within a display. This requires users to always complete a visual search, which takes effort and time. Requiring a few extra seconds to authenticate compared with alphanumeric is not a practical cost given the increase in memorability for intermittent users (e.g., accessing infrequent services: taxes, concert tickets). However, frequent users might be authenticating hundreds of times a week making efficiency a critical usability concern (e.g., accessing your laptop). Those users authenticating with their EaN password regularly, can transfer the password to pro-cedural memory allowing for rapid and effortless logins. They simply enter their password without completing an inefficient visual search, but if they forget their strong password the map provides the necessary clues for recognition.

5 Conclusions

Over the past decade, numerous researchers have proposed various graphical authen-tication schemes, even though most prevent OSAs, they have failed to gain widespread implementation. We propose EaN might be capable of bridging the gap between strong passwords and graphical passcodes. Password authentication is facilitated by providing users with a static map image with an embedded icon passcode path, which helps users remember their strong password. Importantly, the EaN passwords generated from the passcode paths fulfill the recommendations for a strong password [2].

Results indicated the EaN authentication scheme surpassed the security require-ments. And, participants (92%) indicated they would be willing to put forth additional authentication entry effort in order to prevent OSAs. In this case, learning the new EaN authentication scheme could be viewed as an acceptable effort, if they perceive an increase in security. Thus, the proposed hybrid EaN scheme is a promising authentication alternative that incorporates the benefits associated with graphical passcodes and the critical security aspects associated with strong alphanumeric passwords.

References

1. Zyiran, M., Haga, W.J.: Password security: an empirical study. J. Manage. Inf. Syst. **15**(4), 161–185 (1999)
2. Barton, B.F., Barton, M.S.: User-friendly password methods for computer-mediated information systems. Comput. Secur. **3**(3), 186–195 (1984)
3. Still, J.D., Cain, A.A., Schuster, D.: Human-centered authentication guidelines. Inf. Comput. Secur. **25**(4), 437–453 (2017)
4. Paivio, A.: Imagery and Verbal Processes. Psychology Press, New York (2013)
5. Madigan, S.: Picture memory. In: Yuille, J.C. (edn.) Imagery, Memory and Cognition: Essays in Honor of Allan Paivio, pp. 65–89 (1983)
6. Suo, X., Zhu, Y., Owen, G.S.: Graphical passwords: a survey. In: Proceedings of the 21st Annual Computer Security Applications Conference, pp. 463–472, December 2005
7. English, R., Poet, R.: The effectiveness of intersection attack countermeasures for graphical passwords. In: Proceedings of 11th International Conference on Trust, Security and Privacy in Computing and Communications (TrustCom), pp. 1–8. IEEE (2012)
8. Cain, A.A., Still, J.D.: Usability comparison of over-the-shoulder attack resistant authentication schemes. J. Usability Stud. **13**, 196–219 (2018)
9. Wiedenbeck, S., Waters, J., Birget, J.C., Brodskiy, A., Memon, N.: PassPoints: design and longitudinal evaluation of a graphical password system. Int. J. Hum.-Comput. Stud. **63**(1), 102–127 (2005)
10. Hayashi, E., Dhamija, R., Christin, N., Perrig, A.: Use your illusion: secure authentication usable anywhere. In: Proceedings of the 4th Symposium on Usable Privacy and Security, pp. 35–45 (2008)
11. De Luca, A., Denzel, M., Hussmann, H.: Look into my eyes! Can you guess my password? In: Proceedings of the 5th Symposium on Usable Privacy and Security. AMC (2009)
12. Khot, R.A., Kumaraguru, P., Srinathan, K.: WYSWYE: shoulder surfing defense for recognition based graphical passwords. In: Proceedings of the 24th Australian Computer-Human Interaction Conference, pp. 285–294 (2012)
13. Al Ameen, M.N.: The impact of cues and user interaction on the memorability of system-assigned random passwords (Doctoral dissertation) (2016)
14. Braz, C., Robert, J.M.: Security and usability: the case of the user authentication methods. In: Proceedings of the 18th International Conference of the Association Francophone Interaction Homme- Machine, pp. 199–203. ACM (2006)
15. Brostoff, S., Inglesant, P., Sasse, M.A.: Evaluating the usability and security of a graphical one-time PIN system. In: Proceedings of the 24th BCS Interaction Specialist Group Conference, pp. 88–97, September2010
16. Perkovic, T., Cagalj, M., Rakic, N.: SSSL: shoulder surfing safe login. In: 17th International Conference on Software, Telecommunications & Computer Networks (SoftCOM), pp. 270–275 (2009)
17. Belk, M., Fidas, C., Germanakos, P., Samaras, G.: The interplay between humans, technology and user authentication: a cognitive processing perspective. Comput. Hum. Behav. **76**, 184–200 (2017)

18. Brooke, J.: SUS-A quick and dirty usability scale. Usability Eval. Ind. **189**(194), 4–7 (1996)
19. Bangor, A., Kortum, P., Miller, J.: Determining what individual SUS scores mean: adding an adjective rating scale. J. usability Stud. **4**(3), 114–123 (2009)
20. Tiller, L.N., Cain, A.A., Potter, L.N., Still, J.D.: Graphical authentication schemes: balancing amount of image distortion. In: Ahram, T., Nicholson, D. (eds) Advances in Human Factors in Cybersecurity. AHFE 2018. Advances in Intelligent Systems and Computing, vol. 782, pp. 88–98. Springer, Cham. https://doi.org/10.1007/978-3-319-94782-2_9
21. Sun, H.M., Chen, S.T., Yeh, J.H., Cheng, C.Y.: A shoulder surfing resistant graphical authentication system. IEEE Trans. Dependable Secure Comput. **99**, 1–14 (2016)
22. Zangooei, T., Mansoori, M., Welch, I.: A hybrid recognition and recall based approach in graphical passwords. In: Proceedings of the 24th Australian Computer-Human Interaction Conference, pp. 665–673 (2012)
23. Bangor, A., Kortum, P.T., Miller, J.T.: An empirical evaluation of the system usability scale. Int. J. Hum.-Comput. Interact. **24**, 574–594 (2008)
24. Peres, S.C., Pham, T., Phillips, R.: Validation of the system usability scale (SUS): SUS in the wild. In: The Proceedings of the Human Factors and Ergonomics Society, vol. 57(1), pp. 192–196 (2013)
25. Still, J.D., Still, M.L., Grgic, J.: Designing intuitive interactions: exploring performance and reflection measures. Interact. Comput. **27**, 271–286 (2015)
26. Shneiderman, B., Plaisant, C.: Designing the User Interface: Strategies for Effective Human-Computer Interaction, 5th edn. Addison-Wesley Publishers, New York (2010, 2005)

Cybersecurity Awareness and Behavior

From Cyber-Security Deception
to Manipulation and Gratification
Through Gamification

Xavier Bellekens[1(✉)], Gayan Jayasekara[1], Hanan Hindy[1], Miroslav Bures[1,3],
David Brosset[2], Christos Tachtatzis[4], and Robert Atkinson[4]

[1] Division of Cyber-Security, Abertay University, Dundee, Scotland
x.bellekens@abertay.ac.uk
[2] Chair of Naval Cyber Defense, Ecole Navale, Lanvéoc, France
[3] Department of Computer Science, Faculty of Electrical Engineering,
Czech Technical University in Prague, Prague, Czech Republic
[4] Department of Electronic and Electrical Engineering,
University of Strathclyde, Glasgow, Scotland

Abstract. With the ever growing networking capabilities and services offered to users, attack surfaces have been increasing exponentially, additionally, the intricacy of network architectures has increased the complexity of cyber-defenses, to this end, the use of deception has recently been trending both in academia and industry. Deception enables to create proactive defense systems, luring attackers in order to better defend the systems at hand. Current applications of deception, only rely on static, or low interactive environments. In this paper we present a platform that combines human-computer-interaction, analytics, gamification and deception to lure malicious users into selected traps while piquing their interests. Furthermore we analyse the interactive deceptive aspects of the platform through the addition of a narrative, further engaging malicious users into following a predefined path and deflecting attacks from key network systems.

Keywords: Deception · Cyber-security · Manipulation ·
Interactive defense

1 Introduction

Over the last two decades the field of cyber-security has experienced numerous changes associated with the evolution of neighboring fields, such as networking, mobile communications, and recently the Internet of Things (IoT) [7]. Changes in mindsets have also been witnessed, a couple of years ago the cyber-security industry blamed users for their mistakes often depicted as the number one reason behind security breaches. Nowadays, companies are empowering users, modifying their perception of being the weak link, into being the center-piece of

© Springer Nature Switzerland AG 2019
A. Moallem (Ed.): HCII 2019, LNCS 11594, pp. 99–114, 2019.
https://doi.org/10.1007/978-3-030-22351-9_7

security design [9]. Users are by definition "in control" and therefore a cyber-security asset. Researchers have focused on the gamification of cyber-security elements, helping users to learn and understand the concepts of attacks and threats, allowing them to become the first line of defense to report anomalies [19]. However, over the past years numerous infrastructures have suffered from malicious intent, data breaches, and crypto-ransomeware, clearly demonstrating the technical "know-how" of hackers and their ability to bypass the security measures in place [12].

Researchers concentrated on the gamification, learning and teaching theory of cyber-security to end-users in numerous fields through various techniques and scenarios to raise end-user cyber-situational awareness [1, 2]. While empowering the end-users, researchers overlooked hackers, and the potential of using hacker gamification to benefit cyber-security. In this paper, we argue that there is an endemic issue in the understanding of hacking practices leading to vulnerable devices, software and architectures. We therefore propose a gamification platform for hackers. The platform is designed with hacker user-interaction and deception in mind.

The contributions of this paper are threefold:

- Deceptive Interactive Techniques are proposed and defined. This can be transposed to other systems to increase the interactivity of deception systems.
- An Interactive Deceptive Based Platform is presented. The platform is able to deploy scenarios to engage and deceive malicious users in different contexts.
- Deceptive narrative scenarios based on gamification are presented and evaluated. The narrative enables to engage the malicious user to further explore the deceptive scenarios and safeguards key elements of the network.

The remainder of this paper is organised as follows; Sect. 2 discusses techniques to engage malicious users through Gamification, Narrative, Manipulation and Gratification. Section 3 introduces the interactive deception platform and its components, followed by Sect. 4 which discusses 3 different scenarios to evaluate the interactivity and deceptiveness of the platform. Furthermore, Sect. 5 discusses the results obtained through the different scenarios, Sect. 6 highlight the related works, Sect. 7 discusses the key takeaways from the platform and its limitations and the paper concludes with Sect. 8.

2   Interactive Deception Based Defenses

The premise of this research assumes that all networks are vulnerable. This premise is extended to the belief that the attack surface grows alongside the number of devices connected to the network and the applications installed. Defending large attack surfaces is cumbersome and requires extensive maintenance. While IDS, Firewalls and other security appliances enable a high degree of protection and are key to enhance the overall security of a network, they may also contain vulnerabilities, hence, further increasing the attack surface [4]. Deception-based defenses on the other hand enable a system to trick or mislead

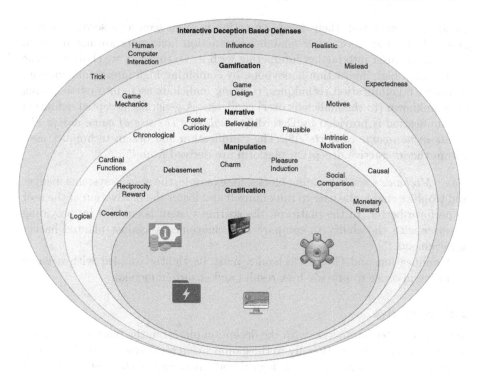

Fig. 1. Inner architecture of the deception framework

an attacker to perform (or not) an action. Two of the most widely accepted definition of deception applied to cyber-security are provided by Yuill [18] and Almeshekah and Spafford [1]. In their manuscript, Almeshekah and Spafford discuss the addition of "confusion" to the widely accepted definition provided by Yuill. In this paper we argue, that deception and confusion in cyber-security is best achieved, through human computer interaction. Static systems, such as described in literature [10,16] often fail to meet the definitions aforementioned. We further argue that high interaction environments are key to deceptive defenses. Low interaction deceptive environments fail to mimic the behaviour of virtualised systems, furthermore, they fail to provide malicious user with a viable challenge and hence, limiting the usefulness of such systems [15]. Our platform, while providing a fully interactive system, further extends this by building upon gamification techniques and story telling (narrative), intrinsically, providing an immersive environment to the malicious user similar to video games (Fig. 1).

2.1 Gamification

Interactive defences, such as honeypots, are often based on real or virtualised systems logging interaction information and queries made by malicious users. While honeypots are effective at detecting and deflecting cyber-attacks or creating malware zoo, their deceptive action is often seen as a secondary purpose [14]. Furthermore, while enabling interaction honeypots are not designed to coerce the user into further interacting with it. To this end, we challenged the definition of high interaction honeypots, by combining high interaction environments with gamification techniques, coercing malicious users into participating in an unknown (to the malicious user) challenge. A generally accepted definition of gamification is provided by Deterding *et al.* as *"The use of game design elements in non-game contexts"* [8]. The gamification and design techniques used within the interactive deception platform are derived from [5].

Game Mechanics act as building blocks, for example, the scoring systems, badges and trophies enable the user to rank himself and foster the motivation of the user to perform better. In the platform, the scoring system is enabled by providing the user with the ability to compare his achievements against planted hacker achievements [5].

Gamification and Game Mechanics must be tightly coupled with a game narrative in order to provide best results and ensure immersion.

2.2   Narrative

In order to foster interaction with the deception platform, the platform builds on an attack narrative, additionally to the gamification techniques used. The narrative enables to construct a causal, logical and chronological chain of events, necessary to the high interaction capabilities of the platform. Barthes [3] described events critical to the coherence of the story as "cardinal functions". Cardinal functions play an important role within story telling as it enables branching into sub-stories, but also allows the malicious user to immerse himself within the challenge provided by the platform. In order to increase the deception aspect of the platform, the narrative follows the intrinsic motivation of a malicious user. Furthermore, the narrative must be plausible, as different network architecture may have different vulnerabilities and rewards, and hence, intrinsic motivations. Furthermore, narratives must cultivate the curiosity of the malicious user as the story unfolds, it is therefore important to align the narrative to the gamification aspect of the platform. To this end, the platform provides a believable chain of events based on potential cyber-attacks and vulnerabilities induced within the systems as scenarios. The stories provided by the platform are linear, and constructed retrospectively, in order to avoid mismatches between the vulnerabilities, the gamification, the rewards and the narrative.

The gamification and reward fully inform the narrative, guiding the malicious user to its next step. While the malicious user can perform an infinite number of action, he is unable to influence the outcome of the game without following the path laid out.

2.3   Manipulation

A unique approach to deceive and mislead users is through manipulation. Manipulation can be defined as the action of controlling someone at your advantage.

Manipulation can take different forms as explored by Buss [6]. In his study, Buss reported 12 different manipulation techniques used in close relationships and interactional context. We identified 7 techniques to work with our deception platform, each leading the malicious user to perform an action at our advantage to either follow the story or to follow another path (i.e. target).

Coercion is the practice of making someone perform a forced action by using threat or force. Through data gathering, and behavioural analysis an operator is able to modify the narrative and gamification element relating to a specific malicious user, enabling to display coercive error message, forcing the hacker to follow any other pre-defined given path.

Reciprocity Reward are provided through a flexible narrative. As aforementioned, the platform can be used to monitor the actions of a malicious user. In order to evaluate the user's competencies, the platform requires manual vulnerabilities testing, hence, the gamification engine provides reciprocal rewards to users that are not using vulnerabilities scanners. Enabling them to continue further discovering key elements within the deceptive environment.

Debasement is the practice of lowering values, to manipulate someone. While unable to work on the emotions of the malicious user, the narrative is able changes by analysing the attacks performed. Vulnerabilities can be loaded in a round robin fashion, in order to keep the malicious user entertained, and therefore exhibit less difficulties. Debasing the platform challenges ensures the continuation of the story and thus the immersion of the malicious user within the deceptive game.

Charm focuses on complimenting someone in order to perform an action. As the platform and the narrative require a logical and believable construct, charming the malicious user is only done through subtle clues, such as comments on the "ability" of a malicious user in code running on the client-side. Those charming "comments" help the user follow the pre-defined path, while believing to follow this path through is own free will.

Pleasure Induction is the ability of demonstrating that an unwanted action can be pleasurable for the malicious user. This is provided by the ability to debase specific vulnerabilities enabling the malicious user to continue is progression through the deceptive platform and earn rewards.

Social Comparison is the act of comparing the malicious user against other hackers or groups. Due to the nature of the platform, obvious comparisons such as leaderboard would annihilate the immersive element of the platform. To this end, comments on client-side and defacing pages are hidden. Website defacement is an attack that changes the appearance of a website, often accompanied by the name of the defacers or the group of defacers. This subtle clue, enables to create a social comparison between the malicious user and other groups or hackers.

Monetary Rewards are core of some scenarios to deceive the hacker. The narrative builds upon potential credit cards, or valuable information available at the end of the quest, hence leading the attacker to follow the narrative to obtain a potential monetary reward.

2.4 Gratification

Luring a malicious user into deception requires to foster its curiosity, in this manuscript, we use gratification to trigger a pleasurable emotional reaction within the malicious user, in order to lure him to perform key deceptive actions. By providing the malicious user, with credit card information, rewards, or key information, we lead the action of the user towards a specific path or target predefined within the platform. The gratification inherently focuses on increasing the deceptive action of the platform.

3 Platform Architecture

This section provides an overview of the deceptive platform architecture. We developed a fully extendable gamification architecture allowing researchers to deploy virtualised hosts on both local networks and the internet. Each virtualised hosts contains a set of specific vulnerability (i.e. web application, software, buffer overflow, etc). Each host is connected to a game engine, an interaction engine and a scoring engine.

Figure 2 depicts the logical architecture of the platform. When a hacker connects to one or more virtual hosts, he is unable to differentiate it from a real-world computer (i.e. running a windows operating system), this is achieved by using port-scanning deception enabling to camouflage the signature of the operating system.

All interactions with the host(s) including time, behavioural data (i.e. Keystroke dynamics, activity tracking, etc.), and engagement are further recorded and processed by the game and the scoring engines. This allows the hacker to be served with polymorphic vulnerabilities which, in turn, can increase or decrease their difficulties over time, keeping the hacker engaged with the platform. Furthermore, Fig. 2 shows that the interaction information gathered through the host(s) is fed to the scoring engine, which provides the hacker with rewards based on pre-defined scenarios. Using a threshold measures, the hacker's interest is further analysed. If his interest scores below threshold, subtle clues are provided to the hacker. The clues are inbuilt in each scenario. The clues vary from wireshark captures, to misleading network scans and vulnerability scans. The clues enable the hacker to seamlessly continue his malicious activity on the network by following a pre-defined path, without suspecting interacting with a virtual environment. The path leads to data being gathered on the attacks, techniques and tools used by hackers to solve each challenges thrown at him. All the gathered information are further analyzed using a circular methodology, enabling the operators to enhance the game engine and the variability of the difficulties.

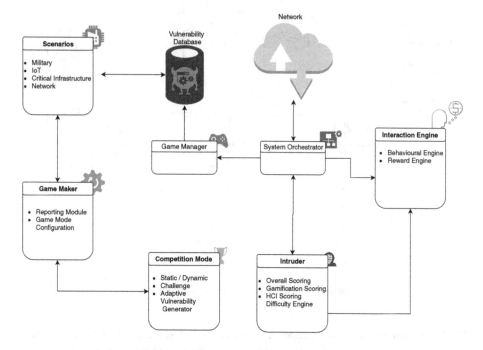

Fig. 2. Logical architecture of the deception framework

Figure 3 provides an overview of the deception framework network architecture. The network can be extended through the Software Defined Network (SDN) controller, enabling an operator to create virtual networks on demand. Information are pulled from the vulnerability database to populate the virtualised hosts running on the virtualised deception host server. Based on the scenario being launched, different network architectures, virtual hosts and vulnerabilities are loaded and spawned on the network. Hacker interactions are made through a load balancer and a Django web server for all web vulnerabilities.

4   Scenarios

4.1   Scenario 1: Shopping Website

77% of web applications have been reported to include a vulnerable JavaScript library enabling malicious users to take advantage of the website and potentially use this vulnerability to launch further attacks. The scenario was evaluated on its own, to identify the state of the narrative, the value of the kernels within the narrative, and the deception, manipulation and gamification aspects.

Figure 4 provides an overview of the deception narrative. The shopping website offers potential monetary rewards if hacked through credit cards stored in the database. To this end, 4 apparent vulnerabilities were created. (I) A "robot.txt" wile containing the path to an unprotected administration page.

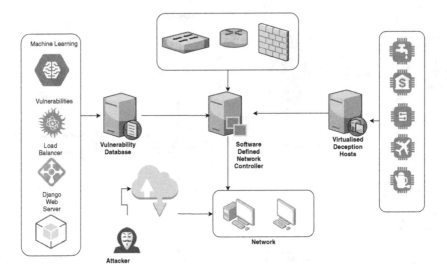

Fig. 3. Network the deception framework

(II) A "JavaScript password checker" library included within the "index.html" page enabling the hacker to bypass the login and password requirements. (III) A "Login SQL Injection" enabling the hacker to use an SQL injection against the password field to gain access to the administration page. (IV) A persistent cross-site scripting (XSS) injection vulnerability.

Through subtle clues, within the code, comments, etc..., the attacker is lead to believe that the website is vulnerable. His interested is further piqued through the manipulation techniques as shown on the edges of Fig. 4. By following the XSS injection vulnerability, the malicious user will quickly discover planted comments from other imaginary hackers, acting as a leaderboard and creating a social comparison between the abilities of the imaginary hackers and the malicious user. Furthermore, by following the first 3 vulnerabilities, the hacker will access an unprotected administration page, which, in turn, will give him access to a "database.db" file containing fabricated credit card numbers and associated CSV numbers. Another file provides information about another shopping website, which simulate similar vulnerabilities with a different design, misleading the hacker to follow another path.

4.2 Scenario 2: Vulnerable FTP

The second scenario is built around a vulnerable version of an FTP application. The FTP contains default credentials enabling a malicious user to read and upload new data on the FTP. The premise of this scenario is to reward the hacker upfront to provide direct gratification.

Figure 5 illustrates the different path the malicious user is able to take. Providing upfront gratification, with clear planted rewards enable to build the

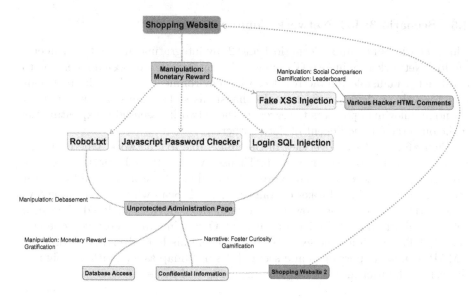

Fig. 4. Web deception narrative

momentum of the narrative. The first file is a database file containing various tables and information. The file contains 2 GB of data, requiring the hacker to spend time analysing and searching for potential information. Within the file, numerous references to a vulnerable WordPress website are made. The link to a defaced page is also provided. The WordPress website is itself vulnerable to SQL injection and XSS attacks and aims at comparing the malicious user skills with the skills of an imaginary planted hacker. The second vulnerability provides the malicious user with a large Nmap scan of numerous machine. One is identified as vulnerable. Upon exploiting the vulnerability the malicious user is able to perform a privilege escalation through a buffer overflow attack (All buffer overflow protections are disabled).

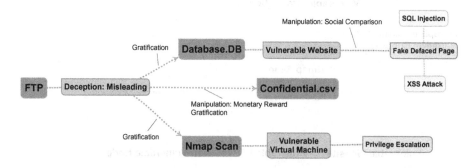

Fig. 5. FTP deception narrative

4.3 Scenario 3: IoT Network Combination

This scenario builds upon Scenario 1 and 2, by integrating them into a vulnerable IoT Network running MQTT nodes. The aggregation of scenarios enable to construct a plausible interactive deception environment, leading the malicious user towards predefined targets and exhaust his skills against known vulnerable nodes allowing operators to segregate the network, essentially, exploiting the malicious user for the benefit of data gathering.

Figure 6 provides an overview of the vulnerable IoT network. One front facing vulnerable IoT device running MQTT uses weak SSH credentials. The device itself contains a file with un-encrypted SSH credentials for a vulnerable "broker server". The root of the broker contains an NMAP Scan which has for objective to lead the malicious user towards the vulnerable devices analysed. The scan contains information about 7 nodes in total. One vulnerable webserver, one vulnerable FTP and 5 IoT nodes with weak credentials but advertised within the NMAP scan as no port open and secured. Using Nmap as an "authority figure" to mislead the user into selecting another proposed target.

5   Evaluation

The platform was built against distinctive scenarios evaluating the narrative, the gamification and the manipulation aspects of the platform. Leading the attacker on a pre-defined path for deception.

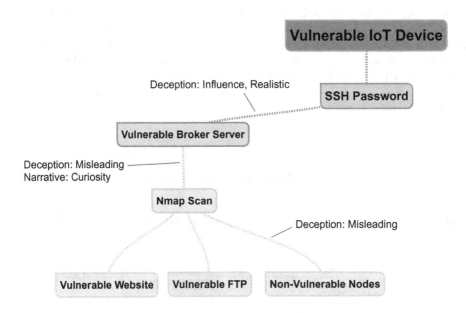

Fig. 6. IoT network deception narrative

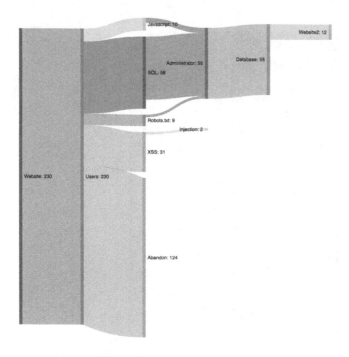

Fig. 7. Website flow narrative

All deception environments have been launched front facing the internet using four different locations (Atlanta, Lyon, London, and Tokyo) for 2 weeks. All interactions with the environment were recorded and the path of the hackers where analysed for each environment. For consistency, all environments were reset at midnight (local time). The path taken by malicious users accessing different systems are recorded using their IP addresses. Furthermore, all malicious users following a path on a predefined scenario have been aggregated.

Figure 7 shows the path followed by malicious users while interacting with the interactive deception web Scenario. A total of 230 users accessed the platform over a period of two weeks. 53.9% of the users did not succeed into accessing the administrative web page, note that in this case no distinctions are made between potential legitimate users and unsuccessful malicious users and bots. 13.4% of malicious users tried XSS injection, but only 0.86% resulted in a successful persistent XSS injection. 3.9% of the users accessed the "robots.txt" file and only 0.86% further accessed the administrator webpage. A surprising result, as this clue was created for debasement purpose (i.e. enabling easy access to the second stage). 24.3% of malicious users performed an SQL attack against the website, however only 23.9% succeeded into accessing the administrator page. 4.34% accessed the JavaScript library, however, only 1.73% of users made it to the administrator page. All users having access to the administrator webpage accessed the database file, however, 21% of the successful users went on to attacking the second deceptive website.

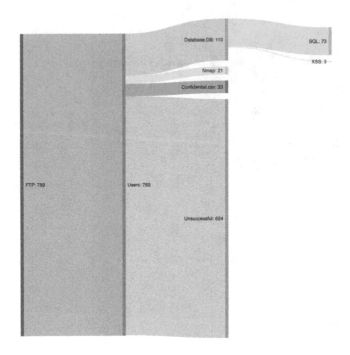

Fig. 8. FTP flow narrative

While the drop-out rate is high, 46% of users carried out at least one attack, with a total of 27.9% carrying out a successful attack. The average time spend by user 29.6 min. The flows presented in Fig. 7 indicate a successful narrative, as successful users tried to proceed with an attack on a pre-defined path, the drop-outs at various stages are indicated by a lack of motivation (i.e. potential gratification) or a lack of skills.

Figure 8 illustrates the path taken by malicious users during their interaction with the interactive deception FTP Scenario. A total of 789 IP addresses were recorded trying to access the FTP over a two week period. 20.7% malicious users successfully logged on the FTP server. 67% of successful users accessed the "Database.DB" file, further leading them to access a planted vulnerable website. 66.36% carried out an SQL attack against the website, while 2.72% carried out an XSS attack. 12.8% of the successful users (at the first stage) accessed the NMAP scan, but none of them carried out any attacks against the vulnerable virtual machine. However 20.12% of the malicious users (at the first stage) accessed the "confidential.csv" containing, fake names, credit card numbers and CSV numbers.

The primary assumption for the high-drop off at the first stage is due to the number of bots that scanned the FTP and abandoned. The low number reported to access the "confidential.csv" file is believed to be due to the too obvious name of the file, hence leading malicious users onto pursuing the "database.DB" file and executing SQL and XSS attacks against the website. Malicious users spend an average time of 9.36 min on the platform.

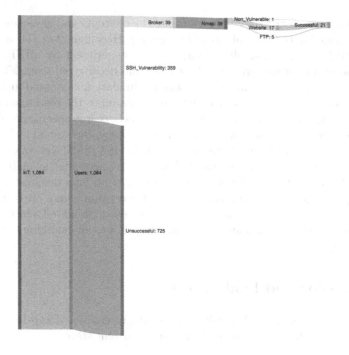

Fig. 9. IoT flow narrative

Figure 9 shows the path taken by malicious users when interacting with the combined environment, through an IoT vulnerable device sending MQTT requests to a vulnerable broker. Out of the 1,084 individual IP recorded 66.88% of requests made to the IoT platform were unsuccessful. 33.11% of attacks succeeded into accessing the IoT virtual sensor by identifying the weak credential uses, however, only 10.8% of the successful users where able to connect to the broker. 100% of the users accessing the broker (stage 3) accessed the Nmap file stored at the root. 2.59% of the successful malicious user accessing the nmap file, attacked the nodes stated as non-vulnerable in the Nmap scan, and successfully accessed the 5 nodes. 56.4% of the users reacted to the misleading information and attacked either the website or the FTP. All malicious users that proceeded to stage 4 performed successful attacks against the deceptive targets. 43.5% also dropped off at stage 3 after having accessed the Nmap file. It is expected that the drop off, might be due to a lack of reward at this stage, clarity in reading the Nmap file provided or a lack of time. The malicious users spend an average time of 41.3 min on the deceptive scenario demonstrating a successful, believable narrative, fostering curiosity.

6   Related Works

McQueen et al. [13] introduced deception defenses in control systems. They defined security through seven abstract concepts, and further defined deception solutions for each abstract security concept. The concepts and associated deception are provided in the form of a broad taxonomy. Heckman *et al.* [11] review the January 2012 real-time red/blue team wargame experiment by MITRE, which included deception at its core, in order to fool and deceive red teams. The main focus of the deception system in place was to simulate a command and control system, which in turn would provide false information to the read team through a fake interface. The system presented by the authors was specifically designed with a wargame in mind, and while proving its efficacy, the system lacks flexibility in order to be deployed in a broader context (i.e. IoT, SME Networks, SCADA Systems, Web, etc...). In [17] Stech *et al.* provide a scientometric analysis of the concepts of deception detection in cyber space. The authors demonstrated that the social, behavioral and cognitive aspects of deception where often discarded from the denial and deception tactics used. They also highlighted a lack of terminology to describe deception and classified deception as an emerging field within cyber-security.

7   Discussion and Limitations

This section introduces the key takeaways of the interactive deception platform as well as the limitations of the platform in its current state.

7.1   Key Takeaways

- **Increased Interaction:** The platform enables malicious users to interact with numerous believable components and focuses on increasing the interaction time between the malicious user and the components.
- **Chronological Events:** The platform builds on the concepts of gamification and narrative, hence, unfolds in a time line fashion.
- **Deflection:** The use of gamification, manipulation, gratification and narrative have demonstrated to be successful in order to deflect attacks from key network components to secondary nodes, or towards the dedicated virtual environment.
- **Platform Flexibility:** The platform is modular and hence enables to fit, and build on numerous scenarios.

7.2   Limitations

- **Scenario Complexity:** Complex environments may require complex scenarios, which may clutter the environments. Furthermore, building believable scenarios and a plausible narrative is time consuming.
- **Distinguishing between legitimate and malicious users:** In its current state the platform is unable to distinguish between users, hence limiting the interaction of the environment with legitimate users.

8   Conclusion

In this paper a successful interactive deception platform based on gamification, narrative, manipulation and gratification techniques is presented. The platform is highly modular and enable users to develop and deploy scenarios to mislead and deceive malicious users on a network, to safeguard key elements of the network, buy time for security operators to isolate the deceptive nodes and malicious user, or to collect and study the behaviour of malicious users. We have also presented a comprehensive model to increase the interaction with deceptive platform. The techniques can easily be transferred across to existing platform. Furthermore, the scenarios presented are based on a plausible narrative encouraging and coercing the user into exploring the environment. In this paper 3 scenarios were presented, demonstrating the efficiency of the narrative, manipulative and gratification components. It was demonstrated that while 2103 individual connection to the platform were recorded over the three scenarios and a high initial drop-out rate, over 75% of users engaging with the platform carry at least one successful attack.

References

1. Almeshekah, M.H., Spafford, E.H.: Planning and integrating deception into computer security defenses. In: Proceedings of the 2014 New Security Paradigms Workshop, pp. 127–138. ACM (2014)
2. Almeshekah, M.H., Spafford, E.H.: Cyber security deception. In: Jajodia, S., Subrahmanian, V.S.S., Swarup, V., Wang, C. (eds.) Cyber Deception, pp. 25–52. Springer, Cham (2016). https://doi.org/10.1007/978-3-319-32699-3_2
3. Barthes, R.: Lecture in inauguration of the chair of literary semiology, collège de france, January 7, 1977. Oxford Literary Rev. 4(1), 31–44 (1979)
4. Bellekens, X.J., Tachtatzis, C., Atkinson, R.C., Renfrew, C., Kirkham, T.: GLoP: enabling massively parallel incident response through GPU log processing. In: Proceedings of the 7th International Conference on Security of Information and Networks, p. 295. ACM (2014)
5. Blohm, I., Leimeister, J.M.: Gamification. Bus. Inf. Sys. Eng. 5(4), 275–278 (2013)
6. Buss, D.M.: Manipulation in close relationships: five personality factors in interactional context. J. Pers. 60(2), 477–499 (1992)
7. Desolda, G., Ardito, C., Matera, M., Piccinno, A.: Mashing-up smart things: a meta-design approach. In: Proceedings of Workshop on End User Development in the Internet of Things Era, CHI 2015 EA, pp. 33–36 (2015)
8. Deterding, S., Dixon, D., Khaled, R., Nacke, L.: From game design elements to gamefulness: defining gamification. In: Proceedings of the 15th International Academic MindTrek Conference: Envisioning Future Media Environments, pp. 9–15. ACM (2011)
9. Faily, S.: Why designing for usability and security is hard. In: Faily, S. (ed.) Designing Usable and Secure Software with IRIS and CAIRIS, pp. 3–8. Springer, Cham (2018). https://doi.org/10.1007/978-3-319-75493-2_1
10. Han, X., Kheir, N., Balzarotti, D.: Deception techniques in computer security: a research perspective. ACM Comput. Surv. (CSUR) 51(4), 80 (2018)

11. Heckman, K.E., Walsh, M.J., Stech, F.J., O'boyle, T.A., DiCato, S.R., Herber, A.F.: Active cyber defense with denial and deception: a cyber-wargame experiment. Comput. Secur. **37**, 72–77 (2013)
12. Hill, G., Bellekens, X.: Cryptoknight: generating and modelling compiled cryptographic primitives. Information **9**(9), 231 (2018)
13. McQueen, M.A., Boyer, W.F.: Deception used for cyber defense of control systems. In: 2nd Conference on Human System Interactions, HSI 2009, pp. 624–631. IEEE (2009)
14. Merien, T., Brosset, D., Bellekens, X., Claramunt, C.: A human-centred model for network flow analysis. In: 2018 2nd Cyber Security in Networking Conference (CSNet), pp. 1–6, October 2018. https://doi.org/10.1109/CSNET.2018.8602913
15. Mérien, T., Bellekens, X., Brosset, D., Claramunt, C.: A spatio-temporal entropy-based approach for the analysis of cyber attacks (demo paper). In: Proceedings of the 26th ACM SIGSPATIAL International Conference on Advances in Geographic Information Systems, pp. 564–567. ACM (2018)
16. Nawrocki, M., Wählisch, M., Schmidt, T.C., Keil, C., Schönfelder, J.: A survey on honeypot software and data analysis. arXiv preprint arXiv:1608.06249 (2016)
17. Stech, F., Heckman, K.E., Hilliard, P., Ballo, J.R.: Scientometrics of deception, counter-deception, and deception detection in cyber-space. PsychNology J. **9**(2) (2011)
18. Yuill, J.J., et al.: Defensive computer-security deception operations: processes, principles and techniques (2007)
19. Zhan, X., Nah, F.F.-H., Cheng, M.X.: An assessment of users' cyber security risk tolerance in reward-based exchange. In: Nah, F.F.-H., Xiao, B.S. (eds.) HCIBGO 2018. LNCS, vol. 10923, pp. 431–441. Springer, Cham (2018). https://doi.org/10.1007/978-3-319-91716-0_34

Gamifying Security Awareness:
A New Prototype

John Russell Cole(✉), Toni Pence(✉), Jeffrey Cummings(✉),
and Elizabeth Baker(✉)

Univeristy of North Carolina at Wilmington, Wilmington, NC 28403, USA
jrc9569@gmail.com,{pencet,cummingsj,bakere}@uncw.edu

Abstract. Data breaches within an organization have many causes. Social engineering attacks, ransom-ware applications and harmful spam email messages are data breach catalysts that are the result of human error. Human error is the leading cause of data breach and is also one of the more difficult factors for an organization to mitigate. Many users are unable to see how their role is impacted by organizational security policy, and therefor see no benefit to abide the policy. When employees use company devices to perform personal tasks, or use personal devices to perform business tasks, lines of ownership can be blurred and important organizational data assets can be put at risk. Training and awareness programs are too often treated as a bandage to fix a wound inflicted by a breach after the fact. If employees were trained effectively, the breach might not have occurred in the first place. This project and accompanying research paper will explore the gamification of the security training and awareness program. By developing role-based game modules to teach secure behavior to all organizational users, incentivizing secure behavior with real rewards that matter to participants and applying the training throughout the year, it can be possible to reinvent security awareness and prevent future data breaches.

Keywords: Virtual environment · Gamification · Security awareness

1 Introduction

According to IBM and the Ponemon Institute's recent release of the 2015 Cost of Data Breach Study: Global Analysis, the average total cost of a data breach for the 350 companies participating in the research study increased from \$3.52 million to \$3.79 million between 2014 and 2015 [6]. The study goes on to state that the average cost paid for each lost or stolen data record containing sensitive and confidential information increased from \$145 to \$154. The study goes into further detail regarding the costs and the root causes of a data breach. Cybersecurity threats are cited throughout the study as primary causes of data breach

Supported by University of North Carolina at Wilmington.

A. Moallem (Ed.): HCII 2019, LNCS 11594, pp. 115–133, 2019.
https://doi.org/10.1007/978-3-030-22351-9_8

and loss. However, when the article addresses the factors that influence the cost of a data breach, either those that accelerate the cost or mitigate the threat and lower the potential cost of a breach, employee training topped the list of factors that decrease the per capita cost of data breach. Along with the extensive use of encryption and an on-site incident response team, employee training is identified as being able to reduce the cost of a data breach by $8 per record, taking the average cost per record from $154 to $146 [6]. According to the 2016 Shred-it Security Tracker information security survey conducted by Ipsos, 78% of small business owners in the U.S. and 51% of senior executive C-Suite respondents only conduct training on information security procedures one or fewer times per year. In addition, 28% of small business owners report that they have never trained their employees on security procedures [4].

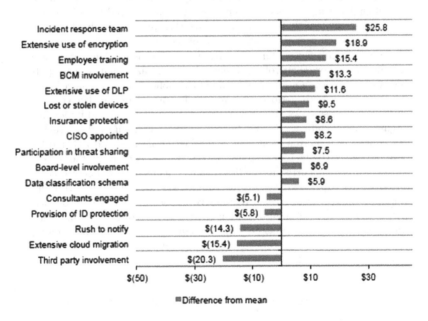

Fig. 1. Employee Training reduced the average cost per record by $15.4. 2016 Cost of Data Breach Study: United States. Ponemon Institute

A more recent study released by the Ponemon Institute entitled 2016 Cost of Data Breach Study: United States, indicates that companies in the United States on average have both a higher cost per stolen record at $221 and a higher average cost of data breach at $7.01 million [7]. The data also indicates that there was a 7% increase in the total cost of breach and a 2% increase in cost per stolen record. It is clear that the cost of data breaches as a trend are on the rise, but the 2016 Ponemon study also indicates that many companies are taking measures to mitigate threats through various means. Improvements in data governance programs will reduce the cost of a data breach. Incident response plans, appointment of a chief information security officer (CISO), employee training and awareness programs and a business continuity management strategy continue to result in cost savings. Employee training reduced the average cost per record by $15.4, shown in Fig. 1 [7].

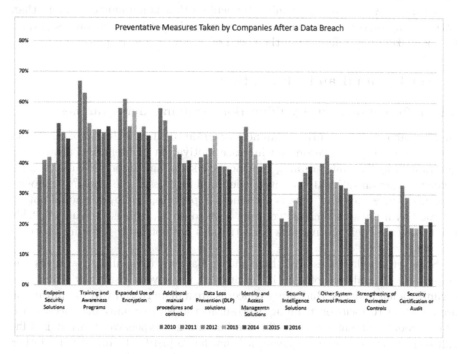

Fig. 2. Employee Training programs implemented after breach decreased by 15%. 2016 Cost of Data Breach Study: United States. Ponemon Institute

However, in that same study there is a different set of data that addresses the methods that companies participating in the survey took to respond to and remediate a data breach. According to this data, since 2010, implementation of employee training and awareness programs as a response to a data breach has decreased by 15%, shown in Fig. 2 [7].

According to Jones, during the same period when organizations are having a difficult time mitigating risk of breaches and developing appropriate countermeasures, employees are seeing more of the technology they use at the work place come into their homes and personal lives [5]. This is a threat to confidentiality because in some cases, the user is performing work related tasks on a non-work machine and non-work related tasks on a work machine. "The security requirements of the user for personal information, if they are considered at all, are normally far lower than those which are required to properly protect an organization's information." Besides the occasional news story surrounding a high profile data breach, home users don't have an understanding of information security requirements to effectively evaluate risks. And if users are giving the same level of consideration to personal assets and resources as they are company assets it could potentially lead to a data breach.

Based on these reports, it is clear that there is serious potential to mitigate controllable security threats by implementing security education and training of end users. A meaningful training curriculum that is administered more than once a year could be the solution to the prevention of future instances of data loss or make a big difference in the speed of discovery and response.

2   Background and Motivation

2.1   Information Security Education, Training and Awareness

Building an effective security awareness program requires inclusion of education and training [10]. Education can increase motivation of users and answer the question "why?", while training can increase skills and improve a user's competence of organizational security policy and addresses the "how?". Siponen explains "Since the 'why' part is extremely important, employees should not be satisfied with answers such as 'you just have to do it', 'this is the rule', or 'this is our policy'. Their motivations and attitudes are not likely to be increased in this way."

Shaw et al. describes the three major barriers to security awareness as employee's general lack of security awareness, employee's computer skills, and organizational budgets. Budgetary concerns are a main reason why organizations are reluctant to focus on training. Certain methods of training like face-to-face or classroom training are very effective but can get expensive. Since it is difficult to measure its potential payoff, it is harder to justify the investment. Other methods of delivery for security training may be cheaper, but less effective. For example, distributing plain text documents to train employees and users about organizational security policy may be the cheapest way to deliver training, but it is less effective and hard to enforce.

In addition to limitations of an organization's budget, certain risk prone behaviors that occur on company equipment and over the company network could also be potentially harmful behaviors, yet are often overlooked by IT and corporate management. Behavior like online shopping and using personal email on corporate devices are good examples of this. Shaw et al. lists some of the most common risk prone behaviors are related to using company resources for non-work related tasks and sharing corporate computing resources with non-employees [9]. These behaviors can be further compounded by the adoption of corporate bring your own device (BYOD) policies. Using company resources with your device can blur the lines of ownership. It is important for an organization to be clear with its employees regarding the correct use of personal devices when used in conjunction with corporate intellectual property.

At its core, information security training and awareness programs are designed to prevent users from violating an organization's security policy. Hu et al. addresses the behavioral reasoning behind a person's decision to violate organizational policy. "We submit that when an individual is presented with an opportunity to commit policy violations, his or her behavior depends on the rational calculus of the costs and the benefits" [2]. Hu goes on to explain that there are three independent forces that control the determination of that cost-benefit evaluation. Individual propensity (which Hu defines as the degree of low self-control), an individual's moral beliefs (defined as the individual's judgment about right and wrong) and the perceived deterrence related to the misconduct (defined as the perceived certainty, severity and celerity of sanctions against the behavior).

2.2 Gamification

Training employees is an important aspect of operations for organizations of all sizes. Traditional training methods often include videos portraying appropriate workplace behavior, electronic learning modules that test a user's understanding of training materials or even posters or newsletters that give information on organizational protocol. In a presentation at the RSA conference in 2014, Ira Winkler and Samantha Manke, the President and Executive Vice President of the security company Secure Mentem compared new training methods involving gamifying security training with traditional methods of training [11]. They discuss the core principles of training gamification: clearly defined goals, rules, ongoing feedback, voluntary participation. They argue that it can't be considered a game if users are "forced" to take it.

Gamification Methods. According to Brian Burke, Research Vice President and analyst at Garner Research, "Gamification is most successful when you are engaging with employees to help them complete their own goals, not organizational goals. Shared goals are achieved as a consequence" [8]. Burke also suggests that making the game more social, like letting employees check their points against each other through leaderboards adds positive reinforcement through incentivization.

The Infosec Institute argues that games in the workplace must be relatable and engaging. They describe an information security training game called "SecurityIQ AwareED", that uses interactive exercises that implements scenarios that employees have likely been in before [3].

The research of Gutzwiller et al. suggests that working in cyber and information security gives very little reward. In fact, the successful performance of your job often rewards you with more work. For example, thwarting an active attack will lead to other issues needing to be resolved and more vulnerabilities to be identified and patched [1]. In fact, they describe the negative performance metric "How did I fail this time?" as a significant source of input to many operator's day-to-day operations and work. They go on to cite that in terms of a cyber environment, the operational interfaces lend themselves to this negative interaction. After performing a task or making a decision, there is little feedback from the interaction and all evidence of the event disappears. "Furthermore, analysts may feel disconnected from their job, and disconcerted that their prior decisions seem of no measurable value or impact. This psychological burden of joyless operation and resulting frustration is contributing to turnover and burnout" [1].

These researchers focus primarily on improving the experience of cybersecurity specialists by improving their day-to-day experience, but their conclusions translate to the defense of gamifying information security training for all employees of an organization. "Hedonomic design approaches suggest that once an interface facilitates safe, effective and usable performance, further design and experimentation should determine how to make these interactions pleasurable" [1].

3   Proposed Application

3.1   Problem

As discussed in the previous sections of this paper, the main problem that my proposed project will address is the issue that human error is still a leading cause in organizational data breaches. These breaches can be mitigated through proper execution of employee training and awareness programs, but many companies don't approach employee training in an effective way. Training is often viewed as a check-box to be filled in on a compliance form during an auditing period. For employees, it's usually a distraction that must be done once a year. There are many forms of training programs that organizations can adopt, each with benefits and drawbacks. One-on-one training sessions are often the most effective, but also the most expensive. Computer Based Training is often the most cost effective, but it can be difficult to reinforce complex topics in an interesting or captivating way.

3.2   Solution

My solution to this issue is to design a gamified security training and awareness program that is adaptive to the organization's needs. The program would feature interactive game-like modules that put the employee into scenarios they will likely have encountered before and will encounter again, in order to better reinforce more secure behavior in those situations. Examples would be working remotely from a hotel room or coffee shop, how to detect and report a social engineering attack, creating an remembering a strong password, among other topics. Each module will have different teachable moments, presenting the employee with choices that they might actually experience in their work day. The game will have multiple sequence paths, and if the employee goes down the wrong path, they will be corrected and allowed to start back over at a checkpoint; this allows them to re-experience the situation again, this time making the correct choice.

The employee's goal is to complete the game module and earn points. Points serve multiple purposes throughout the program. They can be redeemed for real-world rewards and incentives. Your rank on the leaderboard is determined by how many points you have earned. Points help identify your status of mastery within the application. The more points you have, the more opportunities you will have to earn points in the future. See Fig. 3 for an example of this.

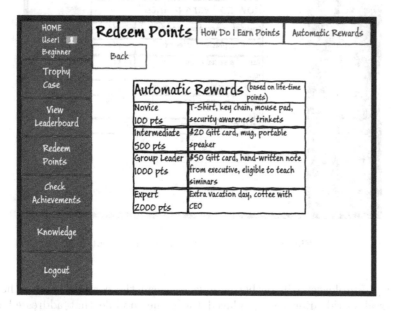

Fig. 3. Example structure of automatic rewards an employee might earn and their corresponding point value

Points can also be earned in other ways. In an effort to make other real-world moments teachable, employees will be subjected to test social engineering and phishing attempts. If they detect the attempt and report it, they are rewarded with points. If they are unable to detect it and the test attack is successful, they experience a teachable moment and their behavior is corrected. There are other ways that employees will be able to earn points as well. See Fig. 4 for more details. In that figure, you'll also see that users will be able to contribute blog articles to the knowledge repository. Rewarding users for sharing their security related experiences from their personal lives or from situations where they failed to detect a social engineering attempt at work will help keep security on users' minds year-round.

Creating an interactive, gamified security training and awareness application that provides real rewards for good performance, has a plan for ongoing training throughout the year and is adaptive to needs of individual organizations can be the solution to the problem presented above.

Scenario-Based Training Modules. It is important to design the gamified modules around scenarios that the employee will likely encounter in an actual

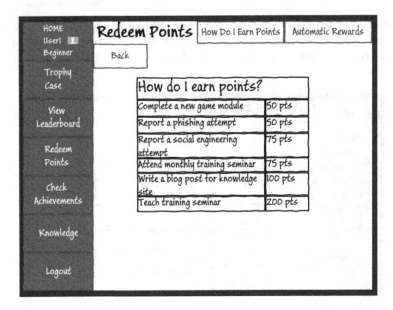

Fig. 4. Example structure of point payout

work day. Employees will be better able to recall the correct secure behavior in the real world after having played the game module that addressed that situation. For example, in a module on working remotely from a coffee shop, if the organizational security policy requires users to connect to the enterprise network through a virtual private network (VPN) connection, their real world behavior will be reinforced by having to perform that action when playing the game module. Something else that could allow employees to better see how their individual role in the organization can impact company data assets is to create learning modules that are role based. If the security training program is identical across the organization, it might be easy for someone in a non-technical role to see how it doesn't apply to them. But if you can design a game module specific to that user's role, showing how a daily activity they do or error they make could be detrimental to the organization's assets, they would likely pay closer attention and have a more security focused attitude going forward.

Incentives and Rewards. Providing real-world incentives and rewards for good security related behavior will add another layer to the gamification of the application. However, it is important to understand that the rewards must be dynamically chosen based on the culture of the organization. Some organizations might want to redeem their points for a gift card, while others might value a ten minute coffee break with the CEO more. When configuring and adapting the training program for an individual organization, this must be part of the design process. Interviewing people in the organization and getting their feedback

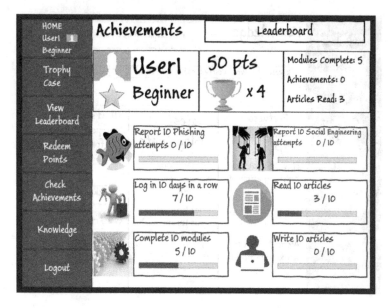

Fig. 5. Example of an employees view of their progress towards a given set of achievements.

would be an effective way to gauge the culture of the employees and would help determine an appropriate reward structure.

Achievements. Achievements can give employees targets to work for. If you have a visual clue indicating your progress towards a given goal, coupled with that knowledge that you'll be granted a bonus point payout if you complete the achievement, you will be more likely to work towards accomplishing this goal. They should increase employee participation in the training program and support the effort to continue the training program throughout the year. You can unveil new sets of achievements every month or every quarter to get people to log back in and try to earn the reward. See Fig. 5.

Knowledge. A smart, user-friendly and complete knowledge repository should be included in the application. An employee needs to be able to access the organization's issue specific security policy with a few clicks of their mouse to insure that every policy is understood and not obfuscated. Having the knowledge repository structured like wiki software would allow for easy navigation. Dedicating a section of the knowledge repository home page to featured articles showcasing important policies that IT wants the organization to focus on, as well as user-submitted blog posts can allow employees to quickly catch up on new and important information, as well as provide them with a chance to earn points by reading articles and writing blog posts. See Fig. 6 for details.

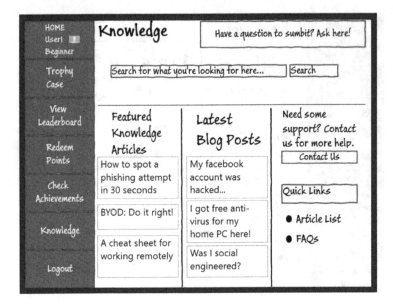

Fig. 6. Example of the knowledge landing page. See sections dedicated to featured knowledge articles and latest user-submitted blog posts

Social Aspects. Allowing users to communicate through the application, while comparing point totals and performance is also important to persuade users to continue using the application throughout the year. Users should be able to post status updates and view other users' updates, view a leaderboard where they are ranked next to their fellow employees based on point totals and other metrics. It can help promote competition throughout the enterprise and might cause some users to work harder to hit the top spot on the board for bragging rights. See Fig. 7. The trophy case will show a quick glance at the leaderboard and display each user's most recently posted status update.

Trophies. Trophies will be similar to achievements, except that they will be surprise rewards. You won't know what actions will earn you a trophy, so it rewards continuing use of the program in order to uncover the trophies and fill up your trophy case. The trophy case screen of the program will serve a few purposes. It will give quick glances at the leaderboard and your standing, show three achievements that you are currently in progress of earning and your progress towards them and a case full of the trophies that you have earned and short descriptions of each one. See Fig. 8.

4   Methodology

In this section I will discuss several factors that influenced my choices in the design process of the application. I chose to include several features in my

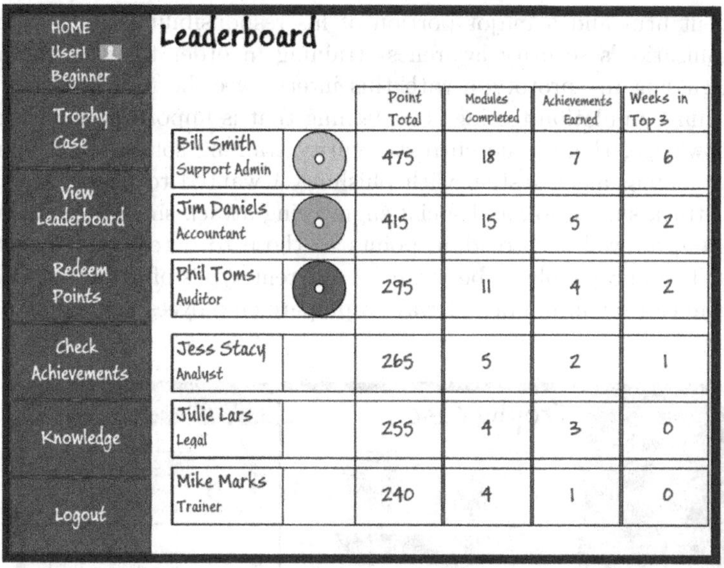

HOME User1 Beginner Trophy Case View Leaderboard Redeem Points Check Achievements Knowledge Logout	**Leaderboard**				
		Point Total	Modules Completed	Achievements Earned	Weeks in Top 3
	Bill Smith Support Admin	475	18	7	6
	Jim Daniels Accountant	415	15	5	2
	Phil Toms Auditor	295	11	4	2
	Jess Stacy Analyst	265	5	2	1
	Julie Lars Legal	255	4	3	0
	Mike Marks Trainer	240	4	1	0

Fig. 7. Example of the leaderboard. Each employee can find themselves on the board ranked by point totals and see how they measure up to other employees in the organization

prototype based on feedback I got from a interviews with professionals, common features and ideas I read about while conducting my background research and inspiration from other existing gamified experiences.

4.1 Background Research

A major concept that I chose to utilize in my program is to practice year-round deployment of new training modules. Suggested by the sources cited in my background research, I consider it to be one of the cornerstone concepts of my proposed security training and awareness program. In order to avoid information security awareness becoming nothing to an organization but a compliance check, it's important to reinforce key security concepts all throughout the year. In addition, another important concept I garnered from my background research, being able to tailor the real earnable rewards and incentives for each organization based on their employee culture. Being able to adapt the rewards dynamically based on what motivates each organization is one of the major keys to this programs successful implementation.

4.2 Interviews

I interviewed a few local professionals seeking some of their advice on what they would look for in an ideal training and awareness program. One of my interviewees is the manager of infrastructure and security operations at a local software development firm and a major portion of his responsibilities is to administer their organization's security awareness training in order to meet compliance. While discussing my prototype with this interviewee, he told me that having good phishing simulation testing is something that is important to include, but to his knowledge, there is no current security training solution that combines a learning management system with phishing. I wanted to be able to provide phishing attack simulation and social engineering attack simulation included in my program, as well as providing points to those to detect and report these attempts. Training people to be aware of different types of attacks and how to report them can be an important way to prepare employees for real attacks.

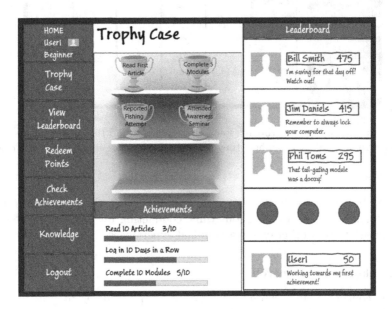

Fig. 8. Example of the Trophy Case. It will allow the user to see quick glances of the leaderboard, achievements they are currently working toward and a case of trophies they have earned.

In addition, this interviewee gave me partial inspiration to create the coffee shop game module by suggesting that he would be highly interested in a module that showed employees proper behavior while working on the road, specifically how to work from a hotel room. This is a module that I would be interested in designing in the future, but it was too similar to the coffee shop module that I was interested in developing for the initial prototype of my application.

I also got the perspective of a user of a large company's cybersecurity training. I observed him while he took the training and we discussed his likes and dislikes of the training modules throughout the process. My main takeaway from this interview was that a well-designed, user-friendly and easy to search knowledge repository should be included in the application. After completing each module, we were presented with a hard to read page with links to knowledge articles for the issue specific security policy. Clicking on the links lead us to the knowledge articles, but we found it hard to search for specific information we were looking for. We also noticed that the videos included in the training had a lot of recycled images and animations, to the point where it was noticeable. The interviewee commented that he would prefer training that was fresh and original. Which gave me the idea to deploy new and original training modules throughout the year.

4.3 Observation of Other Gamified Experiences

Lastly, I was inspired to include elements of my application based on observation of real-world gamified experiences. Nike + uses methods to gamify exercise and encourage fitness by allowing users to track their performance and attempt to beat their previous scores. In addition, they make exercising social by letting you communicate with friends and compete to earn higher scores. You are able to work towards earning achievements and get surprised by trophies. One example of a trophy rewarded in the Nike + application is that if you went for a run on Halloween, you earned a special trophy you might not have known was coming to you. I chose to incorporate all of these elements into my application.

5 Prototype

My approach to developing the application prototype has gone through two iterations. One being a paper phase where I drew out each major screen of the application with pencil and paper, and the second being adapting those paper prototype screens into a more interactive model using Sketchflow, a prototyping tool built into Visual Studio 2013 Expression Blend.

5.1 Tools

After drawing out each necessary screen with pencil and paper, I was ready to begin translating those ideas into Sketchflow. I wasn't too experienced with the tool so it took some time to get acclimated to the software. It has built-in tools like buttons, text boxes and scroll bars that can add interactivity between screens and several ways to program animation to give the application a more game-like feeling. I treated screens like the leaderboard and Trophy Case as early iterations to practice designing with this tool. I treated those early screens as practice for the most important portion of the prototype: the coffee shop game module. By this time I was experienced enough with the tool to confidently add animations and interactive elements, linking multiple screens together to create a short example of what a finalized game might look and act like.

The Sketchflow application interface allows you to access everything you might need to work on your project within a few clicks. See Fig. 9. Adding assets, creating states (used for simulating animation), changing opacity of objects

Fig. 9. A quick glance at the sketchflow user interface.

based on user input to control the flow of the game can all be done in the Sketchflow main editor screen. Sketchflow also has a useful map feature built in. You can see which screens rely on other screens, how the navigation flow of the application will go and can help when the design of your application becomes more complex. See Fig. 10.

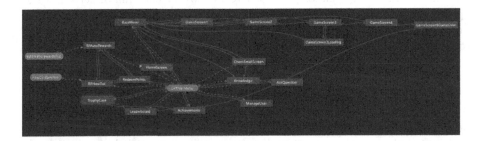

Fig. 10. Map of prototype screens. This layout helped map out the application.

Another tool I found myself using often was a freeware application called GNU Image Manipulation Program or GIMP. In order to get any asset that wasn't already built into Sketchflow, I had to acquire images from elsewhere. In order to edit them down to size and customize to my needs, I would open them in GIMP and use tools to edit, crop, alter color, and remove image backgrounds. After this, it was an easy process to copy the image and paste it into the Sketchflow screen, only needing to move it around and resize it.

5.2   Prototype Screens

When drawing out the initial paper screens, I had a few ideas in mind I had gotten from doing background research into security awareness programs and other gamified applications. Keeping the the game personal was going to be a big part of the application. Making the base menu the perspective of the user from behind their back while sitting at their workstation was really important to me because I wanted the user to feel like they were in the game and could relate to the actions of the in-game player. A goal for later iterations would be to make the base menu even more interactive. I would allow the user to move around the game environment, going to various spots you might find in an office(kitchen, friend's desk, etc), and hiding easter eggs, which are unexpected or undocumented features in software or games, for the user to find and enjoy, giving the game a little more depth and feeling of freedom. For example, allowing the user to click on their phone on the desk and be able to check their messages, and hiding some secret functionality there. See Fig. 11 for a side-by-side comparison of my initial paper prototype screen and a completed Sketchflow screen for the base menu of the application. I had the same strategy when designing the coffee shop module. I wanted to have the user be able to feel like it was actually them making the decisions, so I put the game into a first person perspective. See Fig. 12 for a side-by-side comparison of my initial paper prototype screen and a completed Sketchflow screen for the coffee shop module of the application.

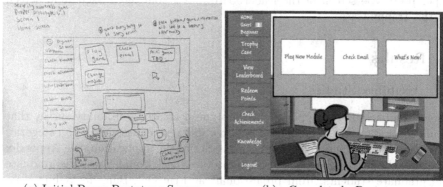

(a) Initial Paper Prototype Screen   (b) Completed Prototype
                                            Screen in Sketchflow

Fig. 11. The base menu prototype screen. Side by side comparison of initial paper prototype screen and completed prototype screen

For some screens, I found myself needing to adapt after originally designing the screen on paper. An example would be my screen for the leaderboard. When designing on paper, I had the idea to show achievements and earned trophies on the same screen. When it came time to develop those screens in Sketchflow, I realized that the leaderboard and achievements would need their own screen,

(a) Initial Paper Prototype Screen   (b) Completed   Prototype
                                            Screen in Sketchflow

Fig. 12. The coffee shop module prototype screen. Side by side comparison of initial
paper prototype screen and completed prototype screen

but that the original screen I designed on paper still would have a place in the
application. It became the Trophy Case screen that gave quick glances at some
of the most important information from both the leaderboard screen and the
achievements screens, as well as displaying the trophies that the user has earned
while using the application. See Fig. 13 for a side-by-side comparison of my initial
paper prototype screen of the leaderboard and a completed Sketchflow screen
for the Trophy Case.

6   Results

6.1   Usability Studies

To get feedback on my application prototype, I created a usability survey that
would evaluate users' experiences in three different categories. The categories
were navigation, functionality and appearance of the application. See Appendix
A to view the survey questions. I sought user feedback from fellow undergraduate
and graduate students, from professionals at Live Oak Bank in Wilmington,
North Carolina and from attendees of the Wilmington Information Technology
Expo, or WITX where I had a booth set up to showcase my application. I
received 23 responses to each survey question. I used a Likert scale for each
question, allowing the user to select a number between 1 and 10 to evaluate
the experience, 1 being the highest rated option and 10 being the lowest rated
option.

Navigation. I wanted to gauge users' feedback on their experience navigating
through the application. I found that the average response to the question "Overall, how would you rate your experience navigating through the application" was

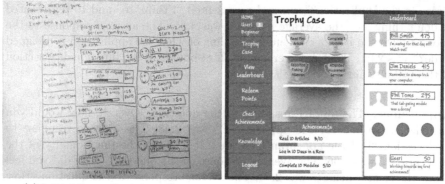

(a) Initial Paper Prototype Screen

(b) Completed Prototype Screen in Sketchflow

Fig. 13. The trophy case prototype screen. Side by side comparison of initial paper prototype screen and completed prototype screen. Originally planned for this screen to be the leaderboard during paper prototyping phase, but ultimately chose to give achievements and leaderboard their own screen and make this the Trophy Case

2.65 where 1 represented "very easy" and 10 was "very difficult". The average response to the question "Overall, I was satisfied with the amount of time it took to complete the application" was 3.22. For the question "When going through the coffee shop module, I found it easy or difficult to navigate to the end" where 1 represented very easy and 10 represented very difficult, the average response was 2.57. The average response to the question "Was navigation through the application intuitive?" was 2.60. The average response for the question "Did you find the screen that let you view how to earn points? If so, how easy was it to get there?" was 4.26. The average response to the question "How often did you find yourself needing to navigate back a screen, but you were unable to do so." was 2.83. For the question "Was it clear where the "Home Screen" was?", the average response was 3.17. The total average for all responses in the navigation section of the usability survey was 3.04.

Functionality. The average response to the question "Overall, how would you rate the functionality of the application?" was 2.43. The average response to the question "How well did you understand the terms/verbiage used in the application?" was 2.22. The average response to the question "How would you rate the consistency of the application?" was 2.48. The average response to the question "When playing the Coffee Shop module, how clear was the distinction between error and success?" was 2.65. The average response to the question "Overall, how satisfied were you with the support information provided by the application? (Help messages, documentation etc.)" was 3.22. For the question "Did you view the trophy case? If so, do you think you know what it is?", where 1 represented "I know what it is" and 10 represented "I don't know what it is/I didn't find it", the average response was 3.74. For the question "Did you view every screen in the application?" where 1 represented "I think so" and 10 represented "I don't think so", the average response was 4.35. The average response to the question "Do you have a clear understanding of what the application is designed to do?" was 2.04. The total average for all responses in the functionality section of the usability survey was 2.89.

Appearance. The average response to the question "Overall, how would you rate the appearance of the application?" was 2.48. The average response to the question "Did the appearance distract at all from the functionality of the application?" was 2.96. The average response to the question "How did you feel about the color scheme?" was 2.74. The average response to the question "How would you rate the layout of the application?" was 2.74. The average response to the question "Did you find the appearance of the application consistent?" was 2.48. The total average for all responses in the functionality section of the usability survey was 2.68.

7   Conclusion

The development of this prototype training application was in response to the fact that human error still ranks as a leading cause of data breach for organizations of all sizes. The goal is to implement a gamified training and awareness program that is applied throughout the year and puts users into real-world situations where they will have to apply secure behavior to pass gamified modules and earn real rewards and incentives by participating. By doing so, it will incentivize the process of executing secure behavior, ensure that information security is more than simply a check box on an auditor's form for executives and allow all employees in an organization to see how their role is impacted by information security policy. If securing an organization's data assets truly lies in the hands of the end user, then empowering the user with the tools and motivation they need to execute secure behavior is the key to preventing and mitigating future data breaches.

References

1. Gutzwiller, R.S., Fugate, S., Sawyer, B.D., Hancock, P.: The human factors of cyber network defense. In: Proceedings of the Human Factors and Ergonomics Society Annual Meeting, vol. 59, pp. 322–326. SAGE Publications, Los Angeles (2015)
2. Hu, Q., Xu, Z., Dinev, T., Ling, H.: Does deterrence work in reducing information security policy abuse by employees? Commun. ACM **54**(6), 54–60 (2011)
3. Institute IT: Gamification of security awareness campaigns, 13 May 2016
4. Shred-it: Five strategies to help companies strengthen information security and get back to business, 16 Aug 2016
5. Jones, A.: How do you make information security user friendly? (2010)
6. LLC PI: 2015 cost of data breach study: Global analysis. Technical report, Ponemon Institute LLC (2015)

7. LLC PI: 2016 cost of data breach study: United states. Technical report, Ponemon Institute (2016)
8. Marvin, R.: How gamified brain science is transforming e-learning, 30 November 2015
9. Shaw, R.S., Chen, C.C., Harris, A.L., Huang, H.J.: The impact of information richness on information security awareness training effectiveness. Comput. Educ. **52**(1), 92–100 (2009)
10. Siponen, M.T.: A conceptual foundation for organizational information security awareness. Inf. Manage. Comput. Secur. **8**(1), 31–41 (2000)
11. Winkler, I., Manke, S.: RSA conference. In: Gamifying Security Awareness, 24 February 2014

Alerting Users About Phishing Attacks

Giuseppe Desolda[1($\boxtimes$)], Francesco Di Nocera[2], Lauren Ferro[3],
Rosa Lanzilotti[1], Piero Maggi[2], and Andrea Marrella[3]

[1] Department of Computer Science, University of Bari Aldo Moro, Bari, Italy
{giuseppe.desolda,rosa.lanzilotti}@uniba.it
[2] Department of Psychology, University of Roma "La Sapienza", Rome, Italy
{dinocera,piero.maggi}@uniromal.it
[3] Department of Computer, Control, and Management Engineering,
University of Roma "La Sapienza", Rome, Italy
{lsferro,marrella}@diag.uniromal.it

Abstract. Cyber attacks are emerging as problems caused not only by technological aspects but also by human factors neglected when designing interactive systems. In this paper, we show how one of the most popular attacks on the Web, phishing, is very much related to UI aspects and how a wrong UI design determines a greater vulnerability of users. We performed a heuristic evaluation to assess the most recent applications such as browsers and mail clients that adopt warning messages as prevention of phishing attacks. The results highlighted that different aspects of UI should be better designed to limit phishing attacks. In addition, as a prevention of cyber attacks, we described an ongoing work of a questionnaire that aims to make users aware of the risks of cyber attacks.

Keywords: Usable security · Cyber security · Phishing · Design patterns

1 Introduction

Cyber attacks are growing very much in recent years. According to the Symantec Annual Threat Report published for 2018, the total number of Web threats were more than 1 Billion, which was 400% more than in 2014 [29]. For example, in 2018 the number of new malware variants increased by 92%, the coinminer detection grew by 8500%, attacks against IoT devices increased by 600%, the malware variants in mobile devices increased by 54% and the number of new vulnerabilities increased by 13%. According to a new report by the Center for Strategic and International Studies (CSIS) and McAfee [21], cybercrime now costs the world almost $600 billion, or 0.8% of global GDP. This problem touches two-thirds of people who use online services (more than two billion individuals), of which have had their personal data stolen or compromised.

Despite these problems appearing to relate to obsolete technologies or to the scarce adoption of preventions (e.g., antivirus, firewall, etc.), close to 95% of all security incidents are due to human errors, as reported by the IBM latest Cyber Security Intelligence Index Report [17]. Wrong human behaviors can and have led to a range of issues from users becoming a victim of phishing attacks to the disclosure of sensitive information.

A. Moallem (Ed.): HCII 2019, LNCS 11594, pp. 134–148, 2019.
https://doi.org/10.1007/978-3-030-22351-9_9

The causes of these cyber attacks inevitably push HCI researchers, as well as companies, to investigate additional aspects related to users' vulnerabilities. Such areas include the user interface and user interaction, which are at the basis of these attacks. Therefore, if we can improve these areas, we can dramatically decrease the number of attacks, with obvious advantages for people, companies and any organization. Consequently, methods and methodologies defined by the HCI research to create successful and pleasurable interfaces must be revised in order to consider the security aspect.

The research work described in this paper focuses one of the most widespread attacks, i.e. phishing. Phishing is a technique used to collect personal information by and/or sending fraudulent emails that appear to be from a reputable or known source to users to induce them to reveal sensitive information (e.g. passwords, bank account details). Moreover, it is important to note that this is an attack that relies on exploiting people via carefully crafted social engineering campaigns. As a result, the dynamic nature of phishing attacks makes it difficult to implement algorithms that automatically detect phishing scams. Therefore, in case of suspicious phishing attacks, specific software (e.g. antivirus, alerts) and system tools (e.g. firewalls) use warnings to alert users. As demonstrated in [10], the design of warning notifications heavily affects the right identification of a phishing attack by users and, consequently, the system's security.

This paper describes an analysis performed on various applications that provide warning messages for phishing attacks to their users.

2 Related Work

The user interface has an influence on aspects of human behaviors, and thus, are the main causes of security incidents. A study conducted by Federal Computer Week reports that almost 59% of security incidents that involve human errors are the result of simple mistakes as opposed to intentional malicious actions [30]. By analyzing more than 300 security incidents, Hosteler found that human error is one of the first cause of cyberattack (37%) [2]. Furthermore, the simplest and fastest way to start an attack is by means of phishing and social engineering attacks, where 91% of all cyber attacks start with some kind of phishing email that manipulates users to provide sensitive information via various methods of social engineering [14]. Because of the risks associated with cyber attacks, it is crucial for Internet users to be aware of when they are being attacked and to be successfully informed on how to combat them.

Usable security is a research area that in the last 10 year has been addressing such issues. Areas of password creation, demographic and workplace culture, security and trade-offs, and real-time assistance, all influence on a user's practice of good cybersecurity and ultimately contribute to their level of online security.

Security issues may increase also when technology is perceived as an obstacle. In such a case, the user may feel overwhelmed, or may not trust the warnings from the system, thus dismissing them [24]. In several contexts security tools are inherently complex, because they rely on knowledge of concepts such as cryptography, access keys, and digital signature. Therefore, securing a system may be not enough if users do not know how to properly use it. For example, firewalls, anti-viruses, and all the other means to reduce vulnerabilities will protect the system as far as it has been activated and properly configured. Password management is a clear example of this tradeoff: strong but complex passwords are easily forgotten, whereas easy but weak passwords are easily remembered and, generally speaking, more convenient [18]. Usability of those systems is a critical security determinant [28] and can make the difference between system security and letting the user be the weakest link in system security [18]. This problem can be considered as a security-usability tradeoff, indeed, security and usability are perceived as mutually exclusive and the user is asked to tradeoff between them [5]. A user-centered approach to security design is therefore needed [23].

An additional area of consideration when it comes to phishing is how cybersecurity is perceived and practiced depending on the demographic and workplace culture of users. With the ubiquity that global offices afford, it is important to consider the cultural differences that influence the attitudes of users' security, especially when it comes to that of eastern and western culture and norms [6]. For example, the location of work environments that exist in areas that are more vulnerable to phishing scams (e.g. financial businesses) should be treated differently than those that are not given the different motivations and cultural aspects that are fueling attacks. In a study conducted by Henshel et al. [16] they explored the addition of a human factor component to Hofstede's [22] cultural dimensions. This sought to explore variations in cultural behavior among six dimensions and how to integrate them within the Human Factors Framework and Ontology to identify cybersecurity risk assessment metrics. The potential of a framework like this can greatly influence the design of solutions towards issues such as phishing since a one size fits all approach will only address a small part of a larger problem that requires tailored solutions. Hence, researchers can use this for modeling to facilitate additional experimentation. In addition, Henshel et al. assert that culture is a key factor with respect to the human element that has been understudied in cybersecurity risk literature and is key to enhancing and exploring areas of concern within cybersecurity of several fronts such as training, adversaries' cultural framework, and cyber defender/operator [27]. This same approach requires exploration within a workplace environment, given that work environments now are multicultural and thus contain a mix of individualistic and collectivist societal cultures (and various degrees between), which inevitably provide context for individual behaviors and norms for groups [27].

In addition to culture, many aspects of the user interfaces that can expose systems to vulnerabilities have been investigated. One of the most critical aspects regards the warning messages for phishing. Since this is a semantic attack that relies on confusing people, it is difficult to implement an algorithm to automatically detect these attacks [14]. Thus, in case of suspicious phishing attacks, tools use passive or active warnings to alert users to potential phishing sites. Passive indicators are typically implemented as toolbars in a web browser and show security-related information about a website to help users detect phishing attacks. However, they often fail because users do not notice them or do not trust them [33]. Active indicators, available in newest web browsers, typically are pop-up windows that force users to notice the warnings by interrupting their navigation. Even if they are more effective than passive approaches, as in [10], the design of warning message communicates the right identification of a phishing attack on users. A recent investigation [26] reports the results of a large-scale study on web browser security warnings, which involved over 6,000 Chrome and Firefox users. They concluded that warnings of these browsers have improved that their effectiveness can be increased by examining contextual factors and a wider variety of users' concerns. Their results also suggest that habituation plays a smaller role in user decision making than previously thought. These results are in line with the one reported in [13] where 7,225 undergraduate students received (benign) phishing emails to elicit either the fear of losing something valuable (e.g., course registrations, tuition assistance) or the anticipation of gaining something desirable (e.g., iPad, gift card, social networks). The study results revealed that contextualizing messages to appeal to recipients' psychological weaknesses increased their susceptibility to phishing. The fear of losing or anticipation of gaining something valuable increased susceptibility to deception and vulnerability to phishing.

3   Analyzing Some Warnings in Current Applications

Many popular and recent applications like desktop browsers, mobile browsers or email clients nowadays include active phishing warnings. Despite in recent years important indications have emerged on how to improve such warning messages [10, 26], all of them still lack effectiveness, since phishing still remains the most widespread and effective cyber-attack [17, 21, 29].

In this section, we report on a review of some active warning messages implemented by the most popular Web browsers, both for PCs and mobile devices and by some email clients. In order to assess their effectiveness, we carried out an expert evaluation based on the heuristics reported in [10, 26].

3.1   Active Warning Messages Review

We started our review by analyzing three types of applications that implement warning messages for phishing attacks, i.e., desktop Web Browsers, mobile Web browsers and email clients.

Figure 1 reports four warning messages related to the desktop Web browsers we selected, i.e., *Google Chrome*, *Mozilla Firefox*, *Windows Edge* and *Opera*. All of them are active warning, i.e., when the browser detects a potential phishing site, instead of opening the Web page, it stops the users task flow by showing a message that reports information to help the users to decide if they can safely continue or if they have to return to the previous (safe) website.

The main differences between them are: the background color, the alert icon, the text of the message, the place/size/type of the button they must click on if they want to go on the phishing site. Regarding the background color, all of them, except Opera, use varying shades of red to warn the users about the potential fraud. In addition, the alert icon involves a different approach where all the browsers present different icons, which express a different meaning. For example, Google Chrome and Mozilla Firefox use two icons inspired by road symbols, a triangle containing an exclamation point and a circle having a horizontal bar, respectively. The last one appears to be stronger since it indicates a prohibition of access. MS Edge uses a rounded shield with an "X" inside it,

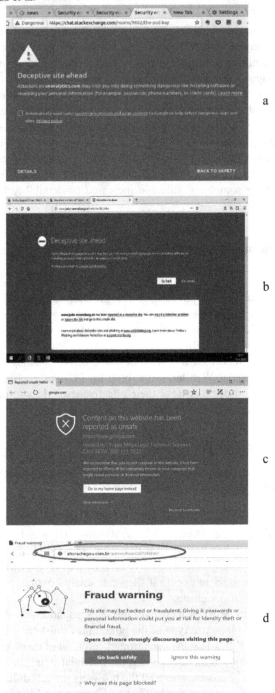

Fig. 1. Warning messages visualized by. (a) Google Chrome, (b) Mozilla Firefox, (c) Microsoft Edge, and (d) Opera. (Color figure online)

while Opera uses a robotic spider. All the messages also include a text reporting additional information about the alert, like the URL of the phishing site (the URL is missing in Opera) or what the consequences could be if the users land on to the phishing site. The last aspect is the button that the users must click on to open the phishing site. Except for Opera, all the warning messages hide this button inside a section that the users can reveal by clicking a button (Details, See details, Additional Information). In this way, it requires that the user takes the time to locate the button before accessing the potentially dangerous website.

Figure 2 shows the warning messages implemented by the browsers for mobile devices we chose, i.e., *Mobile Chrome, Opera Mobile, CM Browser, Internet Samsung, Edge mobile*, and *Firefox mobile*. Like desktop browsers, all of them implement active warnings and their peculiarities are the background color, the alert icon, the text of the message, the place/size/type of the link they must click in case they want to go on the phishing site. Only three of them, i.e., Mobile Chrome, CM Browser, and Firefox use a different shade of red as a background color. Mobile Chrome and Firefox do not use any icon to enrich the warning, while the other browsers visualize a triangle (or a circle in case of Internet Samsung) with an exclamation point inside. All the warnings also report additional information about the alert, like the URL of the phishing site (missing information in Mobile Chrome, Opera and Firefox mobile) or text explaining the risk to open a phishing site. The last aspect is the link the users must click on to open the phishing site. Mobile Chrome, Opera and Firefox mobile show this link in the main page, while the other browsers include it in a section that the users can reveal by clicking a button (Details, See details, Additional Information).

The last type of warning messages we considered are the ones of e-mail clients like *MS Outlook, Windows Mail app, Gmail*, and *Thunderbird*, which are shown in Fig. 3. Unlike the ones analyzed so far, these are passive warning messages, i.e., when the application detects a potential phishing email, it only shows a message, which informs the users that the email can contain suspicious content, like links or attachments. In this case, the main differences between them are the background color, the text of the message, the action the users can do on suspicious contents, the alert icon, and the place/size/type of the button they must click on if they trust the email.

Regarding the first aspect, different background colors are used, like light red on Outlook, orange on Windows mail app, light gray on Gmail and light gray on Thunderbird. The message texts always specify, in different ways, that the email has been detected as potentially unsafe. For example, Outlook says that all the suspicious content are disabled and that the users have to click on a link in the text if they want to enable such contents. The alert icon is used by Windows Mail app, Thunderbird and Gmail. The first two adopt a warning triangle with an exclamation point inside, while Gmail uses a hexagon with an exclamation point indicating the stop. Regarding the button the users must click on to activate the email content, except Gmail, all the warning messages show a link in the text message, while Gmail hides this link inside a section that the users can reveal by clicking the "View Details" button.

Fig. 2. Warning messages visualized by (a) Mobile Chrome, (b) Opera Mobile, (c) CM Browser, (d) Internet Samsung, (e) Edge mobile, and (f) Firefox mobile. (Color figure online)

3.2 Evaluation of Warning Messages

Different warning messages have been already evaluated during controlled experiments [10, 26]. Besides evaluating the efficacy of different solutions, these experiments provided useful indications on how to design and evaluate phishing warning messages. In this paper, given the large number of applications that we considered, rather than doing a controlled experiment, we performed a heuristic evaluation driven by the lessons learned distilled by the previous studies. The aim of our evaluation is to

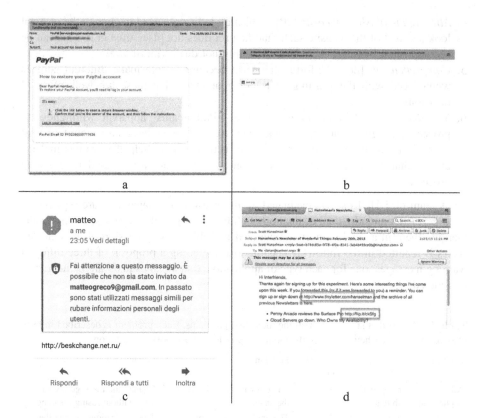

Fig. 3. Warning messages visualized by. (a) MS Outlook, (b) Windows Mail app, (c) Gmail, and (d) Thunderbird.

(*i*) assess the design of a broad spectrum of warning messages, and (*ii*) identify those aspects that still deserve even more attention. This evaluation was driven by two set of heuristics [10, 26]. In the following, we report the list of heuristics used by the evaluators, also specifying the paper they are related to:

1. *Providing clear choices* [10]—Phishing indicators need to provide the user with clear options on how to proceed, rather than simply displaying a block of text. For example, active warnings present choices and recommendations which were largely heeded.
2. *Failing safely* [10]—Phishing indicators must be designed so that users can only proceed to the phishing website after reading the warning message. For instance, active warning prevents users from accessing the page without reviewing the warning's recommendations.
3. *Preventing habituation* [10, 26]—Phishing indicators need to be distinguishable from less serious warnings and used only when there is a clear danger. Polymorphic messages can be adopted to minimize this factor.

4. *Altering the phishing website* [10]—Phishing indicators need to change the original look and feel of the website such that the user does not place trust in it. This can be accomplished by altering its look or simply not displaying it at all.
5. *Comprehension* [26]—Unfortunately, just because people make different choices when faced with the warning, it is not guaranteed that these are well-informed decisions.
6. *Site Reputation, History, and Trust* [26]—Participants' apparent willingness to proceed through a warning because they trust a site or have an account or visit history with a site may be in need of correction. It may help if warnings make it clearer that when a warning appears on a trusted site, it's a good time not to proceed.

A team of 5 HCI experts evaluated all the warning messages that are reported in Sect. 3.1. After an individual evaluation of all the messages, they discussed their results merging them in a single report summarized in Table 1. A discussion of the detected issues is reported in the following section, also including a proposal of three different warning messages, one for each type of application, that ideally satisfy all the heuristics considered.

Table 1. Report that summarizes all the identified problems. Each problem is described in term of severity, violated heuristic, details about the problem and a possible solution.

Application	Heuristic	Severity (1–5)	Problem	Possible solution
All applications	Preventing habituation	4	The error message is always the same	Change the message layout, text, without losing meaning
	Altering website	4	The applications do not change the look and feel of the website	The applications change the look and feel of the website
	Providing clear choices - Site reputation	3	The application does not show the URL of the mimicked site, sometimes only the URL of the fake site	The applications show both the URL so that the users can make more informed decisions by taking advantage of original site reputation
	Comprehension	3	The examples reported in the text are often too vague and general	More concrete examples can be reported, for example depending by the type of phishing site
Edge	Comprehension	3	Text of the message to come back to the previous and safe website is not so clear	Change this text by using a clearer text

(continued)

Table 1. (*continued*)

Application	Heuristic	Severity (1–5)	Problem	Possible solution
Opera desktop – Opera mobile	Site reputation	2	It does not allow to report false positive Web sites	A function to report false positive should be introduced
	Comprehension	5	The background color and the used icon are not adequate for this type of message	The background color should be changed by using the color red; the icon should be replaced with a more effective one
	Failing safely	5	It is possible to ignore the message without reading it. Indeed, the 'Ignore this warning' button is not adequately hidden. It also has the same emphasis of the 'Go back safely' button	The 'Ignore this warning' button should be placed in an internal section, for example in the one the users open by clicking on 'Why was this page blocked'. It should be also changed by using a link instead of a button, to reduce its importance
Opera mobile	Comprehension	4	The message layout and look and feel is very poor	A more professional look and feel can improve the credibility of the message
Internet Samsung	Comprehension	3	Too much information in the same screen, the users will be more prone to avoid reading the text	Short and optimize the text
	Comprehension	5	The background color is not adequate for this type of message	Use the color red as background
Edge mobile	Comprehension	5	The background color is not adequate for this type of message	Use the color red as background
	Comprehension	4	Technical details about the error message are shown and can confuse the users	Remove technical details, in order to speak a language closer to no-technical users
Firefox mobile	Failing safely	5	It is possible to ignore the message without reading it as for Opera browsers	Same suggestion of Opera browsers
All email clients	Failing safely	5	It is possible to ignore the message without reading it	When a phishing email is read, an active warning should be used
	Preventing habituation	5	Phishing indicators are not significantly distinguishable from less serious warnings	More emphasis should be given to these messages

3.3   Discussion

The heuristic evaluation highlighted that there is still much room for improvement to limit a greater number of phishing attacks with more effective warning messages. All the applications we analyzed share some problems.

Desktop browsers are mainly affected by these problems, but Opera also suffers from further critical issues, like the background color that appears not to effectively communicate a danger message, or, more importantly, the link to the phishing page has the same emphasis of the link to go back to the previous and safe site. This last aspect has proven to be crucial for this type of messages since users tend to read the warning messages quite fast and in-turn click on an option that seems more adapt to skip the message, like the button to go on.

Mobile browsers present further critical problems, beyond the ones that we have presented here. For example, Opera mobile has all the problems underlined for the desktop version, but in addition, it also presents a poor look&feel that reduces the users trust. The problem of the background color also affects Samsung Internet and Edge Mobile. In addition, Samsung Internet also reports a long text that can discourage the users in reading it and understand their risks, while Edge mobile shows technical details about the error message, which typically should be included in a hidden section to avoid confusing the users. Another critical problem was detected for Firefox mobile where, like the Opera browser, it is possible to ignore the message without reading it. This situation becomes more dramatic if we consider that most of the Internet access today take place by using mobile phone.

A more problematic situation was highlighted for the email clients. Indeed, all of them are passive warning messages, and it has been proven for over 10 years that they are not very effective for phishing attacks. In addition, their design is not adequate due to the adopted colors, text messages and icons.

In the following, we propose some design indications that could be useful for creating effective warning messages. Polymorphic messages are a solution that is strongly recommended to prevent users from habituation. If warning messages were visualized every time in a slightly different way, changing their content (e.g., the text) and their layout could result in the users being more likely to pay attention to what the message says without skipping it.

Another communal problem regards the information that guides the users in deciding if the suspicious site is dangerous. Users could decide easier if they can see both the URL of the mimicked site and the URL of the fake site, however, none of the applications adopts this strategy, showing only the fake URL. More significant and concrete examples could be used, eventually relate to the exploitation that the phishing attack is trying to initiate (e.g., data or money theft) rather than saying that the phishing site can steal personal data or money. In addition, pictures can be introduced to quickly explain the possible consequences of the attacks, because users often do not read text warning.

4   Toward a Questionnaire to Make Users Aware of Security Issues

Users' vulnerability to cyber-attacks, rather than a matter of tools and policies, is a matter of knowledge about the need of those tools and policies as well as the awareness about the possibilities of intrusions by hackers. This is demonstrated by several cybersecurity breaches (WannaCry ransomware affecting 150 countries is a recent example) in contexts where tools and policies are highly implemented. These breaches rely on social engineering rather than computer science. Enhancing users' awareness and skills on cybersecurity may be a solution to effectively integrate tools and policies with the human factor. In a recent survey regarding the level of risk associated with home users, Furnell et al. [11] found that many responders still lack awareness about cyber-risks. In particular, IT novices, lack the knowledge to protect themselves from Cyber attacks despite they are aware of the fact that they are responsible for.

Empowering users by giving them a better understanding of security issues, possible threats, and how to avoid them is the goal of many intervention programs [7, 19]. This problem has been approached by the military, banking and financial industries and recently it became a priority in healthcare with the adoption of health information technology. Generally speaking, the protection of certain vulnerable groups, for example children, is a societal responsibility [32], but assessing vulnerability is also a crucial variable in cybersecurity research. This area of investigation, tough recognizing in many cases the role of the human factor, has almost exclusively considered demographic and personality factors. Although Rahim et al. [25] reported that the assessment of cybersecurity awareness is not new, to our knowledge no validated, recognized, and general purpose instrument exists for classifying users in terms of cybersecurity awareness.

Some authors of this paper are currently developing an inventory of behavioral markers of the vulnerability to Cyber attacks (CAIN: Cybersecurity Awareness INventory) in a form a questionnaire, which is aimed at investigating both general knowledge about cyber risks and knowledge about specific types of Cyber attacks (such as phishing emails). In this way, it will be possible to use it both in the public and in the private sector and possibly identify specific vulnerabilities. Self-report measures are easy to use, inexpensive, and very useful for obtaining meaningful information from the users that would be inaccessible otherwise. The rating scale will be used for classifying users and correlate the vulnerability score to behavioral outcomes and security threats.

CAIN items are based on scientific and technical literature as well as anecdotal evidence about risky situations for the users. Examples of items are: "My webcam can be accessed by a malicious user", "Permission I have granted to apps on my phone can be exploited by a malicious user", "I use different passwords for different accounts".

A preliminary version of the questionnaire will be administered to a large sample (N > 300) to assess its psychometric properties (reliability and validity). Data will be analyzed using factor analysis to understand whether the scale is mono- or multi-dimensional. The multi-dimensional nature of the questionnaire is very likely as people may cognitively represent threats and secure behaviors differently according to, for example, the type of technology (e.g. desktop vs. mobile). The final version of the questionnaire will retain only those items mostly contributing to the measure of the construct and to the overall reliability. To assess its validity, CAIN will be administered along with other measures in a series of experiments in which the user will face cybersecurity threats. People scoring high on cybersecurity awareness should perform significantly better than the others. This index should provide information about people awareness of cyber risks and about their skills in providing the correct behavior in risky situations. Users need to understand and use systems correctly in order to guarantee the efficacy of any security strategy that has been implemented [11]. Moreover, the possibility to evaluate the level of knowledge and experience that the user has about cybersecurity issues is useful in many ways. In fact, this information could be used to set the right level of security within a system by forcing an inexperienced user to comply with certain protocols, which are necessary for the protection of sensitive information and, at the same time, allowing experienced users to interact with optimized and faster systems.

5   Conclusions and Future Work

In this article, we discussed the problem of cyber security from the perspective of HCI. In particular, we focused on phishing, one of the most effective and widespread cyber attacks that affect the majority of Internet users. We carried out a heuristic evaluation that revealed that warning phishing messages implemented in modern browsers and email clients still lacks in preventing phishing attacks. We also presented an ongoing work on a questionnaire that will make users more aware of the risks of the network.

One of the long-term goals of our research is to define a set of new behavior-based design patterns that support designers by providing indications on how to manage the interface design related to the security aspects. Design patterns have been used in different domains. In computer science, they have used in the design of computer systems of various types [15], including hypertext design [3, 12], e-learning systems design [1, 9], and interaction design [4, 31]. Some authors of this paper have defined a usability evaluation method that uses evaluation patterns [20]. Based on this expertise, a further long-term goal will be to identify evaluation patterns addressing usable security, for traditional systems and more advanced technological solution devoted to web exploration, like mobile cross-device interaction [8] or IoT.

Acknowledgements. The authors are members of ECoNA, an inter-university center for research and services. This collaboration started during the ECONA Workshop that was a Satellite Event of AVI 2018. The authors are grateful to Prof. Tiziana Catarci and Prof. Maria Francesca Costabile for their valuable and constant support.

References

1. Avgeriou, P., Papasalouros, A., Retalis, S., Skordalakis, M.: Towards a pattern language for learning management systems. Educ. Technol. Soc. **6**(2), 11–24 (2003)
2. Is Your Organization Compromise Ready? Data Security Incident Response Report (2016). https://www.bakerlaw.com/files/uploads/Documents/Privacy/2016-Data-Security-Incident-Response-Report.pdf. Accessed 30 Jan 2019
3. Bernstein, M.: Patterns of hypertext. In: Proceedings of ACM Conference on Hypertext and Hypermedia: Links, Objects, Time and Space (HYPERTEXT 1998). ACM, pp. 21–29 (1998)
4. Borchers, J.O.: A pattern approach to interaction design. AI Soc. **15**(4), 359–376 (2001)

5. Braz, C., Seffah, A., M'Raihi, D.: Designing a trade-off between usability and security: a metrics based-model. In: Baranauskas, C., Palanque, P., Abascal, J., Barbosa, S.D.J. (eds.) INTERACT 2007. LNCS, vol. 4663, pp. 114–126. Springer, Heidelberg (2007). https://doi.org/10.1007/978-3-540-74800-7_9

6. Chang, C.-C., Hsueh, W.-Y., Cheng, T.-F.: An advanced anonymous and biometrics-based multi-server authentication scheme using smart cards. Int. J. Netw. Secur. **18**(6), 1010–1021 (2016)

7. de Bruijn, H., Janssen, M.: Building cybersecurity awareness: the need for evidence-based framing strategies. Govern. Inform. Q. **34**(1), 1–7 (2017)

8. Desolda, G., Ardito, C., Jetter, H.-C., Lanzilotti, R.: Exploring spatially-aware cross-device interaction techniques for mobile collaborative sensemaking. Int. J. Hum.-Comput. Stud. **122**, 1–20 (2019)

9. Dimitriadis, Y., Goodyear, P., Retalis, S.: Using e-learning design patterns to augment learners' experiences. Comput. Hum. Behav. **25**(5), 997–998 (2009)

10. Egelman, S., Cranor, L.F., Hong, J.: You've been warned: an empirical study of the effectiveness of web browser phishing warnings. In: Proceedings of SIGCHI Conference on Human Factors in Computing Systems (CHI 2008). ACM, New York, pp. 1065–1074 (2008)

11. Furnell, S.M., Bryant, P., Phippen, A.D.: Assessing the security perceptions of personal internet users. Comput. Secur. **26**(5), 410–417 (2007)

12. Garzotto, F., Paolini, P., Schwabe, D.: HDM—a model-based approach to hypertext application design. ACM Trans. Inform. Syst. (TOIS) **11**(1), 1–26 (1993)

13. Goel, S., Williams, K., Dincelli, E.: Got phished? Internet security and human vulnerability. J. Assoc. Inform. Syst. **18**(1), 22 (2017)

14. Gupta, B.B., Tewari, A., Jain, A.K., Agrawal, D.P.: Fighting against phishing attacks: state of the art and future challenges. Neural Comput. Appl. **28**(12), 3629–3654 (2017)

15. Helm, R., Johnson, R.E., Gamma, E., Vlissides, J.: Design Patterns: Elements of Reusable Object-Oriented Software. Braille Jymico Incorporated, Quebec (2000)

16. Henshel, D., Sample, C., Cains, M., Hoffman, B.: Integrating cultural factors into human factors framework and ontology for cyber attackers. In: Nicholson, D. (ed.) Advances in Human Factors in Cybersecurity. Advances in Intelligent Systems and Computing, vol. 501, pp. 123–137. Springer, Cham (2016). https://doi.org/10.1007/978-3-319-41932-9_11

17. IBM X-Force Threat Intelligence Index (2018). https://microstrat.com/sites/default/files/security-ibm-security-solutions-wg-research-report-77014377usen-20180329.pdf. Accessed 30 Jan 2019

18. Johnston, J., Eloff, J.H.P., Labuschagne, L.: Security and human computer interfaces. Comput. Secur. **22**(8), 675–684 (2003)

19. Kritzinger, E., von Solms, S.H.: Cyber security for home users: a new way of protection through awareness enforcement. Comput. Secur. **29**(8), 840–847 (2010)

20. Lanzilotti, R., Ardito, C., Costabile, M.F., De Angeli, A.: Do patterns help novice evaluators? A comparative study. Int. J. Hum.-Comput. Stud. **69**(1–2), 52–69 (2011)

21. The Economic Impact of Cybercrime—No Slowing Down Executive Summary. https://www.mcafee.com/enterprise/en-us/assets/executive-summaries/es-economic-impact-cybercrime.pdf. Accessed 30 Jan 2019

22. Mintu, A.T.: Cultures and organizations: software of the mind. J. Int. Bus. Stud. **23**, 362–365 (1992)

23. Muñoz-Arteaga, J., González, R.M., Martin, M.V., Vanderdonckt, J., Álvarez-Rodríguez, F.: A methodology for designing information security feedback based on user interface patterns. Adv. Eng. Softw. **40**(12), 1231–1241 (2009)

24. Pfleeger, S.L., Caputo, D.D.: Leveraging behavioral science to mitigate cyber security risk. Comput. Secur. **31**(4), 597–611 (2012)
25. Rahim, N.H.A., Hamid, S., Mat Kiah, M.L., Shamshirband, S., Furnell, S.: A systematic review of approaches to assessing cybersecurity awareness. Kybernetes **44**(4), 606–622 (2015)
26. Reeder, R.W., Felt, A.P., Consolvo, S., Malkin, N., Thompson, C., Egelman, S.: An experience sampling study of user reactions to browser warnings in the field. In: Proceedings of the 2018 CHI Conference on Human Factors in Computing Systems (CHI 2018), pp. 1–13. ACM, New York (2018)
27. Sample, C., Cowley, J., Hutchinson, S., Bakdash, J.: Culture + cyber: exploring the relationship. In: Nicholson, D. (ed.) AHFE 2017. AISC, vol. 593, pp. 185–196. Springer, Cham (2018). https://doi.org/10.1007/978-3-319-60585-2_18
28. Schultz, E.E., Proctor, R.W., Lien, M.-C., Salvendy, G.: Usability and security an appraisal of usability issues in information security methods. Comput. Secur. **20**(2001), 620–634 (2001)
29. Symantec 2018 - Internet Security Threat Report. https://www.symantec.com/content/dam/symantec/docs/reports/istr-23-executive-summary-en.pdf. Accessed 30 Jan 2019
30. Insider Threat Report. https://go.thalesesecurity.com/ESG-Insider-Threat-WP.html. Accessed 30 Jan 2019
31. Tidwell, J.: Designing Interfaces: Patterns for Effective Interaction Design. O'Reilly Media, Inc., Newton (2010)
32. Von Solms, R., Van Niekerk, J.: From information security to cyber security. Comput. Secur. **38**, 97–102 (2013)
33. Wu, M., Miller, R.C., Garfinkel S.L.: Do security toolbars actually prevent phishing attacks? In: Proceedings of SIGCHI Conference on Human Factors in Computing Systems (CHI 2006), pp. 601–610. ACM, New York (2006)

Social Preferences in Decision Making Under Cybersecurity Risks and Uncertainties

Mazaher Kianpour[✉], Harald Øverby, Stewart James Kowalski,
and Christopher Frantz

Norwegian University of Science and Technology, Gjøvik, Norway
{mazaher.kianpour,haraldov,stewart.kowalski,
christopher.frantz}@ntnu.no

Abstract. The most costly cybersecurity incidents for organizations result from the failures of their third parties. This means that organizations should not only invest in their own protection and cybersecurity measures, but also pay attention to that of their business and operational partners. While economic impact and real extent of third parties cybersecurity risks is hard to quantify, decision makers inevitably compare their decisions with other entities in their network. This paper presents a theoretically derived model to analyze the impact of social preferences and other factors on the willingness to cooperate in third party ecosystems. We hypothesize that willingness to cooperate among the organizations in the context of cybersecurity increases following the experience of cybersecurity attacks and increased perceived cybersecurity risks. The effects are mediated by perceived cybersecurity value and moderated by social preferences. These hypotheses are tested using a variance-based structural equation modeling analysis based on feedback from a sample of Norwegian organizations. Our empirical results confirm the strong positive impact of social preferences and cybersecurity attack experience on the willingness to cooperate, and support the reciprocal behavior of cybersecurity decision makers. We further show that more perception of cybersecurity risk and value deter the decision makers to cooperate with other organizations.

Keywords: Social preferences · Behavioral economics ·
Cybersecurity decision making · Structural Equation Modeling ·
Theory development · Perceived Cybersecurity Risk

1 Introduction

As Peter Bernstein states, "The capacity to manage risk, and with it, the appetite to take risk and make forward-looking choices, are key elements of the energy that drives the economic system forward" [1]. While risk taking is driving the modern economics systems forward, uncertainties in cyberspace like the evolving threat landscape and human error, are threatening to slow it down. Nations, organizations and individuals are unsure what a good driving strategy in cyberspace is. Individual preferences and behavioral heterogeneity can play an important role in explaining strategic considerations at organizational levels. Hence, humans play a vital role in cybersecurity

© Springer Nature Switzerland AG 2019
A. Moallem (Ed.): HCII 2019, LNCS 11594, pp. 149–163, 2019.
https://doi.org/10.1007/978-3-030-22351-9_10

strategic decision making, and at the same time, they are often considered the weakest links in this ecosystem [2].

The area of cybersecurity in organizations has three essential properties. First, it consists of heterogeneous interacting, and in some cases, competitive and even adversarial, stakeholders and actors that are characterized by distinct local cultures, structure, machines, and methods [3]. Stakeholders act upon the basis of their own local states at any given time. Second, cybersecurity problems stem from dynamic systems and are driven by the interaction among various stakeholders. These interactions affect future local states and, therefore, create systemic complexity. Third, there are strategic decision makers whose decision processes take into account past actions, potential future actions, and outcomes of other actors. They have heterogeneous motivations, preferences, and benefits. Since these properties are based on the organizations' unique sets of objectives, processes, and resources, it is difficult to see how a one-size-fits-all cybersecurity strategy can be optimal.

The trend toward more globalized production has increased inter-organizational dependencies. Particularly, businesses are forming multi-layered supply chains, as illustrated in Fig. 1. As an externality, security and insecurity can be distributed disproportionately in a supply chain. The coopetition (i.e. organizations may both compete and cooperate at the same time [4]) and interdependent preferences among the organizations face them with a challenge of understanding and measuring the risks that are propagating from them. Recent cybersecurity incidents highlight that it is no longer enough for organizations to focus solely on their in-house cybersecurity defense mechanisms.

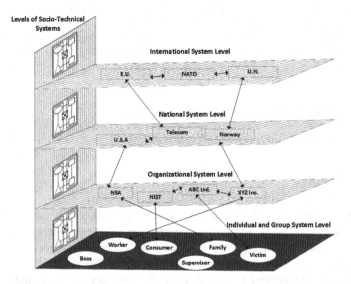

Fig. 1. Interaction among organizations in a socio-technical system is not limited to the organizational level, but also includes different levels of societal actors such as international systems and governments, groups and individuals levels. Each of these actors has their own particular instruments, which can employ different security controls depending on the nature of the system [3].

According to a study from Kaspersky Lab and B2B International, the most costly cybersecurity incidents for businesses result from the failures of their third parties [5]. This means that organizations should not only invest in their own protection and cybersecurity measures, but also pay attention to that of their business partners. To Provide some examples, in December 2018, Managed Health Services (MHS) of Indiana Health Plan announced that a third party data breach potentially exposed up to 31,876 patients' personal data in one of two security incidents the company disclosed [6]. Moreover, attackers expand their reach by targeting third-party services allowing them to steal more data. A new Magecart attack launched through compromised advertising supply chain in November 2018. Attackers loaded their malicious skimming code on 277 e-commerce websites and used their infrastructure of these companies to breach other companies [7].

Different economics models have been employed to address the challenges in the field of cybersecurity in both technical and social aspects [8–10]. In these models, agents are rational, selfish, and have complete information about other agents. However, in real-world scenarios, agents might be irrational, reciprocal, and have incomplete information about their environment. In this his paper we outline empirical cybersecurity economics examples on how these standard models fail to model real-world scenarios because they do not properly model the problems when they ignore social preferences.

The key research question is how to model heterogeneous incentives and preferences at the organizational level. The major aim is to better understand under which conditions the social preferences have significant effects on cybersecurity. To achieve this, we aim at developing an understanding of the important determinants of the socially optimal level of cybersecurity to prevent market failures.

Moreover, the paper investigates which type of social preferences (Reciprocal Fairness, Inequity Aversion, Pure Altruism and Spitefulness or Envy [11]) is stronger and quantitatively a core motive in the domain of cybersecurity. We have designed a survey to address these questions. The respondents of this survey are cybersecurity team members (Chief Information Security Officers, Information Security Analysts, Security Consultants, etc.) and decision makers in Norwegian organizations (Chief Executive Officers, Board Members, etc.).

This work is structured as follows. Section 2 provides a background on behavioral economics and proposed models to analyze behavioral determinants in cybersecurity. Section 3 proposes our research model and hypotheses. The methodological approach and data collection process is explained in Sect. 4. Section 5 presents the empirical results. Theoretical and practical implications are discussed in Sect. 6. Finally, Sect. 7 concludes this study.

2   Related Work

Behavioral Economics sits at the intersection of psychology and economics. Standard economic theories assume fully rational, completely selfish and forward-thinking decision makers. Analytical models based on these assumptions have failed to predict individuals' behavior. However, behavioral economics provides manifold principles considering less rational behavioral choices and other-regarding, interdependent preferences [12].

The application of behavioral economics has become more widespread, most commonly seen in the health domain, and policymakers use it to investigate how predictable deviations from rational behavior can be utilized to steer people to socially desirable directions. This approach is best employed where individuals need to make quick decisions and select the best possible choice.

Thaler and Sunstein [13] and Kahneman [14] popularized the idea that behaviors can be projected into systems and affect the decisions. However, in 1975, Rogers introduced a popular theoretical model of behavior change focusing on the Protection Motivation Theory (PMT) [15]. This model explicitly points out the methods that individuals can assess and counter cyber threats. Dolan et al. [16] proposed a behavior change framework, so-called MINDSPACE, which describes nine behavioral influencers in relation to cybersecurity behavior change paradigm. They discuss that these influencers play important roles in security-related decision making and behavior.

Briggs et al. state that PMT is a useful model in cybersecurity context as it encourages individuals to better protect their cyber assets from cyber threats [17]. They tried to create an effective link between PMT and MINDSPACE to present an integrated framework. This framework can be used to design long term cybersecurity behavioral strategies. It is claimed that the framework can be applied within organizations and provide important insights to managers and practitioners involved in cybersecurity.

There are a variety of psychological models of behavior that address the interplay of attitudes and behaviors. They recognize the importance of psychological traits and attitudes along with the individual's knowledge and experience in decision making. Many of these models are inspired by the Theory of Reasoned Action [18] and Theory of Planned Behavior [19]. The former identifies two factors that determine behavioral intention and assumes that behavior can be completely controlled. The latter, in contrast, differentiates between perceived behavioral control and actual behavioral control.

A survey by Michie et al. [20] shows that there are 80 available models of behavior change in different contexts. The literature review by Sommestad focuses on relevant psychological models for cybersecurity policy compliance [21]. This study identifies 60 different psychological constructs based on established theories including General Deterrence Theory, Neutralization Theory, Social Control Theory, and Theory of Moral Decision-Making. We will focus here on the Theory of Social Preferences, which is studied in behavioral and experimental economics and social psychology. We use this theory in the cybersecurity field to investigate the effects of other-regarding behavior in decision making under cybersecurity risks and uncertainties.

3   Research Model and Hypotheses

This research aims to find the impact of social preferences on the perceived cybersecurity risk, the perceived cybersecurity value, and the willingness to cooperate in third parties ecosystem to mitigate the probability and impact of future cyber incidents. In the following, we explain our research model, illustrated in Fig. 2, and the hypotheses to be tested in the empirical analysis.

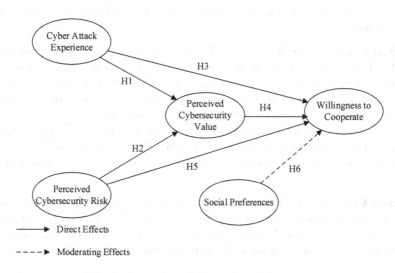

Fig. 2. Research model in path model notation

As Fig. 2 shows, the following hypotheses are proposed to conduct this research:

H1. Cyber attack experience increases the perceived cybersecurity value.

H2. Perceived cybersecurity risk increases the perceived cybersecurity value.

H3. Cyber attack experience increases the likelihood that an organization will cooperate with other organizations to mitigate the probability and impact of future cyber incidents.

H4. Perceived cybersecurity value increases the likelihood that an organization will cooperate with other organizations to mitigate the probability and impact of future cyber incidents.

H5. Perceived cyber risk increases the likelihood that an organization will cooperate with other organizations to mitigate the probability and impact of future cyber incidents.

H6. Social Preferences have moderating effects on the likelihood that an organization will cooperate with other organizations to mitigate the probability and impact of future cyber incidents.

The following latent variables (i.e. research constructs) are used in the proposed model:

Cyber Attack Experience: A cyber attack is a malicious and deliberate attempt by an individual or organization to breach the information system of another individual or organization. Usually, the attacker seeks some type of benefit from disrupting the victim's network [22]. These attacks hit businesses every day and their number is increasing as people are trying to benefit from vulnerable business systems.

According to the third annual report of Ponemon [23], 59% of respondents confirm that their organizations experienced a data breach caused by one of their third parties. 42% of respondents say they had such a data breach in the past 12 months. Additionally, 22% of respondents do not know if they had a third-party data breach in the past 12 months.

Perceived Cybersecurity Risk: Fear of crime consists of two distinct, but highly interrelated, components. First, the rather rational risk perception, which is often stated as the product of the probability of occurrence and the impact of the crime, and second, fear as an emotional feeling of being unsafe [24]. Visser et al. found strong effects of examining prior victimization on perceived risk [25]. Moreover, in a survey by Cisco, 69% of executives indicated that they are not willing to innovate in digital products because of their perceived cybersecurity risks [26]. The finding shows that perceived cybersecurity risk can be a deterrent of cooperation among organizations in digital space.

Perceived Cybersecurity Value: Oscar Wilde said, "A cynic knows the cost of everything and the value of nothing [27]." Cost is a driver for decisions, but not always. Perceived value is what people perceive as the value and worth of a product or service; the higher the perceived value, the more likely it is that they will pay for the product or service.

The reason that we are trying to measure perceived value and understand how it affects the decisions is that they differ from other personal attributes in several ways. Schwartz states that values transcend specific situation and are distinguished from norms, attitudes and specific goals [28]. He also explains that values are observed by subjective importance and they form a unique system of values hierarchies. Values may serve as standards and provide social justifications for behaviors and decisions [29]. Moreover, Sagiv et al. reason that perceived value influences competitive/cooperative behavior and the decisions made [30]. Therefore, to understand and predict the behavior, it is important to consider the perceived cybersecurity value of the agents in the system.

Social Preferences: Game-theoretic predictions are frequently observed in recent experiments on decision making and they have been used to refine behavioral theory. However, explaining decisions outside the laboratory and experimental elicitation of behavior in the context of cybersecurity has not received particular attention in previous studies. We consider that an individual's behavior is affected by three interrelated factors; self-interest, the behavior of others, and the reaction to rewards and punishment.

As a branch of behavioral economics, social preferences describe how economic agents maximize utility considering others' utilities. Differences in social preferences may explain how and why individuals behave in different settings. Social preferences are critical to understand how decision makers scarce resources to themselves and others. These preferences are often dynamic and complex than self-interest.

Willingness to Cooperate: In this study, the willingness to cooperate is defined as the intention of organizations to cooperate with each other to enhance their overall security posture in their third parties ecosystem. These collaborative practices can be performed like creating an incident response team, allocating resources to secure shared critical information, development, and implementation of effective security policies, plans and procedures, etc.

Unlike some studies that only focus on cooperative intentions as the desired behavior, this study also considers the competition among the organizations. The non-selfish motives not only affect cooperation, but also competition incentives. Therefore, we investigate the moderating effects of social preferences on willingness to cooperate in addition to the direct effect of *Cyber Attack Experience, Perceived Cybersecurity Risk* and *Perceived Cybersecurity Value*.

4 Research Method

To test the hypotheses outlined in Sect. 3, we employ Structural Equation Modeling (SEM) [31]. In this section, we describe the reasons behind selecting SEM, data collection and the development of the measurement mode.

4.1 Statistical Method

We live in a complex, multivariate world and studying the impact of one or two variables in isolation would seem relatively artificial and inconsequential [32]. Although modeling always omits some aspect of reality [33], using some approaches (e.g. regression-based approaches) may be too limiting for the analysis of the more complex and realistic situations. Haenlein points out the limitations of the methods such as factor analysis, cluster analysis, and discriminant analysis, which were popular statistical methods in psychology and sociology during the 20th century [34].

To overcome these limitations mentioned above, we apply SEM. This method allows us to model the relationships among multiple independent and dependent constructs, and observable and unobservable variables, simultaneously. There are two approaches to estimate SEM parameters: covariance-based or variance-based. Both approaches are similar, however, the covariance-based approach is more suited for confirmatory theory testing and the variance-based approach rather for theory development [35]. We use the variance-based approach, here and in the following just referred to as Partial Least Squares (PLS), because it is widely used for predictive analysis and is an appropriate technique for theory development as done in this study. This method is furthermore applicable even under conditions of very small sample size. Chin and Newsted indicated that PLS can be performed with a sample size as low as 50 [36]. Moreover, PLS can be used to analyzing models with either reflective, formative or both types of indicators [37].

We use the statistical software SmartPLS 3.0 for parameter estimation as it provides all required features for PLS analysis. First, it supports the PLS Algorithm [38] and bootstrapping, which is considered as the broadly used approach for nonparametric statistics in management, social science, and market research studies. Second, this version supports the consideration of missing values.

4.2 Sample Data

Questback, an affiliated online survey tool with Norwegian University of Science and Technology (NTNU), is used to collect the data. Recall that this study is motivated by a need to understand the effective factors of improving overall cybersecurity in organizations. Therefore, we focused on the individuals who make cybersecurity-related decisions in organizations.

This survey was active for two weeks and the link was inserted in one of the Norwegian Business and Industry Security Council (NSR) news articles[1]. This organization serves the Norwegian business sector in an advisory capacity on matters relating to crime.in different organizations in Norway. Upon clicking the survey link, participants were presented with guidelines and the definition of the terms *Third Parties*, *Retaliatory Actions*, and *Cooperation with third parties*. We provided these definitions in order to prevent ambiguous interpretation of questions. Within the questionnaire, responses to all questions were mandatory, but allowed participants to choose "I have insufficient knowledge to answer this question." if they were unsure about the corresponding question. The survey completion time ranged from 8 to 10 min.

As indicated in Sect. 3, the theoretical constructs identified in our model: *Perceived Cybersecurity Risk*, *Perceived Cybersecurity Value*, *Social Preferences*, and *Cyber Attack Experience* are measured based on different 11 questions in the survey. Answers of 8 questions are reported on 11-point ordinal scales, one question in 5-point frequency scales reporting the update of cybersecurity risk levels in the organization, and 2 questions on the binary scale (Yes, No). These questions are adapted from Ponemon's third annual report [23] and IZA's Preference Survey Module [39].

A total of 66 responses were collected over this period, out of which 62 responses were usable for the study[2]. Table 1 shows the sample demographics of the considered responses.

Table 1. Demographic profile of respondents

Communications	**16**
Manager	4
Senior Executive	11
Staff/Technician	1
Defense and Aerospace	**4**
Director	2
Supervisor	2
Entertainment and Media	**1**

(*continued*)

---

[1] https://www.nsr-org.no/english/category172.html.

[2] We employed Mean Value Replacement, when indicators have less than 10% missing values, and Casewise Deletion, when indicators have more than 10% missing values, as missing value treatment approaches. In this study, we considered "I have insufficient knowledge to answer this question." as missing values.

Table 1. (*continued*)

Manager	1
Financial services	**11**
Director	2
Manager	5
Senior Executive	3
Staff/Technician	1
Industrial and Manufacturing	2
Supervisor	2
Public Sector	**10**
Manager	5
Senior Executive	4
Staff/Technician	1
Retail	**1**
Supervisor	1
Technology and Software	**17**
Consultant	6
Director	3
Manager	2
Senior Executive	4
Staff/Technician	2
Total	**62**

5   Results

To ensure the reliability of the study, we performed the Reliability Analysis to test the internal consistency of related set of questions for each construct. Although Cronbach's alpha is a widely used measurement for internal consistency, it can be easily affected by the number of items in each construct and lead to underestimated results. Hence, we used composite reliability to measure the internal consistency with threshold value of 0.6. Composite reliability is based on factor loadings rather than the correlations observed between the variables.

Convergent validity is another important parameter that refers to the degree which two measures of constructs that theoretically should be related, are in fact related. For convergent validity, the Average Variance Extracted (AVE) of all latent variables should exceed the recommended 0.5 threshold [40].

Table 2 indicates the composite reliability and average variance extracted values of each latent variable. While the values for Perceived Cybersecurity Risk is close to the thresholds, it suggests that the internal consistency and convergent validity of measured variables are acceptable for the study.

After confirming the reliability of the structural model, a complete bootstrapping process was conducted to test the significance of the model at the level of 0.05 confidence interval. We used Bias-Corrected and Accelerated (BCa) bootstrap for estimating nonparametric confidence interval. To ensure the stability of the results, the number of subsamples is 5000. A hypothesis will be accepted only if the test statistics (t-value) is larger than 1.96. Table 3 shows a summary of the hypotheses tests.

Table 2. Composite reliability and average variance extracted values of each latent variable

Latent variable	Composite reliability value	Average variance extracted (AVE)
Cyber attack experience	0.85	0.73
Perceived cybersecurity risk	0.67	0.51
Perceived cybersecurity value	0.94	0.89
Social preferences	0.79	0.58
Willingness to cooperate	0.85	0.73

Table 3. Summary of hypothesis tests

Hypothesis	Original sample (β)	t-Value	Supported?
H1	0.37	2.09	Yes
H2	0.25	1.97	Yes
H3	0.47	4.13	Yes
H4	0.05	0.36	No
H5	0.13	1.59	No
H6	0.30	2.19	Yes

As these results show, Cybersecurity Attack Experience (H1) has a significant positive effect on the Perceived Cybersecurity Value. As for H2, Perceived Cybersecurity Risk has a significant positive effect on Perceived Cybersecurity Value. Cybersecurity Attack Experience (H3) also has a significant positive effect on Willingness to Cooperate. Regarding H4 and H5, Perceived Cybersecurity Value (H4) and Perceived Cybersecurity Risk (H5) have positive effect on Willingness to Cooperate but not statistically significant which suggests that H4 and H5 are rejected. Finally, hypothesis H6 is supported as the results show Social Preferences have significant effect on Willingness to Cooperate.

Finally, to measure the social preferences of the respondents, we used Social Value Orientation (SVO) framework proposed by Murphy et al. [41]. Figure 3 illustrates a graphical representation of the SVO framework.

Figure 4 indicates the ranges within which relevant social preference angles are fallen. These results show that the cooperative behavior among the decision makers in the context of cybersecurity is dominant.

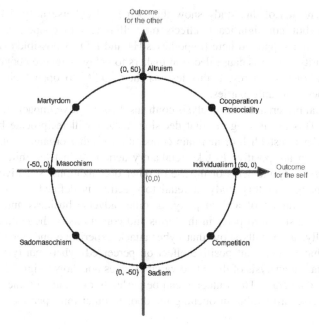

Fig. 3. A graphical representation of Social Value Orientation framework [41].

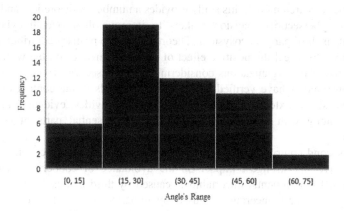

Fig. 4. The ranges of social preference angles

6 Discussion

The significant positive effects of cyber attack experience on willingness to cooperate suggests that organizations that have experienced cyber attacks are more willing to establish or maintain cooperative relationships with other third parties to mitigate the likelihood or impact of future incidents. The consistency between the results of theoretical model and the findings of respondents' social preferences shows that the decision maker's attitude is towards cooperation in the context of cybersecurity.

While the results of this study show that perceived cybersecurity risk and value have positive, but not significant, effects on willingness to cooperate, the related hypotheses are not supported here (hypotheses H4 and H5). A possible explanation is that cybersecurity concerns cause decision makers to delay or ignore cooperation with other organizations. As a result, this lessens their ability to open their network to outside suppliers and third parties.

As for social preferences, the analysis confirms their effective impact on willingness to cooperate. This result suggests that decision makers will reciprocate by adopting positive attitudes to establish or maintain cooperation if other organizations treat them fairly. They even are positive to take retaliatory action against the third parties that cause a cybersecurity incidents or misuse of other organizations' sensitive and confidential information. In this study, a retaliatory action is defined as the discharge, suspension or demotion of a third party, or other adverse business and operational action taken against a third party in the terms and conditions of the contract.

Additionally, the results show that cyber attack experience and perceived cybersecurity risk have significant positive effect on perceived cybersecurity value. However, the mediation analysis of these two variables does not show a significant effect on willingness to cooperate. This outcome can be perfectly explained by the influence of perceived cybersecurity value in opening the door to other third parties.

6.1 Theoretical and Practical Implementation

By testing our research model, this study provides a number of theoretical and practical insights for cybersecurity decision makers to improve their overall cybersecurity posture in their third parties ecosystem. Theoretically, the primary contribution of this study has been to reveal the positive effect of social preferences on the willingness to cooperate among the organizations considering the cybersecurity risks and uncertainties. Previous studies have verified the behavioral models in the context of cybersecurity. This study extends current research and provides evidence that social preferences along with cyber attack experience are essential parts of cooperative willingness.

As the second contribution, this model confirms that perceived cybersecurity risk and value have the strongest impact on the avoidance of cooperation among the organizations. Environmental uncertainties, caused by third parties attacks and weaknesses, and behavioral uncertainty caused by imperfect information or information asymmetry can be two main reasons of this phenomenon. Therefore, our practical implications are mainly directed towards CISOs, but also valuable for other decision makers. To help trusted information sharing, organizations should employ an appropriate, right third party risk management framework based on their structure and business ecosystems. Doing so, they are able to assess the distributed cybersecurity risks in their digital value chain as precise as possible.

7 Conclusions

Cybersecurity decisions are usually not made in a certain, predictable, and isolated environment. Research on the economics of cybersecurity has been largely covered with different perspectives. In this study, we presented a theoretically derived model to explain the impact of social preferences, perceived cybersecurity risk and value, and cyber attack experience on willingness to cooperate in third party ecosystems in the context of cybersecurity. We used variance-based approach of Structural Equation Modeling, so-called Partial Least Square (PLS), to test our research model and analyze the impact of each variable.

The results showed that social preferences and cybersecurity attack experience have significant positive impacts on the willingness to cooperate, and that the dominant preference among the decision makers is towards cooperation and reciprocal behavior. The model also explains that perceived cybersecurity risk and perceived cybersecurity value deter the organizations to cooperate in the context of cybersecurity. The structural equation modeling analysis provides evidence for the small mediating effect of cybersecurity attack experience and perceived cybersecurity risk by perceived cyber-security value. This highlights the importance of the reduction of victimization and improving the defense controls to enhance the overall cybersecurity posture in the ecosystem.

Our results have some limitations: The composite reliability and average variance extracted values of Perceived Cybersecurity Risk is very close to the thresholds. Future research should overcome this limitation by testing the research model using validated instruments suggested in [42]. The analysis of a single Norwegian organizations sample also limits our results. As Dinev [43] demonstrates the importance of cultural aspects when studying cybersecurity behavior, a more comprehensive picture should be compared between different countries.

Since the results of this study show cooperative behavior among the organization in the context of cybersecurity, it is crucial to understand the forces shaping this coop-eration. Moreover, we will investigate the impact of free-riding incentives and exter-nalities of weak cyberdefenses, as the most important problems in cooperation [44], on the overall cybersecurity posture of the ecosystem. Next step of this study is to use the results of this theory to design and develop serious games that help decision makers to understand the cooperation problems and analyze the conditional cooperation and strategic or non-strategic retaliatory actions. The prototype of these games are an extension of CyberAIMs (Cyber Agents' Interactive Modeling and Simulation) [45], a simulation tool for training System and Adversarial Thinking and strategic decision making.

Acknowledgement. We would like to express our special thanks of gratitude to The Norwegian Business and Industry Security Council (NSR) as well as Mr. Adam Szekeres and Mr. EivindKristoffersen Ph.D. Candidates in Information Security, that helped us to design and distribute the survey of this study.

References

1. Bernstein, P.L., Bernstein, P.L.: Against the Gods: The Remarkable Story of Risk. Wiley, New York (1996)
2. Managing Insider Risk Through Training and Culture Report (2016)
3. Kowalski, S.: IT insecurity: a multi-disciplinary inquiry (1996)
4. Øverby, H., Audestad, J.A.: Digital Economics (2018)
5. IT Security: cost-center or strategic investment? (2017)
6. HIPAA Journal: 31,876 Managed Health Services of Indiana Health Plan Members Notified of Impermissible Disclosure of PHINo Title (2019). https://www.hipaajournal.com/31876-managed-health-services-indiana-members-data-breaches/
7. Arghire, I.: New Magecart Group Targets French Ad Agency (2019). https://www.securityweek.com/new-magecart-group-targets-french-ad-agency. Accessed 25 Jan 2019
8. Anderson, R., Moore, T.: The economics of information security. Science (80) (2006)
9. Vishik, C., Sheldon, F., Ott, D.: Economic incentives for cybersecurity: using economics to design technologies ready for deployment. In: Reimer, H., Pohlmann, N., Schneider, W. (eds.) ISSE 2013 Securing Electronic Business Processes, pp. 133–147. Springer, Wiesbaden (2013). https://doi.org/10.1007/978-3-658-03371-2_12
10. Gordon, L.A., Loeb, M.P.: The economics of information security investment. ACM Trans. Inf. Syst. Secur. (TISSEC) 5(4), 438–457 (2002)
11. Cartwright, E.: Behavioral Economics. Routledge (2014)
12. Arney, C.: Predictably irrational: the hidden forces that shape our decisions. Math. Comput. Educ. 44(1), 68 (2010)
13. Thaler, R.H.: Nudge: Improving Decisions About Health, Wealth, and Happiness. Yale University Press, New Haven, London (2008)
14. Kahneman, D., Egan, P.: Thinking, Fast and Slow, vol. 1. Farrar, Straus and Giroux, New York (2011)
15. Rogers, R.W.: A protection motivation theory of fear appeals and attitude change1. J. Psychol. 91(1), 93–114 (1975)
16. Dolan, P., Hallsworth, M., Halpern, D., King, D., Metcalfe, R., Vlaev, I.: Influencing behaviour: the mindspace way. J. Econ. Psychol. 33(1), 264–277 (2012)
17. Briggs, P., Jeske, D., Coventry, L.: Behavior change interventions for cybersecurity. Behav. Change Res. Theor., 115–136 (2017)
18. Fishbein, M., Ajzen, I.: Belief, Attitude, Intention, and Behavior: An Introduction to Theory and Research (1977)
19. Ajzen, I.: The theory of planned behavior. Organ. Behav. Hum. Decis. Process. 50(2), 179–211 (1991)
20. Michie, S., West, R., Campbell, R., Brown, J., Gainforth, H.: ABC of Behaviour Change Theories (ABC of Behavior Change): An Essential Resource for Researchers, Policy Makers and Practitioners. Silverback Publishing (Silverback IS), Croydon (2014)
21. Sommestad, T., Hallberg, J., Lundholm, K., Bengtsson, J.: Variables influencing information security policy compliance: a systematic review of quantitative studies. Inf. Manag. Comput. Secur. 22(1), 42–75 (2014)
22. Cisco: What Are the Most Common Cyberattacks? (2018). https://www.cisco.com/c/en/us/products/security/common-cyberattacks.html. Accessed 25 Nov 2018
23. Ponemon Institute: Data risk in the third-party ecosystem, Ponemon Institute 2016 Research report (2016). http://www.buckleysandler.com
24. Ferraro, K.F., Grange, R.L.: The measurement of fear of crime. Sociol. Inq. 57(1), 70–97 (1987)

25. Visser, M., Scholte, M., Scheepers, P.: Fear of crime and feelings of unsafety in European countries: macro and micro explanations in cross-national perspective. Sociol. Q. **54**(2), 278–301 (2013)
26. Cybersecurity as a Growth Advantage (2016)
27. Wilde, O., Schmalenbach, W., Leonhardi, A.: Lady Windermere's Fan. Library Editions LLP 4001 (1947)
28. Schwartz, S.H.: Universals in the content and structure of values: theoretical advances and empirical tests in 20 countries. In: Advances in Experimental Social Psychology, vol. 25, pp. 1–65. Elsevier (1992)
29. Sagiv, L., Schwartz, S.H.: Value priorities and subjective well-being: direct relations and congruity effects. Eur. J. Soc. Psychol. **30**(2), 177–198 (2000)
30. Sagiv, L., Sverdlik, N., Schwarz, N.: To compete or to cooperate? Values' impact on perception and action in social dilemma games. Eur. J. Soc. Psychol. **41**(1), 64–77 (2011)
31. Kline, R.B.: Principles and Practice of Structural Equation Modeling. Guilford Publications (2015)
32. Jacoby, J.: Consumer research: a state of the art review. J. Mark., 87–96 (1978)
33. Shugan, S.M.: Marketing science, models, monopoly models, and why we need them. Mark. Sci. **21**(3), 223–228 (2002)
34. Haenlein, M., Kaplan, A.M.: A beginner's guide to partial least squares analysis. Underst. Stat. **3**(4), 283–297 (2004)
35. Henseler, J., Ringle, C.M., Sinkovics, R.R.: The use of partial least squares path modeling in international marketing. In: New Challenges to International Marketing, pp. 277–319. Emerald Group Publishing Limited (2009)
36. Chin, W.W., Newsted, P.R.: Structural equation modeling analysis with small samples using partial least squares. Stat. Strat. Small Sample Res. **1**(1), 307–341 (1999)
37. Fornell, C., Bookstein, F.L.: Two structural equation models: LISREL and PLS applied to consumer exit-voice theory. J. Mark. Res., 440–452 (1982)
38. Becker, J.-M., Ismail, I.R.: Accounting for sampling weights in PLS path modeling: simulations and empirical examples. Eur. Manag. J. **34**(6), 606–617 (2016)
39. Falk, A., Becker, A., Dohmen, T., Huffman, D., Sunde, U.: The preference survey module: a validated instrument for measuring risk, time, and social preferences (2016)
40. Fornell, C., Larcker, D.F.: Evaluating structural equation models with unobservable variables and measurement error. J. Mark. Res. **18**, 39–50 (1981)
41. Murphy, R.O., Ackermann, K.A., Handgraaf, M.: Measuring Social Value Orientation (2011)
42. Featherman, M.S., Pavlou, P.A.: Predicting e-services adoption: a perceived risk facets perspective. Int. J. Hum Comput Stud. **59**(4), 451–474 (2003)
43. Dinev, T., Goo, J., Hu, Q., Nam, K.: User behaviour towards protective information technologies: the role of national cultural differences. Inf. Syst. J. **19**(4), 391–412 (2009)
44. Bauer, J.M., Van Eeten, M.J.G.: Cybersecurity: stakeholder incentives, externalities, and policy options. Telecomm. Policy **33**(10–11), 706–719 (2009)
45. Zoto, E., Kianpour, M., Kowalski, S.J., Lopez-Rojas, E.A.: A socio-technical systems approach to design and support systems thinking in cybersecurity and risk management education. Complex Syst. Inf. Model. Q. **18**, 65–75 (2019)

Understanding Perceptions: User Responses to Browser Warning Messages

Heather Molyneaux[1]([✉]), Irina Kondratova[1], and Elizabeth Stobert[2]

[1] National Research Council, Fredericton, NB, Canada
{Heather.Molyneaux, Irina.Kondratova,
  Elizabeth.Stobert}@nrc-cnrc.gc.ca
[2] National Research Council, Montreal, QC, Canada

Abstract. With changes in interfaces resulting from the proliferation of IOT devices and new technologies such as self-driving vehicles, user reactions to browser messages may also change. This paper reviews the literature on user reactions to browser warnings, with emphasis on screen size and form factors. The literature indicates that browser warning message design, habituation, awareness of risk and screen size are aspects that effect user perception of risk. This article surveys the findings while noting challenges and proposed solutions to support effective provision of and user compliance with browser security warnings as well as important user study design considerations for future work – in particular, future work on the effect of screen size on user perception of browser warnings.

Keywords: Survey · User studies · Browser warnings · Screen size · Form factor · Security

1 Introduction

User interfaces are changing. Screen sizes and form factors are, for the most part, shrinking. Smartphone use is growing for not only personal reasons but also for work tasks. Additionally, the proliferation of IOT devices and new technologies such as self-driving cars mean that in the future screens might change again to become larger, smaller or even nonexistent. How do these changes affect how warnings are presented to users? Do these warnings change how users view their own privacy and security? Do people react differently to the same warnings depending on the type of device and the size of the screens on which warnings are displayed? The answers to these questions could have direct implications in designing new interfaces for devices such as driverless cars, to determine appropriate screen sizes for warnings. This study investigates research studies on user perceptions towards browser warnings and outlines best practices for their design. As well, the design for a user evaluation to study screen size and form factor effects in user responses to browser warning messages is presented.

In order to understand the current research we examine the background literature on user reactions to browser warnings and security messages on mobile and desktop computers. There is a gap in the literature whereby the differences between user

© Her Majesty the Queen in Right of Canada 2019
A. Moallem (Ed.): HCII 2019, LNCS 11594, pp. 164–175, 2019.
https://doi.org/10.1007/978-3-030-22351-9_11

attitudes towards browser warnings on mobile compared to desktop or laptop systems are not well examined. As a result, we draw upon the literature review in order to propose a study design that combines observations of any initial differences in a simple user task as well as a self-reported survey asking the same participants to reflect on their mobile vs. desktop and laptop browsing habits and their attitudes towards security and privacy on those devices.

1.1 Background

Improved browser warnings and security indicators can lead to users' improved ability to protect themselves against being cyberattacked online. Phishing and malware attacks are the most prevalent cyberattacks that affect users while Internet browsing, social networking, using online banking services or shopping online. "Phishing refers to use of deceptive computer-based means to trick individuals into disclosing sensitive personal information. Phishing attacks aid criminals in a wide range of illegal activities, including identity theft and fraud. They can also be used to install malware and attacker tools on a user's system" [1]. Malware is defined by NIST [2] as "A program that is covertly inserted into another program with the intent to destroy data, run destructive or intrusive programs, or otherwise compromise the confidentiality, integrity, or availability of the victim's data, applications, or operating system".

To prevent Internet users from falling victim to cybercriminal attacks, W3C's Web Security Context: User Interface Guidelines [3] have prescribed certain best practices for browser security indicators, such as the use of the TLS indicator (https) within the web browser's address bar to indicate secure website. They also give guidelines for designing security warning, caution and danger messages within the browsers, such as:

- Warning messages *must* interrupt the user's current task, such that the user has to acknowledge the message and provide the user with distinct options for how to proceed
- The options *must* be descriptive to the point that their respective meaning can be understood in the absence of any other information contained in the warning interaction
- Danger interactions *must* be presented in a way that makes it impossible for the user to go to or interact with the destination web site that caused the danger situation to occur, without first explicitly interacting with the message.

Borger et al. note that when designing computer warnings the following must be considered: risk needs to be described comprehensively; the warning must be concise and accurate; warnings need to offer users meaningful options; the relevant contextual information must be presented as well as relevant auditing information; and finally, the warning must follow a consistent layout [4].

Borger and colleagues found that browser warnings are an effective way to improve computer security; however there is a need for user studies with larger groups of participants to prove results and improve browser warning effectiveness. Our paper takes a closer look at how people perceive and respond to browser warnings, especially in the context of limited screen space availability of the mobile world, in order to gather best practices and understand gaps to inform future user studies.

1.2   Methodology: A Subsection Sample

In order to investigate the effect of screen size users' perceptions and interactions with browser warnings, we conducted a literature search on the federal science library (FSL) database. The FSL database provides NRC researchers with access to over a thousand databases. Initial searches were conducted on the FSL database using the search terms "web browser" "warning" and "user." Search results were limited to only items from the last 10 years, including only scholarly material, peer reviewed publications and excluding newspaper articles, book reviews and dissertations. We further limited the results to only those containing user studies and evaluations. This resulted in an initial 16 relevant articles. Further articles were gathered and cited as a result of checking more recent articles citing the initial 16. In total 23 articles with user studies and evaluations are referenced in this paper (Table 1).

Table 1. Studies included in the literature review.

Authors	Article	Date
Alsharnouby et al.	Why phishing still works: User strategies for combating phishing attacks	2015
Anderson et al.	Your memory is working against you: How eye tracking and memory explain habituation to security warnings	2016
Balebako et al.	The impact of timing on the salience of smartphone app privacy notices	2015
Böhme and Köpsell	Trained to accept? A field experiment on consent dialogs	2010
Carpenter, Zhu and Kolimi	Reducing online identity disclosure using warnings	2014
Dong, Clark and Jacob	Defending the weakest link: phishing websites detection by analyzing user behaviors	2010
Fagan et al.	A study of users' experiences and beliefs about software update messages	2015
Fagan et al.	How does this message make you feel? A study of user perspectives on software update/warning message design	2015
Herzberg and Ahmad	Security and identification indicators for browsers against spoofing and phishing attacks	2008
Iuga, Nurse and Erola	Baiting the hook: factors impacting susceptibility to phishing attacks	2016
Jorgensen et al.	Dimensions of risk in mobile applications: A user study	2015
Junger, Montoya and Overink	Priming and warnings are not effective to prevent social engineering attacks	2017
Kelley and Bertenthal	Attention and past behavior, not security knowledge, modulate users' decisions to login to insecure websites	2016
Mamonov, Renbunan-Fich	The impact of information security threat awareness on privacy-protective behaviors	2018
Marforio et al.	Evaluation of personalized security indicators as an anti-phishing mechanism for smartphone applications	2016

(*continued*)

Table 1. (*continued*)

Authors	Article	Date
Modic and Anderson	Reading this may harm your computer: the psychology of malware warnings	2014
Purkait, Kumar and Suar	An empirical investigation of the factors that influence internet user's ability to correctly identify a phishing website	2014
Redder et al.	An experience sampling study of user reactions to browser warnings in the field	2018
Redmiles et al.	Asking for a friend: evaluating response biases in security user studies	2018
Schechter et al.	The emperor's new security indicators: An evaluation of website authentication and the effect of role playing on usability studies	2007
Shah and Patil	Evaluating effectiveness of mobile browser security warnings	2016
Silic and Back	The dark side of social networking sites: understanding phishing risks	2016
Virvillis et al.	Mobile devices: A phisher's paradise	2014

2 Findings

Security and privacy are topics of interest to both computer security experts and novice computer users alike; Jorgenson and colleagues note that security experts and regular users of Android devices have similar concerns about safety and security. Personal information privacy – including personally identifying information, password and login credentials and financial information were seen as of the greatest concern, with general users more concerned about data integrity than monitoring risks [5]. However, it can be tricky for users to protect themselves against online risks. Virvilis and colleagues examined popular web browsers on IOS, Android and desktop systems (Windows platforms) visiting 1400 phishing and 1400 malicious URLs to see if browsers warned users of risk. They found most browsers offered limited protection against threats [6].

Even though many users are interested in protecting their own privacy and security online, users still have difficulty making decisions when faced with browser warnings, app permissions, and software update notifications. Below we summarize the findings of user studies into four categories on how the following impact user behavior and beliefs about privacy and security alerts and measures: the role of browser warning messages and alert design; habituation; awareness; and screen size and form factor.

2.1 Browser Warning Messages and Alerts: Design

Why do participants ignore warnings? In a 2015 study Fagan et al. looked at self-reported ratings of software update messages and warnings. Participants were hesitant to apply updates even when reported they cared about security and privacy. A survey on their opinions and experiences with software was coupled with a study whereby users were shown images and asked to rate perception of aspects of the updates and warnings. Annoyance and confusion over update messages lead users towards noncompliance. Also the study found that the user's opinions of the software and vendors affected their decisions regarding applying an update messages [7].

Timing is an important factor in privacy notices and user recall – what the user remembers seeing and reading. Balebako and colleagues studied recall of privacy notice information as a proxy for participants' attention to and the salience of privacy notices. Participants were shown the privacy notice in the app store, at the startup of the app, during app use and afterwards. Those shown the notice during app use had overall increased recall rates [8].

Another avenue of research is examining how what the message say affects the user. Carpenter et al. found that warnings can be successful for countering user "mindlessness", which runs counter to some research indicating that warnings are not generally successful. In their study they found the wording of the warning made a difference; that the term "hazard" rather than "warning" or "caution" was the most effective wording of a warning message. They found that participants were less likely to disclose their driver license number than email address – perhaps due to heuristic, automatic compliance to a request, or "mindlessness" since people are used to revealing email address information online [9]. For future studies the researchers wonder "Are warnings equally effective in other cyber environments, such as smart phones? [9]".

How can the risks of privacy and security disclosures be mitigated? Two of the articles involved user studies with systems designed to complement existing detection systems. Herzberg and colleagues tested three conditions using the Trustbar browser extension – a certificate-derived identification indicator which is user-customized. Trustbar presents a highly visible indication of the security of websites which significantly improved user detection rates within the researchers' experiments [10].

Dong et al. used a user-based phishing system to complement existing anti-phishing solutions. The system alerts users who are about to submit credential information by monitoring user behavior. When users have never or rarely visited a site and the data being submitted is bound to a website other than the current one an alert is sent to the user. They found that their system could detect pharming attacks – attacks similar to phishing, where DNS queries are interrupted, replacing legitimate websites with illegitimate versions designed to trick users into disclosing personal information - which were not detected by existing systems. Also their system fills a gap by alerting the user at the stage when they are at a phishing website and could potentially give out personal information. The researchers show that detecting phishing websites through user behavior is an accurate method which can be used to complement existing detection technologies, and their future work will involve user evaluation to inform future development [11].

2.2   Habituation

The role of habituation in user behaviors was a major theme in many of the findings of research papers examining user responses to browser warnings. Many users are accustomed to entering certain personal information on a daily basis for a variety of reasons, or are asked to consent to a variety of consent dialogs, such as end user license agreement (EULA) dialogues. When promoted for information in a way that seems familiar to them users may fill in personal information and consent without knowing first what they are consenting to, and how their information is going to be used.

In general when asked in a research study participants are quick to disclose personal information. Junger et al. surveyed 100 users in a medium sized town in the Netherlands, asking them to disclose their email information, list products recently purchased, the online shops they make these purchases at and the last 9 digits of their bank account. While only 43.3% disclosed the banking information, a high number of participants disclosed the other information even in the group that were primed not to give out personal information. Priming and warnings did not influence the degree to which participants disclosed personal information. Researchers found that the participants lacked knowledge about what constitutes sensitive information and how it can be used and abused by phishers [12].

Social networking sites (SNS) in particular are places in which users run a high risk of being phished. In their 2016 study Silic et al. directed employees to a fake website. Of the 180 visits the fake website, 122 employees filled in all personal information asked for, and an additional 15 filled in some information. The 15 who did not continue were contacted by email and stated that they felt there was an issue with the website (that the site was not a legitimate site). The researchers found that the "liking" influence technique was a strong incentive for people to reveal personal information, a strong first step in deception interaction They concluded that employees are vulnerable to SNS attacks, that organizations need better control over SNS security threats, SNS security policies need to be strengthened and with social engineering attacks SNS can be a security issue [13].

Böhme's study on online privacy consent dialogs involved showing three type of warnings to 80,000 users. There were three conditions: a neutral condition, a polite request noting a voluntary decision and another condition resembling a typical end-user license agreement (EULA). They found that being polite and asking for voluntary cooperation decreased the probability of users consenting, whereas the condition resembling a EULA saw higher rates of user acceptance. The researchers attribute this to habituation, noting that more than half the participants took less than 8 s – not enough time to read the message. They hypothesize that users are trained to automatically click on "accept" during interruptions typical of EULA – a finding that has repercussions not just with EULAs but also online safety and privacy. The researchers note the importance in interface design in order to prevent habituation of users [14].

However, not all of the research papers pointed to habituation as a major issue in user interactions with browser warnings. Reeder et al. sampled the decisions made by 6,000 Chrome and Firefox users using a browser extension and employing users via Amazon Mechanical Turk – a crowd sourcing marketplace. They found that while users mostly trusted warnings and that habituation was not a major issue, users relied on site reputation, which was a major factor in them proceeding through warnings on trusted sites. They also found that users sometimes downgraded protocols when faced with a warning – proceeding to the site via http when the https site gave them a browser warning [15].

2.3   Awareness

While some of the previously discussed studies noted that awareness of security issues did not seem to have any influence over users prone to habituation, several studies concerned with the susceptibility of users to phishing attacks were interested in seeing if awareness increased user resilience to phishing attacks. These studies had mixed results.

In Alsharnouby et al.'s study participants were asked to identify phishing websites. Only 53% of phishing websites were detected by participants even when users were primed to identify them. The study used eye tracking, and researchers found that users spent little time looking at security indicators – they mainly looked at the content of the website to make their assessment. Gaze time did not correlate with improved detection scores [16]. The findings of this study seem to indicate that habituation (or at least trust of certain websites or content) has greater influence over user behaviors and opinions on suspicious sites than awareness of potential issues.

In an investigation of susceptibility to phishing attacks Iuga and colleagues examined demographics and ability to detect phishing attacks. They found in their study of 382 users only a small group of participants (25%) were able to detect phishing attacks at rates of 75% of the time or more. The average detection score was 65%, indicating that most people have a high risk of succumbing to phishing attacks. Their results suggest that the user's gender and years of PC usage have a statistically significant impact on the detection rate of phishing. They also found that pop-up phishing attacks have a higher success rate than other tested strategies; and that the psychological anchoring effect can be observed in phishing. The anchoring effect occurs when people rely on the first piece of information they are presented with, creating cognitive bias. The researchers state that an approach combining detection tools, training and greater awareness could provide users with increased resistance to phishing attacks [17].

Purkait et al. conducted three experimental tasks and administered surveys in order to examine user awareness of phishing, safe internet practices, users' internet usage and internet skills, cognitive levels and demographic factor. Participants were users who were familiar with online banking and shopping tasks. They found that awareness of phishing had the highest positive effect. Internet skill surprisingly did not have a positive effect. They also found that there was a negative impact for those who used the internet frequently for financial activity, which led them to surmise that those who use the internet for online financial transactions tend to not notice the visual cues for phishing and might be more prone to habituation [18].

Mamonov and Benbunan-Fich examine ways in which users can be motivated to protect themselves from privacy and security threats. In an online experiment they exposed users to news stories about security breaches. Users exposed to such stories chose passwords 500x stronger than the control group, who were exposed to general technology news. The treatment group also limited their disclosure on answers to sensitive information within a survey – in particular questions on drug use, drinking and driving and support for the death penalty. Disclosure of non-sensitive information remained the same. This study suggests that "presenting users with narratives highlighting computer security threats may be an effective way to stimulate adherence to using strong passwords" [19].

Another potential avenue to increase user security could be through the deployment of personalized security indicators. As Marforio et al. note, personal indicators on mobile interfaces may be more effective than on PC platforms due to the simplified interfaces on mobile. They found that within their user study phishing attack success rates decreased 50% when adapting personalized security indicators [20].

Users may not even be aware of some currently employed security measures. In Their 2007 study Schechter et al. evaluated user groups' reactions to removing HTTPS indicators, removing the site-authentication image, and replacing the password entry page with a warning. They found that all participants, even in the user group using their own bank account information, ignored the HTTPS indicators and entered their information. In the second condition, with the site-authentication image removed, 92% of those using their own passwords still entered information. Even in the condition where a warning was presented, 36% present of participants still entered their own password information [21].

These articles suggest that greater awareness of phishing threats, through training, or the necessity of stronger passwords could, in conjunction with other methods, such as detection tools, build user resilience to security and privacy threats. Also the narratives and imagery used to deliver training and present alerts are important tools not only to increase awareness but all combat habituation. At the same time, there are specific challenges to training itself – how and when the training is delivered is as important as the content of that training. There also is a need to be studies of training design and outcomes.

2.4   Screen Size and Form Factor

In addition to human factors that influence the effectiveness of browser security warnings and user compliance, such as user's attention, technical knowledge, past behavior, warning message design, social influence, and memory habituation [22–25], there some additional factors at play, such as screen size and form factor.

Most of the studies reviewed here are concerned with user interaction on desktop and laptop computers. But the importance of smaller devices, such as smartphones, and user awareness of security risk is a growing concern for cybersecurity researchers. Bitton et al. note that security awareness of personal computers is higher than mobile platform awareness levels, and mobile users require a different set of security awareness skills than those needed for PC [26] At the same time, Goel and Jain note that users on mobile devices are three times more vulnerable to phishing attacks. This could be due to a variety of considerations including the smaller screen, awareness issues and lack of user input. Separate techniques are needed to avoid privacy and security attacks on mobile devices [27].

Research demonstrates that the browsers on mobile devices are more limited in availability and visibility of browser security indicators and warnings due to several reasons, including the screen size due to form factor limitations; mobile devices having more limited screen size compared to desktop or laptop computers [28, 29]. For example, in mobile browsers sometimes the edges of pop-ups can extend beyond the side of the display, or buttons can overlap text.

Previous studies of screen size and usability indicate that when the user performs complex tasks, the diminished screen size leads to lower efficiency. Larger device screen sizes are deemed more efficient for information seeking tasks [30]. However, smartphones are increasingly being used for working on the go and social activities, tasks which sometimes require web browsing. With an increase in the use of smartphones for web browsing tasks which involve personal information, such as on SNS sites or financial information, such as online banking, portable devices with smaller screens are becoming more of a target for phishing attacks. Such attacks can lead to identify theft, fraud, and even the installation of malware. Such activities are obfuscated to the user, and due to the limited capacity of some smaller smartphone devices, appropriate countermeasures may not be installed, rendering the user vulnerable.

Research studies indicate that security and privacy can be seen as more of an issue on the smaller screen than a larger screen. In Chin and colleagues' 2012 study of 60 smartphone users it was found that users were more concerned about privacy and connecting to sensitive information on the smartphone compared to a laptop or a desktop, because of fear of physical loss or damage to the device. The users also had concerns over user interface accidents (such as making accidental online purchases), as well as concerns related to the perception of limited security and privacy properties of their phone [31].

3 Discussion

Researchers note that education and training to increase awareness of security and privacy risks is not enough; software solutions are also necessary [27]. For future work Jorgensen et al. call for an evaluation and development of new risk communication methods– more specifically interfaces that allow users to quickly and accurately assess the security and privacy risks of downloading apps for Android devices [5].

Researchers also highlight the need for increased user studies. User studies are far from straightforward: ecological validity is paramount but ethical issues arise when studying users using their own devices and personal information in real world situations. In lab studies the ethical implications are more limited, especially when users are not using their personal devices or personal data, but in lab settings users are particularly primed for awareness. Redmiles et al. state several benefits and biases of self-reported data in the security field. Self-reported measures, most commonly surveys, are characterized by the ease of which information is collected, the control researchers have over the study and the depth of understanding which can be achieved via user responses. However there are many potential biases inherent in self-reported measures, including users having difficulty remembering past events, as well as users shaping their own answers in order to meet perceived expectations of the audience (i.e. the researchers) [32]. In self-reported accounts of security behaviors, instances of phishing attacks can also be underreported, as users may not even be aware that they have fallen for phishing attacks in the past.

In their study Redmiles and colleagues compared real world behaviors to survey results. They found a systematic relationship between the self-reported data and the real world scenarios which only really "breaks down when survey respondents are required to notice and act on minor details of experimental manipulations." Specific insights are difficult to access within self-reported surveys. The data from the surveys closely mirrored the measurement data but users were prone to over report good behaviors. Attention for message details was more difficult to capture in surveys than real life. The researchers suggest that more security studies should involve interview-facilitated data collection, A/B testing, field observations or lab-observation hybrids [32]. Schechter et al. also note that participants using their own personal account information compared to those given assigned information will be more mindful of security issued in studies, indicating a need for study measures not just following role play participation but also asking questions about real world scenarios [21]. However, having participants use their own personal information in studies puts the participants at greater risk – an ethical complication.

Context also makes a big difference in security studies. Some users might be aware of and responsive to security threats in some areas and not others. Researchers noted that while employees are generally trained on security threats there is a need for better training and awareness of the security threats SNS pose to employees and companies [13].

4   Future Work

The articles we reviewed raised a variety of issues about privacy and security that could shape future work concerning user behavior on smaller screens, like smartphones, compared to larger screens of laptops and desktops. For example, are users more likely to disclose personal information on their smartphone or using a desktop or laptop? Are users more likely or less likely to engage in financial tasks, like banking and online shopping, on their desktop than the phone, and are users more prone to dismiss browser warnings on smaller screens like mobile phones compared to larger screens?

More work needs to be done in order to examine if users have different security habits on different form factors. Do they feel different devices have different levels of security and how does that affect their own use of the devices? How do users react to security warnings on smaller screen compared to larger screened devices? And what is the role of design, habituation, and awareness on user perceptions of security on the different form factors?

In order to investigate these questions we constructed a research plan that includes observing users' browsing habits in lab during two role-playing tasks, one involving a smartphone and the other involving a laptop. Users will be directed to a website and a researcher will have them think aloud while they complete a task using each of the devices. The researcher will record the actions of the user while paying close attention to what the user does when faced with a browser notification. Afterwards data will be collected about the users' regular smartphone and laptop browsing habits as well as some questions about the task they just completed.

We coupled the task with the survey to encourage the participants to think about how they react to (or are habituated to ignore) different notices on websites in their everyday browsing. Findings from the survey will give us greater insight into what sort of tasks they do as well as their own perceptions of browser warnings on both smaller and larger screens when they are using their own devices in a real world setting.

5 Conclusions

When examining the relationship between the device form factor and user responses to security and privacy warnings, many factors must be considered, including users' past experience with various device form factors, their online habits for each type of the device, and their perceptions of privacy and security in general.

In order to examine users' reactions to browser warnings and gather self-reported measures of users' experiences with browser warnings on smart phones as well as desktop and laptop computers, our future work will involve a user study with multiple user data collection measures, including a two condition task study followed by a survey on users' past practices and experiences. The study will generate new knowledge on users' online behaviors and develop design recommendations to improve the effectiveness of security warnings on mobile devices.

Relatively little attention has been devoted to studying the effect of screen size and the device form factor on users' responses to security warnings. Our future studies will work towards filling this gap.

References

1. Mell, P., Kent, K., Nusbaum, J.: Guide to malware incident prevention and handling. US Department of Commerce, Technology Administration, National Institute of Standards and Technology 800-83. Gaithersburg, Maryland (2005)
2. Souppaya, M., Scarfone, K.: Guide to malware incident prevention and handling for desktops and laptops. NIST Special Publication 800-83 (2013)
3. W3C: W3C guidelines Web Security Context: User Interface Guidelines, W3C Recommendation, 12 August 2010. http://www.w3.org/TR/2010/REC-wsc-ui-20100812/
4. Borger, W., Iacono, L.L.: User perception and response to computer security warnings. In: Weisbecker, A., Burmester, M., Schmidt, A. (eds) Mensch und computer 2015 Workshopband Stuttgart: Oldenbourg Wissenschaftsverlag, pp. 621–646 (2015)
5. Jorgensen, Z., Chen, J., Gates, C.S., Li, N., Proctor, R.W., Yu, T.: Dimensions of risk in mobile applications: a user study. In: CODASPY 2015, San Antonio, Texas, pp. 49–60, 2–4 March 2015
6. Virilis, N., Mylonas, A., Nikolaos, T.: Security busters: web browser security vs. rogue sites. Comput. Secur. **52**, 90–105 (2015)
7. Fagan, M., Khan, M., Buck, R.: A Study of user's experiences and beliefs about software update messages. Comput. Hum. Behav. **51**, 504–519 (2015)
8. Balebako, R., Schaub, F., Adjerid, I., Acquisti, A., Cranor, L.F.: The impact of timing on the Salience of smartphone app privacy notices. In: SPSM 2015, Denver, Colorado, pp. 63–74, 12 October 2015
9. Carpenter, S., Zhu, F., Kolimi, S.: Reducing online identity disclosure using warnings. Appl. Ergon. **45**(5), 1337–1342 (2014)
10. Herzberg, A, Jbara, A: Security and identification indicators for browsers against spoofing and phishing attacks. ACM Trans. Internet Technol. **8**(4), 16 (2008)
11. Dong, X., Clark, J., Jacob, J.: Defending the weakest link: phishing websites section by analysing user behaviours. Telecommun. Syst. **45**(2–3), 215–226 (2010)
12. Junger, M., Montoya, L., Overink, F.-J.: Priming and warnings are not effective to prevent social engineering attacks. Comput. Hum. Behav. **66**, 75–87 (2017)

13. Silic, M., Back, A.: The dark side of social networking sites: understanding phishing risks. Comput. Hum. Behav. **60**, 35–43 (2016)

14. Böhme, R., Köpsell, S.: Trained to accept? a field experiment on consent dialogs. In: CHI 2010, Atlanta Georgia, pp. 2403–2406, 10–15 April 2010

15. Reeder, R., Felt, A., Consolvo, S., Malkin, N., Thompson, C., Egelman, S.: An experience sampling study of user reactions to browser warnings in the field. In: Proceedings of the 2018 CHI Conference on Human Factors in Computing Systems. ACM (2018)

16. Alsharnouby, M., Alaca, F, Chiasson, S.: Why phishing still works: user strategies for combating phishing attacks. Int. J. Hum.-Comput. Stud. **82**(10), 69–82 (2015)

17. Iuga, C., Nurse, J., Erola, A.: Baiting the hook: factors impacting susceptibility to phishing attacks. Hum.-centric Comput. Inf. Sci. **6**(1), 8 (2016)

18. Purkait, S., Kumar De., S, Suar, D.: An Empirical investigation of the factors that influence internet user's ability to correctly identify a phishing website. Inf. Manage. Comput. Secur. **22**(3), 194–234 (2014)

19. Mamonov, S., Renbunan-Fich, R.: The impact of information security threat awareness on privacy-protective behaviors. Comput. Hum. Behav. **83**, 32–44 (2018)

20. Marforio, C., Masti, R.J., Soriente, C., Kostianinen, K., Capkun, S.: Evaluation of personalized security indicators as an anti-phishing mechanism for smartphone applications. In: CHI 2016 #chiforgood, San Jose, CA, USA, pp. 540–551 (2016)

21. Schechter, S., Dhamija, R., Ozment, A., Fischer, I.: The emperor's new security indicators: an evaluation of website authentication and the effect of role playing on usability studies. In: IEEE Symposium on Security (2007)

22. Kelley, T., Bertenthal, B.I.: Attention and past behavior, not security knowledge, modulate users' decisions to login to insecure websites. Inf. Comput. Secur. **24**(2), 164–176 (2016)

23. Fagan, M., Khan, M.M.H., Nguyen, N.: How does this message make you feel? a study of user perspectives on software update/warning message design. Hum.-centric Comput. Inf. Sci. **5**(1), 36 (2015)

24. Modic, D., Anderson, R.: Reading this may harm your computer: the psychology of malware warnings. Comput. Hum. Behav. **41**, 71–79 (2014)

25. Anderson, B.B., Jenkins, J.L., Vance, A., Kirwan, C.B., Eargle, D.: Your memory is working against you: how eye tracking and memory explain habituation to security warnings. Decis. Support Syst. **92**, 3–13 (2016)

26. Bitton, R., Finkelshtein, A., Sidi, L., Puzis, R., Rokach, L.: Taxonomy of mobile users' security awareness. Comput. Secur. **73**, 266–293 (2018)

27. Goel, D., Jain, A.K.: Mobile phishing attacks and defense mechanisms: state of art and open research challenges. Comput. Secur. **73**, 519–544 (2018)

28. Shah, R., Patil, K.: Evaluating effectiveness of mobile browser security warnings. ICTACT J. Commun. Technol. **7**(3), 1373–1378 (2016)

29. Virvilis, N., Tsalis, N., Mylonas, A., Gritzalis, D.: Mobile devices: a phisher's paradise. In: 2014 11th International Conference on Security and Cryptography (SECRYPT), pp. 1–9. IEEE, August 2014

30. Raptis, D., Tselios, N., Kjeldskov, J., Skov, M.: Does size matter? investigating the impact of mobile phone screen size on users' oerceieved usability, effectiveness and efficiency. In: Mobile HCI, pp. 127–136. ACM (2013)

31. Chin, E., Felt, A.P, Sekar, V., Wagner, D.: Measuring user confidence in smartphone security and privacy. In: Symposium on Usable Privacy and Security (SOUPS), Washington DC, pp. 1–16, 11–13 July 2012

32. Redmiles, E.M., Zhu, Z., Kross, S., Kuchhal, D., Dumitras, T., Mazurek, M.L.: Asking for a friend: evaluating response biases in security user studies. In: CCS2018. Toronto ON, 15–19 October 2018

Understanding Parents' Concerns with Smart Device Usage in the Home

Aarathi Prasad[1]([✉]), Ruben Ruiz[1], and Timothy Stablein[2]

[1] Skidmore College, Saratoga Springs, NY, USA
aprasad@skidmore.edu
[2] Union College, Schenectady, NY, USA

Abstract. Several studies have been conducted to determine parenting strategies in the age of digital technology. However, we are not aware of any qualitative research regarding parents' safety and privacy concerns about their children's use of smart devices in the home. Given the rise in use of smart devices within the home in general, and among children in particular, we wanted to explore the privacy and safety concerns that parents have about their children's device use, their experiences using devices with their children, children's independent use, and restrictions parents place on device use. In this paper, we present findings from an exploratory study of 29 participants through three focus groups and 14 semi-structured interviews. Our study revealed that encouraging device usage may help build familial relationships and foster open communication between parents and children. We also discovered that parents feel it is their responsibility to keep their children from harm when they use smart devices, and that parents do not trust applications, devices, smart device manufacturers or Internet providers to do so. Our findings can help researchers better understand the different device usage scenarios, parents' concerns about their kids' device use, and parent-child relationships, which will help them design better tools that encourage parents and children to work together to develop device usage rules and better safety and privacy practices.

Keywords: Smart home · Smartphones · Tablets · Children ·
Privacy · Trust · Security · Safety · Family

1 Introduction

A survey conducted by CommonSense Media discovered that the number of 0–8 year olds using smartphones have increased from 45% in 2011 to 95% in 2017, tablets 8 to 78% and their own tablet from <1% to 42% in the home [5]. Smart devices have been shown to be useful to child development, and as such, electronic books, tablets, and laptops are used in classrooms across the nation [8, 25]. For example, over the years, researchers have explored different ways to use smart devices to determine whether a child has a learning disability or a

© Springer Nature Switzerland AG 2019
A. Moallem (Ed.): HCII 2019, LNCS 11594, pp. 176–190, 2019.
https://doi.org/10.1007/978-3-030-22351-9_12

developmental disorder [1], and also to enhance children's learning ([4,10,20]). On the other hand, media is rife with stories about the negative impact of smart devices and applications (apps) on children ([19,21–23]). Nonetheless, a national survey of 2300 parents with children under 8 demonstrated that only about 30% of parents were very or somewhat concerned about their children's media usage, and only 3% admitted that media usage caused conflict in the home [28]. Researchers have also addressed concerns about addiction [18], and smartphone safety [29], which raise additional concerns about the well-being of children when using smart devices.

Smart device proliferation within the home, and virtually all aspects of our social and personal lives also raises questions about the confidentiality and security of information transmitted and collected through them. Prior research has explored ways to help users better manage their privacy when using smartphone apps [2,3,24]. Researchers have also demonstrated the risks and recommended ways to mitigate risks when using smart toys [14,31]. Researchers also interviewed experts on teen online behavior, risks and risk mitigation strategies [13]. But there is still a lack of understanding of the security, privacy and safety concerns that parents have about their children's smart device use.

We conducted an exploratory study to understand parents' concerns about safety, security and privacy, children's interactions with devices, and restrictions parents placed on device use. Through focus groups and semi-structured interviews, we address the following research questions:

- How and in what contexts do children use smart devices?
- What kind of security, privacy and safety concerns do parents have about their kids' device use?
- What restrictions do parents place on their children's device use?
- How does smart device use affect familial relationships?

In this paper, we present our findings from the focus groups and interviews. Our findings reveal different device usage scenarios, parents' concerns about their kids' device use, and how device use affects familial relationships.

2   Related Work

In this section, we present prior research on understanding children's smart device usage, and parents' concerns about the device usage, as well as studies on how to protect child safety on the Internet.

Children's Device Use: Common Sense Media conducted studies about media-use patterns among children from birth to age 8 in America as well as surveys about people's use of media use (tweens, college students, and adults) [5,6]; the research showed that media use was a source of tension among parents and children, and that the latest technologies, such as smart toys, often appear first in households with young children. Moreover, Manches et al. analyzed social media sites, conducted home visits to observe children's use of smart devices and conducted workshops to explore children's understanding of video games [12] and discovered that parents and children do not necessarily understand how technology captures their activities. Finally, Magee et al. used diary studies, interviews and creative activities to understand how teenagers use technology and how factors such as relationships and life goals affect their technology use [11].

Concerns About Device Use: A 2016 survey from Common Sense Media found that 50% of teenagers felt addicted to their devices, and 78% checked their devices at least hourly [6]. However, teenagers also had privacy concerns. For example, researchers conducted a two-month, web-based diary study to understand teenagers' online risk experiences when browsing the web on their computers and mobile devices and discovered that teenagers rarely communicated their concerns with their parents [30]. Prior research also offered insights of differing views of parents and children about device use and presented the need for technologies that can support ways to reach agreements on device usage restrictions [15]. Additionally, researchers conducted semi-structured interviews with parents and children to understand their privacy and interaction expectations from Internet-connected toys [14]. Researchers also discovered security and privacy flaws in smart devices. Manches et al. found that commercially successful IoT designs such as the Skylander and Disney Infinity influence children's attitudes and behavior and also reveal information about their daily activities [12]. Valente et al. discovered security flaws in Internet-connected toys [26].

Safety Measures and Parental Controls: In addition to discovering security flaws and privacy leaks, researchers also proposed ways to mitigate risks. For example, Yong et al. proposed risk mitigation strategies against online pedophiles when using Internet-connected robot toys [31]. Prior research has also presented ways to improve security and privacy controls on smart devices. For example, researchers have provided recommendations for mobile apps for online safety that embed better family values [29]. McReynolds et al. gave recommendations for Internet-connected toy manufacturers and policy makers that take into consideration security, privacy and better child-toy interaction [14]. Jang et al. presented design recommendations for IoT device manufacturers to provide fine-grained access control and authentication to multi-user devices in the home [9]. Finally, researchers have also interviewed experts on teen online behavior, risks and risk mitigation strategies and proposed solutions to promote online safety while protecting teen privacy [13].

Our work will complement existing work by exploring different device usage scenarios, presenting parents' concerns about their children's safety, security, and privacy and how and why parents control their children's device usage.

3   Methods

We recruited participants for our exploratory study via flyers posted at childcare centers, and public places such as schools, bookstores and public libraries and via campus-wide emails (at the authors' respective institutions) and emails sent personally to friends and family. Participants were given $10 Amazon gift cards for their participation. We conducted focus groups and interviews with 29 parents about their concerns regarding their kids' use of smart devices (mainly smartphones and tablets) in the home. We conducted interviews in addition to focus groups, since we expected some people to not divulge their true behavior when in the company of others in the focus group because of societal expectations.

Prior to the focus group discussions and interviews, participants were also asked to fill out a brief survey to collect demographic information including, age, sex, race/ethnicity, income, occupation, education level, family form/marital status, number of children, and questions concerning their smart device experience.

Out of the 29 participants, 25 were female, and 4 male. 17 out of the 29 were between the age of 41 and 50; detailed age ranges are shown in Fig. 1a. 24 identified themselves as white, 3 as Asian, 1 as Hispanic or Latino, 1 as white, black and American Indian and one did not wish to disclose their race, as shown in Fig. 1b. All the participants had at least an Associate degree; 2 had Associates degree, 8 had Bachelors, 7 had Masters, 1 had a professional degree and 11 had a doctorate degree, as shown in Fig. 1c. All participants were full-time employees and earning wages. 1 participant had an annual household income of \$35000–\$49,999, 5 between \$50000–\$749,999, 4 between \$75000–\$99,999, 10 between \$100,000–\$149,999, and 7 above \$150,000, as shown in Fig. 1d. 26 out of the 29 participants were married or in a domestic partnership, 2 were separated and 1 was single and never married.

As shown in Fig. 1e, 10 of the participants had one child, 12 had two children, 4 had three and 3 had four children. Out of the 29 participants, 3 had adopted at least one child. Figure 1f shows the age ranges of all the kids of the participants. In the case of all except one participant, the children lived with the parent participating in the study.

4   Findings

Except for one participant, all others had at least one smartphone in the home; the maximum number of smartphones in a home was six. Similarly, all except one participant had at least one tablet at home, the maximum number of tablets in a home was five. 15 participants had at least one gaming console and 11 had at least one smart assistant or appliance at home.

Device Usage Statistics: Out of the 28 that had smartphones at home, children used the participant or their spouse's phone in 20 households and children had their own phones in 7 households. Similarly, out of the 28 that had tablets at home, children used the participant or their spouse's tablet in 15 households and children had their own tablets in 16 households. Similarly, out of the 15 that had gaming consoles at home, children used the gaming consoles in 10 households. Similarly, out of the 11 that had smart assistants at home, children used the smart assistants in 6 households. Children in 20 households started using devices when they were less than 5 years of age, 3 when they were between 5 and 9, 2 when they were between 9 and 13 and 2 when they were between 13 and 18.

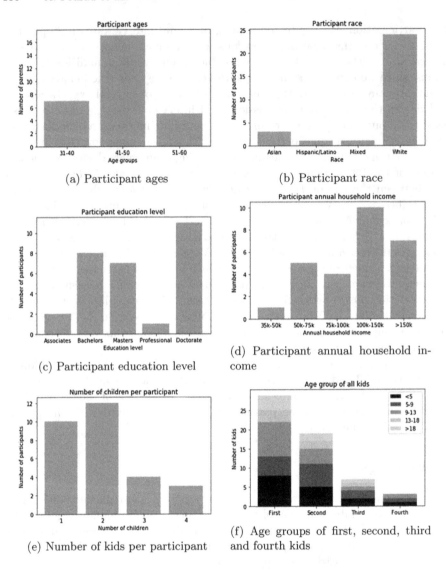

Fig. 1.

Exposure to Devices: Some parents encouraged smart device usage since they found it helped their children. For example, one participant described how her son, who was on the autistic spectrum, used technology as a place of comfort where he was able to express himself without judgment. Other parents wanted their children to use smart devices so they could connect with their family and friends when they could not physically be with them; one participant said "[my daughter] can still be with all her friends who she grew up with [but who go to different schools] through the [online video] game."

Parents also used smart devices to help them take care of their children. One parent noted, "technology becomes a baby sitter. They tend not to fight with one other, especially when they each have [a] device". One participant also used an Internet-connected camera to check in on her son from her office, when he got home from school; "I see when my son gets home. He can talk to me through that. I can see he is sitting on his couch and doing his homework. He is not supposed to have anyone home."

Most children learned about devices from watching their parents use it. Meanwhile, other parents did not want their children to be exposed to devices at a young age, so they often attempted to stop using their smartphones in an obvious way in front of their children. In these cases, young children still noticed when the parents used the phones even for a brief moment, for example, to play music. One participant said, "I try to keep the smart device completely out of her sight. But we are music people. So my husband uses [his phone] as [a speaker]. [Our daughter] recognizes his phone as a speaker."

Some parents were forced to expose their children to technology because of school work that required access to the Internet; the children of some of the participants went to schools that required laptops, as early as middle school. One participant said, "We don't have screen time on the weekends. [But] then [when my daughter] has homework on the weekend, then it's like restricting a textbook."

Younger siblings started using devices at a younger age when compared to the older children. One participant gave phones to all her children at the same time; the older one got a new phone and the younger ones received their parents' older phones. Children's interactions with smart devices also changed with the evolution of technology; one parent reminisced how their child was first exposed to a DVD six years ago, and gradually went on to reading electronic books on a Kindle and then to browsing the Internet on smart devices. Most participants reduced restrictions on their children's device usage when their children became older; one participant mentioned, "As they get bigger, his world gets bigger. We are realizing he needs [access to devices]."

Some parents hesitated buying technology either because they did not see the need for it, they were not sure if their children were old enough to be exposed to the technology, or they could not justify the expense. One participant said "Should we buy it because everybody has it, or should we make do without it. It was initially one of the reasons we were delayed in jumping in sooner. A combination of [my children] are too young and [the device] is expensive."

Parental Concerns: Parents had varying concerns about the effect of technology on their child's physical and emotional development. One parent was concerned about device usage making her child lead a sedentary lifestyle since he spent most of his free time on his gaming console. She said, "We want him active, playing outdoors. I don't know if sitting there all day [in front of the gaming console] is good for anybody". Some parents were concerned about children using a smart device in the bedroom, as it may affect their sleep. Another parent thought the content was too advanced for her toddler and she was not benefiting from watching the videos; "The shows are going fast, and for her age, the images and characters might look fascinating but she gets nothing out of it. [..] Some of them are really cute shows they are perfectly fine, but they are moving rapidly so she might not be able to process. " One parent was also worried about how the devices were affecting social skills as she had observed her daughter play online games with her friends even when they were in the same room. Some parents were also concerned that their children would be exposed to content that was not appropriate to their age, because of lack of regulation on certain apps such as YouTube kids. Parents also believed more time commanding smart assistants would take away politeness from their young children.

Some parents believed even though the devices provided instant gratification, they provided no long-term benefits for the children and also distracted them from the "real world". One participant said "[her son] can use his time to do better things [than use his device] to improve himself, of course." Another participant pointed out that children were often distracted by the devices; "I think it's one of those things that's good in moderation. The things he is watching are educational and that in and of itself are not bad. [However] he gets very into it, and doesn't notice the things going on around him."

Safety, Security and Privacy Concerns: Many parents were worried about their children's safety on social media; some were worried about their children being stalked if they revealed their location information online. Several parents were concerned about their children revealing their location on cooperative games and location-based apps; one participant said, "[My daughter] will be like, 'I have a Snapchat Map and I know where my friends are,' and that's terrifying! I ask, 'Do they know where you are?' and she responds, 'Yes!' and I don't really like that!".

Some parents with younger children were not as concerned about privacy, since they did not think any data about their children were getting disclosed. A participant, whose child was still a toddler said, "That's just me as a person, I'm not that worked up about privacy stuff. I assume that everything about me is public knowledge, and for my kids, I think it's going to be even more true. But I'm not that concerned about privacy, especially because [my daughter] doesn't use it by herself yet. I'm not worried that she is gonna stumble down some darkhole. As she gets older, I can imagine being much more concerned about safety, just who she is interacting with. But right now, I have zero concerns." Similarly another participant, whose child was playing single player games on the gaming console, said, "I think I'll have more concerns when [my son] is older, when he's interacting with people. All the things that he does [right now] is just him viewing content or playing a game. There is no texting, no messaging. I'll be very concerned when he is able to interact with other people, because he may not be screening them the way I would." Another parent, whose children were older and were using smart devices to chat with friends, pointed out, "At this point, given they basically chat with their friends and play games that don't involve revealing their identities, I am comfortable. Once they want to do social media, then I will be more concerned."

Some participants' concerns about privacy was based on their own negative experiences regarding the unintended disclosure of their sensitive data. For example, one participant preferred to stay off any Internet-connected device because a family member's credit card was stolen. Many participants also expressed concerns about Internet-connected cameras recording sensitive video.

Most participants were also concerned with smart assistants being always "on". One participant said, "I am sure Google is listening and collect information about what is going on in everyone's homes, not to the level that it really concerns me. There is nothing going on in my home that is proprietary. They are hearing a family going about in their day to day lives. It's not like I'm shouting out my SSN." Another participant worried that smart assistants were listening in on people's conversations and getting to know them. One participant also mentioned how smart assistants disclosed personal information about her friend when she visited her friend's house; "Her wall device announced she has a package coming. I don't know if anyone coming to my house should know if a package is coming".

4.1 Parental Control

All 29 participants said that they expected parents to be the most responsible for maintaining the safety of their child when using smart devices, compared to smart device companies, games or apps, or internet providers. Parents unanimously agreed that it was their responsibility to keep their children safe by monitoring their children's device use and by being more directly involved when their children used the device. Parents attempted to monitor their kids' device usage either by perusing their search history or text messages, or by sitting with them when they were using the device or by being in the room and near enough to hear what their children were watching on the smart device.

Four parents said they had complete control in keeping their child safe when using smart devices, 17 said they had a good amount of control, 4 said they had some control and 4 had very little control. One participant said, "[Parental controls on smart devices] are capable with human oversight. I don't think the devices are inherently protecting the kid. With my oversight and my involvement, the parameters I set up are sufficient to protect [my children]." Another parent said, "I don't think it's the device, it's more the parent. They need to be more proactive."

Parents trusted the content of apps and devices that they were familiar with and had verified to be appropriate for their children. One parent said, "we know what games [our children] have, so they don't have to [play the games] around us." But only two parents trusted smart device companies to protect their children from harm, while an overwhelming majority of 26 parents said they did not trust smart device companies to do so. Similarly, 25 parents did not trust applications and games and 27 parents did not trust Internet providers to protect their children from harm.

To protect their children, parents control their children's device usage by enforcing restrictions. A majority of parents restrict the time their children spend on smart phones and tablets; 19 parents enforce restrictions on smart phones and 22 restrict usage of smart tablets. 8 out of 9 parents restrict the time their children spend on gaming consoles. 1 out of 7 parents restrict the time their children spend on smart assistants.

Parents used several techniques to enforce their restrictions; some parents used warnings towards the end of screen time, and others used context-based rules. One participant said, "We have a timer app, and when she hears it she knows it's time to get off, or, we'll say, 'OK you can watch four videos and then get off'." Some parents created context-based rules for their children so it was clear to their children when and where they could use smart devices. One parent mentioned that their child got more time with the device when they had guests over while others banned devices at the dinner table and at restaurants, and prevented their children from using devices after 9pm or until after their chores were done.

Some participants would use the device with their children; this was mostly parents with babies and toddlers. One participant said, "We haven't set any controls on [smartphones] so he can really access anything he wants on the Internet. We have no parental controls, but we're always with him when he has it."

Some parents would be in the same room and ask their children to increase the volume when watching videos or listen to their conversations on gaming consoles. One participant said, "Even if she is using YouTube, I do not allow her to wear headphones so that I may hear what she is listening to. If she has a game on her iPhone, it has to [go] through us."

Some parents would explain to their children their reasons for wanting control so that their children would be comfortable with it. One participant said she asked her son who he was talking to every time she heard him talk to someone over the microphone when using the gaming console; "He understands that we will question who he is playing with." Some parents asked their children for passwords to monitor their usage. One participant said, "We keep her passwords so that we can spot check if [..] something is going on, and she knows that we do that."

Reasons for Wanting Control: Parents often made decisions on restricting device usage based on their own experience, podcasts, articles, and from discussions with other parents. One participant said, "I am making a decision by my own feel, and trying to remember back to my own childhood what shows I grew up on". Some parents also mentioned their decisions depended on their own understanding of their children's personalities and needs; one participant made her decision based on "articles I have read, my personal encounter with my daughter and knowing my daughter and knowing who she is and how she engages the world, things in her world." Most parents' need for control stemmed from their belief that devices and apps were bad and addictive; one participant's concern was that "[her child was] just becoming too dependent on them, and life [was] revolving around them".

Some parents also wanted to restrict their children's device usage because of their concerns regarding their own lack of control over their device usage; one participant said, "[My daughter] spends too much time on the internet, and I think this is the way people are becoming. I even notice it with myself. Sometimes [..] in the beginning I would find that I would only go on to search for such and such information. But hours later, you will find yourself sifting through all this content which had nothing to do with your initial purpose. You [lose] hours and that would frustrate me."

Familial Relationships: Restricting device usage often led to conflict in the home. Some children observed their friends' device usage and considered their own parents to be too restrictive. One participant said, "I can see he gets very annoyed and he complains, 'well, I didn't have enough screen-time.' He knows that term, but we don't use that very often! He always almost always complains first." Another parent was concerned that her children would use her spouse's frequent smartphone usage behavior to negotiate for more time. Another participant said her son did not argue, but merely explained why he could not stop; "My son is a little more stubborn. You have to accomplish a goal or mission, mom I am not done, I have to finish the game."

Some parents also identified ways in which device use brought them closer as a family; one participant pointed out her daughters would show her baking videos and say "Mommy, watch this lady make cupcakes.. can we make them this weekend?". Another participant said her children always watched sporting events on their smart TV with the parents.

Open Communication: A few parents of teenagers were also concerned about restricting device use as they wanted to have an open communication with their children. One participant said, "I would rather [she] be home and see, or give her the device and [watch explicit content], and then come to me and say guess what I saw and get some input, than try to shield her and deny access, and then have her secretively find the information and [get] misinformation and not [want] to talk to me about the things she is experiencing."

Some parents discussed good safety practices with their children. One participant said, "[My daughter] understands that the people on the Internet, they are not [her] friends because they are not right here, because [she doesn't] know them". Another participant said "I am always trying to drive home the point that you never want to write or say what you don't want to say to someone's face. In terms of language, what is appropriate, what would you say in front of your teacher."

A parent used an instance when her daughter talked to a stranger while playing a cooperative game as a teaching moment; "She was talking with this boy for quite a long time, and she got off and we asked her who is that. And she said I don't know. And we were like oh my god, you don't know. You are never doing that ever again. " Another parent wanted to "have dialogues with [her kids about safety]" and during one such instance, realized that "[her son] did not understand that [strangers on the Internet] might not be 13 [as they claimed they were] in the game."

One participant noted that it is important for parents to work with their children who grew up with easy access to technology and help them learn the skill of getting work done with distractions that they as adults did not have growing up, he said "I'm sure [my daughter] is getting work done, but she is also getting distracted. It's a skill they have to learn. I have that challenge. I'm getting work done, [then] paper comments [and] notifications [pop] up - a skill they need to learn we never had to learn growing up, to defer jumping on whatever it is you have to jump on." Another participant said she wanted her to children to learn that it is okay to not be on their smart device all the time, for example, it is okay to wait to respond to text messages; she said she wanted them to learn that "just because a text comes through, do you have to stop what you are doing and gauge it? I don't have to check that till we are done."

Our preliminary results provide new insights into device usage restrictions that parents place on their children, the parents' notions of privacy and their lack of trust in smart devices, and also demonstrate the possible failings of existing parental controls, as parents more often take it upon themselves to monitor their children's device use, instead of trusting the parental controls to protect their children.

5   Discussion

Even though most parents found technology to be useful, for example, as a parenting tool and for keeping in touch with family and friends, they were also concerned that unregulated use of technology could be a distraction. Parents felt solely responsible for their children's safety when they used smart devices. So they monitored the content their children were exposed to via apps and devices and also restricted the time the children spent on the devices.

Parents typically enforced time and context-based restrictions on their children's device usage. For time-based restrictions, parents chose a duration that they thought was sufficient for their children to spend on a device; for example, many parents chose one hour. Sometimes, the time restrictions changed depending on the context – for example, children were allowed more screen-time when they were sick, when the parents were busy or when they were traveling. Alternately, some parents banned device use in certain contexts - when children had homework or chores to complete, when it was time for bed, when they were outdoors at a restaurant. However, enforcing the rules often resulted in conflict in the home because children refused to stop using the apps. Okeke et al. showed that reminding users about the time they spend on an app can encourage them to stop using it [16]; similar nudging techniques can be adapted for babies and toddlers who cannot read or do not understand the concept of time. Similarly, apps could also incorporate incentives for older children to stop using the devices, for e.g., children could "collect" badges or stars for every time they stopped using the devices as soon as they had reached their daily device usage limit. It is also possible for apps and devices to use machine learning techniques to learn the different contexts in which the children use the devices; for example, apps can already predict a user's social interactions, daily activities, and mobility patterns [7]. The apps could then associate the context with the restrictions set by the parents and the devices can learn to trigger the nudging techniques based on the context with minimal human intervention.

Another way parents monitored device usage was by monitoring the content consumed by the children, either by using the devices with the children, by vetting apps before hand, by being in the same room when the children use the apps but listening to their conversation or what they are watching, or by going through the text or browser history either because their child's device was on the same account or by borrowing their passwords. It is important that parents explain their reasons behind wanting to monitor their children's device usage so their children do not assume that they need to share personal information in order to gain someone's trust. Parents may also benefit from better privacy tools that they can install on their children's devices to detect and warn users about oversharing when they are about to disclose sensitive information.

Additionally, parents also had concerns about their children sharing sensitive information such as location with strangers; apps could easily send an alert to a parent when a stranger connects with their children, so that parents can have a conversation with their children about safety practices. Parents with younger children were not concerned about their child's safety since they thought their children were not sharing any information. However, even though young children are not intentionally sharing information, several inferences can be made about their habits based on their usage patterns. So it is important for parents of young children to understand how information is collected, stored and shared by the different apps and devices that their children use, and to educate the children on good safety and privacy practices, once they are old enough to understand them.

The usable privacy community has been working on better tools for educating users about data management [17,24,27]. Parental controls should also be improved so it is easier for a parent, not only to be able to monitor the content their children consume, but also to have a conversation with the children about good safety and sharing practices. With better context-sensing and device usage controls, the devices may be able to reduce the responsibility on the parent of controlling their children's device usage.

Exploratory studies, like ours, could benefit from a bigger sample size, better population sampling and longer duration. Nevertheless, the study provided us insights into device usage scenarios, effect of device usage on familial relationships and parents' concerns regarding the security, privacy and safety of their children.

6   Future Research Directions

We identify the following possible research directions for smart device HCI researchers based on the findings from the exploratory study.

Safety and Privacy Controls: We should develop privacy frameworks for smartphone apps that educate users about how data is collected and shared through the app and warn the users when they are about to share information that may be sensitive.

Tools to Encourage Open Communication: Parents should be able to see a summary of their children's smart device usage in a manner that allows them to communicate with their children to develop rules around their device usage and develop better safety and privacy practices.

Nudging Tools: Conflict in the home may be reduced by using devices and apps that detect the contexts in which children use the devices and apps, and gradually nudge the children to stop using devices and apps when it gets close to their screen-time limit.

7   Summary

In this paper, we present findings from an exploratory study of 29 participants regarding the smart device usage restrictions that parents place on their children, the parents' notions of privacy and their lack of trust in smart devices. We conclude the paper by recommending future directions for smart device HCI researchers.

References

1. Anzulewicz, A., Sobota, K., Delafield-Butt, J.T.: Toward the autism motor signature: gesture patterns during smart tablet gameplay identify children with autism. Sci. Rep. **6**, 31107 (2016). https://doi.org/10.1038/srep31107
2. Balebako, R., Schaub, F., Adjerid, I., Acquisti, A., Cranor, L.F.: The impact of timing on the salience of smartphone app privacy notices. In: CCS Workshop on Security and Privacy in Smartphones and Mobile Devices (2015)
3. Benisch, M., et al.: The impact of expressiveness on the effectiveness of privacy mechanisms for location-sharing. In: Proceedings of the Symposium on Usable Privacy and Security. ACM (2009)
4. Cingel, D., Piper, A.M.: How parents engage children in tablet-based reading experiences: an exploration of haptic feedback. In: Computer-Supported Cooperative Work and Social Computing (2017)
5. Common Sense Media: The common sense census: Media use by kids age zero to eight
6. Common Sense Media: Technology addiction: Concern, controversy and finding balance (2016)
7. Harari, G.M., Lane, N.D., Wang, R., Crosier, B.S., Campbell, A.T., Gosling, S.D.: Using smartphones to collect behavioral data in psychological science: opportunities, practical considerations, and challenges. Perspect. Psychol. Sci. **11**(6), 838–854 (2016). https://doi.org/10.1177/1745691616650285. pMID: 27899727
8. Hu, W.: Math that moves: Schools embrace the ipad. https://www.nytimes.com/2011/01/05/education/05tablets.html
9. Jang, W., Chhabra, A., Prasad, A.: Enabling multi-user controls in smart home devices. In: Internet of Things Security and Privacy (2017)

10. Ko, M., Choi, S., Yang, S., Lee, J., Lee, U.: FamiLync: facilitating participatory parental mediation of adolescents' smartphone use. In: ACM International Joint Conference on Pervasive and Ubiquitous Computing (Ubicomp) (2015)
11. Magee, R.M., Agosto, D.E., Forte, A.: Four factors that regulate teen technology use in everyday life. In: Computer-Supported Cooperative Work and Social Computing (2017)
12. Manches, A., Duncan, P., Plowman, L., Sabeti, S.: Three questions about the internet of things and children. In: TechTrends (2015)
13. Marsh, A., Downs, J.S., Cranor, L.F.: Experts' views on digital parenting strategies. Technical report, CyLab Security and Privacy Institute (2017)
14. McReynolds, E., Hubbard, S., Lau, T., Saraf, A., Cakmak, M., Roesner, F.: Toys that listen: a study of parents, children, and internet-connected toys. In: Conference on Human Factors in Computing Systems. ACM (2017)
15. Nouwen, M., JafariNaimi, N., Zaman, B.: Parental controls: reimagining technologies for parent-child interaction. In: European Conference on Computer-Supported Cooperative Work - Exploratory Papers, Reports of the European Society for Socially Embedded Technologies (2017)
16. Okeke, F., Sobolev, M., Dell, N., Estrin, D.: Good vibrations: can a digital nudge reduce digital overload? In: International Conference on Human-Computer Interaction with Mobile Devices and Services (MobileHCI), pp. 4:1–4:12. ACM (2018). http://doi.acm.org/10.1145/3229434.3229463
17. Patil, S., Schlegel, R., Kapadia, A., Lee, A.J.: Reflection or action?: how feedback and control affect location sharing decisions. In: ACM SIGCHI Conference on Human Factors in Computing Systems (CHI 2014), May 2014
18. Schiano, D.J., Burg, C., Smith, A.N., Moore, F.: Parenting digital youth: how now? In: CHI Conference Extended Abstracts on Human Factors in Computing Systems (2016)
19. Singer, N., Valentino-DeVries, J.: Google's marketing of children's apps misleads parents, consumer groups say (2018). https://www.nytimes.com/2018/12/19/technology/google-kids-apps-misleads-complaint.html?smid=tw-nytimes&smtyp=cur
20. Song, S., Kim, S., Kim, J., Park, W., Yim, D.: Talklime: mobile system intervention to improve parent-child interaction for children with language delay. In: ACM International Joint Conference on Pervasive and Ubiquitous Computing (Ubicomp) (2015)
21. (Times): Is Your Child a Phone 'Addict'? (2018). https://www.nytimes.com/2018/01/17/well/family/is-your-child-a-phone-addict.html. A.H.N.Y
22. (Times): Is screen time bad for kids' brains?. https://www.nytimes.com/2018/12/10/health/screen-time-kids-psychology.html. B.C.N.Y
23. (Times): Turn off messenger kids, health experts plead to facebook (2018). https://www.nytimes.com/2018/01/30/technology/messenger-kids-facebook-letter.html. C.K.N.Y
24. Tsai, J.Y., Kelley, P., Drielsma, P., Cranor, L.F., Hong, J., Sadeh, N.: Who's viewed you?: the impact of feedback in a mobile location-sharing application. In: Conference on Human Factors in Computing Systems, pp. 2003–2012. ACM (2009). http://doi.acm.org/10.1145/1518701.1519005
25. University: The digital student: E-books, tablets and even smartphones becoming classroom staples. https://phys.org/news/2012-07-digital-student-e-books-tablets-smartphones.html
26. Valente, J., Cardenas, A.A.: Security & privacy in smart toys. In: Internet of Things Security and Privacy (2017)

27. Vaniea, K., Bauer, L., Cranor, L.F., Reiter, M.K.: Out of sight, out of mind: effects of displaying access-control information near the item it controls. In: Proceedings of the 2012 Tenth Annual International Conference on Privacy, Security and Trust (PST), pp. 128–136. IEEE (2012). https://doi.org/10.1109/PST.2012.6297929
28. Wartella, E.: Parenting in the age of digital technology. Northwestern University Center on Media and Human Development, Technical report (2013)
29. Wisniewski, P., Ghosh, A.K., Xu, H., Rosson, M.B., Carroll, J.M.: Parental control vs. teen self-regulation: is there a middle ground for mobile online safety. In: Computer-Supported Cooperative Work and Social Computing (2017)
30. Wisniewski, P., Xu, H., Rosson, M.B., Carroll, J.M.: Parents just don't understand: why teens don't talk to parents about their online risk experiences. In: Computer-Supported Cooperative Work and Social Computing (2017)
31. Yong, S., Lindskog, D., Ruhl, R., Zavarsky, P.: Risk mitigation strategies for mobile wi-fi robot toys from online pedophiles. In: IEEE Third International Conference on Privacy, Security, Risk and Trust and Third International Conference on Social Computing (2011)

Gamification Techniques for Raising Cyber Security Awareness

Sam Scholefield and Lynsay A. Shepherd$^{(\boxtimes)}$ ⓘ

School of Design and Informatics, Abertay University, Dundee DD1 1HG, UK
lynsay.shepherd@abertay.ac.uk

Abstract. Due to the prevalence of online services in modern society, such as internet banking and social media, it is important for users to have an understanding of basic security measures in order to keep themselves safe online. However, users often do not know how to make their online interactions secure, which demonstrates an educational need in this area. Gamification has grown in popularity in recent years and has been used to teach people about a range of subjects. This paper presents an exploratory study investigating the use of gamification techniques to educate average users about password security, with the aim of raising overall security awareness. To explore the impact of such techniques, a role-playing quiz application (RPG) was developed for the Android platform to educate users about password security. Results gained from the work highlighted that users enjoyed learning via the use of the password application, and felt they benefitted from the inclusion of gamification techniques. Future work seeks to expand the prototype into a full solution, covering a range of security awareness issues.

Keywords: Gamification · Games-based learning · Security awareness · Usable security · Human-centered cyber security

1 Introduction

Society has become increasingly reliant on the Internet for banking, and e-commerce. Typical transactions involve the exchange of personal information such as home addresses, and credit card details. Despite the introduction of biometric authentication mechanisms such as fingerprint-based systems [1], passwords continue to be the primary authentication mechanism for accessing such services, therefore it is important to ensure users remain secure online whilst using passwords. The aim of the research presented in this paper is to raise security awareness and improve password hygiene via the use of gamification techniques.

The following sections of the paper will outline the need to improve end-user security awareness, focusing on the topic of password security. Gamification techniques and their application in the context of the learning environment will also be explored before linking these to the domain of security awareness. Subsequently an overview of the Android-based role-playing quiz application (RPG) is provided. Finally, results will be presented and discussed, allowing conclusions to be drawn as to the usefulness of this approach.

© Springer Nature Switzerland AG 2019
A. Moallem (Ed.): HCII 2019, LNCS 11594, pp. 191–203, 2019.
https://doi.org/10.1007/978-3-030-22351-9_13

1.1 Raising End-User Security Awareness

When browsing the web, there are many ways in which users may potentially place themselves at risk. These can include interacting with poorly coded websites, creating weak passwords, and downloading data from websites containing malicious files [2] There are a number of methods which have been used to raise end-user security awareness when engaging in online transactions, from contextual affective feedback presented in a web browser [3, 4], to visualizing privacy policies [5], and phishing awareness applications [6]. Owing to the ubiquity of passwords, this work focusses on security awareness tools developed to improve password security.

Users often find the creation and retention of strong, secure passwords to be problematic [7, 8], and a number of studies have been conducted to address the issue of security awareness regarding passwords.

A common method of raising password security awareness has involved the use of password meters which are typically placed next to forms on a web page to give users a general indication of password strength. Though meters are widely used, the way in which they measure strength can be poor, meaning trivial passwords can be shown as "safe" [9]. Research has shown additional factors must be considered when using password meters, for example, work by Egelman et al. [10] explored if meters had an impact upon the password created, i.e. if the meter assisted the user in creating a strong password. Results showed that password strength was related to whether the participant felt their account was important, as opposed to the information provided by the password meter. Meters may not necessarily have an impact on raising awareness of creating secure passwords suggesting alternative solutions are needed.

Ciampa [11] also performed a study to explore the impact of different password strength meters, investigating if feedback prompted participants to create stronger passwords. In the study, participants were asked to record four passwords they may use online for accounts. Subsequently, they had to visit websites which offered password strength checking services. Participants also had to record if the password strength checks encouraged them to change their passwords. Results from this experiment showed that *"any feedback mechanism can influence users to create passwords with higher entropy"*. This suggests that user behaviour can be influenced by encouraging users to reflect on their password strength.

Fear appeals are another potential method of raising security awareness. Fear appeals have been described as *"persuasive messages designed to scare people by describing the terrible things that will happen to them if they do not do what the message recommends"* [12]. Vance et al. [13] explored the concept of fear appeals in relation to password security. In this work, participants were asked to register for an account, and the password strength chosen was observed. Multiple groups of participants were used in the study: one group were given no guidance as to how to create a strong password; the static fear appeal treatment group received security information that did not change on user input; another group received an interactive password meter; and a final group received an interactive fear appeal treatment which provided security guidance that updated on user input. Results showed that the interactive fear appeal treatment performed better in terms of choosing stronger passwords, and that such an approach may aid in raising end-user security awareness.

Although previous research has highlighted a number of attempts to raise end-user password security, the prevalence of issues related to password hygiene suggests these are not working. This indicates the need for more effective ways of conveying password security information to the end-user.

1.2 Gamification Techniques and Applications

Gamification can be defined as *"the application of gaming mechanics to non-gaming contexts with the aim of inducing engagement and raising levels of motivation"* [14] and aspects of this can be applied to keep a user engaged in learning. Work by Marczewski [15] cataloged the number and types of mechanics which can be used in the process of developing a gamification-based solution. To date, the work has identified 52 mechanisms which can be used, ranging from signposting (preventing users from becoming lost within an application), to providing users with challenges and physical rewards.

Various gamification techniques have also been discussed by Zichermann and Cunningham [16], who explored the concept of a rewards system which can apply to different contexts, known as SAPS (Status, Access, Power, and Stuff). SAPS utilises gamification in the delivery of rewards. Status is derived from how the user performs or compares to their peers. The mechanism of a leaderboard is one method of integrating status into a gamified application as it allows users to compete against each other. Access can be implemented via the use of a loyalty scheme, encouraging users to remain engaged. A notion of power can be achieved by rewarding a user with moderator duties. Finally, the authors explore the category of "stuff" whereby free rewards are given, providing users with an incentive to continue using a particular application or platform.

Several of these gamification techniques have previously been used in educational games such as Duolingo [17] (for learning new languages), and ClassDojo [18] (for parents and teachers to help teach developmental skills to children).

Gamification in education has also been applied to University level courses. Research conducted by Ibanez, Di-Serio and Delgado-Kloos [19] presented the results of a study in which gamified learning activities were used to teach introductory C-programming at undergraduate level. By using a combination of rewards such as points and badges, and allowing students to show their social standing via the use of a leaderboard, the implementation of gamification in this scenario improved knowledge acquisition. However, gamification did not work for all students, whereby some reached one hundred points within the learning activity and stopped playing rather continuing to engage with additional tasks.

Similar work has been carried out at University level by O'Donovan, Gain and Marais [20] drawing similar conclusions, observing that their *"approach to gamification is effective in a university setting"*. Again, they raise similar issues to Ibanez, Di-Serio and Delgado-Kloos [19], noting that gamification must be implemented with careful planning, to ensure it is beneficial.

Given the success of gamification in an educational context, it seems reasonable to suggest that these concepts have the potential to apply to other domains, such as raising security awareness.

1.3   Gamification and Security Awareness

A number of cyber security-based games have previously been developed to educate users. Many of these games have been aimed primarily at children and young people, such as the Webonauts Internet Academy, an online game designed to educate children about online etiquette [21]. In this game, users travel around space, visiting different planets, learning to deal with different behaviours exhibited on each of them. These skills are synonymous with behaviour on the Internet.

Another educational game is the Cybersecurity Lab, designed to teach young people basic cyber security skills [22]. In this scenario, the user assumes the role of a Chief Technology Officer at a social media company who must defend the application against a number of attacks. Though the game is designed to provide a level of security knowledge, the educator guide for the game suggests it will take 75 min to play through [23], indicating this is a self-contained game which does not promote continuous engagement and ongoing development of cyber security skills. A full browser-based RPG game for children in which they have to save the world from a password crisis [24] was also released.

The role of gamification and cyber security training has also been explored with high school students [25]. Funded by the National Security Agency, and the National Science Foundation, a number of summer camps (named GenCyber) were run in the USA to raise awareness of cyber security, and to encourage interest in computing, covering topics such as secure online behaviour, and social engineering.

Training games in this domain have also been made available for specialist fields, such as law enforcement. Research has been conducted into the use of serious games (i.e. games which are not solely designed for entertainment purposes) examining how these can be used to deliver cybercrime training for law enforcement officers attending a crime scene [26]. A similar game has been made available for Board Members of organisations. Pwc developed Game of Threats [27] which aims to teach the top level of an organisation how to handle a cyber incident.

Pertaining to mobile devices, an Android application targeted towards the general public, called NoPhish [28] was developed to assist users in identifying phishing links. The game consists of multiple levels where users are presented with a URL and are asked to determine its safety. In a subsequent evaluation, participants gave significantly more correct answers when asked about phishing, suggesting this type of application raised their security awareness. A follow-up study was conducted five months later which showed participants still performed well when asking about phishing links however, their overall performance decreased, which suggests issues with retention.

Though many of these games have been created to appeal to children, or specialists, the ubiquity of internet services means that the general population will require security awareness training. The majority of these games are also browser-based, however given the level of worldwide mobile phone ownership [29], it would be beneficial to have a security awareness game application which would appeal to this platform. By creating a level-based approach, this would break learning down into smaller sections, thus ensuring consistency with differing learning attention spans of various age groups [30]. As new cyber security threats are developed, updates could be pushed to the application, keeping end-user knowledge relevant.

Given these factors, the development of a mobile-based application focusing on raising password security awareness has the potential to be an effective tool to help users. In the following section, the methodology behind the research is outlined, explaining how a simplistic password security quiz was turned into a prototype security awareness application via the use of gamification.

2 Methodology

As part of an exploratory study, a Unity role-playing quiz application (RPG) was developed for the Android platform to educate users about password security. With a market share of approximately 75% [31], the Android platform was chosen for the development of the prototype application because it would have the ability to reach a larger target audience in comparison to the iOS platform. Similarly, developing the application in Unity provided a number of advantages. Unity is a multi-platform game engine, and the associated Asset Store allows developers to download free and paid-for assets for use in applications created.

On opening the application (Fig. 1), the end-user is presented with 2 characters on the screen: One is a golden knight (the end-user), the other is a dark knight (the character the end-user is fighting) [32]. The application contains questions related to password security, designed to educate the end-user. These questions cover topics such as choosing a strong password, avoiding the use of commonly used passwords, and practicing good password hygiene. If the end-user answers correctly, the dark knight loses health points. If the user is incorrect, the golden knight loses health points. This continues until one character defeats the other, educating the user regarding password security in the process.

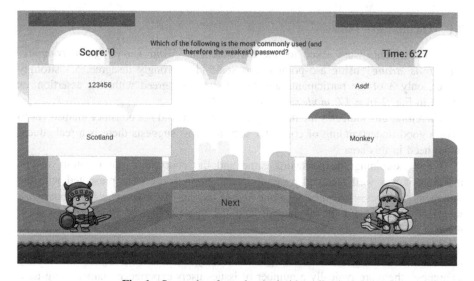

Fig. 1. Screenshot from the Android application

The underlying application is a simplistic multiple-choice quiz. However, aspects of gamification were included, with the goal of motivating users to learn and progress. These features were chosen owning to their suitability to integrate into the context of a quiz-based game, enhancing the experience. Gamification features integrated include a specific theme (RPG-style game with characters), on-screen progress/feedback (the health bar per character), time pressure (timer), consequences (if the user is incorrect, they lose health points), and competition (by means of a leaderboard) [15].

To evaluate the potential impact of the application, 17 participants over the age of 18 years were recruited for the pilot study. Participants varied in gender, and level of education. During the evaluation phase, participants were instructed to play through the application.

Following this, they were provided with a series of statements which they were asked to rate against a 5-point Likert scale (1 - strongly disagree, 5 - strongly agree), providing quantitative data. Statements which the participants were asked to rate included *"Your knowledge in computer security is strong"*, *"The password security game helped increase your knowledge on password security"*, *"The password game was enjoyable"*, and *"Gamification is an effective method of teaching computer security"*. Additionally, a qualitative free-form question was asked, to gather general feedback on the application.

3 Results and Discussion

Overall results highlighted that participants exhibited positive opinions towards the use of an RPG-style quiz application which will be discussed in detail, including quantitative data from the Likert-based questions, and qualitative data from the free-form questions.

3.1 Quantitative Data

When participants were asked to rate the statement *"Your knowledge in computer security is strong"* using a 5-point Likert scale (1 - strongly disagree, 5 - strongly agree), only 3 of the participants agreed, or strongly agreed with this assertion, as shown in Fig. 2 ($n = 17$, mode = 2, mean = 2.7).

Therefore, this indicates the majority of participants did not consider themselves to have a good understanding of computer security. This suggests there is a real educational need in this area.

When examining the password game and the concept of gamification, results indicated it was well received by participants. Participants were presented with the statement *"The password security game helped increase your knowledge on password security"* (Fig. 3), and the mode indicated the majority agreed ($n = 17$, mode = 4, mean = 2.52).

Although participants *felt* their knowledge of password security increased, this needs further investigation with a longitudinal study. When attempting to raise security awareness, there are typically a number of issues users experience, namely long-term retention, long term behavioural change and security fatigue. The term *"security*

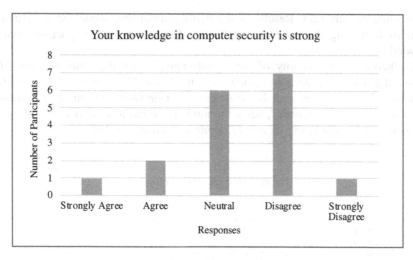

Fig. 2. Participants' self-reported knowledge of computer security

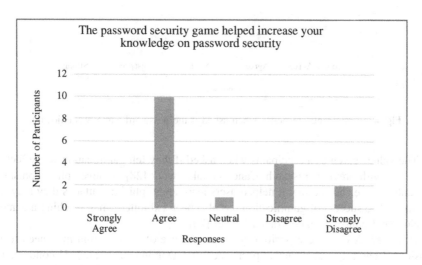

Fig. 3. Participants' response when asked if the password security game helped increase their knowledge of password security

fatigue" is linked to security awareness, highlighting that even though there are programmes to educate people about security, people may still fail to engage with the good practice they have been taught [33]. Essentially, users can tire of being bombarded with security information and may reject the advice they have been given [34].

A longitudinal study comparable to work conducted by Canova et al. [28] would allow the long-term impact of the application to be assessed. After using the password security application for a specified period of time, the participants would complete a questionnaire to assess knowledge gained. A similar questionnaire would be given again some months later. Results of the two questionnaires would be compared to establish if playing the password application had a long-term impact on security knowledge.

Furthermore, the majority of participants agreed with the statement that *"The password game was enjoyable"* (shown in Fig. 4, *n = 17, mode = 4, mean = 3.65*). Regarding the final Likert scale-based statement, *"Gamification is an effective method of teaching computer security"*, again the mode indicated that the majority of participants agreed (shown in Fig. 5, *n = 17, mode = 4, mean = 4.18*).

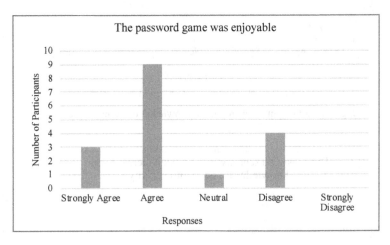

Fig. 4. Participants' response when asked if the password game was enjoyable

The values given by participants when asked if they felt gamification was effective are in line with previous research. Canova et al.'s work [28] on developing a phishing awareness game showed that it helped users learn about phishing attacks they may fall victim to. The success of gamification has also been exhibited when teaching a games-development course at undergraduate level [20].

However, despite these positive findings, the use of gamification may need to be considered carefully regarding impact. Work by Domínguez et al. [35] conducted a study using gamification, providing exercises on an e-learning platform for a general ICT class, some of which were gamified. Results found that students who engaged with gamified content performed poorly on written tasks, but strongly on practical tasks. This suggests that whilst gamification may be effective, it must be used within the right context.

3.2 Qualitative Data

Participants were asked to give an indication as to whether they enjoyed/disliked using the password application. Generally, participants who enjoyed using the application submitted favourable comments relating to the aesthetics of the game, and the implementation of characters. Additionally, these participants claimed it was a fun and

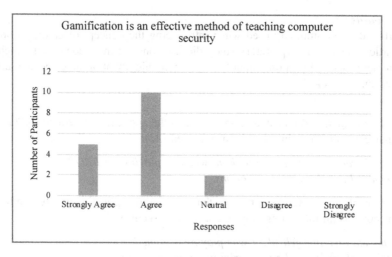

Fig. 5. Participants' response when asked if gamification was an effective method of teaching security

interesting method of learning about password security. Those who disliked using the application indicated this was due to a lack of feedback provided, expressing this would have helped them learn from their errors.

Feedback Provided

Several of the participants pointed to the lack of feedback provided in the prototype game with statements such as:

– *"Maybe explaining why the questions were wrong would have helped?"*
– *"Fun but wanted answers to wrong questions"*

The need to include feedback whilst utilising gamification is concurrent with work by Ibanez, Di-Serio, and Delgado-Kloos [19], stating that feedback is required, particularly in an educational setting as it prevents people from becoming confused about the current task.

The use of specific words may influence user behaviour when providing feedback, for example, in work by Ur et al. [36] when a password was described as "weak", this prompted users to try and create a stronger password. Text-based feedback is seen to be an appropriate method of delivering feedback to the end-user as it is a more direct way of communicating [37]. When applying feedback in the password application, careful consideration must be given as to how this is implemented, ensuring it is helpful to the user.

Gamification Elements

As discussed in the methodology, a number of elements of gamification were included within the application. These comprised of an overarching theme, on-screen feedback, time pressure, consequences, and competition.

Leaderboards
Leaderboards are commonly used when introducing the concept of gamification [16, 20]. Participants in this exploratory study did not consider the leaderboard which had been implemented to be an important factor in their enjoyment of the game, and instead focussed on other elements.

Theme
Many of participants commented on the theme of the application (medieval RPG), with particular comments relating the characters used [32].

- *"The characters were fun to look at, was like playing an RPG"*
- *"I enjoyed the character animations"*

Participants also generally expressed that the overall application was fun, indicating the concept was an interesting way to learn about security.

- *"It looked nice and felt like I was playing a game"*
- *"Learnt information about security in an enjoyable way"*
- *"Was an interesting way to ask questions"*

This result is of interest owing to previous literature establishing how people learn, and the impact which particular themes can have upon the learner. Work by Parker and Lepper [38] examined the use of fantasy contexts in relation to the way children learned to use the Logo programming language. It was found that the use of fantasy contexts such as scenarios involving pirates and detectives motivated children to learn. Given that the password application makes use of a medieval theme, this has the potential to lead to a similar effect. However, others have debated the level of knowledge gained from what is referred to as *"edutainment media"* – games or films which are designed to be fun and educational, and have highlighted the need for longitudinal evaluative studies to be conducted [39].

Overall, qualitative data gained from participants who used the application revealed that, whilst they liked the concept of the application, they felt there were several features missing from the prototype which would have helped their understanding. One such issue was the lack of feedback provided during the game. Ultimately, comments gained from the evaluation were useful for informing how the research work will develop in the future. Before developing a full version of a gamified security awareness application, it is important to consider human-centered design changes following responses from participants.

3.3 Limitations

The research contained a number of limitations. This was an exploratory study, with a small sample size, and no long-term evaluation regarding the retention of knowledge in relation to password security was conducted.

Gender differences also need to be explored as this demographic was not included in the participant questionnaire. Previous work in the field has identified that males find game-based learning more enjoyable than females [25]. This may indicate that the password security application may need to be modified to ensure it is consumed by the maximum number of target users.

4   Conclusion and Future Work

To conclude, the RPG-style application was viewed positively by participants. The results indicated that participants enjoyed playing this type of application, and they suggested it increased their knowledge on password security. Additionally, participants felt gamification was a useful method of raising security awareness. Owing to the positive results derived from this exploratory study, future work seeks to develop the prototype application into a full security awareness application, covering a range of topics including phishing and information sharing. This will also allow a longitudinal study to be developed to compare knowledge gained from the security awareness application against real-word security practices exhibited by end-users.

Some users highlighted that the application still seemed like a quiz, despite the inclusion of several gamification elements. To overcome this issue, placing the quiz within the context of an overarching storyline may make the application more immersive [15].

Finally, future work seeks to adapt the application to ensure it appeals to varying age ranges, such as children and the elderly, helping them learn about password security in a fun, yet effective manner.

References

1. Bhagavatula, C., Ur, B., Iacovino, K., Kywe, S., Cranor, L., Savvides, M.: Biometric authentication on iPhone and Android: usability, perceptions, and influences on adoption. In: Proceedings of the USEC 2015, 8 February 2015, San Diego, CA, pp. 1–10 (2015)
2. Shepherd, L.A., Archibald, J., Ferguson, R.I.: Perception of risky security behaviour by users: survey of current approaches. In: Marinos, L., Askoxylakis, I. (eds.) HAS 2013. LNCS, vol. 8030, pp. 176–185. Springer, Heidelberg (2013). https://doi.org/10.1007/978-3-642-39345-7_19
3. Shepherd, L.A., Archibald, J., Ferguson, R.I.: Assessing the impact of affective feedback on end-user security awareness. In: Tryfonas, T. (ed.) HAS 2017. LNCS, vol. 10292, pp. 143–159. Springer, Cham (2017). https://doi.org/10.1007/978-3-319-58460-7_10
4. Shepherd, L.A., Archibald, J.: Security awareness and affective feedback: categorical behaviour vs. reported behaviour. In: 2017 International Conference On Cyber Situational Awareness, Data Analytics And Assessment (Cyber SA), London, pp. 1–6 (2017)
5. Kelley, P.G., Bresee, J., Cranor, L.F., Reeder, R.W.: A nutrition label for privacy. In: Proceedings of the 5th Symposium on Usable Privacy and Security, p. 4. ACM (2009)
6. Canova, G., Volkamer, M., Bergmann, C., Borza, R.: NoPhish: an anti-phishing education app. In: Mauw, S., Jensen, C.D. (eds.) STM 2014. LNCS, vol. 8743, pp. 188–192. Springer, Cham (2014). https://doi.org/10.1007/978-3-319-11851-2_14
7. Furnell, S., Jusoh, A., Katsabas, D.: The challenges of understanding and using security: a survey of end-users. Comput. Secur. 25(1), 27–35 (2006)
8. Shay, R., et al.: A spoonful of sugar? In: Proceedings of the 33rd Annual ACM Conference on Human Factors in Computing Systems - CHI 2015, pp. 2903–2912 (2015)
9. De Carné De Carnavalet, X., Mannan M.: A large-scale evaluation of high-impact password strength meters. ACM Trans. Inf. Syst. Secur. 18(1), Article no. 1 (2015)

10. Egelman, S., Sotirakopoulos, A., Muslukhov, I., Beznosov, K., Herley, C.: Does my password go up to eleven? In: Proceedings of the SIGCHI Conference on Human Factors in Computing Systems - CHI 2013, pp. 2379–2388 (2013)
11. Ciampa, M.: A comparison of password feedback mechanisms and their impact on password entropy. Inf. Manag. Comput. Secur. 21(5), 344–359 (2013)
12. Witte, K.: Putting the fear back into fear appeals: the extended parallel process model. Commun. Monogr. 59(4), 329–349 (1992)
13. Vance, A., Eargle, D., Ouimet, K., Straub, D.: Enhancing password security through interactive fear appeals: a web-based field experiment. In: 2013 46th Hawaii International Conference on System Sciences, pp. 2988–2997 (2013)
14. Growth Engineering: What is the Definition of Gamification and What Does it Mean? (2018). http://www.growthengineering.co.uk/definition-of-gamification/
15. Marczewski, A.: 52 Gamification Mechanics and Elements. Gamified UK - #Gamification Expert (2018). https://www.gamified.uk/user-types/gamification-mechanics-elements/
16. Zichermann, G., Cunningham, C.: Gamification by Design: Implementing Game Mechanics in Web and Mobile Apps. O'Reilly, Sebastopol (2011)
17. Duolingo: Learn a language for free (2018). https://www.duolingo.com/
18. ClassDojo: Learn all about ClassDojo (2018). https://www.classdojo.com/
19. Ibanez, M., Di-Serio, A., Delgado-Kloos, C.: Gamification for engaging computer science students in learning activities: a case study. IEEE Trans. Learn. Technol. 7(3), 291–301 (2014)
20. O'Donovan, S., Gain, J., Marais, P.: A case study in the gamification of a university-level games development course. In: Proceedings of the South African Institute for Computer Scientists and Information Technologists Conference, pp. 242–251. ACM (2013)
21. LearningWorks for Kids: Webonauts Internet Academy - LearningWorks for Kids (2019). https://learningworksforkids.com/apps/webonauts-internet-academy/
22. Pbs.org: Cybersecurity Lab | NOVA Labs | PBS (2019). https://www.pbs.org/wgbh/nova/labs/lab/cyber/
23. Pbs.org: The Cybersecurity Lab - Educator Guide | NOVA Labs | PBS (2019). https://www.pbs.org/wgbh/nova/labs/about-cyber-lab/educator-guide/
24. TrueKey: World Password Day Game (2017). https://game.truekey.com/EN/
25. Jin, G., Tu, M., Kim, T., Heffron, J., White, J.: Evaluation of game-based learning in cybersecurity education for high school students. J. Educ. Learn. (EduLearn) 12(1), 150 (2018)
26. Coull, N., et al.: On the use of serious games technology to facilitate large-scale training in cybercrime response. In: European Police Science and Research Bulletin, Special Conference Edition, no. 3, pp. 123–130 (2017)
27. PwC: Game of Threats (2015). https://www.pwc.co.uk/issues/cyber-security-data-privacy/services/game-of-threats.html
28. Canova, G., Volkamer, M., Bergmann, C., Reinheimer, B.: NoPhish app evaluation: lab and retention study. In: NDSS Workshop on Usable Security, pp. 1–10 (2015)
29. Statista: Number of mobile phone users worldwide 2015–2020 | Statista (2019). https://www.statista.com/statistics/274774/forecast-of-mobile-phone-users-worldwide/
30. Gómez-Pérez, E., Ostrosky-Solís, F.: Attention and memory evaluation across the life span: heterogeneous effects of age and education. J. Clin. Exp. Neuropsychol. 28(4), 477–494 (2006)
31. StatCounter Global Stats: Mobile Operating System Market Share Worldwide | StatCounter Global Stats (2018). http://gs.statcounter.com/os-market-share/mobile/worldwide/2019
32. Pomazan, A.: Fantasy Medieval Character Pack - Asset Store (2018). https://assetstore.unity.com/packages/2d/characters/fantasy-medieval-character-pack-81647aff

33. Furnell, S., Thomson, K.: Recognising and addressing 'security fatigue'. Comput. Fraud Secur. **2009**(11), 7–11 (2009)
34. Herley, C.: So long, and no thanks for the externalities: the rational rejection of security advice by users. In: Proceedings of the 2009 workshop on New security Paradigms Workshop, pp. 133–144. ACM, September 2009
35. Domínguez, A., Saenz-de-Navarrete, J., de-Marcos, L., Fernández-Sanz, L., Pagés, C., Martínez-Herráiz, J.: Gamifying learning experiences: Practical implications and outcomes. Comput. Educ. **63**, 380–392 (2013)
36. Ur, B., et al.: How does your password measure up? The effect of strength meters on password creation. In: Security 2012 Proceedings of the 21st USENIX Conference on Security Symposium (2012)
37. Dehn, D., Van Mulken, S.: The impact of animated interface agents: a review of empirical research. Int. J. Hum Comput Stud. **52**(1), 1–22 (2000)
38. Parker, L., Lepper, M.: Effects of fantasy contexts on children's learning and motivation: Making learning more fun. J. Pers. Soc. Psychol. **62**(4), 625–633 (1992)
39. Okan, Z.: Edutainment: is learning at risk? Br. J. Edu. Technol. **34**(3), 255–264 (2003)

An Identification Method of Untrusted Interactive Behavior in ERP System Based on Markov Chain

Mengyao Xu[1], Qian Yi[2(✉)], Shuping Yi[1], and Shiquan Xiong[1]

[1] Department of Industrial Engineering,
Chongqing University, Chongqing 400044, China
{xumengyao,ysp}@cqu.edu.cn, xiongshquan@163.com
[2] Department of Mechanical Design and Manufacturing,
Chongqing University, Chongqing 400044, China
yiqian@cqu.edu.cn

Abstract. Enterprise Resource Planning (ERP) software system is widely used in enterprises as an advanced management system. In recent years, the information security problem of ERP software system has gradually attracted people's attention. To solve the information security problem of the ERP software system, we first need to pay attention to the untrusted interactive behavior in the ERP software system. Enterprise network users generate a lot of interactive behavior in the process of using ERP system. Untrusted interactive behavior will cause huge damage to the enterprise if they are not identified. Based on this, this paper proposes a method based on Markov chain to identify untrusted interactive behavior of users in the ERP system, Firstly, a series of network user behavior characteristics are constructed based on the log records of ERP system. Then, the hidden Markov model is used to model the behavior of trusted users based on these behavior characteristics. Next, the forward algorithm is used to calculate the probability of a series of observation sequences of trusted users and untrusted users based on the hidden Markov model of trusted users. Finally, the untrusted users are identified by comparing the observation sequence probability set of trusted and untrusted users. The recognition rate of the model for trusted users is 92.64%, and the false positive rate for untrusted users is 0.76%. This result indicates that the model is effective for identifying untrusted interaction behavior.

Keywords: Hidden Markov model · Untrusted interactive behavior · Behavioral characteristics · ERP system

1 Introduction

With the popularization and development of enterprise information management, ERP system is widely used in enterprises as an advanced management system. Enterprise users are faced with many information security issues while enjoying the convenience of ERP system. The US Department of Homeland Security (DHS) issued a security alert saying that national hackers and criminals are increasingly attacking ERP systems,

© Springer Nature Switzerland AG 2019
A. Moallem (Ed.): HCII 2019, LNCS 11594, pp. 204–214, 2019.
https://doi.org/10.1007/978-3-030-22351-9_14

and they have found evidence that Dridex Trojan attacked bank's ERP system, which brought huge losses to the bank.

One of the methods that can be used to secure information security in ERP systems is intrusion detection. Anomaly detection approach [1] is a key element of intrusion detection that attempts to evaluate the behavior of a user or system and consider intrusive or irregular activities as some deviation from normal patterns. The core of the method is how to identify whether the current behavior is abnormal (intrusive or irregular).

Currently, the traditional studies on identify abnormal behavior of network users are classified into two categories. One is to use network traffic as a characteristic [2–6]. Jain et al. [2] identify abnormal behavior by identifying abnormal network traffic. The other is to use packet as a characteristic [7–11]. Lee et al. [7] identify abnormal behavior by monitoring whether packets are abnormal. However, the characteristics they choose are vitally dependent on computer, moreover, the abnormal behavior identified by these characteristics do not necessarily correspond to the abnormal behavior of users in real life. Therefore, the credibility of the abnormal behavior identified by these methods is open to question.

Trust is typically interpreted as a subjective belief in the reliability, honesty and security of an entity on which we depend for our welfare [12], and these entities contain software, hardware, data, people and organizations. Numerous researchers have conceptualized trust as a behavior, which has been validated in work collaboration and social communications [13]. On the one hand, behavior-based trust models are widely used in e-commerce sites to help consumers assess the quality of their products. Cao et al. [14] studied the trusted third party (TTP) in Australia's business and examined the factors influencing consumers' trust behavior from the perspective of consumers online trust of online shopping. Kaur et al. [15] proposed a model to discern the impact of trust factors pertaining in Indian E-Commerce marketplace on the customers' intention to purchase from an e-store. On the other hand, behavior-based trust models are widely used in software system to ensure information security of software systems. There are two main models in this field. One is to evaluate the factors affecting trust by using continuous or discrete real numbers (trust value) [16–19]. Hosseini et al. [16] proposed a way to measure the user's behavioral credibility by scoring the user's behavior, and also proposed that the score of repeated malicious behavior should be lower than the first malicious behavior. There are some problems in determining whether the behavior is credible by calculating the trust value. When establishing the evaluation system, some untrusted interactive behaviors are preset, so it is impossible to detect untrusted interactive behaviors that are not preset. The other is to model the trusted users by continually optimizing the characteristic framework that describes trusted behaviors [20–22]. Yan et al. [20] built a behavioral characteristic framework of trusted users based on computer trust and the interaction intention between human and computer. However, these articles have only been theoretically studied and have not been further explored in conjunction with actual data.

In this paper, we study how to identify untrusted interactive behavior in ERP software systems based on human factors. Trusted interaction is defined as a predictable and controllable information transformation process through a computer network in a way that people and computers work together in an effective manner. Moreover, trusted interactive behavior refers to behavior that is consistent with an individual's behavioral habits and reflects it in network operations. Hence, we establish a behavioral model of a trusted user by selecting characteristics that reflect individual behavioral habits and then identify untrusted interactive behavior on this basis.

The remainder of this paper is organized as follows: The background is described in Sect. 2. The method for how to identify the untrusted interactive behavior is described in Sect. 3 and an example is given in Sect. 4. Finally, the concluding remarks are addressed in Sect. 5.

2 Background

Hidden Markov Model (HMM) has a wide range of applications in the field of pattern recognition.

2.1 The Concept of Hidden Markov Model (HMM)

HMM is a conceptual model of time series. It describes the process of randomly generating unobservable state sequences from a hidden Markov chain, and then generating an observation sequence from each state.

HMM is a double stochastic process. One is Markov chain, which is used to describe the state of metastasis. Another is to describe each state and observation of the corresponding relation between statistics [23].

HMM has two basic assumptions:

(1) The state of the hidden Markov chain at any time t depends only on the state of its previous moment, regardless of the state and observation at other times, and is independent of the time t.
(2) Observation at any time depends only on the state of the Markov chain at that moment, independent of other observations and states.

2.2 The Parameters of HMM

An HMM is characterized by the following:

(1) Q is a collection of all possible states, V is a collection of all possible observations;
(2) I is a sequence of states of length T, O is the corresponding observation sequence;
(3) N is the number of all possible states; M is the number of all possible observations;
(4) A is the state transition probability distribution;

$$A = \{a_{ij}\} \text{ and } a_{ij} = P[q_{t+1} = j \,|\, q_t = i], 1 \leq i,j \leq N \tag{1}$$

(5) B is the observation symbol probability distribution in state j;

$$B = \{b_j(v_k)\} \text{ and } b_j(v_k) = P[o_t = v_k \,|\, q_t = j], \ 1 \leq j \leq N, \ 1 \leq k \leq M \tag{2}$$

(6) π is the initial state distribution;

$$\pi = \{\pi_i\} \text{ and } \pi_i = P[q_1 = i], \ 1 \le i \le N \qquad (3)$$

For convenience, we usually use a compact notation $\lambda = (A, B, \pi)$ to indicate the complete parameter set of an HMM.

2.3   Three Algorithms of HMM

HMM has three algorithms:

(1) Forward or backward algorithm. Given the model $\lambda = (A, B, \pi)$ and the observation sequence $O = (o_1, o_2, \ldots, o_T)$ to calculate the probability $P(O \mid \lambda)$ of the occurrence of the sequence O under the model λ.
(2) Baum-Welch algorithm. Given the observation sequence $O = (o_1, o_2, \ldots, o_T)$ to estimate the parameters of the model $\lambda = (A, B, \pi)$ and make the observation sequence probability $P(O \mid \lambda)$ maximum under this model.
(3) Viterbi algorithm. Given the observation sequence to find the most likely corresponding state sequence.

3   Method

In our research, we collect the characteristic data of each trusted interactive behavior of the user, and use the hidden Markov model to establish each user's network behavior pattern. Then, each user's online behavior is matched to its network behavior pattern. Matching unsuccessful behavior is considered untrusted interactive behavior.

3.1   Data Collection and Preparation

In this paper, the data comes from the background log of a publishing company. This log records the operational records left by all users of the company when they use the ERP software system. All the characteristics of the log record are as follows (Table 1):

Table 1. The characteristics of the log record

Company related characteristics	Operation related characteristics	Time related characteristics	Individual basic characteristics
Bill code	Dr (delete or not)	Login time	Enter ip
Bill id	Enter button	Logout time	Enter system
Bill type	Enter function	Ts	Operate type
Business log	Enter function code		Operate id
Business type			Operate name
Company name			

When we preprocess this data, firstly, we should filter the entire operation record of the required user according to the operator's name. Secondly, trusted interactive behavior refers to behavior that is consistent with an individual's behavioral habits and reflects it in network operations. However, a single operation can't correctly describe the user's operating habits, and usually a series of operations can represent the user's operating habits. Therefore, the user's ten operations are treated as one unit, and the next unit is obtained by moving one operation down on the basis of the previous unit. Finally, we need to determine which characteristics are selected to describe the behavior patterns of trusted users.

3.2 The Selection of Characteristics

Based on the user's behavioral habits, six characteristics are chosen to describe the behavior patterns of trusted users (Table 2).

Table 2. Selected characteristics

Characteristics	Instructions
The number of IPs	The number of IPs used in a unit
Enter button & function	First combining the enter function and the enter button, then count the categories and encode them, then count the types of each unit and encode them
Time accumulation for each operation	The accumulated value of ts for a unit operation
Operating time period	Dividing 24 h a day into 48 time periods according to a time period of half an hour, and encode each time period
Time difference between before and after operation	First calculating the time difference between before and after operations, and then calculate the cumulative time difference of a unit
The combination of the types of operations	There are two types of operations, calculating the permutation and combination of the operation types of a unit and encoding them

The number of IPs can show that the user likes to use the same IP for a long time while working, or prefers to change frequently. The enter button & function can represent the order of operations. The time accumulation for each operation can reflect the speed of user operations. The operating time period can reflect the user's work schedule. The time difference between before and after operation reflect the user's attitude towards work (like delay or timely processing). The combination of the types of operations can represent the character of the individual.

An example is used to illustrate the meaning of the characteristics: the operation of a unit of a user is (1, 23, 3, 4, 1, 10), that means the user only uses one type of IP to perform this group of operations and the operation sequence number is 23, a total of 3 s was spent to perform this set of operations and the accumulated time difference between before and after operations is 6 min to 8 min, The operating time period is

9:00–9:30 and the operation type combination number is 10 (5 business operations, 2 function operations, 3 business operations).

The relevant original record table displayed in Chinese is shown below (Fig. 1).

ENTERIP	IP数量	LOGINTIME	时间段	OPERATETYP	操作种类	OPRATORN	ENTERBUTTON&ENTEI	TS
192.168.	1	2013-01-29 09:53:37	2	business	2	张静	保存（基本）库存销	2013-01-29 09:53:37
192.168.	1	2013-01-29 09:53:37	2	business	2	张静	推式保存(实发)库存	2013-01-29 09:53:37
192.168.	1	2013-01-29 09:54:02	2	business	2	张静	送审订单管理	2013-01-29 09:54:02
192.168.	1	2013-01-29 09:54:08	2	business	2	张静	审核订单管理	2013-01-29 09:54:08
192.168.	1	2013-01-29 09:54:11	2	business	2	张静	保存（基本）库存销	2013-01-29 09:54:11
192.168.	1	2013-01-29 09:54:11	2	business	2	张静	推式保存(实发)库存	2013-01-29 09:54:11
192.168.	1	2013-01-29 09:54:38	2	business	2	张静	送审订单管理	2013-01-29 09:54:38
192.168.	1	2013-01-29 09:59:19	2	function	2	张静	ennull订单维护	2013-01-29 09:59:19
192.168.	1	2013-01-29 10:10:51	3	business	2	张静	修改订单管理	2013-01-29 10:10:51
192.168.	1	2013-01-29 10:12:30	3	business	2	张静	修改订单管理	2013-01-29 10:12:30
192.168.	1	2013-01-29 10:13:26	3	business	2	张静	新增单据销售订单	2013-01-29 10:13:26
192.168.	1	2013-01-29 10:49:51	3	business	2	张静	修改订单管理	2013-01-29 10:49:51
192.168.	1	2013-01-29 10:50:35	3	business	2	张静	修改订单管理	2013-01-29 10:50:35
192.168.	1	2013-01-29 11:28:09	3	business	2	张静	新增单据销售订单	2013-01-29 11:28:09
192.168.	1	2013-01-29 11:29:24	3	business	2	张静	新增单据销售订单	2013-01-29 11:29:24
192.168.	1	2013-01-29 11:29:32	3	business	2	张静	送审订单管理	2013-01-29 11:29:32
192.168.	1	2013-01-29 11:29:53	3	business	2	张静	修改订单管理	2013-01-29 11:29:53
192.168.	1	2013-01-29 11:30:03	3	business	1	张静	审核订单管理	2013-01-29 11:30:03
192.168.	1	2013-01-29 11:30:04	3	business	1	张静	保存（基本）库存销	2013-01-29 11:30:04
192.168.	1	2013-01-29 11:30:04	3	business	1	张静	推式保存(实发)库存	2013-01-29 11:30:04
192.168.	1	2013-01-29 11:30:12	3	business	1	张静	送审订单管理	2013-01-29 11:30:12
192.168.	1	2013-01-29 11:30:35	3	business	1	张静	审核订单管理	2013-01-29 11:30:35

Fig. 1. The relevant original record

3.3 The Model Parameters of Trusted Users

The untrusted interactive behavior is diverse and we can't fully understand. Based on this, we model the behavior of the user when the system is running normally, which means that each behavior of the user is trusted. The hidden Markov model built for the behavior of trusted users contains only two states: trusted state and untrusted state. The trusted state is represented by 0, and the untrusted state is represented by 1. The number of observations is determined by the type of unit operation in the previous section. Because the model is modeled when the system is running normally, the state transition matrix $A = \begin{bmatrix} 1 & 0 \\ 1 & 0 \end{bmatrix}$, this means that the transition probability from the trusted state to the trusted state and from the untrusted state to the trusted state is 1, that is, regardless of the current state, the next step will be transferred to a trusted state with a probability of 1. The observation probability matrix B refers to the probability distribution of the unit operation of the trusted user. The initial state probability vector $\pi = \{1, 0\}$. Based on this, the hidden Markov model of trusted user behavior is established.

3.4 The Behavior Recognition of Untrusted Users

We need to set a fixed size sliding window for the observation sequence. The distance that the window slides down each time is an operation. Next, the forward algorithm is used to calculate the observed sequence probability set of trusted and untrusted user behavior under the hidden Markov model of trusted user behavior. When we obtain an observation sequence set of trusted user behavior, we need to use a smaller value in the observation sequence set as our decision threshold. The observation sequence exceeding the threshold is determined as a sequence of behaviors of the trusted user, and instead is determined as a sequence of behaviors of the untrusted user.

4   Procedure

There are two network users using the ERP system participated in the experiment. They are from a publishing company in Chongqing, China. User A is defined as a trusted user, user B is defined as an untrusted user.

4.1   Training Phase

Sequences of user A are used as a training set, User A's hidden Markov model is the trusted user's hidden Markov model. The hidden Markov model of the trusted user has been represented in the third section. User A's observation sequence has a window size of three. Using user A's 20,000 observation sequences as training data, the model can obtain the observation sequence probability set of user A. The probability of the observed sequences is so small, so we use a logarithm of the probability of these observations to amplify them. The amount of data is too large. The following Fig. 2 only shows the probability of observation sequence of 1000 data. Thus, the probability threshold of the observation sequence of user A is determined to be −6.389.

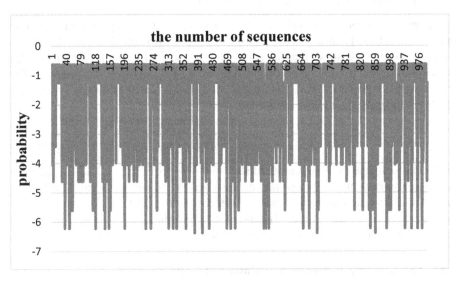

Fig. 2. Observation sequence probability set of training data

4.2   Test Phase

User A's remaining 5000 observation sequences are used as test data 1, which are used to test the recognition rate of the model. The observation sequence probability set of user A's test data is shown in the Fig. 3 below.

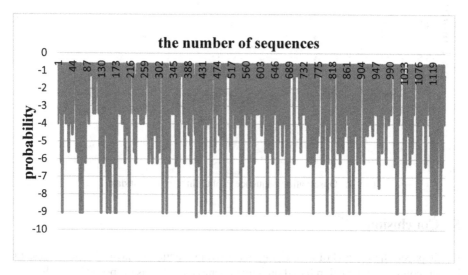

Fig. 3. Observation sequence probability set of test data 1

The test results show that the recognition rate of the model for trusted user behavior is 92.64%, and the false positive rate is 7.36%. This means that in the 4989 pieces of behavior data of trusted users, 4622 pieces of data are judged as behavior data of trusted users, and 367 pieces of data are determined as behavior data of untrusted users.

User B's 5000 observation sequences are used as test data 2, which are used to test the false positive rate of the model. The observation sequence probability set of user B's test data is shown in the Fig. 4 below.

The test results show that the recognition rate of the model for untrusted user behavior is 99.24%, and the false positive rate is 0.76%. This means that in the 4989 pieces of behavior data of untrusted users, 4951 pieces of data are judged as behavior data of untrusted users, and 38 pieces of data are determined as behavior data of trusted users.

Identifying the untrusted user's behavior as the trusted user is more horrible than identifying the trusted user's behavior as the untrusted user. Therefore, we choose a relatively large threshold to ensure a lower false positive rate when selecting the observation sequence probability threshold.

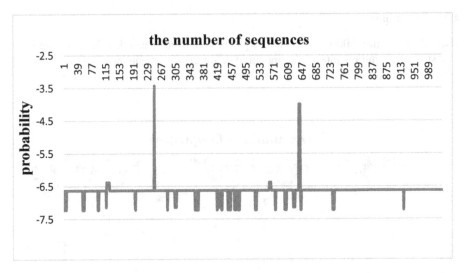

Fig. 4. Observation sequence probability set of test data 2

5 Conclusion

In this paper, the method of identifying untrusted interaction behavior in the process of human-computer interaction based on human behavior habits is proposed by us. Firstly, we analyzed the current information security issues of the ERP software system and reviewed the current methods for solving the information security problems of ERP software systems. Secondly, we propose that to solve the information security problem of ERP software system, we first need to identify the untrusted interaction behavior in the ERP software system. At the same time, we define the trusted interaction and trusted interactive behavior. Thirdly, we introduced the related concepts, parameters and algorithms of the hidden Markov model, then we use Hidden Markov Model to model the behavior of trusted users. Fourthly, we use the forward algorithm in the hidden Markov model to calculate the observation sequence probability set of the trusted user behavior and determine the probability threshold of the observed sequence. Finally, the recognition rate and false positive rate of the model were tested with two test sets.

From the experimental results, the recognition rate of our model is 92.64% and the false positive rate is 0.76%. This shows that the model is effective for identifying untrusted interactive behavior. Moreover, our research provides a new way to identify untrusted interactive behavior and the behavior we define as untrusted user behavior is closer to the abnormal user behavior in real life.

In the future, there is still a lot of work that needs to be done by us. Firstly, we can consider to improve the characteristic framework, such as adding some computer-related characteristics, or the characteristics of the environment's influence on interaction behavior in human-computer interaction etc. Secondly, only the simplest hidden Markov model is used to model the behavior of trusted users. In future research, higher-order hidden Markov models can be considered to model the behavior of trusted users. Finally, the influence of other factors on the experiment wasn't considered when selecting the experimental subjects, for example, the influence of the occupation of the experimental subjects on their operating habits.

Acknowledgments. This work was supported by the National Natural Science Foundation of China under Grant No. 71671020.

References

1. Carter, E.: Intrusion Detection Systems. Cisco Press, Indianapolis (2002)
2. Jain, R., Abouzakhar, N.: Hidden Markov model based anomaly intrusion detection. In: International Conference for Internet Technology & Secured Transactions. IEEE (2012)
3. Lee, D.C., et al.: Fast traffic anomalies detection using SNMP MIB correlation analysis. In: International Conference on Advanced Communication Technology. IEEE (2009)
4. Huang, S.Y., Huang, Y.N.: Network traffic anomaly detection based on growing hierarchical SOM. In: IEEE/IFIP International Conference on Dependable Systems & Networks. IEEE Computer Society (2013)
5. Yan, G.: Network anomaly traffic detection method based on support vector machine. In: International Conference on Smart City & Systems Engineering. IEEE (2017)
6. Yu, Q., Gu, X.: Network traffic anomaly detection based on dynamic programming. In: International Conference on Computing Intelligence & Information System. IEEE Computer Society (2017)
7. Lee, S., Shin, S.-H., Roh, B.-h.: Abnormal behavior-based detection of Shodan and Censys-like scanning. In: Ninth International Conference on Ubiquitous and Future Networks (ICUFN). IEEE (2017)
8. Garg, A., Maheshwari, P.: PHAD: packet header anomaly detection. In: International Conference on Intelligent Systems & Control. IEEE (2016)
9. Wang, K., Kim, H.S.: PCAD: cloud performance anomaly detection with data packet counts. In: IEEE International Conference on Cloud Computing Technology & Science. IEEE Computer Society (2017)
10. Uyyala, S., Naik, D.: Anomaly based intrusion detection of packet dropping attacks in mobile ad-hoc networks. In: International Conference on Control. IEEE (2014)
11. Caulkins, B.D., Lee, J., Wang, M.: Packet- vs. session-based modeling for intrusion detection systems. In: International Conference on Information Technology: Coding & Computing. IEEE (2005)
12. Jøsang, A.: Identity management and trusted interaction in Internet and mobile computing. IET Inf. Secur. **8**(2), 67–79 (2014). Author, F., Author, S.: Title of a proceedings paper. In: Editor, F., Editor, S. (eds.) CONFERENCE 2016, LNCS, vol. 9999, pp. 1–13. Springer, Heidelberg (2016)
13. Anderson, J.C., Narus, J.A.: A model of distributor firm and manufacturer firm working partnerships. J. Mark. **54**(1), 42–58 (1990). Author, F.: Contribution title. In: 9th International Proceedings on Proceedings, pp. 1–2. Publisher, Location (2010)
14. Cao, C., Yan, J., Li, M.: The effects of consumer perceived different service of trusted third party on trust intention: an empirical study in Australia. In: IEEE 14th International Conference on e-Business Engineering (ICEBE). IEEE (2017)

15. Kaur, B., Madan, S.: A fuzzy expert system to evaluate customer's trust in B2C E-commerce websites. In: International Conference on Computing for Sustainable Global Development. IEEE (2014)

16. Hosseini, S.B, Shojaee, A., Agheli, N.: A new method for evaluating cloud computing user behavior trust. In: Information & Knowledge Technology. IEEE (2015)

17. Yang, X., Liu, L., Zou, R.: A statistical user-behavior trust evaluation algorithm based on cloud model. In: International Conference on Computer Sciences & Convergence Information Technology. IEEE (2012)

18. Ma, J., Zhang, Y.: Research on trusted evaluation method of user behavior based on AHP algorithm. In: International Conference on Information Technology in Medicine & Education. IEEE (2015)

19. Jiang, W., Guo, S., Chen, W.: A trust evaluation model and algorithm based on network behavior detection. In: IEEE International Conference on Broadband Network & Multimedia Technology. IEEE (2011)

20. Yan, Z., Kantola, R., Zhang, P.: Theoretical issues in the study of trust in human-computer interaction. In: IEEE International Conference on Trust. IEEE (2012)

21. Liu, W., Ci, L., Liu, L.: Research on behavior trust based on Bayesian inference in trusted computing networks. In: IEEE International Conference on Smart City/SocialCom/SustainCom. IEEE (2016)

22. Yan, Z., Kantola, R., Zhang, P.: A research model for human-computer trust interaction. In: IEEE International Conference on Trust. IEEE Computer Society (2011)

23. Jiang, X.: A facial expression recognition model based on HMM. In: International Conference on Electronic & Mechanical Engineering & Information Technology. IEEE (2011)

Security and Usability

A Framework of Information Security Integrated with Human Factors

Ahmed I. Al-Darwish and Pilsung Choe[✉]

Department of Mechanical and Industrial Engineering,
Qatar University, Al Tarfa, Doha 2713, Qatar
aal709549@student.qu.edu.qa, pchoe@qu.edu.qa

Abstract. Information systems support organizations to achieve strategic competitiveness over other organizations and assist senior management in the decision-making process. In addition, they help organizations in timely implementation of projects and effective risk management. A reliable and coherent Information System requires a solid security framework that ensures Confidentiality, Integrity, Availability, Authenticity and Auditability of the critical information assets; therefore, managing security is essential for organizations doing business in a globally networked and competitive environment whilst seeking to achieve their objectives and goals and ensuring the continuity of business. This paper provides an integrated framework that classifies and holistic view of challenges in Information Security Systems, and their interrelationships. The framework is expected to provide a basis that can be used to evaluate individual organizational members' behavior and the adequateness of existing security measures.

Keywords: Information security management · Information security culture ·
Human factors · Organizational factors · Technological factors ·
Security challenges · Organizational security

1 Introduction

Uncertainty and risks are growing due to increased dynamic, complex and interrelated economy and enhanced threats from a wide range of forces, such as financial instability, political movements and terrorism, societal requirements, extreme nature events due to climate change, cyber-attacks and others. In the past years there were different low-probability and high-impact events, Black Swan events [1, 23], which are almost impossible to forecast (e.g., drought, earthquake, floods, cyber-attacks). Depending on how uncertainty is handled, it can become opportunity or threat. Traditionally, organizations managed risks in "silos" [13, 14, 23], such as finance, market, compliance, regulation, human resources, innovation, Information Security and others. But risks interrelate in a cybernetic way. Recently organizations adopt more comprehensive approaches and aggregate the results of the different risk assessments into an organization-wide risk profile [4, 12, 15, 23, 30].

Organization must protect their information assets from unauthorized access and quickly resume business activities after a security breach. It is necessary to broaden the

A. Moallem (Ed.): HCII 2019, LNCS 11594, pp. 217–229, 2019.
https://doi.org/10.1007/978-3-030-22351-9_15

study of Information Security risk to include not only the technical, but also the non-technical issues [10, 12, 16, 21, 23].

To date, studies have shown that non-technical risks are as important as technical risks in safeguarding an organization's sensitive information and in addressing Information Security management strategies or issues [17–19, 22]. However, little attention has been paid to the role of human factors (e.g. individual choice and behavior) or to organizational factors such as national and organizational culture, environment, and levels of Information Security awareness, and how these factors relate to attitudes about Information Security and its management.

For a long time, Information Security was seen as a technical job and an integral part of the IT department. Corresponding frameworks start at the process level and go down through all technical levels accordingly an IT enterprise architecture approach [23]. Despite the common goals of Information Security and enterprise risk management, we found no systemic framework for extending Information Security management to enterprise risk management. In addition, although there have been studies of specific challenges of Information Security management [1, 6, 7, 20] or sets of challenges along one of the factors, none have provided a comprehensive integrated overview of the challenges faced by Information Security management. A better understanding of how different human, organizational, financial and technological elements interplay could explain how different factors lead to sources of security breaches and vulnerabilities within organizations [5, 8, 20].

This paper provides an integrated framework that classifies and holistic view of these challenges, and their interrelationships (Fig. 1). This framework can help organizations identify their limitations with respect to implementing security standards and determine if they are spending their security resources effectively. It also provides a way to understand how different factors interplay. The integrated Information Security framework described in this paper will provide a sound basis that can be used to evaluate individual organizational members' behavior and the adequateness of existing security measures [20, 22, 25–27].

2 Social Engineering

A major concern within Information Security is the threat of Social Engineering Attacks. Social engineering attacks are made to collect sensitive information, and this information is often used maliciously. Social Engineering Attacks can cause a great deal of disruption to business activities and create financial, social and technical mayhem. Their impacts can extend beyond geographical borders and organizational boundaries. Therefore, dealing with Social Engineering Attacks would be in a great interest of any organization. Janczewski and Fu (2010) identified five main causes of Social Engineering Attacks: people, lack of security awareness, psychological weaknesses, technology and defense and attack methods and provided a conceptual model in order to understand the impact of Social Engineering Attacks on individuals and businesses and present a defensive approach to mitigate these risks [14].

According to the Verizon Report of Data Breach Investigation Report (2016), human factors are a main source of successful attacks, even using the latest security techniques and protocols, most information systems still face numerous security breaches. Human factors are at the heart of the vast majority of security breaches, however, human factors in Information Security are very complex to define because, they are intertwined with organizational culture and individual perceptions and characteristics. Providing a global solution to Information Security is a big challenge in the organizational context. Therefore, this paper define human factors as one of the major components responsible for inadequate Information Security and risk to organizational assets [14].

3   Human Factors in Information Security

People work falls into four categories: individual, team, management and customer/interested party. Human factors within these categories can become uncontrollable forces, because people have different perceptions of security, and their reactions to Information Security procedures are diverse and highly subjective and hard to measure. People have their own culture, attitudes, skills, knowledge, understandings, behavior and interests that depend upon the role that they play within the organization. Individuals' interaction with computers and decisions made with regard to Information Security are certainly very dynamic and complex issues. We can classify human factors into direct and indirect human factors based on the directness of the impact on the Information Security System [31].

3.1   Direct Human Factors

Direct human factors are based on individuals who have a direct impact on the overall Information Security System. These individuals are involved in an organization's efforts to meet its goals and objectives. They are also social entities within the Information Security System and cannot be measured using a technical approach. A socio-technical approach enables these entities to be defined in an Information Security System and is constructed upon social and technical sub-systems alike. These direct human factors include errors, usability, security awareness, training and education, skills, experience, employee engagement, incentive and disincentive policies, ignorance and negligence, and stress as follows [14]:

Errors: Swain and Guttman (1983) distinguish five different types of human factor errors, which can be used to explain Information Security breaches. First, there are acts of omission, in which people forget to perform a necessary action. For instance, in an Information Security domain, this could involve the failure to regularly change passwords. Second, errors are commonly acts of commission, in which people perform an incorrect procedure or action, such as writing down a password. Third, a number of errors are caused by extraneous acts, which involves doing something unnecessary. Fourth, errors can be caused by sequential acts, which involve doing something in the wrong order. Finally, time errors, caused by people failing to perform a task within the required time [16].

Usability: There is a trade-off between security and usability. According to Wilde (2001), there are four motivating factors that influence this trade-off between security and usability. Users are influenced by the expected costs and benefits associated with the risky behavior, and the expected costs and benefits associated with the safe behavior. Hence, if the potential gains associated with undertaking a risky activity are quite high, or if the adherence to a security system is a great inconvenience, then people are less likely to obey the policy, and are more likely to take risks. This is supported by Schneier (2003), who indicates that an understanding of the trade-offs associated with security is essential. Similarly, the security of information technology could be greatly improved through a drastic reduction in users' access and privileges. However, people are unlikely to tolerate such stringent restrictions, and it is therefore necessary to find an adequate balance between security and usability [16].

Security Awareness, Training and Education are some of the most effective countermeasures against the human factor threats to Information Security. According to the National Institute of Standards and Technology (NIST) report on security awareness and training, "learning is a continuum; it starts with awareness, builds to training, and evolves into education". The goal of awareness is to ensure that individuals are aware of potential IT security concerns and know how to recognize and react to such concerns. Training goes a step beyond this and aims to produce the required security skills and competencies. The aim of education is to integrate those security skills and competencies into a body of knowledge, and education "strives to produce IT security specialists and professionals capable of vision and pro-active response" [16, 27, 28].

Besnard and Arief (2004) emphasize the education of staff, stressing that although education may not alter behavior on its own, education makes people aware of the consequences of their actions. It ensures that individuals are conscious of the threats and the potential damages that can result from insecure behaviors.

Skills are one of the main forces in dealing with Information Security issues such as incident response. The absence of adequate and appropriately skilled staff contributes to a weak performance of Information Security policy. Employees are required to possess adequate skills to deal with the requirements of Information Security policy. Education and training are crucial in developing skills and demonstrating a commitment to preserve professionalism and competency [14, 25, 27].

Experience: Scholars have different views on the factor of experience with respect to the Information Security System. Some argue that people's understanding of Information Security procedures relies upon a few human factors, including their experience, whilst some go further and claim that a successful implementation of an Information Security System depends greatly on people's knowledge and experience. Although there is disagreement on the level of influence the factor of experience has, both sides would not deny its important role [14, 25, 27].

Employee Engagement in an organizational context can be seen as the unwillingness of employees to contribute to the achievement of the organization's goals and objectives in situations where they should demonstrate pro-social behaviour. Disengagement will lead to apathy, which creates significant issues in organizations due to a lack of willingness to implement organizational security policies and procedures. It creates an environment in which employees believe they have no responsibilities. Whereas a positive attitude, motivation and optimal working conditions contribute to better performance. Alavi (2016) argues that positive attitude serves the effectiveness of a security system; and the miscommunication between employees and senior management contributes to misunderstanding that leads to employee apathy [14].

Incentive and Disincentive Policies in organizations reward good behaviour and punish bad attitude. There are certain connections between people's attitudes and incentive and disincentive policies; even a little persuasion invariably increases motivation. Kabay (2002) argued that even a simple comment on Information Security policy made by an employee should be considered seriously, considering how it can ultimately affect the entire Information Security System in an organization. This factor has an impact on people's motivation to go along with Information Security policies. Organizations sometimes focus on punishment when instead they should divert their attention towards training and reward policy [14].

Ignorance and Negligence: Employees in organizations, sometimes unintentionally, do not pay enough attention to security policy. One example of user negligence and ignorance is when software piracy occurs because employees have little knowledge of software installation for various reasons such as a lack of training. The impact on an Information Security as a result of ignorance or negligence requires decisive action and must be addressed by Information Security professionals. Organizations pay far more attention to reinforcing technical facilities to overcome this issue, but ignorance and negligence are human issues and must therefore be confronted differently [14].

Individuals' stress in corporations can be caused by heavy workloads and tight project deadlines. People react maladaptive to stress and work overload despite any training programs they may receive. Stress leads to human error. Those under stress may tend to bypass Information Security policies. Stress and fatigue have a direct relationship to Information Security vulnerabilities [14, 25].

Security behavior can be described using a two-factor taxonomy, where the two factors are intentionality and technical expertise, which creates six categories of security behaviors, where two of those behaviors (Aware Assurance and Basic Hygiene) are positive, designed to increase security, and four of the behaviors may result in breaches to security. Intentional Destruction covers the actions of malicious insiders, who have technical expertise and the intent to do harm, whereas Detrimental Misuse involves personnel who have malicious intent, but lack technical expertise. Dangerous Tinkering covers behaviors that require technical expertise, but where there is not an intention to do harm. Perhaps the most common behavior, which will be covered in the most detail in this report, is Naïve Mistakes, in which individuals with low expertise and without malicious intentions perform an action which was not intended to harm the organization, but yet could result in a security breach.

3.2   Indirect Human Factors

Indirect factors have a certain influence on direct factors, as well as on Information Security System. However, these factors affect people through elements that are largely controlled by organizations and which individuals have no jurisdictional power over; therefore, these factors are collective matters managed by organizations. These indirect human factors include budget, return on investment, culture, Information Security and safety climate, communication, security policy enforcement, management support, Information Security business dashboard, risk perception and information processing biases and audit and compliance process as follows [14]:

Budget: Information Security experts widely believe that budgets have a significant impact on the efficiency of Information Security System. To ensure that an Information Security System fulfils its objectives effectively, organizations must have an effective cost strategy, which should be adopted for addressing the technical and personal requirements of the Information System. For instance, organizations will not be able to deal with Information Security System goals sufficiently if an access control mechanism has not been implemented or if employees have not been receiving adequate training. The importance of training emerges when the element of cost effectiveness is highlighted. Some measures to reduce cost, such as automated user access provisioning, require training programs that are less costly. This demonstrates the relationship between budget planning and direct human factors [25].

Return on Information Security Investment: Security cannot tolerate any performance delays in protection mechanisms and requires extra attention to ensure its success and at the lowest possible cost. Cost and urgency in organization's procurement processes thus become a priority, especially dealing with security requirements. Nevertheless, the way security is designed and implemented varies from one organization to another and depends upon the nature of the business, organizational culture and how the business risk management approach is adopted [24]. Information Security management systems are now increasingly based on economic principles such as cost-benefit analysis. Balancing Information Security costs and benefits is essential for organizations. However, organizations will invest in Information Security to a greater extent if the cost of investment is less than the cost of potential risk [14, 25, 27].

Culture: Organization's culture has a strong impact on organizational security. In order to understand security culture, it is important to have a grasp on the wider literature of organizational culture. Culture is defined differently, measured differently and evaluated differently. Schein's model of culture consists of three levels: artifacts and creations, values and beliefs, and basic assumptions. Artifacts and creations comprise the first level and represent the most visible and apparent aspects of an organization. According to Schein (1985), this level includes the elements of culture that can be seen and heard and easily interpreted by employees, customers and the public, including furniture and clothing, symbols, objects, the language used within the workplace, as well as slogans, rituals and stories [32]. The second level of culture comprises values and beliefs that underpin artifacts and creations. Values are the wants and desires that guide behavior; they are devised by senior management to provide direction and guidelines for the behavior of their employees. Third level of culture, basic assumptions, which represents and captures an organization's culture. Basic assumptions are hidden, elusive and invisible, making the core concepts of culture difficult, not only to understand, but also to assess. These basic assumptions include the "assumptions individuals hold about the organization and how it functions, they relate to aspects of human behavior, the nature of reality and the organization's relationship to its environment" [32]. Culture evolves and develops over time and this complexity is a contributing factor to the debate over what the construct of culture represents [16, 27].

Information Security and Safety Climate: The concept of organizational climate is similar to that of organizational culture. Organizational climate is a concept that is described as "shared perceptions of organizational policies, practices, procedures, both formal and informal". The constructs of culture and climate do overlap and share many similarities. They are both used to explain the ways in which individuals make sense of their work environments. Both concepts stress that culture and climate are learned through socialization and interaction with others. Importantly, both attempts to "identify the environment that affects the behavior of people in organizations". Parsons (2010) identified eight dimensions of a safety climate: the importance of safety and training, the effects of safe conduct on promotion, the effects of required workplace safety, the effects of safe conduct on social issues, the management's attitudes towards safety, the level of risk in the workplace, the status of safety officer and the status of safety committee. All eight dimensions are based on employee perceptions of their workplace environment [16].

Chan and colleagues (2005) found a relationship between safety climate and Information Security compliance behaviors. Their findings show that compliant behavior in Information Security is influenced by both organizational factors and personal factors. The overall results suggest that compliant behaviors can be increased by promoting self-efficacy, ensuring that there is a positive perception of Information Security climate, and ensuring that all levels of the organization (co-workers, supervisors and upper management) apply security guidelines to their everyday behaviors. Essentially a positive relationship between safety climate and employee behavior will more than likely improve the level of Information Security within an organization [16, 25].

Communication: O'Neill (2004) describes risk communication as: *"An interactive process of exchanging information and opinions between stakeholders regarding the nature and associated risks of a hazard on the individual or community and the appropriate responses to minimize risks".*

The manner in which Information Security is communicated can strongly influence how it is interpreted and whether it is then acted upon. Communication is far more likely to be effective if there is an adequate understanding of the gaps in current beliefs, and a clear and concise message of what the target audience needs to know [29]. Evidence also suggests that aspects of individuals' personality or cognitive style are likely to influence the manner in which they respond to information regarding risk. Finally, the effectiveness of risk communication could be increased if the message is framed towards the various cognitive styles, with different messages for different styles [16, 27].

Security Policy Enforcement: A security policy is an organizational document in which the Information Security procedures and rules are outlined. Employees at all levels of the organization must understand the security policy and participate in its implementation according to their position [1]. Enforcing a security policy is a major issue for an Information Security System and its successful implementation should be supported by management. Network security, access control, IT personnel job descriptions and password policy are examples of factors that are required to be covered by security policy [14, 25].

Management Support: To enforce policies relating to the Information Security in organizations, management must support it from the design stage through all evaluation stages. The role of management in an Information Security System is not only to advocate but also to deliver a clear message of Information Security policy to the rest of the organization. An obvious example of management endorsement of an Information Security System in organizations is the allocation of an adequate budget, which is entirely under the control of senior management. The general perception of senior management is that an Information Security System is entirely the responsibility of an IT department, who should ensure the installation of appropriate and adequate software systems to preserve the security of information [14, 25].

Information Security Business Dashboard: Information Security management and business decision-making are intimately interconnected with risk management. Executive boards require an understanding and monitoring of the risks that have the potential to obstruct their organization's ability to achieve its goals. These risks are characterized by Key Risk Indicators (KIRs), which stem directly from the organization's long-term strategy. The Business Intelligence Dashboard (BID) guides organizations towards a suitable information security posture whilst providing answers to key questions often raised by executives. Providing a meaningful BID for organizations and their senior executives helps them to receive some extended analytical insights on security metrics and Key Security Performance Indicators (KSPIs), a non-technical method that can be grasped by non-technical senior executives [14, 25].

Risk Perception and Information Processing Biases: When making behavioral decisions, individuals will often decide based on their estimates of the risks associated with the various options. Hence, the manner in which IT users perceive threats will influence their behavioral responses [27]. People often take shortcuts in the decision-making process, by using a number of information processing biases and heuristics to simplify the task. These biases and heuristics can affect risk perception, and evidence suggests that people generally have an inaccurate perception of risk [29]. Although there is a great deal of research in risk perception in general, there is little empirical study examining individuals' perceptions of risk within the Information Security domain. Huang and colleagues (2007) concluded that perceptions of Information Security risks could be described using six factors, namely knowledge, impact, severity, controllability, possibility and awareness. A few other authors have inferred perceptions of security risks from research in other areas. For example, Pattinson and Anderson (2005) suggest that perceptions of security risks are generally influenced by factors such as the individuals' mood at the time, recent media reports, past experiences, and knowledge of technical aspects, such as viruses. A few psychological, social and cultural factors can also affect the way that people perceive risk [16].

Audit and Compliance Process: It is not all that difficult to discover risk exposure gaps, or improvement opportunities. Neither is it that difficult to implement some solutions to address these. The trick, however, is that closing a gap improperly can sometimes be worse than not closing it in the first place. By "closing" a gap one can gain a sense of misplaced confidence and security that may in fact be more damaging than recognizing that a gap still exists and needs to be cautiously managed. What's worse is that improperly/inadequately closing gaps uses up resources and introduces additional variation potentially further destabilizing processes. The lesson here is to focus more on the quality of gap closure and improvement, rather than quantity.

4   Conclusion: Integrated Framework

The Information Security framework is based upon the conceptual understanding of an Information Security System within an organizational context and its integration with other concepts such as security incident, risk, technical and non-technical factors and return on investment within an organizational setting. All these concepts are necessary to determine the adequate and appropriate level of control mechanism required to effectively address risks to information assets through effective Information Security framework. The conceptual Framework address the Information Security from four angles: Business, Enterprise Risk Management, Technology & Human. These four elements are most relevant to achieve a balance between Information Security goals and organizational goals, as a defiance mechanism against attackers' goals and Human Factors [2, 9].

An effective Information Security System depends as much on knowledge of the business as on software architecture. Security professionals require the translation of business requirements and goals into an Information Security System solution capable of meeting those goals and requirements. This also extends to technology, human factors and the specific use of processes that should be aligned with business objectives and security goals. An organization's business goals and IT strategy are two factors that most influence the adoption of security countermeasures. Technology, risks and critical human factors all provide sources for Information Security System requirements (Fig. 1) [9, 11].

The risks and human factors from the business domain are mapped to the functions and objects of the Information Security System. The business processes and functions are understood through IT, which aggregates one or more functions from the Information Security System. The direct and indirect human factors identified include: Errors, Awareness, Skills, Experience, Ignorance and Negligence, Stress, Budget, Culture, Communication, Security Policy Enforcement, and others. These have been mentioned in many academic and professional reports as the source of Security Incidents; this is because they have direct and substantial impacts on Security Incidents [3, 25].

Tools and strategies are essential in keeping organizations cost effective whilst Information Security professionals endeavor to demonstrate the value of and Return on

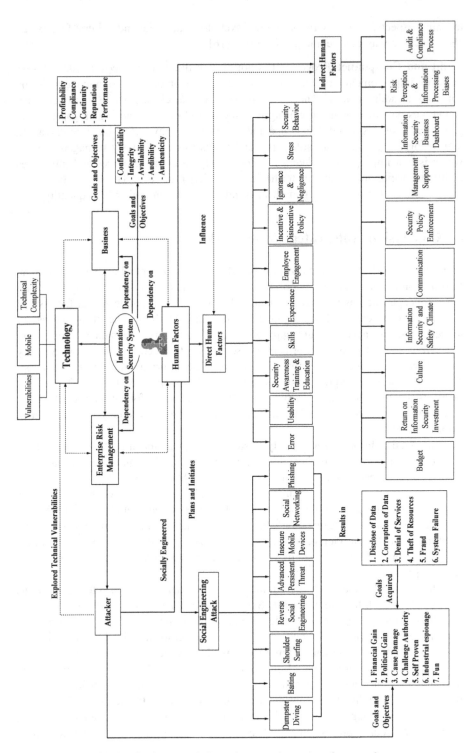

Fig. 1. The integrate information security system framework

Information Security Investment. Information Security Systems research literature indicates that there is a clear relationship between investments in Information Security System and enhanced organizational performance. Available tools and methods allow organizations to calculate and analyze the financial impact of a specific security control but cannot be used to analyze the cost-benefit of other factors such as critical human factors. Information Security management systems are now increasingly based on economic principles such as cost-benefit analysis [25].

Effective risk management practice forms the core of an organization's Information Security System. The risk management process is about identifying, analyzing, evaluating and treating risks and sets the stage for protecting organization's assets. An Information Security System combines business, socio-technical and technology concepts, including critical human factors, risks and investment, at every phase of development. Thus, Information Security System are affected by multidimensional factors during the course of their design, implementation and evaluation. Consideration of the influence of critical human factors, risks and security investment in meeting the goals should be given to construct a more consistent and reliable risk assessment methodology.

This study provides a perspective understanding of the role of human factors in relation to Information Security risks based on a literature review. Our study will continue to validate the applicability of the Information Security framework based on quantitative analyses using real security breach incident data in an industry in Qatar.

References

1. Audestad, J.: Four reasons why 100% security cannot be achieved. Telektronikk **1**, 38–47 (2005)
2. Johan, N., Rossouw, S.: Understanding Information Security Culture: A Conceptual Framwork: Centre for Information Security Studies. Nelson Mandela Metropolitan University, South Africa (2000)
3. Adele, V., Jan, E.: An information security governance framework. Inf. Syst. Manage. J. **24**, 361–372 (2007)
4. Kankanhalli, A., Teo, H.-H., Tan, B.C., Wei, K.-K.: An integrative study of information systems security effectiveness. Int. J. Inf. Manage. **23**, 139–154 (2003)
5. Koskosas, I.V., Paul, R.J.: The interrelationship and effect of culture and risk communication in setting internet banking security goals, New York, NY (2004)
6. Kraemer, S., Carayon, P.: Human errors and violations in computer and information security: the viewpoint of network administrators and security specialists. Appl. Ergon. **38**, 143–154 (2007)
7. Ernst, Young.: Into the cloud, out of the fog, Ernst & Young's 2011 Global Information Security Survey. http://www.ey.com/Publication
8. Siponen, M., Oinas-Kukkonen, H.: A review of information security issues and respective research contributions. SIGMIS Database **38**(1), 60–80 (2007)
9. Rodrigo, W., Kirstie H., Konstantin, B.: An integrated view of human, organizational, and technological challenges of IT security management, University of British Columbia (2008). www.emeraldinsight.com/0968-5227.htm

10. Kirstie, H., David, B., Rodrigo, W., Kasia, M., Gagne, A., Konstantin, B.: Human, Organizational, and Technological Factors of IT Security, Florence, Italy (2008)
11. Salahuddin, A., Karen, N., Kavoos, M.: Information security culture: a behavior compliance conceptual framework. School of Management, Queensland University of Technology, Brisbane (2010)
12. Margareth S.: Information security management to enterprise risk management. In: Sobh, T., Elleithy, K. (eds.) Innovations and Advances in Computing, Switzerland (2015)
13. Margareth, S., Michael, F., Ruth, B.: Information management for holistic, collaborative information security management. In: Sobh, T., Elleithy, K. (eds.) Emerging Trends in Computing, Informatics, Systems Sciences, and Engineering, vol. 151. Springer, New York (2013). https://doi.org/10.1007/978-1-4614-3558-7_17
14. Alavi, R., Islam, S., Lee, W.: A Risk-Driven Investment Model for Analyzing Human Factors in Information Security, The University of East London, Computing and Engineering (2016)
15. Werlinger, R., Hawkey, K., Beznosov, K.: Human, Organizational and Technological Challenges of Implementing Information Security in Organizations, University of British Columbia (2008)
16. Parsons, K., McCormac, A., Butavicius, M., and Ferguson, L.: Human Factors and Information Security: Individual, Culture and Security Environment. Defense Science and Technology Organization (DSTO-TR-2484) (2010)
17. Chan, M., Woon, I., Kankanhalli, A.: Perceptions of information security at the workplace: linking information security climate to compliant behavior. J. Inf. Priv. Secur. 1(3), 18–42 (2005)
18. Huang, D., Rau, P.P., Salvendy, G.: A survey of factors influencing people's perception of information security. In: Jacko, J. (ed.) Hum.-Comput. Interact. Part IV. Springer, Heidelberg (2007)
19. ISO: ISO/IEC 17799 Information technology - Security techniques - code of practice for information security management. Second edition 2005-06-15. Reference: ISO/IEC 17799-1:2005(E). pp. 1–115 (2005)
20. Needle, D.: Culture at the level of the firm: organizational and corporate perspectives. In: Barry, J., Chandle, J., Clarck, H., Johnson, R., Needle, D. (eds.) Organization and Management: A Critical Text. Business Press, London (2000)
21. O'Neill, B.: Developing a Risk Communication Model to Encourage Community Safety from Natural Hazards. Paper Presented at the Fourth NSW Safe Communities Symposium, Sydney, and NSW (2004)
22. Reichers, A.E., Schneider, B.: Climate and culture: an evolution of constructs. In: Schneider, B. (ed.) Organizational Climate and Culture. Jossey-Bass Publishers, San Francisco (1990)
23. Richardson, R.: 2007 CSI Computer Crime and Security Survey. Computer Security Institute, Ritov (2007)
24. Schein, E.H.: Organizational Culture and Leadership. Jossey-Bass, San Francisco (1985)
25. Schultz, E.: The human factor in security. Comput. Secur. 24, 425–426 (2005)
26. Swain, A. D., Guttman, H. E.: Handbook of human reliability analysis with emphasis on nuclear power plant applications, NUREG/CR-1278, Washington, D.C. (1983)
27. Van der Pligt, J.: Risk perception and self-protective behavior. Eur. Psychol. 1, 34–43 (1996)
28. Wilson, M., Hash, J.: Computer Security: Building an Information Technology Security Awareness and Training Program. Information Technology Laboratory National Institute of Standards and Technology, Gaithersburg, MD 20899-8933 (2003)
29. Janczewski, L.J., Fu, L.: Social engineering-based attacks: model and New Zealand perspective. In: 2010 International Multiconference on Computer Science and Information Technology, pp. 847–853. IEEE, October 2010

30. Siponen, M.T.: A conceptual foundation for organizational information security awareness. Inf. Manage. Comput. Secur. **8**(1), 31–41 (2000)
31. Werlinger, R., Hawkey, K., Beznosov, K.: An integrated view of human, organizational, and technological challenges of IT security management. Inf. Manage. Comput. Secur. **17**(1), 4–19 (2009)
32. Wilde, G.J.S.: Target Risk 2: A New Psychology of Safety and Health. PDE Publications, Toronto (2001)

Making Sense of Darknet Markets: Automatic Inference of Semantic Classifications from Unconventional Multimedia Datasets

Alexander Berman[1($\boxtimes$)] and Celeste Lyn Paul[2($\boxtimes$)]

[1] Texas A&M University, College Station, USA
anberman@tamu.edu
[2] U.S. Department of Defense, Arlington, USA
clpaul@tycho.ncsc.mil

Abstract. Darknet Markets are a hotbed of illicit trade and are difficult for law enforcement to monitor and analyze. Topic Modeling has been a popular method to semantically analyze market listings, but lacks the ability to infer the information-rich visual semantics of images embedded within these listings. In this paper we present a relatively fast method using unsupervised and self-supervised machine learning methods to infer image semantics from large, unstructured multimedia corpora, and demonstrate how it may aid analysts in investigating the content of Darknet Markets.

Keywords: Darknet · Semantics · Latent Dirichlet Allocation · Neural networks

1 Introduction

Darknet Markets (DNM) are online marketplaces hosted on anonymous networks, such as Tor, that provide access to buyers and sellers of usually illicit or unregulated goods. A famous DNM, Silk Road, operated from 2011 until 2013 when it was shut down by the FBI for illegal trade [1,11]. Silk Road was the first of dozens of DNMs to operate - and be shut down by law enforcement. Law enforcement is in a constant game of whack-a-mole as two new markets pop up for every one that is taken down.

There is an increasing need to understand the scope and content of DNMs to support law enforcement's efforts to protect public safety. As markets are shut down, new markets will often adopt the abandoned content, making tracking overall trends an essential task. The sheer scope and quantity of DNMs makes this a significant big data analysis problem. Common approaches to this problem include textual content analysis [11,16]. However, these methods fall short of fully characterizing DNM content since listings tend to include multimedia,

© Springer Nature Switzerland AG 2019
A. Moallem (Ed.): HCII 2019, LNCS 11594, pp. 230–248, 2019.
https://doi.org/10.1007/978-3-030-22351-9_16

such as images, to describe the products rather than using solely text. The content itself can be a challenge to parse consistently for use in Natural Language Processing (NLP) analysis [16], requiring manual and time-consuming methods as a fall-back.

Methods that provide automatic semantic organization of DNM listings based on multimedia properties could help make the analysis of these markets more tractable. There has been some success utilizing supervised machine learning algorithms to classify DNM images through training on a large labeled corpus of images from market listings [14]. However, labeling large image corpora and training of new image classifiers is a non-trivial task. To properly label these datasets, analysts must spend many hours distinguishing the semantics between all images in a dataset, or analysts must find an existing labeled dataset that is analogous to their goals. In the case of DNMs, there are few datasets containing labels for illicit object images, such as specific guns and drugs. The labeling process can also be prone to human bias and issues of not sampling less frequent classes or not sampling emerging classes. Reducing the labeling burden on analysts and could allow for more timely and accurate analysis of DNM content.

Other work on analyzing DNMs has utilized tools such as topic modeling to help track activities within these markets [6,11], and bag-of-visual-words methods to classify images [6]. This paper presents a method to automatically identify semantic relationships between text and images for listings in the Gwern Darknet Markets dataset [9], in order to aid analysts in achieving a better understanding of diverse multimedia descriptions from various illicit goods and services. We demonstrate applications of this method on DNM listings, and propose future work to assist with future DNM content analysis.

2   Related Work

Image classification systems with near-human accuracy [22] have increased interest for organizing and inferring classifications of images across many domains. Previous work has taken the approach of labeling large datasets for the purpose of classifying and tracking DNM activity. Fidalgo et al. categorized Darknet images that corresponded with particular illegal activities [6]. They utilized Edge-SIFT features with dense SIFT descriptors to categorize pages on the Darknet by images with high accuracy. This is particularly applicable to law-enforcement and security agencies, which could benefit from being able to automatically flag and sort through illegal Darknet activities.

As new forms of illegal activity become prominent, there is a need from law enforcement to be able to classify those activities promptly. However, these classification systems often require large amounts of labeled data. In many domains, such as identifying product images in niche online markets, it takes large-scale crowd-sourcing [3], or smaller groups of people long periods of time to label enough images to train classification systems to satisfactory performance. In addition, these labeled images may not meet every future analysis need. The only semantic-inference that can be done with the supervised models trained on the labeled dataset is from the pre-defined semantics designated by the labelers. This means that it can take several iterations of labeling entire datasets before being able to predict future images for certain analysis tasks. Also, this predicates that several individuals need to spend non- trivial amounts of time looking through images and determining distinguishable semantic categories of images before labeling each image.

For many applications, the time, specialty, and clearance needed to properly label a dataset may be infeasible. Where possible, automatic labeling of images based on an image's surrounding context could make classification feasible. To accomplish this, descriptive labels from other media such as text must be generated to describe this context. In Porter's analysis of Darknet market terms over time [11], he utilized Latent Dirichlet Allocation (LDA) on text data scraped from Reddit forums that discussed darknet activities. Porter generates high-level topics of these subreddits, and identifies changes in behavior after many darknet markets faced legal action in summer of 2017 [11]. A notable aspect of this change was a shift from casual language to more serious, security-concerned language. He notes that while LDA could give great insight into changes within the darknet community, all insights should be verified with the original textual source. Porter's LDA-driven analysis was much faster than analyzing the text from scratch, as one can form hypotheses quicker; but, the analysis still takes some time. Our work addresses some of these issues by augmenting the topic model latent space with correlated images, which can help inform analysts and further support their hypothesis formation.

Another method for saving time in analysis of webpages is TextTopicNet [7,18], which presents a method to bootstrap image classification and cross-modal retrieval tools by training an instance of CaffeNet [12] to predict semantic meaning of images, optimizing to match images to their source document topic vectors. Using the ImageCLEF Wikipedia dataset [23], Gomez et al. demonstrate retrieval based on LDA topic vector weights, and on the learned visual features from the Convolutional Neural Network (CNN). They show that training CNN's to match broad semantic topics can better support more specific computer vision tasks like image classification, object detection, and multi-modal retrieval. However, the time and expertise needed to train TextTopicNet would be presently infeasible by an analyst not well-versed in neural networks, and without access to a GPU-accelerated workstation to speed up training. Inspired by TexTopic-Net, we utilize a similar method to automatically train a model within a more feasible timeframe, and demonstrate applications of its image topic-composition predictions on Wikipedia articles and Darknet marketplaces.

3   Methodology

Our method for supporting the analysis of DNMs is inspired by previous work in the area. First, similar to TextTopicNet [7,18], we created training image-topic vectors (labels) for each image from the LDA-generated document-topic vectors from where that image originated. Then, we trained a convolutional neural

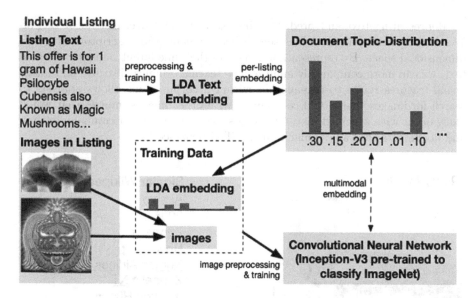

Fig. 1. System for training a CNN to predict Topic Vectors for any given Image, representing what type of text document an image with similar visual/semantic features would be found according to this model.

network (CNN), accelerated by transfer-learning [24], to predict the document topic-vector where a given image could be located. Once the training converged, a matrix of all images in the dataset and the predicted textual topic vectors was created. This model essentially predicts the type of document from which a given image would originate, affording analysts the ability to directly relate images and text in the domain of the training dataset (Fig. 1).

3.1 Latent Dirichlet Allocation

In order to automatically classify images based on associated documents, we make the assumption that images are correlated to probability distributions of topics that generate text documents within the dataset. These compositions of textual topics are generated via LDA topic modeling. LDA is a generative statistical model of a large text collection, where each document is generated as a mixture of k topics (where k is specified by the user). Each topic is represented as a probability distribution over words present in the text collection. The result of this generative process, as defined by Blei et al. [2], is two parameters: word probabilities given each topic, and topic probabilities given each document. All documents in the dataset are represented by topic probabilities, which are in turn represented by word probabilities. Any document, even if unseen during the training of an LDA model, can be represented by a probability distribution over all topics of the learned model. We utilize the MALLET library to train LDA models and tune its hyper-parameters [15].

Representing text and predicting images in topic space, instead of Bag-of-Words representations, provides semantically meaningful descriptors in lower-dimensional space. By representing images in the same latent semantic space as text, we can more comparably analyze how textual semantic features and image visual features relate to one-another within a corpus. This allows analysts to search for images that would co-occur in with other images, images that would likely occur with specified text, documents that would likely accompany images, and documents that are similar to a specified text (see Fig. 2).

Query Image

Similar Wikipedia Articles
Airship
2005
Zeppelin
Hovercraft
Korean Airlines Flight 007
Zeppelin NT
Aviation History
Gimli Glider

Images that have a similar predicted text embedding to Query

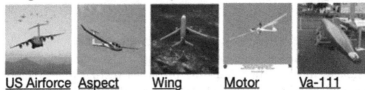

US Airforce   Aspect   Wing   Motor   Va-111   Air Show
               Ratio (Wing)   Glider   Shkval

Fig. 2. The CNN trained in this paper can quickly retrieve documents that a query image may be found within, and identify other images that may be found in those types of documents. The above example demonstrates retrieving Wikipedia articles and images from the ImageCLEF dataset with a 200-topic LDA and CNN model.

3.2   Neural Network Architecture and Training Procedure

To automatically create categories of images within a textual dataset without much human supervision, we adapted TextTopicNet [7,18] to work on Inception-V3 image classification CNN architecture [22]. TextTopicNet took 120,000 epochs (the number of times it trained on the entire image dataset) to converge on the ImageCLEF dataset [23]. This would take an infeasible amount of time on many everyday machines, and still would take a non-trivial amount of time on multi-GPU machines. To combat this, we applied transfer-learning from a model trained on image-classifications from the 'ImageNet' dataset, which contains over 1000 different classifications for everyday images [5]. On top of the convolutional layers of Inception V3 [22], we placed a global average pooling layer, followed by a fully connected layer with 1024 output dimensions, a dropout layer with 0.5 probability, and another fully connected layer that outputs dimensions equal to the k dimensions of the trained LDA model. This network is then optimized with Stochastic Gradient Descent of learning rate of 0.0001 and momentum of 0.9, to minimize sigmoid cross-entropy loss similar to TextTopicNet.

Once an LDA model is trained on a textual dataset, we created a table with rows corresponding to the images, text, and the topic vectors. This is randomly split into a training dataset (80%) and a validation dataset (20%). Training is done in two stages: an initial transfer-learning stage, and an additional fine-tuning stage. The first stage loads the ImageNet-trained weights into the model, initializing the fully-connected layers with variance scaling [10]. All layers besides the dense layers are frozen, so that the dense layers train while utilizing the image-features recognized by the ImageNet-trained convolutional layers. After the validation loss converges or a maximum number of epochs are reached, this stage ends. The set of CNN weights with the best epoch performance are loaded for the fine-tuning stage. The top 172 convolutional layers are then unfrozen and updated by the next round of training. This allows for the higher-level features generated by the convolutional network to be better fit to the training images, which may require different features than ImageNet. Once this stage converges or reaches a maximum number of epochs, training is stopped. The weights with the best overall validation-loss are loaded and then topic vectors are generated for each image. For 40-topic LDA models, we trained with an upper-limit of 25 epochs per the transfer and fine-tuning stages separately (50 combined), ending each stage if validation accuracy increased for three successive epochs. For LDA models with larger topic-dimensions, the upper-limit was increased to 50 epochs. The neural network components of this system were implemented using the Keras python framework [4]. With transfer-learning it typically takes fewer than 40 epochs total to converge rather than the more than one-hundred-thousand epochs used in the original TextTopicNet model [7,18]. This allows for relatively fast training, that could make this method affordable and accessible for future applications in analysis of multimodal data, such as DNM.

3.3 Datasets

To test this neural network training process and to investigate applications of the trained model, we trained on two datasets: ImageCLEF and Gwern Darknet Markets. To provide evidence that our system works similarly to TextTopicNet [7,18], we train and provide results on models from the ImageCLEF dataset [23] which serves as a common link between our papers. We then train models and demonstrate results on Darknet listings to convey this system's potential to aid analysts in navigating more unconventional multimodal datasets. Image-CLEF is a collection of Wikipedia articles with images from 2010–2011 [23]. The Gwern Darknet Markets Archive includes HTML documents of DNM listings and includes images [9]. We utilized a subset of 17 markets from this dataset in all training and demonstrations for this paper.

The ImageCLEF dataset [23], same as the one utilized by TextTopicNet [7,18], has 42,777 English Wikipedia articles between 2010–2011 with 100,785 associated images. All articles have been completely cleaned of HTML artifacts, and only contain article-specific text. Articles and images cover a large semantic range. This paper reproduces those results on the recommended 40 topics, as well as increasing number of topics beyond mentioned in TextTopicNet. A standard English stopword list was applied to this dataset before performing LDA. This dataset was utilized to test our methodology before utilizing the system on the less-studied DNM.

Market	# of Listings	# of Images	Market	# of Listings	# of Images	Market	# of Listings	# of Images
AmazonDark	390	136	DogeRoad	304	103	TheRealDeal	5,080	493
Andromeda	3,884	1,552	DreamMarket	2484	5	TorBazaar	1,352	214
Area51	965	351	Oxygen	6818	2,829	TorMarket	2,054	791
CloudNine	307	1,057	Pandora	23,600	5,399	UndergroundMarket	387	78
CryptoMarket	7,294	2,360	SilkRoad2	169,799	2,268	WhiteRabbit	1,442	320
DarknetHeroes	722	154	TheMarketPlace	14,466	998	Total	241,348	19,108

Fig. 3. Number of Listings and Images analyzed from the Gwern Darknet Markets Archive per market. An image may be referenced in multiple listings within a market.

The Gwern Darknet Markets Archive is a publicly-available dataset gathered by crawling various DNMs [9]. In this paper, we analyze 17 markets from this dataset (see Fig. 3). These markets consist of raw HTML from market listings across various dates. We only processed the latest version of duplicate listings from the crawlers' datasets, ignoring older listings with less text and images. Then we removed HTML tags from the listings. As many artifacts and uninformative text remained in the listings, the top 20% most-frequent terms per market were removed from the respective DNM listings. This removed many missed webpage artifacts, and some repeated other text such as headers and market-wide text. Both images downloaded in the crawler, and embedded images from the HTML were associated with listings. We generated a stoplist of commonly missed HTML artifacts and less-informative terms. Researchers removed the most common images per market that had nothing to do with the listings (e.g. button icons, market banners, etc.). Small images were also removed. A total of 241,348 listings were extracted with 47,101 images. LDA and the CNN were trained with 40 topics and 450 topics.

4   Results

We will first describe what the image textual-topic prediction models can accomplish with a clean dataset like Wikipedia, before moving to the models trained on the noisier Darknet dataset. Insights gained from the Wikipedia data were then applied to the Darknet dataset to help find patterns without much prior knowledge of the markets.

4.1   ImageCLEF

We trained a image to textual-topic prediction model using the method described in 3.2 of the Methodology on 40 topics. A sample of the top-weighted images per topic is shown in Fig. 4. These resemble many of the results from Text-TopicNet [7,18], which was trained on the same Wikipedia dataset. These similar results validate that our differences from TextTopicNet, namely the InceptionV3 CNN architecture [22] and transfer-learning [17], did not noticeably alter the end results for how the model predicts LDA textual topic space that would contain any given image. Many of the images, in each topic, show a mixture of many objects fitting a topical theme. Airplane categories (Fig. 4, Topic 2) include everything from commercial airlines to fighter jets. A topic about animals has images of pets, fish, and dinosaurs. The food topic (Fig. 4, Topic 5) has everything from soup to nuts. The image-classifier is able to properly summarize images belonging to different textual topics, showing dataset-specific semantic similarities between images instead of distinguishing images based on purely visual features or only strict supervised labeling patterns.

While the TextTopicNet demonstrated their network on at most one-hundred LDA topics [7,18], in many practical applications of LDA the number of topics will be significantly larger. Many topics in the Wikipedia 40-topic LDA model contained many different classifications of images, while fitting semantic themes generated by LDA, hinted that there may be more granular themes that LDA could discover within the dataset. The square root of the number of documents

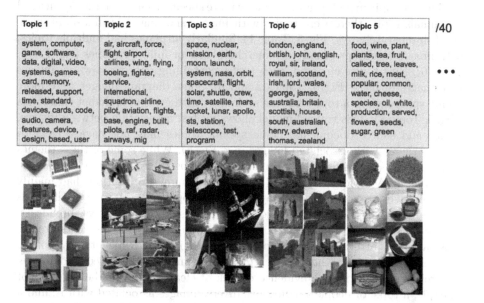

Topic 1	Topic 2	Topic 3	Topic 4	Topic 5
system, computer, game, software, data, digital, video, systems, games, card, memory, released, support, time, standard, devices, cards, code, audio, camera, features, device, design, based, user	air, aircraft, force, flight, airport, airlines, wing, flying, boeing, fighter, service, international, squadron, airline, pilot, aviation, flights, base, engine, built, pilots, raf, radar, airways, mig	space, nuclear, mission, earth, moon, launch, system, nasa, orbit, spacecraft, flight, solar, shuttle, crew, time, satellite, mars, rocket, lunar, apollo, sts, station, telescope, test, program	london, england, british, john, english, royal, sir, ireland, william, scotland, irish, lord, wales, george, james, australia, britain, scottish, house, south, australian, henry, edward, thomas, zealand	food, wine, plant, plants, tea, fruit, called, tree, leaves, milk, rice, meat, popular, common, water, cheese, species, oil, white, production, served, flowers, seeds, sugar, green

/40

• • •

Fig. 4. 5 out of 40 Topics from the ImageCLEF Wikipedia dataset with Top Terms and Top Images by Individual Weight per Topic. Wikipedia articles are a mixture of these topics' terms and image characteristics

Fig. 5. 5 out of 200 Topics from the ImageCLEF Wikipedia dataset with Top Terms and Top Images by Individual Weight per Topic. Both topics and images are more specific than the 40-topic model.

has been recommended as a good number of topics for training LDA models [8], therefore we also trained LDA and the CNN with 200 topics to see the effectiveness of this type of self-supervised network with more granular topics.

The 200 topic model resulted in many more specific topics (see Fig. 5). Instead of animals topic, there were topics with images showing only dinosaurs, pets, and fish separately (e.g. Fig. 5, Topic 1). Similarly airplanes had multiple topics, with images in groups of only commercial planes or military planes (e.g. Fig. 5, Topic 6). New topics emerged, such topics containing only wrist-watch images and images of flags (Fig. 5, Topics 2 and 6). Some diagram images were more evenly split, such as a topic showing all images with grids of alphabet characters (Fig. 5, Topic 8). This trained model allows for fast association between images, terms, and source documents. Some specific topics may not have a clear or obvious theme with associated images (e.g. Fig. 6). While some of these themes do not seem useful at first, they can still provide useful information to analysts. For example, A topic with words describing communist revolutions had mainly black and white photos, which may relate to propaganda. A topic with words related to various media (e.g. radio, align, television, center, news, broadcast, channel, etc.) showed images of fountains, buildings and concerts. These topics show a clear pattern between text and related images, while it may not be obvious without extra thought of why they connect. Other predicted image-text relations may provide evidence of lack of clear themes in the corpus. For example, a topic of people's names has diverse images associated with it, and a topic of scientific terms has many science-related pictures without a clear theme. When inspecting the Wikipedia articles these images originate from, they do contain terms from these topics. Not all topics will have clear patterns associated with the images, especially at higher topic dimensions, but this also can provide

top terms for this text topic: political, movement, revolution, social, national
top images that model would predict would occur in documents made primarily of the this text topic

top terms for this text topic: radio, align, television, center, news, broadcast, channel
top images that model would predict would occur in documents made primarily of the this text topic

top terms for this text topic: bell, wallace, taylor, jones, george, gray, alfred
top images that model would predict would occur in documents made primarily of the this text topic

top terms for this text topic: form, time, called, common, term, modern, include, based
top images that model would predict would occur in documents made primarily of the this text topic

Fig. 6. Top weighted terms and images for topics in the 200-topic ImageCLEF model. Images associated with topics can provide meaningful insight into related source documents, even when that association is not always obvious.

useful information to an analyst. Models with lower topic-dimensionality can provide analysts with more interpretable text-image relations, while models with higher topic-dimensionality will provide more precise relations between text-image relations that may be less interpretable. Both models have advantages, so analysts may desire to utilize both in conjunction to maximize interpretability while still achieving specificity.

Image nearest-neighbor results also leads to more semantically specific image results than when run on fewer topic dimensions. An image of Aaron Rodgers throwing a football was close via Jensen-Shannon Divergence [13] to not only football action-shots, but also an image of the University of Oklahoma's mascot. The closest similarities to a given image or text query constitute a theme, not an exact matching to the query. Analysts utilizing this system will have to find an optimal number of topics, which has been an open question in LDA research [8]. Image summary and retrieval tasks primarily inform semantics based on the granularity and quality of the topic model, meaning the LDA model quality is imperative.

4.2   Gwern Darknet Markets Archives

The Darknet Markets Archive [9] was a much messier dataset than the cleaned ImageCLEF Wikipedia articles, and there were a number of artifacts not captured by our preprocessing that appeared in the topic space, such as some HTML artifacts, common artifacts from markets (e.g., countries where they can ship), multi-language descriptions, and less polished and consistent wording in many listings. The difficulty in interpretability of the top words per topic does make understanding the model more difficult, but the generated groups of images can still deliver insight into the DNM listings. In these ways, the DNM dataset is more representative of many less-structured datasets than the curated Image-CLEF.

Images Inform Context of Text Topics. Despite the extra artifacts, clear image themes emerge from this dataset, in the 40-topic and 450-topic (approximately the square root of the total number of listings) LDA models. From identifying semantic patterns between images and textual topics, an analyst can gain a sense of the types of images that are in different types of DNM listings. Through this process, viewing images associated with textual topics can aid an analyst in understanding multimodal datasets where solely text would deliver incomplete or noisy information.

Training the image model from a 40-topic trained LDA model produces many interesting high-level themes that are not obvious from looking at only the weighted terms per topic. For example (shown in Fig. 7, Topic 2) a topic focused on currencies and shipping information has images of different online audio and video streaming service logos. Some images relate to details of the text, such as images showing "<number> hits" with a letter grade in the bottom-left corner that all very accurately describe a topic concerned with shipping, prices, and quality of drugs.

Some topics have a mixture of easily distinguishable items, similar to the mixture of terms that compose a topic. One topic has terms 'guide', 'make', and 'watch' which is difficult to make what exactly it is talking about alone. With images, which show images of books and watches, we can infer that this topic is about both books and watches separately (Fig. 10). This likely means similar wording is employed to

Topic 1	Topic 2	Topic 3	Topic 4	Topic 5
price, min, candy, stealth, custom, quality, communication, items, grade, extracts, full, europe, melt, cbd, shipping, herb, ago, infused, products, world	usd, btcvendor, crypto, price, bitcoin, shipping, wallet, ships, btc, category, months, purchase, marketplaceprivate, signout, days, message, comrade, delivery, place, orange	btc, shipment, usd, items, browse, sign, escrow, united, orders, description, feedback, seller, drugs, states, price, buy, category, contact, images, build	shipping, package, dream, communication, quality, price, mail, kush, ago, i'm, board, stealth, months, information, sour, svndmvn, don't, medicine, strains, make	usd, btc, user, message, feedback, pills, contentav, ago, options, vendors, listings, orders, feedbacks, xanax, months, free, positive, made, meds, revolutionaries

/40

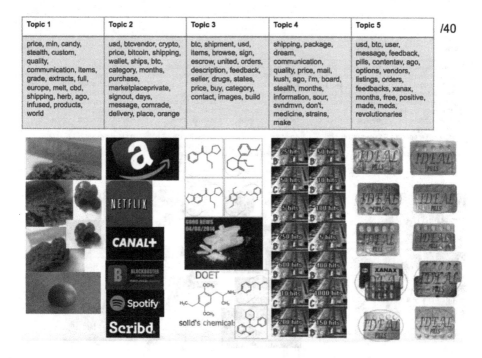

Fig. 7. 5 out of 40 Topics trained on DNM listings

sell watches and books on DNMs. Another example of this is a mushroom-selling topic, which has many more psychedelic images and some images related to money-exchange. The image-inference model can augment analysts' understanding of topics beyond what is represented by words alone.

For the LDA model with 450 topics, the image to textual topic prediction model has many more specific topics (Fig. 8). Individual drugs are now sorted into their own topics (Fig. 9), with topics solely containing images of cocaine, prescription pills, and cigarette variations (Fig. 8, Topic 2). Books gain their own topic, largely associated with hacking terms and the "blackhand". Wristwatches also get their own topic, now separated from books (e.g. Fig. 10). While many of these topics have terms match to images with similar semantic meaning, some images and terms fit semantic themes on their own but not together. For example, a topic showing all images of guns relates to a topic composed of country names (Fig. 8, Topic 4). This likely is due to the inherent messiness of the dataset, but still shows a correlation between terms and semantic content that otherwise would not have been obvious to an analyst viewing the noisy text data on its own. Listings with gun images, for mostly selling purposes, are likely to be on pages that list many different countries. The objective of this LDA-image model is not to link images with semantic labels describing the image, but to better associate images within semantic context surrounding it. In the case of the Darknet data, this context is often different proportions of selling, shipping, and item-quality terms.

Topic 1	Topic 2	Topic 3	Topic 4	Topic 5	/450
information, usps, mail, addresses, make, i'm, it's, note, states, aware, united, orders, righteous, explore, blotter, love, put, don't, receiving, made, names, encrypt, multiple, q&a, adding, acceptable, waiting, list, office, fedex/ups	btc, shipping, guide, buy, gbp, drugs, lsd, eur, ectasy, silk, aud, steroids, usd, cocaine, weed, smoother, worldwide, listing, oil, days, feedback, price, seller, mescaline, dmt, orders, hash, pcs, concentrates, withdraw	usd, price, seller, items, list, latest, digital, orders, upgrade, news, overview, btc, stimulants, opoids, ratings, unit, ecstasy, cannabis, ships, prescription, psychedelics, counterfeits, testing, drugs, kits, miscellanea, average, feedback, eta, dark	islands, republic, united, states, island, saint, french, south, arab, guinea, democratic, british, china, virgin, people's, georgia, korea, netherlands, samoa, congo, france, accounts, czech, vatican, state, cameroon, guyana, jamaica, suriname, polynesia	scan, passport, custom, usa, fakemarket, scans, fake, credit/debit, bill, license, card, products, master/visa/amex, licence, cards, pdf, utility, driving, orders, great, templates, passports, buyers, lsd, buyer, back, drivers, template, escrow, psd	•••

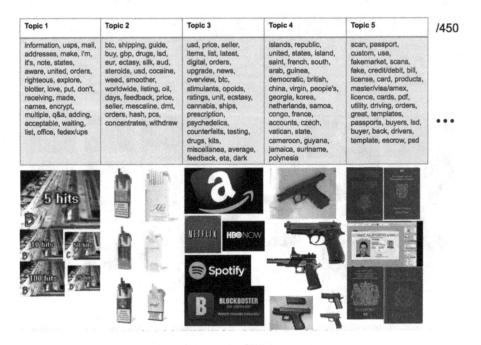

Fig. 8. 5 out of 450 Topics trained on DNMs listings

Top terms for this text topic: pills, usd, meds, btc, buy, philippines, message, ritalin, generic, idealpills, ambien, shipping, xanax, product, codeine, adderall, note, treat, listings, valium, roche, delivered, ship, anxiety, alprazolam

Top terms for this text topic: cocaine, quality, meth, pure, gram, high, crystal, grams, united, uncut, purity, kingdom, price, ice, stimulants, states, speed, free, coke, mdma, usa, shards, canada, sample, methamphetamine, flake, clean, fishscale

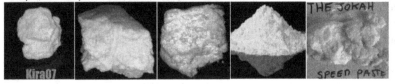

Fig. 9. Drug Images Distinguished via CNN-Predicted association with 450 Textual Topics, allowing analysts the ability to identify items like drugs via images and text.

Top terms for this text topic: watch, guide, make, pictures, book, replica, hacking, digital, security, check,
(1 of 40 topics) windows, onion, optiman, jpg, price, case, blackhand, aaa, ebook, original

**Images with
highest weights
for this topic:**

Top terms for this text topic: blackhand, guide, hacking, complete, policy, digital, collection, orders, goods,
(1 of 450 topics) chemistry, experience, early, book, bulk, finalize, refund, product, edition, ship, lsd

**Images with
highest weights
for this topic:**

Top terms for this text topic: package, goods, days, reship, shipping, gram, product, contact, quality, free, yall,
(1 of 450 topics) provide, funds, feedback, arrival, listing, lost, refund, heroin, orders

**Images with
highest weights
for this topic:**

Fig. 10. Larger-Dimension Topic Models lead to more specific terms and images. The
40-topic model had a topic for books and watches, while the 450-topic model had
separate topics for watches and books individually.

The greater number of topics also creates many topics that cannot be deci-
phered based on the top terms and top images alone. Some single topics contain
terms and images from a wide semantic range, including a mixture of pills, marijuana, counterfeit currency, and various software. These topics may represent a
way to distinguish listings, but they do not provide much information on their
own. It is possible that further cleaning of the text data could make these multimodal relationships more readily decipherable.

Retrieval Tasks. One potential application of this type of neural network on
Darknet marketplace datasets is the ability to see how different images relate in
terms of predicted contextual text topics. Images of guns are near other images of
guns, images of passports are near other images of passports, etc. This trained
model allows not only for comparison of different images present within the

dataset, but allows for querying of nearest neighbors based on any given image unseen during the training process. For example, Fig. 11 illustrates that the 450-topic network predicts that an image of fire not in the training set would be seen in listings associated with images of pipes and marijuana. The network is capable of relating images in the context of the dataset, which could provide valuable threads to pull on and discover new insights.

These threads can be found by utilizing LDA to infer topic distributions based on arbitrary text, and finding nearest neighbors to that text. If an analyst is curious what images would be associated with any collection of terms in the dataset, they can utilize the LDA model to infer the topic distribution for those terms and then find the nearest neighboring images in that space via Jensen-Shannon Divergence [13] the similarity measure. For example, as shown in Fig. 12, an analyst curious about finding hacker materials on the darknet could query "hack exploit script", which retrieves nearest neighbor images that are screenshots that are found within listings. In this case, it is not immediately obvious why the text and the images are related. Upon further analysis of the source listing the screenshots originated from, we see that these screenshot images are part of tutorials explaining how a customer can purchase scripts. From this observation, we can infer that listings that sell scripts and have screenshots may be catering to less experienced customers who may not know how to exchange cryptocurrency for illicit products. Automated predicting of images' positions in the LDA textual topic space allows for analysts to create and refine queries that can lead to revealed relations and further insights into ever-changing listing categories on DNMs.

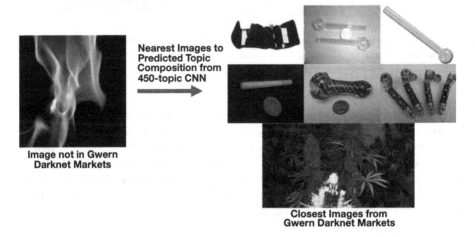

Nearest Images to Predicted Topic Composition from 450-topic CNN

Image not in Gwern Darknet Markets

Closest Images from Gwern Darknet Markets

Fig. 11. Image of Fire (not in the dataset) is predicted to be related to Images from the Gwern Darknet Markets Archive that would be in Listings of the same Textual Topic Composition (i.e. Fire and Smoking)

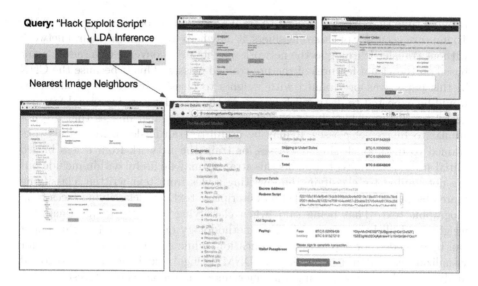

Fig. 12. The LDA-inferred topic composition of the query "hack exploit script" is nearest to predicted topic-compositions (450 dimensions) of screenshots, originating from tutorials detailing steps one would take to purchase a script

5 Discussion and Future Work

The technique of creating image descriptors to associate with textual semantics presents ways to summarize large multimodal datasets without much initial human input. Adding images to visualizations of textual topics could help analysts obtain a more-complete view of what a dataset contains. In addition, the ability to query based on images may allow analysts to help find items that may be more difficult to describe with words accurately.

The methods demonstrated in this paper are not for finding a needle in the haystack, but for finding if a certain color of hay is mixed within the haystack. Viewing topic summaries, and querying all of the topic-inferred media, does not present analysts with complete knowledge of datasets' outliers. The goal is to further support analysts' ability to pull at strings, further learning about the composition until they can form their own generalizations about the data and deepen their explorations. More tools generated from the CNN presented in this paper could help further analysis once analyst generalizations are settled. Image retrieval based on image similarity, not necessarily semantic similarity could be done by retrieving based on the top pooling layer output of the CNN before the fully-connected layers [7,18]. Classifiers could be built with Support Vector Machines or newly trained fully-connected layers, training on the pooling layer output, which is fine-tuned to distinguish visual features within the dataset. These classifiers could identify hand-labeled instances and future data of interest, such as classify images from the TOR Image Categories dataset [6]. Building supervised classifiers would likely take less hand-labeling time and less model training time than what is needed to train a neural network from scratch [7,18]. To improve accuracy of these classifiers, it may help to retrain the neural network without transfer-learning as the network weights may converge to a saddle point based on the visual features of the pre-trained classes. This is because the CNN in this paper was pre-trained with weights to classify ImageNet [5] and thus would be expected to distinguish images in the new datasets via visual features useful for distinguishing ImageNet classes. To distinguish images that are not similar to ImageNet classes, it may be useful to transfer-learn from a network trained to distinguish similar classes, or train the network from a less biased initial state. Examples of domains this strategy may be useful within include but are not limited to: classifying handwriting styles from text written, classifying more abstract illustrations based on descriptive text, and classifying faces from biographic text. That being said, when classifying everyday items, ImageNet weights will likely perform well. The methodology demonstrated in this paper can be extended for supervised classification, while simultaneously allowing for visualizations of domain-specific (e.g. DNM listings) text-image relations to aid analysts in identifying existing and emerging semantic areas of interest.

Many datasets, especially collections of web resources, are multimodal and lend themselves to similar methods of self-supervised learning as mentioned in this paper. Future work could also investigate how other media, and other neural network architecture, could relate more media forms to LDA topic space. This method may be able to bootstrap analysis and classification of many domains and media, potentially linking text, images, video, and audio all to the same semantic space for a more complete view of any given dataset.

Future work may identify how to adapt existing LDA visualization strategies [19–21] to include images in conjunction with the existing textual elements. This could allow for analysts to not only better understand a dataset from LDA-categorization of text and images, but allow for greater exploration of hypothesis' based on the multimodal nature of many datasets. To better understand web content such as Darknet Markets, analysts will greatly benefit from tools that can automatically summarize and can enable the exploration of inter-relations between modalities of a dataset. In this work we propose initial tools for relatively computationally inexpensive, automatic semantic classification of multimodal datasets, and demonstrate these tools' abilities via Darknet Market data.

6   Conclusion

This paper presents tools to support analysts in quickly associating images with textual semantic features, within the context of a multimodal dataset. As demonstrated on Wikipedia and Darknet Market data, one can obtain relatively-fast automatic semantic classification of text and images, with almost no human preprocessing or labeling of the data. This can give analysts more complete knowledge of topics that compose a dataset, where text alone is not always fully descriptive of the multimodal documents' contents. This is especially useful in cases where the text is not very informative on its own, such as the Darknet Market listings analyzed in this paper, where many terms are artifacts of documents that can not be trivially removed. Beyond summarization, we demonstrate how the trained CNN and LDA models in conjunction can retrieve documents and images based on both text and image queries. This can allow analysts to better explore areas not obvious in the topic model, such as the relation between tutorials and hacking scripts found in the Darknet. Additionally, almost no domain knowledge is needed to train these models, meaning the methods in this paper could serve as a "launching point" into exploration of unorganized multimodal datasets. Future work could extend tools and workflows taken from this launching point into more fine-grain tools for supervised classification and visualization of multimodal relations of the data. The combination of transfer-learning and unsupervised topic modeling result in a relatively-quick method for analysts to gain initial understanding of large multimodal datasets' compositions, such as Darknet Markets, without requiring significant analyst experience in the domain of the dataset.

References

1. How the feds took down the Dread Pirate Roberts — Ars Technica. https://arstechnica.com/tech-policy/2013/10/how-the-feds-took-down-the-dread-pirate-roberts/
2. Blei, D., Ng, A., Jordan, M.: Latent Dirichlet allocation. jmlr.org http://www.jmlr.org/papers/v3/blei03a.html
3. Buhrmester, M., Kwang, T.: Amazon's mechanical turk: a new source of inexpensive, yet high-quality, data? journals.sagepub.com http://journals.sagepub.com/doi/abs/10.1177/1745691610393980
4. Chollet, F.: Deep learning with Python (2017). https://dl.acm.org/citation.cfm?id=3203489
5. Deng, J., Dong, W., Socher, R., Li, L.J., Li, K., Fei-Fei, L.: ImageNet: a large-scale hierarchical image database. Technical report. http://www.image-net.org
6. Fidalgo, E., Alegre, E., González-Castro, V., Fernández-Robles, L.: Illegal activity categorisation in DarkNet based on image classification using CREIC method. In: Pérez García, H., Alfonso-Cendón, J., Sánchez González, L., Quintián, H., Corchado, E. (eds.) SOCO/CISIS/ICEUTE -2017. AISC, vol. 649, pp. 600–609. Springer, Cham (2018). https://doi.org/10.1007/978-3-319-67180-2_58
7. Gomez, L., Patel, Y., Rusiñol, M.: Self-supervised learning of visual features through embedding images into text topic spaces. openaccess.thecvf.com http://openaccess.thecvf.com/content_cvpr_2017/papers/Gomez_Self-Supervised_Learning_of_CVPR_2017_paper.pdf
8. Grant, S., Cordy, J.: Estimating the optimal number of latent concepts in source code analysis. ieeexplore.ieee.org https://ieeexplore.ieee.org/abstract/document/5601828/
9. Branwen, G., et al.: Dark net market archives, 2011–2015 (2015). https://www.gwern.net/DNM-archives
10. He, K., Zhang, X., Ren, S., Sun, J.: Delving deep into rectifiers: surpassing human-level performance on ImageNet classification. Technical report. https://arxiv.org/pdf/1502.01852v1.pdf
11. Porter, K.: Analyzing the DarkNetMarkets subreddit for evolutions of tools and trends using LDA topic modeling. Digit. Invest. (2018). https://www.sciencedirect.com/science/article/pii/S1742287618302020

12. Krizhevsky, A., Sutskever, I., Hinton, G.: Imagenet classification with deep convolutional neural networks. papers.nips.cc http://papers.nips.cc/paper/4824-imagenet-classification-with-deep-convolutional-neural-networks
13. Lin, J.: Divergence measures based on the Shannon entropy. ieeexplore.ieee.org https://ieeexplore.ieee.org/abstract/document/61115/
14. Matilla, D., González-Castro, V., Fernández-Robles, L., Fidalgo, E., Al-Nabki, W.: Color SIFT descriptors to categorize illegal activities in images of onion domains. Technical report. https://www.torproject.org/
15. McCallum, A.K.: MALLET: a machine learning for language toolkit (2002). http://mallet.cs.umass.edu
16. Munksgaard, R., Demant, J., Branwen, G.: A replication and methodological critique of the study "Evaluating drug trafficking on the Tor Network". Int. J. Drug Policy **35**, 92–96 (2016). https://doi.org/10.1016/j.drugpo.2016.02.027
17. Pan, S.J., Yang, Q.: A survey on transfer learning (2009). https://doi.org/10.1109/TKDE.2009.191, http://socrates.acadiau.ca/courses/comp/dsilver/NIPS95
18. Patel, Y., Gomez, L., Gomez, R., Rusiñol, M., Karatzas, D., Jawahar, C.V.: Text-TopicNet - self-supervised learning of visual features through embedding images on semantic text spaces, July 2018. http://arxiv.org/abs/1807.02110
19. Paul, C.L., et al.: TexTonic: interactive visualization for exploration and discovery of very large text collections. Inf. Vis. (2018). https://doi.org/10.1177/1473871618785390, http://journals.sagepub.com/doi/10.1177/1473871618785390
20. Sievert, C., Shirley, K.E.: LDAvis: a method for visualizing and interpreting topics. Technical report (2014). http://www.aclweb.org/anthology/W14-3110
21. Singh, J., Zerr, S., Siersdorfer, S.: Structure-aware visualization of text corpora. In: Proceedings of the 2017 Conference on Conference Human Information Interaction and Retrieval - CHIIR 2017, pp. 107–116. ACM Press, New York (2017). https://doi.org/10.1145/3020165.3020182, http://dl.acm.org/citation.cfm?doid=3020165.3020182
22. Szegedy, C., Vanhoucke, V., Ioffe, S., Shlens, J., Wojna, Z.: Rethinking the inception architecture for computer vision, December 2015. http://arxiv.org/abs/1512.00567
23. Tsikrika, T., Popescu, A., Kludas, J.: Overview of the Wikipedia image retrieval task at ImageCLEF 2011. ims-sites.dei.unipd.it http://ims-sites.dei.unipd.it/documents/71612/86377/CLEF2011wn-ImageCLEF-TsikrikaEt2011.pdf
24. Yosinski, J., Clune, J., Bengio, Y.: How transferable are features in deep neural networks? papers.nips.cc http://papers.nips.cc/paper/5347-how-transferable-are-features-in-deep-n%E2%80%A6

Policy Creation for Enterprise-Level Data Sharing

Linda Briesemeister[1], Woodrow Gustafson[2], Grit Denker[1],
April Martin[2], Karsten Martiny[1], Ron Moore[2], Dusko Pavlovic[3],
and Mark St. John[2(✉)]

[1] SRI International, Menlo Park, CA, USA
[2] Pacific Science & Engineering, San Diego, CA, USA
MarkSt.John@pacific-science.com
[3] University of Hawaii, Honolulu, HI, USA

Abstract. Enterprises, including military, law enforcement, medical, financial, and commercial organizations, must often share large quantities of data, some potentially sensitive, with many other enterprises. A key issue, the mechanics of data sharing, involves how to precisely and unambiguously specify which data to share with which partner or group of partners. This issue can be addressed through a system of formal data sharing policy definitions and automated enforcement. Several challenges arise when specifying enterprise-level data sharing policies. A first challenge involves the scale and complexity of data types to be shared. An easily understood method is required to represent and visualize an enterprise's data types and their relationships so that users can quickly, easily, and precisely specify which data types and relationships to share. A second challenge involves the scale and complexity of data sharing partners. Enterprises typically have many partners involved in different projects, and there are often complex hierarchies among groups of partners that must be considered and navigated to specify which partners or groups of partners to include in a data sharing policy. A third challenge is that defining policies formally, given the first two challenges of scale and complexity, requires complex, precise language, but these languages are difficult to use by non-specialists. More useable methods of policy specification are needed. Our approach was to develop a software wizard that walks users through a series of steps for defining a data sharing policy. A combination of innovative and well known methods is used to address these challenges of scale, complexity, and usability.

Keywords: Cybersecurity · Privacy · User interface · Design

1 Introduction

1.1 Enterprise Data Sharing

Enterprises are large, distributed, information-rich organizations, including military, law enforcement, medical, financial, and commercial organizations. Enterprises must often share large quantities of data, some potentially sensitive, with many other

A. Moallem (Ed.): HCII 2019, LNCS 11594, pp. 249–265, 2019.
https://doi.org/10.1007/978-3-030-22351-9_17

enterprises. However, data sharing is rarely, if ever, all or none. Rather, specific types of data are shared with specific partners to achieve specific objectives. Data sharing may be on-going to achieve long-term objectives, or it may be a one-time event to achieve a specific transient objective. For example, financial institutions may regularly share data with the government and with other financial institutions, or they may share data about a specific transaction with law enforcement to track an illegal transaction. Similarly, military organizations may regularly share some data with other militaries to coordinate mutual defense, or they may share specific data with a host nation to support a disaster relief operation. Once the relief operation is complete, the data sharing ceases.

Enterprise data sharing, and personal data sharing, as well, involves two central concerns: deciding whether to accept the risks of any particular sharing of data, and how to correctly specify that sharing of data, including the specific partners to receive the data, and any other parameters, such as a specific time period for data sharing to achieve the enterprise's objectives. Another concern is how to incorporate innovative cryptographic methods, such as multi-party computation and differential privacy, to obfuscate the details of shared data while still achieving the benefits of sharing data. For example, using multi-party computation, data could be shared in encrypted form and combined with encrypted data from other parties to compute results relevant to all the parties. Parties only see their own data, but everyone sees the results [1]. The framework described here provides a path forward for incorporating these technologies, and work on this capability is underway.

2   Data Sharing Risks and Benefits

Deciding whether to share specific data with specific partners involves evaluating two competing values: (1) the risk that the partner will exploit the shared data in unintended ways and cause harm, and (2) the benefit of sharing the data with the partner to achieve an objective. In most cases, the benefits should outweigh the risks in order for data sharing to be acceptable. Even if the risks are high, if the benefit is higher still, then sharing should typically proceed.

The risk of sharing data can be broken down into two factors: the sensitivity of the data, that is, the amount of harm its unintended exploitation could create, and the trust in the data sharing partner to not exploit, or further share, the data.

A simple equation for computing risk from sensitivity and trust is based on the decision making and actuarial formula that risk is the product of the chance of an event and the value of that event. Chance is translated to trust – the likelihood of the recipient keeping shared data safe and not exploiting it. Value is translated as sensitivity – the amount of harm that would result from exploitation. These concepts are captured in formula (1), where (1 − trust) is the likelihood of exploitation.

$$\text{Risk} = (1 - \text{trust}) * \text{sensitivity} \tag{1}$$

Trust in partners, data sensitivity, and data sharing benefits are all subjective assessments. A consensus approach to assessing trust is to assess the ability, integrity, and beneficence of the data sharing partner [5]. Ability involves the technical abilities of the partner to keep the shared data secret. Integrity involves the degree to which the partner abides by law and order and upholds agreements. Beneficence involves the relationship between the enterprise and the partner, and the extent to which the partner is invested in maintaining that relationship by upholding the agreement not to exploit the data. These assessments are then combined into an overall assessment of trust in the partner.

A standard approach to assessing sensitivity is to assess the amount of harm that could be caused if the data were exploited. This harm can be estimated in terms of money, personnel, reputation, equipment lost, and the value of missed or thwarted objectives.

Data sharing benefits can be assessed as a combination of the value of the objective for which the data is being shared and the increased probability of success of the objective given that the data is shared. If sharing the data greatly increases the chances of success, and the objective is valuable, then there is high benefit to the sharing.

Developing reliable and valid methods for assessing trust, sensitivity, and benefits are important challenges. Here, though, we focus on the mechanics of data sharing and several technical challenges to specifying data sharing correctly and effectively.

3 Data Sharing Policy Specification Challenges and Solutions

The mechanics of data sharing can be addressed through a system of formal data sharing policy definitions and automated enforcement. The authors and others have collaborated to develop an experimental enterprise-level system for sharing data in effective, privacy-preserving ways, included tailored data access control based on explicit data sharing polices [6, 8]. In this system, data sharing partners make data requests. Incoming data requests are evaluated at a policy decision point. A policy decision engine assesses the data request against the data sharing policies in force at that time and returns a decision to allow or deny the request. Additionally, policies can be written to include constraints on data sharing, such as only share police record data for residents who are at least 18 years old, or only share a count of residents testing positive for tuberculosis rather than the names of each individual who has tested positive. The sharing decision, to allow or deny the request, and any constraints on sharing are forwarded to a policy enforcement point that creates policy-safe queries to retrieve the requested data from a database. This separation into a Policy Decision Point (PDP) and a Policy Enforcement Point (PEP) follows standard approaches (cf. for example XACML [11]) and ensures that policy decisions can be made without the need to access data—only the policy enforcement point requires accessing data instances.

A first challenge to precisely specifying data sharing policies involves the scale and complexity of data types. Enterprises typically have many different types of data, and these data types are not well represented by a flat list of types that users could scan through and check off to be shared. Further, data types cannot be organized naturally into a hierarchy. Rather, data types bear complex relationships with one another.

Since data types are typically not organized into a hierarchy, there is no root that could be used to start the exploration of data types. Instead, data types can be organized from many perspectives, such as types of entities (people, ships, money, resources) or domains (financial, personal, military). Second, there are loops in the relations among data types such that a data type would appear in multiple locations in a hierarchy (for example, persons are citizens of nations and nations have places of interest to which persons travel, meaning that both persons and nations would appear in multiple locations in a hierarchy). Instead, the relations among data types is better represented as a connected graph or network. A method is therefore needed to visualize a network of data types so that users can navigate among the data types and specify which types to add to a data sharing policy.

A second challenge involves the scale and complexity of data sharing partners. Enterprises typically have many partners involved in different projects, and there are often complex hierarchies among groups of partners that must be considered and navigated to specify which partners or groups of partners to include in a data sharing policy. For example, an enterprise may wish to share data all nongovernmental organizations (NGOs), only with health care NGOs, or only with Doctors without Borders and the Red Cross. Logical expressions, including "AND," "OR," and "NOT" provide a precise way to specify arbitrary sets of partners, but they can be difficult to use. More intuitive methods are needed.

A third challenge is that defining policies formally, given the first two challenges of scale and complexity, requires complex, precise language. This complexity and precision can be achieved in formal logic languages, such as Flora-2, but they are difficult to use by non-specialists, such as members of enterprises who need to define data sharing policies to accomplish their objectives.

Here, we describe three methods for addressing these three challenges. These methods involve (1) representing an enterprise's data as a semantic network and developing a tool that visualizes the network and allows users to navigate the network and designate which data types to share, (2) an attribute-based filter metaphor for specifying sets of partners with whom to share specific data, and (3) a software wizard that walks users through the steps of specifying a data sharing policy, including which data to share with whom, without requiring users to learn complex, formal languages for policy specification.

3.1 Specifying Data Sets

Throughout the system, including the Policy Decision Point and Policy Enforcement Point, the data available for sharing is represented by a common data model (CDM). The CDM specifies the relationships among data classes, their subclasses, and their properties and is represented in Web Ontology Language (OWL). A CDM visualization was developed for the project, called the CDM Explorer, that reads in the CDM specification, and visualizes it as a network to users. Users can navigate around the network to select data classes and properties to add to a data sharing policy. While there are many network visualization tools, the CDM Explorer has several specific capabilities including visualization and navigation of a semantic network, specifically, ability to select data types and properties for inclusion in a data sharing policy, and ability to specify constraints on which data are shared.

To begin exploring the network, the user is first presented with a list of data classes. To keep the list to a manageable length, subclasses are hidden under their superclasses until the superclass is expanded (see Fig. 1). The figure shows that the superclass Physical Entity has been expanded to show two subclasses, Mobile Entity and Stationary Entity. Mobile Entity has also been expanded. Currently, in the CDM, the only subclass of Mobile Entity is Ship.

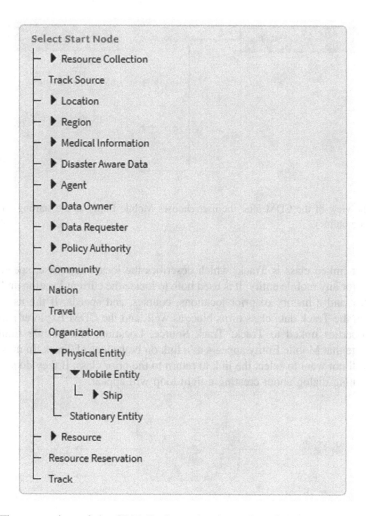

Fig. 1. The entry view of the CDM Explorer showing a list of data classes arranged into superclasses and their subclasses.

If the user chooses Mobile Entity, the CDM Explorer opens a view of the CDM network (see Fig. 2). The Mobile Entity class is shown on the left in blue, indicating that it is a selected data class. Mobile Entity is linked to four other data classes: Nation,

Organization, Resource, and Track. These linked data classes are called object properties of Mobile Entity. Rolling over an object property, such as Nation, reveals the relationship between the two data classes. In this case, the relationship between Mobile Entity and Nation is "Owner Nation." This link specifies the nation, if any, that owns each mobile entity. Similarly, Organization specifies the organization, if any, that owns each mobile entity.

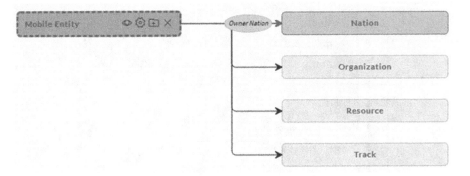

Fig. 2. The view of the CDM after the user chooses Mobile Entity as the starting data class. (Color figure online)

Another linked class is Track, which describes the location, course, speed, and a timestamp for any mobile entity. It is used both to locate the current location and course of an entity and a history of prior locations, courses, and speeds. If the user selects Track, then the Track data class turns blue, as well, and the CDM Explorer shows the object properties linked to Track: Track Source, Location, and Mobile Entity (see Fig. 3). Note that Mobile Entity appears as a link on both sides of Track. In most cases, the user will not want to select the link to return to the prior class. If they do select that link, a warning dialog about creating a tight loop will appear.

Fig. 3. View of the CDM Explorer after Track is selected. (Color figure online)

As shown in Fig. 3, Track has three data properties shown inside the Track box: Course, Speed, and Time. Track also has three object properties shown as links on the right side of the figure. Track is also selected for focus in the CDM Explorer, as indicated by the dashed lines around the box.

The location data for a track is specified through the link to the object property Location. The rationale for this CDM layout choice is that locations are in themselves complex data types. For example, locations can be expressed in different coordinate systems and units. Hence, we have added a hierarchy for these data types into our model. The examples shown here express geographic locations in latitude and longitude via a Location subclass called Geodetic2DLocation.

Users can back up and remove classes by selecting the X in a data class box. Users can also select subclasses by selecting the folder icon next to the X in a data class box. In Fig. 4, the user has selected the Ship subclass of Mobile Entity, and then selected the folder icon again to show subclasses of Ship.

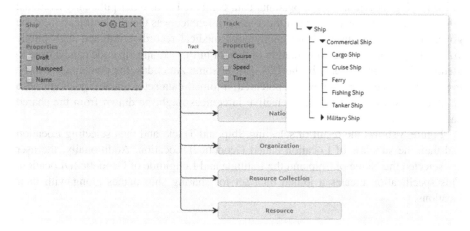

Fig. 4. A snapshot from the CDM Explorer tool showing the Ship data class, it's three data properties (blue box on the left), multiple subclasses of Ship (white box on the right), and five links to other data classes (blue box for Track and grey links in the middle). (Color figure online)

Because Ship is a subclass of Mobile Entity, it inherits each of the Mobile Entity object properties: Nation, Organization, Resource, and Track. If Mobile Entity had any data properties, Ship would have inherited those properties, as well. Similarly, if the user selected the subclass Cargo Ship, then Cargo ship would inherit all five object properties and three data properties of Ship. Cargo Ship might also have its own object and data properties, such as Cargo Tunnage to add.

Joined Data Sets and the CDM. An important realization from the project was that data is almost always shared in joined sets, such as ship names and locations during a military or law enforcement operation or patient names and disease states during a humanitarian crisis. Locations alone have little or no meaning, as do ship names alone. It is only the combination of ship name and location that reveals information and may be sensitive. In other words, ship names alone cannot be exploited; nor can locations; but the combination of ship names and locations can be exploited and therefore are sensitive. For example the names of ballistic missile submarines and their locations is extremely sensitive. Furthermore, the data need to be correlated in the sense that ship names are correlated with their locations rather than simply providing two uncorrelated lists of names and locations. A joined data set specifies this correlated sharing of data.

While joined data sets is the correct level of analysis for assessing data sensitivity, assessing sensitivity is nontrivial. For example, while the names and locations of ballistic missile submarines is extremely sensitive, the names and locations of commercial fishing vessels is not typically very sensitive. One must think carefully about the instances of joined data within a joined data set and whether there are any sensitive instances. Constraints on a joined data set (see below) can significantly change the sensitivity of shared data depending of whether they allow sensitive instances to be shared or constrain them from sharing.

Finally, sensitive data can be inferred from shared data. An example is re-identifying individuals from personal data combined with other publically available information. A famous example of this type of inference was the re-identification of the governor of Massachusetts from anonymous medical records combined with public voter rolls [9]. In fact, the combination of data of birth, sex, and zip code can be used to identify 87% of individuals in the U.S. [9]. In some zip codes, the percentage can be even higher. Due to this inference potential, a joined data set's sensitivity should also be assessed with regard to what sensitive inferences might be drawn from the shared data.

Figure 5 shows the result of selecting Ship and Track, and then selecting Location and then the subclass of Location called Geodetic2DLocation. Additionally, the user has selected the Name of Ship and the Latitude and Longitude of Geodetic2DLocation. This specification creates a joined data set for sharing ship names along with their locations.

Fig. 5. Selection of the data classes Ship, Track, and Geodetic2DLocation and the data properties (Ship) Name, Latitude, and Longitude.

Further, it is not sufficient to specify *that* different data items are correlated. It is also necessary to specify *how* these items are connected. For instance, if the names of nations are to be shared jointly with the names of persons, it is ambiguous how persons are to be related to nations (i.e., on what attribute persons and nations ought to be joined). For instance, among other relations, one can chose to share information about a nation's residents, or its citizens. In both cases the result is a join between the classes Nation and Person, but the affected data instances will usually not be identical sets because nations typically have residents who are citizens of a foreign country, and simultaneous have citizens who are residents in a foreign country. These considerations imply that the set of a nation's citizens and a set of a nation's residents would be considerably different from each other. Thus, to prevent any ambiguities, a joined data set needs to precisely specify how classes are linked by including the linking property (shown as the edge labels in the figures), such as "resident of" or "citizen of", in its specification. Consequently, a joined data set specification must always be expressed as a connected subgraph of the CDM.

Constraints. Constraints on data sharing can also be specified within the CDM Explorer. For example, a user could desire to share the ship name and location of just a single ship of interest, for instance, if it were suspected of some illegal activity. In this example, a constraint would be placed on the Name data property in the Ship data class. Figure 6 shows how this constraint is specified. From the Ship data class, the user chooses the gear icon in the upper right corner of the data class box. This action opens a dialog box where the user chooses which property to constrain (Name), then specifies the nature of the constraint as the logical test Equal, and then defines a String with the value of the name of the ship in question. For example, a user could specify that the ship's name equal "Damanzaihao," the name of the world's largest fishing vessel, which was recently detained by Peru for illegal fishing [7]. This approach to specifying constraints is necessary due to the separation of the architecture into decision and enforcement points. The policy decision point does not have access to any actual data, and thus it is not possible to specify policies directly on specific data instances (such as "location of Damanzaihao"). Instead, the policies need to be specified at the level of the data model (i.e., "locations of ships") and then the additional constraint on the ship's name allows the policy enforcement point to restrict shared data to specific instances, as intended.

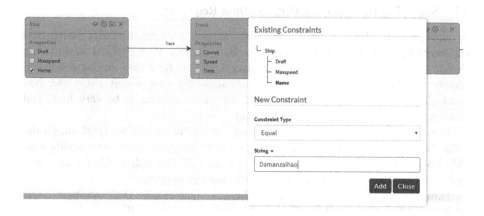

Fig. 6. Adding a constraint on the name of a ship.

In the ship name example, Ship Name is a shared property and part of the joined data set. However, the constraint does not need to be a shared property. Any property can be used as a constraint. For example, a user may have a goal to share persons' names and arrest records but to exclude the arrest records of children. This constraint would involve placing a constraint on the DateOfBirth property in the data class Person. In this case, the constraint is placed on a property that is not shared as part of the policy. That is, if the policy is to share names and arrest records, but no other personal information, then DateOfBirth will not be shared. It can still be a source of constraint on shared data, however. Similarly, the sharing of the names of ships and their locations could be limited to a geographical region of interest or to a particular timeframe, such as immediately preceding and following some event of interest.

Summary for Specifying Data Sets. As the CDM grows to include more data classes and properties, the CDM Explorer becomes a critical tool to visualize sections of the network and specify parts of it for sharing in a policy. Even so, familiarity with the CDM and where data classes are located is very helpful. Within a large CDM, it becomes possible to lose track of one's location and begin having difficulty navigating. For this reason, future versions of the CDM Explorer will contain a search tool where a user can specify a data class or property and have that term highlighted in the network. It may also be necessary to highlight related terms since terminology in very large CDMs could become complex. The user could then choose which highlighted instance of the term to explore further. It is also possible to specify two data classes, and have the CDM Explorer find the shortest path between them. This path is likely to be the desired connection path between the classes, and if not, it provides a useful basis for exploring for the desired path. Finally, a zoom capability should also help with navigation issues.

In sum, the CDM Explorer provides a rich and useful method for visualizating the relations among data within the CDM, specifying joined data sets to share, and specifying any desired constraints to place on that sharing.

3.2   Specifying Data Sharing Partners/Data Requesters

An enterprise is likely to have many data sharing partners, hereafter called data requesters because they make requests for data that are then checked against data sharing policies. Specifying one or more data requesters for a data sharing policy can become unwieldy. For instance, if each data requester were simply listed and then checked off for inclusion in a policy, that list would potentially be very long, and checking requesters would be prone to errors.

Instead, policies are likely to refer to groups of data requesters who perform similar tasks, therefore, choosing requesters based on their attributes could substantially simplify specifying sets of data requesters for a data sharing policy. Useful attributes include the user's role or tasking, nationality, and organization.

However, using logical expressions, such as "[attribute-1 AND (attribute-2 OR attribute-3)] but NOT attribute-4" to write attribute-based specifications is likely to exceed most users' training. The general public is well known to have difficulty both reading and writing complex logical expressions including the correct use of "AND," "OR," and "NOT" [2–4]. Instead, the user interface needs to use a more readily usable metaphor to specify attribute-based specifications of data requesters. We chose a fairly common method of specifying search filters that is more natural and well known for most users. As described in more detail below, users select one or more attributes to filter the set of data requesters. They can also select among members of an attribute, if specific members need to be included or excluding from a policy. For example, a user could select epidemiologists as the role and all nations as the nation. Or a user could select specific nations or even exclude specific nations from a data sharing policy. This method provides similar expressibility as formal logical expressions, but within a more intuitive metaphor for users.

Finally, membership in user groups changes over time, yet policies should still apply to the current membership of a group. For example, if the Centers for Disease Control bring on a new epidemiologist, any policy that shared data with CDC epidemiologists should share data with that new epidemiologist without requiring a change to the policy. This requirement is different from standard uses of search filters. Search filters are typically used to identify an enumerated set of things. Here, the set of search filters itself becomes the data requester specification within a policy, and the enumerated list of things it identifies may change over time as group memberships change.

In sum, there are four requirements that data requester specification must address

- Many data requesters in the system
- Attribute-based specification
- Alternative user interface or metaphor to formal logical expressions
- Dynamic specifications as members of user groups change over time

Details of Search Filters. Figure 7 shows the user interface developed for specifying data sharing partners via attribute-based filters. The attributes, such as role, nation, and organization, are shown in the top row. Users can open an attribute and select all or some of the choices. For example, under "role," there are choices for care providers, response coordinators, situation monitors, epidemiologists, and other more specific roles. These roles were developed for a use-case involving humanitarian assistance, specifically a pandemic. A more generic interface would have many additional roles and include the ability to search for relevant roles.

The currently specified set of filters is shown in the center of the display. Epidemiologist was chosen as the role, and all nations, excluding the United Kingdom, was chosen as the nation. Each filter is represented as a "pill," and the two filters are combined as an intersection. The explicit use of logical operators "AND" and "OR" was avoided, and icons for intersection and union were used in their stead. While these icons are unambiguous, they are more obscure, therefore, a simple explanation and example was provided when a user rolled over them.

The set of data requesters to which the filters resolve is shown at the bottom of the display. This list is provided to give users feedback on the effects of the filters they specify and combine. As filters are specified and combined, the list grows and shinks accordingly. Importantly, however, it is the set of filters and their combination that is provided to the policy rather the enumerated list of partners. By providing the filters, the list is evaluated fresh each time the policy is assessed. As the membership of Epidemiologist changes over time, for example, the list will change as well. This design ensures that a policy consistently refers to the current membership of attributes rather than the membership in effect when the policy was created.

Attribute-based filtering is a fairly common user interface method for narrowing a search. Figure 8 shows an example of filters taken from the website Amazon.com.

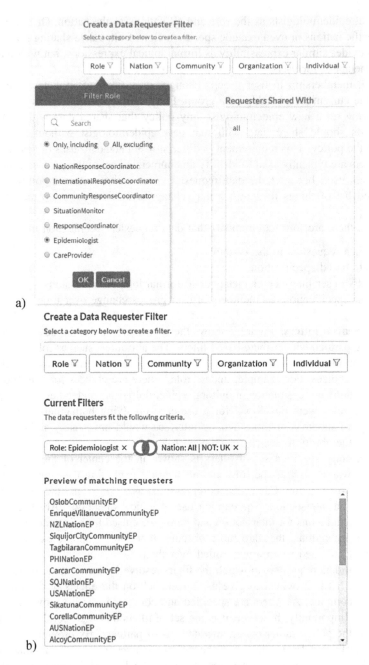

a)

b)

Fig. 7. Data requester search filters. The top figure (a) shows the selection of Epidemiologists from the Role attributed-based filter. The bottom figure (b) shows the creation of two filters, one for Epidemiologists and a second for all Nations except UK. The lower half of the bottom figure shows the list of data requesters who match the two filters.

In the example, attribute categories are shown in bold with their choices shown underneath. Checking multiple boxes within a category is treated as a union, while checking boxes between categories are treated as an intersection, e.g. checking Baldwin and 5 foot leads to just those items that fit both attributes. Selecting a link, an attribute in a category that does not have a checkbox, is treated an a intersection, e.g. under Doorknob function, one chooses either privacy or passage. The revised list of products that meet the filter specification would be shown to the right of the figure.

Fig. 8. Example filters from Amazon.com.

Young and Shneiderman [10] developed an attributed-base filter method that used the filtering of flowing water as a metaphor. Users could create the equivalent of logical queries by selecting attributes and values of attributes, and dragging the attributes to locations on the screen to create a sequence of filters. Their method allowed arbitrary nesting while our simpler method does not.

Summary for Specifying Data Sharing Partners. This method of attribute-based filters avoids formal logical expressions and instead uses a version of a common method for filtering search results. It scales far better than an enumerated list of data sharing partners and allows a clear way to specify meaningful groups of partners.

3.3 Defining Policies

Once the to-be-shared data and the data sharing partners have been specified, there is still the matter of writing the policy so that it can be evaluated by the policy decision engine when requests for data arrive. The engine requires a formal, precise representation of the

```
@!{BoholNationAllowsNationAggregationToRC}
?pa [ po#allow_sa(?req, ?dd) ] :-
?pa = combined#BHLNationPA,
?req [ po#requester -> ?r ],
((?r = po#isDR_type.po#getDR(prime#ResponseCoordina-
tor))),
?polData = ${
?var4 : prime#Person [
prime#medicalInformation -> ?var5 ],
?var5 : medical#DiseaseStatus [
medical#state -> ?var6 ],
?var3 : prime#Community [
prime#resident -> ?var4 ],
?var0 : prime#NationPolicyAuthority [
prime#nation -> ?var1 ],
?var1 : prime#Nation [
prime#name -> ?var2,
prime#community -> ?var3 ]
},
implies_sharing(?polData, ?req.po#requestFormula, ?con-
str),
?id = "BoholNationAllowsNationAggregationToRC"^^\string,
?descr = "Bohol nation PA allows sharing statistically accu-
rate aggregation of disease state data of its residents at the
level of nation with any Response Coordinator"^^\string,
?prio = 0,
?dd = decisionDetails(?pa, ?req, ?constr, ?startTime,
?endTime, ?id, ?descr, ?prio).
```

Fig. 9. An example of a data sharing policy written in Flora-2.

policy, and there are formal languages designed for this type of specification. Flora-2 (http://flora.sourceforge.net/) is a good example.

However, Flora-2 is a complex language, and as with any formal language, it has a complex and detailed syntax. Only a highly trained user would be able to code a data sharing policy directly into Flora-2 without error, and it would still be a time-consuming process. For example, a host country might decide to share disease status data about its residents with international response coordinators. However, the host country may want to protect its residents' privacy by only providing aggregate counts of how many of its residents have the disease. For this example, the host nation is a fictitious county named Bohol, and the Bohol nation policy authority is the individual who has authority to create data sharing policies concerning the Bohol nation's data. In English, the policy could be stated as "Bohol nation policy authority allows sharing statistically accurate aggregations at the level of nation of disease state data of its residents with any Response Coordinator." Figure 9 shows how this policy could be written in Flora-2. Any typo could break all policy specifications in the system.

The alternative method developed by our project was to create a software wizard that walks users through a process of specifying the components of a data sharing policy, including specifying the joined data set and the data requesters. The user interface of the wizard is designed to support a user who is not trained in logical languages to accurately express a desired data sharing policy. The wizard then turns the policy specification into Flora-2 code for evaluation.

The components of a data sharing policy are:

1. Policy Authority – person who had authority to create a policy and created this policy *(individual)*
2. Decision – permissive or restrictive policy *('allow sharing' or 'disallow sharing')*
3. ID – a unique identifier for each policy *(string)*
4. Name – a short natural language name for the policy *(string)*
5. Description – a natural language description of the policy *(string)*
6. Requesters – which data sharing partners are addressed by this policy *(Disjunctive Normal Form (DNF) of RequesterAttributes)*
7. Data – which data are addressed by this policy *(joined data set)*
8. (optional) Constraints of a sharing decision *(Special Constraint Vocabulary)*
9. (optional) Start and end time for this policy *(DateTime)*
10. Precedence – A number that determines which other policies this policy can override and which policies can override it *(integer)*

Step 1 of the wizard is determined by credentials established while logging onto the system. A policy authority has the ability to set data sharing policies only over a specified set of data that is managed through their credentials. Steps 5, 6, and 7 of the wizard are described above. The remaining steps of the wizard are straight-forward dialogs.

In sum, a software wizard including the CDM Explorer and the attribute-based data requester specifier allows a non-specialist to create detailed and unambiguous data sharing policies.

4 Summary and Conclusions

Enterprises need precise and sophisticated methods for specifying which data to share with which of their partners. A useful approach is to write data sharing policies that explicitly and precisely define data sharing. Three challenges to this approach are (1) the scale and complexity of specifying the data, (2) the scale and complexity of specifying the data sharing partners, and (3) users' limited training in using formal languages to write data sharing policies.

Here, we describe three methods for addressing these three challenges. The scale and complexity of specifying the to-be-shared data is addressed by representing data types owned by an enterprise within a network, or graph, formalism called a common data model (CDM). A CDM Explorer tool visualizes the network and allows users to explore the network and designate a connected subgraph of data types to share. The CDM formalism suits the nature of the relations among data types, and the CDM Explorer provides a graphic way to visualize the network and specify data types to share. The CDM Explore also provides a method for specifying constraints on which data to share.

The scale and complexity of specifying data sharing partners, also called data requesters, is addressed by developing an attribute-based filter metaphor for specifying sets of data requesters. While writing logical expressions to specify sets of data requesters would be difficult for many users, attribute-based filters are a common metaphor for searching and filtering items, for example, on Amazon.com. Unlike most such filter tools, however, the filters themselves are written into the data sharing policy rather than the resulting enumerated list of items. Using the filters makes the policy dynamic and sensitive to changes in group membership over time so that a policy will resolve to the correct set of data requesters over time.

Users' limited training in formal languages is addressed by developing a software wizard that incorporates the CDM Explorer tool and the attributed-based filter tool and walks users through the steps of specifying a data sharing policy. The resulting specification is then rewritten into a formal language for evaluation by the policy decision engine.

The structure of the CDM and its visualization within the CDM Explorer and the attribute-based data requester filters scale better than enumerated lists of data types and requesters, and they are much easier to use than formal languages and logical expressions. Together, these tools create an innovative and highly useful system for specifying data sharing policies for enterprises. Given the prevalence of data sharing among enterprises and the risks of inadvertent sharing and exploitation, effective and usable tools to support precise data sharing are essential.

The approach should generalize well. Any types of data and relationships among data types can be represented in a CDM and then visualized in the CDM Explorer. Additionally, there are no in-principle limits to the types of constraints that could be imposed on which data to share, though new constraint types would have to be added to the constraint dialog. The approach is also general in terms of data requesters, groups of requesters, and attributes, though new attributes would have to be added to the dialog, or a method would have to be developed to automatically add attributes from a description. Consequently, the approach should be useful for a wide variety of different types of enterprises and data sharing purposes.

Acknowledgements. This research was developed with funding from the Defense Advanced Research Projects Agency (DARPA). The views, opinions and/or findings expressed are those of the author and should not be interpreted as representing the official views or policies of the Department of Defense or the U.S. Government. Approved for Public Release, Distribution Unlimited.

References

1. Du, W., Atallah, M.J.: Secure multi-party computation problems and their applications: a review and open problems. In: Proceedings of the 2001 Workshop on New Security Paradigms, pp. 13–22. ACM, September 2001
2. Essens, P.J., McCann, C.A., Hartevelt, M.A.: An experimental study of the interpretation of logical operators in database querying. Acta Physiol. **78**(1–3), 201–225 (1991)
3. Greene, S.L., Devlin, S.J., Cannata, P.E., Gomez, L.M.: No IFs, ANDs, or ORs: a study of database querying. Int. J. Man Mach. Stud. **32**(3), 303–326 (1990)
4. Ogden, W., Kaplan, C.: The use of AND and OR in a natural language computer interface. In: Proceedings of the Human Factors Society Annual Meeting, vol. 30, no. 8, pp. 829–833. SAGE Publications, Los Angeles, September 1986
5. Mayer, R.C., Davis, J.H., Schoorman, F.D.: An integrative model of organizational trust. Acad. Manag. Rev. **20**(3), 709–734 (1995)
6. Myers, K., et al.: Privacy technologies for controlled information sharing in coalition operations. In: Proceedings of the Symposium on Knowledge System for Coalition Operations, Los Angeles, CA (2017)
7. Seafoodsource, 9 July 2018. www.seafoodsource.com
8. St. John, M., et al.: Enterprise-level private data sharing: framework and user interface concepts. In: Proceedings of the 2018 Applied Human Factors and Ergonomics Conference, AHFE, Orlando, FL, July 2018
9. Sweeney, L.: Weaving technology and policy together to maintain confidentiality. J. Law Med. Ethics **25**(2–3), 98–110 (1997)
10. Young, D., Shneiderman, B.: A graphical filter/flow representation of Boolean queries: a prototype implementation and evaluation. J. Am. Soc. Inf. Sci. **44**(6), 327–339 (1993)
11. OASIS Standard: eXtensible Access Control Markup Language (XACML) Version 3.0, January 2013. https://www.oasis-open.org/committees/xacml

Classification of Web History Tools Through Web Analysis

João Rafael Gonçalves Evangelista[(✉)],
Dacyr Dante de Oliveira Gatto, and Renato José Sassi

Universidade Nove de Julho – UNINOVE, São Paulo, SP 01504-000, Brazil
jrafal607@gmail.com

Abstract. Web pages may contain various types of sensitive information exposed, such as user login information. Even after these pages have been corrected, the sensitive information, once exposed, can be found through the web history tools. These tools make snapshots of web pages, that is, capture the state of the pages in the most varied periods. Although these tools are widely used, it is not known which web history tool is the most accessed. A method to find out which web history tool is the most accessed is by means of classification using the web analytics technique. Therefore, in view of this scenario, the objective of this work was to classify web history tools through web analysis. The methodology used was the descriptive with quantitative approach. As for the technical procedures, this work is characterized as experimental to verify if the technique of web analysis is able to classify web history tools. The results show that the technique of web analysis produces indicators capable of classifying the web history tools by the total number of accesses received.

Keywords: Web analytics · Web history tools · Open Source Intelligence · Web technologies

1 Introduction

People are increasingly sharing information on the internet. Practices such as publishing employee lists on organizational web pages allow people with bad intentions to identify easily company employees among millions of social media users [1].

In addition to the information shared on the internet by users, other sensitive information may also be exposed. A badly configured web page can leave unprotected information such as user logins, database settings, information about active servers in the domain, services in operation, and other types of sensitive information.

Even after correcting the web pages, we can find the sensitive information exposed using web history tools. Web history tools work like a repository, collecting and archiving web pages periodically [2].

The concept used to describe the collection of information from open sources, as well as the techniques and tools used to acquire this information is Open Source Intelligence (OSINT) [3].

© Springer Nature Switzerland AG 2019
A. Moallem (Ed.): HCII 2019, LNCS 11594, pp. 266–276, 2019.
https://doi.org/10.1007/978-3-030-22351-9_18

Web history tools are available on the internet, but not known which is the most accessed. One method to find out which web history tool is most accessed is through web analytics. Web analytics is a technique that extracts indicators about user interaction with a web page.

Web analytics encompasses a variety of activities, such as measuring web traffic, collecting large volumes of data, analyzing web performance, mining corporate data, and visualizing data strategies [4].

Web analytics provide indicators that can analyze and classify pages on the Internet, for example: The total number of hits received in a given time period, the type of device that accessed the page, the average duration of each access, or even the average number of pages accessed.

In view of this scenario, the objective of this work was to classify web history tools through web analysis technique using the Access Rank indicator, in order to find out which are the most accessed web history tools.

2   Theoretical Background

2.1   Web History Tools

With the evolution of the internet, it is simpler to search information. You can search for any word or phrase, and in a few moments, search engines that are capable of generating results. In addition to searching the internet, another important factor for acquiring information is automated capture [5].

For this, systems and tools are developed to facilitate the proper archiving of content. Among the tools available on the internet, we have the web history tools or archiving tools of web pages [5, 6].

Web History tools have the capability to recover and access previously archived Web pages. For your use, it is enough that the user provides the URL of the desired page and navigate among those archived by the web history tool [7].

Internet Archive [8], for example, is the first web history tool to archive web pages. The tool holds more than 360 billion web pages with files since 1996, making it possible to go back in time to view previous versions of archived web pages [6].

To analyze and evaluate web pages in a determined period, web history tools are commonly used. [9] for example, present the use of the web history tool Wayback Machine [10] to highlight the growth in store sales following the introduction of new policies in Italy.

The authors [11] address another application; they present the use of the historic web tool Wayback Machine [10] to confirm the historical accuracy of a classification of informal financial systems, known as shadow banks, in fintech or non-fintech.

2.2   Open Source Intelligence (OSINT)

Open Source Intelligence (OSINT) involves the collection, analysis, and use of data from open sources for intelligent purposes. So, it can be understood that OSINT involves locating, selecting and extracting information from open sources, such as Twitter and Facebook, and, finally, analyzing extracted information [12, 13].

According to the methodology of tests of information security PTES Technical Guideline [14], OSINT, in the simplest of terms, is to find and analyze open sources. In the area of information security, this information collection process aims to produce current and relevant information that is valuable to an attacker or a competitor.

OSINT can act in several types of open sources, such as global media, blogs on the internet, web pages with government reports, satellite images, academic works, Wikipedia, YouTube and Facebook, as well as a series of other information made available through internet and other media resources [15].

The information discovered by OSINT is defined by [16] as information that is publicly available for anyone to acquire this information legally by request, purchase or observation. Usually the practice of Open Sources Intelligence is seen in positive terms, particularly as a conventional data collection method that does not violate human rights [17].

[15, 17–19] present other concepts that address the collection of information, where OSINT acts directly with each one. The authors as disciplines of intelligence approach the concepts. Table 1 describes the intelligence disciplines along with their ID and description.

Table 1. Intelligence disciplines.

ID	Intelligence disciplines	Description
01	COMINT	Communication Intelligence
02	CULTINT	Cultural Intelligence
03	DFINT	Digital Forensics Intelligence
04	ELINT	Electronic Intelligence
05	GEOINT	Geospatial Intelligence
06	HUMINT	Human Intelligence
07	IMINT	Image Intelligence
08	MARKINT	Market Intelligence
09	MASINT	Measurement and Signature Intelligence
10	SIGINT	Signal Intelligence
11	SOCMINT	Social Media Intelligence
12	TECHINT	Technical Intelligence
13	TELINT	Telemetry Intelligence

The practice of data collection has been discussed since 1941 when an effort to monitor German and Japanese radio broadcasts was launched with the creation of the Foreign Broadcast Monitoring Service, an organization that later became the Open Source Center [16].

From the creation of the Open Source Center to the present, numerous tools and techniques for collecting information from open sources have emerged that self-tune the search and analysis [20]. For example, address the practice of OSINT tools such as Google, Shodan, Sensys, theHarvester, Z-map and Carrot2 to find vulnerabilities in a system.

2.3   Web Analytics

Web analytics is a technique that involves the use of softwares that collect data about the behavior of users while they browse the internet. You get the data by tracking the mouse clicks or even by requesting information for the users [21].

The web analytics technique is responsible for helping to understand how users interact with web pages and mobile applications, automatically registering aspects of user behavior, and then combining, analyzing, and transforming behavior into data [22].

To run a web analytics on a web page, you must have a question or questions to answer. In Fig. 1, its show how the answers are not always as simple as we expect, and when we look at an area, we can discover new discoveries along the way. Semi-structured analysis involves data collection, transformation and analysis [22].

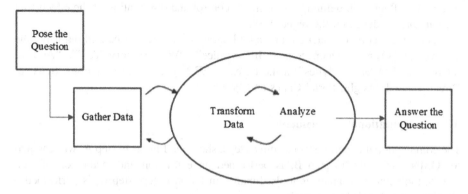

Fig. 1. The flow for performing a web analysis.

An example of web analytics application, is to use it to know information on where web traffic is coming up, what types of products users are interested in, what types of keywords users are typing in search engines for access a website [23].

Web analytics can also analyze user-generated content on social media, such as product reviews. The organization responsible for the product can use these opinions as feedback on their product to improve it, while the customer can use the same opinions to decide whether to buy the product or not [24].

Another example of application addressed by [25] is on the use of web analytics to perform performance measurement in digital marketing. Already [26] presents the web analysis to obtain and evaluate the performance indicators generated by university students inside a library [27]. Present the use of web analysis through the tool Similarweb [28] to develop a categorization of web pages. While [29] also used the Similarweb tool to explore the interest and use of the PhET website in a university.

3   Materials and Methods

3.1   Characteristics of the Studied Process

This research is of the descriptive type with a quantitative approach, since it involves the application of the web analysis in tools of historical web.

The descriptive research has as main objective the description of the characteristics of a certain population or phenomenon or the establishment of relations between variables. Its most significant characteristics are the use of standardized data collection techniques [30].

As for the technical procedures, this research is experimental, as it verifies if the web analytics application is able to classify the web history tools. The experimental research consists in determining an object of study, selecting the variables that would be able to influence it, defining the forms of control and observation of the effects that the variable produces on the object [30].

As for the theoretical background, a bibliographic survey was carried out using the key-words: "Osint", "Open Source Intelligence", "Web History Tool", "Archive Internet" and "Web Analytics" in the bases: IEEE Digital Library, Scopus, Science-Direct, EmeraldInsight, Portal Capes and ProQuest.

3.2   Computational Experiments

The computational experiments has three steps, shown in Fig. 2. In step A, we searched for OSINT Toolkits. In step B, is performed an extraction and evaluation of web history tools and web analysis tools. Finally, in the last step, step C, is performed a classification of web history tools.

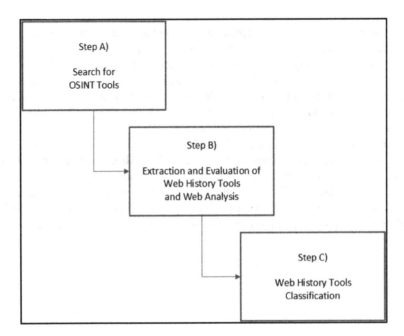

Fig. 2. The figure shows the steps of the computational experiments of this work.

- **Step A: Search for OSINT Tools:** We searched for OSINT toolkits to extract web history tools and web analytics tools. For this, we used the search engines: Biznar [31], Carrot2 [32], Google [33] and Metabear [34]. The OSINT toolkit selected was the "OSINT, Tools and Resources Handbook" of the I-Intelligence company [34].
- **Step B: Extraction and Evaluation of Web History Tools and Web Analysis:** We looked at the OSINT toolkit defined in phase A by web history and web analytics tools.

For the Web History tools, you extracted all the tools that appeared in the OSINT toolkit in the "Web History and Site Capture" category. For the validation of extracted web history tools, selected the link of each tool and performed a search with the URL of the social network domain LinkedIn [35].

For the web analytics tools, we extracted tools that could perform an online web analysis without the need for installation. For evaluation criteria, we verified which web analytics tools could be executed free of charge for a minimum period of 30 days. Selected the tools, a web analysis was done with each tool in the social network LinkedIn [35].

- **Step C: Web History Tools Classification:** A Web analysis was performed on the web history tools extracted in step B with the tool Similarweb, also extracted in step B. After the web analysis, we selected the desired indicators, and finally, we created an attribute "Rank Access", to classify the web history tools by the total number of accesses received.

4 Results and Discussions

In this section, the results of the computational experiments are presented and discussed. The experiments has three steps:

- **Step A: Search for OSINT Tools:** We searched for OSINT toolkits to extract web history tools and web analytics tools. For this, we searched the key words: "OSINT framework", "OSINT Toolkit" and "OSINT platform" in search engines: Biznar [31], Carrot2 [32], Google [33] and Metabear [34].

For the selection criteria of the OSINT toolkits, it was verified which of the toolkits found would bring the greatest amount of OSINT tools grouped by categories and which of them appear in periodicals or books. In Table 2, the OSINT toolkits found, along with their ID, Type and URL.

The toolkits Osintframework and Inteltechniques presented few or even none categorized as web analytics. Thus, the "OSINT, Tools and Resources Handbook" toolkit of the company I-Intelligence [20] was selected for the variety and quantity of categorized tools.

Table 2. OSINT toolkits.

ID	OSINT Toolkit	Type	URL
01	Osintframework	Web Page	https://osintframework.com/
02	Inteltechniques	Web Page	https://inteltechniques.com/menu.html
03	Osint Tools and Resources Handbook	Ebook (PDF)	https://www.i-intelligence.eu/wp-content/uploads/2016/11/2016_November_Open-Source-Intelligence-Tools-and-Resources-Handbook.pdf

– **Step B: Extraction and Evaluation of Web History Tools and Web Analysis:**
We looked at the OSINT toolkit defined in phase A by web history and web analytics tools. For Web History tools, all tools from the "Web History and Website Capture" category found in the OSINT toolkit was extracted. Then, it was verified which tools could be executed online, without the need of installation. Table 3 shows the web history tools extracted along with your ID and URL.

Table 3. Web history tools.

ID	Web history tool	URL
01	Archive.is	http://archive.is
02	Archive.fo	http://archive.fo
03	CashedPages	http://www.cachedpages.com
04	CachedView	http://cachedview.com
05	Common Crawl	http://commoncrawl.org
06	Screenshots.com	http://www.screenshots.com
07	Wayback Machine	http://archive.org/web/web.php

To evaluate previously extracted web history tools, you have accessed each tool and searched the LinkedIn social network domain. All selected tools have managed to bring historical pages of the social network.

For the web analytics tools, we extracted tools that could perform an online web analysis without the need for installation. For selection criteria, it was verified which web analytics tools could be executed free of charge for a minimum period of 30 days. The Table 4 presents the extracted web analytics tools along with their ID and URL.

Table 4. Web analytics tools.

ID	Web analytics tools	URL
01	Similarweb	https://www.similarweb.com/
02	Crunchbase	https://www.crunchbase.com

For the evaluation of the web analysis tools extracted, a web analysis was performed on the LinkedIn social network with each of them. The Crunchbase tool [37] provided much more qualitative rather than quantitative information, being unable to find indicators about users' use of the social network.

The web analytics tool Crunchbase [37] provided values such as: Name of the founders, e-mail addresses of some employees, investors, links to social media, current price of the organization, name of the organization's team, among others.

In addition to the Crunchbase tool [37], the tool Similarweb [28] provided quantitative information on user interaction with the social network, such as: Global rank, total number of accesses received, average monthly accesses, average access time and rate mean of rejection. Thus, the tool Similarweb [28] was selected to perform the web analysis in this work.

The indicators selected to perform the classification of web-based tools by the total number of accesses received were Global rank and total number of accesses received between June 2018 and August 2018, the most recent date available in the tool at the time of execution of this work.

- **Step C: Web History Tools Classification:** A web analysis was performed on the web history tools extracted in Phase B with the tool Similarweb.

The following indicators selected were Total accesses received by the tool between June 2018 and August 2018, in addition to the global rank reported by the tool Similarweb. To perform classification, the attribute "Access Rank" was created based on the indicators selected previously.

Table 5 presents the web history tools sorted by rank access.

Table 5. Web history tools classify by access rank.

ID	Web history tool	Rank global	Total of accessed received	Access rank
07	Wayback Machine	237	301,3 M	1
01	Archive.is	3193	58,74 M	2
02	Archive.fo	9848	18,33 M	3
03	CashedPages	337600	437,821	4
04	CachedView	245786	388,303	5
05	Common Crawl	1199003	78,918	6
06	Screenshots.com	3281034	31,769	7

The web history tool that presented the highest number of accesses received was the Wayback Machine with 301.3 million accesses between June 2018 and August 2018. The Fig. 3 shows the graph of the web history tools and the total accesses of each tool received between June 2018 and August 2018.

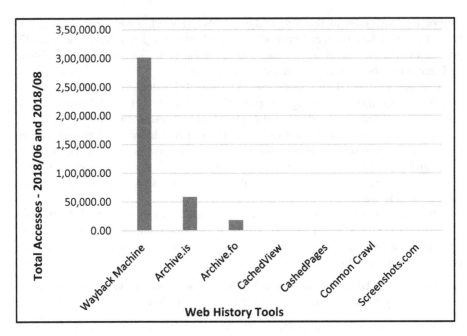

Fig. 3. The figure shows the total number of hits received by web history tools between June 2018 and August 2018.

5   Conclusion

In this work, we approached the classification of tools of historical web by means of the technique of web analysis with the objective of evidencing the ones that are the most accessed.

The application of the web analytics through the tool Similarweb generated important indicators, of which, were used the "Total of incomes received" and "Global Rank". These Indicators, which were able to classify the web history tools by the total access received. Thus, one can see which Web-based tools are the most accessed by the number of accesses received.

As a contribution of this work, the technique to classify the web history tools can be applied not only to classify OSINT online tools, but other types of web pages, in different areas, such as marketing and education. In addition, this work also presents the OSINT toolkits, where one can explore the other categories of tools, such as search engines, geo-localization tools, among others.

As a suggestion for future work, it will be interesting to continue the evaluation of the OSINT tools, since incorporating other categories and not just the web history tools, it becomes possible to develop a framed OSINT framework, tool or platform or information security using the most accessed tools.

References

1. Edwards, M., Larson, R., Green, B., Rashid, A., Baron, A.: Panning for gold: automatically analysing online social engineering attack surfaces. Comput. Secur. **69**, 18–34 (2017)
2. Li, Y., Arora, S., Youtie, J., Shapira, P.: Using web mining to explore triple helix influences on growth in small and mid-size firms. Technovation **76**, 3–14 (2018)
3. Glassman, M., Kang, M.J.: Intelligence in the internet age: the emergence and evolution of open source intelligence (OSINT). Comput. Hum. Behav. **28**(2), 673–682 (2012)
4. Čegan, L., Filip, P.: Webalyt: open web analytics platform. In: 27th International Conference, RADIOELEKTRONIKA 2017, pp. 1–5. IEEE (2017)
5. Singhal, A., Srivastava, P., Dawn, S.: Computational transformation from web to Ebook archiving. In: 5th Uttar Pradesh Section International Conference on Electrical, Electronics and Computer Engineering, UPCON 2018, pp. 1–6. IEEE (2018)
6. Alnoamany, Y., Alsum, A., Weigle, M.C., Nelson, M.L.: Who and what links to the internet archive. Int. J. Digit. Libr. **14**(3–4), 101–115 (2014)
7. Kanhabua, N., Kemkes, P., Nejdl, W., Nguyen, T.N., Reis, F., Tran, N.K.: How to search the internet archive without indexing it. In: Fuhr, N., Kovács, L., Risse, T., Nejdl, W. (eds.) TPDL 2016. LNCS, vol. 9819, pp. 147–160. Springer, Cham (2016). https://doi.org/10.1007/978-3-319-43997-6_12
8. Internet Archive homepage. https://archive.org/. Accessed 31 Aug 2018
9. Carrieri, V., Madio, L., Principe, F.: Light cannabis and organized crime: evidence from (Unintended) liberalization in Italy. Eur. Econ. Rev. **113**, 63–76 (2019)
10. Wayback Machine homepage. https://archive.org/web/. Accessed 31 Aug 2018
11. Buchak, G., Matvos, G., Piskorski, T., Seru, A.: Fintech, regulatory arbitrage, and the rise of shadow banks. J. Financ. Econ. **130**(3), 453–483 (2018)
12. Howells, K., Ertugan, A.: Applying fuzzy logic for sentiment analysis of social media network data in marketing. Procedia Comput. Sci. **120**, 664–670 (2017)
13. Koops, B., Hoepman, J., Leenes, R.: Open-source intelligence and privacy by design. Comput. Law Secur. Rev. **29**(6), 676–688 (2013)
14. Penetration Testing Execution Standard – Technical Guidelines homepage. http://www.Pentest-Standard.Org/Index.Php/PTES_Technical_Guidelines. Accessed 25 Aug 2018
15. Quick, D., Choo, K.R.: Digital forensic intelligence: data subsets and open source intelligence (DFINT + OSINT): a timely and cohesive mix. Future Gener. Comput. Syst. **78**, 558–567 (2018)
16. Clarke, C.S.: Open source intelligence. An Oxymoron or real intelligence? Marine Corps Gazette **99**(8), 22 (2015). Professional Journal of U.S. Marines
17. Hribar, G., Podbregar, I., Ivanuša, T.: OSINT: a "grey zone"? Int. J. Intell. Counterintelligence **27**(3), 529–549 (2014)
18. Akhgar, B., Bayerl, P.S., Sampson, F.: Open Source Intelligence Investigation: From Strategy to Implementation. Springer, Cham (2017). https://doi.org/10.1007/978-3-319-47671-1
19. Chauhan, S., Panda, N.K.: Hacking Web Intelligence: Open Source Intelligence and Web Reconnaissance Concepts and Techniques, 1st edn. Syngress (2015)
20. Lee, S., Shon, T.: Open source intelligence base cyber threat inspection framework for critical infrastructures. In: Future Technologies Conference (FTC) 2016, pp. 1030–1033. IEEE (2016)
21. Salini, A., Malavolta, I., Fabrizio.: Leveraging web analytics for automatically generating mobile navigation models. In: International Conference on Mobile Services (MS), pp. 103–110. IEEE (2016)

22. Beasley, M.: Practical Web Analytics for User Experience: How Analytics Can Help You Understand Your Users, 1st edn. Newnes, Oxford (2013)
23. Reshma, K., Rajendran, V.V.: An enhanced approach for querying integrated web analytics ontology using Quepy. In: International Conference on Intelligent Computing and Control (I2C2), pp. 1–6. IEEE (2017)
24. Rathan, M., Vishwanath, R.H., Murugeshwari, P., Sushmitha, H.M.: Every post matters: a survey on applications of sentiment analysis in social media. In: International Conference on Smart Technologies for Smart Nation, SMARTTECHCON 2017, pp. 709–714. IEEE (2017)
25. Järvinen, J., Karjaluoto, H.: The use of web analytics for digital marketing performance measurement. Ind. Mark. Manage. **50**, 117–127 (2015)
26. Fagan, J.C.: The suitability of web analytics key performance indicators in the academic library environment. J. Acad. Librarianship **40**(1), 25–34 (2014)
27. Choi, D., Han, J., Chun, S., Rappos, E., Robert, S., Know, T.T.: Bit.Ly/Practice: uncovering content publishing and sharing through URL shortening services. Telematics Inform. **35**(5), 1310–1323 (2018)
28. Similarweb homepage. https://www.similarweb.com/pro. Accessed 2 Sept 2018
29. Zhang, M.: Who are interested in online science simulations? Tracking a trend of digital divide in internet use. Comput. Educ. **76**, 205–214 (2014)
30. Gil, A.C.: Métodos E Técnicas De Pesquisa Social, 6th edn. Ediitora Atlas SA, São Paulo (2008)
31. Biznar homepage. https://biznar.com/biznar/desktop/en/search.html. Accessed 1 Sept 2018
32. Carrot2 homepage. http://Search.Carrot2.Org/Stable/Search. Accessed 1 Sept 2018
33. Google homepage. https://Www.Google.Com.Br/. Accessed 1 Sept 2018
34. Metabear homepage. http://www.metabear.com/. Accessed 9 July 2018
35. I-Intelligence homepage. https://www.i-intelligence.eu/wp-content/uploads/2016/11/2016_November_Open-Source-Intelligence-Tools-and-Resources-Handbook.pdf. Accessed 16 July 2018
36. LinkedIn homepage. https://br.linkedin.com/. Accessed 1 Sept 2018
37. Crunchbase homepage. https://www.crunchbase.com/. Accessed 2 Sept 2018

Investigating Visualisation Techniques for Rapid Triage of Digital Forensic Evidence

Gavin Hales[✉] and Ethan Bayne

Division of Cyber Security, Abertay University, Dundee, UK
{gavin.hales,e.bayne}@abertay.ac.uk

Abstract. This study investigates the feasibility of a tool that allows digital forensics (DF) investigators to efficiently triage device datasets during the collection phase of an investigation. This tool utilises data visualisation techniques to display images found in near real-time to the end user. Findings indicate that participants were able to accurately identify contraband material whilst using this tool, however, classification accuracy dropped slightly with larger datasets. Combined with participant feedback, the results show that the proposed triage method is indeed feasible, and this tool provides a solid foundation for the continuation of further work.

Keywords: Digital forensics · Data visualisation · Computer security · File carving · Digital triage

1 Introduction

Digital forensics (DF) is considered an essential practice of law enforcement, often employed when crimes may have been committed with the aid of an electronic device. During the evidence collection phase of a DF investigation, data is recovered from digital devices that are suspected to be involved in a crime. Devices seized may include computers, external storage devices, storage media, and mobile devices—such as a smartphone or tablet. The evidence collection phase includes the recovery of deleted data that may be of forensic significance to the investigation, in a process known as file carving. A frequent objective of file carving when used in law enforcement is to recover photographic evidence that may be important to the case.

The file carving stage of an investigation is generally a hands-off process where software is used to recover data. During recovery, the investigator cannot proceed with reviewing results until the file carving operation is complete. Currently available software that is used to complete file carving operations tend to be slow and often provide the investigator with very little feedback about the content found on a device during processing. Previous work has been conducted that utilised Graphics Processing Units (GPUs) to accelerate computationally intensive pattern matching operations in the file carving process, significantly reducing the time required to perform the reconstruction of evidence. However, visual feedback of evidence discovered during processing is an area that remains relatively unexplored and may benefit from further research.

© Springer Nature Switzerland AG 2019
A. Moallem (Ed.): HCII 2019, LNCS 11594, pp. 277–293, 2019.
https://doi.org/10.1007/978-3-030-22351-9_19

This work examines the possibility of applying information visualisation techniques to the collection stage of the investigation, in unison with GPU accelerated file carving, to allow the DF investigator to rapidly triage datasets. The motivation behind this work is the increasing average workload for DF investigators, specifically in the area of law enforcement. These ever-growing workloads lead to longer investigation times and delays in the processing of cases. Through allowing the investigator to triage and prioritise relevant datasets at an earlier stage of the investigative process, it is hoped that this will reduce the time required to investigate.

In this study, participants were shown 6 videos of a GPU accelerated file carving tool that recovers images from a disk and displays these in near real-time (assuming a small delay caused by on-screen rendering). To simulate a case where a suspect is in possession of illicit images, participants were informed that any photos of birds were to be considered "illegal" content. Half of the videos that were shown contained images of birds in varying proportions, and the other half of the videos only showed non-bird images. This methodology was utilised to assess the ability of the participants (n = 30) to accurately identify datasets with potentially "illegal" content.

The following sections present; the methodology that the study followed in order to answer whether visualisation techniques could be applied to the collection phase of a DF investigation, the results that were gathered from participants who undertook the experiment, followed by an analysis and conclusions based on these results.

2 Background

Over recent years, the number of computing devices owned by people has increased due to the growing adoption of portable devices such as smartphones, smart home products and digital assistants [1]. The ubiquity of such devices implies that they often play a central role in criminal activity such as extortion, cybercrime, identity theft, etc. Even where these devices are not the primary instruments of a crime, they frequently prove to be an invaluable source of information in other cases, providing information such as location history, call records, photo metadata, etc. Therefore, it is not uncommon for law enforcement to seize all digital devices from suspects. These devices, however, have not only become more prevalent, but have also continually grown in terms of storage capacity as shown by combining data in [2–4] (depicted in Fig. 1.). Devices with a storage capacity of 200 GB+ would have previously been restricted to larger devices, such as desktop computers and laptops, but recently developed smartphones regularly come with storage capacity options of 256 GB or more. However, the technology used to examine devices in DF investigations has not kept pace with these increases in device storage, which presents significant challenges for investigators. A report by Her Majesty's Inspectorate of Constabulary (HMIC) in 2015 reported that police investigations involving digital devices were commonly delayed up to 12 months or more after a review of 124 digital forensic cases from six UK police forces [5].

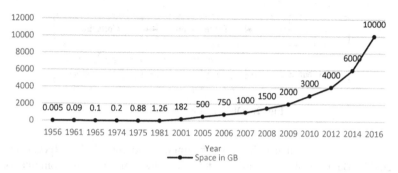

Fig. 1. Consumer hard drive capacity timeline

The digital investigative methodology, as defined by the Digital Forensics Research Workshop [6], proposes 6 stages of DF investigation. The stages, as shown in Fig. 2, include the Examination stage, where the investigator will explore all of the data recovered from devices and identify evidence that is relevant to the case. It is this stage of the investigative process that can take significant human input and time, which may be exacerbated by the increasing volumes of data involved in these cases. The tools frequently used by the investigator to explore the data are traditionally text-based tools that do not lend themselves well to the efficient exploration of large datasets due to the variety of media found in these datasets. Hales [7] suggests the use of exploratory information visualisation techniques to construct a visual timeline of events on the digital device that could assist the investigator in creating a narrative of behaviour. The developed tool – Insight – takes the information from a popular DF tool – Autopsy – and presents it to the user as a visual timeline. Different types of information such as web browsing history and EXIF metadata are all presented on the same timeline; allowing the investigator to see a detailed picture of what the device owner was using the device for at any point in time. The research shows that participants reacted more positively to software that provides a timeline visualisation of the device data when comparing to traditional textual interfaces commonly used. Statistical analysis shows that the use of visualisations improve the ability of the investigator to make accurate conclusions regarding a narrative of suspect behaviour. User experience when utilising visualisation software is also judged to be equal to traditional DF software and sig-nificantly better when performing tasks such as corroborating evidence or determining user behaviour at a specific point in time. Visualisation techniques have also been successfully applied to other areas of computer security; such as network security [8, 9] and malware analysis [10, 11].

The previous research conducted into the application of information visualisation techniques suggests further exploration of the application of these techniques to earlier stages of the DF investigative process; specifically, the Collection phase. During this phase, file carving is performed on data that is retrieved from a device, attempting to recover data using physical information stored on the drive. Tools available to perform this step are generally automatic and require minimal human intervention, with output during the process generally limited to little more than a progress bar. Historically, this has also been a time-consuming process as all data from a device has to be processed

Fig. 2. DF investigative model [6]

on the CPU for patterns that indicate the beginning and end of files. Recent research conducted by Bayne et al. [12] demonstrates how pattern matching – a computationally intensive processes vital to file carving – can be moved to GPUs using an asynchronous processing approach to greatly reduce processing time when compared to traditional CPU processing approaches employed by other DF tools. The tool developed by this research – OpenForensics[1] – showed time reductions of up to 97% when compared to performing the same file carving operation on other established DF tools that employ CPU processing.

To explore the application of information visualisation techniques whilst performing file carving on the data under investigation, the OpenForensics tool was modified to create a visualisation prototype for this work. This prototype displays the images discovered by the tool in near to real-time to the end user in a 4 × 4 grid on screen (Fig. 3). Due to the fast processing speed of the tool, the images displayed within this grid change quickly. The authors hypothesise that the display of near to real-time results within the application could be used to allow investigators to perform rapid triage of a dataset thereby reducing the examination time required to identify datasets that may contain information of forensic interest.

Researchers have suggested machine learning solutions to perform automatic triage of data collected in DF cases by classifying any images found [13, 14]. Whilst it is acknowledged that indeed this may be a worthwhile route to pursue, for the purposes of law enforcement use, it would not be appropriate to allow a computer to be the sole decision maker as to whether datasets contain potentially valuable evidence, or whether any images should be examined in detail by a human or not. There are a number of legal and ethical ramifications potentially raised by such an approach. It should also be noted that whilst advances in machine learning have been significant, there are still areas where there are challenges. One challenge that remains problematic is the ability of these systems to accurately differentiate between children, adolescents and adults. When used in law enforcement settings, in many cases these tools will be used to look for possession of illegal images, such as those depicting minors [15]. The automated recognition of images is an area of ongoing research and, as such, machine learning techniques are not explored as a part of this work at this time.

---

[1] https://github.com/ethanbayne/OpenForensics.

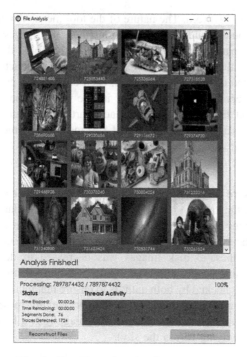

Fig. 3. OpenForensics visualisation interface

3   Methodology

The purpose of this body of work is to ascertain whether end users can accurately identify "illegal" images in a dataset as they are being recovered and shown to them by a GPU accelerated file carving tool. The tool displays the images to the participant as it processes them in a 4×4 grid filling each row from left to right and moving rows upwards as the last row is filled. The approach followed by this research used the OpenForensics tool, which was modified to display acquired images to the end user in near real-time. This allowed the accuracy of the participant's answers to be examined, in terms of the number of correct and incorrect responses.

3.1   Dataset Design

Six datasets were developed for use in this experiment, with the aim of closely reflecting the type of content that may be found on a small USB storage device in an investigation. To create these datasets, a tool was used to scrape random images from Google Images, using several different keywords, including "birds". A USB storage device was securely wiped, and then a sample of these images was placed on the drive. The images were subsequently deleted, and a clone (disk image) of the USB storage device was acquired, as is standard practice in a DF investigation. Following this sequence provided a dataset in a format that the file carving tool could analyse and recover the deleted images from. The nature of the tool means that subsequent runs on different hardware would produce a visualisation where the images change at different speeds. Allowing the participants to use the tool directly would thus produce skewed results depending on the hardware the experiment was conducted on. In order to counteract this, a video of the tool running on each dataset was created to ensure that each participant observed the visualisation in the exact same way, with images appearing onscreen at the same speed for each participant. During the video, each image remains on the screen for an average of 800 ms. As the time taken for a human to perceive the content of an image is around 1/3 of a second (~ 333 ms) [16], the images are ensured not to be appearing at a speed that is outside of the bounds of what can be perceived.

These datasets were designed to have an increasing number of non-bird images, therefore decreasing the ratio of "illegal" bird images in the dataset. In 3 of the 6 datasets, no bird images were included, and in the other 3 datasets, there were varying amounts of bird images included, as shown in Table 1. The ratio of bird images included in each of these 3 disk images was decreased to determine participant accuracy with increasing levels of visual "noise". When creating the datasets, the images were manually checked by both authors to ensure that there were no images that were ambiguous (e.g. a cartoon image of the Linux penguin mascot "Tux") or contained birds that were not the main subject of the image (e.g. a landscape photograph with a few small birds flying across the sky).

Table 1. Data file summary

Dataset	Total number of images	"Illegal" Images Incl?
1	100	Yes – 10 (10%)
2	100	No
3	1000	No
4	1000	Yes – 10 (1%)
5	5000	Yes – 5 (0.1%)
6	5000	No

3.2 "Illegal" Image Detection

Participants (n = 30) were required to have a good knowledge of computing, with regular use of computers as part of their career. Due to the use of pre-recorded videos of the tool, a significant technical ability such as a background in computer science was not required. Each participant reported normal or corrected to normal vision and were asked if they were colour-blind. The participants were given information at the start of the experiment that informed them about the fact that images of birds were to be considered to be "illegal" during the experiment, and they should look out for any images of these in each video. They were told that they were not required to count the number of images they saw, or to try and remember what each image looked like; only that they would be asked to identify if there had been any images of birds, which would indicate it would be worthwhile for law enforcement to investigate further. The videos were played in full-screen mode to eliminate other distractions on screen and were conducted on displays with similar sizes and resolutions at as close to eye level as was feasible.

Each participant was asked to watch each video only once, and to refrain from rewinding or stopping the video once it had started. A video player was used to blank the screen after each video was played so that no images remained on the screen. To control for fatigue, a Latin Square design for the order of the videos was adopted (Table 2). This was essential, as both videos 5 and 6 were over 4 min in length, which could lead to fatigue when concentrating on the images appearing. Participants were allocated to a group when signing the consent form, and all groups had a total of 5 participants each.

Table 2. Participant group video order

Group	Video order					
A	1	2	3	4	5	6
B	6	1	2	3	4	5
C	5	6	1	2	3	4
D	4	5	6	1	2	3
E	3	4	5	6	1	2
F	2	3	4	5	6	1

After watching each video, the participants were asked to complete 2 questions relating to the video they had just watched. The first of these questions was simply "Did you see any pictures of birds?" with possible responses of simply "Yes" or "No". The results of the question were used to determine metrics such as the hit rate and false alarm rate. They were also asked to give an indication of their confidence in their answer. This was presented in the format "How confident are you that you saw/did not see pictures of birds in Video X?" and a response in the format of a Likert scale where 1 represented "Not Very Confident" and 5 represented "Very Confident". The results from this question were used to determine whether there was any correlation between the number of images being shown to the participants and the confidence in their answer, or between false alarms/misses and confidence. Finally, to gauge the participant perception of the tool, and provide additional context to the triage results, the participants were asked to optionally respond to the question: "Now that you have watched all of the videos, how did you find the experience of searching for pictures of birds as they appeared?" Thematic analysis was conducted on the responses to this question.

3.3 Interface Preference

Upon the conclusion of the experiment, the participants were shown a few simple interfaces and asked to indicate their preferred interface. These questions were proposed in order to inform future visualisation design based on the preference of the users. The first interface comparison displayed 2 interfaces to the participant (Fig. 4) and asked; "If you had a large gallery of photos on your computer and wanted to find a specific photo, how would you prefer to do this?" They were presented with 2 responses: "(Interface 1) Show one full-screen photo at a time, and keep pressing the next arrow until you found the photo" or "(Interface 2) Show all of your photos in a file browser with thumbnails and find it from there." This question was asked to determine whether the participants were likely to prefer a "flashcard" approach or view multiple photos at the same time.

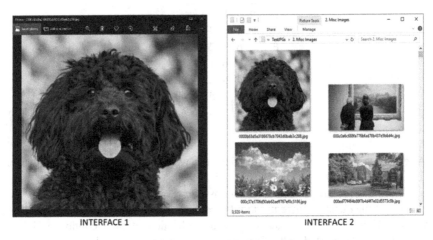

INTERFACE 1   INTERFACE 2

Fig. 4. Flashcard vs Grid layout preference

The second question presented the participant with 3 interfaces (Fig. 5). Each interface depicted an image gallery, with varying sizes of images in each interface. This question was presented to determine whether the user is likely to prefer larger images with fewer shown at a time, or smaller images with more shown on screen at one time. The question was presented as "Which of the following interfaces do you prefer?" with a simple option to select Interface 1 or Interface 2.

INTERFACE 1   INTERFACE 2

INTERFACE 3

Fig. 5. Image browser size preference

4   Results

In this section, results from the experiment where participants were asked to detect images of birds will be presented and discussed, alongside the confidence ratings of participant responses after watching each video. Responses provided on interface design preferences will also be discussed, together with a thematic analysis of the perceptual feedback provided by participants at the conclusion of the experiment.

4.1   File Carving Triage Results

Accuracy

When exploring the results from the file carving tool experiment, the videos were grouped into pairs of datasets with the same number of images; one video with bird images present and one video without bird images present. The pairings, therefore, as per Table 1, are Videos 1 & 2, 3 & 4 and 5 & 6.

The first of these pairs, which contained 100 images, 10% of which were birds in Video 1 showed a hit rate of 93%. The correct rejection rate for this pair is also 93%. These figures are high, as was expected by the researchers, as the relatively high number of bird images in the dataset led to many participants verbally commenting that they were "obvious". The breakdown of participant responses to this video pair can be seen in Table 3. This shows that participants can accurately differentiate between the datasets with and without bird images in a small dataset.

Table 3. Video 1 & 2 detection results

	Responded "Yes"	Responded "No"
Video 1 (Birds Present)	28 (93%)	2 (7%)
Video 2 (Birds Absent)	2 (7%)	28 (93%)

The second of the video pairs, containing 1000 images and 1% bird images in Video 3 shows a hit rate of 83%. The correct rejection rate for this pair was 90%. The breakdown of the participant responses for this pair can be seen in Table 4. Although these figures still show a relatively high level of accuracy amongst the participants in identifying bird images, this is a noticeable decrease from the previous video.

Table 4. Video 3 & 4 detection results

	Responded "Yes"	Responded "No"
Video 4 (Birds Present)	25 (83%)	5 (17%)
Video 3 (Birds Absent)	3 (10%)	27 (90%)

The final pair of videos that contain a total of 5000 images, 0.1% of which are of birds in Video 5, show again a hit rate of 83% and but a lower correct rejection rate of 77%. As can be seen in Table 5, this means that the false alarm rate for this pair of videos is 23%. This value is relatively high and indicates a slightly decreasing level of accuracy from the participants in the longer videos with fewer bird images, this is also shown in Fig. 6.

Table 5. Video 5 & 6 detection results

	Responded "Yes"	Responded "No"
Video 5 (Birds Present)	25 (83%)	5 (17%)
Video 6 (Birds Absent)	7 (23%)	23 (77%)

Participants' answers between varying sizes of datasets were analysed. An exact McNemar's test determined that there was no statistically significant difference in the proportion of answers given between videos with birds present within them—videos 1

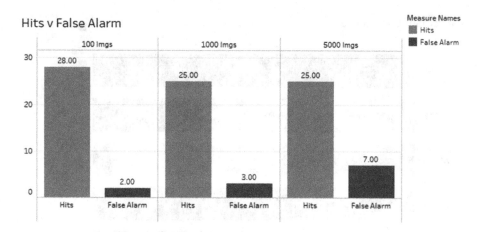

Fig. 6. Hits and false alarm rates for each dataset size

and 4 $(p = .37)$, videos 4 and 5 $(p = 1.00)$, and videos 1 and 5 $(p = .45)$. An exact McNemar's test similarly determined that there was no statistically significant difference in the proportion of answers given between videos without birds present within them—videos 2 and 3 $(p = 1.00)$, videos 3 and 6 $(p = .29)$, and videos 2 and 6 $(p = .12)$.

It is interesting to note that, although not a large enough sample to analyse in depth, one participant that declared themselves as colour-blind (deuteranopia) gave as accurate answers in the experiment as other participants. It was found that colour-blindness did not affect their ability to recognise the bird images. This participant succeeded at correctly identifying all videos with a 100% hit and correct rejection rate. It is not known whether the colour-blindness of the participant influenced their results, or whether this is coincidence. This may be an area for future research.

4.2 Participant Confidence

After watching each video and indicating whether they saw images of birds in the video, the participants were asked to rate on a Likert scale of 1 to 5, the confidence they had in the answer that they had given, where 1 indicated that they were "Not Very Confident" in their answer and 5 indicated that they were "Very Confident" in their answer. Figure 7 shows a breakdown of the responses given by participants for this question for each video. Overall, for many of the videos, participants generally responded that they were confident with their responses. All participants were confident with their answer to Video 1, reinforcing the verbal comments that this video was "obvious", although it was found that 2 participants answered this incorrectly with "no".

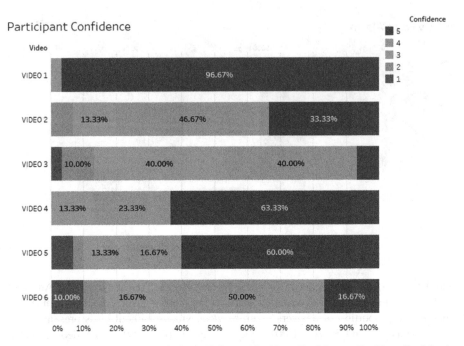

Fig. 7. Participant confidence levels (From left: 1 – Not Very Confident to 5 – Very Confident)

Using Friedman's ANOVA test, the confidence ratings of the participants significantly differed over the six videos $(x^2(5) = 8.00, p < .001)$.

Wilcoxon Signed Rank tests were used to measure the confidence of a participant's answers between videos with bird images to those without. It appeared that a participant's confidence significantly differs between videos 1 and 2 $(T = -3.91, N$ for Test $= 30, p < .001, r = -.5)$, between videos 3 and 4 $(T = -3.96, N$ for Test $= 30, p < .001, r = -.51)$ and between videos 5 and 6, $(T = -2.57, N$ for Test $= 30, p = .01, r = -.33)$. It can be concluded that a participant's confidence significantly differs between videos with birds and videos without birds in them.

Wilcoxon Signed Rank tests were also used to test a participant's confidence in their answers between shorter and longer videos. It appeared that a participant's confidence significantly differs between videos 1 and 4 $(T = -2.89, N$ for Test $= 30, p = .004, r = -.37)$ and videos 2 and 3 $(T = -3.40, N$ for Test $= 30, p = .001, r = -.44)$. However, each participant's confidence did not differ significantly between videos 4 and 5 $(T = -1.20, N$ for Test $= 30, p = .23)$ and videos 3 and 6 $(T = 1.04, N$ for Test $= 30, p = .30)$. It can be concluded that a participant's confidence in their answers weakened between watching the videos with 100 images and 1000 images, but each participant remained as confident with their answers between the videos with 1000 images and 5000 images.

4.3 Interface Preference

At the end of the experiment, the participants were shown different interfaces and asked to indicate which one they would prefer to use if they were looking for a specific photo on their computer (these interfaces can be seen in Figs. 4 and 5). The first of these questions presented the user with a single large full-screen image versus a grid of images. The response to this question was that all participants unanimously preferred Interface 2 that depicted a grid of images. As this was the format used for the visualisation of images in the file carving tool, it reinforces that this design decision was the correct to make instead of rapidly showing the users images one at a time.

The second question was related to the sizing of the images displayed in a grid format, the purpose of which was to determine whether users prefer an interface with relatively large images, average sized images (similar to the interface in the tool), or an interface with relatively small images. The results of this (Fig. 8) show that the majority of participants (86.67%) preferred the interface that showed averagely sized thumbnails, which was similar to the format and size of the images presented by the tool. Again, this reinforces the design decisions made when creating this tool. It should, however, be noted that these preferences may be due to a response bias as the participants were asked these questions after using the tool. In future, it may be of interest to test if these responses vary before exposure to the software.

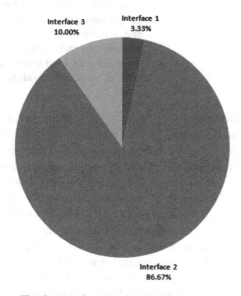

Fig. 8. Interface thumbnail size preference

4.4 Qualitative Feedback

After watching all of the videos in the experiment, the participants were asked to give feedback on how they found the experience of searching for pictures of birds as they appeared in the video. This was a free text field where they could leave any comments they felt were relevant. Of the 30 participants, 29 provided responses to this question. Thematic analysis was conducted on the responses, where five common themes were identified. These themes can be seen in Table 6.

Table 6. Themes in participant feedback

Theme	Participants commenting on theme	Example of comments
Difficult	53%	"Like looking for a needle in a haystack" "Quite difficult"
Length of task	30%	"Longer videos were difficult" "Difficult to keep track of all the images and the longer each video is the harder it was."
Fast image speed	30%	"…rather difficult to keep up with the image flow" "Very hard because the pictures came and went so fast"
Fatigue	23%	"Cognitively demanding" "Quite straining on the eyes during the longer videos."
Variable rate of image appearance	13%	"The rate differences made it more challenging in some of the videos than others - I suspect the images appeared as they were carved rather than at a consistent rate." "Because the bulk image elections [sic] were not a consistent pace I felt it was much harder to see the birds, it would be smooth then jarring"

As can be seen from the analysis of themes, many of the participants commented on how difficult they found the task to be. This comment was often made in combination with one of the other themes; specifically, participants also frequently identified that the difficulty they had with the task was caused by the fast speed that the images appeared onscreen. The difficulty was also caused by the length of the 5000 image videos, which were over 4 min long. The length of the videos also appears as a theme in several responses where the participants mentioned a level of fatigue whilst undertaking the task.

Some participants also commented that the inconsistent rate that the images were displayed on the screen posed a challenge and, in some cases, made it much harder to see the images of birds. This inconsistent rate at which the images appear is due to the way that the tool and file carving work. As images are being recovered from deleted data on a disk, there are times where the tool may find multiple images clustered in co-located blocks of data; other times the tool may not find images for a period of time. This leads to points where the images stop populating, pause for a short time, and then continue populating rapidly. A buffer could be used to attempt to smoothen the display of these images to the end user, however, this was not implemented in the tool as it would add an artificial overhead to the process and make the process longer, which contradicts the motivation for this research.

5 Analysis

As can be seen from the ability of the participants to detect images of birds in a dataset, and correctly triage this dataset, generally the results are indicative of a potential benefit to the digital forensic investigative process, given further refinements based on the outcomes of this work. Participants were found in most cases able to correctly identify the presence of 'illegal' images, however, as also shown by these results, the accuracy of the responses given starts to decline slightly in datasets with more images, and fewer bird images. In the videos with 5000 images, the number of correct hits is still relatively high at 83%, however, as shown in Fig. 6, the number of false alarms is also relatively high at 23%. The threshold at which the detection accuracy is too low is highly dependent on the scenario that the tool is being utilised in. If the tool is being used to triage the data of someone accused of possession of inappropriate images of minors for example, then law enforcement authorities are likely to reasonably demand a hit rate of very close to 100%. However, if the tool is being used to investigate a device in an organisation for an employee accused of photographing confidential property, for example, a slightly lower accuracy rating may be acceptable.

In this study, it was hypothesised that the length of time the investigator was required to watch a video for would have a direct impact on the confidence of their answer; with longer videos leading to lower confidence ratings. However, the findings do not support this hypothesis, as the confidence rating between videos with 1000 and 5000 images were not significantly different. Instead, it was found that there were consistent and significant differences between the confidence ratings of videos including images of birds, and those without, across all dataset sizes. Combined with the increasing false positive rate, it could be conjectured that as the participants become more uncertain whether they may have missed a bird image in the large datasets that did not contain bird images, they are more likely to respond indicating that they did see a bird image so that a dataset potentially containing evidence is not incorrectly dismissed, signifying a possible response bias. This is not necessarily an issue in law enforcement scenarios, as a suggestion of a false positive during the triage stage will lead to further investigation of an irrelevant dataset, thus simply decreasing the efficiency of the investigation. Incorrectly dismissing datasets that contain evidence (a "miss") is more of an issue as in a law enforcement scenario, this could lead to failure to prosecute or acquit a suspect.

Exploration of the feedback given by participants yield several themes that highlight some of the issues encountered by the participants. Notably, a significant number of participants (53%) indicated that they found the tasks "difficult" in some way. Exploring the themes further revealed further core reasons for this difficulty. The speed that the images appeared on screen was mentioned by 30% of the participants, who generally said that the flow of images was difficult to keep up with. Artificially reducing the rate that the images appeared could be a solution to this, however, as mentioned previously, this would delay the overall investigation, which is contrary to the aim of this research. The relatively long time where the participants are required to look at the screen, and the high level of concentration that they must apply to the task led to 23% of the participants mentioning that some form of fatigue was experienced during the experiment. Some participants indicated that this was in the form of high cognitive demand, whilst others indicated it was in the form of eye strain. This would be exacerbated in lengthy DF investigations. Thus, an alternative visualisation may need to be explored that could allow the user to look away from the screen without the risk of missing large volumes of data.

6   Conclusions and Future Work

This work has explored a method of visualising the results of a GPU accelerated file carving tool in real time, to provide a rapid triaging tool for use in DF investigations. It was hypothesised that this tool would provide the user with a way to make accurate and timely decisions about the kind of images contained on a device, and thus decide as to whether investigating it at length would be necessary.

In testing this tool with 30 participants, it was shown that the accuracy of the participants in detecting contraband images is generally good, however, it begins to decline slightly (albeit not statistically significantly) with larger datasets containing fewer contraband images. This has indicated that the underlying idea of rapid triage using such a tool is feasible, however, further work will be required in refining the format of the visualisation tool. This conclusion is reinforced by participant feedback indicating that the task was difficult due to the high speed at which the images appeared and then disappeared from the screen, along with the fatigue experienced from having to concentrate on the screen for an extended period of time. Ideally, future work will allow a visualisation method to be developed where the information is displayed to the investigator for a longer period of time, allowing them to look away from the screen, while maintaining or improving upon the accuracy levels seen in this study.

It would be of interest to apply machine learning techniques to aid identification of contraband material—not as a replacement for human analysis, but to augment it. This approach could allow for certain pieces of data to be drawn more clearly to the attention of the human investigator if deemed by an image recognition algorithm to potentially be of interest. Such an approach would hypothetically reduce the strain on the investigator and allow them to make more accurate and confident triage decisions, whilst still ensuring that no data is hidden; an important feature in DF tools.

Acknowledgements. The authors gratefully acknowledge the support of NVIDIA Corporation with the donation of the Titan X Pascal GPU used for this research. The authors would also like to thank Abertay University's R-LINCS initiative for the funding of a compute server that was used in the development of this processing model.

References

1. OFCOM: Decade of Digital Dependency (2018). https://www.ofcom.org.uk/about-ofcom/latest/features-and-news/decade-of-digital-dependency
2. Vaughan-Nichols, S.J.: Hard drive technology reaches a turning point. Computer **36**, 21–23 (2003). Long. Beach. Calif)

3. Farrance, R.: Timeline: 50 Years of Hard Drives (2006). https://www.pcworld.com/article/127105/article.html
4. Mah Ung, G.: Seagate's 10 TB Barracuda Pro is the world's largest consumer hard drive (2016). https://www.pcworld.com/article/3096292/storage/seagates-10tb-barracuda-pro-is-the-worlds-largest-consumer-hard-drive.html
5. Her Majesty's Inspectorate of Constabulary: Online and on the edge: Real risks in a virtual world (2015)
6. Palmer, G.: A road map for digital forensic research. In: First Digital Forensic Research Workshop, Utica, New York, pp. 27–30 (2001)
7. Hales, G.: Visualisation of device datasets to assist digital forensic investigation. In: 2017 International Conference on Cyber Situational Awareness, Data Analytics and Assessment (Cyber SA), IEEE (2017)
8. Angelini, M., Blasilli, G., Catarci, T., Lenti, S., Santucci, G.: Vulnus: visual vulnerability analysis for network security. IEEE Trans. Vis. Comput. Graph. **25**, 183–192 (2019)
9. Liu, X., Sun, Y., Fang, L., Liu, J., Yu, L.: A survey of network traffic visualization in detecting network security threats. In: Lu, Y., Wu, X., Zhang, X. (eds.) ISCTCS 2014. CCIS, vol. 520, pp. 91–98. Springer, Heidelberg (2015). https://doi.org/10.1007/978-3-662-47401-3_12
10. Nataraj, L., Manjunath, B.S.: SPAM: signal processing to analyze malware [Applications Corner]. IEEE Signal Process. Mag. **33**, 105–117 (2016)
11. Quist, D.A., Liebrock, L.M.: Visualizing compiled executables for malware analysis. In: 2009 6th International Workshop on Visualization for Cyber Security, pp. 27–32. IEEE (2009)
12. Bayne, E., Ferguson, R.I., Sampson, A.T.: OpenForensics: a digital forensics GPU pattern matching approach for the 21st century. Digital Invest. **24**, S29–S37 (2018)
13. Perez, M., et al.: Video pornography detection through deep learning techniques and motion information. Neurocomputing **230**, 279–293 (2017)
14. Platzer, C., Stuetz, M., Lindorfer, M.: Skin sheriff. In: Proceedings of the 2nd International Workshop on Security and Forensics in Communication Systems - SFCS 2014, pp. 45–56. ACM Press, New York (2014)
15. Mayer, F., Steinebach, M.: Forensic image inspection assisted by deep learning. In: Proceedings of the 12th International Conference on Availability, Reliability and Security - ARES 2017, pp. 1–9. ACM Press, New York (2017)
16. Potter, M.C.: Meaning in visual search. Science **187**, 965–966 (1975)

Behind the Façade

Paradigms in Ubiquitous Cryptography

Aaron MacSween[(✉)] and Yann Flory

XWiki SAS, Paris, France
research@xwiki.com

Abstract. Despite continued maturation since the latter half of the last century, cryptography still bears the vestigial traces of its roots as an arcane art. Cryptographers have abandoned any fondness for obfuscation and turned to the irrevocable properties of mathematics and prime numbers to ensure the privacy of those who would wield their tools. Notwithstanding its apparent modernity, the majority of recent cryptosystems have not enjoyed widespread adoption. Usage is limited primarily to the sophisticated elite who possess the time, interest, and inclination required to understand the behaviour of these systems, if not necessarily their inner workings.

While we may find more apt metaphors for conveying the complex properties of ciphers and cryptosystems, the effort behind such ad-hoc approaches will always have to be adapted to suit new algorithms, and will have to contend with their ostensibly simpler plaintext counterparts. mastodon accountt new primitives can continue to be described in terms of progressively more elabortate boxes, locks, and keys, it is difficult to imagine an explanation sufficiently compelling to extend to all those who do not enjoy the luxury of privacy.

Modern cryptographers have embraced Kerckhoffs's principle, that:

A cryptosystem should be secure even if everything about the system, except the key, is public knowledge

We will argue that this is insufficient, and that a second principle is necessary:

A cryptosystem should be secure even if nothing about the system, except the plaintext system it replaces, is familiar to its operator

In simpler language, assuming they seek a future in which everyone is able to control the spread of their personal information, those in the field of cryptographic development must create systems which are difficult to misuse.

We will present CryptPad, an open-source, browser-based suite of collaborative editors which employs end-to-end-encryption to protect the contents of user documents from passive surveillance, including that of the server operators. It implements familiar façades (login and registration forms, document curation facilities, access control policy definition, and a variety of applications) using a small set of common cryptographic primitives.

© Springer Nature Switzerland AG 2019
A. Moallem (Ed.): HCII 2019, LNCS 11594, pp. 294–313, 2019.
https://doi.org/10.1007/978-3-030-22351-9_20

While the underlying mechanisms of the system are not especially sophisticated, their properties are sufficient to facilitate schemes matching existing user expectations as set by established plaintext platforms. Though we will refer to established systems as the initial results of this design philosophy throughout, our goal is to describe in concrete terms the methodology which continues to shape their development. We will outline the benefits of this paradigm of system design, describe the aspects of various cryptographic algorithms which challenge users and developers alike, and recount the results of our iterative user acceptance testing.

We will demonstrate the value of serving an audience which is uninterested in the technical details of the platforms they use, exploring not just the abstract notion of *the network effect*, but detailing the types of social networks through which we have observed the adoption of the platform. By reframing issues of deployment in this manner, we hope to contribute towards the wider accessibility of cryptographic research beyond the purview of its core constituents. In order to move towards our envisioned future of ubiquitous cryptography, we must dissociate the means of securing information from the experience of doing so.

Keywords: Cybersecurity, privacy and trust in computing areas: Web technologies ·
Human factors: communication of security risks to end-users ·
Human factors: user acceptance of security and privacy technologies ·
Human factors: user awareness of privacy threats, legal, ethical, economic and societal issues in cybersecurity: Privacy by design & default

1   Methodology

Our findings are derived from user reports and consultations, anecdotal accounts, and measurements taken from our flagship instance [cry2019b].

User reports were received via email, Matrix/IRC, Twitter [twi2019], Mastodon [cry2019c], the project's GitHub issue tracker [cry2019d], and in person.

We consulted with users in a variety of unstructured formats while demonstrating the software at conferences and meetups, answering questions and taking note of users' first impressions. The nature of these venues didn't afford us the chance to take careful notes, though their conversational nature allowed us to gauge perceptions over time and understand motivations for using privacy-enhancing technologies.

We performed semi-structured remote interviews with a number of self-identified *power users* using VOIP and screen sharing tools, usually taking collaborative notes via CryptPad itself.

Finally, we processed server logs using ElasticSearch and Kibana [ela2019]. These logs included asynchronous HTTP HEAD requests with keywords for specific actions performed by clients using our telemetry API from which users can opt-out. This API exposes general data such as which APIs the client supports, their screen dimensions, and which features they use.

2   Demographics and General Response

Our interviews revealed that most users had been introduced to collaborative editors via Etherpad-lite, which they had used on a regular basis. They noted difficulty managing projects with more than a few documents as they were prone to being lost. Many used a *pad of pads* for such projects, or migrated to platforms like Google's *Drive*.

Most subjects were familiar with the Snowden revelations, Facebook's *Cambridge Analytica* scandal, and the practices of *surveillance capitalism*. They typically employed between two and five browser extensions intended to block ads and trackers, limit the execution of Javascript, and enforce the use of HTTPS when available.

Self-identified *infosec experts* were a vocal minority of those willing to be interviewed. Many were very receptive to the platform, indicating it satisfied their expectations for privacy and functionality, and that it was simple enough to allow collaboration with peers in place of proprietary or unencrypted alternatives.

Some appreciated the software but had concerns as to whether the server operators could be trusted not to insert malicious Javascript. They were often capable of running their own instance, and often enjoyed doing so as a hobby. On the opposite end of the spectrum, some were highly skeptical and objected to the absence of a dedicated client which could run outside of a browser, presumably restricting their workflows to editing alone or using collaborative editors with the assumption that their documents were not private.

The majority reported that their interest in PETs was not professional in nature, but better described as a hobby or a form of activism. They preferred to have their content remain private, but didn't require it. Many of these respondents indicated that they promoted the software to raise awareness of routine passive surveillance. They offered more feedback regarding the ergonomics of the system, as their peers cited those factors as obstacles to their regular adoption. This posed the greatest barrier to own their own adoption, as they used it for its collaborative features more than for solo workflows.

3   Façades

In architecture, the facade of a building is often the most important aspect from a design standpoint, as it sets the tone for the rest of the building [wik2019]

Many features in CryptPad intentionally resemble those offered by services with more conventional architectures. Most logic is implemented clientside, making novel use of encryption to provide the access control functionality usually enforced by a central authority. The following sections will compare these façades against the traditional counterparts they emulate, focusing more on recent insights than the technical implementations covered in our previous paper [mac2018].

3.1 Document Creation

Users access existing documents via their URLs, which encode identifiers and encryption keys into the *fragment identifier* portion of the URL. Colloquially called the URL's *hash*, this data is not sent to the server as a part of the page's HTTP request. Whenever an editor is accessed without a hash already provided, a new one is generated on their device and encoded into their URL bar. This allows users to share access by sharing a URL, an activity which is already familiar to many internet users.

3.2 Document Curation

Initial versions of CryptPad stored references to recently edited documents using the browser's *localStorage* API and displayed them in a table on the home page. URLs generated by the system are not intended to be memorable, and the lack of strong guarantees of browser storage persistence made this a fragile solution. In practice users worked around these limitations by tracking their documents via the *pad of pads* method they'd reported using for Etherpad document curation. Sharing access to this root document allowed them to curate and access their content from multiple browsers and devices, which users noted was critical for their usage.

We implemented the *CryptDrive* application to use the same data structure and present an interface like that of most filesystem browsers. The initial version of this interface simply exposed the hash of the user's drive for the purpose of recovery. Subsequent iterations tied this root key to their login info.

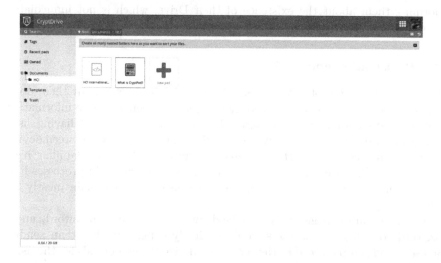

Fig. 1. Document curation via the CryptDrive

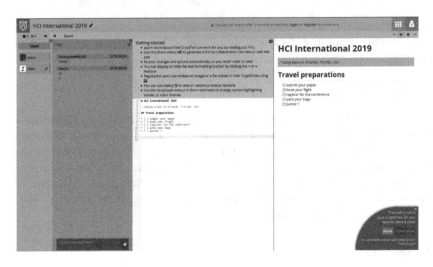

Fig. 2. Storing a pad in a users CryptDrive

Over time we have added many features to improve users ability to organize and retrieve their documents, like tagging, search, and the views which sort files by their various attributes. One of the more significant changes we've made was to stop storing files in the drive automatically when they were viewed. At first we believed that users would see more benefit from the drive if they discovered that it kept their history for them, but it was brought to our attention [cry2019a] that this implicit behaviour was not communicated, and could lead to a privacy breach for users who weren't aware of this default behaviour (Fig. 1).

We implemented a dialog asking users whether they wanted to store the document in their CryptDrive and offered the ability to configure their account to use the legacy behaviour. It offered users more control, while simultaneously informing them about the existence of their Drive, which is not immediately obvious to new users.

3.3 Registration and Login

Since each user's CryptDrive tracks the encryption keys for all their documents, its credentials serve as a root keyring for all their sensitive information, making their handling a particularly risky operation. To avoid having users achieve multi-device workflows by transmitting these credentials between devices in an insecure manner, we chose to make them accessible via a familiar *registration page*. The mechanisms behind the registration and login processes have been modified several times, though the core mechanisms remain mostly the same (Fig. 2).

The registration page features a field for a username, a password, and a password confirmation, as users would typically expect. Rather than sending the username and password to the server, we derive the credentials for the user's

Fig. 3. An overview of user registration

drive from their input in a deterministic manner. The same inputs from any device will derive the same keys, effectively allowing the user to memorize their encryption keys.

For the derivation process, we used *scrypt*, a memory-hard *password-based key derivation function*. Each user's password is salted with their username and an optional server-wide token, ensuring that each user on each instance would have their own unique keyspace, making it difficult to brute-force passwords. After deriving a hash for the user's drive, we cache the derived encryption key in localStorage, leaving them logged in so long their storage was not cleared (Fig. 3).

Logging in is a simple matter of entering credentials and having the client check whether they yield the hash for an existing user account. Logging out requires only that localStorage be cleared.

This scheme is resilient in the event of a serverside compromise, since user credentials are never learned by the server. Users generally understand that they should not share login credentials, and so their typical behaviour is consistent with our desired usage. The main difference between this mode and conventional login procedures is that the service operator has no means of recovering or resetting user passwords. As we were conscious of the risk that users would expect to rely on password reset, we took measures to encourage users to remember their credentials (Fig. 4).

Upon entering a valid username and two matching passphrases, the user is presented with a confirmation dialog. It offers two buttons, but inverts their position and the usual coloring to encourage them to click on the abort button. We intend to shock the user into reading the dialog more carefully, in which case they learn that reset is not possible. The confirmation button's text states *"I have written down my username and password, proceed"*.

Fig. 4. Informing users that we can't recover or reset their passwords

In theory, this should prevent users from losing access, however, it does not have a perfect success rate. According to our telemetry, CryptPad.fr received 1800 registrations within a period of 90 days, while we received fewer than 5 requests for recovery in the same period. On some occasions, users were either able to remember their password or to regain access to their most critical documents by searching their browser's history for its URL.

Understandably, data loss is traumatic, and so we hope to minimize its likelihood further. Users who lose access to their documents are frustrated, and we expect that such experiences are likely to impact their confidence in using platforms which utilize such schemes.

Users who contacted us for the purpose of data recovery tended to offer their username or email as an identifying feature of their account, indicating that they did not understand that neither was ever exposed to us, as we only recognize users by their *Public signing key*.

The belief that usernames are globally unique doesn't tend to affect user security in a negative way, though on several occasions we have received queries from users stating that two different sets of documents were stored in the same *CryptDrive* on multiple devices. After a little troubleshooting it was discovered that they had accidentally registered twice with the same username while intending to log in, though they'd used two different passwords. Once they realized this fact it was relatively simple to merge the complete list of documents into a single drive, though they indicated that it was a stressful situation.

User passwords are required to be at least 8 characters in length by default, though custom lengths can be set by the server administrator. There are no restrictions imposed on the characters used for the password or username, allowing users to choose emojis or any special characters they like. Likewise, users are not required to use capitals, minuscules, numbers or special characters, since such rules often frustrate users [cod2019b] and don't contribute to their security in a meaningful way.

3.4   Authenticated Serverside Actions

A variety of features are either impossible or impractical to implement entirely clientside. These are implemented serverside as *remote procedure calls*, either on-demand or requiring authentication from clients if they are not sensitive in nature.

We consider information public if it is encrypted and does not reveal any information about particular users. Queries for the size of an encrypted document history, its metadata, and similar information can therefore be requested by any client.

Authenticated calls include queries or actions concerning particular users, as identified by their *ed25519 public signing key*. All authenticated requests are signed by the client with their private key, and validated by the server.

The development of this authentication layer was motivated in part by our desire to distinguish between documents stored in users drives and those used by exclusively by unregistered users or noone at all. Our measurements indicate that as many as 70% of the documents created on our server are used only for a short time before being abandoned. Lacking a means of identifying such documents our disk usage would continue to grow indefinitely. Since the software is open-source, we generate income by offering increased quotas to paying users, so this system also serves to track and enforce each user's quota.

Each user's list of documents is tracked using an append-only log, identified by the user's public key, with each line indicating one of three actions:

- *pin* a document (indicate that it should not be removed)
- *unpin* a document (indicate that the user no longer requires it)
- *reset* the user's pin list to a specified list of documents

Pin and unpin commands are sent to the server progressively as the user adds or removes documents from their drive. Each command returns a hash of the sorted list of their pinned documents, allowing the user to confirm that the server's account of their usage matches their own local list. If the client finds that their hash does not match that of the server, they send a reset command. The bearer of a private key is also able to delete their pin log, as we will cover when presenting *account deletion*. This system enables us to track the size of all documents pinned with a given public key, though users have expressed confusion about the reported size which includes the documents' full history.

Document deletion must also be implemented serverside, though the capacity to delete a file must be specified at its creation, otherwise any user could delete any document. Finally, we implement functionality for *encrypted file upload*, and *user password change*, covered below.

3.5   Capabilities and Delegation

The delegation of capabilities described earlier is achieved by sharing a document's URL, which can contain a variety of additional features beyond the basic features defined by its cryptographic keys.

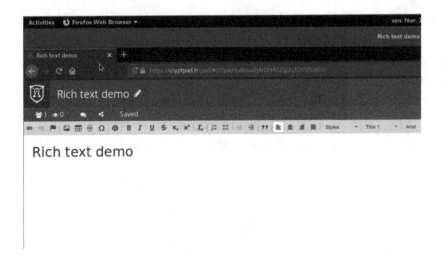

Fig. 5. The 'edit hash' for a document

Many editors also support a variety of modes, and users expressed the desire to share views of those modes directly. These modes include *present mode*, which was most obviously relevant to the slideshow editor. Likewise, documents can be loaded in *embed mode*, which displays the content of the document without the toolbars and other aspects of the platform which would be intrusive if included in an iframe.

We provide a dedicated menu for choosing the attributes and capabilities which users would like to share. Unfortunately, we discovered that some of the heuristics employed by various adblockers (which are very commonly used by our intended audience) caused the button for this sharing menu not to be displayed. We styled the share menu using an icon provided as a part of the fontawesome icon set.

Upon further investigation we determined that it was removed on the basis of its class (fa-share), since that logo is often used by social media sharing buttons which often track users. We worked around this bug by creating an alias for the class (fa-shhare), though the heuristics defined by adblockers are necessarily imperfect and quite likely to interfere with our intended behaviour again in the future.

Beyond the rudimentary capabilites for viewing and editing documents, we also offer support for deletion, automatic expiration, and password protection. These capabilities are exposed only to registered users via the *pad creation screen*, so as to avoid overwhelming new users. Since each user's drive is represented internally as a document itself, some of these capabilities are reused for user account administration as well, though generally through a different interface.

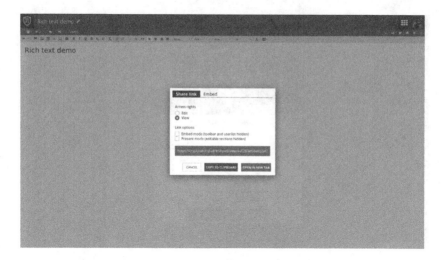

Fig. 6. The *sharing menu*

The owner of a document's log is defined at the time of its creation by including the public key of its creator in the first message of its history, making ownership immutable (and therefore *non-transferrable*) and *public* (Fig. 5).

Ownership of created documents is optional, for those who would prefer not to be linked to their creations. In practice this is the cause of much confusion, as it is difficult to know whether deletion will be desirable at a later time. Future iterations on ownership will most likely feature one-time signing keys, facilitating unlinkability and delegation of the right to delete a document. Going a step further, mutable metadata could be rewritten or amended, allowing an owner to delegate new owners or moderators, as well as allowiing revocation of server-defined rights.

Due to occasional reports of users accidentally and irrevocably deleting their content, we are considering modifying deletion such that files are temporarily moved into cold storage for a set period of time, after which they will be permanently deleted.

Expiration reuses existing deletion functionality, but schedules it for time relative to that of its creation. If a document is owned, it can be deleted in advance of its expiration time, though we do not currently offer the ability for the owner to cancel deletion. Expiration time is distributed to newly joining clients as a part of its metadata, which also indicates whether the document is owned or not (Fig. 6).

The development of *password-protected documents* was sponsored by a contributor who desired an additional level of security in the event that a document's URL was accidentally disclosed. We implemented the functionality clientside in a manner similar to that used for registration, defining a new versioned URL which supported a different scheme for deriving secrets.

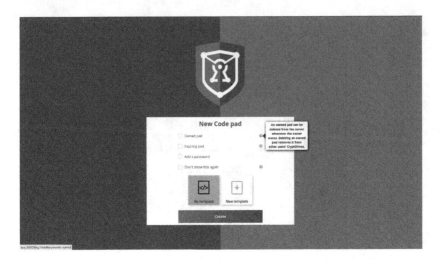

Fig. 7. The pad creation screen as seen by a registered user

The new format uses a cryptographically secure random seed, which is hashed with or without a password, as the creator desires. The resulting hash is divided into a signing key, and a secondary seed which is also hashed. The result of the second hash is then divided into the document's id and symmetric encryption key.

An additional flag is appended to the seed to indicate that a password is required, otherwise the keys are derived without its input. Once a valid password is entered, it is stored within the user's drive (Fig. 7).

This scheme offers an increased level of security, however, it does nothing to prevent brute-force password entry. Similarly, the user who created the document is not notified if someone attempts many passwords. Since our database is considered public, we do not currently have a mechanism for restricting access beyond limiting the accessibility of the secret values noted above.

It is trivial to change the password for owned documents, as the owner need only create a new document with the same content using secrets derived from a new password. Once the new document is in place, the old one is deleted. This implementation was quite simple, however, it has the unfortunate side-effect of having to re-distribute the new password manually. Future iterations will likely remove the notion of a password entirely, and instead track which users should have access, delivering strong secrets directly to their accounts in a secure manner (Fig. 8).

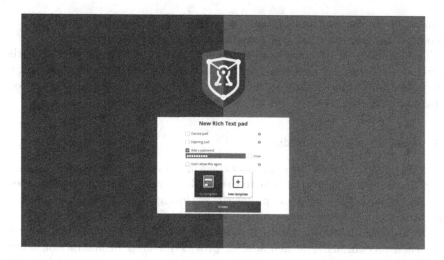

Fig. 8. A document protected by a password

3.6 Account Deletion

Account deletion is supported for users who registered after the introduction of ownership for user accounts. It is exposed via the settings page, and recursively deletes all the user's owned documents, their pin log, and their drive.

Users in possession of accounts which predate ownership can migrate to the newer format by creating a new *owned account*, setting a flag for the old one to mark it as deprecated, and unpinning it. Clientside checks for account

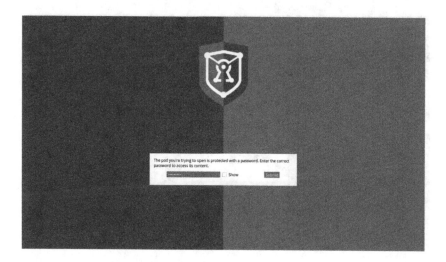

Fig. 9. Password entry for a protected document

deprecation prevent the user from accidentally accessing and modifying their old account data, ensuring that it expires after a period of inactivity.

The locations of user account documents were originally derived from the provided username and password, so the creation of a new account document in a new location required that we modify the scheme for login and registration, detailed below (Fig. 9).

3.7   User Password Change

This functionality differs from *password reset* in that the user is required to know the password which they would like to change. It is primarily meant to serve users whose passwords have been compromised, as through a data breach on another site, or through in-person or remote surveillance (as through a keylogger).

Our original password system derived the secrets for a user's drive directly from their credentials. The new system provided a layer of abstraction which stored existing or randomly generated credentials in an encrypted blob on the server, with its location and encryption keys derived from the supplied credentials. The resulting encryption keys are used only to write and delete blobs at a particular location. Due to our inability to migrate existing data, the new system was deployed in parallel with the legacy system, with additional code to handle the many edge cases.

When attempting to log in or register, we confirm that their credentials match an existing legacy account and that it has not been marked as deprecated. The user is logged in if a valid account is found, otherwise we check for a modern account. If no account is found the user is informed that account exists with the provided username and password (Fig. 10).

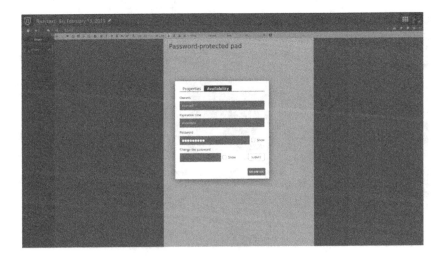

Fig. 10. Password change for a protected document

The actual password change process requests that the user enter their current password, the new password, and a confirmation of the new password. Assuming the old password is correct and the new passwords match, the current state of the user's account document is re-encrypted and written to a new location. The new location and encryption keys are encrypted and written using the keys derived from their new password and their existing username. If the whole process completes with no errors, then the old user account document is either deleted outright if it was owned, or marked as deprecated otherwise.

Our telemetry indicates that user passwords are not changed often, with approximately 20 in any given 90 day period, though it is quite likely that these rare events are motivated by valid security concerns.

3.8   Remote Logout

Remote logout was developed to address cases active sessions on confiscated or inaccessible devuces. Some of our advocates report advising users who lack the privilege of a dedicated device for their regular use, who tend to use the service from libraries or other providers of public terminals.

Should a user forget to log out when they finish using a device, they are able to remotely terminate such lingering sessions. When a user logs in, a token is copied from their account document into the localStorage of the device. The settings page provides an interface which updates the token, triggering its replication to all active sessions. If at any time the client discovers that their local token does not match the account token, they immediately log out.

Admittedly, since this system is implemented clientside it cannot force malicious or custom clients to stop accessing an account. It was implemented before the existence of user password change and the related facilities for user account relocation. We operate under the assumption that it is better to provide some imperfect level of security than to do nothing in the absence of a perfect solution. Now that we have the capacity to actually re-encrypt and relocate a user's account, such a mechanism could provide a stronger guarantee of confidentiality by re-keying and effectively providing *forward secrecy*.

Like password change, remote logout is used very rarely, though in the cases where it is used it may be essential.

3.9   File Encryption

While a number of platforms provide the capacity to encrypt and upload files, CryptPad integrates this functionality into its various applications and implements permission schemes comparable to those of the rest of the platform, such as password protection, expiration, and deletion. Notably, encrypted documents are immutable, making it impossible to edit one file embedded in many places.

At the present date, CryptPad stores over 17000 files for a total 6.9 GB of storage space, with individual files being no larger than 25 MB. 4.1 GB of the total space is consumed by owned files, while the remaining 2.8 GB have no owner. Encrypted files do not seem to pose any serious usability issues, as we have not received any special requests to modify their behaviour.

3.10   Shared Folders

Most security issues in CryptPad are related to the accidental disclosure of keys, and so many features are intended to make this less likely. Shared folders make it possible to delegate ongoing access to a collection once, limiting the opportunities for insecure key management. This functionality was deferred until the introduction of shared workers made it a practical consideration.

Fig. 11. Termination of remote sessions

Like a user's drive, shared folders are identified by URLs, and delegate the capability to edit any document stored within, as the data structure replicates the seeds and passwords used to derive all the keys. This single-tier level of access is reasonable for a single user's drive, but not necessarily so in a group context. We plan to offer shared folders with cascading permissions, such that access to a read-only version of a folder will only provide read-only access to the elements contained within (Fig. 11).

3.11   Chat

Chat in CryptPad was also developed for the primary purpose of offering a secure means to transmit URLs. Two distinct but related chat interfaces are offered by the platform, a dedicated *contacts* application which is not widely used, and *contextual chat* which provides a dedicated chat channel for every pad (Fig. 12).

The contacts application requires that users become friends before being able to message each other, however, such requests must be completed while both

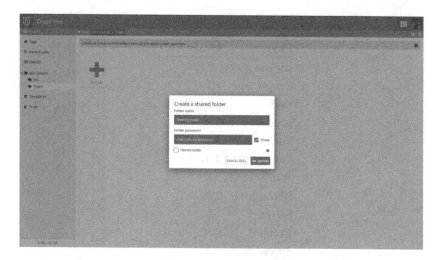

Fig. 12. Shared folder creation

users are online, making it quite fragile in practice. We plan to improve offline friend requests to hook into a well-integrated notification system and use the same messaging functionality to delegate access to pads, making social features a more central part of the platform.

3.12 Editors

Statistics regarding the usage of each editor are suggestive of certain trends on their own, however, combined with user reports we are able to discern more general patterns (Table 1).

The rich text editor, based on CKEditor 4 [cke2019], is by far the most popular application as used on *CryptPad.fr*. We replace the editor's image inclusion functionality with our own, forbidding the inclusion of remote files so as to ensure that user IPs are not exposed to third-party services, preferring to encrypt and upload images to the drive of the user embedding it within the document. We also indicate the location of other users' cursors, making the experience of collaborative editing more tangible.

While we enable all of our applications on our flagship instance, community-hosted instances allow for administrators to restrict usage to particular editors. The instance hosted by the Pirate Party of Germany [25] notably disallows usage of rich text documents, preferring the markdown-based formats which integrate more readily with the rest of their infrastructure.

User reports suggest that rich text editing is preferred by those with an average level of computing experience, or those whose peers match that demographic.

The curation functionality of the CryptDrive is not used especially often. While we consider it natural to simultaneously read or edit multiple text documents, only one browser tab is required to access those documents. We would

Table 1. Application usage

Page	Usage (%)
Rich text	57.32
CryptDrive	15.02
Code	9.34
Kanban	3.93
Slide	3.27
Poll	3.04
Whiteboard	2.55
Contacts	2.46
Settings	1.91
Profile	0.82
Spreadsheet	0.33

Page load percentage by application

expect this to lead to fewer page loads, however, only about one fifth of the users who view pads view the drive, as indicated by counting only unique IP addresses for each type. This seems to indicate that many collaborative session are initiated and managed by a minority of their participants, while the majority edits particular documents but does not actively curate their own collection.

We have seen this number increase considerably since we began prompting users as to whether they would like to store a pad in their drive, suggesting that many prospective users simply weren't aware of its existence.

The code editor (based on Codemirror [cod2019a]) seems most popular among technical users who favour it for its Markdown syntax highlighting and live preview functionality, though it offers a range of other highlighting modes, of which at least a minority of users are aware. Reports indicate that plain and rich text editing are nearly exclusive for any particular user, except when users are invited to collaborate with a peer. Use of Markdown's syntax requires some training, the limiting effect of which is evident in the rate of adoption compared to rich text editing.

The relatively low rates of adoption for the remaining editors could suggest that users consider their text documents to be more sensitive, or simply non-textual use cases are more rare by their very nature. Our *kanban application* (based on jkanban [jka2019]) occupies a small niche among particular users who have reported using CryptPad exclusively for its functionality, as there exist no other competing implementations of encrypted project boards.

Most of our *slideshow* editor's implementation overlaps with that of our code editor. Unlike the code editor, the slide editor only supports Markdown, and implements a few custom extensions to the language so as to delimit sections of content as distinct slides.

One user has noted that the editor seems *"only for geeks"*, and that they expect more functionality for their slideshows. Indeed, the syntax for the application was based on tslide [tsl2019], which is intended to facilitate slideshows from the terminal.

Users have noted that competing presentation platforms which offer similar rendering functionality require a page reload to see the latest content. Our editor renders this content *on the fly*, and as such the final result is viewable in real-time as long as anyone is modifying the content.

Notably, we have received requests for adding support for rendering mathematical equations, as users who are knowledgeable about such subjects are often required to present their knowledge to others. Like our kanban, this editor enjoys a small but loyal user base.

CryptPad's *poll editor* was written without the aid of third-party frameworks with the intent of providing an alternative to *Doodle* [doo2019] and other scheduling applications. While its adoption is not considerably worse than some of our other applications, we are aware of users who employ CryptPad's kanban and slide editors in applicable situations, but persist in using Doodle or other unencrypted alternatives despite being ideologically inclined towards privacy-friendly tools.

The document model currently employed throughout most of CryptPad does not allow for granular permissions for sections of a document. Other polling applications only allow particular users to change their own results, but CryptPad's document model only restricts access on a global scale, allowing anyone with edit rights for the poll to change any of its fields, including other users responses. This severely limits its suitability for groups without some established social norms for cooperation, and generally serves to confuse users.

Overall we conclude that the current implementation of this appliciation was not a good fit for the needs of its prospective users, though a new data model with granular permissions would likely improve adoption.

Like polls, whiteboards (based on our fork of Fabric.js [fab2019]) were implemented primarily as an experiment, and have received relatively little attention from users and the development team alike. The basic features it offers are perhaps insufficient for serious use cases which might warrant the need for privacy, making it an unsuitable candidate for inclusion in the platform.

Supplementary applications like our dedicated encrypted messenger, settings page, and user profiles collectively make up just over 5% of usage. It's entirely possible to use the platform without them, however, we expect that the functionality they offer could be more widely useful if they were more visible. Perhaps the features they offer would receive more attention if they were integrated throughout the platform as with our encrypted files, rather than in dedicated pages.

Our spreadsheet implementation (based upon OnlyOffice [onl2019]) has been very highly requested through the life of the project, however, its use is still low as it has only recently been made available through its beta release. Their implementation differs considerably from our other applications due to technical constraints, making use of APIs which are only available to registered users, which has limited the ease of its adoption.

4 Conclusion

Our proposed principle references two highly subjective terms, *secure* and *familiar*. It is worth considering *against which adversaries* the system must remain secure, and *with which existing systems* the intended audience is familiar. We reference Etherpad and Google Docs, however, neither platform is without its own assumptions which may not hold true in different contexts.

We notice a general conflict between those who want more help from centralized authorities and those who want a fully decentralized solution relying only on cryptography. Two-factor authentication can act as a guarantee against brute-force password-cracking, and centralized oversight can guard against password loss. Which answer is correct seems to depend largely on who is asked.

We struggle to balance the needs of common and high-risk users even while questioning the validity of these terms, as risk itself may not fit neatly into a single spectrum. Accessibility itself is also multi-faceted, necessitating an approach which is aware of a variety of normative assumptions, some of which we are most certainly guilty.

These concerns are not unique to the development of cryptographic systems, but are rather endemic to the field of design. This is not to say that there are not solutions to the problems we face, just that they are not likely to be universal. It is difficult for us to say whether error reports indicate a poor design, or too wide of a demographic. In the absence of such reports we judge that a particular implementation has been a success, but in any case we recognize clear room for improvement in many directions.

The role of finance is unfortunately outside the scope of this paper, despite the extent to which surveillance is motivated by revenue models. Future works may investigate this relationship more closely.

CryptPad's development has centered around this principle of modeling user expectations with cryptography. We have been limited by both the environment which we target, and the ciphers available for that environment, yet on the whole this approach proven very satisfying for our users. Perhaps it is unsurprising to hear that users were surprised by interfaces which behaved in manners contradicting their past experience, yet the majority of the façades presented have achieved better than modest acceptance. By no means do we believe that we have sufficiently dissociated the means and experience of security, yet we are confidant that the conscious effort of separation has driven the success we can claim.

References

[mac2018] ACM DocEng 20118. Association for Computing Machinery (2018). https://doceng.org/doceng2018

[cke2019] Ckeditor4 (2019). https://ckeditor.com/ckeditor-4/. Accessed 26 Feb 2019

[cod2019a] Codemirror (2019a). https://codemirror.net/. Accessed 26 Feb 2019 [cod2019b] codinghorror blog (2019b). https://blog.codinghorror.com/password-rules-are-bullshit/. Accessed 26 Feb 2019

[cry2019a] (2019a) Cryptpad issue 270. https://github.com/xwiki-labs/cryptpad/issues/270; consulted 2019–02-26

[cry2019b] Cryptpad.fr (2019b). https://cryptpad.fr. Accessed 26 Feb 2019

[cry2019c] Cryptpad's mastodon account (2019c). https://social.weho.st/@cryptpad. Accessed 26 Feb 2019

[cry2019d] Cryptpad's source (2019d). https://github.com/xwiki-labs/cryptpad. Accessed 26 Feb 2019

[doo2019] Doodle web application (2019). https://doodle.com/. Accessed 26 Feb 2019

[ela2019] Elastic search (2019). https://www.elastic.co/. Accessed 26 Feb 2019

[fab2019] fabricjs source (2019). https://github.com/fabricjs/fabric.js. Accessed 26 Feb 2019

[jka2019] Jkanban source (2019). https://github.com/riktar/jkanban/. Accessed 26 Feb 2019

[onl2019] Onlyoffice website (2019). https://www.onlyoffice.com/. Accessed 26 Feb 2019

[tsl2019] Tslide source (2019). https://github.com/tslide/tslide. Accessed 26 Feb 2019

[twi2019] Twitter (2019). https://twitter.com/cryptpad. Accessed 26 Feb 2019

[wik2019] Wikipedia facade definition (2019). https://en.wikipedia.org/wiki/Facade. Accessed 26 Feb 2019

Interdependencies, Conflicts and Trade-Offs Between Security and Usability: Why and How Should We Engineer Them?

Bilal Naqvi[1,2]([⊠]) and Ahmed Seffah[3]

[1] Software Engineering, LENS, LUT University, Lappeenranta, Finland
syed.naqvi@student.lut.fi
[2] Mirpur University of Science and Technology, MUST, Mirpur, Pakistan
[3] Green UX Design, Thinking Associates, Paris, France

Abstract. Security and usability are considered as conflicting goals. Despite the recognition that security and usability conflicts pose a serious challenge to achieve effective security, the review of the state of art identifies many gaps in today's practices including, (1) failure of security specialists to address usability, as perceived and defined by the human computer interaction (HCI) community, (2) industry's behavior is being more driven by bug fixing, rather than trying to examine and consider the context and the human experiences in which the bugs occurs, and (3) the lack of HCI skills required for conducting effective user studies. Furthermore, analysis of the existing literature identifies different perceptions concerning the relationship between security and usability. Some researchers have identified existence of trade-offs when it comes to the security and usability conflicts, however, others refer to the trade-offs as mere myths. A four staged process oriented framework to address the security and usability conflict is presented in this paper. The framework governs aspects from identification of the conflicts to elicitation of suitable trade-offs. To support re-use, the outcomes of employing the framework are documented in form of design patterns. A template to standardize documentation of the patterns is also presented along with one example of the usable security patterns.

Keywords: Usability · Security · Usable security · Conflicts · Trade-offs · Framework · Patterns · Usable security patterns

1 Introduction

ISO 25010 model lists security and usability among the eight characteristics of its product quality model [1]. Despite providing guidance on handling each quality characteristic individually, ISO 25010 does not provide guidance when two or more dependent characteristics come into conflict. An example of such a conflict is the conflict between security and usability. As an instance of security and usability conflict consider passwords; despite their role in implementing authentication (a security mechanism), passwords have a human dimension. The password security guidelines suggest passwords to be sufficiently long, frequently changed, have different cases and special characters, etc., however, from user's perspective such passwords are hard to

© Springer Nature Switzerland AG 2019
A. Moallem (Ed.): HCII 2019, LNCS 11594, pp. 314–324, 2019.
https://doi.org/10.1007/978-3-030-22351-9_21

memorize especially when re-use of the passwords is strongly discouraged and an average user has to manage around 22 online password [2].

Password masking is another instance of the security and usability conflict. To protect against shoulder surfing and other similar attacks, almost all authentication implementations mask the password when the user types it. However, for a legitimate user it impacts usability element of 'feedback' as in case of a mistake the user has to re-type long complex password, rather than knowing and correcting the mistake. There-fore, it can be gathered that password masking approach holds good from security perspective, but it has an impact from the usability point of view.

Human factors are perhaps considered as greatest barrier to effective computer security [3]. Most security mechanisms are too difficult and confusing for the average computer user to manage correctly. Furthermore, a common belief is that security and usability are two the opposed quality factors that are related to different components of a system (functionality and user interface respectively). This means that, security of the system and usability of the services can be engineered by two separate teams, mainly by software engineering and user interface (UI)/user experience (UX) teams. However, there are several cases in which security and usability are enhanced by modelling their mutual relationships. Typical examples include online payment and e-banking services, supervision of critical industrial infrastructures, crisis management. This research aims to bridge the gaps between security specialists and UI/UX experts. The following are the key gaps:

One gap explains the failure of security specialists to address usability, as perceived and defined by the HCI community. Security and usability have historically evolved independently or have been considered as two opposite factors. Another historical explanation is that researchers were more driven by technology rather than user problems and perceptions of security. For example, the development of identity management technologies was so demanding in terms of security that it left little time and costs to cater usability and the human factors in general.

A second gap that may be advocated is the industry's behaviors is more driven by bug fixing, rather than trying to examine and consider the context and the user expe-riences in which the bugs occurs. Therefore, most industry efforts have been on automating the process of reporting and handling bugs, rather than looking for human experiences and how they can promote more secure operations overall.

Another gap that demonstrates the lack of alignment between security and usability is the design and innovation approach leading to new security technologies. Most often, the innovation is initiated by a company developing an "in-house technology" addressing a specific problem which occurs in a specific project. Other groups in the same company or others companies may develop their own versions of these solutions. This makes it difficult to ensure the usability of these in-house solutions and several versions of them, while changing the original context of their applicability. Fire-walls, junk mail filters, spyware, and antivirus are good examples.

Finally, the lack of HCI skills required for conducting effective user studies are a serious obstacle. Moreover, user studies are difficult to conduct because regulations governing use of human subjects' in experiments related to safety and security of the systems and services have to be considered.

Despite these gaps and non-alignment between security and usability, the conflict between these two is a recognized problem; the primary question addressed in this paper is why and how to engineer the conflicts and trade-offs between security and usability. One approach that we consider appropriate for engineering the conflicts and appropriate trade-offs involves the use of design patterns. Patterns can be used to document instances of the conflict and balanced solution to address the conflict (right trade-off). Patterns can be disseminated among the community of security and usability developers to influence their decision making when it comes to the conflict between the two characteristics.

The remainder of this paper is organized as follows. Section 2 presents the literature review, which was conducted considering two main objectives. Section 3 discusses the primary question addressed in the paper i.e. why and how to engineer the conflicts and trade-offs between security and usability, both 'why' and 'how' to engineer conflicts and trade-offs are discussed in subsequent sub-sections. A template to standardize documentation of the patterns is also presented along with one example of the usable security patterns. Section 4 concludes the paper.

2 Literature Review

Despite the recognition of security and usability conflict as a challenge, not much has been accomplished for two reasons, (1) security and usability are considered as after thoughts, and (2) security and usability are not considered strategically, and not integrated into to the strategic plans for system development [4].

The literature review was conducted in two stages with objectives as follows.

1. To identify one of the core reasons for non-alignment between security and usability.
2. To identify solutions for addressing security and usability conflicts.

The result of the first stage of literature review revealed inconsistent perceptions about relationship between security and usability as one of the reasons for non-alignment between the two characteristics. However, the findings relevant to both objectives are presented in subsequent sub-sections.

2.1 Inconsistent Perceptions About Relationship Between Security and Usability

Various communities and interest groups have been studying the security and usability conflicts independently from each other, these include: (1) traditional computer security community dealing with the wider scope of quality of services in computer and communication technologies; usability is a minor concern addressed at a cosmetic level in this community, (2) the software engineering community where security and usability have been defined as two among the eight major quality characteristics, and usability is a characteristic of user interfaces and security is a characteristic of the functionality, (3) the HCI community, to name a few. As a result, the available literature on relationships between security and usability can be classified in two categories.

- There are trade-offs when it comes to conflicts between security and usability.
- Trade-offs between security and usability are mere myths.

Most of the research till date argues on existence of the trade-offs between security and usability. The authors [5] conducted a case study on iOS and Android to find an answer for "what is more important: usability or security". The authors identified that importance of security and usability is purely situation based, and that the trade-offs are sometimes in favor of security and vice versa. The authors [6] presented an empirical evidence in favor of existence of the trade-offs between security and usability. The empirical study featured three different schemes for code voting systems. The authors state, "nevertheless, the security gains come at the cost of usability losses". The authors [7] presented an empirical investigation concerning existence of trade-offs between security and usability. The results of within-subjects study to understand and value security and usability trade-offs in end-to-end email encryption were presented. The results of the study identify that the participants in their choice for the preferred system to use deliberately made the trade-offs between security and usability.

In parallel with the research establishing existence of the trade-offs, there is some research classifying security and usability trade-offs as mere myths. A special issue 'the security-usability trade-off myth' features one such discussion between researchers and practitioners in usable security [8]. The participants were of the view that decreasing usability can lead to less security and understanding the context in which solutions are deployed is important. The participants discussed the example of two-factor authentication involving one-time passwords (OTP) and its consequences if the length of OTP is increased from 6 to 8 characters. Overall, the participants were of the view that, "security experts simply invoke the myth of tradeoff between usability and security, and use this as cover to avoid the exercise of saying precisely what security benefit in precisely what scenarios this usability burden is going to deliver." The authors [9] stated that security and usability are not inherently in conflict. The authors suggested that the researchers have to go beyond than just adopting human-centered design principles and consider involving the user in the decision making process.

2.2 Solutions to Address the Security and Usability Conflicts

In line with the second objective of the literature review, we present the solutions that have been proposed to address the security and usability conflict. The author [10] presented a set of guidelines to cater the security and usability conflict. The work is mainly focused on avoiding the conflict by depriving the user from making system security related decisions. The author presented guidelines like, providing a check-list to developers of security systems, hiding security related tasks from users, reducing the user memory load etc. The author also suggested that user should be involved in making security decisions on the system only when the situation is clear to the user; otherwise, the system should take the security decisions itself.

The authors [11] while studying the trade-offs between security and usability presented a set of guidelines to cater the conflict. The authors considered various aspects of usability such as effectiveness, satisfaction, efficiency, learnability and presented different guidelines focusing on each of the mentioned elements in conjunction with security.

The authors [12] suggested to implement security features as a separate service on cloud naming it CaaS "Confidentiality as a Service", which would perform the confidentiality function on behalf of the users even if the credentials are lost. The main theme discussed in their work is to create a level of abstraction, and let the service perform security tasks on user's behalf.

The authors [13] presented an ontological framework for catering the security and usability conflict. The framework is based on identification of usability/security requirements, identifying meaning and system context. After that the conflicts are identified on basis on system requirements, which are characterized on basis of their impact and listed. The nature of the identified conflict is then determined, and based on that the conflict resolution strategy is made in accordance with the system requirements.

The authors [14] presented an 'Assessment Framework for Usable Security' (AFUS), which works by filtering and merging the security and usability requirements, and then applying utility functions for risk analysis. The decision trees are generated to calculate the weight and utility of each attribute of security and usability. The weights determine relative importance of attributes to be considered for requirement specification of software. The authors claim that requirements specified after AFUS have a balance between usability, security and usable security.

3 Interdependencies, Conflicts and Tradeoffs Between Security and Usability: Why and How Should We Engineer Them?

3.1 Why Is It Important to Handle Security and Usability Conflicts?

Security cannot be achieved in real sense unless it incorporates the human element [22]. To establish why it is important to handle security and usability conflicts, we refer to some existing empirical evidences and technical reports. National Institute of Standards and Technology (NIST) report NISTIR 8080 states that "the human element is a critical yet often overlooked component during technology integration [...], it is critical to understand users' primary goals, the characteristics of the users (both physical and cognitive attributes), and the context in which they are operating" [15].

IBM global analysis report on 'cost of data breach' mentions that a data breach caused by human error takes around 162 days to identify and 59 days to contain. Among the root causes of data breaches, the report identifies that 25% of data breaches are caused due to human factors [16]. Considering these stats in conjunction with NIST report, identifies one possible reason for such high number of breaches due to human errors i.e. due to overlooking human factors while designing the security systems. We extend this argument to postulate that security features are unnecessarily complex thereby increasing the chances of error.

As early as in 1998, Whitten and Tygar suggested the need for developers (of security functionality) to think from user's perspective. They further stated that designers of security systems should not assume that the users will read manuals for configuration, instead, the security should be easy to use [17].

The study [18] revealed results of analysis of 32 million passwords for a service, among which 1% were merely "123456" and around 20% of the passwords were the user's name, slang or a common dictionary word. These stats basically describe the user's will, as stated by authors [19], "unless you stand over them with a loaded gun, users will disable, evade, or avoid any security system that proves to be too burdensome or bothersome".

Usable security poses a distinct challenge that needs to be addressed, while working on security of the system. With reference to stats discussed earlier, it is relevant to state that developing a system without incorporating human aspects even being secure against external threats, would be susceptible to: (1) user mistakes ultimately leading to system compromise, (2) increased user disengagement and frustration, (3) users working around anything necessary to do their job [20].

It is important to mention that security and usability conflict is not limited to usability of the interface, and should not also be considered as limited to studies featuring passwords and other authentication mechanisms; however, there are other instances of this conflict beyond just authentication and user interfaces. One such example features conflicts arising with deployment of complex encryption ciphers, which impact 'understandability' of human users while implementing 'confidentiality' (a security mechanism). Furthermore, the authors [20] state, "researchers have identified an increasing number of security mechanisms that are so unusable that the intended users either circumvent them or give up on a service rather than suffer the security". Therefore, it is imperative to consider all aspects of the conflict between security and usability, otherwise we risk building complex secure systems that are susceptible to user mistakes ultimately leading to security compromises.

3.2   How to Engineer the Security and Usability Conflicts?

Figure 1 portrays the proposed four-staged process oriented framework. The framework provides sequence of activities to be followed in order to address the conflict. The framework helps in identifying the conflicts between security and usability while documenting balanced solutions (right trade-offs) in the format of patterns. The four major activities that form basis of this framework are as under.

1. *Analysis* of the diverse human experiences and tasks of the stakeholders and end-users that involve security technologies, modeling of the interaction between stakeholders and user's interaction to accomplish those tasks, and quantifying the possible usability problems.
2. *Modelling* of the relationship between security and usability using as input the descriptions of human experiences, tasks and usability problems identified in the previous step.
3. *Development* of the solutions and their documentation in the format of patterns. The solutions can be used by participating organizations to enhance usability of existing security technologies or the development of new ones.

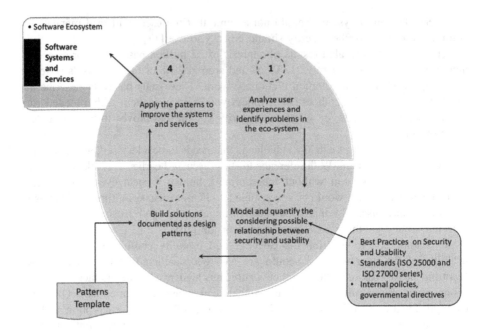

Fig. 1. The proposed process-oriented framework for engineering conflicts between security and usability

4. *Application* of the documented patterns in the software eco-system. Pattern can serve as an effective tool for developers in order to deal with usability concerns in security services. Particularly, the patterns can serve less experienced developers and free-lancers in influencing their decision making abilities when it comes to the security and usability conflicts.

We have been developing and refining this framework using a series of experiments in lab and industry following a design science research (DSR) approach. The main advantage of DSR is the "build-and-evaluate" loop, which allows suggestions from community to be incorporated in the evolved versions of the framework.

As evident from the Fig. 1, the first step involves identification of the conflicts. For this purpose, user studies, cognitive walkthroughs, heuristic evaluations are conducted. Once the conflicts are identified the relationship between security and usability are modelled and quantified. Best practices and standards on security and usability also come into play when modelling the relationship between the two. When do's and don'ts from the perspective of security and usability are known after accessing the underlying best practices, standards and directives, the security and usability professionals brainstorm together to build a balanced solution (the right trade-off) between the two conflicting characteristics. The right trade-offs along with other necessary information are then documented as design patterns. A standardized template for documenting the usable security patterns is presented in Fig. 2.

Once the pattern is documented it can be applied to solve the recurring problem in the software eco-system in similar context of use. The pattern is expected to facilitate

- **Title:** The unique name of name for the pattern. Pattern can be named on basis of the problem it is solving or some names can be attributed to the solution suggested in the pattern.
- **Classification:** What is the category of the pattern, example categories can be: authentication mechanisms, data protection, device protection etc. Classifying patterns and grouping them would assist developers to find them under the relevant category.
- **Prologue:** One sentence that describes the intent behind this pattern.
- **Problem statement:** One or two sentences to summarize the problem addressed by the pattern.
- **Context of Use:** Patterns always have a particular context. A statement describing the context in which the particular patterns can be applied. The context should lack ambiguity so that the pattern is always applied in correct situations.
- **Affected Sub factors:** The sub-factors of usability and security being affected/involved when this pattern is applied.
  - o   Usability:
  - o   Security:
- **Solution:** One or two statements that guide on how to solve the problem.
- **Discussion:** Statements that illuminate the system of forces resolved (forces for us are the dimensions of conflicts) by the pattern.
- **Type of service:** Applicability of pattern from device/infrastructure perspective, e.g. mobile, desktop, web etc.
- **Epilogue:** One sentence per pattern that can be expected to follow this one or simply consequence of applying the pattern.
- **Related Patterns:** The patterns that are related to this pattern; this would provide information about similar patterns that can also be applicable whenever the problem (being addressed in this pattern) occurs.

Fig. 2. Usable security patterns template

developers and designers in making reasonably accurate choices when it comes to the conflicts between security and usability. Both usability and security professionals recognize the importance of incorporating their concerns throughout the design cycle and acknowledge the need for an iterative, rather than a linear design process. Design patterns have shown their effectiveness in supporting a smooth integration and cross-pollination of communities [21]. Patterns also assist in an improved communication among team members from different disciplines by developing a common language or vocabulary when explaining design. For elaborating how a usable security pattern would look like, an example pattern is presented in Fig. 3.

It is pertinent to state that one pattern solves one problem only, therefore, an entire catalogue of patterns is required to support the development of simultaneously usable and secure software systems. The documented patterns can be disseminated among the community of developers and designers using online pages, conducting developer workshops and symposiums, research publications, etc.

- **Title:** Visibility of system status.
- **Classification:** data protection, device protection.
- **Prologue:** To make the user feel satisfied after performing a security task.
- **Problem statement:** The completion of security task leaves the user wondering, if the task was completed to perfection or not.
- **Context of Use:** Whenever security task requires user intervention and user is able to complete the task to perfection. The 'security tasks' would include successful encryption and all other tasks relevant to data and device protection.
- **Affected Sub factors:** The sub-factors of usability and security being affected/involved when this pattern is applied.
  - o   Usability: trust, satisfaction, feedback
  - o   Security: confidentiality, integrity, non-repudiation
- **Solution:** In case of successful completion of a security task, provide the user with feedback followed by clear visibility of the system status. For example, when the communication has been encrypted change the window color that gives the user the protected feel.
- **Discussion:** Providing the user with clear feedback and visibility of status not only preserves system security, but increases the user trust and satisfaction towards the system.
- **Type of service:** mobile, desktop, web.
- **Epilogue:** Increased user satisfaction with no impact on security.
- **Related Patterns:** Can be added later from the catalogue.

Fig. 3. Visibility of system status pattern

4   Conclusion

Security cannot be achieved in real sense unless it is usable by the users. This research advocates an evolving approach from 'user is the problem' to 'user must be a part of technology based solution'. This paper research is an attempt towards aligning security and usability, and for that a process oriented framework is presented. The framework governs the process from identification of the conflicts to documentation of the right trade-offs in form of re-usable design patterns.

Design patterns can also prove to be effective in handling inconsistency of views between different communities, and between academia and industry, by providing shared documentation in form of patterns. The patterns' ability to be improved over the time provides a common ground to incorporate several views i.e. from industry and academia. With the use of patterns, it is imperative to ensure that they are applied in relevant context of use. We have also developed a usable security patterns template to standardize the documentation of the patterns. For standardized documentation, a pattern template encapsulating information like, title, classification, prologue, problem statement, context of use, solution, discussion, is presented in this paper. To instantiate the use of patterns, a novel pattern 'visibility of system status' is also presented. It is worthwhile to state that one pattern addresses only one instance of the conflict, therefore, it is unrealistic to expect a pattern to solve a systems' problem; however, a catalogue of patterns addressing different instances of the conflict between security and usability would be required in this regard.

References

1. ISO 25010, Systems and software engineering – Systems and software Quality Requirements and Evaluation (SQuaRE) – System and software quality models (2011)
2. Password Guidance: Simplifying Your Approach. The National Cyber Security Centre. https://www.ncsc.gov.uk/guidance/password-guidance-simplifying-your-approach
3. Naqvi, B., Seffah, A.: A methodology for aligning usability and security in systems and services. In: International Conference on Information System Engineering (ICISE), pp. 61–66. IEEE (2018)
4. Dhillon, G., Oliveira, T., Susarapu, S., Caldeira, M.: Deciding between information security and usability: developing value based objectives. Comput. Hum. Behav. **61**, 656–666 (2016)
5. Garg, H., Choudhury, T., Kumar, P., Sabitha, S.: Comparison between significance of usability and security in HCI. In: 2017 3rd International Conference on Computational Intelligence Communication Technology (CICT), pp. 1–4 (2017)
6. Kulyk, O., Neumann, S., Budurushi, J., Volkamer, M.: Nothing comes for free: how much usability can you sacrifice for security? IEEE Secur. Priv. **15**, 24–29 (2017)
7. Bai, W., Kim, D., Namara, M., Qian, Y., Kelley, P.G., Mazurek, M.L.: Balancing security and usability in encrypted email. IEEE Internet Comput. **21**, 30–38 (2017)
8. Sasse, M.A., Smith, M., Herley, C., Lipford, H., Vaniea, K.: Debunking security–usability tradeo myths. IEEE Secur. Priv. **14**(5), 33–39 (2016)
9. Cranor, L.F., Buchler, N.: Better together: usability and security go hand in hand. IEEE Secur. Priv. **12**, 89–93 (2014)
10. Hof, H.-J.: User-centric IT security-how to design usable security mechanisms. In: 5th International Conference on Advances in Human-oriented and Personalized Mechanisms, Technologies, and Services (CENTRIC), pp. 7–12 (2012)
11. Sahar, F.: Tradeoffs between usability and security. Int. J. Eng. Tech. **5**, 434–437 (2013)
12. Fahl, S.: Confidentiality as a service—usable security for the cloud. In: 11th International Conference on Trust, Security and Privacy in Computing and Communications (TrustCom), pp. 153–162 (2012)
13. Mairiza D., Zowghi, D.: An ontological framework to manage the relative conflicts between security and usability requirements. In: 3rd International Workshop on Managing Requirements Knowledge (MARK), pp. 1–6 (2010)
14. Hausawi, Y.M., Allen, W.H.: An assessment framework for usable-security based on decision science. In: Tryfonas, T., Askoxylakis, I. (eds.) HAS 2014. LNCS, vol. 8533, pp. 33–44. Springer, Cham (2014). https://doi.org/10.1007/978-3-319-07620-1_4
15. National Institute of Standards and Technology. NISTIR 8080 Usability and Security Considerations for Public Safety Mobile Authentication (2016)
16. IBM: Cost of Data Breach Study: Global Analysis by Ponemon Institute LLC, Sponsored by IBM (2016)
17. Whitten, A., Tygar, J.D.: Usability of security: A case study. School of Computing Science, Carnegie Mellon University. Rep. Technical Report CMU-CS-98-155 (1998)
18. Imperva: Application Defense Center: Consumer Password Worst Practices. http://www.imperva.com/docs/WP_Consumer_Password_Worst_Practices.pdf

19. Ben-Asher, N., Kirschnick, N., Sieger, H., Meyer, J., Ben-Oved, A., Möller, S.: On the need for different security methods on mobile phones. In: Proceedings of the 13th International Conference on Human Computer Interaction with Mobile Devices and Services, pp. 465–473 (2011)
20. Glass, B.D., Jenkinson, G., Liu, Y., Sasse, M.A., Stajano, F., Spencer, M.: The usability canary in the security coal mine: a cognitive framework for evaluation and design of usable authentication solutions. In: Internet Society. Wiley (2003). https://www.wiley.com/en-ad/Multiple+User+Interfaces:+Cross+Platform+Applications+and+Context+Aware+Interfaces-p-9780470854440
21. Seffah, A., Javahery, H.: Multiple User Interfaces: Cross-Platform Applications and Context-Aware Interfaces. Wiley (2014)
22. Garfinkel, S., Lipford, H.R.: Usable security, history, themes and challenges. Morgan and Claypool Publishers, San Juan (2014)

Informing Hybrid System Design in Cyber Security Incident Response

Megan Nyre-Yu[1(✉)], Kelly A. Sprehn[2], and Barrett S. Caldwell[1]

[1] Purdue University, West Lafayette, IN 47907, USA
{mnyre,bscaldwell}@purdue.edu
[2] Draper, Cambridge, MA 02139, USA
ksprehn@draper.com

Abstract. Computer security incident response is a complex socio-technical environment that provides first line of defense against network intrusions, but struggles to obtain and keep qualified analysts at different levels of response. Practical approaches have focused on the larger skillsets and myriad supply channels for getting more qualified candidates. Research approaches to this problem space have been limited in scope and effectiveness, and may be partially or completely removed from actual security operations environments. As low-level incident response (IR) activities move towards automation, context-based research may provide valuable insights for developing hybrid systems that can both execute IR tasks and coordinate with human analysts. This paper presents insights originating from qualitative research with the analysts who currently perform IR functions, and discusses challenges in performing contextual inquiry in this setting. This article also acts as the first in a series of papers by the authors that translate these findings to hybrid system requirements.

Keywords: Cyber security · Incident response · Contextual inquiry · Human-centered design · Human-systems integration

1 Introduction

Cyber security incident response (CSIR) is a critical process in today's rapidly evolving digital landscape. The incident response process, comprised of both humans and systems, provides the first line of defense when a network is attacked, and is responsible for tracking, stopping, and mitigating these attacks in the shortest amount of time possible. These activities require understanding of technology, as well as the ability to collect, correlate, and act upon data within seconds of detection. Despite the importance of CSIR, security operations continue to struggle in finding and retaining qualified candidates for these roles. Traditional approaches in recruitment and education have been unsuccessful in closing this skills gap.

In addition to the labor shortage pressure, systems and attacks alike are becoming more advanced, and CSIR defense strategies must adapt to provide consistent security to businesses, institutions, and governments. An emerging approach is to look to hybrid solutions that combine the creativity and adaptability of humans with the speed and computing power of artificial intelligence (AI). In building hybrid human-automation

© Springer Nature Switzerland AG 2019
A. Moallem (Ed.): HCII 2019, LNCS 11594, pp. 325–338, 2019.
https://doi.org/10.1007/978-3-030-22351-9_22

teams, a key aspect overlooked is the translation of human cognition and decision making into system requirements for cyber security processes and software.

This application area, still in its infancy, is ripe with opportunity, but difficult to study due to the nature of security environments. Considering that the mission of these organizations is to defend the larger network, it makes sense that they are risk averse. In defensive or offensive operations, protecting the tactics and strategy as privileged information is what allows any sort of advantage over an adversary. Thus, security organizations have a responsibility to be cautious regarding their willingness to share information about their own operations in addition to protecting those of the company. Access to security teams and processes is an ongoing problem that prevents supporting sciences, such as human factors, from advancing the current state.

While human factors, psychology, and user experience fields offer us the opportunity to leverage smaller sample sizes in qualitative research, systems to support AI assistance require more vigorously tested models. This is not an uncommon problem for security-critical user groups. Given the challenges of access, this research builds the foundation for continued research, identifying key components of the cyber security team environment. Observational studies and contextual inquiry techniques provide a rich collection of notes, findings, and insights garnered from limited numbers of interactions that can be used to guide more formal development and broader-scope modeling analyses.

The research presented in this paper included an observational field study with three teams to address the above gaps in literature regarding context in cyber security incident response processes. The contextual inquiry included incident response teams from industry, government, and academic organizations. With the focus of a general contextual comparison of incident response by sector, the researchers were able to observe multiple cyber security incident response teams from a large company, state government, and a large university. These teams varied in terms of size, skill, and technical systems to conduct incident response. Elements that affect aspects of incident response, including organizational structure, documentation, and team identity, was also found to differ in these distinct organizational environments, and resulted in identification of insights for consideration in hybrid system design, including how automation is currently viewed and used amongst these diverse teams.

2   Background

2.1   State of Computer Security Incident Response

Cyber security incident response (CSIR) is a critical process in today's rapidly evolving digital landscape [1, 2]. The incident response process includes offensive and defensive operations that, at the core, aim to protect a network from malicious activities. As the parent organization grows in size and capability, the respective network expands in scope and complexity, as do the risks of intrusion and exploitation. Thus, security operations become increasingly important as they provide the first line of defense in this expanding threat environment. Though most organizations today have some form of CSIR coverage, the mission, goals, structure, and protocols of each team may vary greatly, and be dependent on those of the parent organization [1]. These predominantly defensive operations demand long hours, fast processing, and low margin for error from analysts at all levels. Despite the importance, high rates of burnout, and increasing complexity of the job itself, the industry struggles to retain and grow talent [3, 4]. Approaches in widening candidate searches and relaxing formal education constraints have been unsuccessful thus far at closing this skills gap [5].

Technology continues to be instrumental in CSIR. From log aggregation to orchestration platforms [6], software can aid analysts in understanding network activity and making decisions regarding response. As technology is the main medium of incident response activity, the importance of technology design and effectiveness (in conjunction with the human counterpart) is necessary to advancing the field [7]. Current approaches, to be discussed in Sect. 2.2, try to address this problem space from different angles.

2.2   Research Approaches in Addressing Issues in CSIR

Current Approaches. The authors have divided the body of literature on CSIR into two major categories: human-centered approaches, and algorithmic/computational approaches. These categories reflect a trend in this particular technology field that is divided between purely technological approaches and those that incorporate the human user of those technologies. Success of this field relies on expanding the scope of research to become multidisciplinary [8], effectively the integrating these two areas [7, 9–11].

Human-Centered Approaches. Research has recently called for better understanding human demands in CSIR, especially in regards to human capital development and management [12]. Frameworks have been produced to guide knowledge, skills, and abilities (KSAs) of incident response positions [13], and standards now exist to establish incident response processes in organizations [14, 15]. Additional areas of human-centered research in CSIR delve into situation awareness in cyber security settings [16, 17], team-based challenges [18], and social aspects of collaboration between analysts [19–21]. Previous research has made strides in improving interface design and protocol design, as well as recruiting, skills development, and educational curricula.

Contextual information about how these elements may vary by team, industry, or environment can be difficult to obtain due to access challenges, making it challenging to delve further in application and system design using a human-centered approach. Access to incident teams in cyber security is limited due to the nature of security organizations, and their willingness to host individuals who are considered 'outsiders', even if those individuals have provisions for protecting identities of individual participants and parent organizations [22].

Algorithmic and Computational Approaches. Security science is considered as subfield of computer science, and thus tends to focus heavily on computational approaches to security issues. Traditionally, software-based research takes one or more of the following technological approaches: cryptography, programming and semantics, and security modeling [7]. Cryptography is the mathematical derivation of logic structures and technologies behind encryption. Programming and semantics is a very popular approach, and includes development of models, algorithms, and languages for system security. Some applications include insider threat detection [23, 24], incident detection systems [25, 26], and network security assessments using game theory [27]. Lastly, security modeling helps researchers understand the implications of policies as they are enforced across networks, as well as better understanding of threats and system behavior [28, 29]. Despite the scope of these approaches, and the fact that a human will eventually touch the outputs of the algorithms or technologies, many research articles do not explicitly incorporate the human user as an active stakeholder.

Contextual Inquiry in CSIR. Each of the previously described approaches lacks the systems-level view of the interactions between both humans and their technology. Previous literature describes incident response in terms of the scope of processes, skills, and flexibility needed in these teams. However, contextual information about how these elements vary by team or environment is largely missing, making it difficult to delve further in application and system design using a human-centered or systems-level approach. Considering the need for social science perspectives and methods in this area [7], providing a robust contextual review of the CSIR environment helps connect technology design to the users and the application setting [30], and contributes critical findings and evidence towards the introduction of automation, standardization, and smaller improvements of efficiency, training, and general system design.

3   Method

3.1   Securing Access

As with most private organizations, many security organizations are hesitant to involve outside individuals with respect to observing or evaluating their internal processes and performance. Even more so in security organizations, there is sensitivity around disclosing procedures, and the potential security issues and general vulnerabilities that could be inadvertently observed and documented by an outsider. Despite strict ethical research protocol review and approval processes, many security organizations are not comfortable being research participants with unknown, or sometimes non-cleared, observers. Moreover, the authors needed to take additional precautions to assure participants that, should conversations delve into job topics that were not purely process related, there would be no implications on the participants' current job status or performance evaluations. Essentially, the authors were careful to navigate interview topics without inducing stress or concern over participants' relationships with their companies.

Rigorous vetting and leveraging personal connections were critical in securing access to the three teams involved in this study. For each organization, the main researcher was required to speak with directors or Chief Information Security Officers (CISOs), answering very specific questions about the data to be collected and context in which it would be published. There was a general fear of divulging potentially sensitive information about the company and its security profile. Despite Institutional Review Board (IRB) approval and document disclosure, as well as the direct communication with high-ranking security officials, some companies still did not feel comfortable participating. Nevertheless, with the additional clarification and boundary-setting between the researcher and the organizations, three organizations did allow for interviews, and some observations or data collection opportunities. As research matures and proves its relevance and value, more organizations may allow more research, but access is expected to continue to be a challenge during this period of growth and technological advancement.

3.2 Data Collection and Processing

During onsite observations, the researcher generated notes about each organization, including organizational structures, communications, and incident handling processes. Observation and interview notes were reviewed, transcribed, clarified, and codified within several days of observation for organization and researcher reflection.

Collecting Data. The main researcher (the first author of this paper) visited three teams at different sites. Each team was associated with a separate company or organization, and represented the three major sectors: government, industry, and academia. The government team was a security operations team within a state government. The industry team was a security operations team at a large defense company. The academic team was a security operations team at a large research university.

Upon arrival, the researcher established rapport with individual participants by meeting one-on-one to discuss the study and answer questions. The manager of the area was consistently the first participant such that the researcher could transition to organizational and process-related questions directly with management. As discussions transitioned from study description to interviewing, the author recorded handwritten notes to capture data. For subsequent participants, the author continued to verify previous responses, as well as learn about the different participant perspectives, goals, and even potential frustrations as they described their roles and daily routines.

When allowed by the manager, the researcher also spent some time observing analysts performing incident response activities and participating in handoff protocols (such as shift changes). The researcher was able to ask questions during or shortly after these events to clarify the observation. Not all organizations were comfortable with direct observations; thus, simulated incidents were used to walk through past incidents, individuals involved, actions taken, and issues that arose during the actual event. The simulated incidents and talk-throughs are a valuable resource in constrained fields for gathering data.

Data Processing. Observational notes collected with each team were collated with more cursory process notes. The anonymized and de-identified notes were then translated to individual, stand-alone statements. The statements were used in creating the Affinity Diagram (see Fig. 1 below). In total, 227 statements were used to inform the findings and insights as described below.

3.3   Data Synthesis

Several data synthesis methods are available to create visual representations of the qualitative data, and provide a bridge between data and design [30]. This paper utilized affinity diagramming to consolidate statements from all three CSIR teams, and divide the statements into groups that represent the themes between the respective statements. Future work will build on these affinity diagrams to create experience models [30] to represent specific aspects of each team observed, which can be visually compared to understand differences between CSIR teams.

Affinity Diagrams. After data processing, an iterative bottom-up coding procedure was used to group observation statements into higher-level themes [31, 32] using an Affinity Diagramming method [30]. In order to create the Affinity Diagrams, the first two authors utilized virtually collaborative platforms to store, group, and regroup qualitative statements from generated data. The first author was able to create first-round nodes from the raw data in NVivo, and then copy the codes into Google Sheets for shared analysis with the second author. In order to maintain visual grouping of statements, the authors would simultaneously choose a statement, cut it out of the shared spreadsheet, then paste it into an appropriate group within the shared Google Keep platform to help emulate the traditional "post-it note" synthesis exercise used during collocated analysis. As Google Keep allows for collaboration between users to build groups or checklists, this was an effective way to digitally group (or "affinitize") the statements while maintaining a shared picture between the authors. In expanding on the method, the authors could work asynchronously with intermittent meetings to discuss context and meaning of the groupings. The first two authors completed three rounds of arranging and discussing groups to form consensus on meaningful findings.

4   Results

4.1   Affinity Diagram

As mentioned, the Affinity Diagram amalgamates the 227 original statements into eight (8) larger categories, each with 3–7 subcategories. Each subcategory includes no more than ten (10) statements. The section below includes the main and subcategories in outline format, and a summarized graphic can be found in Fig. 1. The authors note that the outline numbers are used solely for organization purposes, and do not indicate importance, priority, or order. These numbers also aid in connecting the outline to the figure, as do the italicized terms in each statement.

The Affinity Diagram contents are as follows:

1. Analyst Day-to-Day
    1.1. The mission of the organization drives the *authority* of the SOC. The security profile drives the scope of the *work*. Conflict between the two creates tension within operations.
    1.2. *Expertise* is necessary (and sometimes replaced by procedures) to appropriately escalate incidents.

1.3. *Shift handoffs*, or day-to-day transitions, should be dynamic and interactive to create accountability and facilitate learning; documentation strengthens these.

1.4. *Conversational interaction* between analysts creates opportunities for learning, feedback, and team rapport; If avoided, these opportunities may be lost.

1.5. Analysts manage information from multiple sources and must quickly switch *(pivot)* between them.

1.6. An active, updated, and accessible *knowledge repository* becomes a critical resource in supporting efficient operations.

1.7. *Procedures* provide a standardized starting point for learning the analyst job, but too much reliance limits the ability to pursue creative solutions and preventions.

1.8. *Shared* situation *awareness* can be created through dynamic meetings, structured communications, or shared system visibility.

1.9. Electronic and connected *systems* play a role in different types of handoffs in CSIR, particularly in facilitating the recording and transmittal of information between people.

2. Communication

   2.1. *Organizational communication* can facilitate wider awareness of security issues and higher-level decision influences; but also create bottlenecks if the communication channels are not efficiently designed.

   2.2. Communication *protocols* should be carefully *designed* to ensure the proper point of contact is in-the-loop, temporally appropriate, and responsive.

   2.3. *Communication* within the *SOC* organization should be bilateral between entities, fluid, and detailed; should facilitate shared understanding and learning.

3. SOC Management

   3.1. 24/7 *coverage* in IR Operations are theoretically needed but can be difficult to justify or maintain.

   3.2. CSIR Teams conduct a variety of tasks amongst members, but coordination, accountability, and growth can fail without strong protocols and norms for *collaboration*.

   3.3. SOC management must conduct *strategic activities*, which does not always involve direct, on-site management.

   3.4. SOC Management must conduct *tactical activities*, sometimes done by leads or deputies, that involve direct interaction with and management of analysts.

   3.5. *Leads* play a coordinating *role* in facilitating handoffs.

4. Automation

   4.1. Opportunities for automation require stakeholder and needs identification prior to development, and should consider maintenance workload per automated task in *cost-benefit* analyses.

   4.2. *Disadvantages* of automated tasks should be carefully evaluated, as they can increase task complexity and overall workload, as well as decrease entry-level analyst opportunities for problem-solving.

   4.3. Automation has some clear *advantages* in helping decrease individual and organization workload with respect to incident response, and some opportunities have been clearly identified based on current perceptions of those advantages.

5. Attrition/Retention
    5.1. Job and market *demands* drive external attrition.
    5.2. *Design* the *organization* for a strong T1 foundation (developed and well-rounded) with appropriate division of labor and consistent rules to promote efficiency and collaboration.
    5.3. There is a natural *progression* from low level analyst to high level analyst that takes time and expertise accumulation; if this progression is inhibited, the organization cannot fully mature.
6. Roles and Responsibilities
    6.1. Security operations are often divided into *tiers* (low to high), which tend to correspond with level of expertise and complexity of investigation or response.
    6.2. Expertise sharing from higher tiers to lower tiers is an opportunity for *knowledge transfer* and apprenticeship; Barriers include culture, collocation, and acceptable communication practices.
    6.3. *Tiered* organizations in incident response can cause issues with system redundancies, disjointed communications, and cultural division; Careful design of communication and information sharing is warranted to assure efficient and effective *interaction*/coordination.
    6.4. *Roles outside* the CSOC support inter-organizational communication and security-related decisions and activities; These individuals may or may not be considered part of the team (by themselves or others), which can inhibit effective coordination and response.
7. Policy
    7.1. Overall *mission* of the organization may drive the perceived importance of security.
    7.2. Territorial *boundaries* of security responsibility can create tension between internal entities and lack of visibility.
    7.3. *Politics* and weak understanding of security *risk* can affect decision making that cascades through the organization.
    7.4. *Organizational design* will drive the authority, scope, and boundaries of responsibilities, awareness, support, and information transfer.
    7.5. Policy drives the *information* that can and cannot be *shared* within and beyond the organization.
8. Definitions and Standards
    8.1. Developing, training, and maintaining consistent *documentation* creates standardized knowledge and can facilitate coordination practices.
    8.2. Evaluating performance of people and processes is needed and challenging; without development of relevant *metrics*, teams can lose sight of their purpose, strengths, and weaknesses.
    8.3. Next generation systems and metrics will include macro-level analysis of incidents and IR performance to develop a larger *operational picture*.
    8.4. There are different indicators of analyst performance, which vary in terms of robustness, quantifiability, priority; *Analyst performance* is not necessarily evaluated.

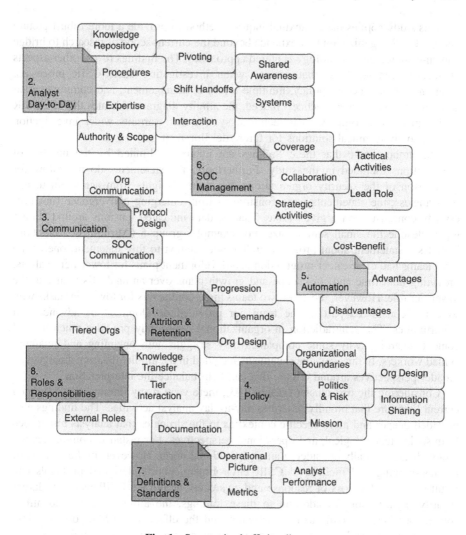

Fig. 1. Summarized affinity diagram

5   Discussion

5.1   Findings and Implications

This study applies the contextual inquiry method to provide a more robust picture into the CSIR organization that expands beyond the current scope of research to bridge human-centered and technology-centered approaches. The findings reveal other aspects of security organizations that emerge when investigating basic CSIR processes, including factors such as policy, multiple levels of management, and communication and information sharing practices. Indeed, the affinity diagram indicates that the CSIR environment is a complex socio-technical system that warrants wider investigation beyond solely technical solutions for future development.

This study applies the contextual inquiry method to provide a more robust picture into the CSIR organization that expands beyond the current scope of research to bridge human-centered and technology-centered approaches. The findings reveal other aspects of security organizations that emerge when investigating basic CSIR processes, including factors such as policy, multiple levels of management, and communication and information sharing practices. Indeed, the affinity diagram indicates that the CSIR environment is a complex socio-technical system that warrants wider investigation beyond solely technical solutions for future development.

The authors note that these findings are inherently limited by the number of organizations included in the study. Furthermore, the statements do not allow for comparison of the security organizations, but rather insights from across all teams. Nevertheless, the statements were constructed from emerging convergence (not necessarily consensus) on a given issue. That is, data indicated tensions around certain topics despite the small sample size. For example, group 5 (Attrition & Retention) includes a statement about progression. To give context to this statement, one of the three teams had clear career progression and development plans for lower-tier analysts, providing both time and skill scope and growth plans over an analyst's tenure in the lower-tier role. However, the other two teams hired contractors for lower-tier tasks who were not considered part of the team nor provided development or advancement opportunities. This contradiction in organizational philosophy provides much needed context regarding why some companies may struggle with obtaining and retaining skilled workers. In this way, the statements included in the affinity diagram amalgamate broader perspectives around a topic that can help balance the interpretation.

Considering the first cluster (groups 1–3), there were many findings that validated current literature that broadly describes day-to-day analyst activities. The findings also provided deeper and more specific context as to the struggles that analysts might face from social, technological, and operational perspectives. For instance, communication protocols are typically considered an organizational norm. However, in the context of the fast-moving and multi-level CSIR environment, poorly designed protocols can result in a complete loss of response and awareness within the CSIR team and larger security organization. In addition to these findings, the affinity diagram identifies connections between daily analyst activities and the effect of the SOC organization, management, and style. Communication norms emerge from this effect and support, or detract from the operations of the analysts.

The second cluster includes only one group (automation), which sits between the day-to-day activities and the broader organizational components. While automation is not at the forefront of the analysts' minds, it does provide an opportunity to reallocate work functions and typically works behind the scenes to filter and correlate data before the analyst sees it. One interesting finding that came out of the contextual inquiry exercise was the contested views regarding automation in different teams. That is, some teams views automation as a solution to the analyst supply problem, while others viewed it as a way to further mature the organizational capability. Additionally, automation tended to be a sore subject from the perspective of training and maintaining the automation to work properly without interruption to the analyst.

Finally, the third cluster (groups 5–8) revealed that the organizational structure, policies, and roles and responsibilities have an effect on each of the above categories, and can possibly lead to lessons learned regarding attrition and retention. Within this cluster, statements touch on more systemic aspects of security operations that can ultimately impact the effectiveness of the CSIR team. Findings revealed that, despite the technological advancements in cyber security, organizations can still struggle with (and even become an inhibitor to) advancing the state of security within a given company.

5.2   Collecting Contextual Data in CSIR Environments

Contextual data is crucial to informing effective design, and could be a key component of advancing the state of cyber security by providing valuable information to hybrid system developers. However, it has been challenging to collection in CSIR, partially due to access issues. Even when researchers are allowed on the premises, management may not allow direct observation of security analysts, making it difficult to capture highly detailed information about how these individuals work independently and together.

Techniques used in this study created some level of flexibility in directly interacting with and collecting data from analysts. For instance, if a firm was not comfortable with direct observation of live events, simulations of past events could be used to observe the process post-mortem. To increase the fidelity of the simulation, the researcher can create multi-monitor visuals on white boards and have the analysts describe what would be on their screen during a given day, then use a think aloud process to describe specific steps while following the documented events on paper. This was an effective method of decreasing pressure on analysts, making it more immersive, and encouraging verbal interaction between analysts in the room (which may not be a standard interaction within the relatively quiet, and sometimes partitioned, security operations center).

Access is a common and recognized problem when conducting human-centered research in the security industry. The above strategies can be valuable in mitigating some of the underlying issues and concerns by security operations groups. Moreover, the authors encourage exercising creativity and flexibility when using traditional methods in order to accommodate these concerns.

5.3   Using Contextual Inquiry in CSIR Technology Design

Contextual inquiry is a powerful method commonly used to collect data directly from the user's environment. Ultimately, purpose of which is guiding design and develop technology [30]. Though the outputs may not directly influence specific software aspects of next generation automation [33], they can help guide additional focus and research efforts in this domain. In addition to system designers, managers may also find the insights useful in reflecting on their teams' goals, performance, and work design.

Drawing Insights from Context. Providing a robust contextual review of the CSIR environment contributes critical findings and evidence towards the introduction (and improvement) of automation and standardization. Moreover, when provided to managers and leadership currently in this setting, context-driven evidence inspires practical improvements of efficiency, training, and general system design.

One important aspect of context-driven research in cyber security is the idea that a one-size-fits-all solution is not always valid or effective. Though the findings presented here encompass data from three very different teams, the dichotomous tensions inferred from the final statements reveal that different teams have different needs that should be considered when designing, evaluating, or implementing new systems that directly or indirectly involve human interaction.

One advantage to collecting and using contextual data is that it is readily available to those who have access to the respective environment. Researchers can expand upon this paper by conducting contextual inquiry techniques to observe and interview analysts in different CSIR settings. As contextual inquiry should include several researchers, temporal and geographic distribution can be overcome with collaborative editing tools.

Future Work in Building Experience Models. Future work by the authors will focus on building experience models, which help capture the complexity of a user's job role and environment without diminishing the important details that drive design decisions. Contextual inquiry literature describes a number of models that can be constructed with qualitative data collected from on-site observations and interviews [30], which provide a deeper understanding of the user's work and environment [34]. Each model represents a perspective of the user's work, and choosing an appropriate model is important for focusing the design actions. System designers can use the models to inspire features and better understand user needs. For this series, the authors will focus on Collaboration Models for each location to act as a comparison across different CSIR teams. The results will help add to team collaboration research in this setting and begin to build understanding of human-machine collaboration needs for hybrid systems.

6   Conclusion

Though somewhat challenging to obtain access to security operations, contextual data collection and analysis can provide insights that reveal differences in organizational, operational, and political aspects of different CSIR teams. Affinity diagramming helped identify emergent topics from qualitative data to understand user-centered aspects of tasks, such as resource usage and problem solving processes. These insights allow researchers to better understand nonlinear assumptions and needs of analysts who perform incident response. Mission and goals of each team were included in data collection to help inform design of system directives and protocols. As automated systems grow in capability and popularity, insights such as these can be used to inform smarter hybrid systems that can execute IR tasks as well as coordinate with human analysts in the system. Ongoing research by the authors will build upon this study to create experience models and provide a systematic methodology for assessing needs of human analysts in cyber security for the purpose of hybrid system design.

References

1. Ruefle, R., Dorofee, A., Mundie, D., Householder, A.D., Murray, M., Perl, S.J.: Computer security incident response team development and evolution. IEEE Secur. Priv. **12**, 16–26 (2014)
2. Chen, T.R., Shore, D.B., Zaccaro, S.J., Dalal, R.S., Tetrick, L.E., Gorab, A.K.: An organizational psychology perspective to examining computer security incident response teams. IEEE Secur. Priv. **12**, 61–67 (2014)
3. Cobb, S.: Mind this gap: criminal hacking and the global cybersecurity skills shortage, a critical analysis. In: Virus Bulletin Conference. Virus Bulletin (2016)
4. Hewlett-Packard Development: Growing the Security Analyst (2014)
5. Bureau of Labor Statistics: Information Security Analysts. https://www.bls.gov/ooh/computer-and-information-technology/information-security-analysts.htm
6. Neiva, C., Lawson, C., Bussa, T., Sadowski, G.: Innovation Insight for Security Orchestration, Automation and Response (SOAR) (2017)
7. National Academies of Sciences Engineering and Medicine: Foundational Cybersecurity Research. National Academies Press, Washington (2017)
8. Proctor, R.W.: The role of human factors/ergonomics in the science of security: Decision making and action selection in cyberspace (2015)
9. Lathrop, S.D.: Interacting with synthetic teammates in cyberspace. In: Nicholson, D. (ed.) AHFE 2017. AISC, vol. 593, pp. 133–145. Springer, Cham (2018). https://doi.org/10.1007/978-3-319-60585-2_14
10. Scharre, P.D.: The opportunity & challenge of autonomous systems. In: Williams, A.P., Scharre, P.D. (eds.) Autonomous Systems: Issues for Defence Policy Makers, pp. 3–26. NATO Communications and Information Agency, Norfolk (2003)
11. Williams, L.C.: Spy chiefs set sights on AI and cyber (2017). https://fcw.com/articles/2017/09/07/intel-insa-ai-tech-chiefs-insa.aspx
12. Hoffman, L., Burley, D., Toregas, C.: Holistically Building the Cybersecurity Workforce (2012)
13. National Initiative for Cybersecurity Careers and Studies: NICE Cybersecurity Workforce Framework. https://niccs.us-cert.gov/workforce-development/cyber-security-workforce-framework
14. Bada, M., Creese, S., Goldsmith, M., Mitchell, C., Phillips, E.: Computer Security Incident Response Teams (CSIRTs): An Overview. Global Cyber Security Capacity Centre, pp. 1–23 (2014)
15. West-Brown, M.J., Stikvoort, D., Kossakowski, K.-P., Killcrece, G., Ruefle, R., Zajicek, M.: Handbook for Computer Security Incident Response Teams (CSIRTs). Carnegie Mellon Software Engineering Institute, Pittsburgh, PA (2003)
16. Staheli, D., Mancuso, V., Leahy, M.J., Kalke, M.M.: Cloudbreak: answering the challenges of cyber command and control. Lincoln Lab. J. **22**, 60–73 (2016)
17. Tyworth, M., Giacobe, N.A., Mancuso, V.: Cyber situation awareness as distributed socio-cognitive work. In: Cyber Sensing 2012, vol. 8408, p. 84080F. International Society for Optics and Photonics (2012)
18. Steinke, J., et al.: Improving cybersecurity incident response team effectiveness using teams-based research. IEEE Secur. Priv. **13**, 20–29 (2015)
19. Werlinger, R., Muldner, K., Hawkey, K., Beznosov, K.: Preparation, detection, and analysis: the diagnostic work of IT security incident response. Inf. Manage. Comput. Secur. **18**, 26–42 (2010)

20. Beznosov, K., Beznosova, O.: On the imbalance of the security problem space and its expected consequences. Inf. Manage. Comput. Secur. **15**, 420–431 (2007)
21. Ahrend, J.M., Jirotka, M., Jones, K.: On the collaborative practices of cyber threat intelligence analysts to develop and utilize tacit threat and defence knowledge. In: 2016 International Conference on Cyber Situational Awareness, Data Analytics And Assessment (CyberSA), pp. 1–10. IEEE (2016)
22. Sundaramurthy, S.C., McHugh, J., Ou, X., Rajagopalan, S.R., Wesch, M.: An anthropological approach to studying CSIRTs. IEEE Secur. Priv. **12**(5), 52–60 (2014)
23. Buford, J.F., Lewis, L., Jakobson, G.: Insider threat detection using situation-aware MAS. In: Proceedings of 11th International Conference on Information Fusion, FUSION 2008 (2008)
24. Bowen, B.M., Devarajan, R., Stolfo, S.: Measuring the human factor of cyber security. In: 2011 IEEE International Conference on Technologies for Homeland Security (HST), pp. 230–235 (2011)
25. Faysel, M.A., Haque, S.S.: Towards cyber defense: research in intrusion detection and intrusion prevention systems. IJCSNS Int. J. Comput. Sci. Netw. Secur. **10**, 316–325 (2010)
26. Kumar, V.: Parallel and distributed computing for cybersecurity. IEEE Distrib. Syst. Online **6**, 1–9 (2005)
27. Roy, S., Ellis, C., Shiva, S., Dasgupta, D., Shandilya, V., Wu, Q.: A survey of game theory as applied to network security. In: 2010 43rd Hawaii International Conference on System Sciences, pp. 1–10 (2010)
28. Memon, M.: Security modeling for service-oriented systems using security pattern refinement approach. Softw. Syst. Model. **13**, 549–573 (2014)
29. Goldstein, A.: Components of a multi-perspective modeling method for designing and managing IT security systems. Inf. Syst. E-bus. Manag. **14**, 101–141 (2016)
30. Holtzblatt, K.: Contextual Design : Design for Life. Elsevier, Amsterdam (2016)
31. Saldana, J.: The Coding Manual for Qualitative Researchers. SAGE, Los Angeles (2009)
32. Auerbach, C., Silverstein, L.B.: Qualitative Data: An Introduction to Coding and Analysis. New York University Press, New York (2003)
33. Hoffman, R.R., Deal, S.V: Influencing versus informing design, part 1: a gap analysis. IEEE Intell. Syst. **23**, 78–81(2008)
34. Holtzblatt, K., Jones, S.: Contextual inquiry: a participatory technique for system design. In: Schuler, D., Namioka, A. (eds.) Participatory Design: Principles and Practices, pp. 177–210. Lawrence Erlbaum Associates, Hillsdale (1993)

Revolutionizing the Visual Design of Capture the Flag (CTF) Competitions

Rukman Senanayake[1]([✉]), Phillip Porras[1]([✉]), and Jason Kaehler[2]([✉])

[1] SRI International, Menlo Park, CA 95125, USA
{rukman.senanayake,phillip.porras}@sri.com
[2] Asylum Labs, 1735 Wharf Road, Suite A, Capitola, CA 95010, USA
j.kaehler@asylumlabsinc.com

Abstract. There are a variety of cyber-security challenge tournaments held within the INFOSEC and Hacker communities, which among their benefits help to promote and identify emerging talent. Unfortunately, most of these competitions are rather narrow in reach, being of interest primarily to those enthusiasts who are already well versed in cyber security. To attract a broader pool of younger generation participants requires one to make such events more engaging and intellectually accessible. The way these tournaments are currently conducted and presented to live audiences is rather opaque, if not unintelligible to most who encounter them. This paper presents an ongoing effort to bridge the presentation gap necessary to make cyber security competitions more attractive and accessible to a broader audience. We present the design of a new but familiar model for capturing the interplay, individual achievements, and tactical drama that transpires during one form of cyber security competition. The main user interface and presentation paradigm in this research borrows from those of established e-sports, such as *League of Legends* and *Overwatch*. Our motivation is to elevate the current format of cyber security competition events to incorporate design and presentation elements that are informed by techniques that have evolved within the e-sports community. We apply the physics models and battlefield visualizations of virtual world gaming environments in a manner that captures the intellectual challenges, team achievements, and tactical gameplay that occur in a popular form of cyber security tournament, called the Capture The Flag (CTF) competition. Our goal is to make these events intellectually accessible to broader audiences, to engage a broader and more diverse talent pool of competitors, and to increase the awareness and interest in cyber security among the general public.

Keywords: Cyber security · Capture the Flag · Visualization ·
Cyber education · National cyber league

1 Introduction

Those who have attended one of the growing lists of INFOSEC or hacking conferences will have likely been exposed to an increasingly competitive skills-building event called a Capture the Flag competition (CTF). CTFs regularly draw security professionals, enthusiasts, government IT specialists, and a wide range of collegiate teams

© Springer Nature Switzerland AG 2019
A. Moallem (Ed.): HCII 2019, LNCS 11594, pp. 339–352, 2019.
https://doi.org/10.1007/978-3-030-22351-9_23

from around the world. Participants pit their skills against each other as they attempt to defend (and in some cases attack) complex applications, computing devices, and even whole computer networks. These competitions have grown in competitiveness and sophistication, even to the height of one venue requiring competitors to create entirely autonomous agents that can discover vulnerabilities, auto-patching their networks, and produce and launch exploits without human assistance [5].

The experiences and skills that result from such competitions help to inspire and develop cyber security talent that the technology-dependent world needs within its workforce [1–4]. In the U.S., these competitions are sponsored by government organizations such as the Defense Advanced Research Projects Agency (DARPA) [5] and the National Science Foundation (NSF), and by leading IT companies across the commercial sector. Internationally, countries in the EU and Asia similarly invest in CTF competitions [6, 7], as part of their strategic investments of building cyber defense skills and identifying desperately needed talent. In fact, ctftime.org tracks more than 200 distinct CTF competitions that take place around the world [9].

No single universally followed model governs CTF competitions. The rules, duration, and the players' network configurations deviate considerably from venue to venue. However, we broadly categorize CTF competitions into three general forms:

- **Blue Team Competitions:** focus entirely on developing defensive skill. In these competitions, participants are granted time to analyze a common configuration of applications and computing assets, derive defenses, and are then evaluated based on their ability to protect these assets from attacks launched by a single Red Team (an offensive cyber-attack team).
- **Red-Team/Blue-Team Competitions:** blend both offensive and defensive objectives. Teams must race to uncover a wide range of vulnerabilities that have been implanted into a common configuration of applications and network components, which each team must administer. Teams must then patch and reconfigure their applications and network to neutralize the vulnerabilities, while weaponizing and launching exploits that compromise the security of those other teams that may have not yet succeeded in protecting their computing assets.
- **Red Team Competitions:** involve individuals, working alone or on teams, who are presented with a common set of applications or computing assets, and are competitively measured by their abilities to construct exploitations against these components.

No matter what the form of competition, CTFs share in the need for participants to conduct in-depth analyses, followed by (either or both) some form of software development or system administration. These phases of a CTF competition involve significant intellectual challenges that are designed to test the participant's technical skills. Unfortunately, for the CTF audience—even one dominated by the technically savvy—viewing these activities is about as engaging as watching small groups of students work on challenging homework problems. These competitions are slow paced, and often take place over an entire day or multiple days. Often, such as at DEFCON [8], the progress that slowly unfolds during the competition is presented to the audience in spreadsheet form, capturing simple statistics as each team progresses in defending their networks or testing exploits. However, embedded within the CTF competition are moments of technical achievement, significant tactical decisions [10], and instances of sophisticated adversarial attacks whose outcomes decide which team will win, and *how* and *why* they have succeeded.

In this paper we present a foray into the design of one form of CTF competition (the Red-Team/Blue Team form) as a visually engaging e-sport tournament. To do this, we impose a structure on the CTF competition, design and develop the visual elements of an intuitive virtual environment in which the players compete, and introduce techniques for isolating individual achievements, team interplay, and scoreboard presentation. We propose a battlefield visualization, which achieves a tradeoff between the number of teams present versus our desire to deliver single-camera presentations of the entire CTF competitions. We offer a novel visualization that captures all elements of the competition.

The contributions of this paper including the following:

- We define a CTF competition framework that deconstructs the event into a series of discrete activities that are performed, often in parallel, by members of each team. We discuss the anticipated sizes of teams and visual elements that are designed to isolate individual skills and team achievements.
- We present a 3-D virtual battlefield paradigm as the landscape on which the CTF competition is played. Our prototype is built using the Unreal game engine [11], which provides full camera virtualized movements that enable a CTF narrator (an event broadcaster) to navigate and visually isolate elements of the competition.
- We introduce a visual ontology of cyber-attacks, network and application architecture, and cyber defense functions. These elements are designed using familiar physics and semantics that enable unsophisticated audiences to grasp major status milestones and dynamic events as initiated by teams and referees.
- We discuss the motivations and challenges of taking a highly complex, slow-paced, and intellectually dense event and re-envisioning it as a visually engaging and intuitively familiar competition. Success in this activity can help CTFs expand their important role in promoting and identify an increasingly critical skill that is globally underserved.
- We design a novel *narrator-centric* presentation layer for the broadcast function, which allows for a subject matter expert to communicate, live, with the audience regarding the actions taking place within the virtual environment. Due to the complexity of the domain, knowing *when* and *where* to look is a substantial issue. Our system gives the narrator a camera 'switcher', enabling the focus to shift to action within the field of play as the competition unfolds.

2   Related Work

In the last decade, a great deal of investment has been made to study the impact of gamifying certain areas of cyber security, such that complex host and network events can be readily understood by a wider audience [14–16]. There are many well-documented advantages to such an approach [17]. Toward a model of cyber gamification, it is possible to focus on sub-domains of cyber security to specialize in skills development [18, 19]. Such efforts can target a range of demographics, from students in high schools [20, 21] to entry-level professionals [22].

CTF and Cyber Grand Challenge (CGC) style competitions are becoming increasingly popular as a means to identify new talent in the cyber security domain [9]. There are many CTF competitions formats, most of which have been studied to understand their efficacy in identifying talent, as well as popularizing the field of cyber security [22–24]. In addition, there is a drive to investigate which competition format can be used most broadly [25–27]. The lessons learned form DARPA's CGC format is also well understood and documented [28–30]. Given the current understanding of the impact we have on the format of CTF competitions and given the many differing formats being used, we hypothesize that in our case, we could exercise a degree of freedom in structuring certain elements of the CTF format to facilitate a visual gamification experience. We also posit that the format we propose simplifies certain logistical and technological pain points.

3 Conceptual Overview

When considering the real-time visualization of a highly complex environment with millions of concurrent events happening for a sustained period, the primary conceptual consideration is one of abstraction. In producing a game design, we have chosen a 'top-down' approach, which is narrator-centric and provides an over-watch perspective that is tailored to provide third parties with a visual understanding of the field of play. To determine best practices here, we looked primarily at e-sport events and traditional broadcast television sports.

The first and most essential challenge one finds when attempting to re-envision a CTF competition is that there exist no universal rulebook that specifies how all such competitions are conducted. CTFs have formed organically, and are subject to the preferences of their sponsors and organizers, including iterative improvement from past experiences. CTF organizers also evolve the rules and structure to adjust the difficulty of the challenges. This is to keep pace with the sophistication of the participants and their hacking tools, which are improving at a remarkable pace.

3.1 The Game Structure

Through our analysis of prior CTF competitions, and from communications with both participants and organizers, we have distilled several important commonalities in rules and competition structure that exist across Red-Team/Blue-Team CTFs. Further, in defining our canonical CTF game structure, we are sensitive to avoid decisions that reduce the applicability of the design, excluding the problem of scalability. The game design presented here will not scale to large-numbers of teams, albeit we are agnostic to the number of players that can participate within a single team [12].

Our CTF is designed as a team-based competition for two or more teams, with an idealized size of between 6 to 8 teams (for visual scale of the battlefield). All teams are provided an identically configured network, which includes host and network misconfigurations that can enable other teams to infiltrate their opponent networks. In addition, each team is given a required set of applications (or *test apps*) that must be run and maintained accessible on the team's network at all times. Access to each team's test apps are continually probed by competition referees, who will penalize a team for any unresponsive or corrupted application. Unfortunately, the test apps are purpose- fully embedded with one or more critical security flaws that render them vulnerable to attack by any other team that can weaponize an exploit faster than the team hosting the test app can patch the vulnerability.

Blue-Team Responsibilities: Each team must demonstrate their administrative security skills by identifying and removing all configuration vulnerabilities from their network. In addition, the team must reverse engineering, discover, and patch all vulnerabilities in each test apps while not degrading the referee's access to the test app. These defensive actions require significant time and skill, and failure to remove a security weakness will render the team's network exploitable, and thereby subject to score reductions. These configuration flaws and test app vulnerabilities are unknown in number, thus removing any certainty from a team that it has fully protected its assets from attack.

Red-Team Responsibilities: In parallel with their defensive challenges, teams must also demonstrate their skills in offensive operations. While each configuration flaw and test app vulnerability represents a threat to the team that must be removed before points are lost, they also represent opportunities to generate exploits that can be launched against the other teams, thereby earning points in the competition depending on the outcome.

Visualizing Tactical Game Play: An essential objective in presenting a CTF compe- tition is that of accurately visualizing the improvement that each team makes to their defensive posture, as well as their progress in constructing and launching exploits. Capturing defensive progress translates to visualizing the installation of patches to the set of vulnerable test apps, and the removal of network flaws that were delivered within each team's network. Exploit construction, network scanning for reconnaissance pur- poses, and exploit execution are also vital to visualize. Combined, these defensive posture changes and offensive actions do not just capture distinctions in the speed and skills of teams, but also capture purposeful tactical game play that teams employ, which may ultimately decide which team will win.

Some teams will focus on the immediate and comprehensive installation of defenses as quickly as possible, while on the other extreme there may be teams that employ their resources toward exploit generation to strike first. However, every exploit and network scan performed by one team enables other teams to observe the exploit or scan pattern, thereby revealing an attack surface that may not have been apparent or properly addressed. Exposing an attack (or scan), particularly one that is unsuccessful, reveals *threat intelligence,* which may help other teams harden their defenses and create their own exploit variants) [10].

3.2 Implementation of the Battle Space

Visualization of a tournament requires an ability to perform fine-grained monitoring of the actions of contestants, referees, and selective events that occur on the hosts and networks in the field of play. The instrumented platform that we use to capture these activities is already integrated into existing contests, but we impose additional surveillance requirements.

Team Assets: Game participants are provided with an instance of a Linux VM running [31]. Kali is a Linux OS Distribution that is designed for the penetration testing community, and includes a wide assortment of hacking tools that are typically used in these competitions. We augment Kali with OS extensions that enable the monitoring of key activities that are used to track each team member: process execution, file IO operations, administrative functions, and network connections. We also introduce a requirement that all teams must post exploit binaries or script that they intend to run into a team-designated exploit directory. All attacks and scans produce process executions that result in connections to external networks. Any process that performs these external connections but is launched from a directory outside the designated directory will result in a penalty.

Game Assets: Hosts that are located in each team's protected network are similarly instrumented with OS extensions that monitor all processes, file IO operations, authentication operations, and network operations. We employ system call monitoring extensions that produce records that are correlated with network flow records (using SRIFlow [32]). A correlated record captures the process ID, application name, the user ID of the participant who launched the process, and the source and target IPs, ports, and protocol involved in the flow. This information drives both visual elements of the game display and is used by the referees to detect various rule violations.

Referee Actions: Referees provide a continual stream of network probes that analyze the state and availability of each team's network assets and test apps. The outcome of these flows is visualized in the game environment as health and status indicators per host and test app. In addition, referees continually analyze all network flows from each team, inspecting each for rule violations that represent out-of-bound probing and exploit executions that are launched from outside the designated attack directories.

4 The Visualization Layer

A natural physical model that captures many of the key aspects of the CTF competition is that of a battlefield, composed of each team's network and test apps visualized as cities. This approach presents a familiar grounding for audiences to interpret the status per contestant, and for understanding when exploits are launched from one team into the cityscape of another team. A successful attack is viewed with a visual indicator of structural damage to the target host or test app, which is represented as a physical structure. We discuss the model and visual elements below.

The Visualization Layer represents the majority of effort in this research as the team had a number of simultaneous goals. The overall visual 'look' needed a strong 'theme' to appeal to casual observers and have a 'cool' factor often seen in video games, including the use of sport team mascots that convey both the organization and the successes and damages incurred. We chose giant robots to represent the Teams, and small cities to represent their networks, with buildings as the machines in the network and abstract spheres to indicate the actual binaries themselves, illustrated in Fig. 1.

There are 4 categories of actor:

Players: are shown as a photograph or live video with icon representing the current tool they are using. Player highlighting is an important aspect of game competitions that is largely absent from current CTFs, and we posit that for widespread popular acceptance, a critical aspect of audience engagement involves the ability to identify and highlight the successes and setbacks of individual players within a team. Thus, our game design pays significant attention toward bringing the competitors themselves forward in game visualizations, with the goal of creating "star players".

Binaries: test apps are a primary game element that provides the central focus for much of the competition. Teams distinguish their strategies and score points based on their ability to produce defensive patches, maintain availability, or succeed in producing exploits against these test apps (binaries).

Flags: the primary scoring indicators in a CTF competition. A team receives a Flag when it penetrates an opponent's binary successfully.

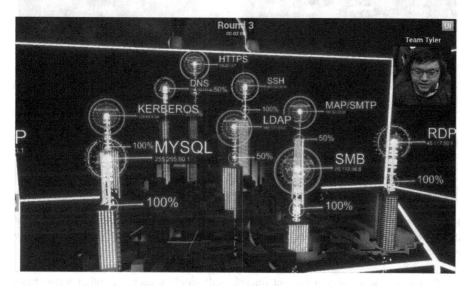

Fig. 1. Illustration of a team's hosts, test-apps, and network. The test-apps are labeled by the binary name and colored based on their patch status.

Exploits: Table 1 presents the *method* a team will use to retrieve an enemy flag. An exploit is launched as an attack, which becomes a central focus of action in the visualization. However, the attack visualization must not just capture the launch, but must also provide a visual indication of what method of attack the audience is witnessing. We represent 6 basic attack types and two types of "network scans".

As a secondary element, we show the patches themselves and the process of them being published to all other teams. This patch-publishing requirement means that teams must share with each other every applied patch, as it is instantiated, in their own test apps. This is due to a rule that was recently added to some mature CTFs (Fig. 2).

Table 1. Seven default attack methods are defined, Column 2 identifies the visual representation of the exploit method defined in Column 3.

Attack 0	Flare bullet	Brute force authentication
Attack 1	Green bullet	Misconfiguration exploit
Attack 2	Red bullet	Unintended data exposure
Attack 3	Red laser	SQL injection
Attack 4	Green laser	Application fuzzing
Attack 5	Missiles	Remote code execution
Attack 6	Robot bug swarm	Denial of service
Attack 7	Network scan	Network scan (green is standard, orange is out of bounds)

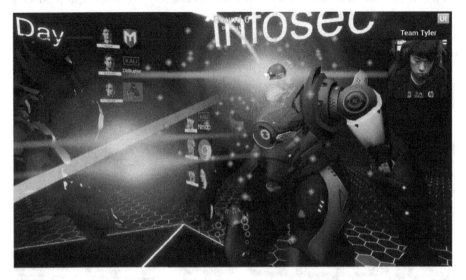

Fig. 2. Illustration of an exploit that is launched and credited to a specific player. Designation of the responsible team is indicated through the mascot, and the exploit method is visually represented by the shape and color.

Teams may also publish corrupt (or infected) patches, such that other teams must take great care. This adds an interesting dynamic to the core decision process teams face during real competitions. We also include the notion of an "infection," in which a team has successfully penetrated an opponent's network.

As the competition progresses and players attack each other's assets, the system ingests the Event Layer information and visually links the action to the appropriate actor:

Team A decides to target Binary 2 and Binary 3 from Team B. Their best SQL team member just completed a SQL vulnerability patch and rapidly pivots to constructing the SQL exploit. The visualization will show him working on that attack, and when he releases it on the network, we will see the Team A giant robot fire a red laser at the Team B buildings that host Binary 2 and Binary 3. If the attack succeeds, the building "explodes" and a flag will be seen flying from that location to the feet of Team A.

The system is live. However, some programmatic attacks that occur in milliseconds are visualized over a synthetic duration for the human audience. This aspect of sequentially staging visual events is incident-based rather than live-traffic based. Once a team has hit a given target (say 20 flags) or the competition clock has hit a predetermined end-point, scores are tallied and results are presented.

4.1   E-Sport Tools Layer

If you watch a professional sporting event (or e-sports), you will notice what a critical role the narrator (broadcaster) plays. Having a subject matter expert (SME) who can talk about the competition while it progresses and point out the nuances, strategies and specifics make the entire spectator experience vastly more rewarding and engaging. However, unlike traditional sports where the 'action' is usually centered around a particular area on the field or court (usually 'the ball'), in CTF's we have a highly decentralized field of play, with many actors performing a wide range of activities in parallel. This presents a substantial challenge for the 'broadcast' aspect of the application. *What should we be looking at?*

This is where the 'Broadcaster's interface' becomes critical. This is a set of onscreen functionalities that only the broadcaster will see. Conceptually, our prototype CTF game engine incorporates a camera 'switcher' (borrowed from broadcast TV facilities), where a variety of cameras allow the broadcaster to quickly pivot the audience to follow the action, and then narrate the particular event or strategy. This view includes both in-game actions and separate 'Data Pages' that provide historical data about players, teams, and the test app challenges. Figure 3 illustrates an example of a broadcaster perspective with camera selection.

'Scoping,' represents another critical component of the Broadcasters Interface. Since these playfields can get quite chaotic, it is often desirable to remove aspects of

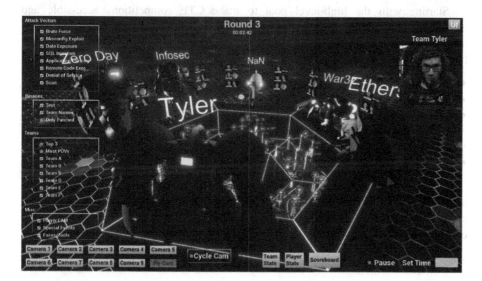

Fig. 3. An example of the broadcaster view with the camera selection options.

the visualization to discuss a particular detail. Broadcasters can toggle the display of each kind of attack, for example to show ONLY Misconfiguration Exploits, or can remove certain teams and to show isolated interactions between Team A and B. Providing these tools during the presentation enables the broadcaster to minimize visual clutter, so that the narration can be translated to the visual display with less confusion.

Finally, Data Pages are analogous to the 'stats' shown in broadcast sports and e-sports. We have seam sheets, leaderboards and individual sheets. The Team-sheets update with game information, for example if a player has been red-carded for illegal activity (such as an out-of-bounds scan or launching external network activity from a process that is launched outside the exploit directory) (Fig. 4).

Fig. 4. Example data pages that highlight team and individual statistics.

4.2   An Example Parameters of a CTF E-Sport Competition

We have designed and constructed demonstration e-Sport games using the design described in this paper. The following briefly summarizes the parameters that were used within this demonstration.

Starting with the high-level goal to make CTF competitions accessible and enjoyable to the widest possible audience, we began by imposing a set of constraints for this particular e-sport inspired visualization. Specifically, we chose to show a red-blue CTF, with the following parameters:

- Number of teams: 6
- Number of members per team: 6
- Which tools are provided: Kali, IDA pro, Nmap, Chrome, Wireshark, Metasploit, DirBuster, SQLmap, Nessus, Burpsuite, and John the Ripper
- Number of binaries per team: 9
- Event duration: 12 h

It is important to note that these constraints are somewhat arbitrary and that the actual world of CTFs has a wide range of possible configurations. With this in mind, our core system is flexible and could support a fair amount of variation if required. We consider this current design as a starting point for a robust and extensible framework.

5 Future Work and Discussion

As the existing CTF game engine framework evolves, there are a several open problems that were deemed beyond the scope of our present design. This section enumerates the limitations of our work and acknowledges several open technical challenges.

Tournament Extensibility and Scalability. An ideal visualization framework should handle a wide range of arbitrary devices and configurations. For example, recently, IoT-based CTF competition have emerged in recognition of the ongoing security challenges that these devices now pose [13], We see natural extensions to our current battlefield motif. However binary test applications, and the network administrative functions involved in Blue-Team activities are less relevant. The system should also visually scale to the number of players, teams, and binaries, in an automated and graceful way. This is perhaps the most significant challenge in CTF game design. Procedural geometry and rule-based modeling offer potential solutions on the 3D layout construction, while more flexible interim data-formats could drive the configuration of the battle space. Finally, the visual ontology of discriminating among exploit classes is currently fixed in number. We would like to extend this vocabulary through better instrumentation and a more robust event description syntax.

A Granular Representation of Traffic Content. The current instrumentation of the hosts and network focus on flow-level analysis, in which the type of attack must be designated by the application from which it is launched. However, the internal size, structure, and content of flows can offer insights into the methods and outcomes of an exploit attempt. Deep packet inspection, which is not performed in the current prototype, would enable the visualization of the responses of the hosts and test apps as they encounters probes and exploits. These responses can offer insights into how Blue-team defenses are performing as new connections from the opponents are parried.

The Semantics of Player Activity. Perhaps one of the most direct ways in which e-sports draw spectators into the game is by their ability to visualize the activities of the individual players. To appreciate the skills, strategies, and the progression of the game, it is important to understand what the players are doing at a given moment in the contest. This point is particularly relevant to the slow-paced, multi-hour duration of a CTF competition. Audiences are more likely to rotate in among multiple tournaments or attend and return to the tournament rather than engage in monitoring the tournament from beginning to end. We would like methods to visually represent the process of attack construction, as well as methods to visualize vulnerability discovery, and security flaw removal.

Post-Game Analytic Services. We currently collect the bare minimum in analytics. One area for future algorithmic extensions is that of conducting automated comparisons of milestones, such as exploit formulation, exploit execution, test app patch deployment, configuration flow removal, and network scans. The rate and timing of these milestones could facilitate additional narratives that explain team strategies and the skills that are exhibited among the competitors. There may be analogies that arise between CTF gameplay comparisons with existing e-sport competitions that can facilitate a better understanding of the skills and strategies that teams employed during the competition.

A Recommendation System for Broadcasters. When and where spectator attention should be focused may not be obvious? As mentioned earlier, regardless of our effort to abstract the assets and applications of a typical CTF into a familiar physical representation (a city-scape battlefield), there remains the potential difficulty for the audience to always know *where* the most interesting events are happening. Even when a competition is slow paced, the ability to identify when background activity becomes notably interesting may not always be immediately apparent. An expert system could be applied to filter and prioritize events through a series of criteria, and then offer recommendations to the broadcaster of scrutiny-worthy fields of play. Camera activations could also be automatically adjusted to capture action and a single button could allow the broadcaster to zoom based on these recommendations. As the number of teams and players increases, such automation will become increasingly valuable.

6 Conclusion

This paper presents the design of a Cyber CTF competition framework, which employs a 3-D virtual battlefield abstraction that is designed to increase the engagement and understanding of the action that transpires. We present the motivations and challenges of taking a highly complex, slow-paced, and intellectually dense event and re-envisioning it as a visually engaging and intuitively familiar competition. Our prototype framework is designed to model CTFs as an e-sport tournament, with a cityscape abstraction of live networks, hosts, and applications, and a visual ontology of defensive and offensive actions that capture the milestones and events as they unfold. Further, we discuss the ability of this framework to capture the strategic decisions made by the teams, as each must decide how to balance its resources on defensive or offensive activities. Finally, we outline the limitations and open problems that we have encountered during this project.

Acknowledgments. This project was funded by the National Science Foundation (NSF) (Award Number DGE-1824258). The views, opinions, and/or findings contained in this paper are those of the authors and should not be interpreted as representing the official views or policies, either expressed or implied, of NSF.

References

1. Tobey, D.H., Pusey, P., Burley, D.L.: Engaging learners in cybersecurity careers: lessons from the launch of the national cyber league. In: ACM Inroads, New York, NY, USA, March 2014
2. Vigna, G., et al.: Ten years of iCTF: the good, the bad, and the ugly. In: Proceedings of the USENIX Summit on Gaming, Games and Gamification in Security Education (3GSE), San Diego, CA, August 2014

3. Cheung, R.S., Cohen, J.P., Lo, H.Z., Elia, F., Carrillo-Marque, V.: Effectiveness of Cybersecurity Competitions (2012). https://www.josephpcohen.com/papers/seccomp.pdf
4. Namin, A.S., Aguirre-Muñoz, Z., Jones, K.S.: Teaching cyber security through competition: an experience report about a participatory training workshop. In: Proceedings of the 7th Annual International Conference on Computer Science Education: Innovation and Technology (CSEIT) (2016)
5. DARPA: Welcome to DARPA's Cyber Grand Challenge – full playlist, July 2016. https://www.youtube.com/watch?v=g5Kt2ayMN0&list=PL6wMum5UsYvZx2x9QGhDY8j3FcQUH7uY0
6. The European Cyber Security Agency: European Cyber Security Challenge. Home page for the EU 2019 CTF Competition. January 2019. https://www.europeancybersecuritychallenge.eu/
7. EY.COM: The Asia-Pacific Cyber Case Challenge, January 2019. https://www.ey.com/cn/en/careers/ey-asia-pacific-cyber-challenge
8. DEFCON: DEFCON 2018 Capture The Flag (CTF) Competition, January 2018. https://www.defcon.org/html/defcon-26/dc-26-ctf.html
9. CTF Time: CTFS, January 2019. https://ctftime.org/ctfs
10. Bao, T., Shoshitaishvili, Y., Wang, R., Kruegel, C. Vigna, G., Brumley, D.: How shall we play a game?: a game-theoretical model for cyber-warfare games. In: Proceedings of the 30th IEEE Computer Security Foundations Symposium, CSF 2017, Santa Barbara, CA, 21–25 August 2017
11. Epic Games: What is the Unreal Engine 4, January 2019. https://www.unrealengine.com/en-US/what-is-unreal-engine-4
12. Samurai CTF Team: We are Samurai CTF and we won Defcon CTF this year (2013). http://www.reddit.com/r/netsec/comments/y0nnu/we_are_samurai_ctf_and_we_won_defcon_ctf_this/c5r9osm
13. Fortinet: Ph0wn: A CTF Dedicated to Smart Devices, November 2018. https://www.fortinet.com/blog/threat-research/ph0wn-a-ctf-cedicated-to-smart-devices.html
14. Boopathi, K., Sreejith, S., Bithin, A.: Learning cyber security through gamification. Indian J. Sci. Technol. **8**, 642–649 (2015)
15. Fink, G., Best, D., Manz, D., Popovsky, V., Endicott-Popovsky, B.: Gamification for measuring cyber security situational awareness. In: Schmorrow, Dylan D., Fidopiastis, Cali M. (eds.) AC 2013. LNCS (LNAI), vol. 8027, pp. 656–665. Springer, Heidelberg (2013). https://doi.org/10.1007/978-3-642-39454-6_70
16. McDaniel, L., Talvi, E., Hay, B.: Capture the flag as cyber security introduction. In: Proceedings of the 49th Hawaii International Conference on System Sciences (HICSS). IEEE (2016)
17. Dabrowski, A., Kammerstetter, M., Thamm, E., Weippl, E., Kastner, W.: Leveraging competitive gamification for sustainable fun and profit in security education. In: USENIX Summit on Gaming, Games, and Gamification in Security Education (3GSE 15) (2015)
18. Adams, M., Makramalla, M.: Cybersecurity skills training: an attacker-centric gamified approach. Technol. Innov. Manag. Rev. **5**(1) (2015)
19. Nakaya, M., Akagi, S., Tominaga, H.: Implementation and trial practices for hacking competition CTF as introductory educational experience for information literacy and security learning. In: Proceedings of ICIA (2016)
20. Chapman, P., Burket, J., Brumley, D.: PicoCTF: a game-based computer security competition for high school students. In: 3GSE, August 2014
21. Dasgupta, D., Ferebee,D.M., Michalewicz, Z.: Applying Puzzle-based learning to cyber-security education. In: Proceedings of the 2013 on InfoSecCD 2013: Information Security Curriculum Development Conference, p. 20. ACM, October 2013

22. Gavas, E., Memon, N., Britton, D.: Winning cybersecurity one challenge at a time. IEEE Secur. Priv. **10**(4), 75–79 (2012)
23. Chung, K., Cohen, J.: Learning obstacles in the capture the flag model. In: 3GSE, August 2014
24. Vigna, G., et al.: Ten years of iCTF: The good, the bad, and the ugly. In: 3GSE, August 2014
25. Chothia, T., Novakovic, C.: An offline capture the flag-style virtual machine and an assessment of its value for cybersecurity education. In: USENIX Summit on Gaming, Games, and Gamification in Security Education (3GSE 15) (2015)
26. Nunes, E., Kulkarni, N., Shakarian, P., Ruef, A., Little, J.: Cyber-deception and attribution in capture-the-flag exercises. In: Jajodia, S., Subrahmanian, V.S.S., Swarup, V., Wang, C. (eds.) Cyber Deception, pp. 151–167. Springer, Cham (2016). https://doi.org/10.1007/978-3-319-32699-3_7
27. Ford, V., Siraj, A., Haynes, A., Brown, E.: Capture the flag unplugged: an offline cyber competition. In: Proceedings of the 2017 ACM SIGCSE Technical Symposium on Computer Science Education, pp. 225–230. ACM, March 2017
28. Song, J., Alves-Foss, J.: The DARPA cyber grand challenge: a competitor's perspective. Proc. IEEE Secur. Priv. **13**(6), 72–76 (2015)
29. Song, J., Alves-Foss, J.: The DARPA cyber grand challenge: a competitor. In: Proc. IEEE Secur. Priv. (1) (2016)
30. Walker, M.: Machine vs. machine: lessons from the first year of cyber grand challenge. In: Proceedings of the 24th USENIX Security Symposium (2015)
31. Kali.Org: Kali Distribution Page - Our Most Advanced Penetration Testing Distribution, Ever, January 2019. https://www.kali.org
32. SRI International: SRIFlow Distribution Page – Network Flow Auditing for Security and Visualization, January 2019. http://sriflow.csl.sri.com

Privacy and Trust

Reciprocities or Incentives? Understanding Privacy Intrusion Perspectives and Sharing Behaviors

Ala Sarah Alaqra[(✉)] and Erik Wästlund

Karlstad University, Karlstad, Sweden
alaaalaq@kau.se

Abstract. The importance and perception of privacy varies from one context to the other. However, everyone values his or her privacy to a certain extent. The subjectivity of that value, attitudes, and behaviors would depend on different entangling factors. It is important to understand the motivation that influences human behavior, whether to protect or share their information. In this paper, we aim at understanding the boundaries of privacy, factors influencing information sharing behavior including experiences (reciprocities of privacy), and efforts taken to protect one's data.

We collected data using quantitative (survey/quiz) and qualitative means (focus groups). In the survey/quiz, our results showed that intrusion experience and awareness have a significant correlation between sharing of data. Furthermore, our focus groups results yielded details on influencing factors for privacy reciprocities and tradeoffs. We discuss our results in terms of privacy incentives and factors influencing the sharing behavior of their information. Finally, we highlight the complexity of behavior where intrinsic and extrinsic motivations could clash and result in a dilemma such as the privacy paradox phenomenon.

Keywords: Incentive · Reciprocity · Privacy · Privacy paradox · Behavior · Motivation

1 Incentives: Motivating Behavior

Understanding human behavior and motivation has been a research goal within different fields. Biologists, psychologists, economists have been exploring human motivation in order to shed a light on understanding decision-making processes. Incentives, used as a motivational technique to stimulate activities and actions, give some insight to prediction modules and strategies [1].

Motivation is generally the reason why people behave in a particular way to achieve their goals, activities, and needs. In psychology, there are two types of motivation: Intrinsic and extrinsic [2, 3]. Intrinsic motivation is related to one's own sense of accomplishment, satisfaction and is closely related to fun, whereas extrinsic motivation is instrumental; dealing with external rewards or consequences [2]. One major theory of motivation is the incentive theory, which focuses on rewards to motivate a behavior. The *Positive* reinforcement (reward) gives a positive meaning to a behavior, and thus the awarded activity is stimulated to occur repeatedly [4].

© Springer Nature Switzerland AG 2019
A. Moallem (Ed.): HCII 2019, LNCS 11594, pp. 355–370, 2019.
https://doi.org/10.1007/978-3-030-22351-9_24

Rewards, can have different effects on behavior, possibly unintended, depending on different factors [1]. The factor of time (past behavioral influence) has been shown to play an important role in human behavior, and social influence to reciprocity when it comes to incentives [5]. However, human behavior has shown to be more complex than just be motivated by monetary incentives [1, 6]. Studies have emphasized the importance of considering different motives for incentives such as the desire to reciprocate, or avoid social disapproval [7].

2 Privacy: Breaking Boundaries

With the growing online activity, exposure to threats and risks of privacy increases. Apart from cyber adversaries and data collectors, users sharing of their personal information (indirectly or by reciprocity) is a key factor to regulating the intrusion of their privacy.

To define privacy is to select a context and understand which factors and actors are involved in that definition. When considering personal freedom, privacy can be defined as "the right to be let alone" [8]. Whereas context and specific norms are key in the concept of contextual integrity [9].

According to Communication Privacy Management (CPM) theory, people's sharing of private information, using the boundary metaphor, is denoted by boundaries [10, 11]. CMP focuses on the motivations behind people's self-disclosure of their private data using the privacy boundaries. When people keep to themselves, is it considered a *personal* boundary, however when they share information that is when it becomes a *collective* boundary. Understanding when and why these boundaries are crossed is one way to understand sharing behaviors.

When dealing with privacy, especially with human factors, privacy aspects may seem subjective. The tendency to give bias positive responses is higher when it comes to the topic of privacy. The incentive of having the privacy of data being protected is desired and when asked, users tend to agree to that. However, according to the privacy paradox, instances have shown behaviors that entails otherwise. The conflict between attitude, showing concerns and behavior is not new as seen in the works of Barnes, Taddicken and kokolakis [12–14]. Privacy paradox show contradictions on users' online behavior, where people would state that they value privacy, however their behaviors might indicate otherwise [12, 13]. It is therefore difficult to tell through empirical research if users are indicating their intention or behavior when it comes to privacy. Hu and Pu compare two preference elicitation methods, the common rating versus personality quiz [15]. They highlight the importance of considering psychological aspects, and indicate that personality quiz could be a powerful tool as alternative to the rating approach for higher accuracy for revealing user's preferences. In the first study, survey/quiz we used a personality test format as a motivational approach by giving users the incentive of "feedback: result of their test", we intentionally avoided monetary incentives due to possible unintended effects [16].

2.1   Scope

In previous research, we have claimed that data privacy is a wicked problem [17], a complex issue with no straightforward solution. An ecosystem of technological, legal, and human factors should be considered when enhancing data privacy. We therefore consider that technological and legal aspects are set, whereas our investigations and contributions of this paper focus on human factors.

The scope of this work is part of the EU H2020 project PRISMACLOUD (Privacy and Security Maintaining Services in the Cloud). The project develops privacy enhancing solutions for avoiding privacy intrusion in the Cloud, such as malleable (redactable) signatures [18]. A malleable signature is a cryptographic scheme that allows specified redaction (removing or blacking out) of fields within a digitally signed document while maintaining the validity of the signature. One of the PRISMACLOUD eHealth use cases allows patients to redact specified fields of documents that were digitally signed by their medical doctor) so that they can share it afterwards. Therefore, it is important to understand user's perspectives as well as which incentives promote their sharing behaviors for the design processes.

2.2   Research Objectives

In our studies, we investigate attitudes toward privacy incentives and privacy boundaries, and focus on the behavior of sharing personal information and factors that influence their behavior: whether it is reciprocation they seek or an incentive that motivates them. Therefore our research questions are:

- What are the *boundaries* of privacy?
- What factors influence information sharing behavior i.e., which reciprocities are privacy being traded for?
- Can intrusion experiences influence privacy behavior?
- What efforts do users take in order to protect their privacy?

3   Methodologies and Approaches

These studies are part of our Value Sensitive Design (VSD) approach, focusing on the privacy value. VSD approach accounts for human values in comprehensive manner throughout the design process [19]. We also followed User-centered Design approach (UCD) approach in our project, where the focus is on exploring users' perspectives and experiences throughout design processes [20, 21]. We aimed to understand users' online behavior and willingness to disclose "sensitive" information. In specific, what information that is considered private and in which context, how do users perceive intrusions, and what are they willing to do in order to protect their sensitive information from intrusions.

Using empirical methods, we have collected data using both quantitative (survey) and qualitative (focus groups) means in order to investigate, in explorative manner, users' perceptions, and behavior to disclose "sensitive" information. A survey will act as a quantitative approach; consequently, we investigated and validated results from the survey with focus groups. The following sections will give an account to the two studies' design and procedure.

3.1 Study 1: Survey/Quiz

The survey was conducted online using SurveyGizmo [22]. Choice of the instrument depended on the functionality that permitted the use of personality quiz alternatives. We recruited participants through online forums, brochures around 5 cities in Sweden, contacts mailing lists (In Germany and Italy), and SurveyGizmo sharing option. Aside from English, we had German, Italian and Swedish as alternatives to answer the survey/quiz. We chose Germany, Sweden, and Italy, due to our resources and project partners who aided in translating the survey into corresponding languages.

Since privacy is a relatable topic, we targeted all types of possible participants, which made up our convenience sample. We mainly distinct them by enquiring about their technical experience. The survey was online for 6 weeks between March and May 2017.

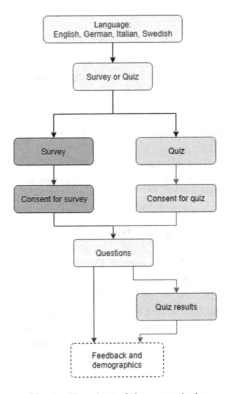

Fig. 1. Flowchart of the survey/quiz

The survey was calculated (by SurveyGizmo) to take 6–10 min to complete. Participants were first given a choice of language: English, Swedish, German, and Italian. Next was the choice to take either a personality quiz or a survey. After that, they were directed to the consent and beginning of the survey/quiz questions, see Fig. 1. The questions consisted of 5 sections corresponding to evaluation criteria (see details in section: Questions and evaluation criteria), and feedback and demographic question-naire which was optional.

Questions and Evaluation Criteria

The questions in the survey/quiz were formulated around the context of privacy, however privacy questions were not asked explicitly. Using indirect enquiry, we used daily situations and metaphors to investigate users' perceptions and attitudes. For example, we used situations which could be interpreted as privacy intrusive and asked about them (e.g., being asked about the content of a shopping bag by a random stranger), or online behaviors that they perform (e.g., filling only mandatory fields in forms). The 5 evaluation criteria, described below, correspond to sections in the survey/quiz.

Attitude and Comfort Toward Intrusion

In this section, there were 5-leveled Likert scale agreement questions varying from "strongly agree" to "strongly disagree". Investigating user's perception of intrusion is crucial in understanding how users perceive privacy. However, how intrusive the behavior may be, it is interesting to investigate the comfort level that users experience when they are put in an intrusive situation. The questions target intrusions to one's information that is more or less private depending on the context and the actors involved. The list of questions describe situations, and subjects are asked to provide feedback by rating their comfort level corresponding to the given situation. The situations are basically regular activities, e.g., shopping, and then an external actor, e.g., stranger, enquires about unexpected information, e.g., what's in their shopping bag. We expect that most users would feel uncomfortable in such situations, and would be aware of the intrusiveness of the situations.

Experience of Intrusive Situations

In this section, there were 4-leveled Likert scale frequency questions varying from "never" to "often". Whether users are consciously aware or not of experiences of intrusion, it is interesting to see if they can relate to the scenarios presented. Specifi-cally if they perceive the intrusion of personal information. We are interested to see if familiarity and experience with intrusion situations have an effect on how users behave with their data. Either they are more privacy aware and careful, so that they would prevent future reoccurrences, or they just accept it and don't see any harm in their experience. We expect the former statement, where users become more careful when they have experienced an intrusive situation. In this section, questions were asked if they have experienced (never, few times, several, and many times) similar situations to the same scenarios of previous section.

Sharing of Personal Data and Contexts

In this section, there were checkbox questions for sharing 5 categories of data in 3 contexts. When addressing personal information, it is difficult to predict what is con-sidered as per se sensitive (independent from the purpose of use) and to what degree for users. We investigated the sharing of personal information of the 5 categories/types of data (medical, political &religious, sexual, income, and demographics) in the contexts of medical staff, employer, and family. The first three listed above categories are regarded as sensitive data according to Art. 9 of the EU General Data Protection Regulation (GDPR), which defines "special categories of personal data" as sensitive for processing [23].

Experience and Effort to Hide Data: Data Minimization
In this section, there were 5-leveled Likert scale agreement questions varying from "strongly agree" to "strongly disagree". Besides being aware of intrusive situations regarding their personal data, we are interested in their prior experience to limit and hide personal information. The latter would indicate higher privacy value and cautiousness when disclosing information. The questions, regarding information disclosure, enquires if they fill out mandatory fields only in forms, or question the need to provide sensitive information in certain situations. We expect that users, who had experiences with cautious information disclosure, are keener to protect their privacy in the future.

Reciprocity and Privacy
In this section, there were 5-leveled Likert scale agreement questions varying from "strongly agree" to "strongly disagree". Considering the abovementioned sections, users who are privacy aware are expected to spend more efforts to protect their data's privacy. The corresponding section's questions investigate users' willingness to spend more time, money, effort to enhance their privacy.

The Quiz: Data-Introvert or Data-Extrovert
When they began the test, they got a disclaimer stating that the two personas are made-up and not official. Throughout the test, the instrument calculated their answers according to their privacy and sharing responses: when users reach a certain threshold of points they are data-extrovert. After answering all questions, they got instant score and a text describing the result i.e., what does data-introvert means.

3.2 Study 2: Focus Groups

Following the survey, we discussed the research criteria from the survey in depth with focus groups. The qualitative approach allows interactivity and freedom of expression among participants, which allows us to investigate their opinions, perspectives, and attitudes.

Considering the scope of the project involved, we included user groups with different technical background and used the knowledge of digital signature as the selection criteria. When recruiting users, they were asked about their knowledge of digital signatures and to what extent, consequently they were put in either the lay user (no knowledge of how digital signatures work) group or technical group (knowledge of how digital signatures work). We had 5 focus groups (6–7 participants in each) totaling 32 participants in Sweden, Germany, and Norway: 3 lay user groups (FG1, FG3, and FG4), and 2 technical groups (FG2 and FG5).

The focus group sessions consisted of two parts (each lasting approximately 45 min), since it was combined with another study [24]. The first part was addressing users perspectives on our research criteria from the survey (we also used the results from the survey as input for discussions), which is reported in this paper, and the second part was mock-up discussions (which is not part of this paper). Participants were given consent forms for participating in the study and for recording the sessions. All participants consented to both, and they were urged to not disclose sensitive identifying information (in which case the recording will stop, and the recording section would be deleted). Two researchers at least were in each session, one took notes and the other moderated the discussion.

3.3 Ethical Considerations

To the best of our efforts, the survey/quiz was anonymous. A disclaimer was included in the survey regarding the personality test analysis being fictional (is not a diagnosis), and that is part of our research. No sensitive or personally identifying information was collected, thus complying with the Swedish Ethical Review Act. As for the focus groups, since the recording of voice might be personally identifying data, we submitted it to the Ethical Review Board at Karlstad University, which was approved in May 2017.

4 Findings and Discussions

4.1 Study 1: Survey/Quiz

In total, there were 165 complete and valid responses, where 162 participants filled in the demographics sections, and 111 filled in the feedback section. There was a good distribution of countries and ages as seen in Figs. 2 and 3. Additionally, we had good distributions of lay and technical users as shown in Table 1. Classification of users into Lay and technical depended on their knowledge and experience of two tools: Digital Signatures and Electronic IDs (selection of tools was dependent on our project's scope).

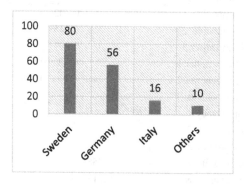

Fig. 2. Demographics showing number of participants in corresponding country

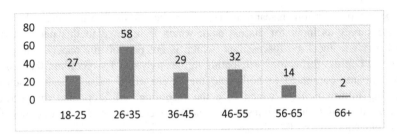

Fig. 3. Demographics showing number of participants in corresponding age-range

Table 1. Demographics showing participants' experience with the two tools as indicators of their technical expertise

Tool/users	Lay	Tech
Electronic ID	60	102
Digital signatures	74	88

In order to investigate the underlying structure of the questions regarding online behavior preferences we conducted a factor analysis (PCA with varimax rotation). The results showed that the questions fell into five factors (see Table 2), namely "Intrusion awareness": being consciously aware of the possibility of the intrusion of one's personal information, "Intrusion experience": the personal experience of privacy intrusion, "Effort for privacy tradeoff": willingness to make an effort to protect their privacy, "Privacy for benefits tradeoff": willingness to trade privacy for benefits, and "Data minimization": the ambition to only enter mandatory information. Table 2 shows the composition of the first to the fifth PCA component, values represent weight of the survey questions in relationship to the factors.

Table 2. The 5 factors and corresponding weights

Rotated component matrix	1	2	3	4	5
Data minimization 1			0,702		
Data minimization 2			0,745		
Data minimization 3			0,797		
Privacy for benefits 1			−0,3	0,63	
Privacy for benefits 2				0,725	
Privacy for benefits 3				0,837	
Effort for privacy 1					0,636
Effort for privacy 2					0,695
Effort for privacy 3					0,733
Intrusion awareness 1		0,758			
Intrusion awareness 2		0,713			
Intrusion awareness 3		0,703			

(*continued*)

Table 2. (*continued*)

Rotated component matrix	1	2	3	4	5
Intrusion awareness 4		0,701			0,324
Intrusion awareness 5		0,671		−0,276	
Intrusion experience 1	0,815				
Intrusion experience 2	0,559				
Intrusion experience 3	0,852				
Intrusion experience 4	0,767				
Intrusion experience 5	0,792				

Extraction Method: Principal Component Analysis.
Rotation Method: Varimax with Kaiser Normalization.

In order to examine to what extent the online behavior preference factors were related to sharing behavior mean scores for each preference factor as well as the sum of all question regarding sharing "Share overall" was calculated for each participant. Pearson correlation coefficients was then calculated between the six variables. The results showed that "Intrusion awareness" and "Intrusion experience" significantly correlated negatively with "Share overall". Additionally, "Effort for privacy" marginally correlated to "Intrusion awareness" (see Table 3 for r and p values).

Table 3. Sharing behavior and online behavior preference factors

		Share overall	Intrution awareness	Intrution experience	Data minimization	Privacy for benefits	Effort for privacy
Share overall	Pearson correlation	1	−,248**	−,286**	−,175*	0,09	0,049
	Sig. (2-tailed)		0,001	0	0,025	0,252	0,531
	N	165	165	165	165	165	165
Intrution awareness	Pearson correlation	−,248**	1	−0,078	0,093	−0,023	0,152
	Sig. (2-tailed)	0,001		0,316	0,233	0,767	0,052
	N	165	165	165	165	165	165
Intrution experience	Pearson correlation	−,286**	−0,078	1	0,021	0,081	−0,008
	Sig. (2-tailed)	0	0,316		0,792	0,302	0,918
	N	165	165	165	165	165	165
Data minimization	Pearson correlation	−,175*	0,093	0,021	1	−0,112	−0,066
	Sig. (2-tailed)	0,025	0,233	0,792		0,151	0,402
	N	165	165	165	165	165	165
Privacy for benefits	Pearson correlation	0,09	−0,023	0,081	−0,112	1	−0,009
	Sig. (2-tailed)	0,252	0,767	0,302	0,151		0,912
	N	165	165	165	165	165	165
Effort for privacy	Pearson correlation	0,049	0,152	−0,008	−0,066	−0,009	1
	Sig. (2-tailed)	0,531	0,052	0,918	0,402	0,912	
	N	165	165	165	165	165	165

** Correlation is significant at the 0.01 level (2-tailed).
* Correlation is significant at the 0.05 level (2-tailed).

To further investigate perceptions of sensitivity of the data types and their willingness to share data we looked at the distribution of participants who were willing to share vs those who were not willing to share. The results showed that perceptions of sensitivity spanned form very sensitive "sexual data" to not sensitive at all "Demographics" (see Fig. 4 for proportions of willingness to share different datatypes).

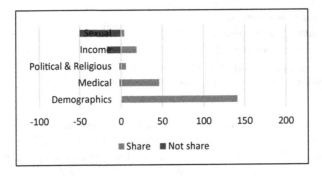

Fig. 4. Willingness to share different datatypes

To follow up on the perceptions of sensitivity of the different datatypes we looked at the specificity of contexts (medical, employer, family) where the datatypes were shared. This was done by calculating the number of different contexts where the datatypes were shared[1]. The results showed that again "Demographics" was the least sensitive datatype as this was shared among **all three contexts by** 85% of participants whereas "Political and Religious" was the most sensitive insofar that it was only shared within **one context** by 88% percent of participants (see Table 4. Willingness to share with up to 3 different contexts).

Table 4. Willingness to share with up to 3 different contexts

Type of data	Number of contexts		
	1	2	3
Demographics	3,05%	10,98%	85,98%
Income	45,95%	41,22%	12,84%
Medical	12,27%	59,51%	28,22%
Political & religious	88,28%	7,59%	4,14%
Sexual	66,96%	29,57%	3,48%

---

[1] The calculations of the proportions of number of contexts is based on those who were willing to share.

4.2   Study 2: Focus Groups

In the discussions of focus groups, all groups shared the opinion regarding the sensitivity of medical, political, sexual, religious, and income data. Most indicated that they would not share sensitive data, whereas they are willing to share demographic data such as age, profession, address.

Sharing Behavior and Factors

Since we were interested in understanding the sharing behavior of the participants, we asked of situations and factors that they see themselves sharing more or less information than they already have. Table 5 summarizes the results of influencing factors to sharing information by the focus groups and shows the distribution of both user types, details of the factors are provided below.

1. Context refers to the environment where participants are sharing information in. For instance, on online dating site, one would reveal different type of information than their professional profile on the web. Additionally, if one is engaging in a specific context e.g., political discussion, then they would have directly/indirectly reveal their political affiliation, which they consider sensitive information.
2. Peer-pressure is the obligation to share certain information due to social pressure: e.g., everyone has shared a piece of information, or due to norms that pressure one to provide some information about one's self.
3. Social acceptance/appeal is wanting to bond with others by sharing information and details based on common grounds and wanting to be liked by others.
4. Duration of interaction refers to time spent with someone, e.g., the feeling of comfort and familiarity will allow sharing more information with the person you have spent more time with.
5. Face to face or offline interaction allows more sharing of information than online, where one lacks control and certainty of whom they are sharing information with and if information is stored somewhere online.
6. Not documented or recorded conversations allows freedom of revealing personal information, whereas one might be more careful in revealing information about themselves in recorded conversations.
7. One on one is more intimate and trustworthy environment to share information than a setting containing a group of people, where one would not feel comfortable sharing with everyone in the group.
8. Experience with age refers to how older generation tend to be more private about their information and sharing behavior/online activity seem to differ from their children.
9. Prior bad experiences tend to make one more cautious when sharing information, since it can also become a personality trait of being more private.
10. Consequences concerns of sharing personal information, especially with health data, could lead to problems such as insurance conflicts. Another concern is profiling through revealing data that is not secretive. Also metadata or derived sensitive information that one is not willing to share.

11. Cultural influences refers to a cultural/social stance on some information that is considered private, e.g., sharing income data in Germany is considered a taboo and thus no one would share that type of data.

Table 5. Factors affecting sharing behavior among lay and technical participants: more (+), more vs. less (±), and less (−)

No.	Factor affecting sharing behaviors	Lay	Tech.
1.	Context	+	+
2.	Peer-pressure/norms	+	+
3.	Social acceptance/appeal		+
4.	Duration of interaction	+	
5.	Face to face vs. online	±	±
6.	Not documented vs. recorded		±
7.	One on one vs. groups	±	±
8.	Experience with age	−	
9.	Prior bad experiences	−	
10.	Consequences concerns: profiling, metadata	−	−
11.	Cultural influences	−	−

Efforts to Protect/Hide Information

In the discussion about the willingness of participants to protect or hide their data and what efforts they undertake, many indicated that they actively try to limit their exposure. Means and efforts mentioned by participants (lay and technical) are clustered into the three following categories.

Rejection the Use of Services

Participants indicated that they would not use the following services for privacy and security reasons. They stated that it is part of their efforts to protect their data's privacy.

- Social media,e.g., Facebook, WhatsApp (lay and tech)
- Free services, e.g., public Wi-Fi (lay and tech)
- Cloud services, e.g., storing photos (lay).

Limitation of Information Exposure

According to participants, one way to protect their data is to limit their exposure to privacy intrusive possible portals. Limiting the exposure of one's information online by using ad-blocks for browsing online, or controls to limit online access and sharing of data, and paying for avoiding customized advertisements.

- Using Ad-blocks (lay)
- Controls for online exposure, e.g., sharing pictures (tech)
- Using cash for anonymity (lay)
- Using fake emails (tech)
- Paying for services: Wi-Fi, non-Ad Apps (tech).

Taking on Inconvenient Alternatives

Another approach was to find alternatives for limiting one's possible exposure, however it was noted that not many alternatives exist, and the current ones are inconvenient/cumbersome. Many indicated that they would try to use alternative services that are more privacy friendly, or that they would implement their own service to ensure they have more control.

- SMS instead of chats that require profiles (lay)
- non-smart phone for communication (lay)
- Offline shopping, avoiding ads (lay)
- Using own domain for emails (tech)
- Implement own service (tech).

4.3 Discussions

Privacy Boundaries, Attitudes, and Experience

According to our results, participants showed more or less reservation regarding sharing information, which indicated their boundaries of privacy. In the focus groups, many indicated further reservations in normal settings (outside the context of a focus group discussion where they share their opinions and experiences). Our discussions mainly focused on voluntary self-disclosure (sharing information and crossing the privacy boundary willingly), thus excluding external enforcements of disclosure e.g., law enforcement. The value of having one's data being private (personal boundary) holds true for many especially when they have control over it (voluntary disclosure).

However, participants indicated that they would share more or less information depending on the type of data, which varies in sensitivity; that sensitivity is confirmed by both studies to be affected by the context the information is being shared in. For example, the case of declaring political affiliation as sensitive data, yet revealing that information in a political discussion. This indicates that privacy is situational, and exchange of information is a balance between risks and benefits at that specific point [6]. Experiences and privacy awareness significantly correlated to sharing behavior in our survey/quiz. Similarly, in the focus groups, participants indicated experience with age and bad experiences are factors for having concern to sharing information. However, despite having a privacy-concerned attitude, that does not ensure privacy correct perception or behavior. In the work of Joinson et al. [25], where they addressed the relationship between privacy concerns and users disclosure (behavior) online. They concluded that privacy concerns do not necessary influence the perception of privacy-related situation.

Privacy: Incentives and Reciprocities

From the 5 factors of the survey/quiz, there was a distinction between: "Effort for privacy tradeoff": willingness to make an effort to protect their privacy and "Privacy for benefits tradeoff": willingness to trade privacy for benefits. While in many cases there are efforts to protect and enhance privacy, there are also instances where privacy is being traded for other benefits. Consequently, indicating that privacy is not necessary the most important incentive at all times. The voluntary act of sharing one's information was discussed in the focus groups, and reciprocity was key factor in sharing information. That happens when one is trading their privacy for other benefits (intrinsic and/or extrinsic) such as social acceptance and likability, engaging and interacting, and performing certain settings (context).

Influencing factors to sharing information, mentioned in the focus groups, contained both intrinsic and extrinsic values. While in many cases the values were directly associated with the benefit, the complexity of sharing information was further highlighted in the focus groups. Some participants mentioned that they chose to share more information online to mitigate false profiling, thus by sharing correct information about themselves, they control how they are profiled online. Also, a couple of participants indicated that hiding information might be perceived as suspicious and thus chose to share information in certain occasions consequently to avoid false image. The above-mentioned instances show behaviors of sharing more information because of limited control over the environment and fearing consequences of protecting their own privacy. The contradiction in behavior (sharing information) and situation is an instance where extrinsic (the situation) and intrinsic (privacy-aware) values are mismatching thus affecting the behavior.

Similarly, related work by Li et al. addressed the entanglement of information as non-independent activity from other happenings [6]. In their study, they addressed the sharing of information as secondary exchange to a primary online shopping exchange. Fairness and relatedness of information has shown to be important factor to the information exchange. They also showed that monetary incentive (extrinsic value) could have undermining effects on user's willingness to share information if the information is not relevant.

Discussions in the focus groups revealed a general attitude for having high regard to privacy, however only some active efforts to protect one's privacy were mentioned. The main issue highlighted was that despite the acknowledgement of one's privacy being important, it fades when other incentives or needs are present, thus trading one's privacy in reciprocity for a service or functionality. Additionally, all the mentioned efforts were perceived as inconvenient and the lack of suitable and usable alternatives was a major issue. This indicates that efforts to protect one's privacy are hindered by the lack of suitable alternatives and not only attitudes; also, they fall short depending on the situation and needs.

Limitations

Due to our empirical research, one main limitation is the sample size and scope. We had only the countries involved in our both studies limited to our available resources, and lacked international representatives of the sample. However since the research is explorative, this could act as starting point to expand the study and perform some comparative study with regions outside the European Union, where rules and regulations differ and might influence voluntary sharing of information.

5   Conclusions

Privacy has always been regarded as important, whether it is a personal freedom, right, or preference. However, it is not always the most important incentive, which explains why human behavior, as in the privacy paradox, contradicts to privacy concerns. External influences and other factors are contributing to the perceived privacy unfriendly behaviors. Future solutions should consider providing alternatives to existing incentives that are being traded for one's privacy. Reciprocity is key when addressing privacy behaviors and considerations for different influencing factors are crucial for future research and applications.

Acknowledgements. This work is supported by the EU Horizon 2020 research project № 644962 PRISMACLOUD "Privacy and security maintaining services in the Cloud". We extend our thanks to Simone Fischer-Hübner for her valuable input, our project partners who aided our studies, and to the volunteers who contributed to this research.

References

1. Kamenica, E.: Behavioral economics and psychology of incentives. Annu. Rev. Econ. **4**(1), 427–452 (2011)
2. Ryan, R.M., Deci, E.L.: Intrinsic and extrinsic motivations: classic definitions and new directions. Contemp. Educ. Psychol. **25**(1), 54–67 (2000)
3. Vallerand, R.J.: Toward a hierarchical model of intrinsic and extrinsic motivation. In: Zanna, M.P. (ed.) Advances in Experimental Social Psychology, vol. 29, pp. 271–360. Academic Press, Cambridge (1997)
4. Killeen, P.R.: Incentive theory. Nebr. Symp. Motiv. **29**, 169–216 (1981)
5. André, J.: The evolution of reciprocity: social types or social incentives? Am. Nat. **175**(2), 197–210 (2010)
6. Li, H., Sarathy, R., Xu, H.: Understanding situational online information disclosure as a privacy calculus. J. Comput. Inf. Syst. **51**(1), 62–71 (2010)
7. Fehr, E., Falk, A.: Psychological foundations of incentives. Eur. Econ. Rev. **46**(4), 687–724 (2002)
8. Warren, S.D., Brandeis, L.D.: The right to privacy. Harv. Law Rev. **4**, 193–220 (1890)
9. Nissenbaum, H.: Privacy as contextual integrity. Wash. Rev. **79**, 119 (2004)
10. Petronio, S.: Boundaries of Privacy: Dialectics of Disclosure. SUNY Press, Albany (2012)
11. Petronio, S., Ellemers, N., Giles, H., Gallois, C.: (Mis)communicating across boundaries: interpersonal and intergroup considerations. Commun. Res. **25**(6), 571–595 (1998)
12. Kokolakis, S.: Privacy attitudes and privacy behaviour: a review of current research on the privacy paradox phenomenon. Comput. Secur. **64**, 122–134 (2017)
13. S.B. Barnes: A privacy paradox: social networking in the United States. First Monday **11**(9) (2006)
14. Taddicken, M.: The 'privacy paradox' in the social web: the impact of privacy concerns, individual characteristics, and the perceived social relevance on different forms of self-disclosure. J. Comput.-Mediat. Commun. **19**(2), 248–273 (2014)
15. Hu, R., Pu, P.: A comparative user study on rating vs. personality quiz based preference elicitation methods. In: Proceedings of the 14th International Conference on Intelligent User Interfaces, pp. 367–372 (2009)

16. Tietje, B.C.: When do rewards have enhancement effects? An availability valence approach. J. Consum. Psychol. **12**(4), 363–373 (2002)

17. Alaqra, A.S.: The wicked problem of privacy : design challenge for crypto-based solutions (2018)

18. Chase, M., Kohlweiss, M., Lysyanskaya, A., Meiklejohn, S.: Malleable signatures: complex unary transformations and delegatable anonymous credentials. IACR Cryptol. EPrint Arch. **2013**, 179 (2013)

19. Friedman, B., Kahn P., Borning, A.: Value sensitive design: theory and methods. University of Washington technical report, no. 2–12 (2002). Citeseer

20. Anderson, N.S., Norman, D.A., Draper, S.W.: User centered system design: new perspectives on human-computer interaction. Am. J. Psychol. **101**(1), 148 (1988)

21. Abras, C., Maloney-krichmar, D., Preece, J.: User-centered design. In: Bainbridge, W. (ed.) Encyclopedia of Human-Computer Interaction. Sage Publications, Thousand Oaks (2004)

22. Rattray, K.: SurveyGizmo | Enterprise Online Survey Software and Tools. SurveyGizmo. https://www.surveygizmo.com/. Accessed 11 Feb 2019

23. Vollmer, N.: Article 9 EU General Data Protection Regulation (EU-GDPR), 05 September 2018. http://www.privacy-regulation.eu/en/article-9-processing-of-special-categories-of-personal-data-GDPR.htm. Accessed 13 Feb 2019

24. Alaqra, A.S., Fischer-Hübner, S., Framner, E.: Enhancing privacy controls for patients via a selective authentic electronic health record exchange service: qualitative study of perspectives by medical professionals and patients. J. Med. Internet Res. **20**(12), e10954 (2018)

25. Joinson, A.N., Reips, U.-D., Buchanan, T., Schofield, C.B.P.: Privacy, trust, and self-disclosure online. Hum. Comput. Interact. **25**(1), 1–24 (2010)

Trust in Autonomous Technologies

A Contextual Comparison of Influencing User Factors

Teresa Brell$^{(\boxtimes)}$ ⓘ, Hannah Biermann ⓘ, Ralf Philipsen ⓘ,
and Martina Ziefle ⓘ

Human-Computer Interaction Center, RWTH Aachen University,
Campus-Boulevard 57, 52074 Aachen, Germany
{brell,biermann,philipsen,ziefle}@comm.rwth-aachen.de

Abstract. Faced with an increasing automation of everyday life, users' trust in autonomous technologies is a key factor for its successful adoption. Automation of processes, at home or in the transport sector, can offer great advantages (e.g., more comfort and safety), however, transferring control from a human to technology is also a serious challenge for users. Hence, in this study, we examined user diverse trust perceptions and evaluations in contextual comparison. An online questionnaire study was conducted (N = 129), focusing on trust in and the intention to use autonomous driving and smart home environments with regard to different user groups. Results reveal that trust was context sensitive: in particular gender and technical affinity influence users' decision to (dis)trust autonomous technologies. Also, incentives for the usage differed depending on the context. Test environments were perceived as most important incentive for the context of autonomous driving, whereas users strongly appreciated energy efficiency referring to smart home. These results contribute to a deeper understanding of user needs towards the acceptance of autonomous technologies.

Keywords: Trust in automation · Autonomous driving · Smart home ·
Technology acceptance · User diversity

1 Users' Trust in Autonomous Technologies

In view of technical influence on everyday life, automation plays an important role in the current technological development. Today, automation is integrated in numerous contexts like mobility, ambient assisted living, or energy supply. Assistance systems that aim to support people in certain situations in their everyday lives contribute to the introduction of autonomous technologies.

They represent the highest degree of automation, because they are supposed to solve tasks without human control [1]. Therefore, they offer great potential and risks at the same time. Among other things, they can improve the quality of life of potential users by taking over everyday tasks for them [2]. Here, application contexts vary from autonomous driving, industrial production, health care to smart homes.

However, there are still legal and also technical challenges to be solved, in order to guarantee a failure-free usage of autonomous technologies (e.g., [3, 4]). Also, the use of

© Springer Nature Switzerland AG 2019
A. Moallem (Ed.): HCII 2019, LNCS 11594, pp. 371–384, 2019.
https://doi.org/10.1007/978-3-030-22351-9_25

new technologies might cause uncertainties among future users regarding their perceived protection of privacy, controllability, and loss of autonomy (cf. [5]).

For autonomous technologies to be successful, they must be secure, function properly, and be accepted by users. A major obstacle in acceptance of technology is the users trust in the given technology. Since trust as a human social interaction is not only intuitively important [6], but has an significant influence on (technology) acceptance, this factor should be examined in different technology contexts focusing on further possible influencing user factors (cf. [7]). In addition to that, trust is a key factor, on which usage intention is dependent – which was also shown in other contexts before [8]. Therefore, this research focused on: a context comparison with regard to users' disposition to trust. Privacy, security, and trust play an especially important role in the field of **mobility** and **smart home** and are therefore addressed in this work. The following chapter will introduce both contexts and give a definition of the technology as it is understood for this research.

1.1 Autonomous Driving

The technological developments in driving are without any doubt evolving at a high pace. Over the last years more and more advanced driver assistance systems have been introduced, like the adaptive cruise control as well as parking assistance systems, Which steer the vehicle into the desired parking spot automatically [9].

During the next years *autonomous driving* (or highly automated/driverless/self-driving) will be introduced. Here, vehicles equipped with highly connected sensor systems, longitudinal and lateral guidance, cameras, ultra-sonic technology, and more are supposed to "drive themselves on existing roads and can navigate many types of roadways and environmental contexts with almost no direct human input" [10].

Currently there are different systems that classify different degrees of automation to declare a vehicle as autonomous. The National Highway Transport Safety Administration (NHTSA) standard, the SAE standard, or the German Federal Highway Research Institute standard (BASt) are used to classify a vehicle automation level from no intervening vehicle system activity to the system taking over the complete driving task [11, 12]. This study examined vehicles technology at the highest level of automation (no human input necessary).

The possible advantages of integrating autonomous driving technology in our everyday life are enormous: traffic safety and travel efficiency could be increased, CO_2 consumption reduced, and mobility made much more flexible for people with limited mobility [13].

On the other side, the fear of failure of the technology is relatively high as several studies showed [14, 15]: The question of the *ethics of use* has not yet been finally clarified and the legal regulation debate has not reached a consensus yet. Also, the technical facets still show many (perceived) barriers: Attacks by hackers, mistrust in data protection, and the question of who may use and store the (partly personal) data has not been answered yet [15].

Research focused on user-centered factors, to identify the most influential characteristics. In that way, the user factors may be integrated into the early stages of technology development. Here, it could be shown that user factors (e.g., age and gender) impact acceptance decisions [16, 17] as well as the perceived loss of control or distrust of vehicle dependence, which are seen as serious barriers [15].

Considering the increasing automation of driving, further research is needed to explore if and which user factors – here focusing on trust – are influencing factors for increasing automation, even in different usage contexts: e.g., smart homes.

1.2   Smart Home

In recent years, the domestic integration of information and communication technologies (ICT) has increased and encountered great interest in research [18, 19]. Based on ambient intelligence [20], modern living spaces serve as "digital environments that are sensitive, adaptive, and responsive to human needs" [21], also referred to as *smart home* [22]. In general, smart homes realize the interconnection, collaboration, and automation of infrastructure by means of wireless networks to support residents in their daily life [23]. Technically, smart homes are equipped with sensor and actuator technologies that are unobtrusively integrated into the living environment to collect data (e.g., temperature, pressure, motion) and perform action, respectively [23, 24]. For example, lights can turn on automatically when residents get out of bed [25].

Major fields of application are the automation of domestic tasks (e.g., automatic door opening), energy management (e.g., heating control), communication and entertainment (e.g., smart speaker), security and safety enhancement (e.g. camera monitoring), as well as health care assistance (e.g., floor sensors for fall detection) [18, 26]. Besides pre-programmed tasks, users can control and interact with their smart home environment through natural communication (e.g., voice control) and well-known interfaces (e.g., smartphones) [26]. Hence, residents can, for example, open the front door remotely when a camera displays visitors at the entrance [25].

Smart home environments facilitate daily activities, provide more comfort, flexibility, and sustainability, even though their acceptance is not given without restrictions. In fact, it is dependent on, the type of monitoring system and recorded data (e.g., visual vs. auditive) as well as the usage location (e.g., bathroom vs. living room), which may cause distrust due to the feeling of "being observed" [27, 28]. Major perceived barriers are privacy concerns and the system's reliability, as data transfer and technical errors pose serious uncertainties for users [29–31]. Hence, trust in smart technology is a key factor to its successful adoption at users' home [32].

Previous studies showed that the perception and evaluation of a smart home system's trustworthiness differ with regard to diverse user factors, such as gender, living situation, and family background [33–35]. However, the focus so far has been predominantly on medical technologies for the elderly to support aging in place. Yet, research intensity concerning trust in autonomous technologies for daily use, in particular with regard to younger users, who have learnt and experienced the use of technology from an early age and may have different perspectives, is comparatively sparse. Considering the increasing automation of domestic tasks, further research is needed to explore under which conditions and to what extent diverse user groups trust smart systems in their personal living environment.

2   Method

The aim of this study was to examine user factors that influence trust in autonomous technologies, with special regard to autonomous driving and smart home environments. For this purpose, a quantitative online questionnaire study was conducted addressing the following research questions (RQ):

RQ1 Does users' trust in and intention to use autonomous technologies differ with regard to autonomous driving and smart home?

RQ2 Does user diversity impact users' trust in and intention to use autonomous technologies with regard to autonomous driving and smart home?

The empirical study was conducted in Germany. Participation was on voluntary basis, and data security and anonymity were guaranteed. The participants were predominately acquired by social media and were not compensated in any way. Pretests ensured an overall understanding of the material and a maximum response time of 20 min.

2.1   Empirical Design

Based on preliminary qualitative studies in form of focus groups, two different user scenarios were identified to understand the influence of context (autonomous vehicles vs. smart home) towards trust and the intention to use a technology. The further research presented here shows the results of the online study, which was constructed to look closely into user patterns. With former results in mind, we questioned different user dispositions: trust, privacy, and control (see Fig. 1).

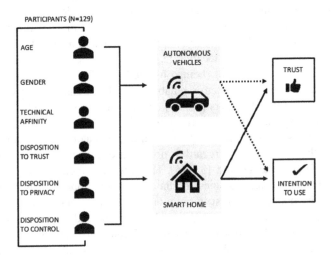

Fig. 1. Empirical design of the online study.

Demographics. The first part of the questionnaire addressed demographic data: age, gender, information about the highest education level, and area of living (city, rural area). In addition to the area, the current state of living (single, flat-sharing community, etc.) and the monthly income was questioned. Given the technological context, the perception of the participants of their self-assessment in handling technology was measured (according to [36]).

User Perception Towards Trust, Privacy, and Control. The second part focused on the participants according to their perceptions. A set of nine items (6-point Likert scale, 6 = full agreement) questioned the participants' disposition to trust. Further, a set of nine items (also 6-point Likert scale) measured the disposition to privacy (see Table 1).

Table 1. Items of disposition to privacy.

To what extent do you agree with the following statements regarding the use of your data?
It is important to me to know what happens to my data
I do not mind, if my data is shared with third parties
I am happy to provide information on my habits and preferences, so that products and services can be developed that really interest me
I want an overview at all times about which data is stored about me
The idea that detailed profiles of me exist, scares me
It is important to me that politics attaches a high priority to privacy
There are situations where it is important that information about me is on the internet
I have no problem revealing my data
I would disclose information, if I could get any financial benefit from its use

A last set of six items (6-point Likert scale) questioned the participants' disposition to control. All disposition sets (based on [37–39]) had a high internal consistency, as the reliability analysis with Cronbach's α reveals: trust ($\alpha = .788$), privacy ($\alpha = .827$), and control ($\alpha = .713$).

Scenarios. The third part was divided into two beforehand identified user scenarios with autonomous driving (I) and smart home (II) technology. First, a short introduction to the technology and the understanding of the level of automation was given. After that, a scenario description helped the participants envision the possibilities of the addressed technology (see Figs. 2 and 3):

AUTONOMOUS VEHICLES

"Imagine you have booked a holiday and have to be at the airport by 04:30 the next morning. You order a self-driving car the evening before, which will be with you the next morning as requested. You load your luggage and then sit down in the autonomous vehicle. The vehicle drives off and uses sensors, cameras, laser scanners and GPS to communicate with the infrastructure. You use the remaining travel time to catch up on the missing sleep. (…)"

Fig. 2. Short version of the scenario introduction for the autonomous driving scenario.

A further detailed description of possible actions (e.g. traffic light stop, traffic-jam recognition or electronic door lock, camera surveillance etc.) was given as well as a conceptual sketch to deepen the users' understanding of technology-based possibilities.

SMART HOME

"Imagine you wake up in the morning, the roller shutters in the house automatically raise via your voice command, the coffee machine switches on automatically like every morning at 7:30 a.m. and makes you a coffee. Once in the kitchen, you tell your fridge that you want to make pizza tonight. It orders all the ingredients for you and has them delivered at the desired time. To be able to warm up after work from the cold temperatures outside, you switch on the heating at home during the lunch break from work via your smartphone or a similar control unit(...)"

Fig. 3. Short version of the scenario introduction for the smart home scenario.

2.2 Participants

In total, 129 participants took part in the online survey. The age ranged from 18 to 77 years (Mean (**M**) = 29.87; Standard Deviation (**SD**) = 13.60). The gender distribution was asymmetrical with 69.8% women (n = 90) and 30.2% men (n = 39). The sample contained 28.7% with a university degree or higher education level (n = 37). 13.2% had completed a vocational training (n = 17), while further 47.3% (n = 61) answered to have the A-level. The remaining participants reported a secondary school diploma.

When asked about the area of living, 27.1% stated to live in the inner city, 30.2% in the suburban area, 18.6% in outlying districts near the city and 24.0% in rural areas. Further, a large part of the sample stated own a driver's license (97.7%). The mean of the technical affinity was M = 4.01 (SD = 1.23) on a scale from 1 to 6 (max.). Therefore, the sample can be assumed to be slightly tech-savvy.

For a better understanding of possible influencing user factors, the beforehand described disposition to trust (M = 3.59, SD = 0.66), privacy (M = 4.37, SD = 0.86), and control (M = 4.56, SD = 0.65) was also questioned on a scale from 1 to 6. A closer look was also given to the correlations between the investigated user factors and the trust in automation and usage intention (as can be seen in Table 2):

Table 2. Correlation (r_s) between user factors and trust in automation (TiA) as well as use intention ($^{**}p < 0.01$).

	Gender	Age	Technical affinity	Trust disposition	Privacy disposition	Control disposition
TiA	$-.270^{**}$	.030	$.285^{**}$	.124	$-.235^{**}$	$-.073$
Use intention	$-.240^{**}$	$-.060$	$.222^{**}$	.002	$-.228^{**}$	$-.040$

3 Results

This chapter summarizes the obtained research results. First, general findings are outlined with regard to the whole sample. Then, the influence of gender, technical affinity, and privacy disposition on users' trust in and intention to use autonomous technologies is presented in detail.

Next to descriptive analyses, inferential statistics were conducted to measure context differences and user diversity effects. Regarding technical affinity and privacy disposition as independent variables, user groups were formed based on median split.

The level of significance (p value) was set at 5%. For effect sizes, the partial eta-squared (η^2) was reported. Mean values above the scale center (M > 3.5) indicated acceptance, whereas mean values below the average (M < 3.5) were interpreted as rejection.

3.1 General Findings

In general, with regard to the whole sample, results revealed that the participants were willing to use autonomous technologies. In particular, the intention to use smart home environments was slightly higher compared to autonomous driving, whereas trust concerning both contexts was rather low (see Table 3). Faced with a decision scenario, the majority preferred to use a living environment equipped with smart home applications (64.3%; n = 83) in contrast to an autonomous car (35.7%; n = 46).

Table 3. Evaluation of the intention to use and trust by context (N = 129).

	Intention to use	Trust
Smart home	M = 3.60; SD = 1.18	M = 3.29; SD = 0.92
Autonomous driving	M = 3.51; SD = 1.30	M = 3.06; SD = 1.04

To validate these context differences, a repeated measures analysis of variance was conducted. Results revealed a significant main effect of trust ($F_{1,128}$ = 49.063; p = .000; η^2 = 0.277). Hence, users' trust differed significantly in both contexts, provided that smart home environments achieved higher evaluation patterns than autonomous driving. However, both contexts failed to reach the trust threshold of M > 3.5 (see Table 3).

Besides from that, the participants evaluated incentives for use, based on preceding focus group discussions, for both contexts (see Fig. 4). Considering autonomous driving, the opportunity to experience an autonomous car ride in a *test environment* was mostly appreciated (M = 4.33; SD = 1.48), followed by *environmental benefit* (M = 4.01; SD = 1.57), *free provision* (M = 3.96; SD = 1.66), and *cost benefit* (M = 3.61; SD = 1.53), whereas *trust in the manufacturer* (M = 3.30; SD = 1.54) and *recommendation* (e.g., by the media or friends) (M = 3.28; SD = 1.46) were not perceived as fitting incentives for use. For comparison, *energy efficiency* (M = 4.20; SD = 1.38) was identified as a major incentive to use smart home environments, next to *free provision* (M = 3.88; SD = 1.64), *cost benefit* (M = 3.73; SD = 1.46), and *test environment* (e.g., smart house visiting) (M = 3.55; SD = 1.57), provided that *trust in the manufacturer* (or installer) (M = 3.34; SD = 1.41) and *recommendation* (M = 3.40; SD = 1.42) were not considered as incentives as well.

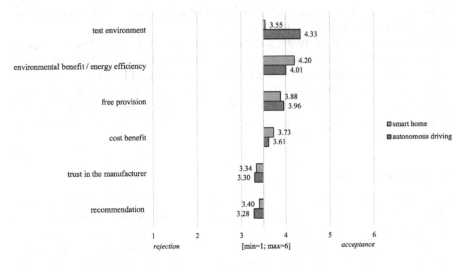

Fig. 4. Evaluation (mean) of incentives for use by context.

3.2   Gender

Trust. Analyses revealed a connection between gender and trust in smart home (r_s = −.211; p = .016) as well as trust in autonomous driving (r_s = −.260; p = .003), indicating that trust was more important to men than women in both contexts. MANOVA measurements confirmed a significant main effect of gender ($F_{2,126}$ = 5.150; p = .007; η^2 = .076). In detail, trust perceptions of women and men varied significantly regarding either smart home ($F_{1,127}$ = 6.300; p = .013; η^2 = .047) and autonomous driving ($F_{1,127}$ = 9.153; p = .003; η^2 = .067). Overall, men trusted autonomous technologies to a greater extent, whereas women were more likely to express distrust, in particular, concerning autonomous driving (see Table 4).

Table 4. Trust evaluation of context by gender.

	Smart home	Autonomous driving
Men (n = 39)	M = 3.59; SD = 0.91	M = 3.47; SD = 1.09
Women (n = 90)	M = 3.16; SD = 0.90	M = 2.88; SD = 0.98

Intention to Use. According to analyses, gender was related to the intention to use autonomous driving (r_s = −.249; p = .004), indicating that men were more willing to use autonomous cars than women. MANOVA measurements confirmed a significant main effect of gender ($F_{2,126} = 3.692$; $p = .028$; $\eta^2 = .055$), and, in detail, with regard to autonomous driving ($F_{1,127} = 7.226$; $p = .008$; $\eta^2 = .054$). Hence, the use intention was greater with men (M = 3.96; SD = 1.46), whereas women (M = 3.31; SD = 1.17) rather rejected autonomous driving.

3.3 Technical Affinity

For the analysis of group differences, based on technical affinity (Mdn = 4.25; SD = 1.24), participants with low (M = 3.15; SD = 0.88) and high technical affinity (M = 5.13; SD = 0.55) were compared.

Trust. Correlation analyses revealed a connection between technical affinity and trust in smart home technology ($r_s = .265$; $p = .002$) as well as trust in autonomous driving ($r_s = .230$; $p = .009$). The greater the affinity for technology, the more trust could be observed. MANOVA measurements confirmed a significant main effect of technical affinity ($F_{2,126} = 4.547$; $p = .012$; $\eta^2 = .067$). In detail, the participants evaluated trust significantly differently depending on their technical affinity regarding either smart home ($F_{1,127} = 8.094$; $p = .005$; $\eta^2 = .060$) and autonomous driving ($F_{1,127} = 5.578$; $p = .020$; $\eta^2 = .042$). Overall, participants with high technical affinity trusted autonomous technologies to a greater extent, whereas participants with low technical affinity were more likely to express distrust, in particular, concerning autonomous driving (see Table 5).

Table 5. Trust evaluation of context by technical affinity (KUT).

	Smart home	Autonomous driving
KUT low (n = 73)	M = 3.09; SD = 0.91	M = 2.88; SD = 0.91
KUT high (n = 56)	M = 3.55; SD = 0.88	M = 3.30; SD = 1.16

Intention to Use. Technical affinity correlated with the intention to use autonomous driving ($r_s = .223$; $p = .011$), indicating that participants with high technical affinity were more willing to use autonomous technologies in this context. However, MANOVA measurements revealed no significant omnibus effect of technical affinity on users' intention to use autonomous technologies ($F_{2,126} = 2.349$; $p = .100$; n.s.).

3.4 Privacy Disposition

For the analysis of group differences, based on privacy disposition (Mdn = 4.33; SD = 0.86), participants with rather low (M = 3.61; SD = 0.56) and high privacy concerns (M = 4.96; SD = 0.53) were compared.

Trust. Based on correlation analyses, privacy disposition was related to trust in smart home ($r_s = -.283$; $p = .001$), indicating that participants with low privacy concerns expressed higher trust levels in this context. However, MANOVA measurements revealed no significant omnibus effect of privacy disposition on users' trust in autonomous technologies ($F_{2,126} = 2.881$; $p = .060$; n.s.).

Intention to Use. Privacy disposition correlated with the intention to use smart home environments ($r_s = -.251$; $p = .004$), indicating that participants with low privacy concerns were more willing to use autonomous technologies in this context. Again, MANOVA measurements revealed no significant omnibus effect ($F_{2,126} = 2.087$; $p = .128$; n.s.).

4 Discussion

In this chapter, the obtained research results are summarized and interpreted. In addition to that, an overview of limitations and future research tasks is given.

4.1 Interpreting Results

This study's aim was to examine trust in automation under consideration of influencing user factors in two contexts: autonomous driving and smart home. Key findings revealed that trust was context sensitive, provided that users' perception and evaluation differed with regard to gender and technical affinity.

In general, the intention to use autonomous technologies was affirmative, whereas users' trust in automation was comparatively low. Our study revealed that trust differed significantly with regard to context, with greater trust in smart home than autonomous driving (RQ1). This could lead to the conclusion that there is a sense of attachment to the technology: the technology is used at home and not in public space. This may lower the threshold of trust in the technology.

For comparison, no significant context difference could be found for the intention to use, which was positive overall. Hence, users' trust seemed to rely to a greater extent on the specific usage situation and type of technology, provided that autonomous driving appeared as a more polarizing issue than smart home.

Considering incentives for use, the opportunity of a test environment was mostly agreed upon in the context of autonomous driving, whereas energy efficiency was perceived as the strongest motivation for smart home. One implication here is, that potential users of autonomous vehicles primarily focused on the experience, which complements studies that have also found an impact of user experience on the perceived benefits and barriers (e.g., risk perception) in this context [40]. Also to keep in mind: autonomous driving cannot be tested "at home". There are spacial requirements to use the technology properly, indicating that the test environment is a logical choice for users as an attractive incentive.

Regarding smart home, participants were predominately concerned with energy management, which goes in line with previous findings (e.g., [30]). In this case, future smart home users emphasized resource motives more strongly, probably for cost and environmental reasons, but also because they were not confronted with the perceived necessity to use technology due to high safety risks, as frequently reported in ambient assisted living scenarios [28]. Overall, trust in the manufacturer or installer as well as recommendations by the media or friends did not influence the decision to use autonomous technologies in either context.

Concerning user diversity, significant effects of gender and technical affinity were found (RQ2), according to which men and participants with high technical affinity expressed stronger trust in autonomous technologies, especially in the context of smart home. In contrast, women and participants with low technical affinity showed limited trust levels and were particularly suspicious of autonomous driving. In this respect, especially men were willing to use autonomous cars, which confirms previous research in the field of new automotive technologies and their adopters [41]. Concerning the participants' privacy disposition, no significant group differences were found. However, a trend could be seen that participants with low privacy concerns were more willing to trust and use autonomous technologies compared to participants with high privacy concerns, in particular with regard to smart home. A reason for that could be the group of low privacy concerns already has profound understanding of the benefits of the technology. Therefore, cross-analysis should look upon a connection of low privacy concerns and high technical affinity. An important point for follow-up studies, focusing on more and different influencing user-diversity factors. Interestingly, trust disposition and trust in automation were not related at all in this study, indicating that interpersonal and human-computer trust depict individual processes, which in turn emphasizes the relevance of research in this area.

4.2 Limitations and Future Research

The research results revealed profound insights into users' trust in automation with regard to different contexts. Yet, the study involved few limitations, which are discussed below, together with future research tasks.

First, regarding the sample, the number of participants and age distribution were adequate, as they allowed to complement previous research, especially in the context of smart home, which was so far rather health care and aging oriented (cf. [35]). However, the proportion of women was considerably high. In particular with regard to the obtained gender effects, our results should be validated in a broader sample, which also addresses further user factors, such as privacy and trust disposition, as well as individual needs for data security. Another point concerns that most of the participants hold a driver's license. Regarding autonomous driving, it would be interesting to know, how people without a driver's license or ability to drive (e.g., because of mobility restrictions) perceive and evaluate trust and use intention in this context.

Furthermore, it was particularly striking that the participants were willing to use autonomous technologies, while indicating at the same time that they rather distrust them in both contexts. This implies, on the one hand, that follow-up studies should investigate the influence of trust on the intention to use automation more closely, also with regard to other contexts (e.g., work and industrial production). On the other hand, the scenario-based questionnaire used in the present study may influenced the participants' response behavior. To prevent method bias (cf. [31]), additional approaches should be used, in particular experimental research designs and simulations, in which participants can experience and evaluate the use of autonomous technologies in real life settings.

Finally, the study was conducted in the western part of Germany. Therefore, the obtained results are to be understood against the cultural background of Germany with its specific system of norms and values. For example, this could be relevant as regards the image of cars and traffic, which might differ from other countries, as well as the perception and dealing with privacy concerns. In this respect, it would be interesting to see, how participants with diverse cultural perspectives, which are probably also expressed in people's perception and behavior, evaluate trust in and the intention to use autonomous technologies according to their increasing integration in everyday life.

Acknowledgements. The authors thank all participants for their openness to participate in the study and to share their opinions regarding trust in autonomous technologies. The authors want to thank Jessica Gerlitz and Luca Liehner for research assistant. This work has been funded by the Federal Ministry of Transport and Digital Infrastructure (BMVI) within the funding guideline "Automated and Networked Driving" under the funding code 16AVF2134C.

References

1. Dumitrescu, R., et al.: Studie "Autonome Systeme" (No. 13-2018). Studien zum deutschen Innovationssystem [Study "Autonomous Systems" (No. 13-2018). Studies on the German innovation system] (2018)
2. van Berlo, A.: Smart home technology: Have older people paved the way? Gerontechnology **2**, 77–87 (2002)
3. Beiker, S.A.: Legal aspects of autonomous driving. Santa Clara Law Review, vol. 52, pp. 1145–1156 (2012)
4. Theoharidou, M., Tsalis, N., Gritzalis, D.: Smart home solutions: privacy issues. In: van Hoof, J., Demiris, G., Wouters, E.J.M. (eds.) Handbook of Smart Homes, Health Care and Well-Being, pp. 67–81. Springer, Cham (2017). https://doi.org/10.1007/978-3-319-01583-5_5
5. Jeschke, S., Jakobs, E.-M., Dröge, A.: Exploring uncertainty: Ungewissheit und Unsicherheit im interdisziplinären Diskurs [Uncertainty and uncertainty in interdisciplinary discourse]. Springer, Wiesbaden (2013). https://doi.org/10.1007/978-3-658-00897-0
6. Slovic, P.: Perceived risk, trust, and democracy. Risk Anal. **13**, 675–682 (1993)
7. Pavlou, P.: Consumer acceptance of electronic commerce. Integrating trust and risk with the technology acceptance model. Int. J. Electron. Commer. **7**, 101–134 (2003)
8. Kim, G., Shin, B., Lee, H.G.: Understanding dynamics between initial trust and usage intentions of mobile banking. Inf. Syst. J. **19**, 283–311 (2009)
9. Wada, M., Yoon, K.S., Hashimoto, H.: Development of advanced parking assistance system. IEEE Trans. Ind. Electron. **50**, 4–17 (2003)
10. Fagnant, D.J., Kockelman, K.: Preparing a nation for autonomous vehicles: opportunities, barriers and policy recommendations. Transp. Res. Part A Policy Pract. **77**, 167–181 (2015)
11. U.S. Department of Transportation: Federal Automated Vehicles Policy, p. 116, September 2016
12. Gasser, T.M., et al.: Rechtsfolgen zunehmender Fahrzeugautomatisierung – Gemeinsamer Schlussbericht der Projektgruppe Bundesanstalt für Straßenwesen (BASt) [Legal consequences of increasing vehicle automation – Joint final report of the project group Federal Highway Research] (2012)
13. Ross, P.E.: Robot, you can drive my car. IEEE Spectr. **51**, 60–90 (2014)
14. Sommer, K.: Continental mobility study 2011. Continental AG (2013)

15. Schmidt, T., Philipsen, R., Themann, P., Ziefle, M.: Public perception of V2X-technology - Evaluation of general advantages, disadvantages and reasons for data sharing with connected vehicles. In: IEEE Intelligent Vehicles Symposium (IV) Gothenburg, Sweden, June 19–22. pp. 1344–1349 (2016)

16. Hohenberger, C., Spörrle, M., Welpe, I.M.: How and why do men and women differ in their willingness to use automated cars? The influence of emotions across different age groups. Transp. Res. Part A Policy Pract. **94**, 374–385 (2016)

17. Ziefle, M., Beul-Leusmann, S., Kasugai, K., Schwalm, M.: Public perception and acceptance of electric vehicles: exploring users' perceived benefits and drawbacks. In: Marcus, A. (ed.) DUXU 2014. LNCS, vol. 8519, pp. 628–639. Springer, Cham (2014). https://doi.org/10.1007/978-3-319-07635-5_60

18. Mendes, T.D.P., Godina, R., Rodrigues, E.M.G., Matias, J.C.O., Catalão, J.P.S.: Smart home communication technologies and applications: wireless protocol assessment for home area network resources. Energies **8**, 7279–7311 (2015)

19. Robles, R.J., Kim, T.: Applications, systems and methods in smart home technology: a review. Int. J. Adv. Sci. Technol. **15**, 37–48 (2010)

20. Cook, D.J., Augusto, J.C., Jakkula, V.R.: Ambient intelligence: technologies, applications, and opportunities. Pervasive Mob. Comput. **5**, 277–298 (2009)

21. Rashidi, P., Mihailidis, A.: A survey on ambient-assisted living tools for older adults. IEEE J. Biomed. Heal. Inform. **17**, 579–590 (2013)

22. Cook, D.J.: How smart is your home? Comput. Sci. **335**, 1579–1582 (2012)

23. Cook, D.J., Das, S.K.: How smart are our environments? An updated look at the state of the art. Pervasive Mob. Comput. **3**, 53–73 (2007)

24. Dengler, S., Awad, A., Dressler, F.: Sensor/actuator networks in smart homes for supporting elderly and handicapped people. In: 21st Conference on Advanced Information Networking and Applications Workshops (AINAW 2007), vol. 2, pp. 863–868. IEEE Computer Society (2007)

25. Lê, Q., Nguyen, H.B., Barnett, T.: Smart homes for older people: positive aging in a digital world. Future Internet **4**, 607–617 (2012)

26. Kleinberger, T., Becker, M., Ras, E., Holzinger, A., Müller, P.: Ambient intelligence in assisted living: enable elderly people to handle future interfaces. In: Stephanidis, C. (ed.) UAHCI 2007. LNCS, vol. 4555, pp. 103–112. Springer, Heidelberg (2007). https://doi.org/10.1007/978-3-540-73281-5_11

27. Himmel, S., Ziefle, M.: Smart home medical technologies: users' requirements for conditional acceptance. I-Com. **15**, 39–50 (2016)

28. Biermann, H., Offermann-van Heek, J., Himmel, S., Ziefle, M.: Ambient assisted living as support for aging in place: quantitative users' acceptance study on ultrasonic whistles. JMIR Aging **1**, e11825 (2018)

29. Steinke, F., Fritsch, T., Hertzner, A., Tautz, H., Zickwolf, S.: Expected reliability of everyday and Ambient Assisted Living technologies: results from an online survey. Int. J. Adv. Comput. Sci. Appl. **4**, 17–22 (2013)

30. Wilson, C., Hargreaves, T., Hauxwell-Baldwin, R.: Benefits and risks of smart home technologies. Energy Policy **103**, 72–83 (2017)

31. Wilkowska, W., Ziefle, M., Himmel, S.: Perceptions of personal privacy in smart home technologies: do user assessments vary depending on the research method? In: Tryfonas, T., Askoxylakis, I. (eds.) HAS 2015. LNCS, vol. 9190, pp. 592–603. Springer, Cham (2015). https://doi.org/10.1007/978-3-319-20376-8_53

32. Falcone, R., Castelfranchi, C.: The socio-cognitive dynamics of trust: does trust create trust? In: Falcone, R., Singh, M., Tan, Y.-H. (eds.) Trust in Cyber-societies. LNCS (LNAI), vol. 2246, pp. 55–72. Springer, Heidelberg (2001). https://doi.org/10.1007/3-540-45547-7_4

33. Steinke, F., Fritsch, T., Silbermann, L.: Trust in Ambient Assisted Living (AAL) - a systematic review of trust in automation and assistance systems. Int. J. Adv. Life Sci. **4**, 77–88 (2012)

34. Steinke, F.: Influence of Trust in Ambient Assisted Living Technologies. Humboldt University Berlin (2015)

35. Wilkowska, W., Ziefle, M.: User diversity as a challenge for the integration of medical technology into future smart home environments. In: Ziefle, M., Röcker, C. (eds.) Human-Centered Design of E-Health Technologies: Concepts, Methods and Applications, pp. 96–126. IGI Global, Hershey (2011)

36. Beier, G.: Kontrollüberzeugungen im Umgang mit Technik: Ein Persönlichkeitsmerkmal mit Relevanz für die Gestaltung technischer Systeme [Locus of Control in a Technological Context]. Humboldt-Universität zu Berlin, Berlin (2004)

37. Li, Y.: A multi-level model of individual information privacy beliefs. Electron. Commer. Res. Appl. **13**, 32–44 (2014)

38. Morton, A.: Measuring inherent privacy concern and desire for privacy – a pilot survey study of an instrument to measure dispositional privacy concern. In: Proceedings on International Conference on Social Computing (SocialCom) 2013, pp. 468–477. IEEE (2013)

39. Xu, H., Dinev, T., Smith, H.J., Hart, P.: Examining the formation of individual's privacy concerns: toward an integrative view. In: Proceedings on International Conference on Information Systems (ICIS) 2008, 6 (2008)

40. Brell, T., Philipsen, R., Ziefle, M.: sCARy! Risk perceptions in autonomous driving: the influence of experience on perceived benefits and barriers. Risk Anal. **39**, 342–357 (2018)

41. Plötz, P., Schneider, U., Globisch, J., Dütschke, E.: Who will buy electric vehicles? Identifying early adopters in Germany. Transp. Res. Part A Policy Pract. **67**, 96–109 (2014)

Privacy Preserving System for Real-Time Enriched-Integrated Service with Feedback to Providers

Kaisei Kajita, Kazuto Ogawa$^{(\boxtimes)}$, and Go Ohtake$^{(\boxtimes)}$

Japan Broadcasting Corporation, Tokyo, Japan
{ogawa.k-cm,ohtake.g-fw}@nhk.or.jp

Abstract. We have developed a secure data-providing system for an enriched-integrated service with feedback to providers featuring a verifiable attribute-based keyword search (VABKS). One potential application of the system is the Integrated Broadcast-Broadband (IBB) service, which acquires information related to broadcast programs via broadband networks. One of the services IBB provides is a recommendation service that delivers recommended information matching user preferences (such as TV programs) based on user viewing history. Another application is in mobile environments featuring smart-phone usage, where services based on user location can be suggested. In this study, we propose a secure system that adds the functions of privacy preservation and feedback to providers. Thereby the functions provide increased business benefit to users of the IBB service for mobile usage, and feedback property provides another benefit to the providers of IBB services.

Keywords: Privacy preserving · Secure systems ·
Attribute-based keyword search · Attribute-based encryption ·
Integrated Broadcast-Broadband service

1 Introduction

1.1 Background

The environment surrounding electrical media has changed significantly in recent years, and the Internet and mobile terminals have now come into everyday use. Providing users (viewers) with valuable experiences through communication devices is an important issue concerning service providers. Many systems for integrated services, such as Hulu, Netflix, and Amazon, have been developed. For example, by referencing a user's *purchasing, sightseeing, and viewing history*, a service provider can provide personally recommended goods, places, and programs according to that user's preference.

Access to traditional broadcasting was mainly limited to inside buildings. It was not possible to provide personalized services because there was no Internet environment. In light of the current circumstances, the broadcast industry has

© Springer Nature Switzerland AG 2019
A. Moallem (Ed.): HCII 2019, LNCS 11594, pp. 385–403, 2019.
https://doi.org/10.1007/978-3-030-22351-9_26

developed the *Integrated Broadcast-Broadband (IBB)* system, and the International Telecommunication Union (ITU) has approved several recommendations related to IBB [1]. Many IBB systems have been developed on the basis of these recommendations, such as Hybridcast in Japan, Freeview Play in the UK, Hybrid broadcast broadband (Hbb) TV in Europe, and Ginga in Brazil, which enable information related to a broadcast program to be transmitted via a broadband network. It is expected that new user experiences will be provided in IBB services.

The basic architecture of a mobile IBB system is shown in Fig. 1. As shown, a broadcast reaches a TV set through the broadcast channel and a broadband channel. The companion screen device (e.g., a smart phone or a tablet) is connected to the TV set via a home LAN network and can be taken out of the building. As a result, IBB services are able to provide recommended broadcast programs that match the user's preference according to the viewing history of the broadcast program he or she has viewed in the past.

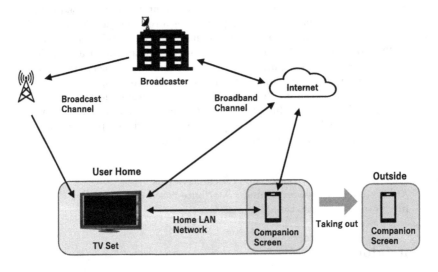

Fig. 1. Basic architecture of a mobile IBB system

Most IBB systems for mobile will use a cloud server, primarily because the space for hardware can be reduced, and all parts of the data can be managed centrally at the cloud server. When using the cloud server, one of the most important issues is how to protect personal information. A cloud is considered an untrusted environment when its resources are publicly used and communication is performed over an untrusted network. A report from the Cloud Security Alliance [12] shows that the security problems are the threats in the cloud; these threats along with solutions to them have been summarized by Tang et al. [17]. When using a cloud server, one of the most crucial issues is how to protect personal information. One way to protect it is by encryption when a data user puts their personal information on the cloud. However, using an IBB system with a general encryption scheme, in which an encryption key and a decryption key are one-to-one, is not efficient. In the case of transmitting personal information to multiple service providers, it is necessary for users to use a different encryption key each time, as each service provider uses a different key. As a result, when the number of users becomes large, this becomes inefficient.

As a solution to the above, we focus on a scheme called *verifiable attribute-based keywords search (VABKS)* [16], which associates secret keys or ciphertexts with a set of attributes and enables access to be controlled in accordance with the decryption condition (policy). Furthermore, since the VABKS scheme has functions to search keywords while encrypting them and to verify the search results, it can fulfil the requirements for our proposed IBB service model (described in Sect. 3). With the above characteristics, we can satisfy the requirements of our service model by using VABKS. One disadvantage is that, although VABKS is highly functional, the search time is lengthy and it is not possible to construct a system with a real-time property. Due to the properties of VABKS, privacy preservation cannot be completely ensured at this point because only limited entities can generate ciphertexts without ingenuity. In this paper, we propose an efficient and secure system that outsources a large amount of data to a cloud server and preserves multiple kinds of personal information by using VABKS.

1.2   Related Works

We focus on VABKS because of its high affinity with IBB services. VABKS can trace its roots to *attribute-based encryption (ABE)* [7], which does not need to generate a distinct encryption key for each entity, and a *searchable encryption* [11], whose ciphertexts can be searched while encrypted.

In the case of an ABE scheme, only entities having an attribute that satisfies an access-control policy can decrypt a ciphertext, where decryption keys or ciphertexts are generated based on attributes (residential place, sex, age, membership type, industry type, reputation, etc.). Therefore, one of the solutions for combatting illegal access is to use an ABE. The first ABE scheme was proposed as an extension of identity-based encryption (IBE) by Sahai et al. [7]. By using VABKS, data such as personal information is encrypted only once. That is, because only the attributes of the service provider that can decrypt at the time of encryption are specified, it is possible to efficiently distribute personal information to multiple service providers. ABE schemes are classified as either key-policy ABE (KP-ABE) [8] or ciphertext-policy ABE (CP-ABE) [9]. In the case of the KP-ABE scheme, a ciphertext is associated with a set of attributes, and a private key is associated with a policy. In the case of the CP-ABE scheme, a ciphertext is associated with a policy, a private key is associated with a set of attributes, and a ciphertext can only be decrypted by a user whose attributes satisfy the policy that is attached to the ciphertext. Ohtake, Ogawa, and Safavi-Naini proposed a privacy preserving system for IBB services using CP-ABE [19]. One of the solutions for security threats in a cloud is to use a searchable encryption. As for the notion of searchable encryption, in a method proposed by Song,

Wagner, and Perring [11], a client stores a set of encrypted files, as well as an encrypted list of keywords for each file, on an untrusted server, and later, in the search phase, the client can efficiently retrieve some of the encrypted files containing specific keywords while keeping the keywords and the files secret. Searchable encryption schemes can be classified as either searchable symmetric encryption (SSE) [11] or public-key encryption with keyword search (PEKS) [6]. PEKS was integrated by Wang et al. [13] into CP-ABE to create a new cryptographic primitive called "ciphertext-policy attribute-based encryption with keyword search function" (KSF-CP-ABE) based on Waters' CP-ABE [10]. However, it is inefficient because it requires composite-order bilinear groups. *Attribute-based keyword search (ABKS)*, proposed in [13–15], satisfies the properties of both ABE and searchable encryption. An ABKS scheme with efficient user revocation was proposed by Sun et al. [15]. A novel cryptographic primitive *verifiable* ABKS called VABKS was proposed by Zheng et al. [16], who proposed a generic construction of VABKS that enables anyone to verify the result of a keyword search.

1.3   Contributions

In this work, we propose a data-providing system with feedback to providers while preserving personal information by applying VABKS. There are three contributions: a secure IBB system, an efficient keyword search system, and an interactive system with feedback to providers.

Privacy-Preserving IBB System. A secure IBB system with cryptographic techniques has not yet reached the point of practical application. We construct a secure IBB system by applying VABKS, which has many functions. The first is to control user access to a cloud. The users have attributes and they can access the database only if their attributes satisfy an access-control policy, since access is controlled by the attributes in our system. Our system also has functions to search keywords, while keeping the viewing history and location data encrypted, and to verify the result of the keyword search.

The proposed system preserves privacy by encrypting the user's personal information as search tokens. When a data owner outsources his or her data to a cloud server, our system protects the data by means of the symmetric encryption algorithm included in the VABKS scheme. We can then achieve a secure system that exploits personal information while personal information is preserved.

Two-Stage Keyword-Search System. Although VABKS is highly functional, its heavy computing and searching load means we cannot obtain a real-time property just by applying VABKS to a system without any ingenuity. We therefore construct an efficient *two-stage* system that incorporates the VABKS scheme. It is assumed that a viewer has two kinds of personal information: viewing history and location data. Viewing history is used for narrowing down the keywords and data files in the database to make the user's unique database, and location data is used for queries to the user's unique database. We implement a two-stage system and a one-stage (normal) system with VABKS. In the one-stage system, the time required for the search increases linearly. This can be a fatal defect for IBB services since virtually all of them require quick responses in real-time. In our two-stage keyword-search system, we narrow down data relevant to the user in advance. As a result, if the number of keywords is about fifty, it takes about 1 s to search for keywords. Therefore, the proposed system is more efficient than a system that only repeats keyword searches at one stage.

Feedback to Provider. In our proposed service model, we consider not only the business operator that provides the information to the user but also the feedback that is given to the business provider. Concretely, in the service model without feedback, a business operator only provides data and can not know who uses the data or how many users are accessing it. If the business operator knows that, it is possible to provide a personalized service or a new service utilizing statistical analysis. This would also enable interactive communication between users and service providers.

2 Envisioned IBB Service

We assume a case where an IBB service is enjoyed in a mobile environment and a viewing history is stored in a mobile communication device that can be moved around. It is possible to use not only information related to the viewing history of the broadcast program but also the location information of the user by using other functions (e.g., the GPS installed in the mobile device). As the information that can be provided increases, better services will be possible. For example, when a user is physically located in a place related to a broadcast program that was previously viewed, services will soon be able to provide the user with information about this place, namely, to provide on-the-spot information etc.

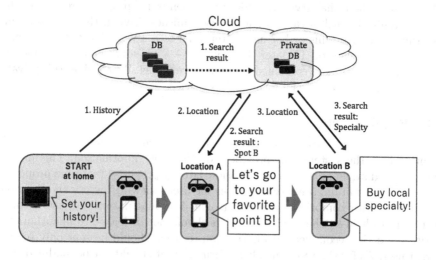

Fig. 2. Service model

2.1 Service Model

Users obtain the service in the mobile environment and we extend existing services to integrated services with mobile (see Fig. 2). For example, when a user drives somewhere related to the viewed broadcast program, he or she is provided with on-the-spot information about that place.

There are four entities involved in this model: providers, users, cloud, and manager. Each provider provides data to the cloud and each user uses the data. It is natural to use the cloud to reduce costs, but there are risks of information leakage.

Users send their histories and their location data to the cloud and the cloud chooses some data to recommend from among all the data provided by providers in accordance with the user's history and location. The user's location data is obtained by using the GPS function of the mobile device. As the provided data increases, better services will be possible, but the time it takes to choose what data to recommend will also increase. In addition, there still remains the crucial issue of preserving personal information (such as user histories).

We assume that all subscribers (users) can enjoy an IBB service by using a mobile terminal and that each user's viewing history is stored in his or her own mobile device, as shown in Fig. 2. It is possible to use not only information related to the viewing history of the broadcast program but also the location data of the user by using other functions such as GPS. For example, when the user is physically located in a place related to the viewed broadcast program, the services will inform the user of nearby places related to the program.

In addition, the service provider provides information on recommended programs and the like according to the user's preference from the viewing history. When a user drives a car, the provider provides certain information based on both the user's viewing history and the current location of the car. Private navigation-guide services like that provide on-the-spot information. There are other cases, where the service provider recommends TV programs related to the driving route. In such a case, when the user finishes driving, the programs can be transmitted from his or her mobile terminal to a TV set back at home, and the user can watch it on TV later. Two systems—a TV set at home and a mobile terminal in the car—are combined in this service model. We consider this private navigation guide service as a form of IBB service.

2.2 Requirements

Since the proposed IBB service involves driving a car, high latency will significantly affect the system that provides "on-the-spot" information. This means the proposed system needs to satisfy a low-latency property: real-time property, as we say. In addition, the service utilizes the user's viewing history and location data. Such data comprises critical personal data and naturally must be protected. Data held by the service providers should not be leaked to unauthorized entities and the recommended information to users should be sent only to the target user. As for the recommended information, it should not be modified. We thus define the requirements of this service as follows.

- **System requirements**
  - Light load: The user can access the service in real-time without high latency.
  - Efficient key management: Key management costs of each entity should be light.
  - Secret searchability: The cloud server can search without decryption.
  - Feedback possibility: The service provider can know which users access the data.
- **Security requirements**
  - Privacy preservation: There are three considerations here. One, the user's personal data should not be leaked to any entities. Two, the source data held by service providers should not be leaked to any unauthorized entities. Three, the personalized data sent to a certain user should not be leaked to any entity other than that user.
  - Verifiability: The personalized data sent to a certain user should be verifiable by that user as to whether the information is correct.
  - Unforgeability: The cloud server should not be able to forge any valid data.

3 Preliminaries

3.1 Cryptographic Tools

We describe the cryptographic schemes and algorithms used in our proposed system. Let $a \leftarrow S$ denote selecting an element a from a set S uniformly at random.

Symmetric Encryption. Let SE be a symmetric encryption, such that $SE = (KeyGen_{SE}, Enc_{SE}, Dec_{SE})$, where $KeyGen_{SE}$ is used for generating a symmetric key, Enc_{SE} is used for encrypting a message, and Dec_{SE} is used for decrypting the ciphertext.

Digital Signature. Let Sig be a digital signature, such that $Sig = (KeyGen_{Sig}, Sign_{Sig}, Verify_{Sig})$, where $KeyGen_{Sig}$ is used for generating a pair of public and private keys, $Sign_{Sig}$ is used for generating a signature for a message, and $Verify_{Sig}$ is used for verifying whether the message matches the signature.

Attribute-Based Encryption. CP-ABE is defined as follows.

Let $Setup_{ABE}$ be an algorithm that generates public parameter pm_{ABE} and master key mk_{ABE}. Let $KGen_{ABE}$ be an algorithm that takes pm_{ABE}, mk_{ABE}, and attribute $\mathcal{A}$ as inputs and outputs secret key sk_{ABE}. Let Enc_{ABE} be an algorithm that takes access-control policy $\mathcal{P}$ and data d as inputs and outputs ciphertext c. Let Dec_{ABE} be an algorithm that decrypts d from c by using sk_{ABE}. As a result, $ABE = (Setup_{ABE}, KGen_{ABE}, Enc_{ABE}, Dec_{ABE})$ is given as the attribute-based encryption scheme.

In this study, we consider CP-ABE, since the ciphertext should be decrypted on the basis of an access-control policy in the proposed system.

Verifiable Attribute-Based Keyword Search. A verifiable attribute-based keyword search scheme (VABKS) can verify the correctness of search results. Let data collections (also referred to as "data sets") $D = (KS, MP, FS)$ denote a set of data files, keyword sets, and their indexes. $KS = \{KS_1, \ldots, KS_n\}$ is a set of n keyword sets, in which elements are encrypted with the same access-control policy. $MP = \{MP(w) | w \in \bigcup_{i=1}^{n} KS_i\}$ is the set of $MP(w)$ that consists of a set of identifiers for identifying data files associated with keyword $w \in \bigcup_{i=1}^{n} KS_i$. $FS = \{F_1, \ldots, F_N\}$ is a set of N data files. VABKS consists of six algorithms ($\mathsf{Setup_{VABKS}}$, $\mathsf{KeyGen_{VABKS}}$, $\mathsf{BuildIndex_{VABKS}}$, $\mathsf{TokenGen_{VABKS}}$, $\mathsf{SearchIndex_{VABKS}}$, $\mathsf{Vrfy_{VABKS}}$) defined as

- $(\mathsf{mk_{VABKS}}, \mathsf{pm_{VABKS}}) \leftarrow \mathsf{Setup_{VABKS}}(1^l)$ takes system parameter l as input, and generates public parameter $\mathsf{pm_{VABKS}}$ and a master key $\mathsf{mk_{VABKS}}$.
- $\mathsf{sk_{VABKS}} \leftarrow \mathsf{KGen_{VABKS}}(\mathsf{mk_{VABKS}}, \mathcal{A})$ takes $\mathsf{mk_{VABKS}}$ and $\mathcal{A}$ as inputs and generates a secret key $\mathsf{sk_{VABKS}}$.
- $(\mathsf{Au}, \mathsf{Index}, \mathsf{D_{cph}}) \leftarrow \mathsf{BuildIndex_{VABKS}}(D, \mathcal{P}, \mathcal{P}')$: Auxiliary information Au, Index and data ciphertext $\mathsf{D_{cph}}$ are obtained by running this algorithm by encryption of $D = (KS, MP, FS)$, where $\mathcal{P}$ is a set of access-control policies to encrypt n keyword groups in KS and $\mathcal{P}'$ is a set of access-control policies for encrypting N data files in FS.
- $\mathsf{tk_{VABKS}} \leftarrow \mathsf{TokenGen_{VABKS}}(\mathsf{sk_{VABKS}}, w)$ issues a search token $\mathsf{tk_{VABKS}}$ with credential $\mathsf{sk_{VABKS}}$ and a keyword w.
- $(\mathsf{proof}, \mathsf{rslt}) \leftarrow \mathsf{SearchIndex_{VABKS}}(\mathsf{Au}, \mathsf{Index}, \mathsf{D_{cph}}, \mathsf{tk_{VABKS}})$ searches Index and outputs search result rslt and a proof proof.
- $\{0, 1\} \leftarrow \mathsf{Verify_{VABKS}}(\mathsf{sk_{VABKS}}, w, \mathsf{tk_{VABKS}}, \mathsf{rslt}, \mathsf{proof})$ verifies $(\mathsf{rslt}, \mathsf{proof})$ with respect to search token $\mathsf{tk_{VABKS}}$.

Correctness of VABKS requires that, given $(\mathsf{mk_{VABKS}}, \mathsf{pm_{VABKS}}) \leftarrow \mathsf{Setup}(1^l)$, $\mathsf{sk_{VABKS}} \leftarrow \mathsf{KGen_{VABKS}}(\mathsf{mk_{VABKS}}, \mathcal{A})$, for any keyword-based data collections D and a keyword w, $(\mathsf{Au}, \mathsf{Index}, \mathsf{D_{cph}}) \leftarrow \mathsf{BuildIndex_{VABKS}}(D, \mathcal{P}, \mathcal{P}')$, $\mathsf{tk_{VABKS}} \leftarrow \mathsf{TokenGen_{VABKS}}(\mathsf{sk_{VABKS}}, w)$, and $(\mathsf{proof}, \mathsf{rslt}) \leftarrow \mathsf{SearchIndex_{VABKS}}(\mathsf{Au}, \mathsf{Index}, \mathsf{D_{cph}}, \mathsf{tk_{VABKS}})$, $(\mathsf{rslt}, \mathsf{proof})$ always holds $1 \leftarrow \mathsf{Verify_{VABKS}}(\mathsf{sk_{VABKS}}, w, \mathsf{tk_{VABKS}}, \mathsf{rslt_{VABKS}}, \mathsf{proof})$.

3.2 Preparations for Design

Here, we define the necessary entities and security requirements for the system construction.

Entities. In this service, there are four entities: a trusted authority (TA) that is a trusted third party such as a system administrator, a data owner (DO) such as a broadcasting station, a data user (DU) who is both a subscriber and a driver, and a cloud server (CL). We define the roles of these four entities as follows.

DU: DU obtains personalized data from DO. This data is based on DU's personal information. DU does not want to leak his personal information to anyone else. DU has his own attribute. If the attribute satisfies DO's access-control policy, DU can access the data provided from DO.

DO: DO has a large amount of data. A data collection consists of data files, keyword sets, and their indexes. DO has an access-control policy and controls which users can access the data it provides. DO does not provide DU with the data directly; instead, it passes the data to DU via CL. DO does not give the data to anyone except for the authorized DUs.

CL: CL makes a bridge between DU and DO. CL receives DU's personal information and DO's data. All data sent from DU and DO are encrypted.

TA: TA authorizes all DUs and DOs.

3.3   Security Model

Here, we show the security model for the proposed system. We define the security requirements and attack models on the basis of the service requirements described in Sect. 2.2. The definitions are specified for the proposed system.

We need to consider the security requirements assuming the worst case. A malicious model is thus adopted for CL. It assumes that CL might not follow the protocol and might illegally modify the data. Moreover, it might analyze the data stored on the cloud server in order to learn personal information about DU or obtain data files belonging to DO.

It is assumed that DUs are honest-but-curious entities, which means they follow the protocols but try to access the data in CL. If DU do not follow the protocols, they cannot enjoy the service, but they might illegally obtain another user's data in CL. From the viewpoint of privacy preservation, DU's personal information should not be leaked anywhere. DUs have several types of personal information that is used as search keywords, and they want to obtain data files possessed by DO according to DU's personal information.

In the proposed system, DO plays the role of service provider. If DO is not an honest entity, the system does not stand. If DO provides incorrect data files, incorrect information will be sent to DU and the service will not work. Thus, an honest model is adopted for DO.

The following properties are defined as the security requirements concerning the system.

1. **Data secrecy:** The cloud server should not deduce any keyword from the encrypted data files and search tokens. Data secrecy requires data sets whose data files and keyword sets should be unrecoverable from encrypted data.
2. **Unlinkability of search tokens:** CL cannot link one search token to another even if they are for an identical keyword. Unlinkability of search tokens requires a non-deterministic search-token-generation function, and queries must be properly represented and securely encrypted.
3. **Data unforgeability:** The malicious CL cannot forge any correctly encrypted data files.
4. **Verifiability of search results:** If the malicious CL returns an incorrect search result, DU can detect the cheating behavior.
5. **Collusion resistance:** The honest-but-curious DU can collude with other DUs in order to obtain another DU's secret key or access a personal database

in CL. Collusion resistance requires that no DU be able to decrypt another DU's ciphertexts in an encrypted personal database even if all DUs except for the authorized DUs collude.

Attack Models. In terms of level of privacy preservation, we consider two threat models depending on the information available to CL and DU.

1. **Known ciphertext model.** The cloud server can only access the encrypted data and the submitted search tokens, which are encrypted as ciphertexts. It can also receive and record the search result. The semantic meanings of this threat scenario are captured by the non-adaptive known ciphertext attack model, in which a cloud server attacks with intent to forge encrypted data, or to obtain information concerning DU's keywords or DO's data files.
2. **Collusion attack model.** In addition to the known ciphertext model, DU colludes with another DU. They collude with the aim of obtaining another user's data possessed by the DO or another user's secret key.

In the following section, we show the concrete construction of our proposed system. It uses a VABKS scheme and meets the above security requirements against the above attack models.

4   Proposed IBB System

We propose a secure and efficient system for the above service (see Fig. 3).

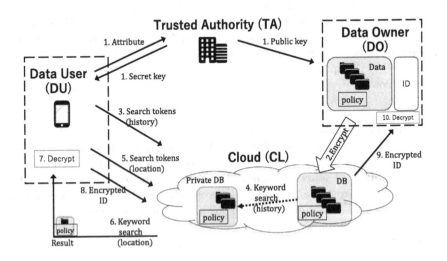

Fig. 3. Proposed system

4.1   System Overview

The system utilizes the VABKS scheme. The algorithms of key generation, encryption, decryption, and keyword search outlined below are those of VABKS.

TA generates public information including an encryption key, generates decryption keys using DU's attributes, and distributes each decryption key to a distinct DU. The data is encrypted by DO, who also determines its access policy. The encrypted data and DO's public key, which is its original one and not identical with that of VABKS, are outsourced to CL. When DU accesses the data, he generates search tokens from his history and sends them to CL. CL searches for encrypted data that matches the tokens and uses it to construct DU's private database. If DU's attributes satisfy the policy, the correct search results are obtained. We should point out here that the tokens are encrypted and the DU's attributes are embedded in the tokens, and that the size of the private database is typically small. When DU travels somewhere and uses the service, he or she makes another token from his location data and sends it to CL. CL searches the matched data from the private database and returns it to DU. DU decrypts the data and uses it. He or she also encrypts his or her ID and the data's ID by using the public key attached to the data and then sends it to CL. CL adds the encrypted ID to the data that DU used. DO can know which DU that accessed the data.

4.2   Construction

Here, we show the concrete construction of our proposed system with VABKS. The basic idea underlying this construction is two-stage keyword searching. The first is a preliminary stage to narrow down the large size of the original data collections into a small size more suitable for DU's personal database. The second is a real-time stage to search personalized data, hence enabling high-speed retrieval from the smaller database on the basis of DU's keywords (e.g., personal information). DO's access-control policy $\mathcal{P}$ for the data and keyword search can be specified by DO when it encrypts data in CL. DU possessing attribute $\mathcal{A}$ satisfying $\mathcal{P}$ can search encrypted data.

The proposed system consists of Sig, SE, ABE, and VABKS. This system, called "SYSV", is shown below. Let $\{l_1, l_2, l_3\}$ be the security parameters. In this system, we assume $\mathcal{P} = \mathcal{P}'$.

Set-up phase: Given security parameters l_1, l_2, the TA executes $(\mathsf{mk}, \mathsf{pm}) \leftarrow \mathsf{Setup}_{\mathsf{VABKS}}(1^{l_1})$ and $(\mathsf{mk}_{\mathsf{ABE}}, \mathsf{pm}_{\mathsf{ABE}}) \leftarrow \mathsf{Setup}_{\mathsf{ABE}}(1^{l_2})$. It then sets $\mathsf{mk} = (\mathsf{mk}, \mathsf{mk}_{\mathsf{ABE}})$ which the TA keeps secret, and $\mathsf{pm} = (\mathsf{pm}, \mathsf{pm}_{\mathsf{ABE}})$, which is publicly known.

Key-generation phase: TA obtains $\mathcal{A}$ from DU, then generates $\mathsf{sk} = (\mathsf{sk}, \mathsf{sk}_{\mathsf{ABE}})$ such that $\mathsf{sk} = \mathsf{KeyGen}_{\mathsf{VABKS}}(\mathsf{mk}, \mathcal{A})$ and $\mathsf{sk}_{\mathsf{ABE}} = \mathsf{KeyGen}_{\mathsf{ABE}}(\mathsf{mk}_{\mathsf{ABE}}, \mathcal{A})$. TA returns sk to DU.

Data-encryption phase: DO executes the following algorithm.
   1. Generate a symmetric encryption key $\mathsf{sk}_{\mathsf{SE}} \leftarrow \mathsf{KeyGen}_{\mathsf{SE}}(1^{l_3})$.

2. Encrypt data $(d_1, \ldots, d_N)$ by $c_{d_i} \leftarrow \mathsf{Enc_{SE}}(\mathsf{sk_{SE}}, d_i)$ and generates encrypted data set $\mathsf{CD} = \{c_{d_1}, \ldots, c_{d_N}\}$.

3. Encrypt symmetric key $\mathsf{sk_{SE}}$ by $c_{\mathsf{sk}} \leftarrow \mathsf{Enc_{ABE}}(\mathsf{sk_{SE}}, \mathcal{P})$ using DO's policy $\mathcal{P}$.

4. Execute $(\mathsf{Au}, \mathsf{Index}, \mathsf{CPH}) \leftarrow \mathsf{BuildIndex_{VABKS}}(D, \mathcal{P}, \mathcal{P}')$ and encrypt each keyword $(w_{i,1}, \ldots, w_{i,n})$ of the data d_i, which is in keyword set KS, and then generate encrypted keywords $\mathsf{CPH} = \{\mathsf{cph}_{i,j}\}_{i,j}$ and auxiliary information $\mathsf{Au} = (\sigma, \mathsf{BF}, \mathsf{vk_{Sig}})$, where σ is a digital signature for each keyword set, BF is a bloom filter and $\mathsf{vk_{Sig}}$ is a verification key for SIG.

5. Set index set MP, which represents the relation between CD and CPH, and send $c = (\mathsf{CD}, c_{\mathsf{sk}}, \mathsf{CPH}), \mathsf{MP}, \mathsf{Au}$ to CL.

Narrowing-down phase (preliminary stage): CL narrows down the encrypted database as follows.

1. After CL receives c, MP, and Au from DO, they are stored in a database on CL. Note that all data in the database are encrypted, except MP and Au.

2. DU takes keywords $\mathbf{v} = \{v_1, \ldots, v_q\}$ and sk as inputs, generates $\mathsf{tk}_v \leftarrow \mathsf{TokenGen_{VABKS}}(\mathsf{sk}, v)$, and sends $\mathsf{tk_v} = \{\mathsf{tk}_{v_1} \ldots, \mathsf{tk}_{v_q}\}$ to CL.

3. CL executes the search algorithm of VABKS for $\mathsf{cph}_{i,j}$ by using a search token $\mathsf{tk_v}$, and it outputs $(\mathsf{proof'}, \mathsf{rslt'}) \leftarrow \mathsf{SearchIndex_{VABKS}}(\mathsf{Au}, \mathsf{cph}_{i,j}, \mathsf{tk_v})$, where $\mathsf{proof'}$ is a certification that includes σ, and $\mathsf{rslt'}$ denotes the result of the search.

4. Let encrypted data set $\mathsf{CD}_{DU} = \{c_{d_1}, c_{d_2} \cdots\}$ be in the user's personal database which corresponds to $\mathsf{cph}_{i,j}$ by using the index set MP. Let $\mathsf{CPH_{DU}} = \{\mathsf{cph}_{\mathsf{DU},1}, \mathsf{cph}_{\mathsf{DU},2}, \cdots\} \subseteq \mathsf{CPH}$. Then, CL stores $c_{DU} = (\mathsf{CD_{DU}}, \mathsf{CPH_{DU}})$ in DU's personal database.

Query phase (real-time stage): DU queries CL with DU's personal database, which is smaller than the original encrypted database, as follows.

1. DU takes a keyword g and sk as inputs and generates search tokens $\mathsf{tk}_g \leftarrow \mathsf{TokenGen_{VABKS}}(\mathsf{sk}, g)$. DU then sends tk_g to CL.

2. CL searches with DU's personal encrypted data c_{DU} by using tk_g and obtains $(\mathsf{proof}, \mathsf{rslt}) \leftarrow \mathsf{SearchIndex_{VABKS}}(\mathsf{Au}, \mathsf{cph}_{\mathsf{DU},i}, \mathsf{tk}_g)$, where proof denotes a certification, and rslt denotes the result of the search.

3. CL returns c_{sk} and c_{d_i} to DU corresponding to $\mathsf{cph}_{\mathsf{DU},i}$.

Decryption phase: DU decrypts $(c_{\mathsf{sk}}, c_{d_i})$ as follows.

1. DU verifies whether the results of searching by CL are forged; namely, $\{0, 1\} \leftarrow \mathsf{Verify_{VABKS}}(\mathsf{sk}, (\mathbf{v}, g), (\mathsf{tk_v}, \mathsf{tk}_g), (\mathsf{proof}, \mathsf{proof'}))$.

2. If Verify outputs 0, DU terminates decryption phase; otherwise, DU decrypts $\mathsf{sk_{SE}} \leftarrow \mathsf{Dec_{ABE}}(\mathsf{sk_{ABE}}, c_{\mathsf{sk}})$ only when DU's attribute $\mathcal{A}$ satisfies DO's policy $\mathcal{P}$. DU then obtains $d_i \leftarrow \mathsf{Dec_{SE}}(\mathsf{sk_{SE}}, c_{d_i})$ according to $\mathbf{v}$ and g.

Feedback phase: DO obtains DU's ID ID_u as follows.

If DU uses d_i, DU encrypts ID_u, $c_{\mathsf{ID}} \leftarrow \mathsf{Enc_{PKE}}(\mathsf{pk_{PKE}}, \mathsf{ID}_u)$ and send it to CL with the index i.

CL add the c_{ID} to the line of c_{d_i}.

DO accesses CL and obtains c_{ID} added to the data CD. DO knows who uses DO's data by executing $\mathsf{ID} = \mathsf{Dec_{PKE}}(\mathsf{sk_{PKW}}, c_{\mathsf{ID}})$.

As long as DU keeps accessing the service, it repeats the procedures from query phase to decryption phase.

4.3   System Security

We show that SYSV has the properties of data secrecy, unlinkability of search token, data unforgeability, verifiability of search results, and collusion resistance. Consequently, the proposed system for IBB service has high security.

Theorem 1. *If* VABKS *is selectively secure against chosen-keyword attack (CKA) in the generic bilinear group model and* ABE *and* SE *are secure against chosen-plaintext attack (CPA), SYSV achieves data secrecy and unlinkability of search tokens in the known ciphertext model.*

Proof. We show that if there exists a polynomial-time algorithm A that breaks SYSV's data secrecy and search token unlinkability with the advantage ε, we can construct a polynomial-time algorithm B that breaks CPA security for either ABE or SE with the advantage of $\frac{\varepsilon}{N^2}$, or selective security against the CKA game of VABKS with the advantage of $\frac{\varepsilon}{(NM)^2}$, where N is the number of data files to be encrypted and M is the maximum number of keywords in one data file; i.e., the number of keywords to be searched is bound to NM.

We consider two cases: (i) the challenger proceeds with a conventional CPA security game with A, or (ii) it proceeds with a selective security against CKA game with A. In the challenge phase, suppose A presents two data collections $D_0 = (KS_0 = \{KS_{(0,1)}, \ldots, KS_{(0,M)}\}, MP, FS_0 = \{FS_{(0,1)}, \ldots, FS_{(0,N)}\})$, $D_1 = (KS_1 = \{KS_{(1,1)}, \ldots, KS_{(1,M)}\}, MP, FS_1 = \{FS_{(1,1)}, \ldots, FS_{(1,N)}\})$ and policy $\mathcal{P}$.

(i) The challenger selects $\lambda \leftarrow \{0,1\}$ and encrypts FS_λ with ABE and $\mathcal{P}$. Now let us consider the advantage of A correctly guessing λ. The advantage of distinguishing which message was encrypted by the hybrid encryption of ABE and SE is equal. Therefore, given two sets of data files FS_0 and FS_1, if the advantage of distinguishing which data collection was encrypted is ε, then the advantage of distinguishing which data file was encrypted is $\frac{\varepsilon}{N^2}$ by selecting one data file from FS_0 and one from FS_1.

(ii) The challenger selects $\lambda \leftarrow \{0,1\}$ and encrypts KS with VABKS. Since ABE is CPA-secure, the probability of A inferring λ is negligible. Then, let us consider the advantage of A correctly guessing λ from keyword ciphertexts. The advantage of distinguishing two keywords encrypted by VABKS is equal. Therefore, given two keyword sets KS_0 and KS_1, if the advantage of distinguishing which keyword set was encrypted is ε, then the advantage of distinguishing which keyword was encrypted is bounded by $\frac{\varepsilon}{(NM)^2}$ by selecting one keyword from KS_0 and one from KS_1.

Therefore, we can construct B whose advantage is $\frac{M^2+1}{(NM)^2}\varepsilon$ in a known ciphertext model if there exists a polynomial-time algorithm A that breaks SYSV's data secrecy and search token unlinkability with the advantage ε.   □

Theorem 2. *SYSV achieves data unforgeability and verifiability of search results if* Sig *is non-adaptively unforgeable against a known ciphertext attack.*

Proof. This theorem can be proved from the security definition of Sig directly. Given correct (rslt, rslt′, proof, proof′) and $(\mathbf{v}, g, \mathsf{tk_v}, \mathsf{tk}_g)$, DU executes the verification algorithm and outputs 1 with overwhelming probability from the verifiability of secure Sig. Moreover, we assume CL attacks in the known ciphertext model. If Sig is non-adaptively unforgeable, CL cannot forge new encrypted date files. □

Theorem 3. *SYSV achieves collusion resistance in the collusion attack model if Theorem 1 holds.*

Proof. This theorem can be proved from the security definition of ABE and VABKS directly. Attackers can recover data only if they have enough attributes to satisfy the tree T_0, so at least one user should be valid to satisfy the privilege tree. Even if multiple users collude in the collusion attack model, they are not able to recover the other user's secret key sk or to obtain the other user's personal database c_{DU} since each secret key sk is randomized by secure key generation algorithms $\mathsf{KeyGen}_{\mathsf{ABE}}$ and $\mathsf{KeyGen}_{\mathsf{ABKS}}$. □

5   Properties

The system makes it possible to search keywords, while keeping the history and location data encrypted, and to securely provide more interesting and suitable information for users by preventing leakage of personal information despite using a cloud. In addition, the provider can know which user is accessing its data. Concretely, it realizes the following properties:

Efficient Two-Stage Keyword-Search: We construct a *two-stage* system. In the preliminary phase, the history is used for narrowing down the database in the cloud and making a small, unique database for the user. This small size is what makes the real-time service possible. This two-stage search is not limited to the above application, and if the search process is divided into two processes, the same construction is possible. Moreover, it is possible to construct a multiple-stage search.

Privacy-Preservation: The search tokens from users are encrypted and the data provided to the users are also encrypted. Hence, even the cloud cannot know the information related to the users.

Data Secrecy: Users can access the database only if their attributes satisfy an access-control policy.

Feedback to Provider: Only the provider who handles data used by a variety of users can know exactly who the users are. When the provider charges the user, this function is indispensable.

An integrated service with access control, privacy preservation, data secrecy, and feedback to the provider has not yet reached practical application, so the

Table 1. Property evaluation: comparison of proposed system with conventional system

	Conventional	Proposed
Encryption and decryption load	light	heavy
Key management cost	heavy	light
Secret searchability	—	$\checkmark$
Privacy preservation	$\checkmark$	$\checkmark$
Verifiability	—	$\checkmark$
Unforgeability	—	$\checkmark$

work we report is the first such system. In addition, we implemented the proposed system and made sure of the real-time property.

We evaluate the proposed system from the viewpoints of both properties and performance.

5.1 Property Evaluation

First, we evaluate the system from the viewpoint of properties. We compare our proposed system, SYSV, with the most trivial system using only a symmetric encryption scheme (as shown in Table 1). We found that the encryption and decryption load of the trivial system was very light and its processes very fast due to its use of the symmetric encryption scheme. Regarding CPU load, the trivial system is superior to ours because it only uses the symmetric key encryption scheme. DO has to manage all DUs' encryption keys and its cost increases in proportion to the number of DUs in the trivial system; however, the proposed system, SYSV, can efficiently manage keys by using its unique attributes and policies. Moreover, SYSV can search for the keywords and data files without decryption. In both systems, CL cannot obtain any plaintexts (such as search keywords and data files) from encrypted data since both systems protect data by encryption. However, if all entities share the same secret keys, all data may be leaked, since CL is a malicious entity. In this sense, the trivial system is a secure system only when CL is not malicious. As we mentioned earlier, the proposed system satisfies both verifiability and unforgeability.

5.2 Implementation

We next evaluate the proposed system from the viewpoint of performance. Specifically, we implemented a two-stage searching system to achieve a real-time property and evaluate its effects. Figure 4 shows the relationship between the number of keywords in DO's database and the search time, and the details are shown in Table 2. All algorithms are implemented on a PC whose specifications are as follows: CPU: Intel Core i7-4790(3.60 GHz), memory: 8 GB, OS:

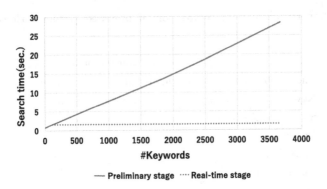

Fig. 4. Relationship between the number of keywords and search time

Cent OS 7.2, and browser: Firefox 38.3.0. Almost all of the encryption algorithms are written in JavaScript (some of them are written in C/C++ due to the limitation of the crypto library). As shown in Figs. 4 and 2, the search time is proportional to the number of keywords. The maximum number of data files used in the experiments was 884 and the number of keywords was 3672. The results show that it took 27.7 s to search data files matched to one token. Actually, the number of data files provided by DOs is very large in the IBB system, and the number of tokens may be more than one. We assume that data files of DOs consist of program title data and time along with related keywords (title, genre, cast members, etc.). Therefore, in the case where DO is a broadcaster, the number of data files will increase in accordance with the number of broadcast programs. For example, Ch.1 in Japan has about 300 programs per week and each program has its own keywords. The number of keywords depends on the program and there are at least four keywords per program. The number of all keywords per year is about $62400(keywords/year) = 300(programs/week) \times 52(weeks/year) \times 4(keywords/program)$ for the Ch.1. When the data files of n channels are collected on CL, the number of keywords would become its n-fold ($\approx n \times 62400$). From the experimental results, it takes roughly $n \times (62400/3672) \times 27.7$ sec ($\approx 8n$ min) to search data files matched to one token. When the number of tokens is m, the time rises another m-fold ($8nm$ min). Although the large size of data files enables a better recommendation, it takes too much time to search the recommended data files. If the reply to a query takes a long time, the service will not stand. In the preliminary stage, the number of data files are narrowed down. If CL can narrow down the size to 25 data files including 100 keywords, DU can obtain the data files within about 1.5 s after DU sends a token to CL. Such services would be acceptable to DU.

Table 2. Experiments results (sec). #Keywords denotes the number of keywords in a database of DO. Encryption denotes the process time for encryption algorithm. Token-Gen, SearchIndex, Verify, and Decrypt denote TokenGen, SearchIndex, Verify, and Dec algorithms, respectively. Search denotes the summation of TokenGen, SearchIndex, Verify, and Decrypt.

#Keywords	Encryption time	Search (total)			
		TokenGen	SearchIndex	Verify	Decrypt
1	0.657	0.778			
		0.027	0.730	0.012	0.010
114	24.897	1.534			
		0.030	1.348	0.086	0.070
918	196.078	7.059			
		0.028	5.835	0.663	0.532
1836	401.522	13.345			
		0.029	10.941	1.319	1.057
2476	524.732	17.666			
		0.028	14.482	1.753	1.403
3672	804.076	27.674			
		0.029	21.165	3.608	2.871

6 Conclusion

We proposed an IBB system that provides users with information related to TV programs while preserving their personal information by encryption of personal information such as viewing history and location data. We apply a VABKS scheme to the proposed IBB service. As yet, there is no system that preserves personal information such as viewing history in an IBB service. In our system, it is possible to preserve personal information appropriately by cryptographic technology and to eliminate information leakage on a cloud server. As a result, users can access services with peace of mind. A malicious cloud server cannot steal personal information since all the information sent to the cloud server is encrypted.

Multiple different secret keys for each user's attributes are generated in the proposed system, and only one public key is used for encryption due to an access-control policy. For this reason, it is necessary to encrypt the data of a broadcast program only once using the public key, regardless of the number of users. There-fore, the burden of key-storage management and key distribution can be reduced compared to that in a system using a one-to-one cryptographic technique such as TLS communication. Also, since keyword search is possible while data are being encrypted, the cloud server does not need to ask the data owner for permission for every search and can efficiently answer the user's inquiries without leaking information.

In addition, since **VABKS** can verify the validity of the search result, it is possible to detect if data has been forged. The algorithm loads on **VABKS** are heavy, so if it is used straight-forwardly in the system, the IBB service will need a lot of time to search for recommendation results, which is generally not acceptable to users. We therefore proposed a two-stage keyword search system to achieve faster real-time service. The proposed system with heavy load is run at the preliminary stage, and the process with light load is run at the second real-time stage. This is what enables the provision of real-time services. Subsequently, we can construct a system that satisfies both high security and efficiency.

Future Works. In this paper, we did not address how DU generates keywords from viewing history. A smart selection of keywords may enable DO to provide the IBB service with higher satisfaction. Another future work is to consider the optimum size of a personal database that can satisfy the user's preference. The reduction loss in Theorem 1 is loose, since the size of N and M are possibly very large in the proposed system, so another future work is to minimize the security reduction loss.

References

1. Recommendation ITU-R BT.2075-1 (2017). http://www.itu.int/dms_pubrec/itu-r/rec/bt/R-REC-BT.2075-1-201701-I!!PDF-E.pdf
2. IPTVFJ STD-0010 STD-0011. http://www.iptvforum.jp/download/
3. DigitalUK. Freeview play - technical specification (2016)
4. Etsi technical specification 102 796 v1.4.1. European Telecommunications Standards Institute (2016)
5. ABNT NBR 15606 series (2016). http://www.abntcolecao.com.br/coltv.aspx?Q=CING45WV08&ID=361862
6. Boneh, D., Di Crescenzo, G., Ostrovsky, R., Persiano, G.: Public key encryption with keyword search. In: Cachin, C., Camenisch, J.L. (eds.) EUROCRYPT 2004. LNCS, vol. 3027, pp. 506–522. Springer, Heidelberg (2004). https://doi.org/10.1007/978-3-540-24676-3_30
7. Sahai, A., Waters, B.: Fuzzy identity-based encryption. In: Cramer, R. (ed.) EUROCRYPT 2005. LNCS, vol. 3494, pp. 457–473. Springer, Heidelberg (2005). https://doi.org/10.1007/11426639_27
8. Goyal, V., Pandey, O., Sahai, A., Waters, B.: Attribute-based encryption for fine-grained access control of encrypted data. In: Proceedings of the 13th ACM Conference on Computer and Communications Security, pp. 89–98. ACM (2006)
9. Bethencourt, J., Sahai, A., Waters, B.: Ciphertext-policy attribute-based encryption. In: 2007 IEEE Symposium on Security and Privacy, SP 2007, pp. 321–334. IEEE (2007)
10. Waters, B.: Ciphertext-policy attribute-based encryption: an expressive, efficient, and provably secure realization. In: Catalano, D., Fazio, N., Gennaro, R., Nicolosi, A. (eds.) PKC 2011. LNCS, vol. 6571, pp. 53–70. Springer, Heidelberg (2011). https://doi.org/10.1007/978-3-642-19379-8_4
11. Song, D. X., Wagner, D., Perrig, A.: Practical techniques for searches on encrypted data. In: 2000 IEEE Symposium on Security and Privacy. S&P 2000, Proceedings, pp. 44–55. IEEE (2000)

12. The Notorious Nine: Cloud Computing Top Threats in 2013 (2013). https:// downloads.cloudsecurityalliance.org/initiatives/top_threats/The_Notorious_Nine_ Cloud_Computing_Top_Threats_in_2013.pdf

13. Wang, C., Li, W., Li, Y., Xu, X.: A ciphertext-policy attribute-based encryption scheme supporting keyword search function. In: Wang, G., Ray, I., Feng, D., Rajarajan, M. (eds.) CSS 2013. LNCS, vol. 8300, pp. 377–386. Springer, Cham (2013). https://doi.org/10.1007/978-3-319-03584-0_28

14. Shi, J., Lai, J., Li, Y., Deng, R.H., Weng, J.: Authorized keyword search on encrypted data. In: Kutyłowski, M., Vaidya, J. (eds.) ESORICS 2014. LNCS, vol. 8712, pp. 419–435. Springer, Cham (2014). https://doi.org/10.1007/978-3-319-11203-9_24

15. Sun, W., Yu, S., Lou, W., Hou, Y.T., Li, H.: Protecting your right: verifiable attribute-based keyword search with fine-grained owner-enforced search authorization in the cloud. IEEE Trans. Parallel Distrib. Syst. **27**(4), 1187–1198 (2016)

16. Zheng, Q., Xu, S., Ateniese, G.: VABKS: verifiable attribute-based keyword search over out- sourced encrypted data. In: INFOCOM, 2014 Proceedings IEEE, pp. 522–530. IEEE (2014)

17. Tang, J., Cui, Y., Li, Q., Ren, K., Liu, J., Buyya, R.: Ensuring security and privacy preservation for cloud data services. ACM Comput. Surv. (CSUR) **49**(1), 13 (2016)

18. Ohtake, G., Safavi-Naini, R., Zhang, L.F.: Outsourcing of Verifiable Attribute-Based Keyword Search. In: Lipmaa, H., Mitrokotsa, A., Matulevičius, R. (eds.) NordSec 2017. LNCS, vol. 10674, pp. 18–35. Springer, Cham (2017). https://doi. org/10.1007/978-3-319-70290-2_2

19. Ohtake, G., Ogawa, K., Safavi-Naini, R.: Privacy preserving system for integrated broadcast-broadband services using attribute-based encryption. IEEE Trans. Consum. Electron. **61**(3), 328–335 (2015)

The Automatic Detection of Sensitive Data in Smart Homes

Mahsa Keshavarz and Mohd Anwar[(✉)]

North Carolina A&T State University, Greensboro, NC 27411, USA
manwar@ncat.edu

Abstract. Smart homes are increasingly becoming popular because they make living comfortable, enjoyable, and secure. People can remotely control various aspects of their smart home environments. However, smart home appliances can pose threats to privacy. The reason is that smart appliances collect and store sensitive information, and if hackers gain access to this information, user privacy may be breached. It is difficult for users to constantly monitor and determine which data is sensitive to them and which one is not. Also, a user's identity can be leaked during sharing of information with different service providers such as health care providers and utility companies. In this paper we address one important privacy issue in smart homes, which is lack of users' control over their desired privacy. We propose a privacy decision framework which considers this problem. In this framework, active learning (machine learning) technique is used to help users detect sensitive information according to their privacy preferences.

Keywords: Smart home · Privacy violation · Pool-based active learning

1 Introduction

Smart home is a dwelling incorporating a communications network that connects the appliances and services, and allows them to be remotely controlled, monitored or accessed [1]. A statistic shows that in 2015 more than 60,000 people search for "smart home" term per month and more than 250 companies invested in this technology [2]. The smart homes offer utility, economy, and comfort [3]. Smart devices perform some of the household tasks and simplify household activities [2]. There is no need to be close to these devices; for example, people are able to cook when they are at work. These smart appliances not only provide comfort but also provide safety inside the home. People can watch and monitor their family and the house from anywhere and anytime [4].

In the context of smart home, privacy is about controlling sharing of information collected by smart appliances. Gathering and sharing information about a person without permission is a violation of privacy. Smart homes collect data such as one's activity levels, sleeping patterns or food intake behaviors from various smart devices and share the information with health care providers or family members [5]. These devices interact with one another and display and analyze the data that they receive in order to exchange information with users or to provide services [6]. Although these services make life easier, they raise concerns about violation of privacy. Studies show

© Springer Nature Switzerland AG 2019
A. Moallem (Ed.): HCII 2019, LNCS 11594, pp. 404–416, 2019.
https://doi.org/10.1007/978-3-030-22351-9_27

that users are concerned about privacy. Due to the privacy issues in smart homes, people have concerns about releasing their private information [7], and they may be hesitant to use the smart devices and live in smart homes. In smart home, users do not have adequate control over their privacy. In November 2018, there was a survey by Deloitte that showed 40% of respondents said that they felt smart home technology "reveals too much about their personal lives," while another 40% said they were worried about their usage being tracked [8]. Smart devices collect various types of user information, and the collected data needs to be categorized into sensitive and non-sensitive data in order to decide which data (non-sensitive data) users want to share and which ones (sensitive data) they do not. Different users have different privacy preferences. When a user desires a high level of privacy, they do not want to share their information; on the other hand, some users may share their information for some reasons such as for medical research. Therefore, some data may be sensitive to some users, but not to some other users. As a result, labeling of collected data into sensitive and non-sensitive category is a non-trivial task.

In this research we study the lack of users' control over their privacy in smart homes. We address this issue by developing a privacy decision framework, and a machine learning technique, active learning, is employed to classify the information into sensitive and non-sensitive categories. With data classification, users' privacy preferences can easily be handled. In this research, we simulated different sensors and gathered sound, light, motion and timestamp data in smart homes to create a dataset of sensitive and non-sensitive data.

2 Related Work

The data shared from smart homes can be stored and later analyzed for extracting users' identity information. To protect released data from such privacy attack, statistical privacy techniques may be used. Statistical privacy computes statistics, answer queries or perform other processing of sensitive datasets without revealing sensitive information [9]. One of the notions in statistical privacy is differential privacy. Differential privacy (DP) is a technique that we can use to mask sensitive information before releasing. This technique helps to minimize the chances of revealing personally identifiable information about the users and violating their privacy [10]. If someone (e.g., a researcher) issues some queries about the dataset for different purposes (e.g., analyzing data to reveal the beginnings of disease outbreak), no one can understand about individual's data in dataset just by looking at the responses to the queries by implementing DP algorithm. The outcome of this algorithm on a database containing some individuals' information is the same as it comes from a database without those individuals' information, which is helpful to balance the utility of released data as well as privacy of the individuals in the dataset.

Another notion of statistical privacy is k-anonymity, which guarantees that the individuals included in an aggregate cannot be identified when the data is released. In other words, k-anonymity property is a property of the released data if the information for each person is indistinguishable from at least $k - 1$ individuals who are also included in the released dataset [11, 12].

The other notion of statistical privacy is l-diversity which can reduce the granularity of data by using different techniques such as generalization and suppression. Suppression is a method that purges some values of the attributes of released data. Generalization is a method that replaces individual values of attributes by a broader category. The l-diversity reduces the weakness of the k-anonymity such as homogeneity attacks (this attack discloses the case where all values of a sensitive attribute are identical within k records) by adding the diversity for sensitive data in the anonymization mechanism [13–15]. These notions are complementary and we need to consider all of them in order to implement security and privacy in smart homes.

Human labor has significantly been replaced by domestic appliances in homes [16]. In smart homes, smart appliances communicate with each other through IoT technologies. These smart appliances capture data about users by using different sensors such as light, sound and temperature. All the capture data transmitted by various communication technologies such as ZigBee and cellular model [17] over the IP network to the Data Management System (DMS) for storage. With user permission, data can be delivered for different usages such as health care, energy management and security. Figure 1 illustrates different domains of the smart home infrastructure, including consumer domain, communication, data management system and various companies that use the data collected from smart devices.

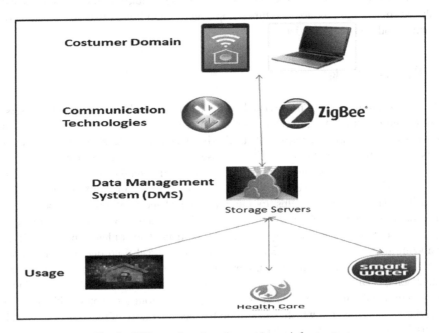

Fig. 1. Different domains of smart home infrastructure

2.1 Privacy Issues with Collected Personal Data

As we mentioned before one privacy problem in the smart homes is that the users are not able to express their preferences, control the sharing of information and choose who can access to this information and for what purposes (See Fig. 2). For example, Zero-Conf configuration in smart homes forces users to accept the vendor's specified default security [18]. As a result, users have very little opportunities to configure their own devices and control the sharing of information or to choose which devices collect what data.

Different users have different expectations of privacy [19]. Different people have different understanding of privacy and they react to issues not in the same way. People can be categorized into 3 different groups based on their levels of privacy concerns: privacy unconcerned users, privacy pragmatist users, and privacy fundamentalist users [20]. In other words, we have different types of users with different expectations of privacy. Some users are very strict about their privacy and they do not want to share data with other people in any cases (i.e., privacy fundamentalist). Some users do not have a problem about sharing their information with other users for different purposes such as medical research (i.e., privacy pragmatist). If a user's privacy expectation is not considered during collecting data, Personal Identifiable Information (PII) can be released. PII is any data that could release some information about a user that helps us to identify a specific individual [21]. PII includes: (1) any information that help attackers to distinguish or trace an individual's identity, such as name, social security number, date and place of birth, mother's maiden name, or biometric records; and (2) any information that is linked or linkable to an individual, such as medical, educational, financial, and employment information. If user preferences are not considered during sharing of data for a service, privacy violation could happen. That is why, users in smart homes should be able to express their preferences and have options to manage their own privacy.

The other way of breaching the privacy is analysis of the user behavior (See Fig. 2). A careful observation of user activities and behavior can leak sensitive information. Some information is not sensitive and if hackers access to this information they cannot identify the user. However, if the observed information connects to other unobserved information, someone may be able to link the information from the two databases and identify individual by accessing to both databases with different PII elements. In fact, the attacker can see data flows generated in a target home by wireless sniffing tools. The encryption cannot protect data because it just protects all the transmitted information, not the source and the destination. For example, the flow between the MAC address of the smart TV and the access point would allow guessing when the users watch TV or goes to sleep by analyzing the flow of the traffic [22].

Table 1 displays some sensitive PII information that the collected data from smart devices may release. Based on preferences, users can label the collected data as sensitive and non-sensitive to express their privacy preferences. However, lacking of users' technical knowledge of smart home devices [23] and an understanding of how the data of smart devices can be accessed by other people [19] will make that task impossible.

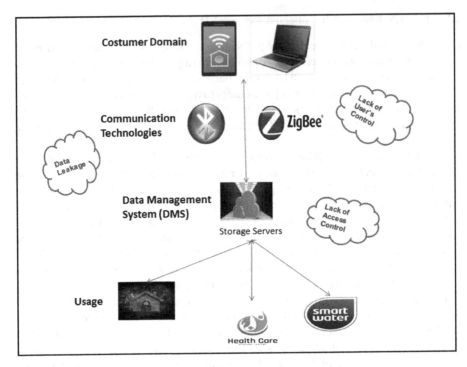

Fig. 2. Privacy issues with collected data

Table 1. Some examples of sensitive data that can be gathered from smart devices

Device	Information collected	Sensitive/Non-sensitive
Gate reminder	Use RFID system to detect the users' objects	Sensitive (PII): Personal attributes and belongings
Smart bed	Sensors track heart rate, breathing and movement	Sensitive (PII): Medical information
Smart thermostat	Use motion sensor, and it can understand when occupants leave the home or go to sleep	Sensitive (PII): Geographical indicators
Smart dressing	Light level information	Non-sensitive

2.2 Existing Solutions

The collected data from smart devices can be used for different usages such as safety, smart health care and energy management. We can see a lot of privacy violations happened during sharing the smart data for these purposes. In this section we surveyed several solutions on privacy issues in smart homes.

One of the usages of collected data from users is providing services for smart home users' safety and comfort. A smart refrigerator helps users easily track the items in the refrigerator that helps them in shopping by the use of RFID tags that attached to user's purchased items. As mentioned before the privacy violations can happen during the communication between the smartphone and the home server. One solution to protect the communication is through HTTPS communication protocol that uses cryptographic tunneling. However, with HTTPS communication users face other threats. There are powerful RFID readers outside of smart homes that attacker can impersonate a genuine RFID reader-enabled smart device inside the home. In this case, the home server would need to generate a private key and public key certificate for a new RFID reader-enabled device. Fernandes et al. propose for the problem that for device and home server to successfully establish HTTPS communication, user need to configure the smart device with its private key and public key certificate and install the public key certificate of the home server [24, 25].

Some devices such as smart camera and smart baby monitor are used for providing safety of users, but there are some reports of eavesdropping attacks, access remote attacks, identity spoofing attacks, and linking attacks by using these security devices. For example, some cases of hackers breaking into smart baby monitors to intrude on the family and speak obscenities are reported [26]. One attack can be man-in-the-middle attack because all the data exchange is transmitted in plain-text [27]. Also some researchers (e.g., Chattopadhyay et al. [28]) studied the security and privacy of smart cameras such as PrivacyCam. This device is a Digital Signal Processor (DSP) based system that motion regions are encrypted before images are streamed. Dufaux et al. [29] scramble regions of interest as part of MPEG-4 and MJPEG encoding instead of relying on cryptography. Baaziz et al. [30] also ensured data integrity by embedding water marks into images. Tansuriyavong et al. [31] performed face recognition and obscure silhouettes of persons. Most of these researchers are focused on identifying privacy relevant image regions.

The other usage of data collected from smart devices is using them for providing healthcare services. In this case, users can regularly monitor their own health in their own homes at their own convenience. Previously, users have to frequently visit their personal doctors for health services and the accumulated visits can be costly. This scenario allows users to reduce their health care costs by eliminating the needs to visit the doctors. However, health information privacy is so important. Disclosure of private health information such as physical and mental health status, behaviors and relationships may cause discrimination, stigma and embarrassment. Therefore protecting medical records of users from different attacks such as eavesdropping attacks and linking attacks is essential.

Although there are some solutions to reduce the risk of privacy violations during transforming the collected data for those usages, still we have a problem about different levels of user's privacy concerns or identifying sensitive data. User privacy preference is an illustration of how all data related to the users in the smart homes can be managed based on user's expectation. There are some solutions for the issues in smart homes such as configuring their privacy setting by themselves but some challenges exist with this solution. In this solution users need to label all of data and identify which information is sensitive for them and which one is non-sensitive. However, the accuracy of the privacy setting relies on user input and all the burdens are on the users. The user input is unpredictable and so laborious that users will not do it. The alternative solution is based on the active learning that users label some data, and a machine learning classifier labels other data on the basis of those user-labeled data. In this solution users are able to determine to whom and with what level of details the information will be shared.

3   Methodology

In this section we implement a solution for the problem of lack of users' control over their sensitive data (privacy) by developing a privacy decision framework (Fig. 3).

The first step of this framework is Data Collection. In this step all smart devices send the collected data to Data Management System for storage. The next step is sending data to machine learning module. In this step we will address the problem of lack of users' control over their privacy by considering different levels of privacy concerns. By using a technique of machine learning, which is called pool-based active learning [32], users are able to label a small amount of the collected data as sensitive and non-sensitive then by using this technique, the model will learn the user's privacy concerns and label the rest of the data. After labeling data as sensitive and non-sensitive we can identify which data can be shared and which cannot. In this way we can protect user's privacy in smart homes.

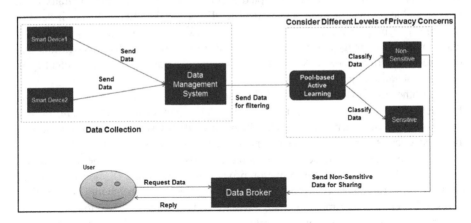

Fig. 3. Privacy decision framework

3.1   Data Collection

We simulated the smart home environment by using different sensors such as light, sound, motion and also timestamp and two individuals played the role of users in smart homes. In this simulated environment we collected data such as their movements, when they turn on or off the light and the amount of sound in the simulated smart home environment to create a dataset. All the data are collected form these sensors by communication through a Raspberry Pi, a single board computer that runs on Raspbian OS. The dataset includes 2079 instances, four features (sound, light, motion, and timestamp) and two classes (Sensitive and Non-Sensitive). The class of instances will be determined based on the user's privacy preferences. Users classify the instances based on their desire for privacy as a sensitive or non-sensitive data.

Table 2 represents the range of sound sensors which can be divided into 3 categories based on decibel (dB) values and how many data points are collected in what time period (morning, midday and night).

Table 2. Sound sensor and timestamp

Sound	Range (dB)	Timestamp	Range
Quiet	20–39	Morning	0–900
Conversation	40–50	Midday	901–1797
Loud	50–70	Night	1798–2079

Light can be divided into different groups based on LUX values (Table 3).

Table 3. Light sensor

Light	Range (LUX)
No light	0–20
General light in the morning	21–130
Office light	131–140
Very bright	141–150

Table 4 presents the categories of motion sensor and the class.

Table 4. Motion sensor and class

Motion	Range	Class	Range
No movement	0	Sensitive	1
Movement	1	Non-sensitive	2

After we collected data from different sensors, we classified data into two groups: sensitive and non-sensitive. We labeled data into sensitive or non-sensitive category based on user's privacy expectations. Table 5 is a small sample of collected data. For example, for the first record in the dataset the sound intensity is 33.97 dB, which it means the environment is quiet, the light intensity is 7 lx, which means the environment is dark, there is no light, motion sensor shows 0 that means no movement and the timestamp is 557 that means the data was collected during early in the morning. The users looked at the first record and realized that this specific data is not sensitive to them so they labeled it as non-sensitive one.

Table 5. A sample of smart home sensor dataset

Sound data	Light data	Motion data	Timestamp	Class
33.97142125	7	0	557	2
41.91279507	138	0	849	2
34.72463897	141	1	1125	1
46.97244913	140	0	1352	1
36.76028213	133	0	822	2

3.2   Consider Different Levels of Privacy Concerns

In this step we address the problem of lacking user's control over their privacy. Active learning technique is implemented on the collected data to consider different levels of users' privacy concerns and giving them options to express their desired privacy. We used pool-based sampling scenario to label data as sensitive and non-sensitive. In the pool-based scenario, users are asked to label a small amount of data as a training dataset and the rest of data is considered as a pool of unlabeled data. Then this training dataset is used to build and train a model and get an initial accuracy. After that a data record for which the model has the least confidence in its label and mostly likely to label is selected and asked from users to label this data. After labeling data by users, the labeled data is added to the training dataset, removed from the pool of unlabeled data and used to retrain the training dataset. This iteration continues until the performance does not significantly improve.

4   Experiment and Results

We used Python language and active learning libraries to build a model for labeling data as sensitive and non-sensitive. The Python libraries that we used in our implementation are SciPy, NumPy, matplotlib, pandas, and Scikit-learn, we used ModAL to use the features of active learning such as pool-based sampling and query strategies. KNN and Random Forest are two classification algorithms we used in order to train the model.

4.1   Accuracy Results of Passive Learning Techniques

Before implementing the active learning technique we use passive learning technique in which we split the data into training dataset and test dataset. As shown in the Table 6, we started with 50% of training dataset in order to train the classifier and obtain 99.6% accuracy. In each time we added 10% of data to the training dataset and realize that the accuracy has increased. At the end we obtained 99.8% of accuracy with 90% of training dataset.

Table 6. Classification accuracy with the passive learning technique

Percentage of training dataset	Accuracy result
50%	0.996309
60%	0.997154
70%	0.997769
80%	0.998077
90%	0.998261

4.2 Accuracy Results of Active Learning Technique

First, we divided the dataset into training (10% of data) and test (90% of data) datasets. We then trained the model with KNN and Random Forest classifiers, tested the dataset with the accuracy result of 99.4%.

After the initial training dataset, in each iteration one query is asked from the oracle to label data and added to the training dataset in order to retrain the model. As we can see in Table 7, the accuracy is increased after the 10 queries and the final accuracy is 99.8%. The reason for increase in accuracy is that in the active learning technique the training dataset was not chosen randomly. We chose the instances from the pool of unlabeled dataset that we are not sure about the labels and added to the training datasets and retrained the model until the performance does not significantly improve.

Table 7. Accuracy result after each query

Accuracy after query number	Result
1	0.994463
2	0.994463
3	0.994463
4	0.996678
5	0.997785
6	0.997785
7	0.998154
8	0.998893
9	0.998893
10	0.998893

After each query the accuracy result has increased, and the final accuracy result is 99.7% (Table 8).

In our research the precision is 0.998 and the recall is 0.997 (Table 9) which means the model classifies data into sensitive and non-sensitive categories with a higher accuracy.

Table 8. Accuracy result after each query

Accuracy after query number	Result
1	0.992617
2	0.992986
3	0.992986
4	0.994832
5	0.994832
6	0.995939
7	0.995939
8	0.998154
9	0.997785
10	0.997785

Table 9. Model evaluation

Accuracy	Precision	Recall	F1-score
0.998	0.998	0.997	0.9898

4.3 Comparison of Active Learning and Passive Learning

As we can see, in the first iteration with a smaller training set, passive learning technique achieved higher accuracy than the active learning technique. However, the initial data that we need to label for training dataset in active learning is 207 instances and in passive learning is 1039 instances. In order to improve the accuracy result in passive learning we need to use 60% of data from the dataset as a training dataset which means the users need to label 1247 instances in a dataset and add them to the training dataset. But for the next iteration, in active learning, the system just choose one data instance at the time from pool of unlabeled data and ask from human oracle to label it. At the end, the final accuracy results with passive learning is 99.8% with 1871 data out of 2079 training instances and the final accuracy result with active learning is 99.9% with just 217 examples for training instances. As a result, in active learning technique, the fewer amounts of data instances are needed to label and use for training and obtain higher accuracy than the passive learning technique. For this reason, we prefer to use active learning technique to build a model of labeling sensitive and non-sensitive smart home data for user's privacy concerns. It gives more accurate result and also saves the time of labeling.

5 Conclusion

Users have significant privacy concerns in smart homes. In order to deliver high quality services to users or for various research communities that require user information, user data is needed which may cause privacy violation. We present an implementation of a data labeling solution. In this work, we consider different levels of privacy concerns by using active learning machine learning technique, which can prevent the privacy violation in smart homes by considering user preferences in order to label data as sensitive or non-sensitive. The machine learning model is implemented to label the collected data automatically. Also in this research we compared two machine learning techniques, which are passive learning and active learning techniques to show that the active learning technique is a promising method for data labeling for privacy.

References

1. Han, D.-M., Lim, J.-H.: Smart home energy management system using IEEE 802.15. 4 and ZigBee. IEEE Trans. Consum. Electron. **56**, 1403–1410 (2010)
2. Pătru, I.-I., Carabaş, M., Bărbulescu, M., Gheorghe, L.: Smart home IoT system. In: 15th RoEduNet Conference: Networking in Education and Research, pp. 1–6 (2016)
3. Wang, M., Zhang, G., Zhang, C., Zhang, J., Li, C.: An IoT-based appliance control system for smart homes. In: Fourth International Conference on Intelligent Control and Information Processing (ICICIP), pp. 744–747 (2013)
4. Kumar, P., Pati, U.C.: IoT based monitoring and control of appliances for smart home. In: IEEE International Conference on Recent Trends in Electronics, Information & Communication Technology (RTEICT), pp. 1145–1150 (2016)
5. Bauer, K.A.: Home-based telemedicine: a survey of ethical issues. Camb. Q. Healthc. Ethics **10**, 137–146 (2001)
6. Zhang, M., Liu, Y., Wang, J., Hu, Y.: A new approach to security analysis of wireless sensor networks for smart home systems. In: International Conference on Intelligent Networking and Collaborative Systems (INCoS), pp. 318–323 (2016)
7. Bennett, C.L., Silver, S.M., Djulbegovic, B., Samaras, A.T., Blau, C.A., Gleason, K.J., et al.: Venous thromboembolism and mortality associated with recombinant erythropoietin and darbepoetin administration for the treatment of cancer-associated anemia. Jama **299**, 914–924 (2008)
8. Baumeister, T.: Adapting PKI for the smart grid. In: IEEE International Conference on Smart Grid Communications (SmartGridComm), pp. 249–254 (2011)
9. Kifer, D., Lin, B.-R.: Towards an axiomatization of statistical privacy and utility. In: Proceedings of the Twenty-Ninth ACM SIGMOD-SIGACT-SIGART Symposium on Principles of Database Systems, pp. 147–158 (2010)
10. Dinur, I., Nissim, K.: Revealing information while preserving privacy. In: Proceedings of the Twenty-Second ACM SIGMOD-SIGACT-SIGART Symposium on Principles of Database Systems, pp. 202–210 (2003)
11. Finster, S., Baumgart, I.: Privacy-aware smart metering: a survey. IEEE Commun. Surv. Tutor. **16**, 1732–1745 (2014)
12. Cavoukian, A., Polonetsky, J., Wolf, C.: Smartprivacy for the smart grid: embedding privacy into the design of electricity conservation. Identity Inf. Soc. **3**, 275–294 (2010)
13. Aggarwal, C.C., Yu, P.S.: A general survey of privacy-preserving data mining models and algorithms. In: Aggarwal, C.C., Yu, P.S. (eds.) Privacy-Preserving Data Mining. Advances in Database Systems, vol. 34, pp. 11–52. Springer, Boston (2008). https://doi.org/10.1007/978-0-387-70992-5_2
14. Li, N., Li, T., Venkatasubramanian, S.: t-closeness: privacy beyond k-anonymity and l-diversity. In: IEEE 23rd International Conference on Data Engineering, ICDE 2007, pp. 106–115 (2007)

15. Machanavajjhala, A., Gehrke, J., Kifer, D., Venkitasubramaniam, M.: l-diversity: privacy beyond k-anonymity. In: Proceedings of the 22nd International Conference on Data Engineering, ICDE 2006, p. 24 (2006)
16. Hamill, L.: Controlling smart devices in the home. Inf. Soc. **22**, 241–249 (2006)
17. Han, D.-M., Lim, J.-H.: Design and implementation of smart home energy management systems based on ZigBee. IEEE Trans. Consum. Electron. **56**, 1417–1425 (2010)
18. Bai, X., Xing, L., Zhang, N., Wang, X., Liao, X., Li, T., et al.: Staying secure and unprepared: understanding and mitigating the security risks of Apple ZeroConf. In: IEEE Symposium on Security and Privacy (SP), pp. 655–674 (2016)
19. Kaaz, K.J., Hoffer, A., Saeidi, M., Sarma, A., Bobba, R.B.: Understanding user perceptions of privacy, and configuration challenges in home automation. In: IEEE Symposium on Visual Languages and Human-Centric Computing (VL/HCC), pp. 297–301 (2017)
20. Urban, J., Hoofnagle, C.: The privacy pragmatic as privacy vulnerable (2014)
21. McCallister, E., Grance, T., Scarfone, K.A.: Guide to protecting the confidentiality of personally identifiable information (PII) (2010)
22. Sanchez, I., Satta, R., Fovino, I.N., Baldini, G., Steri, G., Shaw, D., et al.: Privacy leakages in Smart Home wireless technologies. In: International Carnahan Conference on Security Technology (ICCST), pp. 1–6 (2014)
23. Pappachan, P., Degeling, M., Yus, R., Das, A., Bhagavatula, S., Melicher, W., et al.: Towards privacy-aware smart buildings: capturing, communicating, and enforcing privacy policies and preferences. In: IEEE 37th International Conference on Distributed Computing Systems Workshops (ICDCSW), pp. 193–198 (2017)
24. Fernandes, E., Jung, J., Prakash, A.: Security analysis of emerging smart home applications. In: IEEE Symposium on Security and Privacy (SP), pp. 636–654 (2016)
25. Konidala, D.M., Kim, D.-Y., Yeun, C.-Y., Lee, B.-C.: Security framework for RFID-based applications in smart home environment. J. Inf. Process. Syst. **7**, 111–120 (2011)
26. Notra, S., Siddiqi, M., Gharakheili, H.H., Sivaraman, V., Boreli, R.: An experimental study of security and privacy risks with emerging household appliances. In: IEEE Conference on Communications and Network Security (CNS), pp. 79–84 (2014)
27. Sivaraman, V., Gharakheili, H.H., Vishwanath, A., Boreli, R., Mehani, O.: Network-level security and privacy control for smart-home IoT devices. In: IEEE 11th International Conference on Wireless and Mobile Computing, Networking and Communications (WiMob), pp. 163–167 (2015)
28. Chattopadhyay, A., Boult, T.E.: PrivacyCam: a privacy preserving camera using uCLinux on the Blackfin DSP. In: IEEE Conference on Computer Vision and Pattern Recognition, CVPR 2007, pp. 1–8 (2007)
29. Dufaux, F., Ebrahimi, T.: Scrambling for video surveillance with privacy. In: Conference on Computer Vision and Pattern Recognition Workshop, CVPRW 2006, p. 160 (2006)
30. Baaziz, N., Lolo, N., Padilla, O., Petngang, F.: Security and privacy protection for automated video surveillance. In: IEEE International Symposium on Signal Processing and Information Technology, pp. 17–22 (2007)
31. Tansuriyavong, S., Hanaki, S.-i.: Privacy protection by concealing persons in circumstantial video image. In: Proceedings of the 2001 Workshop on Perceptive User Interfaces, pp. 1–4 (2001)
32. Hossain, H.S., Khan, M.A.A.H., Roy, N.: Active learning enabled activity recognition. Pervasive Mob. Comput. **38**, 312–330 (2017)

Privacy Preservation for Versatile Pay-TV Services

Kazuto Ogawa[1]([✉]) and Koji Nuida[2]

[1] Japan Broadcasting Corporation, Tokyo, Japan
ogawa.k-cm@nhk.or.jp
[2] The University of Tokyo, Tokyo, Japan
nuida@mist.i.u-tokyo.ac.jp

Abstract. In pay-TV services, content is encrypted and transmitted to subscribers. Each subscriber has a security module that holds a decryption key(s) for the encrypted content. A set-top box or a smart card is often used as the security module. When a subscriber wants to obtain the same services outside the home, the subscriber has to bring the security module. However, even if the security module is a card, it is not easy to take it out because of the structure of TV sets and set-top boxes.

As a way of improving current pay-TV services, Ogawa, Tamura, and Hanaoka (OTH17) proposed a system using an attribute-based encryption scheme (ABE). ABE is used to restrict the time and location at which a subscriber can obtain the service.

However, OTH17 requires a third trusted party (TTP) for key and ciphertext generation; thus, the TTP knows the time and location of the subscriber. This means that the subscriber's private information is disclosed to the party.

Here, we propose a system that avoids disclosure of private data by adding a multi-party computation (MPC). In addition, MPC makes the TTP unnecessary.

Keywords: Pay-TV services · Attribute-based encryption · Multi-party computation · Privacy preserving · Non-trusted party

1 Introduction

1.1 Background

Broadcasting and cable TV services encrypt content for the purpose of copyright protection before distributing it to subscribers. Each subscriber needs a decoder with a decryption module for decrypting the content. In Japan, a smart card or a LSI (card what it follows) is used as a security module, and a decryption key is generated in the card [32,33]. Moreover, pay-TV services use the same card to control subscribers' access to their content. The card holds a subscriber's contract information, and the decryption keys are generated on the basis of the information in the card.

© Springer Nature Switzerland AG 2019
A. Moallem (Ed.): HCII 2019, LNCS 11594, pp. 417–428, 2019.
https://doi.org/10.1007/978-3-030-22351-9_28

If the card were be able to be taken out of the TV set or set-top box, subscribers would be able to get identical services outside the home, but it is not easy to take the card out of the receivers, because manufacturers produce receivers, considering breakage of cards.

If the decryption key(s) could be removed electronically and stored in such devices as a mobile phone or tablet PC, the subscriber would not need to take the card out; this would improve quality of service.

Nowadays, there are hybrid systems, such as youview [38], HbbTV [36], Hulu [37], and Hybridcast [35], that offer broadcasting services through the air and network services through the Internet. These systems consider cooperation of receivers and mobile terminals, meaning that it is easy to transmit data from the receiver to the mobile terminal. However, when a third party who can access and use the data transmitted to the mobile terminal illegally use the system in a way that the copyright would be infringed, for example. Hence, in cases in which data can be transmitted to the mobile terminal, countermeasures against possible illegal use of that data should be taken.

Ogawa, Hanaoka, and Imai (OHI07) [26] proposed a method in which a decryption key is updated periodically and a temporal decryption key can be taken out, as a way of improving the currently offered services. That is, the subscriber can obtain identical services outside the home only during a limited period. In this case, even if the decryption key is leaked, the damage caused by the leakage will not extend beyond the valid period of the key. Ogawa, Tamura, and Hanaoka (OTH17) proposed another countermeasure in which an attribute-based encryption scheme (ABE) is used and the location and time are used as attributes. That is, the subscriber can obtain services outside only during a limited period and in restricted area. Even if the decryption key is leaked, the damage would not extend beyond the valid period and the restricted area.

1.2   Contributions

The services considered in this paper are the same as those in OTH17. First, we consider a situation in which subscribers bring the decryption keys with them and obtain identical services outside their homes. The situation corresponds to one of traveling on business or sightseeing. In such a situation, the location where the subscriber stays during the period is usually decided before leaving the home. Moreover, it would likely be a hotel or similar establishment where the subscriber would most want to obtain the services. Furthermore, the time during which the subscriber would obtain the services at the hotel would be limited. Then, by generating a decryption key that can be used at the hotel during the time of stay and storing the key in the mobile terminal electronically would make it possible for a subscriber outside the home to obtain identical services to those received at home when he or she wants them.

OTH17 uses ABE to control accesses to content, and the location and time are used as its attributes. In addition, a trusted third party (TTP) is needed to issue certain decryption keys, and private information, such as the place where the subscriber is and the period of the stay, is sent to the party in plaintext.

That the TTP gets such information is not preferable from the viewpoint of privacy preserving. Moreover, if the party is untrusted, there is a risk that the subscriber's private information will be disclosed. Such a system lacks versatility.

We propose a system that overcomes the above drawback. In order to reduce the risk, we add the multi-party computation protocol (MPC) [1,7,14,24,25,29, 30] to OTH17. In MPC, it is impossible to recover original private data from the share provided to each party. Thus, MPC improves the OTH17 system into one that does not disclose any private information.

1.3 Related Works

The system we propose uses time and location data to control access to the content. As far as we know, there has not been any related proposal except for OHI07 and OTH17 regarding access control to pay-TV services. However, these systems do not consider privacy preservation. Although OHI07 cannot control the location at which the decryption key is used, OTH17 can do so, making it superior to OHI07 with regard to content copyright protection. However, OTH17 is still poor from the viewpoint of privacy preservation, because the user has to tell the place where he or she will use the decryption key.

A position based cryptography scheme (PBC) [6,8–10,16,20,28], which controls the decryption of a ciphertext according to the location the message sender specifies, and a time released encryption scheme (TRE) [3,13,15,18,19,21,22, 27,31], which controls the decryption of a ciphertext according to the time the message sender specifies, can be used for the same purpose. However, the use of such schemes entails sending private data, such as the place and time of stay, in plaintext to certain parties; they too are not preferable from the viewpoint of privacy preservation. The use of PBC and TRE with homomorphic properties may make it possible to eliminate the above risk, but their use requires two encryptions or decryptions; moreover, homomorphic properties seem to raise computational costs.

2 Preliminary

2.1 Current Broadcasting System and OTH17

There are a lot of pay-TV services in North America, Europe, and Asia. The systems in North America and Europe vary from broadcaster to broadcaster, and their details are not disclosed. Although the Common Descrambling System of Digital Video Broadcasting (DVB-CSA) [34] is standardized in Europe, a non-disclosure agreement must be signed in order to see its details, and naturally, the details cannot be disclosed. On the other hand, the Japanese broadcasting system has been disclosed. Figure 1 shows the current broadcasting system used in Japan [32,33].

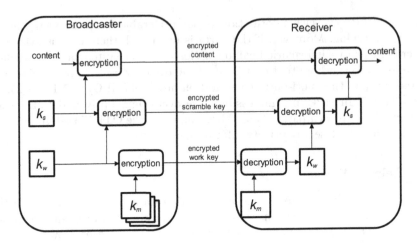

Fig. 1. Japanese Broadcasting System: k_s is the content (scramble) key, k_w is the work key, and k_m is the master key.

The broadcaster encrypts the content M by using a scramble key k_s. It broadcasts the encrypted content $C_M = Enc(k_s, M)$. $Enc(k, M)$ denotes that the plaintext M is encrypted by using a key k. k_s is encrypted by using a work key k_w, and the broadcaster generates an encrypted scramble key $C_{k_s} = Enc(k_w, k_s)$. In addition, k_w is encrypted by using a master key k_m, and the broadcaster generates an encrypted work key $C_{k_w} = Enc(k_m, k_w)$. C_M, C_{k_s}, and C_{k_w} are multiplexed and transmitted to the subscribers.

The Japanese system has multiple symmetric encryption schemes. That is, the scrambling scheme used for content encryption is different from the encryption scheme used for encrypting k_s and k_w. This difference does not affect the proposed system. Hence, we will use the same notation $Enc(\cdot, \cdot)$ as in symmetric encryption.

Each receiver needs a smart card or LSI as a security module to hold a k_m. Each security module has a distinct k_m, and broadcasters can transmit private contract information to each subscriber (receiver) by using k_m. C_M, C_{k_s}, and C_{k_w}, which are transmitted through the air, are demultiplexed in the receiver. k_w is decrypted by using k_m in the security module as follows: $k_w = Dec(k_m, C_{k_w})$. $Dec(k, C)$ denotes that a ciphertext C is decrypted by using a key k. k_s is decrypted by using k_w: $k_s = Dec(k_w, C_{k_s})$. k_s is sent to the receiver, and M is decrypted (descrambled) by using k_s: $M = Dec(k_s, C_M)$ in the receiver.

Since all the encryption schemes are symmetric, their encryption and decryption keys are identical. In the Japanese broadcasting system, the descrambling scheme used for content decryption is different from the scheme of decrypting k_w and k_s, but this difference does not affect the proposed system. Hence, we will use the same notation $Dec(\cdot, \cdot)$.

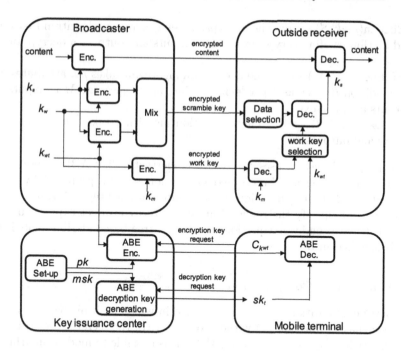

Fig. 2. OTH17 system

OTH17 is constructed on the basis of the above Japanese system. Figure 2 shows this system. It introduces a new work key k_{w_t}, and ABE is used to control accesses to broadcast content.

The broadcaster generates k_{w_t} and encrypts k_s by using k_{w_t}. Receivers receive k_{w_t} from the mobile terminals and decrypt k_s by using k_{w_t}. The key issuance center gets k_{w_t} from the broadcaster, sets up the ABE scheme, generates a decryption key sk_t, encrypts k_{w_t}, and generates $C_{k_{w_t}} = \mathsf{ABE\_Enc}(pk, \beta, k_{w_t})$. The mobile terminals need to store sk_t securely, obtain $C_{k_{w_t}}$ from the key issuance center, and decrypt $k_{w_t} = \mathsf{ABE\_Dec}(sk_t, C_{k_{w_t}})$.

2.2 Attribute-Based Encryption

ABE [2,5,12,17] can prescribe the logic of encryption or decryption by embedding attributes or conditions of attributes into a ciphertext or a decryption key. Arbitrary functions, described as combinations of AND gates, OR gates, NOT gates, and threshold gates, are possible conditions.

Ciphertext-policy ABE is a kind of ABE that embeds attribute data into a decryption key and a policy (condition), such as Boolean formula, into a ciphertext. It consists of four algorithms ($\mathsf{ABE\_Setup}, \mathsf{ABE\_Gen}, \mathsf{ABE\_Enc}, \mathsf{ABE\_Dec}$).

– $\mathsf{ABE\_Setup}(1^\lambda) \to (msk, pk)$: The set-up algorithm takes a security parameter 1^λ as input and outputs a master key msk and a public key pk.

- ABE_Gen$(msk, S) \rightarrow sk$: The decryption key generation algorithm takes msk and attributes of a decryption key S as inputs and outputs a decryption key sk.
- ABE_Enc$(pk, \beta, M) \rightarrow C$: The encryption algorithm takes pk, attributes, and its condition β, such as a Boolean function, and a message M as inputs and outputs a ciphertext C.
- ABE_Dec$(sk, C, \beta) \rightarrow M$: The decryption algorithm takes sk, C, and β as inputs and outputs M.

The proposed system uses the above ciphertext-policy ABE. More specifically, it employs the attribute-based encryption scheme proposed by Attrapadung et al. [2] that can assign an attribute with a range. Attrapadung et al.'s scheme can specify the range of an attribute by a direct expression $\{a, b\}$ and can calculate condition equations by using a tree-based attribute label. The range is included in β.

2.3   Multi-Party Computation

Multi-party computation (MPC) is a method in which multiple parties collaborate to calculate a function $f()$ without disclosure of the secret shares (information) that each party holds. By using MPC, it is possible to modify an arbitrary algorithm (function) into an information-theoretically secure one under certain conditions [4,11]. In MPC, a secret sharing algorithm makes secret shares from an input x to f, and multiple servers obtain distinct shares and execute some calculations. The user gets output shares from the servers and calculates the output $y = f(x)$. The original input x cannot be revealed from any of the secret shares or from any of the information communicated between the servers.

Here, we will assume a semi-honest model. That is, all entities execute their roles without any error. The secret sharing scheme and client-aided client-server model [23,24] used in this paper are described below.

Secret Sharing. A secret sharing scheme consists of two algorithms: Share and Reveal. Share takes as input x and outputs shares $([\![x]\!]_1, \cdots, [\![x]\!]_N)$, $([\![x]\!]_1, \cdots, [\![x]\!]_N) \leftarrow$ Share(x), where N is the number of parties and $[\![x]\!]_i$ denotes a share for the i-th $(i \in [1, N])$ party. Reveal takes as input $([\![x]\!]_1, \cdots, [\![x]\!]_N)$ and outputs $[\![x]\!]$, $[\![x]\!] \leftarrow$ Reveal$([\![x]\!]_1, \cdots, [\![x]\!]_N)$. In this paper, we set $N = 2$. That is, we will use the $\binom{2}{2}$-secret sharing scheme, where Share generates two shares and REVEAL takes input two shares.

Client-Aided Client-Server Model. We employ Morita and et al.'s secret-sharing based MPC in the client-aided client-server model [24]. Its procedure is as follows:
Suppose there are N servers and t clients.

1. Client-$j(j \in [1, t])$ takes input $a_j \in \mathbb{A}$ and generates shares $[\![a_j]\!] = ([\![a_j]\!]_1, \cdots, [\![a_j]\!]_N) \leftarrow$ Share(a_j) for N servers. Client-1 generates a set of aiding information (Beaver triple) $BT_1, \cdots, BT_N$ that helps each server's calculation.

2. Client-j sends $[\![a_j]\!]_i$ to Server-i and Client-1 sends BT_i to Server-i.
3. Server-i calculates its output $[\![b_i]\!]$ from t inputs $([\![a_1]\!]_i, \cdots, [\![a_t]\!]_i)$, communicating with the other servers.
4. Server-i sends $[\![b_i]\!]$ to all clients.
5. Each client takes n inputs $([\![b_1]\!], \cdots, [\![b_N]\!])$ and obtains $b = f(a_1, \cdots, a_t)$ by performing $b \leftarrow \mathsf{Reveal}([\![b_1]\!], \cdots, [\![b_N]\!])$.

3   Proposal

OTH17 employs a trusted third party (TTP) and subscribers' private information; e.g., the subscriber's travel destination is disclosed to the TTP. In contrast, we construct a system that preserves subscribers' private information while maintaining the other properties of OTH17.

Let us suppose that a subscriber carries keys and obtains services outside his or her home (at a hotel). Furthermore, the period of stay at the hotel is limited. Accordingly, a decryption key that can only be used during the stay at the hotel and that can be stored in the subscriber's mobile terminal would make it possible to obtain the expected services.

From the viewpoint of privacy preservation, the data supplied by the subscriber should be kept secret from every other party. To ensure this, we employ the multi-party computation protocol (MPC). In particular, the calculation of TTP in OTH17 is divided up into multiple parts and each part is performed by a separate distinct party. The output of each party is sent to the subscriber. MPC is secure if the original data cannot be recovered from the share of any party. Hence, due to the MPC, no party can obtain original data from its share and the subscriber's privacy is preserved.

3.1   System

Figure 3 shows the proposed system using MPC. There are four entities.

- Mobile terminal: It belongs to a subscriber who has a contract with a broadcaster.
- Broadcaster: It encrypts content and transmits it to all subscribers.
- Server-1, 2: It plays the role of a key issuance center. It generates pk and msk of ABE and issues sk_t and C_{kw_t}.
- Outside receiver: It is a receiver at a hotel, for example.

The broadcaster encrypts k_s by using k_{w_t} and broadcasts the encrypted $C_{k_s} = Enc(k_{w_t}, k_s)$ through the air. k_{w_t} is also encrypted and sent to the outside receiver through communication channels. MPC is used for k_{w_t}'s encryption.

Before the subscriber gets k_{w_t}, the decryption key sk_t of ABE is generated from the location and date attributes of where and when the subscriber plans to obtain the service. This key is generated by using MPC. That is, the subscriber generates multiple shares from his or her attributes (Gen. Shares for MPC-ABE Enc.) and sends each share to a distinct party. Each party generates an output

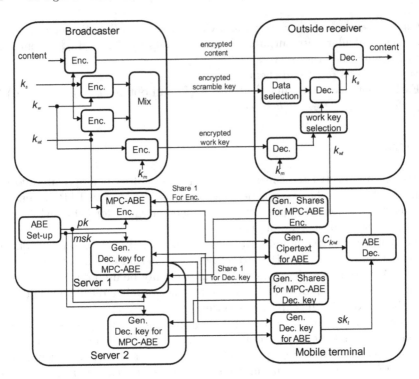

Fig. 3. Proposed System: pk and msk are public and master keys for ABE. MPC-ABE Enc. and Gen Dec. key for MPC-ABE are encryption and decryption-key generation functions of ABE using a multi-party computation. Gen. Shares for MPC-ABE Enc. is a share-generation function for MPC-ABE Enc. and Gen. Shares for MPC-ABE Dec. key is a share-generation function for Gen. Dec. key for MPC-ABE. Gen. Ciphertext for ABE and Gen. Dec. key for ABE are ciphertext-generation and decryption-key-generation functions for ABE.

share from its input and returns it to the subscriber. This algorithm (Gen. Dec. Key for MPC-ABE) is for generating sk_t. The subscriber generates sk_t from the outputs of all parties. The subscriber stores sk_t in the mobile terminal and brings it to the travel destination.

A ciphertext of k_{w_t} is necessary at the hotel. The subscriber generates multiple shares from his or her attributes (Gen. Shares for MPC-ABE Enc.) and sends each share to a distinct party. Each party generates its output share from its input and transmits it through communication networks to the mobile terminal. The algorithm (MPC-ABE Enc.) is for generating the ciphertext. The terminal generates a ciphertext of k_{w_t} from the outputs of all parties. Finally, the subscriber gets the service at the hotel by using sk_t and the ciphertext of k_{w_t}.

This system enables subscribers to enjoy enriched services without having to disclose any of their private information.

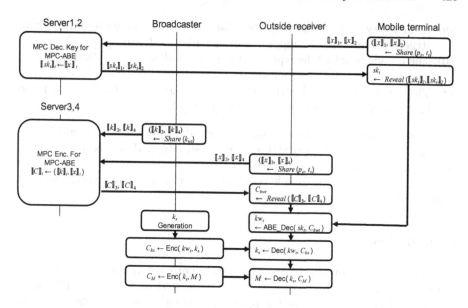

Fig. 4. Service procedure

3.2 Service Procedure

Figure 4 shows the service procedure in the system.

(1) The subscriber obtains a token β from the broadcaster after its authentication and saves it in the mobile terminal.

(2) The subscriber inputs its private information, the place (p_x, p_y) and time t_p at which the subscriber will obtain the service, to its mobile terminal.

(3) The mobile terminal performs $\binom{2}{2}$-secret sharing protocol with (p_x, p_y) and t_p, generates shares $(\llbracket p_1 \rrbracket, \llbracket p_2 \rrbracket) \leftarrow \mathsf{Share}(p_x \| p_y \| t_p \| \beta)$, and sends $\llbracket p_i \rrbracket$ to the server-i($i \in \{1, 2\}$). In addition, aiding shares BT_1 and BT_2 are generated and BT_i is sent to server-i.

(4) After receiving $\llbracket p_i \rrbracket$ from the mobile terminal, server-i generates a share $\llbracket sk_{t_i} \rrbracket$ to calculate a function $f_{kg}(p_x \| p_y \| t_p \| \beta \| \alpha)$ and returns it to the mobile terminal, where α is secret data that all servers share.

(5) After receiving $\llbracket sk_{t_1} \rrbracket$ and $\llbracket sk_{t_2} \rrbracket$ from the servers, the mobile terminal calculates a secret key $sk_t \leftarrow \mathsf{Reveal}(\llbracket sk_{t_1} \rrbracket, \llbracket sk_{t_2} \rrbracket)$.

(6) The broadcaster generates k_{w_t}, and sends it to server-1 and 2.

(7) At the destination, the mobile terminal generates shares of the current place (p_{cx}, p_{cy}) and time t_{cp} by performing $\binom{2}{2}$-secret sharing protocol ($\llbracket p_{c1} \rrbracket$, $\llbracket p_{c2} \rrbracket) \leftarrow \mathsf{Share}(p_{cx} \| p_{cy} \| t_{cp} \| \beta)$, and sends $\llbracket p_{ci} \rrbracket (i \in \{1, 2\})$ to server-i. In addition, the terminal generates shares BT_{c1} and BT_{c2}, and sends $BT_{ci} (i \in \{1, 2\})$ to server-i.

(8) After receiving k_{w_t} from the broadcaster, $\llbracket p_{ci} \rrbracket$ and $\llbracket BT_{ci} \rrbracket$ from the mobile terminal, server-i generates a share $\llbracket c_i \rrbracket$ to calculate a function $C_{k_{w_t}} = f_{cg}(p_{cx} \| p_{cy} \| t_{cp} \| \beta \| \alpha, k_{w_t})$ and returns it to the mobile terminal.

(9) After receiving $[\![c_1]\!]$ and $[\![c_2]\!]$ from the servers, the mobile terminal reconstructs the encrypted temporal work key $C_{k_{w_t}} \leftarrow \mathsf{Reveal}([\![c_1]\!], [\![c_2]\!])$.

(10) The mobile terminal decrypts the temporal work key $k_{w_t} = Dec(sk_t, C_{k_{w_t}})$ and sends it to the outside receiver.

(11) The outside receiver decrypts the scramble key $k_s = Dec(k_{w_t}, C_{k_s})$ and finally decrypts the content $M = Dec(k_s, C_M)$.

As can be seen, the set (p_{px}, p_{py}) at the subscriber's home should be the same with (p_{cx}, p_{cy}) obtained at the travel destination. If this is not the case, the subscriber cannot get the service.

Steps (8) to (11) of the mobile terminal are performed only once at the start of the service at the travel destination.

4   Conclusion

We proposed a method that enables the subscriber to obtain services at a travel destination. In the system, a secret key is generated on the basis of location and time information. That is, the place and time are used to control the subscriber's access to the content. In addition, this system does not require a TTP and it preserves the subscriber's private information; thus, the system can use an untrusted server. Moreover, there are some information-theoretically secure MPCs, and when the system uses such an information-theoretically secure MPC, it becomes secure against attacks from quantum computers.

References

1. Araki, T., Furukawa, J., Lindell, Y., Nof, A., Ohara, K.: High-throughput semi-honest secure three-party computation with an honest majority. In: Proceedings of ACM SIGSAC CCS 2016, pp. 805–817 (2016)

2. Attrapadung, N., Hanaoka, G., Ogawa, K., Ohtake, G., Watanabe, H., Yamada, S.: Attribute-based encryption for range attributes. In: Zikas, V., De Prisco, R. (eds.) SCN 2016. LNCS, vol. 9841, pp. 42–61. Springer, Cham (2016). https://doi.org/10.1007/978-3-319-44618-9_3

3. Baek, J., Safavi-Naini, R., Susilo, W.: Token-controlled public key encryption. In: Deng, R.H., Bao, F., Pang, H.H., Zhou, J. (eds.) ISPEC 2005. LNCS, vol. 3439, pp. 386–397. Springer, Heidelberg (2005). https://doi.org/10.1007/978-3-540-31979-5_33

4. Ben-Or, M., Goldwasser, S., Wigderson, A.: Completeness theorems for non-cryptographic fault-tolerant distributed computation. In: Proceedings of STOC 1988, pp. 1–10 (1988)

5. Bethencourt, J., Sahai, A., Waters, B.: Ciphertext-policy attribute-based encryption. In: Proceedings of IEEE S&P 2007, pp. 321–334 (2007)

6. Brands, S., Chaum, D.: Distance-bounding protocols. In: Helleseth, T. (ed.) EUROCRYPT 1993. LNCS, vol. 765, pp. 344–359. Springer, Heidelberg (1994). https://doi.org/10.1007/3-540-48285-7_30

7. Catrina, O., de Hoogh, S.: Improved primitives for secure multiparty integer computation. In: Garay, J.A., De Prisco, R. (eds.) SCN 2010. LNCS, vol. 6280, pp. 182–199. Springer, Heidelberg (2010). https://doi.org/10.1007/978-3-642-15317-4_13

8. Capkun, S., Hubaux, J.: Secure positioning of wireless devices with application to sensor networks. In: Proceedings of IEEE Infocom 2005, pp. 1917–1928 (2005)

9. Chandran, N., Goyal, V., Moriarty, R., Ostrovsky, R.: Position based cryptography. In: Halevi, S. (ed.) CRYPTO 2009. LNCS, vol. 5677, pp. 391–407. Springer, Heidelberg (2009). https://doi.org/10.1007/978-3-642-03356-8_23

10. Chandran, N., Goyal, V., Moriarty, R., Ostrovsky, R.: Position-based cryptography. SIAM J. Comput. **43**(4), 1291–1341 (2014)

11. Chaum, D., Crépeau, C., Damgård, I.: Multiparty unconditionally secure protocols. In: Proceedings of STOC 1988, pp. 11–19 (1988)

12. Chen, J., Wee, H.: Semi-adaptive attribute-based encryption and improved delegation for Boolean formula. In: Abdalla, M., De Prisco, R. (eds.) SCN 2014. LNCS, vol. 8642, pp. 277–297. Springer, Cham (2014). https://doi.org/10.1007/978-3-319-10879-7_16

13. Cheon, J.H., Hopper, N., Kim, Y., Osipkov, I.: Provably secure timed-release public key encryption. ACM Trans. Inf. Syst. Secur. **11**, 4:1–4:44 (2008)

14. Damgård, I., Fitzi, M., Kiltz, E., Nielsen, J.B., Toft, T.: Unconditionally secure constant-rounds multi-party computation for equality, comparison, bits and exponentiation. In: Halevi, S., Rabin, T. (eds.) TCC 2006. LNCS, vol. 3876, pp. 285–304. Springer, Heidelberg (2006). https://doi.org/10.1007/11681878_15

15. Dent, A.W., Tang, Q.: Revisiting the security model for timed-release encryption with pre-open capability. In: Garay, J.A., Lenstra, A.K., Mambo, M., Peralta, R. (eds.) ISC 2007. LNCS, vol. 4779, pp. 158–174. Springer, Heidelberg (2007). https://doi.org/10.1007/978-3-540-75496-1_11

16. Dziembowski, S., Zdanowicz, M.: Position-based cryptography from noisy channels. In: Pointcheval, D., Vergnaud, D. (eds.) AFRICACRYPT 2014. LNCS, vol. 8469, pp. 300–317. Springer, Cham (2014). https://doi.org/10.1007/978-3-319-06734-6_19

17. Goyal, V., Pandey, O., Sahai, A., Waters, B.: Attribute-based encryption for fine-grained access control of encrypted data. In: Proceeding of ACM CCS 2006, pp. 89–98 (2006)

18. Hwang, Y.H., Yum, D.H., Lee, P.J.: Timed-release encryption with pre-open capability and its application to certified e-mail system. In: Zhou, J., Lopez, J., Deng, R.H., Bao, F. (eds.) ISC 2005. LNCS, vol. 3650, pp. 344–358. Springer, Heidelberg (2005). https://doi.org/10.1007/11556992_25

19. Kasamatsu, K., Matsuda, T., Emura, K., Attrapadung, N., Hanaoka, G., Imai, H.: Time-specific encryption from forward-secure encryption: generic and direct constructions. Int. J. Inf. Secur. **15**(5), 549–571 (2016)

20. Kuno, S., Attrapadung, N., Kitagawa, T., Imai, H.: Position-based encryption. In: Proceedings of SCIS 2012, 1A1-4 (2012). (in Japanese)

21. Matsuda, T., Nakai, Y., Matsuura, K.: Efficient generic constructions of timed-release encryption with pre-open capability. In: Joye, M., Miyaji, A., Otsuka, A. (eds.) Pairing 2010. LNCS, vol. 6487, pp. 225–245. Springer, Heidelberg (2010). https://doi.org/10.1007/978-3-642-17455-1_15

22. May, T.: Time-release crypto (1993). http://www.cyphernet.org/cyphernomicon/chapter14/14.5.html

23. Mohassel, P., Zhang, Y.: SecureML: a system for scalable privacy-preserving machine learning. In: Proceedings of IEEE Symposium on Security and Privacy 2017, pp. 19–38 (2017)

24. Morita, H., Attrapadung, N., Teruya, T., Ohata, S., Nuida, K., Hanaoka, G.: Constant-round client-aided secure comparison protocol. In: Lopez, J., Zhou, J., Soriano, M. (eds.) ESORICS 2018. LNCS, vol. 11099, pp. 395–415. Springer, Cham (2018). https://doi.org/10.1007/978-3-319-98989-1_20

25. Nishide, T., Ohta, K.: Multiparty computation for interval, equality, and comparison without bit-decomposition protocol. In: Okamoto, T., Wang, X. (eds.) PKC 2007. LNCS, vol. 4450, pp. 343–360. Springer, Heidelberg (2007). https://doi.org/10.1007/978-3-540-71677-8_23

26. Ogawa, K., Hanaoka, G., Imai, H.: Traitor tracing scheme secure against key exposure and its application to anywhere TV service. IEICE Trans. Fundam. **E90–A**(5), 1000–1011 (2007)

27. Paterson, K.G., Quaglia, E.A.: Time-specific encryption. In: Garay, J.A., De Prisco, R. (eds.) SCN 2010. LNCS, vol. 6280, pp. 1–16. Springer, Heidelberg (2010). https://doi.org/10.1007/978-3-642-15317-4_1

28. Sastry, N., Shankar, U., Wagner, D.: Secure verification of location claims. In: Proceedings of ACM Wireless Security 2003, pp. 1–10 (2003)

29. Schneider, T., Zohner, M.: GMW vs. Yao? Efficient secure two-party computation with low depth circuits. In: Sadeghi, A.-R. (ed.) FC 2013. LNCS, vol. 7859, pp. 275–292. Springer, Heidelberg (2013). https://doi.org/10.1007/978-3-642-39884-1_23

30. Schoenmakers, B., Tuyls, P.: Practical two-party computation based on the conditional gate. In: Lee, P.J. (ed.) ASIACRYPT 2004. LNCS, vol. 3329, pp. 119–136. Springer, Heidelberg (2004). https://doi.org/10.1007/978-3-540-30539-2_10

31. Yoshida, M., Mitsunari, S., Fujiwara, T.: A timed-release key management scheme for backward recovery. In: Won, D.H., Kim, S. (eds.) ICISC 2005. LNCS, vol. 3935, pp. 3–14. Springer, Heidelberg (2006). https://doi.org/10.1007/11734727_3

32. ARIB: Conditional Access System Specifications for Digital Broadcasting, ARIB STD-B25 (2007)

33. ARIB: Conditional Access System (Second Generation) and CAS Program Download System Specifications for Digital Broadcasting, ARIB STD-B61 (2017)

34. ETSI: DVB common scrambling algorithm-distribution agreements. Technical report (2013)

35. http://www.nhk.or.jp/hybridcast/online/

36. http://www.hbbtv.org/

37. http://www.hulu.com/

38. http://www.youview.com/

Company Privacy Dashboards: Employee Needs and Requirements

Svenja Polst, Patricia Kelbert[(⊠)], and Denis Feth

Fraunhofer IESE, Fraunhofer-Platz 1, 67663 Kaiserslautern, Germany
{svenja.polst, patricia.kelbert,
denis.feth}@iese.fraunhofer.de
http://www.iese.fraunhofer.de

Abstract. As work becomes increasingly digital, companies store and process more personally identifiable information of their employees. This is typically beneficial for both employees and employers, who take advantage of simplified digital work processes and tools. The problem is that there is typically no opt-out option for employees, and employers can misuse collected data for productiveness tracking and other analyses that might be problematic with regard to privacy. Furthermore, employees oftentimes do not know (lack of transparency) and cannot influence (lack of self-determination) which personally identifiable information the employer collects and uses. As a result, many employees have a variety of privacy concerns. While various online services have recently successfully implemented so-called "privacy dashboards" for their users, comparable services are virtually unknown in the workplace. In this paper, we present employees' needs and requirements with regard to transparency and self-determination in the company context. The elicitation was based on a requirements model we introduce. We conducted two workshops with participants from four research institutes and one company. The results were compared to the state of the practice and used to build models that serve as a baseline for company privacy dashboards.

Keywords: Privacy · Privacy needs · Privacy requirements · Transparency · Self-determination · Privacy dashboard · Employee privacy

1 Introduction

With the rise of digital technology, companies are increasingly processing personally identifiable information (PII) to offer services to their customers, company members and partners. Thus, the management of PII is now an integral part of companies' daily activities. Requirements for the management of PII are, at least partially, addressed by legal regulations, such as the EU-GDPR [1]. However, data protection is not only a matter of legal compliance. Individuals are becoming more and more sensitive to the risks associated with the handling of their data. In this context, data protection has become mandatory to both attract and retain customers. Nowadays, data protection is a prerequisite for every relationship (of trust) between a company and, for example, its customers and partners. Hence, it is mandatory for a company to be trustworthy towards all the stakeholders it deals with.

© Springer Nature Switzerland AG 2019
A. Moallem (Ed.): HCII 2019, LNCS 11594, pp. 429–440, 2019.
https://doi.org/10.1007/978-3-030-22351-9_29

However, when looking at the state of the art and the state of the practice, one stakeholder group is still not much considered—namely, the company's own employees. Management of recruitment files or personnel records, use of RFID badges, video surveillance or geolocation tracking—all these are examples of employees' PII that are processed by employers. Of course, companies have an intrinsic interest in legal compliance and in trust as the basis for a fruitful employment relationship. However, this does not necessarily mean that employees do not have (potentially unfulfilled) needs and requirements regarding transparency and self-determination with respect to the processing of their data.

In this paper, we aim to elicit these needs and requirements. This helps us to understand the issues and challenges employees face in that respect. Eventually, we aim to build a central "company privacy dashboard" that meets the employees' demands. The results presented in this paper are a first step towards this direction, and our project is still work in progress. The approach we took, as well as the structure of this paper, follows the process shown in Fig. 1.

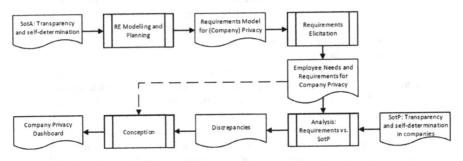

Fig. 1. Conception process for company privacy dashboards

First, we created a requirements model that serves as a baseline for the requirements elicitation and helps us to structure the employees' needs and requirements. This model is, among other factors, based on the state of the art, which is presented in Sect. 2. We then planned the requirements elicitation. Section 3 presents both the requirements model and the elicitation process. Section 4 summarizes the results of the requirements elicitation. In Sect. 5, we investigate the state of the practice regarding the implementation of transparency and self-determination in companies. The comparison between the as-is situation and the requirements we elicited shows that there are major discrepancies. All these insights are the baseline for a generic dashboard model, described in Sect. 6.

2   Related Work

There is a variety of tools tackling transparency issues, so called Transparency Enhancing Technologies (TETs). Hedbom [2] and Janic et al. [3] provide overviews of different (generic) TETs. In addition, Hedbom provides a classification of TETs.

Besides generic TETs, there is some related work in the area of privacy cockpits or privacy dashboards. However, none of the following work explicitly covers the company use-case that we have in focus.

Angulo et al. [4] developed a user interface prototype of a transparency tool that displays an overview of a user's data disclosures to online service providers and allows the user to access its personal data stored at the services' sides. In [5], they also explain how 'Data Track' can help to technically enforce the principles of ex-post transparency (i.e., "providing users with insights about what data have been processed about them and what possible consequences might arise after their data have been revealed" [6]). The focus and stakeholders differ from our work, as we target employees.

The aim of the project myneDATA [7] is to create a personal data cockpit. Matzutt et al. propose a transparent and user-controlled data market in which users can directly and consensually share their personal data with interested parties for monetary compensation. They define a simple model for such an ecosystem and identify pressing challenges arising within this model with respect to the users and data processor demands, legal obligations, and technological limitations. They propose a conceptual architecture for a trusted online platform to overcome these challenges.

The SeDaFa project [8] presents a theory-driven approach to design a vehicular privacy application that is thought to foster self-determined privacy control. Thereby, they draw back on the privacy calculus model and present potential benefits and privacy risk-related information when users have to make privacy decisions. In this study, users acknowledged the dichotomy between functional benefits and privacy-related risks. Both myneDATA and SeDaFa base their model on privacy calculus theory.

The DaSoMan [9] project aims to provide end users of apps or web applications with more transparency and decision-making options regarding the use of their data, where the system should nonetheless support legally compliant data usage. DaSoMan manages data and permissions of the end users, informs them if a data transfer allows conclusions to be drawn about their identity and enables them to change their user settings accordingly. Again, in contrast to our work, the emphasis of the project has not been put on employees' data privacy but on "connected user" data privacy.

3 Elicitation Method

In order to elicit employees' needs and requirements, we created a requirements model that covers all relevant aspects for building a solution to achieve transparency and self-determination in a company (i.e., a privacy dashboard). This model is based on the state of the art regarding transparency and self-determination and prior experiences we gained from the application of different requirements elicitation methods.

3.1 Requirements Model

The requirements model (cf. Fig. 2) describes all aspects that have an impact on the privacy dashboard concept. In the following, we define and describe all aspects of the model.

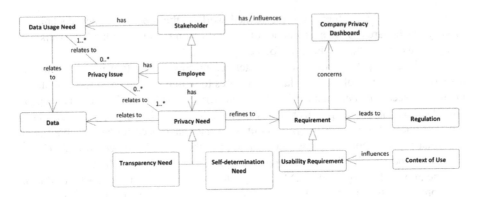

Fig. 2. Requirements model

As depicted in the model, there are several aspects that influence the *Requirements* concerning the *Company Privacy Dashboard*. The requirements stem from stakeholders, regulations, privacy needs and the context of use. *Stakeholders* are all persons that have an interest in the company privacy dashboard. Among others, employees, managers and workers councils are stakeholders. Stakeholders have requirements, or at least they influence them. Managers, for instance, decide how much financial resources are provided, thus affecting the number of features that actually will be implemented in the final dashboard. The key stakeholder in our concept is the *Employee*. Employees have privacy needs. We define *Privacy Needs* as an individual's desires or needs regarding the preservation of its privacy. There are at least two types of privacy needs: transparency needs and self-determination needs. *Transparency Needs* relate to demands for a clear visibility of aspects relevant to the employees' data and privacy [10]. *Self-Determination Needs* relate to demands that enable employees to decide on their degree of informational privacy. All privacy needs relate to the collection, storage, usage, sharing and deletion of PII. In contrast, stakeholders whose tasks depend on PII have *Data Usage Needs* with respect to PII. However, these data usage needs may conflict with the employee's privacy needs related to these data. For example, employers would like to optimize work processes based on data referring to employees, but employees would worry about being tracked and assessed. We call such a conflict a *Privacy Issue*.

The privacy needs are refined into requirements for the company privacy dashboard. While privacy needs are abstract and could also be met by organizational measures, requirements are more precise and refer to the technical solution, i.e., to the company privacy dashboard. Requirements not only emerge from privacy needs, but also from the *Context of Use* and from *Regulations*. The context in which a company privacy dashboard is intended to be used particularly affects the *Usability Requirements*. Regulations include all legal obligations, as well as internal company rules (e.g., company agreements). Our requirements model guides the elicitation of requirements.

3.2   Elicitation

The requirements elicitation is based on the requirements model presented in Sect. 3.1. Thus, we mainly need to elicit *Data, Data Usage Needs, Privacy Issues, Privacy Needs, Context of Use* and *(Usability) Requirements*. The elicitation can be done by means of workshops; except for the elicitation of data usage needs: they should be elicited by analyzing the processes inside a company. For the workshop, we defined a set of five questions that guide the elicitation.

1. "What PII do you consider worth of protection at your working place?"
   The answers to this question relate to *Data*.
2. "What are the privacy issues you see in your company?"
   The answers to this question relate to *Privacy Issues* and *Privacy Needs*.
3. "Suppose there is a tool you can use to define and monitor your company-wide privacy settings: What will be better than today in terms of respecting your privacy with the tool?"
   The answers to this question relate to *Privacy Needs* and *Requirements*.
4. "What are your wishes for the use (usability) of such a tool?"
   The answers to this question relate to the *Context of Use* and *Usability Requirements*.
5. "What would prevent you from using such a tool?"
   The answers to this question relate to *Requirements and Usability Requirements*.

Workshops can be conducted with different stakeholders as long as there is no conflict of interests. For example, employees and the CEO likely have different interests and should not participate in the same workshop in order to prevent problems like overruling. In addition, the participants should reflect diversity regarding certain characteristics that might affect their needs and requirements. We consider the following characteristics in the participant selection process:

- gender
- seniority of service and professional experience
- type of position (trainee, scientific staff, non-scientific staff)
- department (since processes might differ among the departments)
- role (e.g. department head, equal opportunities officer, member of workers council)

Ideally, larger groups are split into smaller groups of three to five persons, and the groups work in parallel in the workshop.

During the workshops, it is likely that questions and uncertainties concerning the processing of PII in the participants' companies emerge. If possible, these issues should be clarified directly at the end of the workshop—in particular, if the company already implements corresponding privacy controls. In our opinion, such a closure is beneficial so that the employees to not leave the workshop worrying that their PII are insufficiently protected.

3.3 Conduction

So far, we conducted two workshops: the first one took place with representatives from four research institutes and one company, whereas the second one took place with representatives from a single institute. The number of participants was eleven and nine, respectively. The duration of the workshop was three to four hours. The workshop will be repeated within other companies and research institutes in the near future to complement our findings and evaluate our hypotheses. The data usage needs will also be conducted in near future.

4 Elicitation Results

In the following, we present a summary of the workshop results. We present data employees consider valuable, as well as their needs and requirements with respect to the protection of these data.

4.1 Valuable Data from the Employees' Point of View

A variety of examples were named during the workshops, which can be categorized as follows:

- master data (e.g., personal contact data, bank account information)
- family-related information (e.g., marital status, children's birth certificate)
- contract information and details (e.g., fixed-term vs. permanent contract, salary)
- official certifications/documents (e.g., driver license)
- health data (e.g., number of sick notes and similar statistics, biometrics)
- photos showing the employee (e.g., snapshots taken at events)
- logs (e.g., access logs, video surveillance, time tracking, browser history)
- data that gives insights into the employees' attitudes and convictions (e.g., religion, sexual orientation)
- communication data and meta-data
- all data that can be used for location tracking or performance monitoring
- private data (i.e., data that stem from private use of company devices).

4.2 Employees' Needs and Requirements

During the workshops, participants expressed many needs and requirements. In this section, needs and requirements regarding transparency, self-determination and usability are summarized. We do not describe data usage needs, as explained in Sect. 3.1.

Transparency. Participants want to have an overview of all their PII existing within the company, including storage locations. They would like to see which person in their company has which usage permission for which of their data and for which purpose. In addition, they want to be actively informed when certain data are actually used (e.g., accessed, forwarded, deleted). In some situations, for example, when pictures depicting them are supposed to be uploaded to social media, employees even want to be informed before the actual usage happens in order to have the chance to veto.

Participants request an overview and management capabilities for all privacy-relevant information, including permissions, usages, (missing) consents and data retention times. Appropriate search functions (e.g., reverse search by data) are also demanded.

Self-determination. In general, participants expect their employers to handle their data in a legally compliant and trustworthy manner. This includes secure defaults (esp. regarding privacy) for all security measures. Besides, the most frequently demanded requirement was the possibility to give explicit consent for certain usages. This consent may be given for individual actions (e.g., uploading a particular photo to social media) or bound to a specific purpose (e.g., only for internal evaluations). The consent may include different kinds of usage constraints (e.g., anonymization, limited data retention). Furthermore, participants want to have the option to delete or correct their data.

Usability. Participants want to have a centralized tool with a GUI to manage all of their privacy settings and information and to directly access their PII. However, some of them also want privacy-relevant information to be shown outside the dashboard, directly integrated into their work processes. Critical information should always be explicitly highlighted in the dashboard. Data export functionality and barrier-free accessibility to the dashboard was also demanded by some participants.

Participants want their data to be protected. However, they themselves do not want to spend much time and effort on protecting their data. Thus, they want to be informed actively by configurable notifications. They also mentioned, though, that they do not want to get irritated by overly frequent notifications and that their work should not be disturbed by the privacy dashboard. Thus, the number of notifications needs to be limited. Alternatively, notifications could be provided on demand. Participants require default settings to be in the interest of the employee and not the employer. Changes to these settings should be possible for individual data items, as well as simultaneously for numerous data sets (batch processing). Individual settings can become very fine-grained.

Participants also want to be able to decide about the use of their PII, even if they are on a business trip. Therefore, they ask for a mobile application and offline capabilities. Moreover, they want to access the system easily. For this purpose, they are asking for single sign on, and no extra device should be required.

Our findings reflect the current state of our project. The needs and requirements were elicited mainly from employees working for research institutes. Employees in industrial and commercial enterprises might have other needs and requirements regarding a company privacy dashboard. For the elicitation of their needs and requirements, further workshops are necessary.

5 Fulfillment of Needs and Requirements in Practice

In general, dashboards are used to present a global view of a system: overview of clients, overview of applications and overview of activities (logs). These dashboards usually contain graphical representations of these entities. Regarding data protection, users are getting more and more used to set their privacy preferences on the web. Dedicated privacy dashboards are becoming increasingly common, especially for large providers such as Google, Microsoft, Instagram or Twitter. These dashboards are more or less explicit, but typically integrated into the user's profile management interface. They allow users to protect their personal sphere in a more or less detailed way by allowing or denying certain data usages by the service provider and third parties.

The requirements we obtained from the workshops revealed that employees want a similar tool in the workplace in order to determine and understand what is happening with their PII. Our preliminary results revealed that transparency is the most important functionality that a dashboard for employees PII should fulfill. Unfortunately, we could not find any reference to such privacy dashboards used within companies for employees' PII. Of course, this does not mean that employees' privacy is currently unprotected or unregulated. Thus, we compared the needs and requirements with other measures used in practice that enable transparency or self-determination.

Indeed, most of the European medium and large-sized companies have worker councils and define rules for protecting employees' rights. Regulations, such as company agreements, internal rules and organizational instructions establish boundaries, guidelines and best practices. They allow employees and employers to see where and how PII is used and are thus a transparency measure. However, due to the number and length of materials to go through, and also due to the legalese used in the regulations, searching for the information is not an easy task. For an employee, the first difficulty lies in finding the right document, then sometimes hundreds of pages have to be skimmed through, which is very time consuming. The burden of this task is the first major mismatch between the state of the practice and the requirements from the workshop participants.

Options for self-determination are even rarer in practice. Our discussions revealed that most of the time there is at best a verbal agreement, but no traceability and no fine-grained access or usage permissions are available. Explicit agreement, for example via forms, only occurs very rarely.

6 Company Privacy Dashboard Models

From our workshop results and derived requirements, we developed different models that, in combination, consider all aspects described in the previous sections. They serve as a baseline for information to be presented and measures to be controlled in the privacy dashboard. The *Data Usage Model* reflects how data is or can be used. The *Document Model* reflects where data are stored and categorized.

The *Data Usage Model* (cf. Fig. 3) describes how *Data Consumers* use *Data*, in particular *Personally Identifiable Information*. Data consumers can be either *Persons* or *Systems*. The *Usage* of *Data* is bound to a certain *Purpose*. *Usages* can be either the

Collection, Storage, Processing, Sharing or Deletion of *Data*. If some data is owned by a person (either because it is *Personal Data* or because certain processes or regulations define the ownership), the usage requires an explicit *Consent*, which is technically implemented by *Permissions*. For our dashboard, both usages and permissions are important concepts. While permissions describe what a data consumer can potentially do with the data, usage describes what a data consumer has actually done. In general, usage is a special type of *Action*. At work, a lot of actions are executed (e.g., as part of *Processes* or *Projects*) that do not include the technical usage of data, such face-to-face communication. However, these actions can still be relevant from a privacy perspective.

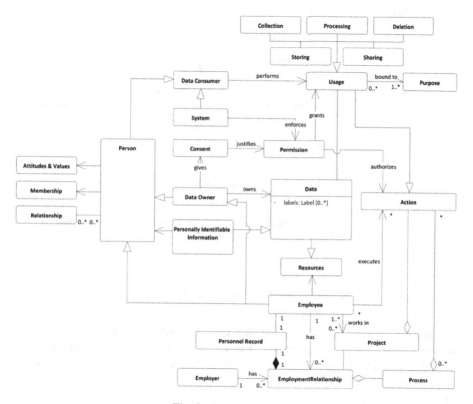

Fig. 3. Data usage model

Obviously, privacy always relates to individuals with certain *Attitudes and Values*. Also, persons have *Relationships* to other persons, and *they* are both data consumer and *Data Owner*, depending on the use case and the data. As we are focusing on company privacy dashboards, the main *Person* of interest is the *Employee*. An *Employee* is in an *Employment Relationship* with an *Employer*, which gives the legal justification for many data usages. In particular, the *Personnel Record* contains a variety of documents containing *Personal Data*.

Different *Labels* can be assigned to data. They characterize data in more details and enable employees to define privacy rules based on these labels (e.g., inhibit access to 'secret' data). Examples for labels include the classification of data (e.g., whether data are secret), the scope (i.e., whether it is personal or business data) and the category. For example, the EU-GDPR defines 'special categories of personal data, as "ethnic origin, political opinions, religious or philosophical beliefs, or trade union membership, and the processing of genetic data, biometric data for the purpose of uniquely identifying a natural person, data concerning health or data concerning a natural person's sex life or sexual orientation" [1].

A *Document Model* (cf. Fig. 4), which describes where data are stored, complements the *Data Usage Model*.

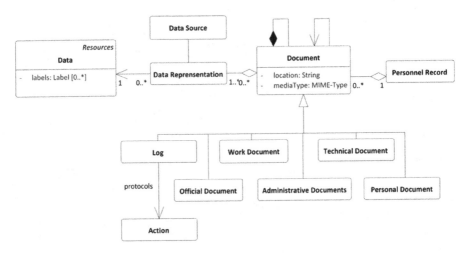

Fig. 4. Document model

The core element is a *Document* that contains *Data Representations* of *Data*, stemming from a particular data source. The idea is that the same data can be contained in different documents (i.e., copies or derivatives). Documents can contain or relate to other documents and have a certain *MIME type*. They can be part of the *Personnel Record*.

For our dashboard concept, we consider the following document types: *Personal Documents, Official Documents, Work Documents, Administrative Documents, Technical Documents* and *Logs*. *Personal Documents* are documents that stem from personal use of the company's infrastructure or systems (e.g., if business email is allowed to be used for personal purposes). *Official Documents* are documents that stem from public or similar authorities (e.g., driver's license). *Work Documents* are documents an employee produces during work (e.g., project results). *Administrative Documents* are documents that the employer produces about an employee (e.g., payroll). *Technical Documents* are documents that relate to IT systems (e.g., configurations). Finally, *Logs* are special documents that contain data that protocolize certain activities.

7 Conclusion and Future Work

We elicited and presented data protection needs of employees and their privacy requirements on their employers. Our research showed that, especially in larger companies, the enforcement of privacy protection is rather mature. Measures are regulated in company agreements, instructions, and security concepts, and they have to be aligned with the local workers councils. However, when comparing the state of the practice with the needs and requirements we elicited, there are still major discrepancies with respect to transparency and self-determination. Even though the above-mentioned agreements and regulation exist, they are oftentimes hard to find, to follow and to understand for the average employee. Of course, this leads to some kind of lose-lose situation. While companies spend a lot of time on effective data protection, they fall short in communicating these efforts to their employees. Also, static documents cannot implement one of the most urgent needs employees reported during our elicitation—namely, there desire to be informed about certain events (such as data sharing) and to have a veto option. In summary, our main conclusion is that a central technical system for the management of privacy (i.e., a privacy dashboard) would be a major advantage for employees and employers alike, as it would strengthen both transparency and self-determination.

We presented two models that are meant to serve as a baseline for the implementation of such dashboards. However, many aspects are still open and need to be further explored. These open issues include a detailed user interface and interaction concept, leading to high levels of usability and user experience. Also, the technical integration into current company infrastructure is a challenging open issue. While this integration might be rather straightforward for transparency, enforcement of privacy settings (i.e., self-determination) presumably requires major changes in the current IT systems. Finally, another interesting issue is whether the introduction of a central privacy management tool also entails new risks, especially regarding privacy. All of these questions need to be resolved for a comprehensive privacy dashboard concept and are thus part of our future work.

Acknowledgment. The research presented in this paper is supported by the German Ministry of Education and Research project "TrUSD – Transparente und selbstbestimmte Ausgestaltung der Datennutzung im Unternehmen" (grant number 16KIS0898). The sole responsibility for the content of this document lies with the authors.

References

1. European Union (2016): REGULATION (EU) 2016/679 OF THE EUROPEAN PARLIAMENT AND OF THE COUNCIL of 27 April 2016 on the protection of natural persons with regard to the processing of personal data and on the free movement of such data, and repealing Directive 95/46/EC (General Data Protection Regulation). http://eur-lex.europa.eu/legal-content/EN/TXT/HTML/?uri=CELEX:32016R0679. Accessed 15 Feb 2018
2. Hedbom, H.: A survey on transparency tools for enhancing privacy. In: Matyáš, V., Fischer-Hübner, S., Cvrček, D., Švenda, P. (eds.) Privacy and Identity 2008. IAICT, vol. 298, pp. 67–82. Springer, Heidelberg (2009). https://doi.org/10.1007/978-3-642-03315-5_5

3. Janic, M., Wijbenga, J.P., Veugen, T.: Transparency enhancing tools (TETs): an overview. In: Workshop on Socio-Technical Aspects in Security and Trust, STAST (2013)
4. Angulo, J., Fischer-Hübner, S., Pulls, T., Wästlund, E.: Usable transparency with the data track: a tool for visualizing data disclosures. In: Proceedings of the 33rd Annual ACM Conference Extended Abstracts on Human Factors in Computing Systems - CHI EA 2015, pp. 1803–1808. ACM Press, Seoul (2015)
5. Fischer-Hübner, S., Angulo, J., Karegar, F., Pulls, T.: Transparency, privacy and trust – technology for tracking and controlling my data disclosures: does this work? In: Habib, S. M., Vassileva, J., Mauw, S., Mühlhäuser, M. (eds.) IFIPTM 2016. IAICT, vol. 473, pp. 3–14. Springer, Cham (2016). https://doi.org/10.1007/978-3-319-41354-9_1
6. Murmann, P., Fischer-Hubner, S.: Tools for achieving usable ex post transparency: a survey. IEEE Access 5, 22965–22991 (2017)
7. Matzutt, R., et al.: myneData (2017)
8. Walter, J., Abendroth, B., Agarwal, N.: PRICON: self-determined privacy in the connected car motivated by the privacy calculus model. In: Proceedings of the 16th International Conference on Mobile and Ubiquitous Multimedia - MUM 2017, pp. 421–427. ACM Press, Stuttgart (2017)
9. DaSoMan - Daten-Souveränitäts-Manager. https://dasoman.de/
10. Hansen, M.: Marrying transparency tools with user-controlled identity management. In: Fischer-Hübner, S., Duquenoy, P., Zuccato, A., Martucci, L. (eds.) Privacy and Identity 2007. ITIFIP, vol. 262, pp. 199–220. Springer, Boston (2008). https://doi.org/10.1007/978-0-387-79026-8_14

Privacy and Power Implications of Web Location of Personal Data Authenticators

Kirsten E. Richards[⊠]

United States Naval Academy, Annapolis, USA
krichard@usna.edu

Abstract. Knowledge of personal data enjoys a long history of use in authentication. Given expanding personal data availability, authentication systems are at risk from sharing data online. This study explores the discoverability of the data – specifically, whether individuals tasked with finding the data were able to accurately identify it using public online sources. The location of successfully located data reveals patterns of data availability and demonstrates vulnerabilities of personal data, which inform current and future models of authentication from a human computer interaction (HCI) perspective. Data location suggests the control users exert of their personal data availability in the United States. The impact of personal control is vital to understanding privacy behaviors, human computer interaction around privacy and authentication, building usable authenticators, and providing meaningful advances in security and privacy.

Keywords: Authentication and identification ·
Privacy implications of authentication technologies ·
Authentication and identification: security and usability of combinations
of authentication factors · Human factors: behavior-based cybersecurity ·
Human factors: human identification of websites

1 Introduction

HCI around personal data significantly influence privacy and security. User behavior has long flummoxed studies in this area leading to the well-known "weakest link" and "privacy paradox" problems (cite). Meanwhile, privacy perspectives have widely shifted from a "right to be left alone", to "control" to "obscurity" (cite), highlighting the lack of personal self-determination in online data privacy.

The exploration of online personal data highlights the problems of data availability that compromises the integrity of authentication systems and personal efficacy in data protection as revealed by the location of personal data. The data selected for the study focused on personal data used in authentication as a subset of more general data to improve understanding of personal influence on data that is generally significant to human computer interactions (HCI) and speaks to broader privacy interests.

A. Moallem (Ed.): HCII 2019, LNCS 11594, pp. 441–451, 2019.
https://doi.org/10.1007/978-3-030-22351-9_30

2 Background

Key to understanding the current issues around privacy, power and authentication is the coalescence big data, personal data, data control and personal data use in authentication.

2.1 Personal Data Availability

The web and evolution of big data revolutionized personal data availability. As companies and governments use, and make data available, they contribute to personal data availability. Individuals also have unprecedented abilities to self-propagate personal data [1]. "Neither criminal skill, nor advanced technical knowledge, nor even rudimentary understanding of password cracking tools, is required to access this personal information which is believed to be attainable readily" [2].

Personal data is exposed on online social media, where seemingly insignificant data could compromise security [3]. Previous studies have indicated that personal data exposure may vary widely and while many studies have explored privacy attitudes and sharing behavior [4, 5].

A movement towards real identities online requirement altered the nature of online identity and made individuals identifiable by name across platforms [6, 7]. One study demonstrated links in social networks reveal private information that users do not wish to reveal, such as political affiliation [8]. Although users may take steps to obscure specific data, such as the names of children, this information may also be revealed secondarily, for example, by other members of the social network [6]. While some research looks at personal data sharing, less attention has been dedicated to empirically understanding what data is available and where it is located and who controls it, particularly with a direct link to security considerations.

It is known that specific information of interest to authentication protocols is available online. Data used in authentication and security protocols, such as a mother's maiden name, can be retrieved from public records [9]. Pet's names were slightly harder to guess than human names, but are also vulnerable to statistical analysis. [10, 11]. In summary, we know that a vast amount of personal data is publicly available online and that the user does not always directly control this data.

2.2 Personal Data Use in Authentication

The contribution of personal data to account compromise are recognized and well addressed in the literature [1, 12–14]. However, personal data continues in use for authentication because of user behavior and by design.

There is a fundamental gap between "good" passwords and human cognition [15–18]. The design of a "good" password is a superb example of failure to attend to the "human" aspect of HCI. Changing how humans interact with passwords is an unlikely solution with users most often compensating by the use of personal data [16]. According to Richards, 2017, the problem of personal data use in authentication is not limited to password authenticators, "some points of personal data connected to other various authentication schemes" [2]. For example, knowledge of social relationships is discoverable online and useful in determining social information used in some types of 5th factor authentication [19].

2.3 Personal Data Control

Control of personal data is clearly an important factor influencing data availability. Individually certainly, and often copiously share their personal data online. Compounding the security problem presented by wide spread personal data sharing through online venues, is the failure of privacy controls on popular Social Networking Sites (SNS) to accurately reflect user intentions [20]. Limits to privacy control render some aspects of availability, and by extension, security, meaningless on an individual user level.

On a broader social level, control over data is also evident in secondary parties, such as government and corporations. Personal information is increasingly collected in a wide variety of circumstances [21]. At times, this data has been reverse engineered to reveal personal information [22, 23], demonstrating the secondary nature of data control. Many different entities may actually be responsible for personal data proliferation on the web [24].

2.4 Background Summary

Lacking in research is a clear relationship between personal data stored online in a variety of public or semi-public venues such as SNS and personal information used in authentication protocols. Furthermore, the ease of discovering personal data by other individuals and the Web locations posing the greatest practical threat are unknown. Thus, while personal information online poses a credible threat to security accomplished through password protection and secondary authentication using personal data; the empirical extent of the threat is unknown.

The study described seeks to clearly connect specific personal data to web locations most likely to reveal accuracy. By establishing this connection, the power dynamic of personal data becomes more readily recognizable.

3 Methods

The study was designed to reflect previous models based around acquaintances, friends, or family members guessing personal data of other individuals [25]. Replacing the acquaintances in the model, strangers to the participants volunteered to search public, online spaces and make their best guess about the personal data.

3.1 Participants

Two different groups of participants were recruited to a multiphase study. One group provided permission to search for their data and one group to look for the data online. These two groups replace acquaintance pairs in previous study models.

Four source participants provided basic demographic data, photograph and verification of data retrieved. Four source participants were recruited to represent a variety of backgrounds, particularly with regard to age and gender. Two female and two male recruits from a variety of age groupings are recruited, reflecting recruitment patterns in similar studies [25]. Pew's research study groupings for studies of social media use which include adults ages 18–29, 30–49, 50–64 and over 65 [26]. One adult was recruited from each age group to represent a spectrum of online engagement and data exposure across various generations. Participant DK is a 58-year-old female. OV is a 31-year-old male. GC is a 26-year-old female and KT is a 65 year old male.

Seeker participants, all unacquainted with the source participants, used free, online resources to look for the particular personal data. They reported the personal data they found – their best guess at the answer, along with a location, the time taken to find the data and their perception of the difficulty of locating the data. Between 35 and 50 seeker participants were recruited for each source yielding up to 205 responses to each data point.

3.2 Personal Data

The personal data points include commonly used questions for secondary authentication as well as the personal data most commonly used in passwords derived from currently available literature on the topics of password creation and secondary authentication. The participants attempted to locate the following data: mother's maiden name, middle name, mobile phone number, pet's names, children's names, and nicknames. These data points were selected based on their significance in authentication protocols and previous studies of guessable authenticators. Seeker participants used a survey to record the personal data found, location of data, the time searched, and the seeker's perception of the difficulty of discovery on a Likert scale.

3.3 Procedure

The seeker participants were first recruited and provided with the IRB approved consent. After consent, they provided their name, city and state location and a photograph. Personal data was not collected at this time. This decision was made to protect seeker participants. If personal data was not recovered from publicly available web information, then that personal data would remain protected in the course of the study and could not be compromised.

The seeker participant was provided with the name and city and state of the source participants and asked to identify the source participant as a stranger, that is, someone with which they have not previously communicated directly either in person or online. The data provided the seeker participant included a photograph of the source participant, determined necessary in the pilot study. None of the biographical description includes any part of the personal data sought. For each point of personal data, the seeker participant provides the requested personal data and may supply multiple guesses, if desired. This design is reflected in other studies as well [25]. Additionally, the approximate time as reported by the seeker spent locating the data, the location of the data, and the perceived difficulty of locating the data were obtained. The web based survey allowed for timing the beginning and end of the web survey. Following seeker participant data collection, the source participants verified the accuracy of collected data.

4 Analysis

Analysis of the data collected included an in-depth exploration of accuracy, time and difficulty, the results of which can be found elsewhere [2]. To understand the data control dynamics associated with data availability, the data location is highlighted here with references to accuracy.

Location was evaluated post facto with analysis of similarities and differences between source participants to providing insight into areas of vulnerability in personal data on the web [27]. The data was then categorized by the researchers. A detailed summary by each data point is discussed in the results. Due to space limitations, the data set is not provided here. The detailed data is available elsewhere [2].

The methodology design allows for examinations of multiple aspects of HCI in personal data. One of the most interesting was the exploring the sources of the personal data online provided by a variety of actors such as the source participants themselves, family and friends, government entities, businesses and employers.

5 Results

Every personal data point was discovered, although not for every source participant. One of the more interesting discoveries was that several important personal data points were not directly self-propagated by source participants, but instead were primarily made available by government entities and commercial enterprises for several of the data points. Official state record systems were utilized to provide accurate answers, as were commercial enterprises such as Ancestory.com, online newspapers, and even RateMyProfessor. Although social media, particularly Facebook, social media was the most searched location, it was not a consistent source of accurate information for several of the data points. Detailed results of location data are provided for each source participant followed by a discussion of the significance with reference to each data point. Data location is non-specific and anonymized to protect source participants.

Data locations were most frequently reported as direct Uniform Resource Locators (URLs). For this reason, data locations were not published directly, as this would reveal the identities of the participants. Rather, all the data locations were tabulated and summarized. The locations are reported both as individual, unique entities, such as "Facebook" or "Ancestery.com" and also as groupings for analysis. At times, participants also reported non-specific locations, such as "checked everywhere" or "Google search". These types of identifies occurred most frequently when reporting failure to find information – such as concluding that a participant did not have children or a pet.

5.1 Detailed Results by Source Participant

Each source participant's location data are provided below and are organized by datapoint. "Most searched" location refers to the most frequently reported source of data, even when that data is most accurate. Accuracy is not the primary focus of this particular analysis, but a brief discussion of accuracy designations are necessary to understand the locations described.

In analysis, it became impractical to categorize data as "correct" or "incorrect", as there were multiple instances of partially correct data, such as identifying two of three children's names correctly or in cases were multiple guesses were provided, some of which were correct. To clearly report these types of cases, multiple categories were developed. "Correct" referred to completely, complete data accurate data. No erroneous guesses were made for "correct" data and no data was mission. For data designed as "Correct/incomplete", all the guesses provided were correct, but not all the data possible was identified. This category was particularly prevalent with Children's Names and Pets, when multiple correct guesses were necessary for a complete set of data. "Partially correct" designates situations were both correct and incorrect data were provided, for example, Children's names were identified correctly, but additional names were included that were not correct. Finally, "Incorrect" is differentiated from "Not Found". "Incorrect" data was reported as accurate by seeker participants while "Not found" data were acknowledge by seeker participants as unidentified. A detailed analysis of accuracy can be found elsewhere [27].

Mother's Maiden Name. For mother's maiden name, all correct data was located only on government or commercial sources. In every case, Facebook was the most popularly searched location, but in only one case did any social media lead to a correct result. Official state record systems, commercial birth record systems and obituary notices provided accurate answers in three of four cases. Facebook was the most frequently searched location in all cases.

DK – No correct results were identified.

GC – The only correct result originated from a government source, the Minnesota Official Marriage System.

KT – Correct results came exclusively from commercial sources including a Newspaper Obituary and commercial genealogy source: familysearch.org.

OV – Mother's Maiden Name was searched for and discovered in a variety of locations. 31 total distinct locations were reported. When compared to accuracy, all the correct answers, save one, were located using social media. The remaining correct answer was located using commercial genealogy site Moose-Roots Birth Records.

Nickname. Facebook was the most popular search location and the most frequently cited for correct answers, however, the rate of accuracy was lower than other search locations. Many different sources provided correct results.

DK – Facebook the most popular search location and was correct in some instances. Correct answers were also located using Google, Newspaper Obituary Notices and Truthfinder.

GC – All correct answers were located on Facebook

KT – Correct answers were supplied from a variety of locations, including Facebook, Rate my Professor, Google, and Truthfinder and an employer's website. The rate of accuracy was lower for Facebook with an accuracy of Interestingly, while Facebook was the most searched, it did not provide the most consistent correct answers. 21.43% of answers supplied from Facebook were correct compared to 75.00% correct guesses from Rate My Professor.

OV – Correct answers were located via Facebook, Linkedin and Twitter. Finally, unspecified "Birth Records" also provided accurate results.

Child(ren's) Name(s). The only correct answer containing accurately identified children across all seeker participants for all source participants was located on intelius. com and applied to KT. In the case of OV, "none" and synonyms or variants such as "doesn't have any" were coded by the researchers and considered correct answers. All other answers ranged from partially correct to incorrect.

DK – The partially correct/incomplete and correct/incomplete answers were derived exclusively from Facebook. No correct answers were discovered by searchers.

GC – The partially correct/incomplete and correct/incomplete answers were derived exclusively from Facebook. No correct answers were discovered by searchers.

KT – The one accurate answer was provided from a commercial source intelius.com. Partially correct/incomplete and correct/incomplete were located using Facebook. Some non-specific data was also supplied, such as "Public Records", "People search" and "Image search" that yielded correct data. At some points, participants provided more insight into the search process, "circular queries using bits of information mined by google search links > [Newspaper website with obituary]" and, "her wife's Facebook page" [2].

OV – "None" was considered a correct answer for Children's Name, rendering it a particularly interesting search. Searchers support correct conclusions in a variety of ways, including citing Facebook, White Pages, Twitter, Quanki, Spokeo and Google. "Lack of evidence" and "Search on multiple sites".

Pet's Name. Facebook was the most frequent source for correct answers. It was also the most cited as a source for lack of evidence leading to a "None" conclusion by seeker participants. Some reported locations also gave insight into the search process for a "None" conclusion - "lack of evidence on social media". Accurate answers were also obtained from blogs, Snap chat, Twitter, unspecified "social media", Twitter, Bing, Google, My Heritage, Pipl, Spokeo, Snapchat, Truthfinder and Yahoo also yielded accurate results.

DK – Correct answers were obtained from a variety of sources including Google, Yahoo, Pipl and Bing and My Heritage, unspecified, "Social Media", and Facebook.

GC – Correct sources included Google, Truthfinder and Facebook.

KT – One successful search yielded a correct result from Facebook.

OV – Correct data was discovered in 8 total distinct locations were reported. Facebook, Twitter, nonspecific, "His Blog", LinkedIn. The commercial source Google was also a frequently reported source. Two participants also added "no evidence on multiple sites" in their responses. Uniquely for this point and participant, all given answers were correct.

Middle Name. This data point was accurately reported from employers, government records, social media and commercial enterprises. It was by far the most accurately discovered data.

DK – White Pages is the most popular search location. Correct answers were located using White Pages, 411 and an employer's website.

GC – The Ohio Resident Database is the most popular search location, followed by Nuwber. Been Verified, Google, White Pages, MyLife, Truthfinder, VoterRecords, Peoplesmart, Whitepages, Quanki, and Instant Checkmate provided accurate answers as well.

KT – Correct answers were located via Facebook, White Pages, Truthfinder, Youtube, Public Records 360, Nuwber, Mylife, Spokeo, Been Verified, Google, White Pages, and Yellow Pages. Facebook was the most frequently searched source.

OV – White Pages is the most popular search location. Two participants also "guessed" after discovering an initial. One of these guesses was correct and one was incorrect. Correct answers included White Pages, Been Verified, an employer's website, Academia.edu, and "Guess" provided accurate information.

Mobile Phone Number. Correct answers were located on social media venue Youtube for KT. Commercial venues Been Verified, Facebook, Pipl, Spokeo, and White-Pages each provided a correct answer for OV. Finally, a partially correct answer was located using commercial venue Truthfinder.

DK – No correct answer was located.

GC – No completely correct answer was located. Facebook remained the most popular search location, followed by WhitePages and Google, but the popular searches did not yield correct answers. A Partially Correct/Incomplete answer was found via commercial source, Truthfinder.

KT – Nuwber and Been Verified were the most popular search locations. Correct answers were only successfully located on Youtube. The researchers viewed the video using the link and discovered that it was a video introducing a course taught by the source participant in the course of employment.

OV – Facebook remained the most popular search location, followed by White Pages and Google. Correct answers were discovered using Facebook, Been Verified, Pipl, Spokeo, and White Pages.

6 Discussion

Data availability and the location of data reveal key factors in privacy, particularly as they relate to data used in authentication models. Facebook was the most frequently cited source of personal data searching, it did not always lead to most accurate results for some data points. This was particularly true of data points that were more difficult to find, such as mother's maiden name.

Some the effects of obscurity through data volume were observed in the data. Many data points involved some amount of "too much" data to find actual accurate answers. This was particularly true of the female search participants, where there were many inaccurate guesses compared to mobile phone number, which most seekers realized they did not find accurately. Obscurity seemed to be more effective in the social media than in other sources.

With regard to data location, source participants had direct power or influence over some of their data placement. *Mother's maiden name* did not appear to be self-propagated in most instances, with primary correct locations of discovery on government and commercial sites. In contrast, *Pet's names, Nicknames, Children's names and Middle names* were very discoverable via social media as well as from numerous other venues as compared to *Mother's maiden name* and *Mobile phone number*. *Mobile phone numbers* were only discovered on one social media source (Youtube) and on multiple commercial venues.

One of the most interesting observations, therefore, is that highly available data is highly availability from a wide variety of sources. However, less available data, which would therefore be better candidates as potential authenticators, were not primarily self-propagated. A key lesson therefore, is to design authentication systems around data that is more difficult to locate and assure, as much as possible, that this data is not propagated outside of the user's control. Users may also be cautioned about self-propagation of data that are used in authentication models.

Future research is needed to establish more clarity on other data used for authentication. Data which is used for authentication should not be propagated on government websites or by employers and that authentication models should be designed around data which is empirically more obscure on the web. There may be some reason to believe that there is a level of protection for individuals in the vast array of data in online social media. More empirical research is needed to discover which data can safely be used in authentication models and what data needs to be considered private, and treated as private by all entities involved in online data publication, both individual users and governments and corporations.

7 Limitations

Many limiting factors were present in this study. A desire to protect source participants – therefore, the study avoided any deeply sensitive data and did not collect personal data from source participants in advance of the search process. As a result, it was not feasible to reward correct guesses, however, theoretically most people would have some motivation for some kind of reward for searching for personal data.

All participants were volunteers, and so privacy attitudes of source participants and the skills of seeker participants also influenced outcomes in unknown ways. Studies that examine privacy attitudes and data availability are currently planned.

Personal data for search were selected on the basis of their significance to authentication. Additional data points were ruled out because of privacy concerns. Repeated experimentation with additional data points are recommended for understanding more about availability of personal data and its significance to authentication.

8 Future Work

Current work by the researchers is seeking to provide additional studies with approximately 60 source participants to expand an understanding of the patterns revealed in this study. More work is needed to establish more clearly which individuals or organizations control data availability and how this data may be protected on the context of authenticators.

As new authenticators are explored, it is recommended that serious consideration be given to the availability of data and how the availability may change over time. It will also be vital to attend to ownership of authenticating data and insure that the data is not easily obtained and perpetuated.

In an era of big data, understanding how data relates to authentication and whom is in control of authenticating data is vital to continued security. The development of new models of authentication and the improvement of current models need to consider the context of publicly available data and seek at a minimum to make the data required to deceptively authenticate more difficult to obtain. Understanding privacy and security related behaviors in the context of data sharing may help elucidate complex user sharing behaviors.

Current studies are planned or underway that explore gender differences in data availability, personality as related to data privacy, control and sharing behaviors, and education and income as context for data availability and sharing behaviors.

Acknowledgements. The study described was conducted while the author was a GAANN fellow at the University of Maryland, Baltimore County. The support and mentorship of Dr. A.F. Norcio is gratefully acknowledged.

References

1. Schneier, B.: Schneier on security: privacy and control. J. Priv. Confidentiality **2**(1), 3–4 (2010)
2. Richards, K.E.: Risk analysis of the discoverability of personal data used for primary and secondary authentication. University of Maryland Baltimore County, MD, US (2017)
3. Reeder, R., Schechter, S.: When the password doesn't work: secondary authentication for websites. IEEE Secur. Priv. Mag. **9**(2), 43 (2011)
4. Acquisti, A., Gross, R.: Imagined communities: awareness, information sharing, and privacy on the Facebook. In: Danezis, G., Golle, P. (eds.) PET 2006. LNCS, vol. 4258, pp. 36–58. Springer, Heidelberg (2006). https://doi.org/10.1007/11957454_3
5. Beldad, A., de Jong, M., Steehouder, M.: A comprehensive theoretical framework for personal information-related behaviors on the internet. Inf. Soc. **27**(4), 220–232 (2011)
6. Schau, H.J., Gilly, M.C.: We are what we post? Self-presentation in personal web space. J. Consum. Res. **30**(3), 385–404 (2003)
7. van Dijck, J.: 'You have one identity': performing the self on Facebook and LinkedIn. Media Cult. Soc. **35**(2), 199–215 (2013)
8. Lindamood, J., et al.: Inferring private information using social network data. In: Proceedings of the 18th International Conference on World Wide Web, pp. 1145–1146. ACM, Madrid (2009)
9. Griffith, V., Jakobsson, M.: Messin' with texas deriving mother's maiden names using public records. In: Ioannidis, J., Keromytis, A., Yung, M. (eds.) ACNS 2005. LNCS, vol. 3531, pp. 91–103. Springer, Heidelberg (2005). https://doi.org/10.1007/11496137_7
10. Bonneau, J., Just, M., Matthews, G.: What's in a name? In: Sion, R. (ed.) FC 2010. LNCS, vol. 6052, pp. 98–113. Springer, Heidelberg (2010). https://doi.org/10.1007/978-3-642-14577-3_10
11. Rabkin, A.: Personal knowledge questions for fallback authentication. In: ACM International Conference Proceeding Series, p. 13 (2008)
12. Oravec, J.A.: Deconstructing "personal privacy" in an age of social media: information control and reputation mangement dimensions. Int. J. Acad. Bus. World **6**(1), 95–104 (2012)
13. Dlamini, M.T., Eloff, J.P., Eloff, M.M.: Information security: the moving target. Comput. Secur. **28**(3/4), 189–198 (2009)

14. Pavlou, P.A.: State of the information privacy literature: where are we now and where should we go? MIS Q. **35**(4), 977–988 (2011)
15. Bonneau, J., et al.: The quest to replace passwords: a framework for comparative evaluation of web authentication schemes. In: IEEE Symposium on Security and Privacy, pp. 553–567 (2012)
16. Brown, A.S., et al.: Generating and remembering passwords. Appl. Cogn. Psychol. **18**(6), 641–651 (2004)
17. Vu, K.-P.L., et al.: Improving password security and memorability to protect personal and organizational information. Int. J. Hum Comput Stud. **65**(8), 744–757 (2007)
18. Sasse, M., Brostoff, S., Weirich, D.: Transforming the 'weakest link' a human-computer interaction approach to usable and effective security. BT Technol. J. **19**(3) (2001)
19. Polakis, I., et al.: All your face are belong to us: breaking Facebook's social authentication. In: Proceedings of the 28th Annual Computer Security Applications Conference, pp. 399–408. ACM, Orlando (2012)
20. Madejski, M., Johnson, M., Bellovin, S.M.: A study of privacy settings errors in an online social network. In: 2012 IEEE International Conference on Pervasive Computing & Communications Workshops, p. 340 (2012)
21. Il-Horn, H., et al.: Overcoming online information privacy concerns: an information-processing theory approach. J. Manag. Inf. Syst. **24**(2), 13–42 (2007)
22. Lee, N.: Consumer privacy in the age of big data. In: Lee, N. (ed.) Facebook Nation: Total Information Awareness, pp. 139–147. Springer, New York (2014). https://doi.org/10.1007/978-1-4614-5308-6_4
23. Lo, B.: Sharing clinical trial data: maximizing benefits, minimizing riskbenefits and risks of sharing clinical trial databenefits and risks of sharing clinical trial data. JAMA **313**(8), 793–794 (2015)
24. Benson, V., Saridakis, G., Tennakoon, H.: Information disclosure of social media users: Does control over personal information, user awareness and security notices matter? Inf. Technol. People **28**(3), 426–441 (2015)
25. Schechter, S., Brush, A.J.B., Egelman, S.: Its o secret: measuring the reliability of authentication via 'secret' questions. In: Proceedings of the 2009 30th IEEE Symposium on Security and Privacy, pp. 375–390 (2009)
26. Brenner, J., Smith, A.: 72% of online adults are social networking site users. Pew Internet & American Life Project, Washington, DC (2013)
27. Richards, K.E., Norcio, A.F.: Exploring the discoverability of personal data used for authentication. In: Nicholson, D. (ed.) AHFE 2017. AISC, vol. 593, pp. 97–105. Springer, Cham (2018). https://doi.org/10.1007/978-3-319-60585-2_11

Trust in Automated Software Repair

The Effects of Repair Source, Transparency, and Programmer Experience on Perceived Trustworthiness and Trust

Tyler J. Ryan[1(✉)], Gene M. Alarcon[2], Charles Walter[3],
Rose Gamble[3], Sarah A. Jessup[2], August Capiola[2],
and Marc D. Pfahler[1]

[1] General Dynamics Information Technology, Dayton, OH, USA
`tyler.ryan.ctr@us.af.mil`
[2] Air Force Research Laboratory, Wright-Patterson AFB, Dayton, OH, USA
[3] University of Tulsa, Tulsa, OK, USA

Abstract. Automation and autonomous systems are becoming increasingly pervasive in society, as are the software systems that control them. There is a need for safe and secure software systems. Automated code repair provides a promising solution. The present research investigates programmers' perceptions of trustworthiness and trust in automated code repair, how those perceptions and intentions differed from code ostensibly repaired by a human, and the effects of repair transparency. The present research comprises two studies, each with a unique sample. The first sample included inexperienced developers ($N = 24$), and the second sample included experienced developers ($N = 24$). Participants were presented with five different pieces of code before and after being repaired by an automated code repair program, and were asked to rate the trustworthiness of the repairs and whether they would endorse using the code. Each study was a 2×2 between-subjects design with repeated measures. The first factor manipulated the purported source of the repairs (human vs automated code repair program). The second factor manipulated the transparency of the repairs (deleted vs commented out). Results suggest that inexperienced developers find automated code repair more trustworthy than repairs made by a human. Both experienced and inexperienced developers trusted the human repairer less after reviewing the repairs, but did not significantly differ in their intentions to trust the automated code repair program after reviewing the repairs.

Keywords: Computer code · Automated code repair · Cyber security · Trust · Genetic algorithms

1 Introduction

Cyber security has become a topic of major concern since the rise of computing and the internet. The loss of personally identifying information (e.g., [1]), accidents due to code issues (e.g., [2]), and banking errors (e.g., [3]) have increased the demand for safe, secure, and resilient systems. However, no system is completely secure if it operates on

This is a U.S. government work and not under copyright protection in the U.S.;
foreign copyright protection may apply 2019
A. Moallem (Ed.): HCII 2019, LNCS 11594, pp. 452–470, 2019.
https://doi.org/10.1007/978-3-030-22351-9_31

an outward facing network. Security vulnerabilities have led computer programmers to work on minimizing threats in a timely manner, reducing the down time of systems and reducing the amount of information an outsider threat can access. One response to cyber-attacks is the use of automated code repair tools that can patch vulnerabilities, such as Clear View [4], ARMOR [5], and GenProg [6]. Although these tools are still in their infancy and not yet deployable to use at runtime, the design of such systems is critically important for human operators. If operators do not trust the automated code repair tool, they will not deploy the tool, leading to vulnerabilities not being patched in a timely manner. Research on psychological principles that influence trust can help software engineers understand what design aspects lead to proper trust calibration (i.e., increasing user trust as a function of system effectiveness; see [7]), which can improve automated code repair tool accessibility and usability. The current study seeks to explore the factors that influence human trust in the GenProg [6] automated code repair tool.

1.1   Automated Code Repair Tools

Software is now embedded in almost every aspect of modern life from industrial control systems, banking software, "Internet of Things", and wearable technology. This ubiquity of software has led to a need for secure, efficient, and timely code repairs. However, the number of defects in software often exceeds the number of assets available to deal with them [8]. Technology exists for automatically detecting vulnerabilities in software such as through the use of static analysis [9, 10], intrusion detection [11], and software diversity methods [12]. However, identifying the issue is only half of the problem; the issue must still be fixed. Research in computer science has started employing evolutionary computation [13] and genetic programming [6] to repair code when predefined test cases fail. Genetic programming utilizes genetic mutations to change and test repairs to software, reducing the time and money spent on code repair [14]. Potential repairs are constructed offline and retested before being placed into the code.

Advances have been made in the field of genetic programming over the course of the past decade, with the GenProg program expanding from the C programming language to include the Java language [15]. However, little research has explored genetic programming from a human factors perspective. As the code repair software uses genetic mutations to find adequate solutions for bugs, it remains to be seen how programmers perceive such patches and repairs. As noted in the human factors literature, users must trust a system or the system will not be implemented [7].

1.2   Trust in Automation

Trust has been defined as the willingness to be vulnerable to another with the expectation of a positive outcome [16]. Although this definition was originally adopted for studying human-human trust, research has extended the definition of trust to human-automation relationships. Trust is an important issue in automation design as trust can facilitate reliance behaviors [7]. Sheridan [17] noted that the level of trust an operator has in an automated system can significantly influence how the automated system is used. The use of automation and its reliability does not always follow a one-to-one relationship. People may rely too little on capable automated systems (under trust) or too much on systems that do not operate at their assumed level (over trust). Over-trusting automation can lead to accidents, such as when drivers do not pay attention to the autopilot functions of Tesla cars [18]. Conversely, under-trust can also lead to accidents, such as not utilizing automation that helps alleviate driver fatigue when the human operator is too tired to drive safely (e.g., driver lane assist). As such, proper trust calibration is desired in contexts in which humans interact with automated aids.

1.3   Trust in Code

Recently, the findings from interpersonal and automation trust literatures have been applied to research on computer programming. Research in the computer and psychological sciences has explored how programmers perceive computer code [19]. However, until recently no research has explored how programmers perceive the trustworthiness of computer code and the psychological processes behind these perceptions. Alarcon et al. [20] performed a cognitive task analysis and found three factors influence perceived trustworthiness and decisions to reuse code, namely reputation, transparency, and performance. Research has been conducted on these three factors, empirically demonstrating the factors are present in code and that researchers can manipulate them [21, 22].

To understand the psychological processes occurring when programmers review code, the heuristic-systematic processing model [23] was applied to perceptions of code [19]. The model hypothesizes that two process occur when a decision is being made to trust code: heuristic and systematic processing. Heuristic processing comprises the use of rules or norms to form judgements and make decisions about a referent. In contrast, systematic processing constitutes more effortful processing by performing critical thinking about the referent to reach a decision. For example, Alarcon et al. [21] found reducing the readability or credibility of computer code led to quicker decisions to abandon code, indicating heuristic processing. In contrast, degrading the organization of computer code led programmers to spend more time on the code, indicating systematic processing. Results indicated that programmers trusted code that was degraded in organization because they spent more time evaluating the code and found it was functional. Additionally, the authors replicated these effects in an additional sample in the same paper.

A key tenet of the HSM is the sufficiency principle [23]. Perceivers are motivated to perform efficient processing, not wanting to process more information than necessary. This efficiency is coupled with confidence. The model posits that there is an actual confidence level and a desired confidence level that humans possess. If the actual level is at or above the desired level, processing stops. However, if actual confidence is below the desired level then processing continues. In the HSM, perceivers are motivated to exert the least amount of processing to determine a particular confidence level. The balance between being efficient but attaining enough information to meet the desired confidence level is called the sufficiency principle [23].

1.4   Trust in Automated Code Generation

Research in the field of trust in automation has burgeoned in the last two decades. Hoff and Bashir [24] conducted a comprehensive review of the trust in automation literature and found three factors influence trust in automation: human factors, situational factors, and learned trust factors. Biases in trust beliefs—such as perceived trustworthiness—may influence both the human and learned trust factors. Human factors aspects, such as certain personality and dispositional variables, may impact perceived trustworthiness [25]. These trust perceptions are important, as they lead to reliance behavior [7, 26].

There is a great deal of literature covering aspects of the trust process in automation, such as in ground collision avoidance software [27], solider detection [28], and x-ray screening tasks [29]. However, the authors are not aware of any research that has explored these aspects in automated computer code. As mentioned above, research on automated code is growing rapidly. It is important to determine the psychological aspects of the human user that facilitate trust in the automated software code repair tools so that when the system is ready to deploy, programmers will appropriately trust in the system and use it when needed.

1.5   Deleting vs Commenting Out Changes

Humans are more sensitive to errors made by automation, with trust declining sharply when automation commits errors compared to when a human commits errors [30]. In initial interactions with automation, users typically monitor the automated system to ensure the system is functioning properly. Transparency is a key aspect when determining whether to trust a system, as transparency conveys information to the user about the decision/task the automation is performing [7]. Lyons et al. [31] found that trust in the automatic ground collision avoidance system in fighter jets increased when information about the system was added to their display, providing greater transparency. Similarly, Alarcon et al. [21] found transparency was a key factor in assessing whether programmers would reuse code, such that more transparent code was reused more often by programmers. Research has consistently demonstrated that transparency is a key factor in software contexts [22, 32]. As such, one of the code functions that may be important for adaptive computer programs is whether they delete or comment out code. Deleting the code can be problematic as the user will have to refer to older versions of the architecture to retrieve the code that was deleted, reducing transparency of the program. In contrast, when the program comments out pieces of the code, the modified section remains in the architecture and can be easily reviewed, providing greater transparency. A commented out section may be reintroduced if needed by removing the comment characters.

1.6   Human vs Computer Repair Trustworthiness

Another important factor to consider when using the code is reputation. Reputation is defined as "perceived code trustworthiness cues based on external information," such as, "the source of the code, information available in reviews, and the number of current users of the software" [20, p. 112]. As such, trust in the code repair may depend on whether an automated aid or a human completed the repair. The complexity of truly autonomous systems comes at a cost. Greater system complexity often means less control and predictability of system behavior [33], all of which may challenge human trust in that system. The ability to adapt, learn, and dynamically respond to environmental stimuli are foundational attributes of a truly autonomous system, yet such capabilities come with inherent expectations and a need for traceability regarding the appropriateness of the system's decision logic [34]. Automated systems capable of learning and adapting may have the capability to perform tasks themselves, but the operator must trust the system to perform the task with little oversight in order for a "reliable" system to achieve maximum benefit. However, trust in automation may differ from trust towards humans [7].

Programmers generally trust other programmers when they review and accept code revisions from those other programmers [21]. Accepting a code revision may be based on aspects such as experience of the programmer who receives the code, experience of the programmer that made changes to the code, or the reputation of the repository from which the code was retrieved. However, there may be differences in how programmers trust a computer program that repairs software compared to a human that repairs software. Lewandosky and colleagues [35] found that automation faults reduced a user's self-confidence in performing a task and reduced trust in their partner when participants perceived they were being paired with an automated system. In contrast, when the participant perceived they were paired with a human partner, self-confidence was not affected, even though all participants were paired with an automated system. These results demonstrate extreme polarization of trust and distrust in human-machine teaming but not in human-human teaming, as performance faults influence trust more in the former compared to the latter. These results are consistent with other research that has found that people are less extreme in their assessments of human-human distrust relative to human-human trust in word elicitation, questionnaires, and paired comparison studies [36]. In contrast, assessments in human-machine trust are less extreme, yet human-machine distrust is more extreme [36]. In other words, humans are more extreme in their distrust of machines and more extreme in their trust of humans.

In the current study, we hypothesize that there are differences in how people trust humans compared to automated systems and the changes made by each to software. Specifically, we expect programmers to want more transparency from automation, such that commented out changes to the code will lead to higher perceptions of trustworthiness and higher use endorsement rates compared to deleted code. We also expect programmers to trust human repairs more, compared to an automated repair program.

2   Study 1

2.1   Study 1 Method

Participants. A total of 24 student programmers from a Midwest university were recruited to participate in the study in exchange for $50 (USD) in financial remuneration. Participants were required to have a minimum of four years of experience with software development and a sufficient knowledge of the C programming language. The sample was primarily male (70.1%) with a mean age of 24.38 ($SD = 3.50$) years, a mean of 6.29 ($SD = 3.37$) years total programming experience, and 58% stated they use C on a weekly basis.

Design. Participants were asked to review and assess repairs made to source code written in C. The study utilized a 2 × 2 between-subject design, with 5 within-subject trials. The between-subject factors consisted of the type of repair made (i.e. deleting lines of code vs commenting out lines of code) and the reported source of the repairs (i.e. human vs automation). The 5 within-subject trials consisted of 5 different pieces of source code and their repairs. Participants were randomly assigned to one of the four conditions and completed each of the five trials. A fully balanced design was achieved with 6 participants in each condition and 5 trials for each participant.

2.2 Study 1 Measures

Trustworthiness. We used a single-item measure to asses overall perceived trustworthiness, consistent with previous studies on trust in code [21, 22]. Participants indicated their perceptions of trustworthiness with the item "How trustworthy do you find this repair?" on a scale ranging from 1 = Not at all Trustworthy to 7 = Very Trustworthy. Research has indicated single item measures are appropriate when the construct is well-defined and multiple items are likely to result in response fatigue [37].

Review Time. The time spent on the code was assessed with HTML timestamps from each page. A timestamp was used to assess when a participant started reviewing the code repairs and when the participant left the code repair to write their assessments. Each page contained only one stimulus.

Trust Intentions. We adapted Mayer and Davis' [38] trust intentions scale to assess intentions to trust the referent (i.e., the software repairer). The scale consists of four items. All items were rated on a 5-point Likert scale (1 = Strongly Disagree to 5 = Strong Agree). The first and third items were reverse coded. We adapted the scale to reflect the referent being assessed. An example item is "I would be comfortable giving [Bill, GenProg] a task or problem which was critical to me, even if I could not monitor their actions. Participants rated their intentions to trust the referent once before beginning the experiment and once after they had finished reviewing all code stimuli. Additionally, participants were asked with a single item whether they would endorse the code repair for use with "Use" or "Don't Use" as response options. This provided a single measure of reviewers' intention to trust for each of the code repairs.

2.3 Study 1 Stimuli

An HTML testbed was created for participants to review the five pieces of code written in C. The testbed presented the code by emulating a diff utility, which provides a side-by-side comparison of two different files, typically source code, and highlights the differences between the two (see Fig. 1). Shortcut buttons were provided at the top of the test bed for participants to quickly navigate to the sections of the code where changes were made.

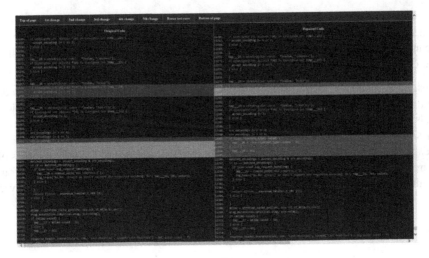

Fig. 1. Example of diff stimuli.

Fig. 2. Example of test cases stimuli.

Before and after seeing each code repair, participants were shown a list of test cases and whether they passed or failed (see Fig. 2). Stimuli consisted of 5 successful patches that were produced by the GenProg program. The stimuli consisted of code samples ranging from 7874 to 16779 lines of code with between 3 and 18 repaired lines across 1 to 5 locations within the code. The code artifacts were ordered such that the simplest changes were shown first, with changes becoming progressively more complex (based on the number of modified lines) as the participants moved through the study. Changes included replacing lines of code with code found elsewhere in the sample, deleting lines of code, and copying lines of code from elsewhere in the sample. Before and after code comparisons (i.e., diffs) were presented in the color scheme used by Visual Studio Code (a popular, free software development tool). All samples were shown in the format provided by GenProg, which was modified from the original by expanding multiple single-line commands into multi-line commands.

2.4   Study 1 Procedure

Participants completed demographic information and background surveys on a locally hosted website. Participants were then informed of their task and were given a brief description of the source of the code repairs (i.e., GenProg or a human programmer named Bill). After being read the description of the source, participants completed an initial trust intentions survey. Participants then conducted the task, reviewing 5 pieces of repaired code. Unbeknownst to the participants, all repairs were produced by GenProg and were the same across both referent conditions (i.e., Bill vs GenProg). After reviewing each repair, participants rated their perceived trustworthiness of the repair, indicated whether they would endorse the repair for use, and wrote any remarks they had about the code repair in provided textboxes. After reviewing all 5 code patches, participants completed the trust intentions questionnaire in regards to their assigned referent for a second time.

2.5   Study 1 Results

Missing data was observed for one participant for their fifth and final trial when providing responses for trustworthiness, use endorsement, and trust intentions. Values were multiply-imputed with 20 datasets to replace the missing data via the bootstrapped EM algorithm provided by the Amelia package [39] in R[1]. Reliabilities, means, standard deviations, and zero-order correlations for trust intentions and perceived code trustworthiness in Study 1 are available from the first author.

Trustworthiness. A repeated-measures analysis of variance (RM ANOVA) was conducted to analyze differences in perceived trustworthiness of the code repairs, factored by the source, type of repair, trial, and their interaction. The design was counter-balanced with six subjects in each condition and 5 observations per subject. Mauchly's test of sphericity was non-significant, $\chi^2(4) = 0.42$, $p = .069$, indicating equal variances across the repeated measurements. Type III sum of squares was used for interpretation of the effects. Source of repair, $F(1, 20) = 5.14$, $p = .035$, $\eta_p^2 = .20$, significantly predicted perceived trustworthiness. Estimated marginal means, presented in Fig. 3, suggest that repairs made by GenProg ($M = 4.87$) were significantly higher in perceived trustworthiness than repairs made by Bill ($M = 3.44$). Neither the type of repair, $F(1, 20) = 0.00$, $p = .993$, nor the trial number, $F(4, 80) = 1.13$, $p = .348$, provided significant explanation of the variance in perceived trustworthiness. Finally, the two-way interactions between source of repair and type of repair, $F(1, 20) = 0.00$, $p = .993$, source of repair and trial, $F(4, 80) = 1.42$, $p = .235$, type of repair and trial, $F(4, 80) = 1.37$, $p = .250$, and the three-way interaction between source of repair, type of repair, and trial, $F(4, 80) = 0.02$, $p = .823$, were all non-significant.

---

[1] Details of the multiple imputation procedure are available from the first author.

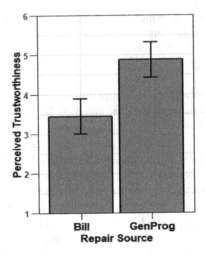

Fig. 3. Student programmers' perceptions of trustworthiness marginal means and standard errors.

Review Time. Previous studies have analyzed time taken to review code to investigate increased engagement with computer code [21, 22]. Thus, we conducted a second RM ANOVA to analyze differences in review time, factored by source of repair, type of repair, and trial. Mauchly's test of sphericity, $\chi^2(4) = .36, p = .025$, indicated significant differences in variances between the repeated measures. As such, a Greenhouse-Geisser correction was applied to the degrees of freedom for interpreting the model effects. Neither source of repair, $F(1, 20) = 0.13, p = .719$, nor type of repair, $F(1, 20) = 0.01$,

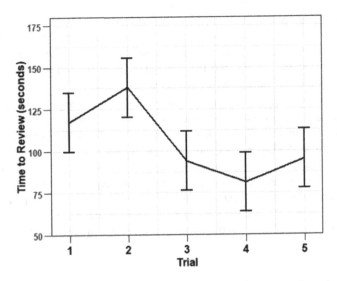

Fig. 4. Student programmers' time to review code marginal means and standard errors.

$p = .941$, were significant. However, trial, $F(2.80, 56.02) = 2.98$, $p = .042$, $\eta_p^2 = .13$, had a significant main effect on review time. A post-hoc analysis of estimated marginal means revealed linear, $b = -100.80$, $t(80) = -2.45$, $p = .017$, and cubic, $b = 91.37$, $t(80) = 2.22$, $p = .029$, trends in the average time taken to review code across the five time points, averaging across levels of source of repair and type of repair. The linear trend indicates participants took less time to review code with each successive piece of code, as illustrated in Fig. 4. The cubic trend suggests an initial increase in review time followed by a decrease.

Probability of Use and Trust Intentions. A generalized linear mixed effects regression analysis was conducted to analyze the probability that participants would endorse each code repair for use, factored by the source of repair and type of repair. The main effects of source of repair, $b = -1.09$, $SE = .62$, $z = -1.78$, $p = .076$, type of repair, $b = -0.39$, $SE = .58$, $z = -0.67$, $p = .502$, and the two-way interaction between repair source and type of repair, $b = 0.11$, $SE = .57$, $z = 0.19$, $p = .848$, were all non-significant. Next, we examined intentions to trust the referent with the trust intentions scale using a RM ANOVA. The scale reliabilities were .48 and .72 for the first and second assessments, respectively. The main effect of trial, $F(1, 20) = 8.71$, $p = .008$, $\eta_p^2 = 0.30$, and interaction between trial and source of repair, $F(1, 20) = 12.59$, $p = .002$, $\eta_p^2 = 0.39$, were both significant. Intentions to trust the referent declined between the initial ($M = 3.04$) and final assessments ($M = 2.49$), illustrated in Fig. 5. The decay in trust was moderated by the source of the repair, such that trust in Bill significantly declined between the initial ($M = 3.31$) and final ($M = 2.10$) assessments, $t(20) = -4.60$, $p < .001$, trust in GenProg did not significantly change between the initial ($M = 2.76$) and final ($M = 2.88$) assessments, $t(20) = 0.42$, $p = .997$, and the differences in change between Bill ($M = -1.21$) and GenProg ($M = 0.11$) across the two time points was significantly different, $t(20) = 2.95$, $p = .039$. The main effect of repair source, $F(1, 20) = 0.32$, $p = .576$, type of repair, $F(1, 20) = 2.12$, $p = .161$ and

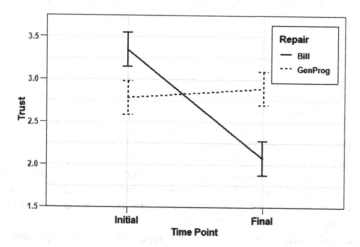

Fig. 5. Student programmers' intentions to trust estimated marginal means and standard errors.

the interactions between repair source and type, $F(1, 20) = 0.79$, $p = .385$, repair type and trial, $F(1, 20) = 0.80$, $p = .381$, and repair source, type, and trial, $F(1, 20) = 0.80$, $p = .381$, were all non-significant.

2.6   Study 1 Discussion

In Study 1, student programmers perceived the code repairs as more trustworthy when GenProg was the source of repair rather than the human programmer, Bill. This result may have occurred because of how the code was repaired. All code stimuli were originally repaired by GenProg, which often does so in a way that is not intuitive. This method of repair often violates conventional approaches and may therefore inhibit perceived trustworthiness. This effect may be diminished for participants in the Gen-Prog condition because they do not have strong expectations for how automated repair should be accomplished.

Over the sequential trials, the student sample spent less time reviewing each of the code repairs. This finding contrasts with our a priori expectations. Although not a specific hypothesis, one may expect programmers would have spent more time reviewing the code repairs, as those repairs became more complicated over the course of the experiment. The cubic trend that emerged indicates students spent more time reviewing code in the beginning of the experiment, but eventually they decreased the time they spent reviewing code over the course of the study. It may be that as the repairs became more complex, students leveraged their previously established heuristics for code review, leading to less time spent scrutinizing the code. However, this supposition is merely speculation until more data can be gathered.

Intentions to trust the repairer, or referent, decayed between the initial and final assessments. However, the source of the repair must be taken into consideration. Intentions to trust Bill declined sharply while intentions to trust GenProg did not change. Similar to perceptions of repair trustworthiness, trust in GenProg was less affected by the unconventional repairs than trust in Bill. Participants may not hold strong beliefs about how GenProg should have conducted the repairs.

3   Study 2

Alarcon et al. [21] CTA postulated that individual differences should play a role in the perception of and decision to trust code. Indeed, research on dual process models in psychology has focused on individual differences in information processing (e.g., [40]) and personality traits characterizing more or less enjoyment in thinking (e.g., need for cognition; [41]). One important individual difference that has been studied in both the psychology and computer science literatures is experience of the perceiver. A majority of research in psychology, and to a degree computer science, has utilized university students in their experiments. However, researchers have cautioned against using students as they may not be representative of the target population [42]. Indeed, research and theory has supported this idea.

Experts and novices perform different types of cognitive processing when reviewing code, namely top-down and bottom-up [43]. Top-down processing is the development of pattern recognition through the use of contextual information [44]. The contextual information helps in the perception of the referent as previous knowledge helps to make predictions of current stimuli. In the context of programming, top-down processing involves reconstructing information about the domain of the program and mapping this knowledge to the referent code [45]. In contrast, bottom-up processing is driven by data that is first perceived and then interpreted [46]. Bottom-up processing in program comprehension theorizes programmers first read code snippets and then cluster these snippets into higher level abstractions [47].

Research has demonstrated that experts more accurately recall code that is properly structured compared to unstructured code [48, 49], indicating a top-down processing approach as the structured code fits their schemas and thus is easily remembered. Ichinco and Kelleher [50] found experienced programmers recalled larger percentages of code snippets. Experienced programmers used schemas to chunk critical data, but novices did not perform the same processes. Additionally, novices have more trouble with static typing than more experienced programmers. In a study of lambda use in C++, compared to novice programmers, experienced programmers completed projects more rapidly accounting for 45.7% of the variance in completion time [51]. The authors concluded that lambdas are harder to use in the first few years of working with C++, but with experience, programmers begin to comprehend them.

As the first sample utilized students, we attempted to replicate the findings of Study 1 with professional programmers. As described above, more experienced programmers should perform top-down processing and should be more experienced with reading code. In addition, there has been a call in the social sciences, and all sciences to a degree, to replicate findings to ensure results are not by chance. By using the same stimuli in the same order, we were able to test the replicability of our findings, as replication with code stimuli may depend on the actual code itself, not just the experimental manipulations to the code [21, 22].

3.1 Study 2 Method

Participants. A total of 24 professional programmers, 2 active duty military personnel and 22 contractors on Department of Defense contracts, were recruited to participate in the study in exchange for $50 (USD) in financial remuneration. Participants were required to have a minimum of four years of experience with software development and know the C programming language. The sample was primarily male (83%) with a mean age of 40.75 ($SD = 11.20$) years, a mean of 16.12 ($SD = 10.02$) years total programming experience, and 50% stated they use C on a weekly basis. A set of t-tests indicated that the professional sample was significantly older, $t(27.45) = -6.72$, $p < .001$, and significantly more experienced, $t(28.15) = -4.48$, $p < .001$, than the student sample. The study design was counter-balanced with 6 participants in each condition.

3.2 Stimuli and Procedure

The same stimuli and procedure were used as in Study 1.

3.3   Study 2 Results

No missing data was observed for Study 2. Means, standard deviations, and zero-order correlations for perceived trustworthiness and review time in Study 2 are available from the first author.

Trustworthiness. A RM ANOVA was conducted to analyze differences in perceived trustworthiness between source of repair, type of repair, and trial. Mauchly's test of sphericity, χ^2 (9) = 15.71, p = .07, found no significant differences in variance between trials. The main effects of source of repair, $F(1, 20)$ = 1.23, p = .281, type of repair, $F(1, 20)$ = 1.70, p = .207, and trial, $F(4, 80)$ = 1.44, p = .228, were all non-significant. The two-way interactions between source of repair and type of repair, $F(1, 20)$ = 0.61, p = .443, source of repair and trial, $F(4, 80)$ = 0.47, p = .757, type of repair and trial, $F(4, 80)$ = 1.33, p = .265, and the three-way interaction between source of repair, type of repair, and order, $F(4, 80)$ = 0.28, p = .893, were all non-significant.

Time. Next, we conducted a repeated measures analysis of variance on review time, factored by source of repair, type of repair, and trial. Mauchly's test of sphericity, χ^2 (9) = 44.31, p < .001, found significant differences in variability between trials. A Greenhouse-Geisser correction was applied to the degrees of freedom for interpreting the model effects. Neither source of repair, $F(1, 20)$ = 0.23, p = .637, nor type of repair, $F(1, 20)$ = 0.41, p = .532, nor the interaction between the two, $F(1, 20)$ = 0.21, p = .649, were significant predictors of review time. The within-subject effects revealed no significant effects for trial, $F(2.06, 41.11)$ = 0.82, p = .449, trial and repair source, $F(2.06, 41.11)$ = 1.11, p = .339, trial and repair type, $F(2.06, 41.11)$ = 1.07, p = .356, or trial, repair source, and repair type, $F(2.06, 41.11)$ = 0.32, p = .736.

Probability of Use and Trust Intentions. A generalized linear mixed effects model was used to analyze participant endorsement of code for use, and the effects of repair source and type. The main effects of both source of repair, b = 0.79, z = 1.17, p = 0.243, and repair type, b = 0.34, z = 0.50, p = .617, were both non-significant. The interaction between source of repair and type of repair, b = −1.94, z = −1.92, p = .056, was also non-significant.

Next, we examined the trust intentions toward the referent. The scale reliabilities for trust intentions for both time points one and two were .62 and .66, respectively. The between-subject effects of source, $F(1, 20)$ = 0.00, p = .954, type, $F(1, 20)$ = 0.41, p = .530, and their interaction, $F(1, 20)$ = 3.24, p = .087, were all non-significant. The within-subjects effects of trial, $F(1, 20)$ = 29.92, p < .001, η_p^2 = 0.60, and trial x repair source, $F(1, 20)$ = 14.71, p = .001, η_p^2 = 0.42, were both significant. Results indicate that overall trust intentions were higher at the initial assessment (M = 3.05) than the final assessment (M = 2.15). This was moderated by repair source, such that trust in Bill significantly decreased, $t(20)$ = −6.58, p < .001, between the initial (M = 3.38) and final assessments (M = 1.83), while trust in GenProg did not significantly differ, $t(20)$ = −1.16, p = .597, between the initial (M = 2.73) and final assessments (M = 2.46), illustrated in Fig. 6. The difference in the change across time points between Bill and GenProg was also significant, $t(20)$ = −2.56, p = .043.

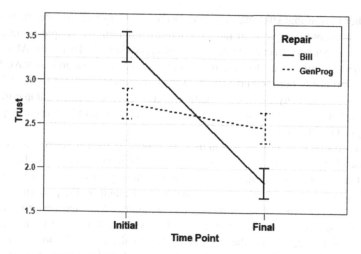

Fig. 6. Experienced programmers' intentions to trust.

3.4   Study 2 Discussion

In Study 2, we assessed whether the source and type of code repair influenced the trust process in a sample of professional software developers. There were no significant effects for perceived trustworthiness, amount of time spent on code review, or use endorsement. With regard to trust intentions, participants trusted Bill less after reviewing the code, while their intentions to trust GenProg did not change significantly. This coincides with the findings on trust and trust intentions in study 1.

4   General Discussion

As society's dependency on software increases, so too will the demand for functional code that is both safe and reliable. Based on a dearth of manpower, software demands will necessitate humans leveraging automated repair tools to help with vetting and repairing software. The current paper investigated the biases programmers have towards code that is repaired by either another human or an automated repair aid. All participants received code that was repaired by GenProg, but half of the participants were told that a human performed the repairs. By investigating these biases, the present research aimed to decipher the difference in human trust towards human repairs versus automated repair tools when the repairs vary in transparency.

In Study 1, student programmers perceived the repaired code as more trustworthy when they believed the code was repaired by the automated repair software (GenProg) compared to a human programmer (Bill). Participants also trusted Bill far less after reviewing the code, while trust in GenProg was not significantly affected. Even though the repairs were identical for both Bill and GenProg conditions, student software developers may have different expectations for how humans versus automation should function [30, 36], as GenProg does not repair code in a way that a human would repair software [52].

Another reason that students may have perceived GenProg as more trustworthy in the student sample compared to the experienced programmer sample is because the students were younger (mean age difference of approximately 16 years). Although we did not measure propensity to trust in automation, previous researchers have found a negative relationship between propensity to trust automation and age [25], such that as age increases, propensity to trust automation decreases. The younger sample may have had a higher propensity to trust automation and therefore would be more likely to trust the changes GenProg made.

Similar to study 1, study 2 showed that intentions to trust Bill decreased, regardless of the type of repair, as the experiment progressed. This was not the case for GenProg, such that trust intentions remained stable across time points. Previous research has shown that trust in automated agents is largely determined by the performance of the automated system, while trust in humans incorporates other non-performance-based factors such as perceptions of integrity and benevolence [16]. The information presented by the test cases and the code diff allowed the reviewers to verify that the patches were effective. This verification of sufficient performance may be the predominant factor in trusting GenProg. Conversely, assessments of trust in a human repairer would necessitate other information and greater scrutiny of non-performance factors related to the patches, such as readability or maintainability of the patch. This would explain why trust in Bill declined sharply while trust in GenProg did not change.

In contrast to our hypotheses, the student sample spent less time reviewing each of the code repairs. As the repairs became more complex, students may have leveraged their previously established heuristics for code review which require less time spent scrutinizing code. When students were more familiar with the task over time, they spent less time looking over how the changes were made, possibly utilizing select-out heuristics more with each successive trial. On the contrary, no significant differences in review time were observed for the professional sample. Experienced developers may be more studious in understanding the code they are reviewing, opting for a more systematic approach to processing information about the stimuli, regardless of their familiarity with the task or method of repair.

4.1   Limitations

Study 1 and study 2 were limited in a few ways. The effect sizes for the manipulated factors were smaller than anticipated. This may, in part, be due to the novelty of the stimuli. Because the patches produced by GenProg are often unintuitive and unconventional, trust in the patch itself would be less influenced by manipulations to the source and type of repair. In the extreme case, participants examining changes made by a human may not have believed that it was a human that made the changes, affecting our results in adverse ways. Finally, the trust intentions scale displayed less than adequate reliability. This may be because of the brevity of the scale, or the items may require a more concrete context with which to assess the referent.

4.2 Implications

The present research has implications for human/automation teaming, specific to software development contexts. As shown in past research [30, 36], humans have different expectancies for human versus automated partners (see also [7]). Though our studies were underpowered, we have provided an impetus for future work to further investigate human biases towards human/automation teammates in software development contexts with larger sample sizes. The present work identified the biases that may shape intentions to reuse software, regardless of the software content and performance specifics. Identifying humans' biases, which may fluctuate depending on supposed source of repair, provides another useful variable that shapes human trust in software development.

As more technology is introduced into our lives, our reliance on computer code will need to increase. Computer programmers who do not trust computer code from others or computer code that is computer-generated will either have to re-write the code from scratch or spend several hours on the code reading it line by line to ensure there are no issues. Computer generated code offers an efficient solution to programmers without sacrificing functionality. This study is, to the authors' knowledge, the first study to examine how transparency influences the way computer programmers perceive how trustworthy code repair tools are when manipulating factors such as source and types of repairs.

4.3 Conclusion

In conclusion, novice programmers are more accepting of unconventional software patches when they believe the patches were generated by an automated tool rather than a human. The time that novice computer programmers spent reviewing code pieces decreased over time, regardless of condition, indicating they may have had greater reliance on heuristics in contrast to the more experienced programmers. Finally, the present study provides evidence that trust in an automated repair tool may be predominantly influenced by its performance, while trust in a human that makes similar repairs is influenced by other non-performance factors.

References

1. Fung, B.: 145 million social security numbers, 99 million addresses and more: every type of personal data Equifax lost to hackers, by the numbers. The Washington Post (2018). https://www.washingtonpost.com/news/the-switch/wp/2018/05/08/every-type-of-personal-data-equifax-lost-to-hackers-by-the-numbers/?noredirect=on&utm_term=.aa92dfb95b08. Accessed 20 Dec 2018
2. Reuters: Lion Air reviewing Boeing jet purchases after crash that killed 189: report. Business Standard (2018). https://www.business-standard.com/article/international/lion-air-reviewing-boeing-jet-purchases-after-crash-that-killed-189-report-118120301164_1.html. Accessed 20 Dec 2018

3. CBS Interactive Inc.: Wells Fargo computer glitch blamed as hundreds lose their homes. CBS News (2018). https://www.cbsnews.com/news/wells-fargo-loan-modification-error-homeowners-who-went-into-foreclosure-seek-answers/. Accessed 20 Dec 2018

4. Perkins, J.H., et al.: Automatically patching errors in deployed software. In: 22nd Symposium on Operating Systems Principles, SOSP, Big Sky, pp. 87–102 (2009). https://doi.org/10.1145/1629575.1629585

5. Carzaniga, A., Gorla, A., Mattavelli, A., Perino, N., Pezzè, M.: Automatic recovery from runtime failures. In: Proceedings of the 2013 International Conference on Software Engineering, pp. 782–791. IEEE Press, Piscataway (2013)

6. Le Goues, C., Nguyen, T., Forrest, S., Weimer, W.: GenProg: a generic method for automatic software repair. J. IEEE Trans. Soft. Eng. **38**, 54–72 (2012). https://doi.org/10.1109/TSE.2011.104

7. Lee, J.D., See, K.A.: Trust in automation: designing for appropriate reliance. Hum. Factors J. Hum. Fac. Erg. Soc. **46**, 50–80 (2004). https://doi.org/10.1518/hfes.46.1.50_30392

8. Anvik, J., Hiew, L., Murphy, G.C.: Coping with an open bug repository. In: Proceedings of the 2005 OOPSLA Workshop on Eclipse Technology Exchange, pp. 35–39. ACM, New York (2005). https://doi.org/10.1145/1117696.1117704

9. Ball, T., Rajamani, S.K.: Automatically validating temporal safety properties of interfaces. In: Dwyer, M. (ed.) SPIN 2001. LNCS, vol. 2057, pp. 102–122. Springer, Heidelberg (2001). https://doi.org/10.1007/3-540-45139-0_7

10. Hovemeyer, D., Pugh, W.: Finding bugs is easy. ACM SIGPLAN Notices **39**, 92–106 (2004). https://doi.org/10.1145/1052883.1052895

11. Denning, D.E.: An intrusion-detection model. J. IEEE Trans. Soft. Eng. **SE-13**, 222–232 (1987). https://doi.org/10.1109/tse.1987.232894

12. Cox, B., et al.: N-variant systems: a secretless framework for security through diversity. In: Proceedings of the 15th Conference on USENIX Security Symposium, pp. 105–120. USENIX Association, Berkeley (2006)

13. Arcuri, A.: Evolutionary repair of faulty software. J. App. Soft Comput. **11**, 3494–3514 (2011). https://doi.org/10.1016/j.asoc.2011.01.023

14. Le Goues, C., Dewey-Vogt, M., Forrest, S., Weimer, W.: A systematic study of automated program repair: fixing 55 out of 105 bugs. In: 34th International Conference on Software Engineering, pp. 3–13. IEEE Press, Zurich (2012). https://doi.org/10.1109/icse.2012.6227211

15. Yuan, Y., Banzhaf, W.: ARJA: automated repair of java programs via multi-objective genetic programming. J. LaTex Class Files **14**, 1–30 (2015). https://doi.org/10.1109/TSE.2018.2874648

16. Mayer, R.C., Davis, H.C., Schoorman, F.D.: An integrative model of organizational trust. J. Acad. Manag. Rev. **20**, 709–734 (1995). https://doi.org/10.5465/amr.1995.9508080335

17. Sheridan, T.B.: Humans and Automation: System Design and Research Issues. Wiley, New York (2002)

18. Lambert, F.: Tesla driver was pulled over by cops after allegedly sleeping drunk on autopilot for 7 miles. Electrek (2018). https://electrek.co/2018/12/01/tesla-pulled-over-cops-sleeping-drunk-autopilot/. Accessed 20 Dec 2018

19. Alarcon, G.M., Ryan, T.J.: Trustworthiness perceptions of computer code: a heuristic-systematic processing model. In: Proceedings of the 51st Hawaii International Conference on System Sciences, pp. 5384–5393 (2018). https://doi.org/10.24251/hicss.2018.671

20. Alarcon, G.M., Militello, L.G., Ryan, P., Jessup, S.A., Calhoun, C.S., Lyons, J.B.: A descriptive model of computer code trustworthiness. J. Cog. Eng. Dec. Making **11**, 107–121 (2016). https://doi.org/10.1177/1555343416657236

21. Alarcon, G.M., et al.: Application of the heuristic-systematic model to computer code trustworthiness: the influence of reputation and transparency. J. Cogent Psych. **4**, 1–22 (2017). https://doi.org/10.1080/23311908.2017.1389640
22. Alarcon, G.M., et al.: The influence of commenting validity, placement, and style on perceptions of computer code trustworthiness: a heuristic-systematic processing approach. J. App. Erg. **70**, 182–193 (2018). https://doi.org/10.1016/j.apergo.2018.02.027
23. Chaiken, S.: Heuristic versus systematic information processing and the use of source versus message cues in persuasion. J. Pers. Soc. Psych. **39**, 752–766 (1980). https://doi.org/10.1037/0022-3514.39.5.752
24. Hoff, K.A., Bashir, M.: Trust in automation: integrating empirical evidence on factors that influence trust. J. Hum. Fact. **57**, 407–434 (2015). https://doi.org/10.1177/0018720814547570
25. Merritt, S.M., Ilgen, D.R.: Not all trust is created equal: dispositional and history-based trust in human-automation interactions. J. Hum. Fact. **50**, 194–210 (2008). https://doi.org/10.1518/001872008X288574
26. Ryan, T.J., Walter, C., Alarcon, G.M., Gamble, R.F., Jessup, S.A., Capiola, A.: The influence of personality on code reuse. In: Proceedings of the 52nd Hawaii International Conference on System Sciences, University of Hawaii, Manoa, 8–11 January 2019
27. Lyons, J.B., et al.: Trust-based analysis of an air force collision avoidance system. J. Erg. Des. **24**, 9–12 (2016). https://doi.org/10.1177/1064804615611274
28. Dzindoleta, M.T., Peterson, S.A., Pomranky, R.A., Pierce, L.G., Beck, H.P.: The role of trust in automation reliance. J. Hum. Comput. Stud. **58**, 697–718 (2003). https://doi.org/10.1016/S1071-5819(03)00038-7
29. Merritt, S.M., Heimbaugh, H., LaChapell, J., Lee, D.: I trust it, but I don't know why: effects of implicit attitudes toward automation on trust in an automated system. J. Hum. Fact. **55**, 520–534 (2013). https://doi.org/10.1177/0018720812465081
30. Dzindoler, M.T., Beck, H.P., Pierce, L.G., Dawe, L.A.: A framework of automation use. Technical report, Army Research Laboratory (2001)
31. Lyons, J.B., et al.: Trust of an automatic ground collision avoidance technology: a fighter pilot perspective. J. Mil. Psych. **28**, 271–277 (2016). https://doi.org/10.1037/mil0000124
32. Ryan, T.J., Walter, C., Alarcon, G.M., Gamble, R.F., Jessup, S.A., Capiola, A.A.: Individual differences in trust in code: the moderating effects of personality on the trustworthiness-trust relationship. In: Stephanidis, C. (ed.) HCI 2018. CCIS, vol. 850, pp. 370–376. Springer, Cham (2018). https://doi.org/10.1007/978-3-319-92270-6_53
33. Chen, J.Y.C., Barnes, M.J.: Human-agent teaming for multirobot control: a review of human factors issues. IEEE Trans. Hum. Mach. Syst. **44**, 13–29 (2014). https://doi.org/10.1109/THMS.2013.2293535
34. Arkin, R.C., Ulam, P., Wagner, A.R.: Moral decision making in autonomous systems: enforcement, moral emotions, dignity, trust, and deception. In: Proceedings of IEEE, pp. 571–589. IEEE Press, New York (2012). https://doi.org/10.1109/jproc.2011.2173265
35. Lewandowsky, S., Mundy, M., Tan, G.P.A.: The dynamic of trust: comparing humans to automation. J. Exp. Psych. **6**, 104–123 (2000). https://doi.org/10.1037//1076-898X.6.2.104
36. Jian, J., Bisantz, A.M., Drury, C.G.: Foundations for an empirically determined scale of trust in automated systems. Int. J. Cog. Erg. **4**, 53–71 (2000). https://doi.org/10.1207/S15327566IJCE0401_04
37. Wanous, J.P., Reichers, A.E., Hudy, M.J.: Overall job satisfaction: how good are single-item measures? J. App. Psych. **82**, 247–252 (1997). https://doi.org/10.1037/0021-9010.82.2.247
38. Mayer, R.C., Davis, J.H.: The effect of the performance appraisal system on trust for management: a field quasi-experiment. J. App. Psych. **84**, 123–136 (1999). https://doi.org/10.1037/0021-9010.84.1.123

39. Honaker, J., King, G., Blackwell, M.: Amelia II: a program for missing data. J. Stat. Soft. **45**, 1–47 (2011). https://doi.org/10.18637/jss.v045.i07
40. Epstein, S., Pacini, R., Denes-Raj, V., Heier, H.: Individual differences in intuitive-experiential and analytical-rational thinking styles. J. Pers. Soc. Psych. **71**, 390–405 (1996). https://doi.org/10.1037/0022-3514.71.2.390
41. Cacioppo, J.T., Petty, R.E.: The need for cognition. J. Pers. Soc. Psych. **42**, 116–131 (1982). https://doi.org/10.1037/0022-3514.42.1.116
42. Henrich, J., Heine, S.J., Norenzayan, A.: The weirdest people in the world. J. Behav. Brain Sci. **33**, 61–83 (2010). https://doi.org/10.1017/S0140525X0999152X
43. Adelson, B.: When novices surpass experts: the difficulty of a task may increase with expertise. J. Exp. Psych: Learn. Mem. Cogn. **10**, 483–495 (1984). https://doi.org/10.1037/0278-7393.10.3.483
44. Dror, I.E., Basola, B., Busemeyer, J.R.: Decision making under time pressure: an independent test of sequential sampling models. J. Mem. Cog. **27**, 713–725 (1999). https://doi.org/10.3758/BF03211564
45. Brooks, P.B.: No Silver Bullet. Elsevier Science Publishers B.V, North-Holland (1986)
46. Gibson, J.J.: The Senses Considered as Perceptual Systems. Houghton Mifflin, Oxford (1966)
47. Storey, M.: Theories, methods and tools in program comprehension: past, present and future. In: 13th International Workshop on Program Comprehension, pp. 181–191. IEEE Press, New York (2005). https://doi.org/10.1109/wpc.2005.38
48. Shneiderman, B.: Exploratory experiments in programmer behavior. J. Comp. Info. Sci. **5**, 123–143 (1976). https://doi.org/10.1007/BF00975629
49. Tait, P., Vessey, I.: The effect of user involvement on system success: a contingency approach. MIS Q. **12**, 91–108 (1988). https://doi.org/10.2307/248809
50. Ichino, M., Kelleher, C.: The need for improved support for interacting with block examples. In: IEEE Blocks and Beyond Workshop, pp. 69–70. IEEE Press, Raleigh (2017). https://doi.org/10.1109/blocks.2017.8120415
51. Altadmri, A., Brown, N.C.C.: 37 million compilations: investigating novice programming mistakes in large-scale student data. In: 46th ACM Technical Symposium on Computer Science Education, pp. 522–527. ACM, New York (2015). https://doi.org/10.1145/2676723.2677258
52. Nakajima, H., Higo, Y., Yokoyama, H., Kusumoto, S.: Toward developer-like automated program repair – modification comparisons between GenProg and developers. In: 23rd Asia-Pacific Software Engineering Conference, pp. 241–248, IEEE Press, Hamilton (2016). https://doi.org/10.1109/apsec.2016.042

Measuring Network User Trust via Mouse Behavior Characteristics Under Different Emotions

Biao Wang[1], Shiquan Xiong[1(✉)], Shuping Yi[1], Qian Yi[2],
and Fangfei Yan[1]

[1] Department of Industrial Engineering, Chongqing University,
Chongqing 400044, China
{wangbiao,ysp,201707131206}@cqu.edu.cn,
xiongshquan@163.com
[2] Department of Mechanical Design and Manufacturing, Chongqing University,
Chongqing 400044, China
yiqian@cqu.edu.cn

Abstract. Authentication based on mouse behavior is a guarantee for network information security. But the mouse behavior is affected by the user's emotions. Therefore, this study aims to analyze the user's mouse behavior characteristics to measure the identity trust of users under different emotions, and to verify whether there is a significant difference. To achieve this goal, an experiment was conducted. A total of 18 college students participated in this study. The results show that there are differences in the accuracy of authentication based on the user's mouse sliding behavior in three different emotional states, but the difference is not significant. The average accuracy of authentication under neutral, positive and negative emotions were 83.6%, 80.3% and 81.9%, respectively. The results also show that although the user performs human-computer interaction under different emotions, it will not essentially affect user authentication. Therefore, it can conclude that measuring network user trust via mouse behavior characteristics under different emotions is credible.

Keywords: Mouse behavior characteristics · Emotion ·
Accuracy of authentication · Network user

1 Introduction

With the rapid development of Internet technology and the implementation of "Internet +" actions, a variety of web applications are widely used. However, there are also many information security issues which cause huge economic losses. In recent years, identity authentication based on user behavior has become a hot topic in the field of network user authentication research. The approach only needs to use the human-computer interaction device to collect the data of the end user behavior, and then analyze the network user behavior characteristics to perform the user identification.

Most researchers have analyzed user behavior from different perspectives for user authentication [1, 2]. For example, researchers analyze the user's mouse dynamics to

© Springer Nature Switzerland AG 2019
A. Moallem (Ed.): HCII 2019, LNCS 11594, pp. 471–481, 2019.
https://doi.org/10.1007/978-3-030-22351-9_32

achieve static or continuous authentication of user identities. Although the authentication based on user's mouse behavior characteristics has a good accuracy rate, the emotional state of the user's human-computer interaction is not considered.

In many scenarios, users will perform human-computer interaction under different emotions even for the same task [3, 4]. It becomes more difficult to authenticate the network user by behavior data under different emotions, because it is not sure whether the network user' behavior pattern will be affected by emotions, and also the extent to which different emotions change the network user' behavior. Therefore, this study analyzes the user's mouse behavior characteristics to measure the identity trust of users under different emotions, and to verify whether there is a significant difference.

2 Literature Review

Authentication based on user's biological characteristics is another guarantee of network information security. Researchers analyze the data of users' mouse and keyboard to build a biometric system [1, 5]. Therefore, most researchers require users to use the mouse to complete a specified task, then extract velocity vector features and detect mouse movements to identify the user [6, 7]. The results of the study show that although the same task is completed, the mouse movements of different users are different. Then, researchers extract more mouse behavior characteristics to build user models. Mondal and Bours [8] extracts five characteristics (type of action, direction, speed of the mouse action, reciprocal acceleration of the mouse action, traveled distance in bins) of mouse behavior, and uses algorithms to establish different levels of trust models to achieve continuous identity authentication. Feher [9] divides the mouse operation into three levels, extracts features according to motion state and mouse function, and then constructs a classifier for each action type to construct a multi-level model for continuous authentication. In the experimental control environment, static authentication can be performed based on mouse behavior characteristics. However, Jorgensen and Yu [10] believed that the mouse operating environment should not be controlled, and the user's natural behavior should be collected for continuous authentication. Whether or not in the experimental control environment, authentication based on mouse behavior is to analyze whether the deviation of mouse behavior is within the normal range. Although the authentication based on user's mouse behavior characteristics has a good accuracy rate, the emotional state of the user's human-computer interaction is not considered.

In addition, users have different emotions, which is very important in the process of human-computer interaction. Some researchers explore the changes of users' emotions to design human-machine interface for higher user experience and satisfaction [11]. And scholars have conducted research on emotion recognition in human-computer interaction [12, 13]. However, at present, most of the research is to collect the digital content (text, audio, pictures, etc.) of user interaction and establish an emotional recognition model [14], so that emotional content can be divided into positive or negative, or objective (neutral) [15]. Although most researchers agree that behavior in human-computer interaction can distinguish the user's emotions, it is difficult to analyze from mouse behavior. There are only a few studies based on mouse behavior to measure user emotions, and few mouse behavior features are selected in the exploration [16]. In the current study, it is more to analyze the mouse behavior from the time dimension to predict the change of emotion, instead of analyzing the motion characteristics of mouse movement. However, simple dimensions make it difficult to get accurate results in a complex website operating environment. To deal with this problem, considering the complex environment of using computers and selecting more mouse behavior characteristics to build a model, the relationship between emotion and mouse is more clearly reflected.

Therefore, this study considers the emotional changes in human-computer interaction, and explores the impact of different emotional states of users on the accuracy of authentication based on mouse behavior.

3　Methodology

3.1　Independent and Dependent Variables

The independent variable was emotional state in the experiment, and was designed in group. Emotion state had three levels: neutral emotion, positive emotion, negative emotion. In the experiment, participants need to complete tasks after their emotions were aroused, so the extend of emotional arousal was the focus of consideration. Therefore, video was used to arouse user's emotional changes, and Facereader was used to detect participants' emotional changes and duration. In order to achieve the purpose of human-computer interaction after the participants' emotions were aroused.

The dependent variable was the accuracy of authentication based on the characteristics of the mouse sliding behavior. The accuracy of authentication was the result of classifying the characteristics of mouse sliding by random forest classifier.

3.2　Participants

In the early stage of the study, ten postgraduates majoring in laboratory-related subjects were invited to conduct multiple emotional tests and pre-experiments. Eighteen college students (9 males and 9 females) form Chongqing University were recruited to be participants during the formal experiment. Their average age was 22.67 (SD = 0.796). They have the ability to operate computer skillfully, and the average year of experience is 4.48 (SD = 1.167). Moreover, 90.47% of participants believed that video could stimulate human emotions, and 9.53% of participants expressed uncertainty.

3.3　Equipment

Preliminary experiments and formal experiments were conducted in the human factors engineering laboratory of Chongqing University. In the preliminary experiment, participants' emotions were detected by installing facereader software on a laptop (HP ProBook 440 G4). Facereader is a software that automatically analyses facial expressions (Neutral, Happy, Sad, Angry, Surprised, Scared, Disgusted). Facereader can get the percentage value of the corresponding emotion based on the user's facial expression. In order to create a real user operating environment (experimental environment) without changing participants' usual mouse operating habits, participants used their own computers and mouse. Finally, interactive data were collected using experimental equipment (HP ProBook 440 G4).

3.4 The Design of Emotional Arousal

In this experiment, three videos were selected to stimulate users' neutral, positive and negative emotions. Previously, 10 participants were invited to test and facereader was used to detect the effect of video on emotional arousal and to verify the duration of emotional arousal. Facereader analyzed participants' facial expressions while watching videos to get percentages of seven basic emotions (Neutral, Happy, Sad, Angry, Surprised, Scare, Disgusted). Neutral was classified as neutral emotions, Happy and Surprised as positive emotions, and the rest as negative emotions.

After repeated tests and adjustments, video 1, video 2 and video 3 were finally used to stimulate users 'neutral, positive and negative emotions. The effect of emotional arousal was showed using percentage of Facereader tests (as shown in Fig. 1). For the first 120S, the percentage of emotions was more than 50%, so the three videos were considered to be successful in stimulating participants' emotions. From 130S to 330S, neutral emotions and negative emotions remained, while positive emotions showed a downward trend in 290S. Therefore, the emotions stimulated by the video can last for about 2.5 min. The mouse operation data in the 2.5 min was also collected in the formal experiment.

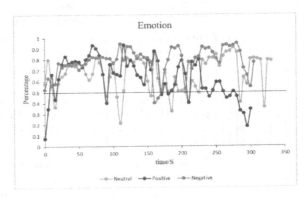

Fig. 1. The percentage and duration of video-inspired emotions

3.5 Experimental Systems and Tasks

The experimental system was a self-built academic exchange website of the research group (http://www.cquieaml.com/). The front-end web page (as shown in Fig. 2) was developed using HTML and javescript and consists of seven parts (academic research, scientific research results, corporate communication, forum interaction, research team, resource sharing, management center). The structure of the website was well structured and the content of the website was rich. Users can browse papers, post or comment on the website. Therefore, this experiment can create a real user operating environment and get the most realistic user behavior data. Javascript codes recorded users mouse data, like click and move, and then transformed the data into back-end sever and saved them.

Each participant needs to complete two tasks in the event that one emotion was activated, each task needs to be operated on the website using the mouse. For example, browsing the post content and posting, this is a simple task. Participants open the specified post, browse, and then copy a piece of text for evaluation and posting. The more difficult task was to test the participants' familiarity with the site. Participants need to answer questions set in advance, and the answers to the questions require the user to find them in the seven sections of the website. In order to avoid the learning effect, the tasks in different emotions had the same form, but the content was different.

Fig. 2. Interface of experimental system

3.6 Procedures

The whole experiment process was as follows: First, the experimenter introduces the purpose, content and precautions of the experiment to the participants. Second, participants were required to fill out a basic information questionnaire, including basic personal information (age, gender, etc.), computer mouse operation, and so on. The experimenter introduced the experiment task to the participants and instructed the participants to complete all the tutorial operations. Participants were required to perform continuous task operations immediately after watching the video, and there was no mandatory sequence for completing two tasks.

After completing the tutorial, enter the formal experiment, the experimental sequence was as follows: It was conducted in four days (four times). On the first day, the participants completed the tutorial independently, familiar with the task flow and the structure of the website, and avoided the influence of the experiment on the mouse operation due to unfamiliar experiments. Then, in three days, watching the video to stimulate different emotions to complete the task to avoid the interference of the subject's fatigue or emotional changes. After the video 1 was watched the next day, the task operation was performed. After video 2 was watched on the third day, the task operation was performed, and after the video 3 was watched on the fourth day, the task operation was performed. The whole experimental process creates a real user operating environment (experimental environment), in order not to change the usual mouse operation behavior habits of the test.

3.7 Data Processing

The original mouse data collected by participants interacting with the website includes five values: the type of mouse event, the x-coordinates of mouse pointer, the y-coordinates of mouse pointer (y), the time (t) of mouse event and user ID. Most researchers believe that the basic events of mouse behavior were click and slide. This paper focuses on move sequences to better illustrate user mouse behavior. Firstly, data of mouse behavior were cleaned, classified, and featured through R programing, and the mouse data with emotional tags (2.5 min) was sorted out. Then, according to the mouse action, the move sequences characteristics (as shown in Table 1) were calculated.

The participant's move sequences characteristics values were calculated according to the formula, and then the average of each of the above feature values was taken to reflect the mouse behavior. The accuracy of authentication was based on the characteristics of mouse movement to establish model calculation results. Several machine learning methods were compared, and the random forest algorithm was chosen to build the model because of the high precision. Firstly, the whole mouse sliding operation characteristics value of eighteen participants on the first day was used as the training set, and the random forest algorithm was used to establish the model. Then the mouse sliding characteristics value (2.5 min) under different emotions was tested as the data of the test set. The accuracy of authentication based on the characteristics of the mouse sliding behavior under different emotions was obtained. Finally, the accuracy rate of eighteen participants under different emotions was conducted using repeated ANOVA.

Table 1. Description of Mouse move sequences characteristics

Operation category	Characteristics name	Description	Formal definition
Movement sequence (MS)	Duration of movement	The sum of mouse sliding time	t_n
	Traveled distance	The sum of mouse sliding paths	$S_n; S_1 = 0$
	Horizontal velocity	Mouse movement speed on screen horizontal axis	$v_x = \delta x/\delta t$
	Vertical velocity	Mouse movement speed on screen longitudinal axis	$v_y = \delta y/\delta t$
	Velocity	Tangential direction speed of mouse movement curve	$v = \sqrt{v_x^2 + v_y^2}$
	Acceleration	The rate of change of the tangential velocity of mouse movement to time	$\dot{v} = \delta v/\delta t$
	Angle of movement	Path angle between mouse movement and screen horizontal axis	$\theta_i = \arctan(\delta y_1/\delta x_1) + \sum_{j=1}^{i} \delta\theta_j$
	Angular velocity	Time variation rate of angular displacement of mouse movement	$w = \delta\theta_t/\delta t$
	Curvature	Rotation rate of arc length in tangential direction of mouse movement	$c = \delta\theta/\delta s$
	Jitter	Ratio of slip displacement to sliding path distance	$S = \frac{\sqrt{(x_1-x_n)^2 + (y_1-y_n)^2}}{S_n}$

4 Results and Discussion

4.1 Influence of Emotion on the Accuracy of Authentication

First, the confusion matrix of 18 participants in neutral emotions, positive emotions, and negative emotions was obtained by random forest classifier (as shown in Figs. 3a–c). The average accuracy of authentication under neutral, positive and negative emotions were 83.6%, 80.3% and 81.9%, respectively. At the same time, the accuracy of authentication based on mouse sliding behavior of 18 participants in three different emotions was obtained (as shown in Table 2). Then, the accuracy of 18 participants' authentication under three emotions was analyzed by variance analysis. The results show that different emotional states of users have no significant impact on the accuracy of authentication. Then, the accuracy of authentication of the 18 participants in the three emotions was analyzed by ANOVA. The results show that there was no significant difference in the accuracy of user authentication under different emotional states $(F_{(2, 34)} = 0.551, p = 0.582 > 0.05)$.

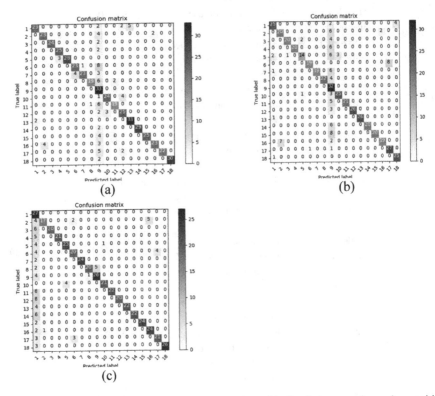

Fig. 3. (a) Confusion matrix under neutral emotion. (b) Confusion matrix under positive emotion. (c) Confusion matrix under negative emotion.

Table 2. Accuracy of authentication of 18 participants in three emotions

Participant number	Accuracy rate in neutral emotions	Accuracy rate in positive emotions	Accuracy rate in negative emotions
1	0.719	0.806	1.000
2	0.793	0.714	0.654
3	0.923	0.769	0.769
4	0.926	0.769	0.808
5	0.903	0.560	0.852
6	0.719	0.704	0.714
7	0.767	0.731	0.923

(continued)

Table 2. (*continued*)

Participant number	Accuracy rate in neutral emotions	Accuracy rate in positive emotions	Accuracy rate in negative emotions
8	0.704	0.846	0.741
9	1.000	1.000	0.839
10	0.828	0.862	0.840
11	0.731	0.808	0.786
12	0.833	0.897	0.769
13	0.943	0.963	0.846
14	0.935	0.769	0.786
15	0.862	0.714	0.923
16	0.767	0.679	0.889
17	0.815	0.931	0.875
18	0.938	0.962	0.897

4.2   Discussion

This study examined the use of the mouse in neutral, positive, and negative emotional states. Then, the trust of the user authentication is measured based on the user's mouse sliding behavior under different emotional states.

It can be seen from Table 2 that the accuracy of user authentication based on the mouse sliding characteristics under different emotions is different. Most participants have a high accuracy of authentication, and only a few participants have low accuracy of authentication under different emotional states. It can be seen from the results that some participants have similar and higher accuracy of authentication in neutral and positive emotions, while their accuracy in negative emotions is lower. For example, participants 9 and 13. Participants No. 13 achieved 100% accuracy in authentication under neutral and positive emotions. It may be because the mouse operations of these participants are more affected by negative emotions. Some participants had a very high accuracy of authentication in negative emotions, but very low in positive emotions. For example, participants such as No. 1, No. 5 and No. 15 may be because their bodies are relaxed at the same time when they have a positive emotional state, thus affecting the mouse operation. Among them, the accuracy of authentication of participants 6 in the three emotions is basically the same and low, around 0.71. It may be that emotional changes have a greater impact on the mouse behavior of participant 6. As to the accuracy of authentication, the average accuracy of 18 participants was 83.6% in neutral emotional state, 80.3% in positive emotional state and 81.9% in negative emotional state. The accuracy of authentication fluctuates slightly under different emotions. Although the user's authentication accuracy is different under different emotions, the credibility of authentication based on mouse behavior is not affected.

In general, the user identification model based on the mouse movement feature calculates that the accuracy of authentication is different under three different emotional states. And this difference is the content of experimental research. However, the user's mouse behavior data with different emotions for human-computer interaction has no significant effect on the results of the identification research.

5   Limitations and Future Work

Three limitations of this study are noted. First, the study was to stimulate user emotions through video, but different participants may be induced with different emotional intensities, which may bias the results. Future studies may explore the effects of different intensity levels of different emotional states.

Second, this study recruited participants who were students from Chongqing University, regardless of age or occupation. Future studies may extend this study to other populations to check generalizability of findings from this study.

Third, this study only considers a few classification algorithms. Future studies should try to use different classifiers and prediction methods to improve accuracy and reliability.

6   Conclusions

Authentication based on mouse behavior is a guarantee for network information security. But the mouse behavior is affected by the user's emotions. Hence, this study aims to explore the effect of user emotions on the accuracy of authentication based on user mouse behavior. In order to achieve this goal, this study conducted an experiment to explore the user's mouse behavior under different emotions.

The experiment results show that there are differences in the accuracy of authentication based on the user's mouse sliding behavior in three different emotional states, but the difference is not significant. Although the accuracy of the authentication of the 18 participants in neutral emotions, positive emotions, and negative emotions fluctuated greatly, the average accuracy rates were 80%, 81%, and 84%, respectively. The results also show that although the user performs human-computer interaction under different emotions, it will not essentially affect user authentication. Therefore, it can conclude that measuring network user trust via mouse behavior characteristics under different emotions is credible.

Acknowledgments. This work was supported by the National Natural Science Foundation of China under Grant No. 71671020.

References

1. Bailey, K.O., Okolica, J.S., Peterson, G.L.: User identification and authentication using multi-modal behavioral biometrics. Comput. Secur. **43**, 77–89 (2014)
2. Monrose, F., Rubin, A.: Authentication via keystroke dynamics. In: ACM Conference on Computer & Communications Security (1997)

3. Chmiel, A., Sobkowicz, P., Sienkiewicz, J., Paltoglou, G., Buckley, K., Thelwall, M., et al.: Negative emotions boost user activity at bbc forum. Phys. Stat. Mech. Appl. **390**(16), 2936–2944 (2011)

4. Maehr, W.: eMotion: Estimation of User's Emotional State by Mouse Motions. Elsevier (2008)

5. Kang, P., Cho, S.: Keystroke dynamics-based user authentication using long and free text strings from various input devices. Inf. Sci. **308**, 72–93 (2015)

6. Gamboa, H., Fred, A.L.N., Jain, A.K.: Webbiometrics: User Verification Via Web Interaction. Biometrics Symposium (2008)

7. Bours, P., Fullu, C.J.A.: Login system using mouse dynamics. In: International Conference on Intelligent Information Hiding & Multimedia Signal Processing (2009)

8. Mondal, S., Bours, P.: A computational approach to the continuous authentication biometric system. Inf. Sci. **304**, 28–53 (2015)

9. Feher, C., Elovici, Y., Moskovitch, R., Rokach, L., Schclar, A.: User identity verification via mouse dynamics. Inf. Sci. **201**, 19–36 (2012)

10. Jorgensen, Z., Yu, T.: On mouse dynamics as a behavioral biometric for authentication. In: [ACM Press the 6th ACM Symposium - Hong Kong, China (2011.03.22–2011.03.24)] Proceedings of the 6th ACM Symposium on Information, Computer and Communications Security - ASIACCS 2011, p. 476 (2011)

11. Calvo, M.G., Lang, P.J.: Gaze patterns when looking at emotional pictures: motivationally biased attention. Motiv. Emot. **28**(3), 221–243 (2004)

12. Cowie, R., Douglas-Cowie, E., Tsapatsoulis, N., Votsis, G., Kollias, S., Fellenz, W., et al.: Emotion recognition in human-computer interaction. IEEE Signal Process. Mag. **18**(1), 32–80 (2001)

13. Rashid, M.: Human emotion recognition from videos using spatio-temporal and audio features. Visual Comput. **29**(12), 1269–1275 (2013)

14. Prabowo, R., Thelwall, M.: Sentiment analysis: a combined approach. J. Inform. **3**(2), 143–157 (2009)

15. Mitrovi, M., Paltoglou, G., Tadi, B.: Networks and emotion-driven user communities at popular blogs. Eur. Phys. J. B **77**(4), 597–609 (2010)

16. Saini, T.S., Bedekar, M.: Inferring user emotions from keyboard and mouse. In: Bhalla, S., Bhateja, V., Chandavale, A.A., Hiwale, A.S., Satapathy, S.C. (eds.) Intelligent Computing and Information and Communication. AISC, vol. 673, pp. 591–601. Springer, Singapore (2018). https://doi.org/10.1007/978-981-10-7245-1_58

Author Index

Printed in the United States
By Bookmasters